Travellers' Health

How to Stay Healthy Abroad

SECOND EDITION

devised and edited by

Dr RICHARD DAWOOD

Oxford New York Tokyo

OXFORD UNIVERSITY PRESS

Oxford University Press, Walton Street, Oxford 0X2 6DP

Oxford New York Toronto
Delhi Bombay Calcutta Madras Karachi
Petaling Jaya Singapore Hong Kong Tokyo
Nairobi Dar es Salaam Cape Town
Melbourne Auckland

and associated companies in
Berlin Ibadan

First published 1986
Reprinted 1986
Reprinted (with revisions) 1987
Second edition 1989
Reprinted (with corrections) 1990

British Library Cataloguing in Publication Data
Travellers' Health.—2nd ed.
1. Travel. Health aspects—Practical information
I. Dawood, Richard
613.6'8
ISBN 0–19–261831–8

Library of Congress Cataloging-in-Publication Data
Travellers' Health/devised and edited by Richard Dawood.—2nd ed.
Includes index Bibliography
1. Travel. Health aspects. 2. Tropical medicine. I. Dawood, Richard M.
RA783.5.T68 1989 613.6'8'0913—dc19 88–37309
ISBN 0–19–261831–8

Typeset by Promenade Graphics Ltd, Cheltenham
Printed in Great Britain by
The Guernsey Press Co. Ltd,
Guernsey, Channel Islands

Preface

This book is intended for travellers who wish to make informed decisions about their own health abroad.

From the moment they leave the security of their accustomed environment, travellers are at risk. Hazards arise not just from strange diseases they encounter on their travels, but from other factors too: home comforts such as a safe water supply, sanitation and public hygiene controls, legal safety standards for motor vehicles and road maintenance, to give just a few examples, may not seem very inspiring, and are easily taken for granted when they are present, but simply do not exist in many popular travel destinations. Environmental factors such as arduous conditions, adverse climate, and high altitude may constitute a hazard; and so may travellers' own behaviour while away—on holiday, free from the restraints of the daily routine, and determined to have a good time with scant regard for the consequences.

When illness or injury occurs abroad, travellers are again at a disadvantage—from inability to communicate with a doctor on account of language or cultural difficulties, inability to find a doctor owing to ignorance of the local medical system, inability perhaps to pay for skilled care in a sudden emergency. There may be a complete absence of skilled medical care, or of medical facilities of a standard acceptable to travellers from technologically sophisticated countries.

When symptoms of an illness acquired abroad do not appear until *after* return home (up to a year later, for example, in certain cases of malaria) a final hazard becomes apparent: the symptoms may be unfamiliar, may pass unrecognized, and the correct diagnosis may not be considered until it is too late.

This book offers neither an exhaustive catalogue of obscure tropical diseases nor a course of training in first aid; it *is* an anthology of invited, *specialist* opinion on a wide range of problems of concern to travellers; concern, either because a genuine hazard exists that travellers should know about, and should take precautions to avoid, or because a disease or hazard which in fact constitutes no real threat has been the potential source of unwarranted anxiety.

It is a popular misconception that exotic infections pose the principal danger to travellers' health. While this book presents detailed information and advice about disease hazards and their prevention, other, no less important hazards have not been neglected. Accidents, for example, are the single most frequent cause of death in travellers abroad, causing 25 times as many deaths as infectious diseases. Some accidents and disasters are indeed indiscriminate, and like the sabotage of the Pan American Boeing 747 over Scotland and the multiple rail crash in South London, both in December 1988, raise issues of safety and security that concern all of us. Most accidents involving travellers, however, like the majority of travellers' health problems, are in fact preventable or under a considerable degree of individual control. People worry increasingly about the dangers of blood transfusion and other forms of medical treatment abroad; prevention of accidents is the most effective way of reducing these risks as well.

Travel may have other unexpected implications for health, not traditionally encompassed by Travel Medicine: an unwanted pregnancy, the possible consequence of failure of absorption of the Pill during a severe bout of traveller's diarrhoea, can ruin the memory of a holiday no less surely than a tropical disease.

The scope of this book largely reflects the range of problems which I have come across during my own travels—often without having been able to deal with them to my own satisfaction at the time—and many subjects discussed here have not previously been given detailed attention in books for travellers. A specialist view is presented on each topic, because the range of subjects considered extends beyond the first-hand experience and expertise of any one individual, and because when travellers are most in need of information or advice about health, they need advice that they can trust and depend on, not myth that has simply been handed on.

Like the rest of medicine, however, travellers' health is not an exact science, and consensus is lacking on many crucial issues. A recent survey found visitors from different countries to the same part of East Africa following no fewer than *eighty* different antimalarial regimes (but an alarming 30 per cent of the visitors were taking no precautions at all). Some of the problems raised in this book have no satisfactory solution, or have solutions that remain a matter of opinion or the subject of debate. Readers will therefore detect differences of opinion between contributors to this book, or may disagree with their conclusions, and we hope that this will stimulate and encourage further debate.

In general, the quality of advice on health matters customarily given to travellers has not been good: adequate pre-travel information and advice are the exception rather than the rule—or this book would not be necessary.

Doctors in developed countries receive minimal training in, and remain largely unfamiliar with, hazards outside their own environment. In a report on the deaths of seven travellers who succumbed to acute mountain sickness while trekking in the Himalayas, Dr John Dickinson pointed out that three of the seven who died were themselves doctors. As Dr Dickinson explains on p. 273, all of those deaths could readily have been avoided. And enough doctors were stricken with diarrhoea on a recent British Medical Association Congress in Egypt, to make headline news at home. Worse still, a third of the doctors attending a gastroenterology convention in Mexico were also stricken.

Deaths still occur in developed countries from malaria, and occur in previously fit, healthy young travellers; initial symptoms are all too easily confused with influenza and deterioration is often rapid without prompt treatment. In the past decade, some 50 000 cases of malaria have occurred in travellers entering Europe. Each year, there are now more than 2000 cases of malaria in travellers entering the UK, and around 1000 cases in travellers entering the USA—for both countries, these figures have trebled over the past ten years. Most of the travellers either did not seek or receive appropriate advice, or did not follow it; many of them, however, knew about the dangers, but simply could not be bothered with precautions. The number of people coming home with malaria rises steadily every year.

Doctors tend to be poor educators; we have depressingly little to show for our efforts to educate the general public on even such a clear cut issue as the effects of cigarette smoking on health. How much more difficult, then, is it for doctors to provide large numbers of departing travellers with detailed information and effective advice for their trip when the usual forum for doing so is a single, hurried consultation, just before departure. There are limits to what can be achieved in or should be expected from a medical consultation under the best of circumstances, even when the doctor is well-motivated and well-informed about the subject, and the traveller is receptive, has a perfect memory, and is good at doing what he or she is told.

What kind of advice should travellers receive? A list of rules and instructions given without explanation or justifications carries the implication that travellers are incapable of understanding the principles involved, are not interested, or do not 'need' to know. It is hardly surprising that advice offered on such condescending terms is seldom followed for long.

The best advice is not a list of do's and don'ts, but is based on information, a clear, rational explanation from which a conclusion is obvious. Information is a powerful weapon, and I believe that travellers should have the opportunity to choose for themselves how much they 'want' or 'need' to know; to an extent, this book is a personal statement of the kind of information I believe should be readily available to anyone interested.

Throughout this book, we have studiously avoided giving blanket advice to consult a doctor without stating the reason for doing so. 'Consult your doctor' is a useful formula to enable advice-givers to evade difficult issues, but is a particularly unhelpful one when it relates to a problem which may arise abroad. It is not easy to find a doctor in a remote place, or to communicate with one in an alien land. Merely finding a doctor does not guarantee that correct advice or treatment will be given. Some 85 per cent of the world's population have never seen a doctor, and never will; advice for travellers must take account of the fact that travellers to many parts of the world will be in the same position.

Advice from doctors, travel agents, embassies, or immunization centres too often goes no further than to provide details of statutory vaccination certificate entry requirements. Few legal requirements now remain, and they are generally no more than public health measures, designed to protect countries from imported disease; they should not be confused with, and are no substitute for, clear advice and instruction on staying healthy abroad. All those who dispense 'advice' which is in fact limited to information about statutory requirements have a responsibility to make it clear that additional precautions are almost always necessary for personal protection. Such further precautions need to be spelt out in detail: advice to 'take care with food hygiene' is practically meaningless to anyone who has never given serious thought to the problems of travelling or living in an environment where total absence of 'basic' sanitary measures is the norm;

there is growing public awareness of food safety and hygiene issues, however, which can only help for the future.

Statutory requirements are creeping back in another context—some countries now require a medical certificate showing a negative AIDS antibody test before granting certain kinds of visa. This practice is contrary to WHO policy and regulations, and deserves to be vigorously opposed.

In the three years since this book first appeared, there has been undoubted growth in interest and awareness of the health problems of travel, and it would be gratifying to think that this book might have made even a small contribution to the process. One group has patently failed to make any large scale contribution, however: the travel industry still views health information for travel as bad for business, or not its concern, and few travel agents appear to see farther than the commission on their next sale. They argue that, since they are not doctors, it is not their responsibility to dispense health advice; but they belittle the problems instead of pointing out the need for advice and directing travellers to suitable sources.

> 'I cannot for the life of me understand the logic in your telling readers about the pollution problem in Rio de Janeiro. Somehow it seems a very self-destructive tack for a publication supposed to encourage, not discourage, world travel. You are doing both your readers and your advertisers a disservice.'
>
> New York advertising agency executive for VARIG,
> writing to withdraw all further advertising
> from Condé Nast *Traveler* magazine.
>
> 'We rejoice in the enrichments of travel, but our aim is to give readers the fullest information, frankly and fairly. They know it's a big world, where sometimes it's sunny and sometimes it rains. Isn't travel just as likely to be discouraged when it begins in illusion and ends in frustration and disappointment?'
>
> Harold Evans
> Editor
> Condé Nast *Traveler* magazine, New York
> (from an editorial on 'Truth in travel')

A major international conference on travel medicine in Zurich in April 1988, the first of its kind, made a concerted effort to involve the travel industry; but fewer than a dozen of the 500 delegates who attended had any connection with the travel industry, and most of these were airline medical staff; there was not a single representative from the travel trade press.

An American survey showed that only 28 per cent of travellers to malarial areas had received any kind of notification from their travel agent that malaria might be a possible hazard. A British victim of malaria, which was acquired on a holiday in the Gambia, was actually told by the travel agent who made the booking that there was no malaria in the Gambia. A Dutch survey showed that travellers who had used travel agents as their sole source of advice were in fact at even greater risk than those who had not troubled to seek advice from any source. There are cases on record where elderly people have been booked on tours to Peru, without any warning about the dangers of high altitude, and have died as a result. One third of British travel brochures make no reference to health whatsoever, according to another recent survey, while only 10 per cent give any useful specific health information.

More problems for travellers means more work for consular officials, who now receive a record number of requests for assistance. In 1988, in an attempt to reduce the burden, the British Government made repeated requests to the Association of British Travel Agents to include information leaflets with tickets. These requests were turned down.

There have been well-substantiated reports in the British Press of injured and sick tourists, in many resorts, being taken for treatment not to the nearest or most suitable hospital, but to the one that pays the largest commission to the local representative of the tour company. London's *Sunday Times* identified a number of representatives who had received 'backhanders'. In most cases this is against company policy, and the newspaper reports resulted in staff dismissals; however travel companies appear to be doing little to stamp out what is still believed to be a widespread practice. Journalists from the *Sunday Times*, posing as tour representatives, were easily able to discover the going rates of commission paid by local hospitals, doctors, ambulance services, and even undertakers. In many resorts, representatives also receive commissions from companies that hire mopeds and motorcycles to tourists—that cause many of the injuries in the first place.

Tour companies are in a position to influence, monitor, and enforce hygiene and safety standards in hotels and resorts; the opportunity to do so is currently being ignored, even though many companies are fully aware of the hazards. Instead, travellers face shabby attempts to disclaim legal liability for the consequences, thinly concealed in the fine print of the brochures.

There are occasional praiseworthy exceptions: one of the best immunization centres anywhere in the world is owned and operated by an airline, the British Airways Immunization Centre in London. Another excellent centre is operated by Thomas Cook, and there are a few more such centres. Most of the travel trade has far to go, however, to the extent that those who care about travellers' health still cannot regard them as partners with shared objectives. It is probably a vain hope, but I would wish to find cause to change these views over the next three years. Meanwhile, judge your travel agent by the extent of visible concern for your health and safety.

If the foregoing gives a rather gloomy view of the state of affairs confronting today's traveller—for whom it is tempting, though incorrect, to assume that advances in medical technology at home have been matched by like progress in combating disease abroad—it is because gloom is justified. Close to *half* of all international travellers experience some kind of adverse effect upon their health as a result of their trip. The majority of problems are inevitably minor ones; but Britons now take over 25 million trips abroad every year, Americans take almost 40 million trips, and more than a million Americans now travel by air every day. The scale on which international travel is now taking place lends perspective to the problem (see also p. 12).

Travellers' health has been a neglected corner of medicine for too long, but more attention from doctors and anyone else can only be a partial solution; ultimately travellers have to look after themselves, and this book aims to give them the power to do so. In this book, the problems have been addressed by experts. It is my fervent hope, and has been my sole purpose in initiating and presenting this project, that travellers will take note of its conclusions.

London R.M.D.
April 1989

Note on second edition

On each occasion that the first edition of this book was reprinted, the opportunity was taken to make minor amendments. This new edition has been thoroughly revised and updated, and includes several new chapters. Despite its slight growth in size, however, its cover price has been reduced. A new production method has also been employed that will enable rapid updating of the text in future as necessary, making it easier to ensure that each impression of this book will be up-to-date at the time of printing.

R.M.D.

Acknowledgements

I would like to thank all of the contributors for their role in making this book a reality, and for their continuing patience and support. It gives me much pleasure to welcome 9 new contributors to this edition.

This project could not have been completed without the assistance and goodwill of many. They include the large number of colleagues and friends who generously advised on specific points and provided constructive criticism; numerous colleagues around the world who assisted with Appendix 3; and Dr Michael Barer and Dr John Naponick whose practical help has been invaluable. The original insect illustrations were drawn by Amanda Callaghan, and Robert Dinwiddie assisted me in preparing the typescript for the first edition.

I would also like to thank Professor D.R. Laurence for his helpful advice; Professor D.A. Warrell, Anthony Dawton, Ronald Hyams, and Anna Giles, for their good counsel; the staff of Oxford University Press, for all their hard work; and many erstwhile travelling companions.

It is with deep regret that I have to record here the deaths of Dr David Haddock and Dr Stanley Browne, contributors to this book who did not live to see it published; I owe them a debt of gratitude for their encouragement and participation.

I remain especially grateful to my parents and to my brothers Norman and Andrew, for their forbearance and formidable support both throughout this project and during my travels.

R.M.D.

Contents

Contributors

Dr **James M. Adam,** OBE, OStJ, BSc, MB, ChB, PhD, FRCP
Colonel (Retd) Royal Army Medical Corps
Lately, Consultant Physiologist, National Institute for Medical Research, and Army Medical Services; and Senior Lecturer, Institute of Environmental and Offshore Medicine, Aberdeen University, UK

Andrew N. Agle, MPH
Child Survival Co-ordinator; Assistant Director for Operations, International Health Program Office,
Centers for Disease Control, Atlanta, Georgia, USA
Formerly of the Bureau for Smallpox Eradication

Dr **Christopher L.R. Bartlett** MSc, MB, BS, FFCM
Consultant Epidemiologist, PHLS Communicable Disease Surveillance Centre, Colindale, London
Honorary Lecturer, Department of Environmental and Preventive Medicine, The Medical College of St Bartholomew's Hospital, London

Dr **Michael R. Barer,** BSc, MB, BS, PhD
Lecturer in Microbiology, University of Newcastle upon Tyne, UK

Dr **Alan J. Benson,** MSc, MB, ChB, FRAeS
Senior Medical Officer (Research), Royal Air Force Institute of Aviation Medicine Farnborough, Hampshire, United Kingdom

Professor **Herbert A. Brant,** MD, FRCP(Ed), FRCS(Ed), FRCOG
Professor of Clinical Obstetrics and Gynaecology, University College Hospital, London

Dr **Stanley G. Browne,** CMG, OBE, MD, FRCP, FRCS, DTM
Formerly Secretary, International Leprosy Association
Formerly Consultant Adviser in Leprosy to the Department of Health and Social Security, UK

Dr **Elphis Christopher,** MB, BS, DObstRCOG, DCH
Senior Medical Officer (Family Planning), Haringey Health Authority, London
Doctor-in-charge, Psychosexual Problem Clinic, University College Hospital, London

Dr **Jonathan H. Cossar,** MD, ChB
General Practitioner; Research Associate, Communicable Diseases (Scotland) Unit, Ruchill Hospital, Glasgow

Dr **Christopher Curtis,** BA, PhD
Medical Research Council, London
London School of Hygiene and Tropical Medicine

Andrew J.S. Dawood, BDS
Department of Conservative Dentistry, Guy's Hospital, London

Dr **Richard M. Dawood,** BSc, MB, BS, FRCR, DTM&H, DRCOG
St Mary's Hospital, and the Hospital for Sick Children, London
Dr **John G. Dickinson,** DM(Oxon.), FRCP, DTM&H, RAMC
Formerly Medical Superintendent, Patan Hospital, Kathmandu, Nepal
Professor of Clinical Physiology, Institute of Medicine, Tribhuwan University, Nepal
Consultant Physician, Queen Elizabeth Military Hospital, London
Dr **H. Elizabeth Driver,** BSc, MB, BS, DipTox, MRCPath
Litigation adviser, McKenna & Co, Aldwych, London
Honorary Clinical Lecturer, University College and Middlesex School of Medicine
Consultant, Medical Research Council Toxicology Unit, Carshalton
Dr **Peter Drotman,** MD, MPH, FACPM
Medical Epidemiologist, AIDS Program, Centers for Disease Control, Atlanta, Georgia, USA
Clinical Assistant Professor of Community Health, Emory University School of Medicine, Atlanta, Georgia, USA
Dr **C.J. Ellis,** FRCP, DTM&H
Consultant Physician, Department of Communicable and Tropical Diseases, East Birmingham Hospital, Birmingham, UK
Dr **Richard Fairhurst,** MB, BS
Chief Medical Officer, The Travellers Medical Service, London
Honorary Clinical Assistant, Department of Accident and Emergency Medicine, University College Hospital, London
Mr **Peter Fison,** MA, MB, FRCS, FCOphth
Consultant Ophthalmic Surgeon, Sutton Eye Unit, Honorary Senior Lecturer, St George's Hospital Medical School, London
Hemda Garelick, BSc, MSc
Research Fellow, Department of Medical Microbiology, London
School of Hygiene and Tropical Medicine
Dr **David Haddock,** MD, FRCP, DTM&H
Formerly Senior Lecturer in Tropical Medicine, Liverpool School of Tropical Medicine
Formerly Consultant Physician in Tropical Medicine, Liverpool Area Health Authority
Dr **Anthony Hall,** FACP, FRCP (Ed)
Consultant Physician, Hospital for Tropical Diseases, London
Honorary Senior Lecturer, London School of Hygiene and Tropical Medicine
Squadron Leader **Richard Harding,** PhD, BSc, MB, BS, DAvMed, MRAeS, RAF
Consultant in Aviation Medicine, Royal Air Force Institute of Aviation Medicine, Farnborough, UK
Dr **John L.M. Hawk,** MRCP, FRACP
Consultant Dermatologist, St John's Hospital for Diseases of the Skin, London
Honorary Senior Lecturer in Photobiology, Institute of Dermatology, London

Mr **Basil Helal,** M.ChirOrth, FRCS, FRCSE
Consultant Orthopaedic Surgeon, The London Hospital, the Royal National Orthopaedic Hospital, London, and the Enfield Group of Hospitals

Dr **Peter Janke,** MA, DPhil
Director of Research, Control Risks Information Services Ltd, London

Dr **Arnold F. Kaufmann,** DVM, MS
Chief, Bacterial Zoonoses Activity, Division of Bacterial Diseases, Centers for Disease Control, Atlanta, Georgia, USA

Dr **Gil Lea,** MB, BS
Senior Medical Officer, British Airways, London

Thomas A. Leonard
Senior Public Health Advisor, AIDS Program, Center for Disease Control, Atlanta, Georgia, USA

Roger Lewis, MA, DipEd
Visiting Professor, National Research Council—IEROSS, Salerno, Italy
Former trustee, 'Release', and National Council for the Welfare of Prisoners Abroad

Dr **P.E. Clinton Manson-Bahr,** MD, FRCP, DTM&H
Lately Senior Lecturer in Clinical Tropical Medicine, London School of Hygiene and Tropical Medicine; and Senior Physician Specialist, Colonial Medical Service

Professor **Denis Mitchison,** CMG, FRCP, FRCPath
Lately Director, Department of Bacteriology, Royal Postgraduate Medical School, London; and Honorary Director, Medical Research Council Unit for Laboratory Studies of Tuberculosis

Dr **Martin Mitcheson,** MB, FRCPsych
Clinical Director, Drug Problem Team, Glenside Hospital, Bristol, UK

Dr **John Naponick,** MD, CM, MPH&TM
Medical Adviser, US AID, El Salvador

Group Captain **Anthony N. Nicholson,** OBE, DSc, FRCP(Edin), FRCPath, RAF
Consultant in Aviation Medicine
Royal Air Force Institute of Aviation Medicine Farnborough, Hampshire, United Kingdom

Dr **Peter O. Oliver,** RD, MD, FFOM, DPH
Group Medical Director, Cunard Steam-Ship Co. plc, Southampton, UK
Surgeon Lieutenant Commander, RNR (Retd)

Dr **John H.S. Pettit,** MD(Lond), FRCP
Visiting Lecturer in Dermatology, Liverpool School of Tropical Medicine
Visiting Lecturer in Dermatology, National University of Malaysia School of Medicine, Malaysia

Ellen G. Poage, RN, MPH
Embassy of the United States of America, El Salvador

Dr **Thomas Quan,** PhD, MPH
Research Microbiologist, Plague Branch, Centers for Disease Control, Fort Collins, Colorado, USA

Dr **Daniel Reid,** OBE, MD, FRCP(Glasg), FFCM, FRSH, DPH
Director, Communicable Diseases (Scotland) Unit, Ruchill Hospital, Glasgow
Honorary Clinical Lecturer, Department of Infectious Diseases, University of Glasgow, UK

Surgeon Commander **Simon S. Ridout,** MB, BS, MSc, AFOM, RN
Principal Medical Officer, RNAS Culdrose, Helston, Cornwall, UK

Rod Robinson, BSc, MIBiol, FRES, FRSH
Senior Research Officer, The Medical Entomology Centre, University of Cambridge, UK

Dr **George P. Schmid,** MD
Clinical Research Investigator, Center for Prevention Services, Centers for Disease Control, Atlanta, Georgia, USA

Professor **Gordon Seward,** MDS, FDSRCS, MB, BS, FRCS(Eng), FRCS(Edin), FFARCS
Director, Department of Oral and Maxillo-Facial Surgery, The London Hospital Medical College
Honorary Consultant in Oral and Maxillo-Facial Surgery to The London Hospital

Professor **David A. Warrell,** MA, DM, FRCP
Professor of Tropical Medicine and Infectious Diseases, University of Oxford, UK
Honorary Clinical Director, Alistair Reid Venom Research Unit, Liverpool School of Tropical Medicine, UK

Dr **Tony Waterston,** MB, ChB, MRCP, DCH, DRCOG
Consultant Community Paediatrician, Newcastle General Hospital, UK
Formerly Consultant Paediatrician, Godfrey Huggins School of Medicine, Harare, Zimbabwe

Dr **Peter J. Watkins,** MD, FRCP
Consultant Physician, Diabetic Department, King's College Hospital, London

Louise Weiss
Travel writer, New York

Dr **Philip D. Welsby,** FRCP (Ed)
Consultant Physician in Communicable Diseases, The City Hospital, Edinburgh, UK

Dr **George B. Wyatt,** FRCP, FFCM
Senior Lecturer in Tropical Medicine, Liverpool School of Tropical Medicine
Consultant Physician, Mersey Regional Hospital Board

Professor **Arie J. Zuckerman,** MD, DSc, FRCP, FRCPath
Professor of Microbiology in the University of London
Director of the Department of Medical Microbiology, and of the WHO Collaborating Centre for Reference and Research on Viral Hepatitis, London School of Hygiene and Tropical Medicine

About this book

• This book contains more information than most people need, so would less information suffice? Rabies, for example, is a serious disease spread by animal bites, and that is all most people actually need to know. If you are unlucky enough to be bitten, however, your life may suddenly depend upon detailed information you would not wish to carry in your head: how to treat the bite, what vaccine to insist upon, and what to do. In 1987, a surprise heatwave struck in the Mediterranean: hundreds of people died, including several holidaymakers. Detailed information about extreme conditions suddenly became important to large numbers of people in a way that could not have been predicted. A major purpose of this book is to make that information available, ready for when you might need it.

• This book is mainly about prevention, which is why you should try to become familiar with it before you travel. It will also help you deal with problems that do occur, though diagnosis of infectious diseases may be difficult even when skilled care is available.

• Don't be put off by the names of strange diseases you have not come across before, or by passages that seem a little technical; you do not have to know everything, and the important practical points are summarized at the end of each chapter, but I believe it is wrong to offer advice without presenting the background information on which it is based.

• *If you are travelling only within North America, Northern Europe, and Australia*, most of the infectious and parasitic diseases referred to in the first half of this book will not be a significant hazard. All travellers should be immunized against tetanus (p. 87), however, and the chapters on diarrhoea (p. 21), rabies (p. 193), and insect bites (p. 178) may also be relevant to you. There is much more to the subject of health problems in travellers than infectious diseases, as you will see from the second half of this book.

• If you are travelling elsewhere, especially to *Africa, Asia, or Latin America*, the sections on diseases of poor hygiene and diseases spread by insects will be particularly relevant. An indication of the geographical distribution of specific diseases is summarized in Appendix 3.

- Remember that accidents are the commonest cause of death in travellers, and most of them are preventable (p. 249); malaria is the most serious infectious hazard that travellers are likely to come across, and full details about prevention appear on page 117; hepatitis is common, but is also preventable (p. 56); diarrhoea and sunburn are the two problems that most often interfere with travel plans, and they too are preventable.
- Depending on the nature of your trip, the risk of other diseases is probably small anyway, but simple precautions can often dramatically reduce or eliminate the risks altogether; this book is for travellers whose health abroad is too important to be left to chance.

Warning

Every effort has been made to ensure that the information presented in this book is accurate. Advice from a book has its limitations, however, and cannot always take account of the particular circumstances of each individual traveller. Advice offered here is not intended to be a substitute for skilled medical care, when such care is available.

1

Staying healthy abroad

Introduction: staying healthy abroad

Prevention is the only approach to travellers' health that makes sense.

Dr Richard Dawood *devised this project and is the editor of this book. He has travelled in almost 70 countries around the world—and has survived.*

Staying healthy abroad is not a question of luck, and indeed is too important to be left to chance; the purpose of this book is to give you the information you need to *prevent* health problems when you travel, before they occur.

Why prevention?

Of the diverse battery of hazards and infectious diseases to which travellers are exposed abroad, some are lethal, many are dangerous, and several have long term effects upon health and well-being; some, also, may be passed on to family, friends, and contacts on return home.

The majority of health problems in travellers, however troublesome at the time, tend to be relatively minor in their long term implications—which is just as well, in view of the substantial numbers of travellers who experience illness abroad, and the meagre attention that such problems generally receive.

A problem need not be serious, however, in order to have a devastating effect upon one's enjoyment of a trip. Even an undignified three-day bout of diarrhoea can force an inconvenient change of travel plans, can mar a holiday, or can interrupt the most carefully calculated business deal.

Health problems in travellers are common. The risks are not decreasing, and we are all susceptible. Health care abroad is costly, travel is expensive, our leisure is precious and some business travellers have much at stake; if for no other reason than the most mercenary ones, prevention is a strategy for health that no traveller can afford to neglect.

Prevention: devising a strategy

Don't delegate responsibility for *your* health abroad to others, however busy or preoccupied you may be with more pressing preparations for your trip; take personal charge. Business travellers are consistently at fault in this regard: they are often less well-informed about health than the average holiday-maker, perhaps because they become complacent, and do not update their knowledge.

Intelligence, good health, and a broad knowledge of world affairs do not absolve you from the need to obtain careful advice and up-to-date information about the health risks of travel that apply to your particular circumstances and travel plans, from a reliable source. This book is intended to help you do that.

Remember that not all doctors are equally able to provide the information you need, and many will probably not provide more than a part of it unless you ask specifically about each point that concerns you. 'Most physicians are remarkably ill-informed about health risks abroad and appropriate protective measures', according to a senior American public health official. Doctors are *not* the sole source of reliable health advice: nurses and other staff at immunization centres and student health centres frequently have considerable experience and more time to talk to you. Listen carefully to them.

Specific prevention measures

Immunization offers protection from several important diseases, and should not be neglected (see pp. 473–88). Be aware of the limitations, however: vaccination *regulations* are designed to protect countries rather than travellers, and not all individuals to whom you may turn for advice are able to make this important distinction. A list of regulations and *recommendations* for each country in the world is given in Appendix 1, but these are liable to change from time to time, and so should be confirmed before departure (see Appendix 6).

Immunizations don't work if they have not been given or are allowed to lapse, and their timing requires thought; not all of them offer 100 per cent protection. Nor can all diseases be prevented by immunization: no traveller who has undergone even a full course of immunization should ever be allowed to assume that no further precautions will be necessary.

Prevention (prophylaxis) with drugs is an essential protective measure for travellers to malarious areas (see pp. 122–6)—malaria is the most dangerous infectious disease hazard to which you are likely to fall victim, and is a potential killer that should never be underestimated. Malaria prophylaxis is not infallible, however, and measures to avoid mosquito bites are of the utmost importance.

Drug treatment can sometimes also be used to prevent certain diarrhoeal diseases, but this subject is a controversial one (see p. 34); the desired result is more likely to be achieved by careful precautions with food, water, and hygiene.

The use of drugs to prevent individual diseases is not a precaution upon which travellers can always rely.

General precautions

In most cases, each disease of concern to the traveller does not have its own, unique, specific preventive measure. There is, after all, a limit to the number of possible ways in which diseases can spread. The same approach to food hygiene provides protection against dysentery in Manila as against giardiasis in Leningrad; and insect repellents assiduously applied protect the traveller against dengue fever in the Caribbean as well as against filariasis in West Africa and unpleasant diseases in many other countries around the world.

Although detailed information about a large number of diseases appears in this book, and the list of hazards may at first glance appear frightening, the important point to realize is that prevention is not only feasible in virtually every case, but is usually not difficult and follows logical principles which relate directly to how the disease is spread. The mode of spread holds the key to prevention of each disease, but this book presents further details as well—to add interest, provide perspective, and for the sake of completeness, to give purpose to precautions that might otherwise seem obscure, unreasonable, or not really necessary.

Because some preventive measures are common to many diseases, a degree of overlap between chapters in a book of this type is inevitable; I make no apology, for the repetition serves to emphasize their importance.

Food hygiene A recent survey of visitors to East Africa showed that only 2 per cent of them were taking adequate dietary precautions. Nothing less than a process of education or re-education in the fundamental principles of hygienic food preparation will protect travellers to most countries outside northern Europe, North America, or Australia. Appetite is a poor guide to food safety, and food should never be assumed to be safe unless it is known to have been freshly and thoroughly cooked (heat sterilized)—in the case of meat, until no red colour remains. Let this rule guide your choice from even the most tempting menu. Satisfy yourself that today's lunch is not yesterday's evening meal, re-heated and re-arranged. Intricate delicacies that have received much handling during preparation, and cold platters left out in the open, are highly likely to have been contaminated. Shellfish should be boiled vigorously for at least ten minutes, or preferably avoided altogether. Fruit and vegetables should be freshly cooked or freshly peeled. This means that you won't always be able to eat what you want or what is on offer when you are hungry. These principles are of crucial importance to travellers, and are discussed again at length in the next chapter and elsewhere throughout the book (see also Appendix 5).

Expensive hotels offer no absolute guarantee of safety from diseases of poor hygiene, and it is a grave error to assume that the food they serve is automatically safe. A recent, serious outbreak of amoebic dysentery and amoebic liver abscesses in a group of Italian tourists was traced to raw vegetables served on ice at a luxury hotel in Phuket. A survey in 1988 by the British consumer magazine *Holiday Which?* found appalling examples of poor hygiene standards and contaminated food in hotel kitchens at popular European resorts; it concluded that a hotel's star-rating bore little relation to the standard of food hygiene in its kitchen. If in doubt, have a look at the kitchen yourself, and check for flies; do you see any food left lying around exposed?

> A 1988 survey of ten thousand chefs in Taiwan found that more than two thirds had athlete's foot; most chefs smoked whilst cooking bare-chested over hot stoves. The local food hygiene department, with praiseworthy candour, described 90 per cent of kitchens in Taiwan as 'hotbeds of germs'.

Flies cannot discriminate between the plate of a wealthy tourist and any of their other preferred habitats. African flies carry African diseases. Do not allow luxurious surroundings to lull you into a false sense of security, and be prepared to *insist* on safe food.

Low budget travellers are not necessarily at greater risk of illness than travellers who stick to luxury hotels. Whether you eat in a street market or anywhere else, you can rely on the same principles of food hygiene to protect you. Do you enjoy eating bread fresh from the oven, food that you have selected and watched cooking, and fresh fruit, peeled carefully yourself? (I always travel with a small spoon and a sharp knife for just this purpose). Food like this is easy to find, is cheap, appetizing, and is almost always safe to eat.

Water safety and purification are discussed in detail on p. 73. In most countries outside northern Europe, North America, and Australia, water from the public drinking supply is likely to be just a very dilute solution of sewage, and should be regarded as such unless known to be safe.

Hospitality is a dangerous pitfall for the unwary. It takes diplomacy and determination to refuse food prepared (unhygienically) by someone who has clearly gone to great lengths in order to please an honoured visitor. This can be an extremely delicate problem in rural areas in developing countries. My personal advice is not to relax your standards of food hygiene under any circumstances; plead illness, use any excuse, and if necessary, even permit the food to be put on your plate and toy with it, but *do not eat* food you consider to be suspect. The momentary embarrassment of offending one's host (and genuine offence is rarely taken) has to be balanced against the risk of illness that may ruin your trip or put you out of action for several days.

Insects transmit a multitude of diseases, not all of which can be prevented individually, and their bites can be a painful nuisance. Personal protection from insects is an important measure, and is discussed in depth on p. 178. Travellers to some infected areas can expect to be bitten by malaria-bearing mosquitoes at least once a day. Simple precautions can reduce the risk of picking up an insect-borne disease—including malaria—by a factor of ten;

to put this another way, if you fail to take these precautions you increase your risk tenfold. Yet roughly half of all travellers to malarial areas take no precautions at all against insect bites.

Sex It has been estimated that there are as many as 2 million prostitutes in Thailand alone, most of whom have had 5000 sexual partners by the age of nineteen: and that one third of male visitors to Thailand have sex with prostitutes, around 70 per cent of whom are thought to be infected with sexually transmitted diseases at any one time. Sex abroad has always been a risky business, but the spread of AIDS now means that the risks from casual sex are much more serious. There are now well-documented cases of HIV transmission to travellers following heterosexual contact abroad. Estimates of numbers of AIDS cases in different countries are often of dubious accuracy, and, as Thomas Leonard and Dr Peter Drotman explain elsewhere in this book, are not a reliable basis for decisions about which countries are 'safe'. As far as the risks of AIDS are concerned, where you go is less important than what you do when you get there.

Sun Since people from temperate climates have been taking holidays in sunny places in ever greater numbers, the incidence of skin cancer has risen significantly—to a level that recently prompted the Royal College of Physicians in London to prepare a special report on the problem. Skin cancer is now known to have a clear relationship not just with long-term exposure to ultraviolet light, but also with acute episodes of sunburn.

The environment holds many hazards, including heat, cold, the effects of high altitude, the bites of wild animals, and accidents—the biggest hazard of all. A large part of this book is devoted to such subjects. Remember to travel unobtrusively, be discreet with your possessions, and avoid flourishing large sums of money in poor areas: as the late Dr Alistair Reid, an expert on hazards from wild animals, once pointed out, the greatest animal danger to travellers is man.

Illness abroad

When prevention fails or the unavoidable occurs, coping with illness abroad and, if necessary, getting yourself or someone else home again quickly, demands resourcefulness and judgement. It helps if a doctor can be found, and knowledge of the local language is a valuable asset. Often, though, self-help is everything.

Medical treatment abroad may itself be dangerous. Publicity about AIDS has drawn attention to some of the potential hazards: unscreened blood transfusions, non-sterile needles, syringes, and medical and dental instruments, acupuncture, and surgery may all spread the AIDS virus (see p. 396); hepatitis B however is much more common, and is also spread by these routes. There are numerous examples of travellers undergoing immunization in poor countries and subsequently developing hepatitis. Not all medical attention is undertaken voluntarily. Have a car accident in Turkey, and you will almost certainly have to provide a blood sample for measurement of your blood alcohol level; the sterility of the needle that is used will probably depend on precisely where you are unfortunate enough to have your accident.

Other hazards include drugs and vaccines that may be ineffective or dangerous; in some poor countries, where the likelihood of being bitten by a dog, and the frequency of rabies, are both high, the locally-produced rabies vaccine may be almost as lethal as the disease itself. Medical skills and standards of practice also vary, and in particular, women should always make sure that a chaperone is present when they are examined. In some countries, there may be an over-enthusiasm for surgical treatment, and this is undoubtedly the case in many European ski resorts; other than in a desperate emergency—a situation that is usually self-evident—repatriation is usually possible prior to any surgery.

The most usual problems, however, are inadequacy of emergency services, and scarcity of skilled medical facilities.

Adequate insurance may remove anxiety about expense, and should provide for emergency repatriation if necessary, but it is also important to have enough cash available to cover immediate costs. A general awareness of the main, likely health risks will be invaluable. Specific advice for coping with individual diseases is given in each of the chapters on the main diseases.

In my view, *all travellers to remote areas with limited medical facilities should also have a knowledge of basic first aid*—both for their own benefit, and the benefit of others—and should attend a course of instruction if necessary.

Coming home

The value of a post-tropical check-up is discussed in Appendix 4. All travellers should realize, however, that it is possible for symptoms of infectious diseases—especially malaria—not to appear until several weeks, or even longer, after return home. When symptoms do appear, their significance may not be recognized immediately. If illness does develop after a trip, make sure that your doctor knows that you have been away.

Attitude

A positive attitude to health, and perception of one's health as a vital element in the success of a trip—rather than as an inconvenient obstacle to enjoyment—are powerful weapons indeed for any traveller.

And finally . . .

The message of this book is not that you should worry about each and every disease that is mentioned here, every time and wherever you travel; or, worse still, that you would be better off staying at home. It is simply this: by informing yourself of the nature of the hazards that travellers face and how these hazards can be overcome, you will learn healthy travel habits that will protect you wherever you go. You could, of course, learn them the hard way, as I have had to do on many of my own travels, in which case you need read no further . . .

The size of the problem

The unprecedented scale and speed of contemporary, international travel means that ever-increasing numbers of travellers are exposed to unfamiliar infections and other hazards. An appreciation of the size and range of the problems can alert the unwary traveller, and help minimize the risks from preventable illnesses associated with travel.

Dr Daniel Reid *is the Director of the Communicable Diseases (Scotland) Unit (CDSU)* at Ruchill Hospital, Glasgow.
Dr Jonathan H. Cossar *is a general practitioner and research associate at the CDSU. Since 1973, epidemiological surveillance has been conducted at the CDSU on illnesses affecting returning travellers. This has helped to define the perspective of illnesses associated with travel, to evaluate the effectiveness of pre-travel health advice, and to develop a computerized database designed to give advice on suitable antimalarial drugs and appropriate immunizations for travellers.*

Undoubtedly most illnesses encountered by travellers are not recorded, and this is especially the case with less serious (though still troublesome) afflictions such as gastrointestinal problems. Statistics from national and international bodies such as the World Health Organization and the World Tourism Organization provide a valuable background to the problem, and increasing numbers of studies are being carried out in many countries to determine the frequency and types of illness encountered by travellers, and to place these in perspective. Although much of the data is incomplete, and depends for its quality on such factors as the enthusiasm of the researcher, meaningful conclusions are still possible, and attack rates can be calculated for different places and different categories of traveller. Over the years, trends can be observed and some tentative conclusions reached.

Historical background

Awareness of the dangers from infection imported by travellers is not new. It was in response to outbreaks of plague during the Middle Ages following the arrival of ships from the east, that

Venice and Rhodes introduced the first regulations. On arrival, ships were kept at a distance and travellers detained in isolation for 40 days (*quaranta giorni*) before they were allowed to proceed to their final destination. First imposed by the Venetian Republic in 1377, this was the origin of the concept of quarantine, with other cities and countries following its example until some form of sanitary regulation became general in many countries during the next five centuries.

More recent records are also of interest. A study by Dr J. Cossar of the fate of 1427 Scottish Presbyterian missionaries who worked abroad between 1873 and 1929, revealed that 25 per cent had to return prematurely due to their own or their family's ill health, and a further 11 per cent died in service. In addition it was noted that the numbers adversely affected were greater for those appointed during the earlier years, when less was known about tropical diseases, and that the problems were more severe for those appointed to the most climatically arduous areas, such as West Africa. Missionaries with a medical background experienced fewer health problems, presumably as a result of their knowledge of disease and its prevention. The effects of local climate and environment on health, and knowledge about disease prevention, remain relevant to the contemporary traveller.

Volume of international travel

The number of travellers crossing international boundaries has increased tremendously in recent years. In 1949, 26 million international tourists were recorded (Table 1.1) whereas by 1986 this had risen to 341 million, with 30 per cent of these travelling to the Mediterranean area. If domestic tourists are included, it has been estimated by the World Tourism Organization that the world total of arrivals at all destinations is now approximately 1000 million. Between 1949 and 1986, there has been a thirteen-fold increase in the number of international arrivals to the United Kingdom, a thirty-one-fold increase in numbers of scheduled air passengers, and a fifteen-fold increase in United Kingdom residents travelling abroad, the proportion of those travelling beyond Europe has increased twenty-three-fold. International tourist arrivals in North America have also increased spectacularly, with 6 180 000 in 1950, and more than 43 million in 1987.

Groups contributing to the growth in travel include tourists,

Table 1.1 Growth in international travel

	1949 (millions)	1960 (millions)	1970 (millions)	1986 (millions)
Total numbers of international tourists	26	72	201	341
Total numbers of air travellers throughout the world	31	106	386	955
Total visits abroad by United Kingdom residents	1.7	6	11.8	25.1
	(%)	(%)	(%)	(%)
Visits by United Kingdom residents (European destinations: rest of world)	92:8	94:6	89:11	88:12
Mode of travel used by United Kingdom residents (sea: air)	—	60:40	43:57	37:63
Proportion of package holiday visits abroad by United Kingdom residents	—	30	30	54

business travellers, technical experts, pilgrims, migrant workers, refugees, immigrants, military personnel, political representatives, sporting participants and spectators, and the travel support services. Of particular significance has been the growth of the 'package tour'.

Speed of international travel

In former times, when sea voyages were the customary method of travelling long distances, the period spent at sea was nearly always longer than the incubation period of the most likely infections. This provided an effective safeguard for the inhabitants of the countries to which infected travellers were bound, and also made it easier to appreciate the significance of any symptoms that appeared during the voyage.

Today, this mode of travel has become relatively much less frequent (Table 1.1). Moreover, with modern air transport the infected patient may well arrive home some days before the appearance of clinical signs of disease. Between 1948 and the present time, the fastest passenger aircraft cruising speed has risen from 340 miles per hour to 1356 miles per hour (in Concorde).

Table 1.2 Some infections imported by travellers

Acquired Immune Deficiency Syndrome	Legionnaires' disease
Amoebiasis	Leishmaniasis
Brucellosis	Leptospirosis
Campylobacter infection	Malaria
Cholera	Poliomyelitis
Cytomegalovirus infection	Rabies
Diphtheria	Salmonellosis
Dysentery	Schistosomiasis
Giardiasis	Sexually transmitted diseases
Helminthic infection (parasitic worms)	Shigellosis
Hepatitis A and B	Tuberculosis
Lassa fever	Typhoid/Paratyphoid

Spectrum of disease associated with travel

Some illnesses may be induced by travel itself, such as motion sickness and upsets to the circadian rhythms; unaccustomed exercise or the effects of altitude may exacerbate pre-existing cardiovascular or respiratory problems. Exposure to unfamiliar infectious agents and the stress of altered climate and environment may also cause problems for the unwary traveller which may be compounded by the differing medical practices encountered overseas.

The spectrum of serious illness acquired abroad is wide. Table 1.2 shows some examples of diseases that have been acquired abroad and imported into the United Kingdom during the past decade.

Extent of illness associated with travel

Since 1973, following an outbreak of legionnaires' disease affecting a group of package holidaymakers returning from Benidorm to Glasgow, several multi-disciplinary collaborative studies of imported illnesses associated with travel have been conducted at the CDSU.

From a total of 14 227 travellers, 37 per cent gave a history of illness. The attack rates ranged from a low of 19 per cent amongst summer visitors to Scotland in 1980 and 20 per cent amongst winter package holidaymakers, to 75 per cent amongst summer package holidaymakers to Romania in 1981 and 78 per cent

Table 1.3 Age of travellers and reports of illness

Age group (years)	Total	Unwell
0–9	550	33%
10–19	1974	41%
20–29	3033	48%
30–39	2028	38%
40–49	2297	32%
50–59	2381	28%
60+	1239	20%
not known	725	32%
Total	14227	37%

amongst 375 tourists from Spain who wrote or telephoned the CDSU following media publicity on legionnaires' disease and travel in 1977.

Age distribution

An analysis of travellers by age group and illness (Table 1.3), shows that the highest attack rates were recorded in the under 40 year age groups. Thereafter attack rates show a progressive diminution with increasing age.

Type of illness

Gastro-intestinal problems, predominantly diarrhoea and vomiting, are the major cause of illness among travellers from abroad and results from our studies are shown in Fig. 1.1.

These results are very similar to those recorded by other researchers. Steffen and his colleagues noted a 30 per cent attack rate for diarrhoeal illness among 16 568 randomly selected Swiss travellers. The highest attack rates were 37 per cent in the 20–29 year age group. Moreover, it has been estimated by Cvjetanovic that in Mediterranean countries of the European Region of the World Health Organization, the yearly incidence of diarrhoea is 12 million in a population of 242 million. Tourists coming to the Mediterranean areas from the rest of Europe run a risk of developing diarrhoea 20 times greater than in their home countries.

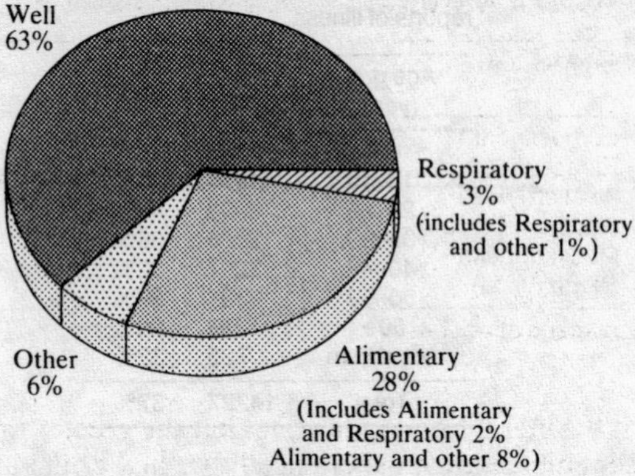

Fig. 1.1 Reports of illness in holidaymakers (number in survey = 14 227; 1973–85).

Risk relative to destination

Different areas of the world have different hazards for travellers and it is prudent to be familiar with the worldwide distribution of the major tropical diseases; elsewhere in this book the risk areas for many diseases are described. The World Health Organization and other agencies also provide assistance in publishing maps showing the world prevalence of malaria, the yellow fever endemic zones, and other more specialized data maps.

In general, the risk from communicable diseases to the traveller in northern Europe, North America, Australia, and New Zealand does not differ greatly from that in the United Kingdom. However, those who travel to more remote destinations may visit, stop over in, or may be unexpectedly diverted to, places with a higher risk of infection. In southern Europe, especially popular with tourists, there is an increased danger of gastro-intestinal infection, including typhoid and paratyphoid fevers, and also potential for the spread of hepatitis A.

In many places where infectious diseases are frequent, and where antibiotics and other drugs are sometimes used excessively or are freely available without prescription, drug-resistant strains of bacteria and parasites are common, so that infections acquired in these areas can be more difficult to treat.

Table 1.4 Area visited, season, and reports of illness

Area visited	Summer attack rate	Winter attack rate
Europe (north)	19%	20%
Europe (east)	57%	12%
Mediterranean (southern Europe)	34%	19%
Mediterranean (North Africa)	77%	32%
Average attack rates	37%	20%

There is a general trend indicating that the greater the cultural and the climatic contrast experienced, the higher the attack rate (Table 1.4). This remains generally true both in summer and in winter. Swiss and Finnish studies corroborate the higher attack rates among those travelling to the southern Mediterranean coastal areas—57 per cent in the Swiss reports and 54 per cent in the Finnish.

Other risk factors

Relaxed attitudes and reduced inhibitions are natural elements of holiday enjoyment. The traveller may thus accept risks that would be avoided in everyday life, such as experimentation with unfamiliar food and drink or participation in a hazardous sporting pursuit. Alcohol may potentiate such behaviour, contribute to road traffic accidents, lead to neglect of precautions against mosquito bites or of regular antimalarial prophylaxis, and to acceptance of risk of exposure to sexually transmitted diseases. Narcotic drug abuse can have similar influences in addition to the risk of hepatitis B from intravenous drug injections. Tobacco smokers also seem to be at greater risk—37 per cent of 2784 smokers in the Glasgow studies were unwell compared with 32 per cent of 7294 non-smokers.

An analysis of the various studies points to the particular vulnerability of certain kinds of traveller: the ‘package holidaymaker’, the inexperienced traveller, those visiting southern Mediterranean countries and especially North Africa, those aged between 20 and 29 years, and those who smoke.

Economic aspects

From information supplied by 3049 travellers from the United Kingdom who became unwell whilst abroad, 1 per cent required hospital admission on their return and 14 per cent consulted a doctor. The cost per travel-associated hospital admission in the UK in 1985 was given as approximately £550 (US$1000). If the survey figures for Scottish travellers mentioned earlier are used as a basis for calculating the cost of admission to hospital for all ill travellers, it is estimated that over £11 million was spent in 1986 in the United Kingdom (US$20 million). This amount does not take into account the considerable additional costs involved with primary care consultations, laboratory investigations, specialist consultations, drug prescriptions, loss of working days and loss of vacation time due to such illness, and of course the considerable expense incurred by travellers and their insurance companies from medical treatment obtained abroad.

Summary of information for travellers

The growth of travel and travel-related illness means that this subject will increasingly demand attention from the medical profession, the travel trade, and travellers themselves.

- Younger travellers are at greater risk from illness.
- The greater the climatic and the cultural contrast between the traveller's country of origin and the destination country, the higher the risk of illness.
- By far the commonest affliction that the traveller is likely to experience is a bout of self-limiting, gastro-intestinal upset—travellers' diarrhoea.
- Increased knowledge and awareness of the hazards and their prevention are needed to reduce the high rate of illness in travellers, and its large cost.

2

Diseases spread mainly by food, drink, and poor hygiene

Diarrhoea and intestinal infections

'Travel broadens the mind and loosens the bowels.' Besides being a favourite comment of specialists in diarrhoeal diseases, this statement represents the unfortunate truth for substantial numbers of travellers all over the world.

Dr Michael Barer *worked and studied at the London School of Hygiene and Tropical Medicine and is a medical microbiologist at Newcastle University, where he conducts research into diarrhoeal disease.*

If you already have diarrhoea and want help, turn to *What to do about diarrhoea* on p. 31.
If you want quick, simple advice on how to avoid getting diarrhoea in the first place, turn to *Prevention* on p. 38.
If you want to understand why these measures may or may not work, read on!

No fewer than two fifths of all international travellers suffer from diarrhoea abroad. Travellers' diarrhoea is not merely a trivial inconvenience: some 30 per cent of sufferers are confined to bed, and a further 40 per cent are forced to change their itinerary.

Diarrhoea: not just a problem for travellers

As far as most healthy western travellers are concerned, a diarrhoeal episode is uncomfortable, at worst debilitating, and may last for up to a few weeks. But for malnourished children in the developing world, diarrhoeal illnesses are life-threatening: at a rough estimate, such illnesses kill at least five million children around the world each year; the true figure may be much higher than this.

The principal cause of death is severe dehydration, and as I shall explain, administration of fluids is now the mainstay of treatment. In addition to appalling mortality rates, diarrhoeal diseases contribute substantially to chronic ill health, increased susceptibility to other diseases, and poor economic performance in countries where they are uncontrolled. Addressing such problems is, not surprisingly, one of the World Health Organization's most pressing concerns.

How diarrhoeal diseases are spread: the cornerstone of prevention

Most cases of travellers' diarrhoea are caused by micro-organisms that either damage the gut or interfere with the normal mechanisms that control water flow across the gut wall. Many different micro-organisms including bacteria, viruses, and protozoa may be responsible. Fortunately, at least for the purposes of this chapter, all the agents of major concern to adult travellers are transmitted in the same manner: you must actually swallow contaminated material to contract the disease.

This has two important practical consequences. First, you should identify and take pains to avoid food, drink, or anything else you might swallow that has a high risk of being contaminated. Second, you should ensure that you do not touch the food you eat, or (if you must use your fingers) that your hands are scrupulously clean and as dry as possible (if necessary, use clean paper tissues or napkins to handle food while eating); plates and cutlery should also be clean and dry.

If your appetite is at its strongest when confronted with mysterious, aromatic, alien delicacies, then you have a simple choice: either to accept the risks involved in satisfying your gastronomic curiosity, or to establish whether or not the food is safe, and to choose something else if it isn't.

Food-poisoning is by no means uncommon, even in developed countries such as the UK. In most outbreaks, investigation usually reveals that a breakdown in recommended food preparation or storage practices is responsible.

Thus, even in a country where organisms that cause diarrhoea are not common in the environment and virtually never contaminate the water supply, the diseases they cause remain inadequately controlled despite widely disseminated knowledge of hygienic catering practices.

Unfortunately, the micro-organisms responsible for diarrhoeal disease do not mark their presence in the food they contaminate by making it look or smell rotten. Instead, the reverse may occasionally be true, since organisms that cause food spoilage can prevent the growth of diarrhoea-causing organisms. In practice, well-cooked food, that is to say food whose temperature has exceeded the boiling point of water for at least fifteen minutes, is nearly always safe.

If not eaten straight away, cooked food should be protected from possible sources of contamination, and refrigerated immediately. Small numbers of surviving bacteria may grow at phenomenal rates if left in a slowly cooling medium (i.e. recently cooked food). In addition, room temperature in tropical countries is much closer to that required for optimal bacterial growth, so safe storage times without refrigeration are much shorter.

Bacteria of the type relevant to this discussion may divide once every twenty minutes: a single bacterial cell weighing one millionth of a gram could (under optimum conditions) divide enough times in twenty-four hours for its offspring to weigh around four million kilograms—or about the weight of a small ship. Clearly bacterial growth of this magnitude could never occur, but these figures serve to illustrate that even minimally contaminated food that has been stored at tropical room temperatures for brief periods cannot be considered safe.

Specific food hazards

So far we have seen that well-cooked food eaten immediately after preparation is generally safe, and that appearance is not a good guide to the likelihood of contamination. In addition, some foods are more risky than others, and I shall attempt to give some guidance in this area.

Shellfish have been the source of many outbreaks of food-borne disease. In many instances this is a consequence of their mode of feeding, which involves filtration of large volumes of sea water, predisposing them to the accumulation of micro-organisms. This is a problem only where sea water is contaminated, but in many parts of the world it is usual for untreated human excreta to be deposited close to areas where shellfish are collected.

Vegetables, salads, and fruit The use of human faeces as fertilizer (nightsoil)—a practice widespread in the tropics—makes salads and uncooked fresh vegetables risky unless they have been carefully washed with clean water. Even where nightsoil is not used, salads and fresh fruit are still quite common sources of infection because they frequently become contaminated during transit, storage, or preparation.

In contrast, travellers to remoter areas who peel fruit themselves without contaminating the contents and eat the fruit immediately are at little risk of infection from this source. One almost suspects that the Almighty created bananas especially for this purpose.

Rice Freshly cooked rice is also generally safe. However, it is common practice in many restaurants and communities for the leftovers to be reheated at the next meal. *Bacillus cereus*, a bacterium that often contaminates rice even in the UK, is able to survive the initial cooking process by producing heat-resistant spores. Left to their own devices in the interval between meals, these spores germinate and the subsequent bacterial growth converts the surrounding rice into a deadly emetic cocktail, lying in wait for the unwary consumer. It is now known that, by this stage, the emetic toxin is so robust that even pressure-cooking will not destroy it.

Drinks Water purification is dealt with in detail in a subsequent chapter (pp. 73–80). However, as I have already suggested in relation to salads, water contamination is not a matter that can be ignored by those who do not drink water: ice, ices, and anything else prepared locally from suspect water supplies should be considered contaminated, since freezing will kill only a fraction of any organisms present. Remember also that even the most stylish breaststrokers swallow small quantities of water while swimming.

Milk Unpasteurized milk (and ice-cream or yoghurt made from it) should always be avoided. Diarrhoeal diseases are rarely contracted this way, but other diseases such as brucellosis and tuberculosis are a real problem in some regions. Listeriosis is a disease that has received much recent publicity and has been linked to certain dairy products; some further details are given on p. 422, but there is no particular increased risk in relation to travel.

Eggs The importance of eggs as a possible source of salmonella infections has received extensive coverage in the UK media but is a problem in many countries where intensive farming methods are used, including the USA. Salmonella infections predominate in growing chickens and are much less frequent in the egg-laying population. Where individual eggs have been tested the infection rate is no greater than 1 in 1000 eggs. There is no evidence to suggest that travellers are at greater risk of acquiring egg-associated salmonellosis at present. In fact it is possible that less intensive egg production methods that do not involve large flocks and battery conditions are less likely to produce contaminated eggs. The greatest risk is related to bulk catering where large numbers of pooled eggs are used. Uncooked or lightly cooked eggs, and foods made with them, such as mayonnaise, sauces, mousses, milk shakes, ice cream, and sandwiches, are frequently incriminated. Thorough cooking kills the organisms.

Alcohol Due caution should also be taken with alcoholic drinks, which should not be assumed to be self-sterilizing. Furthermore, excessive alcohol intake may itself cause diarrhoea by an irritant action. Alcohol within a drink has a dehydrating effect, and reduces the amount of water actually available for rehydration. For these reasons, alcoholic drinks are not recommended as a source of water intake in hot countries.

Flies

Flies live with equal happiness on dung and on food. If you allow flies to walk on your food and then you eat it, for all practical purposes you are eating excrement. Flies may therefore act as important vectors in the 'faecal-oral' transmission of infection.

Hands

Micro-organisms sticking to your hands easily contaminate food if you are careless. A conscious effort not to bring your hands up to your mouth unless they are clean is therefore worthwhile. Proper hand drying after washing is an equally important part of the cleansing process.

Other modes of transmission

Several diarrhoea-causing organisms can probably be transmitted directly from person to person or from animals. However, in most cases this will still involve swallowing contaminated material, so the precautions outlined above will remain effective. Transmission via fine droplets produced by coughing or sneezing is a possible route for the viral agents of diarrhoea. Rotaviruses, the most important of these, remain largely uncontrolled worldwide and are notorious for evading even the most careful cross-infection precautions in modern hospitals.

Organisms responsible for travellers' diarrhoea

Identifying and understanding the organisms that cause diarrhoea are very important steps in developing rational treatments and control measures. The brief details given here are intended to help the reader understand the various patterns of infections and choose the right treatment. The organisms concerned differ greatly in their geographic distribution, as well as in the frequency and severity of the diseases they cause. The principal agents are listed in Fig. 2.1 and prominent causes of travellers' diarrhoea are described below. Details of treatment are given on p. 34.

Enterotoxigenic *Escherichia coli* (*E. coli*)

E. coli bacteria multiply in the small intestine and make toxins, which are responsible for most, if not all of the symptoms. They are responsible for up to 40 per cent of cases of travellers' diarrhoea.

The toxins interact with cells called enterocytes situated in the inner surface of the alimentary tract ('gut') and cause an uncontrolled activation of the mechanisms by which water is normally moved across the gut wall. The result is a dramatic net flow of salt and water *into* the gut.

The large intestine normally absorbs one or two litres of water passing down from the small intestine daily. It has a reserve absorbing capacity of a further two to three litres which must be exceeded before diarrhoea appears. Given that in severe cases several litres of fluids may be lost in the stools, the level of disturbance is impressive, to say the least.

Enterotoxigenic *E. coli* diarrhoea is self-limiting and rarely lasts more than 48 hours.

Shigella

Organisms of the *Shigella* group, along with some strains of *E. coli* that don't produce the toxins mentioned above, are responsible for bacillary dysentery. Shigella organisms are responsible for up to 15 per cent of travellers' diarrhoea.

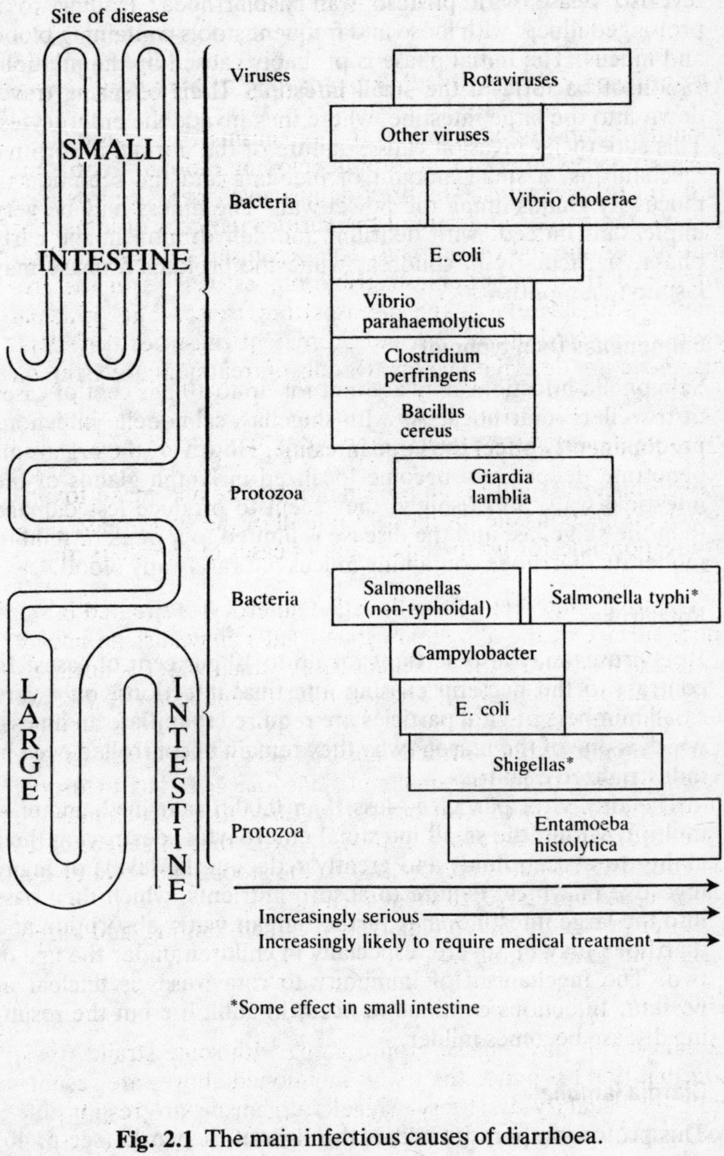

Fig. 2.1 The main infectious causes of diarrhoea.

The disease occurs characteristically in two phases: an initial feverish phase with profuse watery diarrhoea, leading to a prolonged illness with loose and frequent stools containing blood and mucus. The initial phase is probably caused by the multiplication of bacteria in the small intestine. Their offspring travel down into the large intestine, where they invade the enterocytes. This superficial invasion causes failure of the normal absorptive mechanisms, a small amount of bleeding and the secretion of mucus by glands lining the bowel wall. The illness may be very unpleasant indeed, with delirium and dehydration in the early phase, particularly in children, while the prolonged phase may last up to a month.

Salmonellas (non-typhoid)

Salmonella infections may account for up to 10 per cent of cases of travellers' diarrhoea. As with shigellas, salmonella infections predominantly affect the large intestine. However, the organisms penetrate deeper and become localized in lymph glands of the intestinal wall. Surprisingly, they seem to produce less damage than the shigellas, and the disease is limited to a week of mild to moderate diarrhoea containing mucus but rarely any blood.

Rotaviruses

Rotaviruses may also account for up to 10 per cent of cases. In contrast to the bacteria causing intestinal infections, only very small numbers of viral particles are required to initiate an illness, which is one of the reasons why they remain uncontrolled even in industrialized countries.

The tiny viral particles—less than 0.0001 mm in diameter—multiply within the small intestinal enterocytes, destroying their ability to absorb fluids and greatly reducing the levels of many digestive enzymes. Failure to absorb nutrients, which then pass into the large intestine, may further impair water absorption and diarrhoea may be severe, especially in children under the age of two. The mechanism of immunity to rotaviruses is unclear at present. Infections continue to occur in adult life but the resulting disease becomes milder.

Giardia lamblia

This protozoon parasite occurs throughout the world (see p. 46) and is able to stick firmly to the wall of the small intestine. It probably accounts for less than 3 per cent of cases of travellers' diarrhoea, though it accounts for a much larger proportion of cases of diarrhoea persisting after return home.

In prolonged infections it destroys the inward projections of the gut (called villi), which are responsible for absorbing digested food. If untreated, this may lead to a state of malnutrition characterized by a number of vitamin deficiencies.

The early phase of the disease varies from a self-limiting mild condition to an extremely unpleasant profuse watery diarrhoea succeeded by a chronic phase with bulky, extremely foul-smelling, pale grey stools that indicate failure to absorb digested food. The second phase may persist at various levels of severity for months or even years.

Entamoeba histolytica

E. histolytica is another protozoon parasite, related to free-living amoebae so commonly studied in school biology classes. Like *Giardia* it is a relatively uncommon cause of travellers' diarrhoea, accounting for less than 3 per cent of cases. *E. histolytica* occurs in most tropical countries and causes amoebic dysentery (see p. 45), a disease of the large intestine that superficially resembles the 'bacillary dysentery' mentioned above.

The active disease-producing stage of this organism's life-cycle, the 'trophozoites', invade the intestinal wall, causing bleeding and mucus production. Tissue destruction may be extensive and leads to the formation of deep ulcers. Trophozoites may spread to the liver (in about one in five cases) and occasionally (in about one in 1000 cases) produce abscesses there. Over the course of several months or even years, further spread can occur to other parts of the body, notably the lungs and the brain, with fatal consequences.

From the sufferer's point of view, this diarrhoea may be distinguished from that of bacillary dysentery by its gradual onset, absence of fever and delirium, and considerable pain associated with defecation. However, absence of these features does not exclude the possibility of amoebic infection and in view of the rare and serious consequences anybody with a prolonged change in bowel habit after a visit to a tropical country should have themselves carefully examined. Both of these parasites are discussed further in the next chapter.

Unidentified causes

In surveys attempting to establish the cause of diarrhoeal illness in almost any group of individuals, no clearly defined infecting agent may be found in up to 40 per cent of cases. It seems likely that there are several as yet unidentified causative organisms involved.

Over the last fifteen years, no fewer than four 'new' major infectious causes of diarrhoeal disease have been brought to light (rotavirus, *Campylobacter*, *Clostridium difficile*, and *Cryptosporidium*) and we have no reason to suspect that the next fifteen years will not bring similar discoveries.

Enteropathogens

Several other agents of diarrhoeal disease (enteropathogens) are known to be important, although their exact significance to travellers is not established. They are all considered causes of 'food-poisoning', a rather loose term that denotes any acute illness attributable to recent consumption of food. Information regarding these is summarized in Table 2.1. They can to a certain extent be differentiated by the sufferer on the basis of the interval between eating contaminated food and the onset of the symptoms, and the nature of the symptoms themselves.

Two very important enteropathogens are those which cause typhoid and cholera.

Typhoid

The bacterium responsible for typhoid is called *Salmonella typhi*, and shows a pattern of invasion similar to that seen with the other salmonellas. However, after localizing in the lymph glands of the large intestine and terminal small intestine, there is further spread into the blood along with ulcer formation in the bowel wall. Symptoms take around seven days to appear after exposure (but may range from three to sixty days) and include fever, headache, abdominal pain, constipation, and diarrhoea. Typhoid is a serious illness and a fatal outcome is common without treatment.

Cholera

This cataclysmically dehydrating disease is caused by a bacterium called *Vibrio cholerae*. A toxin almost identical in structure and action to one of the *E. coli* toxins, combined with a number of other less well-defined toxic products, precipitates dramatic fluid

Table 2.1 Types of bacterial food-poisoning

Causal agent	Incubation period	Symptoms	Comments
Salmonellas (non-typhoid)	6–72 hrs (usually 12–36 hrs)	diarrhoea, abdominal pain, vomiting, and fever	see text
Clostridium perfringens	8–22 hrs (usually 12–18 hrs)	diarrhoea, abdominal pain (vomiting is rare)	toxin formed in small intestine
Staphylococcus aureus	1–7 hrs (usually 2–4 hrs)	nausea, vomiting, abdominal pain, prostration, dehydration, low temperature, sometimes diarrhoea	preformed toxin in the food (hence rapid onset)
Campylobacter	1–11 days (usually 2–5 days)	abdominal pain, diarrhoea occasionally with blood, malaise (vomiting is uncommon)	similar to shigellosis; probably very common
Bacillus cereus	1–5 hrs or	predominantly vomiting	preformed toxin
	8–16 hrs	predominantly diarrhoea	toxin made in small intestine
Vibrio parahaemolyticus	2–48 hrs (usually 12–24 hrs)	abdominal pain diarrhoea, sometimes nausea, vomiting, fever, and headaches	toxins made in small intestine; classically caught from uncooked seafood

loss, commonly exceeding half a litre per hour in the early stages (in adults). Given that the total water content of an adult is about 45 litres and that loss of more than 10 per cent of this is usually fatal, a simple calculation reveals that cholera may be fatal as early as nine hours after the onset of symptoms unless rehydration is approached vigorously.

What to do about diarrhoea

Practical help for diarrhoea starts with a description of stool quality.

A simple approach based on such descriptions is presented in Fig. 2.2. The various courses of action—oral rehydration, seek-

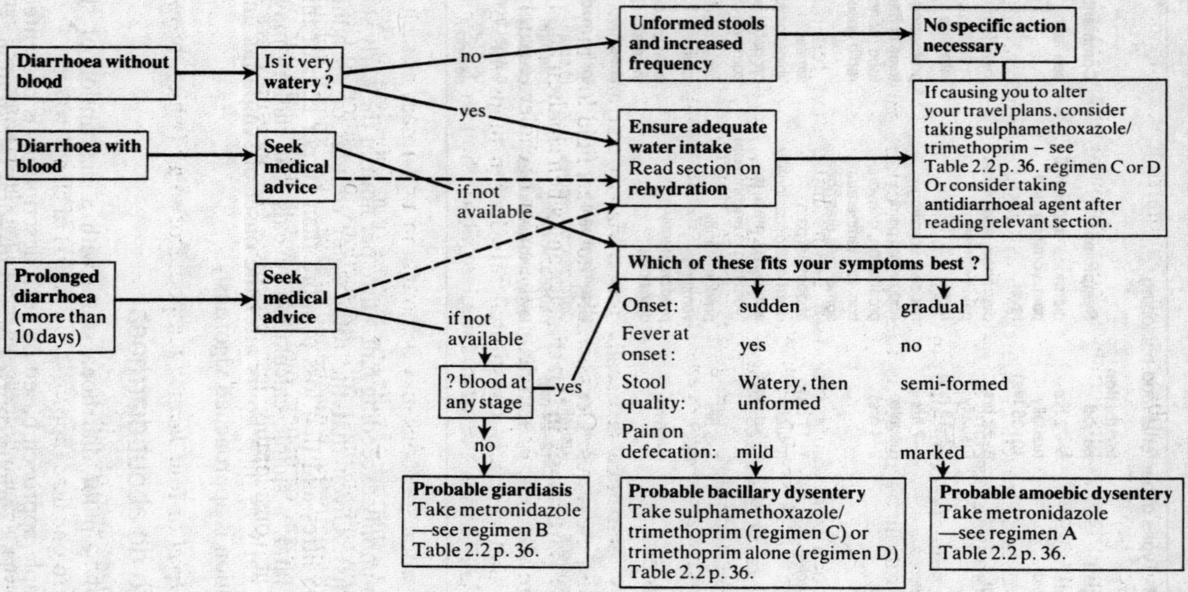

Notes: 1. There are many non-infectious causes of diarrhoea and blood in the faeces (e.g. anxiety and haemorrhoids respectively). These make medical attention advisable wherever these symptoms are prolonged or recurrent.
2. Typhoid does not usually cause severe diarrhoea; fever is always present — see p. 30.

Fig. 2.2 What to do about diarrhoea.

ing medical advice, antibiotics, and antidiarrhoeal medicines—are detailed below.

Four important points should be borne in mind when considering appropriate action;

- Most cases of travellers' diarrhoea will resolve within 48 to 72 hours without any specific treatment.
- Severe illness is commoner in children.
- Rehydration by mouth is the most important part of treatment.
- Diarrhoea containing blood or lasting more than ten days should always be taken seriously.

In the rare instances where travellers' diarrhoea is severe enough to be life-threatening, it is *adequate fluid intake, not antibiotics, or antidiarrhoeal agents*, that proves life-saving.

Rehydration

Travellers' diarrhoea is usually too trivial to warrant specific rehydration measures. Occasionally, however, fluid loss may be disastrous, particularly in hot climates and when children and the elderly are affected. Research into the action of cholera toxin has revealed that carefully constituted rehydration fluids not only replace fluid losses but also stimulate absorption in the small intestine.

Rehydration solutions may be bought in a pharmacy as sachets containing a mixture of salts and glucose (e.g. Dioralyte or WHO rehydration salt sachets) with instructions for adding to clean* water. Alternatively, with the aid of a vessel of known volume, teaspoon, sugar or honey, and salt you can make up your own solution at considerably less expense. The measures are as follows:

- Eight *level* or four *heaped* teaspoons of sugar (white, brown, or honey)
- plus $\frac{1}{2}$ teaspoon of salt
- added to one litre (approx 1 US quart) of clean* water.

* Clean water is obviously desirable, but rehydration with suspect water is better than no rehydration at all.

It has recently been discovered that rehydration becomes even more efficient if certain other substances are added to the solution, such as glycine and citrate. Sachets containing these additives are becoming commercially available, and are recommended if they can be obtained. A similar effect can be achieved by *substituting* 30–40 grams (10–15 teaspoons) per litre of powdered rice for the sugar (above). (The powder should be boiled in a small volume of water first.)

Oral rehydration should be initiated early rather than late. If you are treating yourself as the illness proceeds, your judgement may be impaired and you may become too weak to take appropriate action.

For healthy adults with mild to moderate attacks, an adequate intake of most non-alcoholic drinks will normally suffice. Rehydration fluids should *always* be prepared for infants.

When ministering to others, look for any evidence of significant dehydration such as dry tongue, dark yellow urine in small quantities, or no urine, or loss of skin elasticity (failure of abdominal skin to spring back after pinching and lifting). If such evidence is found, particularly in children, the sufferer should be badgered into drinking as much as possible until he or she starts to urinate normally. A sensible regime is to visit every five to ten minutes, day and night, insisting on some intake at each visit.

These measures are not intended to replace appropriate medical care. Anyone who is showing signs of dehydration would be well advised to seek medical attention. As soon as someone you are caring for ceases to be able to drink then *this is a medical emergency*, and they should receive attention as soon as possible since intravenous rehydration will be needed (see also pp. 430–2 and 492–3).

Antibiotics

Most forms of diarrhoeal disease will resolve without the use of antibiotics. Antibiotics are completely useless when the cause is a virus, are usually irrelevant with non-typhoid salmonellas (they may actually prolong carriage of the organism after the illness is over) and constitute quite a significant cause of diarrhoea in their own right.

Just as the world's grasslands and forests have their own flora, so too does the human large intestine. Like indiscriminate weedkillers, antibiotics often kill off bacteria normally resident in our gut (there are about one hundred million million of them) with which we have an important natural relationship. Their absence may lead to transient diarrhoea until the normal ecology is restored, or more seriously their elimination may pave the way for 'unfriendly' organisms to invade.

With these warnings in mind, there are a number of fairly clear circumstances where antibiotics are needed in gut infections. Any antibiotic treatment should preferably be prescribed by a doctor. However, in an emergency the following regimes may be considered after consultation with Table 2.2 (p. 36):

Metronidazole (Flagyl) is an effective and safe drug and can be used in the treatment of suspected amoebiasis and giardiasis. Minor side-effects (compared to the illness you are treating) are fairly common and include: an unpleasant metallic taste, nausea, and a furry tongue. Unless you want a remarkably bad hangover you should not drink alcohol during treatment. The regimens for use of metronidazole in suspected amoebiasis and giardiasis are shown in Table 2.2, (regimens A and B).

Sulphamethoxazole with trimethoprim (Bactrim, Septrin) is of use in bacillary dysentery (shigellosis). Side-effects related to use of this drug are usually due to the sulphamethoxazole component. Although generally rare, if they occur you should stop taking the tablets at once. Important signs of toxicity are skin rashes, blood in the urine, and jaundice. The drug should never be given to someone who is dehydrated. The regimen for treatment of suspected bacillary dysentery (shigellosis) is shown in Table 2.2 (regimen C).

There is now considerable evidence suggesting that trimethoprim alone, in the regimen in Table 2.2 (regimen D), is equally effective in treating bacillary dysentery.

Recently it has been shown that the two regimes for trimethoprim with sulphamethoxazole and trimethoprim alone shown in Table 2.2 are fairly effective in shortening up to two thirds of diarrhoeal episodes in travellers. But for reasons I shall discuss in the section on prevention, I do not consider such treatment justified unless an important part of the trip will be ruined if the episode continues too long.

If differentiation between probable amoebic and bacillary dysentery proves impossible, then it would be perfectly reasonable

Table 2.2 Antibiotic regimens for treatment of various suspected causes of diarrhoea*

Suspected cause	Regimen	Antibiotic	Age	Amount per dose	Doses per day and duration
Suspected amoebiasis	A	metronidazole (Flagyl, Zadstat)	adult	750–800 mg	one dose three times per day for five days
			8–12 yrs	400–500 mg	
			4–7 yrs	375–400 mg	
			2–3 yrs	200–120 mg	
			under 2	80–120 mg	
Suspected giardiasis	B	metronidazole (Flagyl, Zadstat)	adult	200–250 mg	one dose three times per day for five days
			8–12 yrs	200–250 mg	
			3–7 yrs	100–125 mg	
			under 3	50–62 mg	
*Suspected bacillary dysentery (shigellosis)	C	sulphamethoxazole (smx) with trimethoprim (tmp) (Bactrim, Septrin etc.)	adult	800 mg smx 160 mg tmp	one dose two times per day for five days
			6–12 yrs	400 mg smx 80 mg tmp	
			2–6 yrs	200 mg smx 40 mg tmp	
			under 2	100 mg smx 20 mg tmp	
	or				
	D	trimethoprim alone	adult	200 mg	one dose two times per day for five days
			6–12 yrs	100 mg	
			6 months –5 yrs	50 mg	
Suspected typhoid	E	chloramphenicol (Chloromycetin)	12–adult	500 mg –1 g	one dose for times per day
			8–12 yrs	250 mg	
			3–7 yrs	125 mg	
	or				
	F	sulphamethoxazole (smx) with trimethoprim (tmp) (Bactrim, Septrin etc.)	12–adult	1200 mg smx 240 mg tmp	one dose two times per day
			8–12 yrs	800 mg smx 160 mg tmp	
			3–7 yrs	400 mg smx 80 mg tmp	

*Notes

1. Any antibiotic treatment should preferably be prescribed by a doctor. The above regimens are for *emergency use only*.
2. Use of the above regimens should be considered *only* after reading the accompanying text on antibiotics (p. 34) and consulting Fig. 2.2 (p. 32).
3. For regimens A and B, the choice of doses given allows for different tablet sizes.

to take a course of sulphamethoxazole with trimethoprim and metronidazole simultaneously.

Antidiarrhoeal agents

Although these agents may give some measure of relief they may also prolong infections, particularly amoebic and bacillary dysentery. In principle, they hold back part of the body's natural and appropriate response, which is literally to flush out the infection. They also cause constipation if used in excess or when stool frequency is normal. I would recommend their use only when sanitary arrangements are difficult (e.g. on long bus journeys) or to permit attendance at important meetings, and then limited to two to four doses. They should never be used when the sufferer has bloody diarrhoea.

With the above warnings in mind, the three antidiarrhoeal agents that might be considered are: codeine phosphate, diphenoxylate with atropine (Lomotil), and loperamide hydrochloride (Imodium, Arret). Dosages for adults and children are shown in Table 2.3 overleaf.

All three drugs are chemically related to morphine, and may *constitute a serious risk* to children if the *recommended dose is exceeded*. They should never be given to a drowsy or dehydrated child. When antidiarrhoeal treatment for a child is considered essential, loperamide is the safest choice, because it has fewer side effects and a greater margin of safety between effective dose and overdose.

I can envisage few circumstances where the administration of these drugs is absolutely necessary, but if you really feel obliged to give them, adhere closely to the regimes presented.

Kaopectate (a bit like kaolin and morphine without the morphine!) is safe but not very effective. One dose of one to two tablespoonfuls (four to eight teaspoons) may be given to children above two years of age after every bowel movement. Kaopectate is not recommended for children aged under two years.

Typhoid

Typhoid is not necessarily a diarrhoeal illness. When it does occur, diarrhoea is not usually present when symptoms start. Typhoid often begins like a cold or flu with a headache, sore throat, and a gradually increasing fever. If a patient has a pulse of

Table 2.3 Antidiarrhoeal agents*

Drug	Age	Amount per dose	Doses per day
codeine phosphate*	13–adult	30 mg	one dose up to four times daily
	9–12 yrs	15 mg	one dose up to four times daily
	under 9 yrs	*do not give*	—
diphenoxylate 2.5 mg with atropine sulphate 25 μg (Lomotil)*	adult	two tabs	two doses (four tabs) initially then one dose (two tabs) every six hours
	13–16 yrs	two tabs	one dose (two tabs) three times daily
	9–12 yrs	one tab	one dose (one tab) four times daily
	4–8 yrs	one tab	one dose (one tab) three times daily
	1–3 yrs	one tab	one dose (one tab) two times daily
loperamide hydrochloride (Imodium, Arret)*	13–adult	2 mg	two doses (4 mg) initially then one dose (2 mg) every four to six hours
	9–12 yrs	2 mg	one dose (2 mg) four times daily
	4–8 yrs	1 mg	one dose (1 mg) for times daily
	1–3 yrs	1 mg	one dose (1 mg) two or three times daily

Notes
1. Do not take any of the above drugs without first reading the accompanying text on antidiarrhoeal agents (p. 37).
2. The above drugs may constitute a *serious risk* to children *if the recommended dose is exceeded.*

only 80 beats per minute or less despite an obvious high fever, then typhoid is more likely. The illness is more severe in the second week and the victim may become delirious.

Medical help should always be sought. In an emergency, antibiotic treatment with chloramphenicol or sulphamethoxazole/trimethoprim in the doses shown in Table 2.2 (regimens E and F) may be used.

Prevention

The most important preventive measures are outlined in the section on transmission, and the principal precautions necessary are summarized in Figure 2.3, opposite.

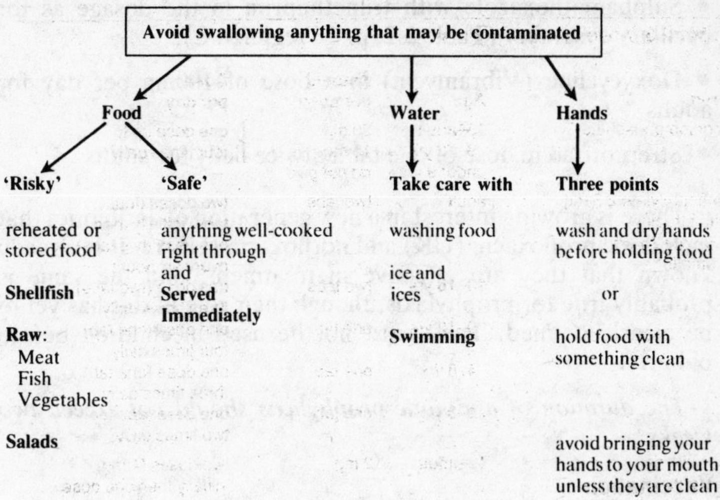

Fig. 2.3 Preventing diarrhoea.

Antibiotics are often advocated for prevention and their use remains somewhat controversial. The main arguments against this practice are:

1. Some of the rare side-effects of antibiotics are considerably worse than the diseases they may prevent.
2. Widespread, indiscriminate consumption of antibiotics promotes the development of antibiotic-resistant bacteria. This may make other infections more difficult to treat.
3. Antibiotics make diagnosis difficult when infection does occur.

The main arguments *for* the prophylactic use of antibiotics are:

1. Several regimes are known to be effective.
2. The personal cost of being out of action may outweigh the risks involved in taking antibiotics.

My personal feeling is that antibiotics should be taken as a preventive only when important meetings or other plans are at risk, or when the traveller is already weakened from some long-standing illness (e.g. heart disease).

The following may be considered:

• Sulphamethoxazole with trimethoprim in the dosage as for bacillary dysentery (Table 2.2, p. 36 regimen C).

• Doxycycline (Vibramycin) in a dose of 100mg per day for adults.*

• Streptotriad in dose of one tablet twice daily for adults.

There is growing interest in a new generation of antibiotics that includes ciprofloxacin (UK) and norfloxacin (USA). It is already known that they are effective in treatment, and the same is probably true for prophylaxis, though their role in this has yet to be clearly defined. They must not be used in children before puberty.

The duration of antibiotic prophylaxis should not exceed two weeks.

Vaccination

Typhoid An effective injected vaccine is available against typhoid (see p. 480), and this vaccine is recommended when travelling to areas where sanitation may be poor. An oral typhoid vaccine based ingeniously on freeze-dried bacteria which 'come of life' briefly in the small intestine and then 'commit suicide' is currently being evaluated. Despite initial optimistic reports, its effectiveness is now in doubt and the prospects for widespread introduction seem distant.

Injectable vaccines for the related diseases, paratyphoid A and B, also exist but their use in combination with the typhoid vaccine (TAB vaccine) is no longer recommended.

Cholera An injectable cholera vaccine has been widely used for many years (see p. 479). The protection it offers is poor and it is of questionable value unless you are visiting an area where there are currently many cases, or in the occasional event of a cholera vaccine certificate being required for entry to the country you are visiting.

At present, determined efforts are being made to develop vaccines based on the toxins of *E. coli*, vaccines against rotaviruses

* Doxycycline is a tetracycline and should not be used by children or pregnant women.

and a new cholera vaccine. However, I would be surprised if any of these became widely available within the next five to ten years.

Other diarrhoea medicines

The traveller will find a host of tempting preparations offered to the current or potential sufferer in any local or foreign pharmacy. Many of these are useless, or actually damaging. For example clioquinol (Entero-Vioform) is still a surprisingly popular remedy in some countries—despite being toxic and ineffective.

Some, like bismuth subsalicylate (Pepto-Bismol) are known to be effective; but it would demand considerable ingenuity from any traveller to arrange sufficient supplies to comply with the rather energetic dose regimes. The vision of a Victorian explorer followed by hordes of porters bearing crates of Pepto-Bismol does however have its appeal! In fairness, tablet preparations of bismuth subsalicylate have recently been shown to be moderately effective for both prevention and treatment.

Persisting symptoms

Most diarrhoeal episodes in travellers last between 48 and 72 hours, but a significant proportion of the self-limiting illnesses (salmonella, shigellosis, cryptosporidiosis, and *Campylobacter*) may be expected to last up to 10 days. *Giardia lamblia* and *Entamoeba histolytica* are not self-limiting and, although relatively uncommon among the overall causes of diarrhoea, are relatively more common in the returning traveller.

Several other even rarer illnesses also became relatively more important in this context. These include tropical sprue, a poorly understood condition in which the normally sparsely populated small intestine contains large numbers of bacteria; and several of the parasitic worms dealt with in the next chapter. These illnesses are rarely life-threatening but they are definitely sufficiently serious to warrant careful investigation.

Other, non-infective disorders, unrelated to travel other than by coincidence, may also cause diarrhoea, bleeding, and abdominal symptoms. Careful investigation is of the utmost importance.

Summary of advice for travellers

- Diarrhoeal illnesses are avoidable.
- Most travellers' diarrhoea is the result of swallowing contaminated food, drink, or other material.
- The contaminating micro-organisms are rendered harmless by adequate cooking (temperatures above the boiling point of water, all the way through, for at least 15 minutes).
- Food only remains safe if eaten immediately after cooking or if sealed and refrigerated without delay.
- Precautions with food are summarized in Appendix 5.
- Diarrhoeal episodes are usually self-limiting, get better after one to three days, and require no specific treatment.
- When required, replacement of water losses is the first consideration of treatment, especially with children (p. 33).
- Guidelines for the place and use of antibiotics, antidiarrhoeal medication, and other drugs are given on pp. 34–41.

Intestinal parasites

Travellers to rural areas in the tropics are at greatest risk from parasitic diseases, though all travellers should choose their food with care, because complications are occasionally serious.

Dr David Haddock *was a Senior Lecturer in Tropical Medicine at the Liverpool School of Tropical Medicine. He also worked for long periods in Tanzania, Ghana, Nigeria, and Saudi Arabia, and was a WHO consultant in Ghana and the Sudan.*
Dr George Wyatt *is a Senior Lecturer in Tropical Medicine at the Liverpool School of Tropical Medicine.*

Most people who live in developing countries harbour one or more varieties of intestinal parasite, and travellers to those countries are at risk of infection. 'Host' and parasite usually co-exist in reasonable harmony, and most often no serious condition results from the relationship. In a few cases, however, serious illness and even death may occur unless treatment is given.

Intestinal parasite infestations usually follow the swallowing of infective forms of the parasite (eggs or larvae) in food or water contaminated with human or animal faeces containing excreted parasites. The frequency and severity of infection with intestinal parasites is therefore highest in areas with low standards of hygiene, poor sewage disposal, and unsatisfactory water supplies. Flies are abundant in such areas and are able to carry infective parasites on their feet directly from faeces to food. Some types of intestinal worm cause infection when their larvae penetrate the skin (bare feet especially), when the skin comes into contact with soil contaminated with faeces. Tapeworm infections follow eating infected meat that has not been properly cooked.

Intestinal parasites and the traveller

The traveller usually has to rely on food prepared by others, and it is difficult to influence other people's standard of food hygiene or preparation. Even seemingly good-class establishments may be sources of infection. Water supplies are often contaminated, and should be regarded with suspicion. In many countries intestinal infections with bacteria, viruses, and parasites are the commonest health hazards to visitors; such infections are difficult to avoid completely but sensible precautions greatly diminish the risks.

As mentioned in the previous chapter and on pp. 73–80, all drinking water should be boiled or sterilized; cold drinks or ices should not be bought from street vendors. Raw salads and vegetables are notorious sources of parasitic infections, and are usually best avoided completely. Meat should be thoroughly cooked until all trace of red colour is lost. Fruit should be peeled carefully. In addition to such general precautions, the possibility of infection by parasitic skin penetration makes it unsafe to walk around without shoes in many tropical areas.

Types of intestinal parasites

Parasites of the intestinal tract fall into two groups—the *protozoa* and the *metazoa* (worms).

The protozoa are microscopic, single-celled creatures which multiply by simple cell division to produce more adult parasites within the gut. As in the case of infection with bacteria, an initially small infection can rapidly build up to a heavy one. The protozoa include *amoebae* and *giardia*.

The second group of parasites, the metazoa, or worms, are complex multicellular animals which may be as small as a few millimetres or, in the case of tapeworms, up to several metres long. Generally, intestinal worms excrete eggs in the faeces but cannot reproduce adult worms inside the body. Their eggs have to undergo development outside the body, often in the soil.

The gravity of human infection often depends upon the number of adult worms in the intestine, and light infections are often relatively harmless. The number of adult worms depends upon the number of infective forms that have been swallowed, or that have penetrated the skin. Worms can damage the lining of the intestine, causing haemorrhage or ulceration. They can also cause mechanical disturbances in the gut, or can migrate into the side-alleys of the intestine.

Unlike many bacterial and viral infections, parasitic infections do not lead to immunity from further infection with the same parasite. So repeated infection is common, and chronic infection is also a problem because the worms may survive for several years—indeed a beef tapeworm may survive in the intestines for twenty-five years.

Some protozoal infections of the intestine

Amoebic dysentery (amoebiasis)

This infection is caused by an amoeba called *Entamoeba histolytica*. This single-celled creature secretes enzymes to digest particles of food in the gut and then absorbs the products by engulfing them. The amoeba usually lives in the large intestine and is about five times the size of a red blood cell. Sometimes amoebae invade the gut wall by digestion of the tissues and so cause dysentery, or they may be carried to the liver or other organs and cause abscesses. Different strains of amoebae vary in their capacity to cause disease.

Amoebae living in the cavity or on the surface of the intestine cause no symptoms, but as they are passed out in the faeces they round up and secrete a thick protective wall to form resistant infective cysts. In the absence of proper hygiene, food or water may be contaminated by these cysts, and the amoebae reform when the cysts reach the large intestine of another person.

Amoebae that invade the wall of the large intestine cause ulceration and bleeding. The patient suffers from a slowly developing and often recurrent dysentery with blood and slimy mucus in the motions. Dysentery may persist or recur for months and may occasionally lead on to perforation of the gut and peritonitis. Amoebic liver abscesses sometimes occur in people who already have dysentery; more often, however, there are no gut symptoms, just severe pain over the liver and high fever. These abscesses are very dangerous and require urgent treatment.

Amoebiasis is a frequent infection in travellers or expatriates resident in the tropics and infection may be present in up to 20 per cent of local residents. Most of these people have no symptoms, but they pass cysts in their motions and are therefore potentially infective to others. Once infected, carriage of amoebae may last for months or many years and it is possible to develop disease many years after initial exposure so that even asymptomatic expatriate carriers usually need treatment.

Intestinal infection with *E. histolytica* is usually readily detected if stool specimens are examined by a competent technician. Effective drug treatment is available usually with metronidazole (Flagyl) and diloxanide furoate (Furamide) but, since many other conditions may simulate amoebiasis, laboratory confirmation before treatment is always advisable.

Giardiasis

The cause of giardiasis is a tiny one-celled parasite called *Giardia lamblia*, which is about three times the size of a red blood cell. It lives in the small intestine and may damage the lining. *Giardia* is present in European and North American countries, but infection is much more common in countries with a low standard of hygiene. Several thousand people who are infected abroad return to the United Kingdom with this parasite each year. As with *E. histolytica* resistant infective cysts are passed in the stools and infection is acquired by swallowing these cysts in contaminated water or food.

Some infected individuals have no symptoms, but excrete infective cysts in their stools for weeks or months. Others have moderate diarrhoea often with the passage of excess gas and a distended abdomen; this may persist for several weeks though rarely for longer than six months (see also diarrhoea p. 21). A very small proportion of those infected have severe diarrhoea with fatty stools and marked weight loss, weakness, and anaemia. This is due to a loss of the ability to absorb food from the intestine properly (malabsorption).

Giardiasis is the commonest cause of diarrhoea persisting for weeks after return home. The diagnosis is made by microscopic examination of stool specimens and treatment with metronidazole or other drugs is usually highly effective.

Some worm infections of the intestine

Hookworm infection (ankylostomiasis)

About 600 million people around the world are infected with hookworms. These worms live in the small intestine, and attach themselves to its lining by means of teeth or cutting plates. The worms suck blood from their hosts and periodically shift their position, leaving a small bleeding point.

Each worm causes a blood loss of 0.03–0.1 ml of blood daily. There may be 100 or more worms in the intestine, and chronic blood loss eventually leads to anaemia, particularly if iron intake is also low.

Hookworm eggs are voided in the stool, and if soil conditions are warm and moist, infective larvae take about a week to hatch. They can survive in the soil for several weeks. The larvae can penetrate intact skin, sometimes producing an itchy rash, and find their way to the lungs through the blood stream. The larvae undergo further development in the lungs for several days, causing a cough, before migrating through the air passages and the oesophagus to the small intestine, where they mature to form 1 cm long adults, which may survive for up to nine years.

Barefooted farmers working in tropical areas are particularly liable to heavy infection, and severe anaemia due to hookworm infection can cause cardiac failure and death.

Visitors to rural areas in the tropics may acquire light infections, especially if they wander around with bare feet.

Diagnosis and treatment Diagnosis is made by microscopical examination of the stools and identifying hookworm eggs. The anaemia is treated with iron preparations and the worms are eliminated with drugs such as mebendazole (Vermox) or pyrantel (Combantrin).

Creeping eruption Certain hookworm larvae, which normally parasitize dogs, are able to penetrate human skin but unable to mature further. These larvae wander around aimlessly under the skin for several months. In the course of their migration, the worms produce an itchy, red, moving, worm shaped trail. (See also larva migrans, p. 103 and skin problems, p. 341.)

This condition is called creeping eruption and causes considerable irritation; secondary infection with bacteria may occur as a result of scratching. The rash is usually on the feet or legs, and cure is obtained by treatment with thiabendazole (Mintezol) tablets or ointment.

Creeping eruption is not uncommon in tourists, who become infected on beaches befouled by dogs in the Americas, the Caribbean, Africa, and Asia.

Strongyloides stercoralis (strongyloidiasis)

Strongyloides is common in many tropical areas. Like hookworm, larvae of *Strongyloides* are excreted in faeces, develop in the soil, and cause infection by penetrating the skin.

The larvae reach the small intestine in the same way, mature and reside in its lining. Infection is often harmless, but sometimes causes intestinal ulceration with abdominal pain, diarrhoea, and failure to absorb certain nutrients. However, the larvae are also able to mature in the intestine and penetrate the lining of the intestine or the skin around the anus, perpetuating the infection. Infection may last for a lifetime. Larvae wandering beneath the skin may produce a creeping eruption on the trunk (see also larva currens, p. 104). If someone with strongyloidiasis is given cortisone-like drugs which suppress immunity, the infection can rapidly become generalized and cause death.

Diagnosis is made by finding larvae in the faeces, and treatment is with thiabendazole (Mintezol).

Roundworm infections (ascariasis)

About 1000 million people in the world and perhaps one third of the inhabitants of tropical Africa are thought to harbour the common roundworm *Ascaris lumbricoides*. Roundworms are large, stout, whitish worms 15–30 cm long and 2–6 mm in diameter. Infection is acquired by swallowing infective eggs often on vegetables. Eggs are passed in the stools of infected persons especially children and need to mature in suitable soil before they become infective.

Heavy infections with roundworms in local children can cause serious disease ranging from abdominal colic and distension to nutritional disturbance and even blockage of the small intestine by a tangled mass of worms. Infection with a few worms in an expatriate rarely causes trouble but they should always be expelled because very occasionally they can enter a bile duct or other orifice and cause disease.

The diagnosis is made by finding the eggs on microscopy of the stool. A number of drugs are available for treatment; one such is mebendazole (Vermox).

The beef tapeworm

The beef tapeworm *Taenia saginata* is long and ribbon-like, about 1 cm broad and up to several metres in length. Each worm has hundreds of segments, each of which is a hermaphrodite creature. *Taenia saginata* resides in the small intestine, attached to the intestinal lining by suckers at its head. It usually causes surprisingly little disturbance to its host, who may be unaware of its

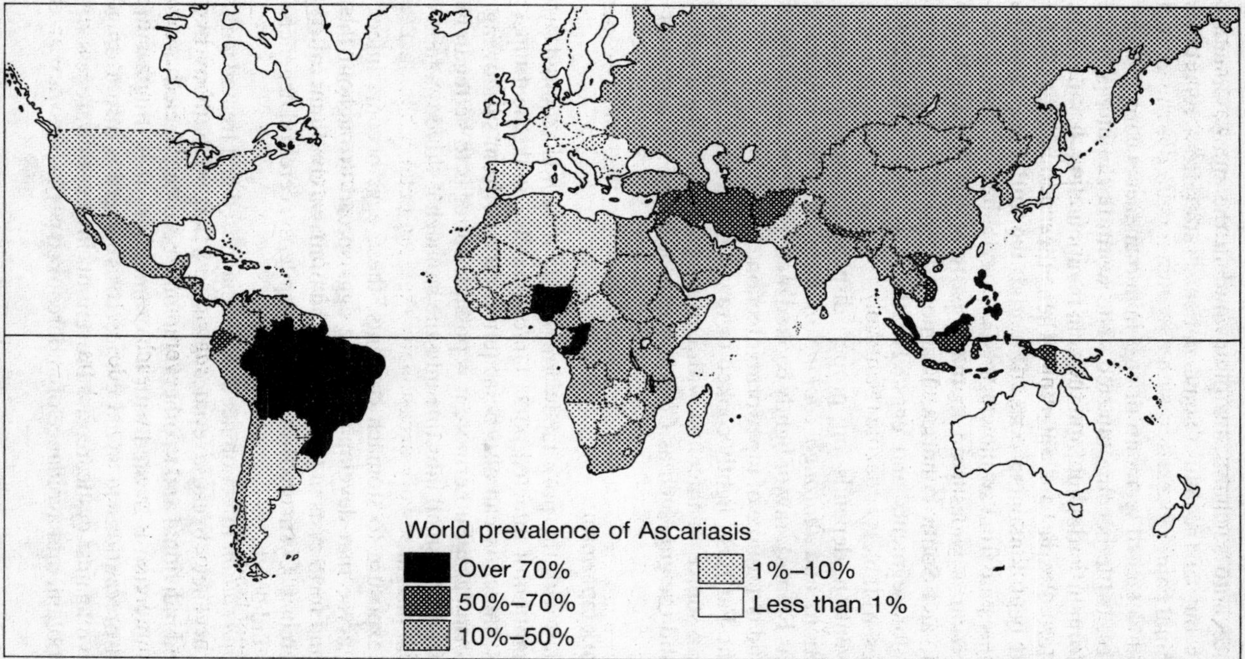

Map 2.1 World distribution of ascariasis. Percentage figures refer to the proportion of the local population affected. (Reproduced, with modifications, by kind permission of the Editor, *Parasitology Today*.) The prevalence of ascariasis varies considerably *within* countries; more detailed information is given in: Crompton, D. W. T. (1989). Prevalence of ascariasis. In *Ascariasis and its prevention and control* (ed. D. W. T. Crompton, M. C. Nesheim, and Z. C. Pawlowski). Taylor and Francis, London.

presence until segments are discovered in the stools, or even wriggle out of the anus. Some patients suffer from recurrent abdominal pains.

When detached segments or eggs in human faeces contaminate pastures, cattle become infected. The worm does not reach its adult form in cattle, but forms cysts in their muscles—0.5–1 cm in diameter. People are infected when they eat inadequately cooked beef containing cysts. The adult worm develops in the small intestine from swallowing cysts.

Infection is widespread in many parts of the Middle East, Africa, and South America. Diagnosis is made by examining stools for segments and eggs. Treatment is with niclosamide (Yomesan) tablets.

Prevention depends on proper disposal of sewage, meat inspection, and *thorough cooking of meat.* In some countries (such as France), raw or lightly cooked meat is regarded as a delicacy and is a source of tapeworm infection.

In the Far East, lightly cooked or raw fish is consumed widely and is a source of infection with certain parasites infecting the liver and the gut, such as *Clonorchis sinensis* (the Chinese liver fluke).

The pork tapeworm

Infection with the pork tapeworm *Taenia solium* is acquired by consumption of infected pork. Unfortunately, unlike beef tapeworms, infection can also be acquired directly from swallowing tapeworm eggs. Futhermore it is possible for eggs to be regurgitated from the small intestine into the stomach if there is a tapeworm in the gut.

On exposure to stomach contents, these eggs become infective. Larvae that develop from the eggs spread throughout the body and form cysts in the muscles and brain—a condition called cysticercosis. Cysticercosis may cause epilepsy, cerebral degeneration, and death.

Taenia solium infection needs to be diagnosed and treated with some urgency, because cysticercosis is a hazard both to the infected individual and to others who may become infected.

The infection is treated with niclosamide or other drugs, with special precautions to avoid cysticercosis. There is also a drug effective against cysticercosis. Prevention involves awareness of the problem, and avoidance of undercooked pork.

Hydatid cysts

Hydatid cysts are caused by *Echinococcus granulosus*: the adult form of this parasite is a small tapeworm that lives in the intestines of dogs. Its eggs are infective to man, sheep, goats, camels, and horses, and are passed in dogs' faeces. Larvae develop from any eggs that are eaten, and these form slowly growing larval cysts in the tissues. Dogs become infected when they eat organs of sheep or other animals that contain these larval cysts. Humans usually become infected by stroking dogs: eggs from the fur adhere to the fingers, and are subsequently swallowed.

In humans, larval cysts form most often in the liver, but the lungs, brain, bones, and other tissues may also be affected. The cysts grow very slowly but behave like expanding tumours that may not become obvious for five to ten years after infection. Surgical excision is necessary, and is sometimes difficult. Drug treatment has been disappointing. Prevention depends upon avoiding contact with dogs in endemic areas, proper disposal of animal carcasses, deworming dogs, and food hygiene.

Other parasitic worms

There have been recent cases of a form of meningitis caused by the larvae of the parasitic worm *Angiostrongylus cantonensis*. The disease occurs in South East Asia and the Pacific, and complications are serious. The disease is spread by eating undercooked snails. Escargots prepared by the traditional French methods, at high temperature, are safe.

Summary of advice for travellers

- Travellers to rural, tropical areas are at greatest risk from intestinal parasites. Most parasitic infections are not life-threatening, but they may occasionally be very dangerous. Symptoms of infection may not appear for months or even years after leaving an endemic area. Most infestations can be avoided by commonsense precautions—so follow this book's advice on food and water hygiene, wear shoes, and avoid handling dogs.

- At the moment no drugs or vaccines are available for preventing these infections, but effective treatment exists for most if given sufficiently early. Travellers who have spent prolonged periods abroad or who have 'lived rough' are advised to have a stool examination on return home to detect possible hidden infection.

Poliomyelitis

Polio is common in countries with poor hygiene, and is a serious hazard to travellers who have not been immunized.

Dr George Wyatt *is a Senior Lecturer in Tropical Medicine at the Liverpool School of Tropical Medicine.*

Poliomyelitis, or polio, was once widely known as 'infantile paralysis' because it caused paralysis chiefly in young children. As hygiene improved in many parts of the world, infection became more common later in life, when its effects tend to be more serious; in Europe, major epidemics of polio caused death and severe disability in young adults during the 1940s and 1950s.

With the introduction and widespread use of polio vaccines polio has now been largely eliminated from developed countries. However, it remains common in many developing countries, and is especially common in young children; in many areas up to 1 per cent of school-children may be lame from previous polio.

Infection

Polio is caused by a virus, which is spread from person to person either in mucus from the nose and throat, or by contamination of food or drink with infected faeces. There are three varieties of polio virus. After infection a person may become a 'carrier', and continue to excrete the virus in his stools for many weeks.

Once the virus has travelled to the motor nerve cells in the spinal cord and brain, it damages these cells and causes paralysis of the muscles they control.

Poliomyelitis occurs in two phases—an initial non-specific illness of fever, headache, muscle pains, and perhaps a stiff neck, followed after a short interval by a return of muscle pains and the rapid development of paralysis over the next twenty-four hours. The paralysis may be limited to a single limb or may spread rapidly to involve much of the body. Very severe polio is sometimes fatal because the muscles used in breathing or swallowing are affected. In those who survive, recovery of muscle power takes place over the next few months, but some permanent disability often remains.

Fortunately most young children infected with polio virus escape with little or no damage, although a few are left with a wasted paralysed limb. Infection in adults all too often produces severe paralysis.

Polio and the traveller

Polio is a serious hazard for non-immunized travellers in developing countries, and many tragedies have occurred, resulting in death or permanent paralysis. Polio virus still circulates constantly in areas with low levels of hygiene and low immunization rates in local inhabitants.

Most travellers will have received a full primary course of immunization as a child, but some may have missed immunization and older people may never have been offered the vaccine. Because so little polio virus has been circulating in the last twenty years, unvaccinated persons should never assume that they are *naturally* immune whatever their age.

Immunization

There are two types of polio vaccine (see p. 481). The type most often used is a modified live virus vaccine given by mouth as drops or on a sugar lump. There is also a killed vaccine given by injection, which is also highly effective and is preferred for travellers who are pregnant or who have a depressed immune system because of disease or drugs (such as high doses of corticosteroids).

People who have never been immunized or who have no record of immunization should receive three doses of polio vaccine, preferably at monthly intervals before they travel. People who have been fully immunized at any time in the past need only a single booster dose of oral polio vaccine every ten years, if they intend to travel.

Oral polio vaccine is both highly effective and very safe. There is, however, an extremely small risk of the vaccine virus causing paralysis in unvaccinated close contacts of the person being immunized. This is why it is usual for all members of the same household who have not been immunized before to be offered immunization at the same time.

Whilst there are theoretical objections to immunization with two live virus vaccines at the same time, I have never heard of anyone coming to any harm from being immunized against polio and yellow fever together. This theoretical objection should not stop people from receiving both vaccines on the same day if there is not sufficient time for the usual three-week interval between vaccines. Normal immunoglobulin (gamma-globulin) for protection against viral hepatitis may also contain antibodies against polio, so it is therefore usually given last, shortly before travel and at least two weeks after the last dose of oral polio vaccine (see p. 481).

If there is insufficient time, however, polio and immunoglobulin may be given together.

Summary of advice for travellers

- Full immunization against polio is essential for anyone travelling to a developing country and advisable for those travelling anywhere outside Northern Europe and North America. Although good general hygiene may somewhat reduce the risk of catching polio, it is unreliable and cannot replace immunization.

Viral hepatitis

Hepatitis is common in travellers to areas outside North America, Northern Europe, and Australia, and may result in an unpleasant prolonged illness. All travellers should understand how the different types of hepatitis are spread.

Professor Arie J. Zuckerman *is Director of the Department of Medical Microbiology at the London School of Hygiene and Tropical Medicine, and of the WHO Collaborating Centre for Reference and Research on Viral Hepatitis.*

Viral hepatitis is common thoroughout the world and is a major public health problem. At least six different viruses are capable of causing the infection, and the illnesses associated with each (which are all very similar) are as follows:

1. Hepatitis A, also known in the past as infectious hepatitis or epidemic jaundice
2. Epidemic non-A hepatitis
3. Hepatitis B, also known in the past as serum hepatitis
4. Hepatitis D, (Delta hepatitis)
5. Non-A, non-B hepatitis, which is caused by several different viruses, (although, by definition, not by the viruses responsible for hepatitis A and B).

The viruses responsible for hepatitis A and hepatitis B have been 'characterized', i.e. a great deal is known about their size, structure, and biology. Sensitive laboratory tests are available for detecting components of the viruses (viral antigens) and immune products against the viruses (antibodies) in the blood or tissues of people who have been infected with these viruses—and hence a diagnosis of infection can be made with precision.

The viruses responsible for non-A, non-B hepatitis have not, on the other hand, been fully characterized, and specific laboratory tests are not available for detecting them. The diagnosis of non-A, non-B hepatitis is thus made (as the name implies) in cases of hepatitis where hepatitis A, hepatitis B, hepatitis D, and other viruses known to cause liver damage have been excluded.

The illness

The illness seen in all forms of hepatitis is similar, and results from acute inflammation of the liver. It is frequently heralded by symptoms such as fever, chills, headache, fatigue, generalized weakness, and aches and pains. A few days later, there is often loss of appetite, nausea, vomiting, right upper abdominal pain or tenderness, followed closely by dark urine, light-coloured faeces, and jaundice of the skin or the sclerae (outer coating of the eyeballs). Many infections, particularly in early life, are without specific symptoms, or without jaundice. In others, jaundice may be severe and prolonged; complete liver failure may occur, and the patient may lapse into a coma.

Hepatitis A

Hepatitis A is common in all parts of the world, but the exact incidence is difficult to estimate because of the high proportion of asymptomatic cases, infections without jaundice, and differing patterns of disease. Surveys of antibody to hepatitis A have shown that while the prevalence of hepatitis A in industrialized countries (particularly northern Europe, North America and Australia) is decreasing, the infection is virtually universal in most other regions, particularly in warm climate countries.

Only one form of hepatitis A has been identified, and the antibody that develops against it persists for many years, frequently for life, providing immunity.

An epidemic illness similar to that caused by hepatitis A, and commonly transmitted by contaminated water, has recently been noted in India, Burma, the eastern USSR, parts of the Middle East, and North Africa, but this illness is not caused by the recognized form of hepatitis A virus—since in the areas mentioned most people have already been infected with hepatitis A in early life, and are immune. The illness is due to a virus which is quite distinct from hepatitis A, and is referred to as enteric non-A, non-B hepatitis. No specific tests are available for detecting this virus.

How it is spread

Hepatitis A virus is spread by the faecal-oral route, usually by person to person contact, and infection is particularly common in conditions of poor sanitation and overcrowding. Outbreaks result most frequently from faecal contamination of drinking water and food (although water-borne transmission is not a major factor in industrialized countries, or where the piped water supply has been adequately treated and chlorinated).

Food-borne outbreaks, which have become more important and frequent in developed countries, may be due to the shedding of the virus in the faeces of infected food handlers during the incubation period of the illness: the source of the outbreak can often be traced to cooking. Raw or inadequately cooked shellfish cultivated in sewage-contaminated tidal or coastal water, and raw vegetables grown in soil fertilized with untreated human faeces and excreta, are associated with a high risk of infection with hepatitis A virus. Hepatitis A infection is frequently contracted by travellers from areas of low to areas of high prevalence.

Hepatitis A virus is very rarely transmitted by blood transfusion or by inoculation.

The incubation period of the virus is between three and five weeks with an average of twenty-eight days.

Age incidence and seasonal patterns

All age groups are susceptible to infection. The highest incidence is observed in children of school age, but in North America and in many countries in northern Europe most cases occur in adults, frequently after travel abroad. In temperate zones the characteristic seasonal trend is for an increase in incidence in the autumn and early winter months, falling progressively to a minimum in midsummer; but recently this seasonal trend has been lost in some countries. In many tropical countries, the peak of reported infection tends to occur during the rainy season with low incidence in the dry months.

Consequences of infection

The illness caused by hepatitis A is described above. Although the disease has a low mortality, patients may be incapacitated for many weeks. There is no evidence of persistence of infection with hepatitis A virus nor of progression to chronic liver disease.

Enterically transmitted non-A, non-B hepatitis is very severe during pregnancy and is associated with high maternal mortality.

Like hepatitis A, there is no evidence that it progresses to chronic liver disease.

Prevention and control

Control of the infection is difficult. Since faecal shedding of the virus and therefore infectivity is at its highest during the incubation period, strict isolation of cases is not a useful measure. Spread of infection is reduced by simple hygienic measures and the sanitary disposal of excreta.

Normal human immunoglobulin, commonly referred to as gammaglobulin, contains the hepatitis A antibody and will prevent or lessen the severity of the illness, while not always preventing excretion of the virus or the development of asymptomatic hepatitis. Immunoglobulin injections may be required every four to six months for people at risk such as close personal contacts of patients with hepatitis A, and those exposed to contaminated food.

In such cases a 16 per cent solution of immunoglobulin in a dose of 2 i.u. hepatitis A antibody/kg body weight may be given intramuscularly before exposure to the virus or early during the incubation period.

Current preparations of immunoglobulin do not afford protection against enterically transmitted non-A, non-B hepatitis.

Hepatitis A and the traveller

Prophylaxis with immunoglobulin is recommended for persons without hepatitis A antibody* who are visiting highly endemic areas. Anyone can be given immunoglobulin—there are no general contradictions for its use (see also pp. 55 and 481).

Immunoglobulin prepared for intramuscular administration by cold ethanol fractionation according to the Cohn method is safe and without any risk of transmitting blood-borne infections including HIV (the virus causing AIDS). This is the method of preparation used by all reputable manufacturers in industrialized countries.

Vaccines against hepatitis A are being developed and clinical trials are in progress.

Other preventive measures include strict personal hygiene, avoiding eating raw or inadequately cooked shellfish, avoiding

* Immunity to hepatitis A can be checked with a blood test—see p. 481.

raw vegetables, and avoiding drinking untreated water and raw milk.

Hepatitis B

Like hepatitis A, hepatitis B occurs throughout the world. Its continued survival is ensured by the large number of individuals who are carriers of the virus, estimated to be at least 300 million worldwide. Hepatitis B can be spread either from carriers or from people with inapparent infection, or during the incubation period, illness, or early convalescence.

A person is defined as a carrier if hepatitis B surface antigen—a marker of the virus—persists in their circulation for more than six months following infection. A person may be a lifelong carrier and remain apparently healthy, although variable degrees of liver damage can occur.

The prevalence of hepatitis B carriers varies from one region of the world to another. In northern Europe, North America, and Australia, 0·1 per cent of the population are carriers (at least among blood donors); in central and eastern Europe up to 5 per cent; in southern Europe, countries bordering the Mediterranean and parts of Central and South America a higher frequency; and in parts of Africa, Asia, and the Pacific area, 20 per cent or more of the apparently healthy population may be carriers.

The incidence of hepatitis B tends to be higher among adults living in urban communities and among those living in poor conditions. The infection may become established in closed institutions such as institutions for the mentally-handicapped.

Certain groups of people—recipients of unscreened blood transfusions and infusions of certain blood products, health care and laboratory personnel, staff in institutions for the mentally handicapped, male homosexuals, prostitutes, and abusers of injectable drugs and narcotics—are at considerably increased risk of contracting hepatitis B because of the means of transmission. Travellers or expatriates belonging to any of these groups are at higher risk in countries where the carrier rate is high.

How it is spread

Before the development of laboratory tests for hepatitis B, this infection was diagnosed whenever a hepatitis-like illness occurred about 60–180 days after the injection of human blood or plasma fractions or the use of inadequately sterilized syringes and needles. The development of specific laboratory tests for hepatitis B confirmed the importance of transmission by skin penetration, and infectivity appears to be especially related to blood.

Transmission of the infection may result from accidental inoculation with minute amounts of blood which may occur during medical, surgical, or dental procedures; during immunization with inadequately sterilized syringes and needles; sharing of needles during intravenous drug abuse; during tattooing, ear piercing, and nose piercing; during acupuncture, during laboratory accidents and accidental inoculation with razors and similar objects that have been contaminated with blood.

However, hepatitis B is not spread exclusively by blood or blood products. Hepatitis B surface antigen has been found in other body fluids such as saliva, menstrual and vaginal discharges, and seminal fluid, and these have been implicated as vehicles of transmission of the infection. In certain circumstances the virus may be infective by mouth, and there is much evidence for the transmission of hepatitis B by sexual contact. The sexually promiscuous, particularly male homosexuals, are at high risk.

In the tropics and in warm climates, additional factors may be important for the transmission of hepatitis B. These include traditional tattooing and scarification, blood-letting, ritual circumcision, and repeated biting by blood-sucking insects. Results of investigations into the role that biting insects play in the spread of hepatitis B are conflicting. Hepatitis B surface antigen has been detected in several species of mosquito and in bed-bugs that have either been trapped in the wild or fed experimentally on infected blood, but no convincing evidence of multiplication of the virus in insects has been obtained. However, mechanical transmission of the infection via an insect's biting parts is a possibility.

Hepatitis B also tends to occur within family groups, although the precise mechanism of intrafamilial spread is not known.

Transmission of hepatitis B virus from carrier mothers to their babies can occur around the time of birth and appears to be an important factor in determining the prevalence of the infection in some regions, particularly in China and South East Asia.

The carrier state

Progression to the carrier state is commoner in males, more likely to follow infections acquired in childhood than in adult life, and more likely to occur in people with natural or acquired immune deficiencies. The carrier state becomes established in approximately 5 to 10 per cent of infected adults. In countries where hepatitis B infection is common the highest prevalence of surface antigen is found in children aged four to eight, with steadily declining rates among older age groups.

There is an urgent need to define the mechanisms which lead to the carrier state and to introduce methods of interruption of transmission. This is a complex and vexed issue, with considerable personal, social, and economic implications.

Consequences of infection

The symptoms and manifestations of hepatitis B are similar to those of the other types of viral hepatitis. However, the picture is complicated by the carrier state and by chronic liver disease, which may follow the infection. Chronic liver disease may be severe and may progress to primary liver cancer. In many parts of the world primary liver cancer is one of the commonest human cancers, particularly in men.

Prevention and control

Immunization against hepatitis B can be carried out in two ways. *Passive* immunization involves the inoculation of hepatitis B immunoglobulin (hepatitis B gamma-globulin) containing antibody against hepatitis B. However, for hepatitis B, there is now also the possibility of *active* immunization, because a vaccine containing hepatitis B antigen has been developed. In active immunization the inoculation of inactivated antigen 'primes' the body's immune system for production of its own antibodies.

Passive immunization Prevention with hepatitis B immunoglobulin is not required for travellers.

Hepatitis B immunoglobulin is of the greatest value as a protective measure in situations involving a single acute exposure to hepatitis B, as when blood or other material containing hepatitis B surface antigen is accidentally inoculated, swallowed, or splashed in the eyes. Two doses administered thirty days apart are required for efficacy: the first dose should preferably be administered within forty-eight hours of exposure. It should not be administered later than seven days following exposure.

Active immunization Hepatitis B vaccines have been prepared from antigen purified from the plasma of carriers of the virus, inactivated to ensure freedom from all infectious organisms and harmful contaminating material. Newer hepatitis B vaccines have been developed using recombinant DNA technology (genetic engineering). They are safe and effective, and have been licensed in many countries, including the UK and USA.

Among the groups who might benefit from the vaccine are patients who require multiple transfusions, patients with immune deficiencies, patients with malignant disease, health-care personnel, homosexual men, drug addicts, and prostitutes.

In regions where transmission of hepatitis B from mothers to infants is common, protective immunization of susceptible women of child-bearing age and infants would be desirable. Immunization should also be considered by non-immune persons living in certain tropical and non-tropical areas where the prevalence of hepatitis B infection is high and where the carrier rate may reach 10–20 per cent of the population, and where primary liver cancer is common.

The currently available vaccines are expensive, costing $100–150 for a course of immunization. Vaccination of travellers is not necessary unless: (1) they belong to a high risk category; (2) they will remain in an endemic area for longer than about six months; (3) they will reside in rural areas or engage in sporting or other activities that carry an increased risk of accidents, injury, or occupational exposure to blood.

Travellers likely to need medical treatment abroad—such as kidney dialysis or blood transfusion—should also receive the hepatitis B vaccine.

Hepatitis B and the traveller

Travellers should take commonsense precautions to reduce the risk of hepatitis B. They should employ great caution in any intimate or sexual contact (particularly male homosexual contact) with possible hepatitis B carriers; they should where possible avoid any procedure involving penetration of the skin, for example, tattooing, ear piercing, any sort of injections, blood transfusions, and many medical, surgical and dental procedures carried out under dubious sanitary conditions.

The delta virus is a defective infectious agent that can only infect actively in the presence of hepatitis B. The infection is common in parts of Southern Europe, the Middle East, parts of tropical Africa, and in parts of South America. The virus is spread in the same way as hepatitis B and precautions against it are identical. Immunization against hepatitis B will also protect against Delta hepatitis.

Non-A, non-B hepatitis

Improved laboratory diagnosis of hepatitis A and hepatitis B has enabled a previously unrecognized form of hepatitis, unrelated to either type A or B, to be identified. It is referred to as non-A, non-B hepatitis, and it is now known to be the most common form of hepatitis occurring after a blood transfusion and the administration of blood-clotting factors in some countries. It has been found in every country in which it has been sought, has some features in common with hepatitis B, and has been detected in patients on dialysis and among drug addicts. In several countries a significant number of cases are not associated with transfusion, and such sporadic cases have been found to account for up to 15–20 per cent of all adult patients with viral hepatitis.

In general, the illness is mild, often without jaundice or other symptoms. However, there is evidence that the infection may be followed by the development of a persistent carrier state: chronic hepatitis may occur in as many 40–50 per cent of patients after infection associated with blood transfusion or treatment by renal dialysis. About 10 per cent of patients with the sporadic form of the infection may progress to chronic liver damage.

There are no known methods of preventing non-A, non-B hepatitis (beyond precautions applicable to hepatitis B).

Treatment of viral hepatitis

No specific treatment is available for any of the types of viral hepatitis. A number of antiviral substances are under study for the management of chronic liver disease associated with hepatitis B. Bed rest is required during the acute phase. A low fat diet is usually preferred during the acute phase of the disease. Alcohol should not be consumed for six months after recovery.

Women using oral contraceptives (the Pill or progestogen-only Pill) can carry on with this contraceptive method during convalescence and recovery from hepatitis.

Evacuation of a patient with acute hepatitis is not usually necessary unless serious complications develop, when special facilities may be required.

Summary of advice for travellers

- Hepatitis A and the enteric form of non-A, non-B hepatitis are a risk to travellers in areas of the world where hygienic and sanitary conditions are poor. Passive immunization with gammaglobulin should be considered for non-immune travellers anywhere outside northern Europe, the USA, Canada, Australia, and New Zealand. This should be given shortly before departure and provides reasonably complete protection. Long-term travellers may require further injections every four to six months. Strict personal hygiene, avoidance of untreated water and raw or inadequately cooked food, particularly raw vegetables, shellfish and milk, can help prevent infection.
- Hepatitis B is a risk to certain groups of people in industrialized countries, notably health-care personnel and male homosexuals. The risk increases in developing countries, where there are generally more carriers. Caution should be observed with regard to intimate or sexual encounters with inhabitants of these countries. Passive immunization with hepatitis B immunoglobulin is not necessary for travellers. Active immunization with hepatitis B vaccine is expensive but is advisable for health-care personnel, members of other risk categories working in the subtropics or tropics, and long stay travellers to endemic areas.
- Penetration of the skin by any object that may have come in contact with someone else's blood or other body fluids—as in tattooing, ear piercing, sharing of razors, acupuncture, sharing of needles by drug abusers, and any medical, dental, or surgical procedure, including blood transfusion and donation under dubious hygienic conditions—should be avoided.
- Non-A, non-B hepatitis is principally a risk of blood transfusion. No preventative immunization is available, and avoidance is by measures similar to those advised for hepatitis B.
- Travellers who develop a general malaise and symptoms such as right upper abdominal pain, jaundice, and dark-coloured urine either abroad or after their return should suspect viral hepatitis, and should seek medical advice immediately.

Poisons and contaminants in food

Certain foods need to be treated with caution while abroad: in the tropics, fish and shellfish pose a particular hazard.

Dr Elizabeth Driver *is currently a medical adviser in a law firm in London. She has worked as a toxicologist at the Medical Research Council and in the Tropical Metabolism Research Unit in Jamaica.*

One of the most enjoyable aspects of visiting a foreign country is the opportunity to sample the local cuisine—and provided such food is carefully prepared and cooked, this usually carries little risk.

Unfortunately, some foreign delicacies or even staple foodstuffs contain contaminants and biological toxins in their raw or uncooked form, and although local culinary methods have usually evolved for dealing with such contaminants prior to consumption, cases of poisoning still occasionally occur. This risk of poisoning is in addition to the hazards of food-borne infection considered elsewhere in this section.

Travellers should therefore know which foods carry a significant danger, and either avoid them completely or exercise extreme caution. The foods themselves range from cassava, eaten as a staple throughout the tropics, to 'fugu' or puffer fish, considered a delicacy in Japan and much of the Indo-Pacific.

Types of poisoning

The variety of potential food contaminants and toxins is vast and their effects range from the trivial and inconvenient to the frankly dramatic. In general, however, poisoning can be classified into 'acute' and 'chronic' varieties. *Acute* poisoning, is more or less immediate in onset and may follow consumption of a single portion of contaminated food. *Chronic* poisoning is a long-term process which generally follows the repeated consumption of small amounts of a toxic substance over an extended period—so it is unlikely to appear in travellers on a short trip.

Acute poisoning

Acute poisoning may be produced by foods of either plant or animal origin.

Plant toxins

Local customs have generally developed to allow the consumption of potentially poisonous plant material by the use of particular methods of preparation which minimize the hazard. Travellers should be wary of preparing unusual foods for themselves, but may be reasonably confident that food prepared by local people will be innocuous. Poisoning is much more likely to result from eating wild berries or fungi. The two most toxic flowering plants are the castor bean (*Ricinus communis*) and the rosary pea (*Abrus precatorius*). The latter is sometimes encountered in bead necklaces, usually of African origin, and should be confined to this decorative use. If seeds with broken coats are swallowed, persistent diarrhoea, often with bloody mucus, begins after a latent period of up to three days. Death may result. Many mushrooms are toxic, but generally produce gastro-intestinal symptoms, sweating or headache, which will resolve spontaneously after a few hours of discomfort. A few mushrooms have an alcohol-sensitizing effect, whilst others induce hallucinations. Only *Amanita phalloides* and similar types are likely to be fatal.

Cassava (manioc) is a dietary staple in many tropical countries. The tubers may be eaten whole, rather like sweet potatoes, or may be processed to produce a flour which is used to make bread. The problem is that cassava, particularly the 'bitter' varieties, contains poisonous hydrocyanic acid. When the tubers are damaged, an enzyme accelerates the release of the cyanide.

The poisonous nature of cassava has long been recognized in every country where it is used, and traditional ways of preparing the tubers minimize the amount of cyanide that reaches the table. These methods include soaking, washing in running water, boiling and pounding.

Consumption of improperly prepared cassava results in the dramatic onset of abdominal pain and vomiting, progressing to mental confusion, muscle paralysis, and ultimately to respiratory failure in fatal cases.

Ackee Travellers to Jamaica or Nigeria may be introduced to the delights of the fruit of *Blighia sapida*, known as the *ackee* in Jamaica and *isin* in Nigeria.

In Jamaica, this strange fruit is served up with bacon or salt-fish as a kind of scrambled egg look-alike. Problems arise if the fruit is eaten unripe or has been improperly prepared, as it contains a potent toxin that rapidly lowers the blood sugar level. The victim succumbs rapidly to vomiting, followed by convulsions, coma, and death in the majority of cases. This is more likely to occur in the already malnourished, but unripe fruit can be lethal to anyone. Correct preparation involves boiling the fruit and then discarding the water.

Animal Toxins

The vast majority of poisonings are the result of eating fish or other forms of sea food. There are approximately 1200 marine species known to be poisonous or venomous. They are found throughout the world but only pose a medical or socio-economic hazard in a few areas.

Animal toxins fall into two categories. First, a normal constituent of the animal or one of its organs may be toxic. For example Eskimos have always known of the toxicity of polar bear liver, which contains immensely high levels of vitamin A. Second, the animal itself may be contaminated with toxins.

Puffer fish The puffer fish—known as 'fugu' in Japan—is a kind of culinary Russian Roulette. It is said to be sufficiently delicious to warrant the considerable risk attached to its consumption. Japanese chefs have to be specially licensed to carry out the delicate operation of removing the roe, liver, and skin which contain the lethal *tetrodotoxin*, but every year several deaths occur from eating fugu. About 40 per cent of those who develop significant signs and symptoms die. Death is said to be preceded by a tingling sensation of the lips . . .

Paralytic shellfish poisoning Rather less dramatic in onset, but nonetheless unpleasant, is the poisoning caused by eating fish, or more often shellfish, which have ingested plankton containing *saxitoxin*. In some areas of the world, such as the Caribbean, dinoflagellate protozoa may be present in such large numbers that the sea looks red and the amount of saxitoxin in the flesh of fish or shellfish will be correspondingly high. Fishermen in areas which are commonly affected know not to harvest the fish when there is a 'red tide'. Symptoms of poisoning are slowing of the heart rate even to the point of heart failure, and muscle paralysis. Mild poisoning may result from ingesting just 1 milligram of the toxin, which could be found in a single clam. Without treatment 4 milligrams of the toxin would be fatal.

Ciguatera Another form of fish poisoning is *ciguatera*. Many fish, in particular the red snapper, grouper, and barracuda, in a broad circumglobal belt from 35 degrees North to 35 degrees South, particularly in the tropical Pacific and Caribbean, are capable of accumulating *ciguatoxin* from their foodstuffs. The toxin is present in the entire flesh of the fish. Unfortunately, the problem may suddenly appear in any one location after years of absence, and is not signalled by any visible change in the sea. Symptoms appear one to six hours after consumption of the fish and include abdominal pain, nausea, vomiting, numbness, and tingling of the lips and tongue, and shooting pain in the extremities. In severe cases, blood pressure falls and respiratory paralysis can lead to death. Treatment is difficult.

Scombroid poisoning Some fish of the mackerel or tuna varieties may be the cause of poisoning if they are inadequately refrigerated and preserved. Cooking does not destroy the toxin. A toxic substance, originally thought to be histamine, is formed by the action of enzymes on the muscle of the dead fish. Recent research suggests that another toxin, *saurine*, is also formed. This causes nausea, vomiting, diarrhoea, and epigastric pain. The face of the victim becomes flushed and burning and there may be numbness, thirst, and generalized urticaria. Fortunately all these signs and symptoms, which arise within about 2 hours of the meal, subside within 12–16 hours. No treatment is required. It is said that the flesh of the fish becomes rather peppery. This type of poisoning may occur anywhere in the world.

Chronic poisoning

The long-term effects of food toxins are of rather less importance to travellers than acute poisons, but travellers should none the less be aware of the dangers of certain moulds and metals.

Mycotoxins

Mycotoxins, the toxins produced by moulds, have been implicated in several diseases both in tropical and in temperate climates. Improper food storage frequently causes problems, because moulds grow well in warm damp conditions. Mould-contaminated food may be consumed directly by man, or by domestic animals reared for food—pigs for example—which are capable of accumulating toxins in their flesh. Balkan nephropathy, a strange and serious disease of the kidneys confined to areas of Yugoslavia, Rumania, and Bulgaria, was first recognized thirty years ago. Only recently has it been linked to consumption of a mould that grows on maize.

Aflatoxin is the toxin of *Aspergillus flavus*, which grows on peanuts and other crops. The toxin is highly carcinogenic, and consumption of mouldy peanuts explains the high incidence of liver cancer in some parts of Africa—particularly West Africa. This has serious economic implications for many of the countries involved.

Eating mouldy cornmeal may be one of the factors involved in the high incidence of cancer of the oesophagus (gullet) found in areas of China. Excessive consumption of pickles and preserved foods containing nitrites may also be contributing factors.

Poor nutritional status, particularly combined with deficiency of vitamins A and C, probably increases susceptibility to mycotoxins. The well-nourished traveller may be at rather less risk than the indigenous population, but would still be well advised to avoid mouldy foods.

Metals

Various metals can be toxic. Lead from cooking pots is found in high levels in home-brewed beers in various parts of Africa, and can lead to chronic poisoning. Mercury present in seed dressing has caused poisoning in starving peasants in Iraq, forced by hunger to eat the grain intended for planting.

Summary of advice for travellers

- Food toxins and contaminants are so diverse that there are no really hard-and-fast rules for the traveller to follow. Generally, where food is known to be hazardous—such as with cassava or puffer fish—traditional local methods of preparation have evolved to minimize the risk.
- Most such traditions have a basis in fact, and are best observed. Obviously decayed or mouldy foods, either plant or animal, are likely to cause toxic effects.

The Guinea worm

Guinea worm is an alarming and distasteful infection, not particularly dangerous in itself but liable to cause bacterial skin infection and serious sepsis. Unusual in travellers, the infection is avoided by careful choice and treatment of drinking water supplies.

Dr David Haddock *was a Senior Lecturer in Tropical Medicine at the Liverpool School of Tropical Medicine. He also worked for long periods in Tanzania, Ghana, Nigeria, and Saudi Arabia, and was a WHO consultant in Ghana and the Sudan.*
Dr George Wyatt *is a Senior Lecturer in Tropical Medicine at the Liverpool School of Tropical Medicine.*

The total eradication of guinea worm infection from the world was adopted as a goal by the World Health Assembly in 1986. It is hoped that this ancient disease will follow smallpox into oblivion; but at present it is alive and well in parts of Africa where there are estimated to be about 3 million new cases each year. India has made considerable progress towards eradicating this disease and control programmes are also under way in Pakistan. It is an infection of poor people in rural areas who drink water from infected pools or step wells. Because infection does not confer immunity against reinfection many people suffer from the disease each year and much time is lost from growing food or attending school.

About the disease

The female worm is 60–100 cm long and 2 mm in diameter. It travels under the skin and usually appears in the legs. The male worm is much smaller and dies after accomplishing his life's work—impregnating the female!

The female worm reaches maturity about one year after initial infection, and secretes chemicals that cause ulceration of the overlying skin in the region of the creature's head. The worm's uterus protrudes through the resulting ulcer, and millions of living larvae are discharged like drops of milk each time the ulcer is exposed to water. After about three weeks, birth of the larvae is complete and the worm dies. It is reabsorbed, emerges from the ulcer or is extracted. This may be the end of the infestation, but unfortunately secondary bacterial infection of the ulcerated skin is common and may lead to serious sepsis in adjacent tissues, infection of neighbouring joints, or even tetanus.

Many villagers are incapacitated for weeks at a time by guinea worms. After the worm has discharged her larvae the old method of attaching the worm to a stick and winding it out of the ulcer slowly day by day is still useful; but the ulcer must be kept clean, well covered, and away from water sources used for drinking. Several drugs are available to facilitate extraction of the worm and antibiotics may be needed for bacterial infection.

How infection is spread

Larvae that escape from the worm through the skin ulcer and reach fresh water may be swallowed by tiny shrimp-like creatures called cyclops. Within cyclops the larvae develop and grow, and become infective to humans about four weeks later. Once swallowed in contaminated water the cyclops are digested freeing the larvae, which then burrow through the intestinal wall; they find their way to the subcutaneous tissues and become adult in about a year.

Contamination of water supplies occurs when people with Guinea worm ulceration stand in drinking water or bathe their ulcers there. The larvae can then reach and infect cyclops which are later swallowed. Transmission is especially common during the dry season when water supplies in ponds and wells dry up or become small in volume.

Guinea worm and travellers

Travellers are at risk if they drink untreated water from primitive water supplies in areas where Guinea worm infection exists. Guinea worm is an unusual infection in travellers unless they are living rough or travelling in poor rural areas in the tropics.

Prevention

- Guinea worm is one of many diseases spread by polluted water. Travellers should be as careful as possible about the water they drink (see next chapter). Water should be boiled or filtered to remove the cyclops which transmit the disease. Because of the danger of tetanus, tetanus precautions are advisable if a guinea worm ulcer develops (see tetanus, p. 88).

Safe water

Careful choice or treatment of water—whether for drinking, washing, preparing food or swimming in—is one of the most important health precautions a traveller can take.

Hemda Garelick *is a Research Fellow at the London School of Hygiene and Tropical Medicine.*

Water is essential for our survival: according to our size, activity, culture, health status, climate, and choice of clothing, we require between two and five litres of water (four and ten US pints) every day.

In the developed world, the availability of safe water in more or less unlimited quantities is taken for granted. This does not apply in the developing world: in many countries, easy access to a safe water supply—and that does not necessarily mean a piped water supply—is available to only about 70–80 per cent of the urban population and to about 40 per cent of the rural population. Figures for access to sanitary facilities are even worse, so it is hardly surprising that water-related diseases remain a major problem in the developing world and that travellers to such countries are at risk.

Water and disease

Water-related infections can be divided into four groups, according to how they are transmitted;

1. Those spread by drinking contaminated water;
2. Those spread through lack of hygiene and sanitary facilities (lack of water);
3. Those spread through *direct* contact with contaminated water (e.g. swimming) or *indirect* contact (e.g. eating fish that carry infection from contaminated water);
4. Those spread through bites of insects that need water in order to breed (see particularly malaria, pp. 117–28);

In the first two categories, the infections of greatest importance to the traveller are those transmitted by the faecal-oral route, that is from one person's faeces to another person's mouth.

These include diarrhoeal diseases, dysenteries, typhoid, poliomyelitis, hepatitis A, and worm infections, discussed in earlier chapters.

In the third category, diseases transmitted through direct or indirect contact with water include schistosomiasis (see pp. 90–4), guinea worm (p. 71), fish tapeworms, and liver flukes.

Chemical contamination (unless gross) is likely to affect travellers far less than the local population, because the harmful effects tend to be cumulative and related to duration of exposure. In contrast, biological contamination (e.g. pathogenic micro-organisms) has a more acute effect on travellers than on local people who may have acquired partial or full immunity to locally prevalent infections.

Water and the traveller

Contamination of water supplies is usually due to poor sanitation close to water sources, sewage disposal into the sources themselves, leakage of sewage into distribution systems or contamination with industrial or farm waste. Even if a piped water supply is safe at its source, it is not always safe by the time it reaches the tap. *Intermittent* tap-water supplies should be regarded as particularly suspect.

Travellers on short trips to areas with water supplies of uncertain quality should avoid drinking tap water, or untreated water from any other source. It is best to keep to hot drinks, bottled or canned drinks of well-known brand names—international standards of water treatment are usually followed at bottling plants. Carbonated drinks are acidic, and slightly safer. Make sure that all bottles are opened in your presence, and that their rims are clean and dry.

Boiling is always a good way of treating water. Some hotels supply boiled water on request and this can be used for drinking, or for brushing teeth. Portable boiling elements that can boil small quantities of water are useful when the right voltage of electricity is available. Refuse politely any cold drink from an unknown source.

Ice is only as safe as the water from which it is made, and should not be put in drinks unless it is known to be safe. Drinks can be cooled by placing them on ice rather than adding ice to them.

Alcohol may be a medical disinfectant, but should not be relied upon to sterilize water. Ethanol is most effective at a concentration of 50–70 per cent; below 20 per cent, its bactericidal action is negligible. Spirits labelled 95 proof contain only about 47 per cent alcohol. Beware of methylated alcohol, which is very poisonous, and should never be added to drinking water.

If no other safe water supply can be obtained, tap water that is too hot to touch can be left to cool and is generally safe to drink.

Those planning a trip to remote areas, or intending to live in countries where drinking water is not readily available, should know about the various possible methods for making water safe.

Water treatment

The choice of processes used in a public water treatment plant depends on the physical, chemical, and microbiological characteristics of the water, but the main steps generally necessary are these:

1. The removal of suspended solids by precipitation, sedimentation, or filtration.
2. Disinfection—usually by chlorination—to inactivate and kill the possible pathogens (disease-causing infective agents).

Treating small quantities of water is based on similar principles but is rather easier, and a wider range of processes is possible.

Begin by choosing the purest possible source. This is likely to be tap water, well water, spring water, or collected rain water, all of which are preferable to surface water e.g. rivers, streams, or pond water, which tend to be polluted. Rain water can be collected from roofs, which should be clean and made of tiles or sheeting, not of lead or thatch.

Boiling

Boiling is the most effective way of sterilizing water. It kills all infective agents including amoebic cysts, which are resistant to chlorine.

This treatment is not affected by the turbidity or the chemical characteristics of the water. The only limitation of boiling is that it is not always practical and is generally suitable only for small quantities. The water should be boiled vigorously for five minutes (this is sufficient even at high altitude).

Boiling tends to make water taste flat, because it reduces the amount of dissolved gases. To improve the taste, drinking water should be allowed to cool in a covered, partially filled container for a few hours, in the same container in which it has been boiled.

Filtration

Filtration is a process that should be used when boiling is not practicable. It is either an initial step or can produce safe water in a single step when the right equipment is used.

Removal of suspended solids In order to make disinfection (with chlorine or iodine) as effective as possible, suspended solids and organic matter must be removed. Organic matter interferes with the process of chemical disinfection, and pathogens adsorbed to suspended solid are less susceptible to disinfection.

Filtration through a closely woven cloth is adequate, and filtration bags such as the Millbank bag are available commercially. These can take from five to twenty-five litres (about one to five gallons). However, it is important to remember that although the water may look clear it has not yet been made safe, and requires further treatment.

Removal of pathogens Ceramic filter 'candles' of a very fine pore size (which can be as fine as 0·5 μ, the finer the better) are available commercially, and some units can be attached to piped water supplies. They remove most pathogens found in water (bacteria, amoebic cysts, and some viruses). Some of the filters are impregnated with silver, which acts as a bactericide and may also destroy certain viruses.

Manufacturers' instructions on the operation and maintenance of fiiters should be followed. Filters should be examined regularly for cracks and leaks. They should be cleaned by scrubbing, and boiled (unless impregnated with silver) when clogged and at weekly intervals.

Disposable paper cartridge filters are also available. They should be kept wet when in use, or the paper filter may shrink or crack.

Most carbon filters are not recommended for making water safe. They are normally used to improve the taste of clean water. They remove organic matter, dissolved chlorine, and pathogens by a mechanism of adsorption, not by mechanical straining. When overloaded they can shed the adsorbed material, and unless impregnated with silver, bacteria may even grow on the filter. The efficiency of the filter over a period of time will depend on the organic load of the water: travellers may find it difficult to determine when the filter is exhausted. Some ceramic filter candles have the option of adding activated carbon to improve the taste. It is important to ensure that any such combined filter does not rely on the carbon for removal of pathogens. Only in cases of high chemical contamination will addition of activated carbon to the filter be advantageous to health.

Filtered water should always be boiled or disinfected before being given to babies and small children.

There are a great many convenient-looking purification devices on the market based on filtration, and they are often recommended to travellers. The manufacturers frequently make extravagant claims about the effectiveness and safety of their products without producing any objective and convincing evidence to support their claims—such as precise details of how and by whom microbiological tests were performed. Without this evidence, such gadgets must always be regarded with suspicion, however attractive they may seem. The safest purification methods remain boiling and chemical disinfection.

Chemical disinfection

Chemical disinfection is recommended when boiling or fine-pore filtration is not possible, or when extra safety is required.

Chlorine This is the most widely used water disinfectant. It kills living organisms by inactivating biologically active compounds. However, it also reacts with any other organic matter that may be present in the water, and this reduces the amount of chlorine available to kill pathogens. Pathogens adsorbed to suspended solids may also be protected from disinfection. Water should thus be filtered before disinfection (see above).

Chlorine is an effective disinfectant against bacteria and some viruses, although less effective against amoebic cysts. The amount of chlorine needed for inactivation of amoebic cysts is 10 times that needed for inactivation of bacteria.

Iodine This works in a similar way to chlorine and is thought to be a more effective disinfectant, especially against amoebic cysts.

Both chlorine-based and iodine-based disinfection tablets are available commercially. When these are used, it is important to follow manufacturers' instructions carefully, and to make sure that water to be treated is clear.

Liquid chlorine laundry bleach and first aid tincture of iodine can also be used. The exact constituents and concentration of the solutions should be determined before use. Liquid chlorine laundry bleach usually contains 4–6 per cent available chlorine, and one to two drops (1 drop = 0·05 ml) of such a solution (or alternatively four to eight drops of a 1 per cent solution) should be added to each litre of water. Tincture of iodine usually contains 2 per cent iodine, and four drops of the solution should be added to one litre of water.

In both cases, the treated water should be allowed to stand for 20–30 minutes before use, although very cold water should be allowed to stand longer (a few hours if possible).

The use of iodine in this way is *not* thought to be harmful, though regular long term use should probably be avoided on theoretical grounds; likewise, use in pregnancy has not been associated with harmful effects, but is probably also best avoided on theoretical grounds; anyone with a thyroid problem should consult their doctor first.

Storage of treated water

Treated water should be stored in conditions that will prevent recontamination, and preferably in the same container in which it has been treated. If this is impractical, make sure that storage containers are either sterile or disinfected. They should always be covered, and should ideally have a tap at the bottom or a narrow opening, thus minimizing the risk of contamination when drawing off the treated water. Store water in a cool place, away from children.

Sanitation and hygiene

Sanitary facilities should be kept as far away as possible from water and food. Hands must always be washed before handling food and drink. Personal hygiene should be maintained at the highest standard possible.

Food hygiene

Food—especially fresh food obtained locally in areas where sanitary conditions are poor—should always be regarded as contaminated.

Fruit and vegetables should be washed thoroughly in clean soapy water and then rinsed with treated water. Rinsing alone is not enough—sterilizing chemicals in treated water will not kill pathogens on fruit and vegetables because contact time is not long enough.

Soaking in chlorine (e.g. using Milton tablets) or iodine—the concentration of either should be roughly 3 times that normally used for drinking water purification—is usually also effective, though the contact time necessary depends on how badly contaminated the food is.

Soaking in potassium permanganate, traditionally recommended for this purpose, is less reliable; permanganate has few medical uses these days.

Dipping in boiling water is a simple and effective alternative.

Avoid eating any raw vegetables or cold food prepared by others—especially in restaurants and hotels, and especially salads. (If you really must eat a salad that looks suspect, plenty of lemon juice or strong vinegar in the dressing will slightly reduce the risk.)

Seafood, fish, and meat should always be well cooked, and unpasteurized milk should be boiled or avoided.

Swimming

Swimming in the sea is usually safe, unless it is close to sewage works or highly populated areas with no proper sanitary facilities (see also p. 458). Swimming in fresh surface water is not advised, especially in areas where schistosomiasis (bilharzia) (see pp. 90–4) and Guinea worm (p. 71) are found.

Suppliers

1. Chlorination or iodination tablets

Boots Co. Ltd, Nottingham NG2 3AA, England (Chlorination tablets)

Survival Aids Ltd, Morland, Penrith, Cumbria CA10 3AZ, England

Wisconsin Pharmacal Co. (Potable Aqua iodination tablets), 6769 North Industrial Road, Milwaukee, Wisconsin 53223, USA

2. Filtration bags (Millbank)
   Johnson-Progress Ltd, Carpenters Rd, Stratford, London E15 2DA, England
3. Ceramic candle filtration units and pumps
   Fairy Industrial Ceramic Ltd, Filleybrooks, Stone, Staffs ST15 OPU, England

   Filopur, Resource Development & Engineering Systems, 7 Rue Muzy, 1207 Geneva, Switzerland

   Katadyn Filters, 37 Town End, Wilsford (nr. Grantham), Lincs, NG32 3NX, England, Tel. 0400–30285 (also supplies industrial and ultra-violet purification units)

   Katadyn USA Inc., 12219 St James Road, Potomac, MD 20854, USA, Tel. 301 251–0570

   Performance Filters (NA) Inc., 2940 Portsmouth Avenue, Cincinnatti OH 45208, USA.
4. Paper cartridge filters
   Victoria Industrial Contract Ltd., 443–445 Holloway Rd, London N7 6LW, England
5. Boiling elements
   Pifco Mini-boiler
   Pifco Ltd, Princess St, Failsworth, Manchester M35 OHS, England

For further advice:

Departments of Medical Microbiology and Tropical Hygiene,
London School of Hygiene and Tropical Medicine, Keppel St, London WC1E, 7HT, England

3

Diseases of 'contact'

3

Diseases of contact

Routes of infection

[illegible]

Tuberculosis

Tuberculosis is mainly a risk to children of expatriates living in the tropics. The BCG vaccine provides valuable protection.

Professor Denis A. Mitchison *conducts extensive collaborative research with centres in East and Central Africa, India, Hong Kong, Singapore, and Algeria, to which he travels. He is a WHO Expert in Tuberculosis.*

The risk of getting tuberculosis (TB) from travel is small, even if you intend to live abroad for a long time in an area where the disease is common. TB is found most frequently in the tropics, particularly in South-East Asia, where in many countries about one in 500 of the population suffer from severe disease. TB is also fairly common in Africa, the Middle East, and Central America.

In poor developing countries there has been little or no change in the amount of disease over the past two or three decades. In contrast in the developed countries, the number of people infected with tubercle bacilli has fallen steadily by about 14 per cent each year.

Sources of infection

TB is caused by tubercle bacilli and usually affects the lungs. It is almost always spread by the airborne route. People with severe disease harbour numerous tubercle bacilli in their sputum (often 1 million bacilli per cc). On coughing they produce a fine mist of sputum particles that dry quickly, leaving a cloud of tiny 'droplet nuclei'. These can remain suspended in the air and are small enough to carry bacilli into the innermost parts of the lungs, where they cause a primary focus of disease; a skin test (Heaf, Mantoux, or Tine tests) with tuberculin, a product of tubercle bacilli, now becomes positive, indicating developing immunity.

TB does not always cause serious illness and in most individuals, the primary focus heals without overt signs of disease, although the risk in young unvaccinated children is much higher than in adults.

TB can also be contracted by drinking milk from cows that have TB in their udders, in which case tubercle bacilli usually enter the body through the tonsils and the lymph glands of the neck. (Although these 'bovine' bacilli are slightly different from the bacilli that normally produce human TB, they are still capable of producing disease in humans; human bacilli, however, never cause disease in cows.)

Bovine tubercle bacilli are rarely found in patients in tropical countries, so transmission of the disease by the milk-borne route appears to be uncommon. This may be because the Zebu cattle found in the tropics are relatively immune to TB or because milk in these countries is boiled as a matter of routine. In most other countries bovine tuberculosis has been eliminated and milk is pasteurized.

People do not catch the disease by contact with infected objects.

Active disease

On the unusual occasions when an infection with tubercle bacilli becomes established, the bacilli in the primary lesions may grow to produce active disease locally, or may travel in the bloodstream to produce disease elsewhere. Active TB, with symptoms such as a chronic cough with production of sputum which may be bloodstained, and fever, may start at any time from a few weeks to many years after the initial infection, although the risk decreases with time.

Treatment with antituberculous drugs is very effective, but must be continued for at least six to nine months because the bacilli multiply much more slowly than other bacteria, and a correspondingly longer period of contact with the drugs is needed to kill them.

Immunization

Immunization against TB (see p. 485) is with tubercle bacilli of the BCG strain (Bacille Calmette Guérin, for the French bacteriologists who introduced it). These bacilli are of a special 'attenuated' type: although they are alive and provoke the development of immunity, they cannot cause disease.

The vaccine goes into the skin, after which a small ulcer develops that can take several weeks to heal. Conversion of the tuberculin skin test to positive and development of immunity are thought to occur about six weeks after vaccination. This is why vaccination should take place well before the date of departure.

In the UK, BCG is offered to children aged twelve to fourteen if they are tuberculin negative and are therefore not already immune from previous contact with tubercle bacilli.

BCG has been shown to provide a very valuable degree of protection against TB, lasting at least ten years, and reducing the number of cases by 80 per cent. After this, however, protection appears to decline; the reasons for this are not clear.

In many other countries BCG is given at birth or soon after; its overall effectiveness in infancy is not known, but it appears to prevent the most serious complications of childhood TB.

Summary of advice for travellers

- No special precautions are necessary for those travelling in Europe or North America.

- For travellers to areas of high prevalence, BCG vaccination needs to be considered. In essence, the younger the person and the longer he or she intends to stay abroad, the stronger the case for vaccination. I would suggest that it is mandatory in children under about twelve, even for fairly short visits. However, it would be of doubtful value in adults over about thirty-five (for whom we have no evidence of its efficacy), even if they are tuberculin negative.

- For short-term travellers to areas of high prevalence, special precautions in taking milk or milk products are not usually necessary. However, expatriate families should ensure that their milk is boiled, and that butter is made from pasteurized milk or at least comes from a herd that is well looked after. When yoghurt or cheese is made, the souring of the milk kills tubercle bacilli and removes the risk.

- Domestic staff can get infective TB and be a real risk for an expatriate family. Anyone who develops a chronic cough for three or four weeks or more (often the only sign of TB) should be sent to the local government chest clinic for chest X-ray and sputum examination, which will usually be done free. Should infectious disease be diagnosed, the risk of TB developing in any child not previously BCG vaccinated is greatly diminished if he or she is started immediately on chemoprophylaxis with antituberculosis drugs. The drug usually given is isoniazid, either in tablet or syrup form, and it must be taken for at least six months.

- **Travellers from the USA** are not normally offered BCG vaccination, because of a fundamentally different public health policy towards TB, and should discuss prevention of this disease with their own doctor before departure.

  If a high risk of TB is anticipated, they may sometimes be offered chemoprophylaxis with isoniazid instead. It is not usually given for more than one year, so that it cannot be relied upon to provide protection for the long term expatriate.

  The risk of liver damage occurring during treatment with isoniazid increases with age; it is negligible in children, but sufficiently large in those aged thirty-five or more as to make chemoprophylaxis inadvisable.

Tetanus

All travellers should be immunized against tetanus, because the risks are widespread and correct treatment following injury may be difficult to obtain.

Dr David Haddock *was a Senior Lecturer in Tropical Medicine at the Liverpool School of Tropical Medicine. He also worked for long periods in Tanzania, Ghana, Nigeria, and Saudi Arabia, and was a WHO consultant in Ghana and the Sudan.*
Dr George Wyatt *is a Senior Lecturer in Tropical Medicine at the Liverpool School of Tropical Medicine.*

Tetanus is a leading cause of death in many developing countries, particularly in hot, moist tropical areas. Probably 500 000 people die each year from tetanus, though 90 per cent of these are newborn infants—who are at special risk owing to unhygienic methods of cutting and dressing the umbilical cord after birth, with contamination and infection.

Today, tetanus is about 100 times more common in tropical Africa than in the UK; sixty years ago it used to be common in Europe and the USA, but immunization and good medical care have greatly reduced its incidence. Globally, it is an important disease because it is common, often fatal, and although difficult to treat, is easily prevented.

How infection occurs and how disease is spread

Tetanus is caused by infection of wounds with a bacterium called *Clostridium tetani*, which damages the nervous system and muscles with a powerful toxin. The toxin causes forceful, continuous muscle contraction and severe spasm, often leading to death from respiratory problems and exhaustion. As little as 0·1 mg of toxin may be fatal to an adult and the fatality rate from tetanus is about 40–50 per cent in the absence of highly specialized treatment. The first sign of disease is often spasm of the jaw muscles—which is why the disease is often called 'lockjaw'. The muscle spasm interferes with swallowing.

Clostridium tetani lives in the intestinal tracts of man and animals, where it does not cause disease; but the bacteria produce spores, which are passed in the faeces and contaminate the environment. Spores of *C. tetani* persist for years in soil and dust, and are resistant to heat, drying, chemicals, and sunlight; steam heat under pressure (autoclaving) at 115°C for five minutes is necessary to destroy them.

Most outside environments are contaminated with tetanus spores, particularly in agricultural areas where animal manure is used.

Tetanus bacilli can develop from the spores and produce toxin in the absence of oxygen, and they multiply in deep, dirty wounds containing foreign material and dead tissue, where the local oxygen levels are very low. Many different kinds of injury favour multiplication of tetanus bacilli, and some are listed below, *although in about 30 per cent of cases the injury is probably a small puncture wound, too small to attract attention.*

Wounds and injuries associated with tetanus

- Deep, dirty wounds
- Compound fractures (fractures with broken skin)
- Bites of animals and humans
- Non-sterile injections
- Operations
- Tattooing, ear piercing, and traditional circumcision
- Chronic ulcers and ear infections
- The uterus following childbirth, miscarriage, or abortion
- Infected umbilical cords in the newborn

The symptoms of tetanus usually begin seven to fourteen days after injury.

Many wounds causing tetanus occur on the feet or legs. Walking around bare-footed is inadvisable because of the tetanus hazard, and also because of the dangers of skin-penetrating worm larvae (p. 46) and jigger fleas (p. 171).

Prevention

The best method of prevention is by immunization with tetanus toxoid in infancy, with booster doses every ten years (although immunity probably lasts for longer than this). Those who suffer an injury may require a further dose, especially if it has been longer than 5 years since their last immunization.

Injured persons who have not been immunized previously or are unsure of their immunization status need to be given ready-made tetanus antibodies in the form of human tetanus immunoglobulin (HTIG) in one arm and tetanus toxoid in the other. If HTIG is not available anti-tetanus serum (ATS) produced in horses can be used, but there is an increased risk of allergic reactions particularly if the person has been exposed to horse serum before. Another important preventive measure is the proper cleaning of wounds with removal of any dead tissue. Professional treatment of dirty or deep wounds should be obtained if possible. First-aid treatment includes washing the wound with clean water and soap or weak detergents soon after the injury. Strong antiseptics may damage the tissues and should be avoided. Antibiotics cannot be relied upon to prevent tetanus by themselves.

Travellers should make every effect to ensure that they receive protection against tetanus after any serious injury—this protection may not be offered routinely in some areas.

Summary of advice for travellers

- Tetanus is rare in travellers taking a conventional holiday, but is a greater hazard for those going on safari, trekking, climbing, or exploring.

- All travellers should check that they have received a primary immunization course against tetanus and that they have had a booster injection within the last ten years. Since routine immunization against tetanus in infancy, as part of DPT (diphtheria, pertussis, tetanus) triple vaccine, was only introduced in 1961 in the UK, many older people will not have received primary immunization, unless for instance they have served in the armed forces.

- Primary immunization against tetanus is obtained by three injections of tetanus toxoid. Intervals of 6–8 weeks between the first and second doses and 4–6 months between the second and third dose are best. After this immunity is maintained by booster doses of toxoid every ten years, or sooner if there is an injury. Too frequent injections of toxoid should be avoided as allergic reactions may occur. It is safe to have tetanus toxoid injections at the same time as other immunizations.

Schistosomiasis (bilharzia)

Schistosomiasis is an unpleasant disease spread by contact with fresh water. Travellers are at risk in most tropical areas.

Dr Clinton Manson-Bahr *taught and practised in Africa and the Western Pacific for twenty-three years. He is a descendant of Sir Patrick Manson, the founder of modern Tropical Medicine, and is the editor of Manson's* Tropical Diseases*—the foremost medical textbook on the subject.*

Schistosomiasis, or bilharzia as it is also called, is found throughout the tropics and subtropics. It is a grave problem in countries where it is common, because although not a 'killer' disease in the usual sense, it gnaws insidiously at the general health of entire populations. The geographical distribution of the disease is shown in Map 3.1 opposite.

At least 200 million people around the world are afflicted, and this figure is rising rapidly; ironically, the dams, irrigation schemes, and agricultural projects so necessary for the fight against world poverty and hunger themselves create conditions in which the disease thrives. Schistosomiasis is a special problem in young children; it hinders development, and reduces life expectancy. It remains a problem in China despite an attempt at eradication that involved the entire nation.

How infection is spread

Schistosomiasis is an infection with one of three kinds of worm, called *Schistosoma haematobium* (urinary schistosomiasis), *Schistosoma mansoni* (intestinal schistosomiasis), and *Schistosoma japonicum* (Far Eastern schistosomiasis).

The fully grown worms live in the veins of the urinary bladder (*S. haematobium*), or the wall of the intestine (*S. mansoni* and *S. japonicum*). The worms produce large numbers of eggs which leave the body through the lining of the bladder or intestines. On contact with fresh water, larvae hatch from the eggs and infect certain varieties of snail in which they develop further, and multiply. More larvae are produced (called *cercariae*), which swim freely in fresh water, and actively seek out and penetrate the skin of a human host.

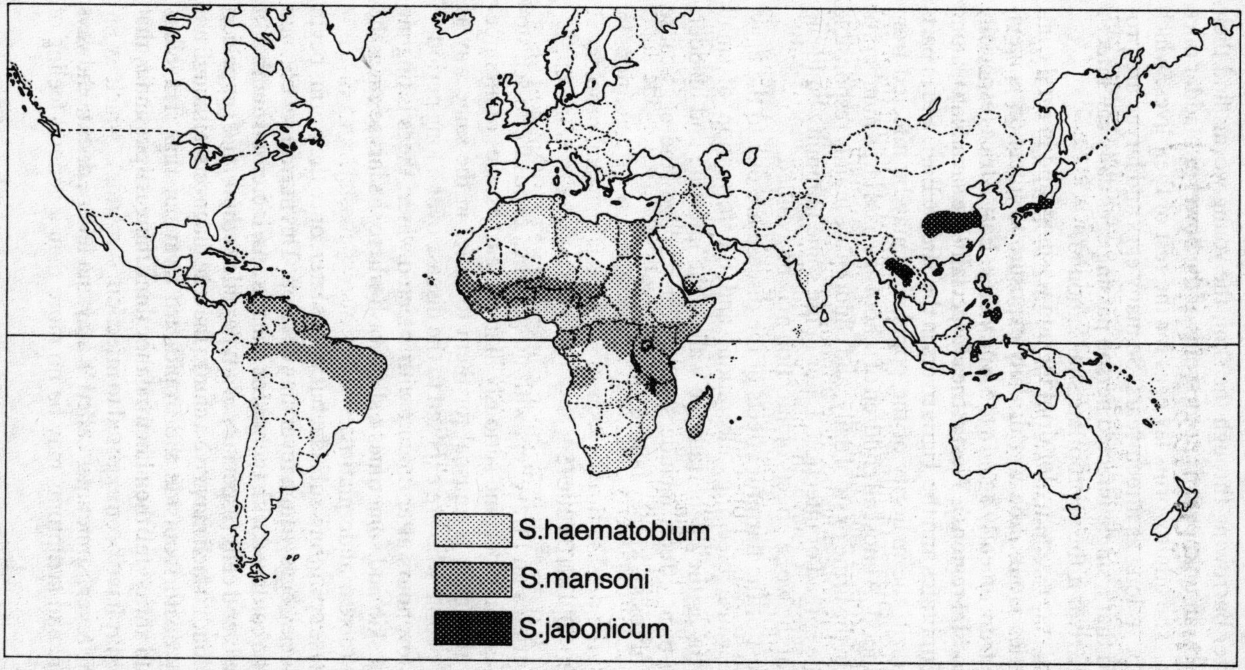

Map. 3.1 Geographical distribution of schistosomiasis (bilharzia). The disease occurs in 74 countries. Travellers requiring specific, localized information may wish to consult the WHO Atlas listed under 'Further reading'.

After burrowing through the skin, the young worms find their way (by an unknown route) to veins of the bowel or bladder once again. The adult worms lay eggs for the rest of their lives, which may be as long as fifteen years. So many eggs and larvae are produced that a single infected person passing eggs daily can infect a whole river if the appropriate snails abound.

Water is necessary for drinking and washing, and in rural communities around the world, daily exposure to infection is inevitable from an early age. In the Nile valley, East Africa (especially the coastal regions), West Africa (especially the savannah), along the Euphrates and the Tigris rivers in the Middle East, and in parts of Brazil, the majority of the population may be infected from childhood. Almost all children of school age pass large numbers of eggs in the urine or stool daily, and children are mainly responsible for the spread of infection. Later in life some immunity builds up so that the worst effects of infection may be avoided.

Most of the harmful effects of the disease are due to the eggs; these cause bleeding, ulceration, and the formation of small growths as they penetrate the wall of the intestine and bladder. Long-term effects include severe liver damage (the eggs cause liver fibrosis), kidney failure, and cancer.

Disease in travellers

Expatriates and travellers with no previous exposure to schistosomiasis may become seriously ill in the early stages of an infection, though it is unusual for them to suffer in the same way as local people who are exposed to the disease over a long period.

A few hours after contact with infected water, there is tingling of the skin and sometimes a slight rash where the larvae enter the body (cercarial dermatitis).

These symptoms subside, but weeks later, once the worms begin producing eggs, a high fever may develop. This may be severe, and may be confused with typhoid or malaria. An increased number of white blood cells (especially of a type called *eosinophils*) appear in the blood, which may give a clue to the true diagnosis, although not many doctors outside the tropics are aware of this. Travellers should always tell their doctor if they think there is a possibility that they may have been exposed to infection.

The fever, sometimes called 'Katayama fever', does not always occur, and symptoms may be no more than a general feeling of lassitude and ill health. Once the infection becomes established, abdominal pain and blood in the urine or stool are common.

Treatment

A new drug is now available for treatment of all forms of schistosomiasis, and is very effective. Praziquantel tablets are given, usually as a single dose, and side-effects are rare.

Travellers at risk

Travellers to all countries shown on Map 3.1 (p. 91) may be in danger of infection. Especially at risk are those who bathe in streams, rivers, or lakes, or who indulge in watersports such as water-skiing and wind-surfing in fresh-water areas; watersports are particularly dangerous because they may involve exposure to surface water over a large area. Activities such as snipe and duck shooting and cross-country walking safaris where streams have to be crossed are also hazardous.

Some areas are especially risky: the Nile valley, Lake Victoria, the Tigris and Euphrates river systems, and artificial lakes such as Lake Kariba in Zimbabwe and Lake Volta in Ghana, which are both notorious. Even small collections of water far from human habitation can give rise to serious infections since baboons can harbour *S. mansoni*, the commonest cause of Katayama fever.

Personal protection

No vaccine is available and none is foreseen in the near future.

Never assume fresh water to be free from bilharzia in an endemic area. Infection can occur on contact with infected water from streams, rivers, and lakes. Even deep water, far offshore, cannot be regarded as safe, and it is dangerous to swim from boats in infected lakes. Salt water and brackish water are safe from schistosomiasis, however, and so is heavily polluted water.

Since the larvae die quickly on removal from water and cannot survive drying, quick drying of exposed skin and clothing does offer some protection. Rubber boots and wetsuits are protective also, but must be dried quickly in the sun after use. Water that has been chlorinated or stored in a snail-free environment for forty-eight hours is safe, since any cercariae present will have died off.

Swimming-pools that are snail-free are safe, but care must be taken that any water entering the pool has been treated. Neglected swimming-pools can rapidly become colonized with snails. Dams are especially dangerous and invariably become infected within ten years of construction.

Check-up on return home (see Appendix 4)

A check-up should involve examination of the urine and stool for the presence of eggs. Remember that eggs take 30–40 days to be produced following initial infection, so tests made earlier than this will be negative. Samples should be taken at least forty days after the last possible exposure. Modern egg concentration methods should always be asked for specifically.

A white blood cell count is advisable, and there is now also a specific and highly accurate serological test (ELISA) for schistosomiasis.

Swimmers' itch

Swimmers' itch is an intensified variety of cercarial dermatitis caused by schistosome larvae which die in the skin and do not develop further. This condition can occur in temperate as well as in tropical countries—recent outbreaks have occurred in the USA. Some hours after exposure to the water an itching sensation develops on the exposed skin surfaces, followed by a rash composed of small red intensely irritant papules which fade after twenty-four hours. No further symptoms occur and no harm results. Antihistamine tablets (p. 349) or ointment are all that is necessary for treatment.

If contact with water cannot be avoided, always observe the following precautions:

- Do not cross streams at points where there is much human contact, such as village river crossings; always cross upstream of a village.
- Wear long trousers and sleeves and dry out immediately in the sun after crossing.
- Wear waterproof footwear when possible.
- Always take particular care to avoid contact with water and remember the risks of baboon-contaminated water. Resist the temptation to strip off and swim after a long hot march.

Diphtheria

Diphtheria is a potentially serious infection, rarely seen in developed countries these days, but still an important hazard to travellers who have not been immunized. All travellers should know or find out if they are immune to diphtheria, and if necessary, should have this checked by a skin test a few weeks before departure.

Dr Clinton Manson-Bahr *taught and practised in Africa and the Western Pacific for twenty-three years. He is a descendant of Sir Patrick Manson, the founder of modern Tropical Medicine, and is the editor of Manson's* Tropical Diseases*—the foremost medical textbook on the subject.*

Diphtheria is caused by a bacillus which in many people lives quite harmlessly in the throat or on the skin without causing disease. People who harbour the bacillus in this way are known as 'carriers'; they are unaffected either because they have been immunized against diphtheria or because they have previously come in contact with the bacillus and have acquired immunity.

Problems arise only when the bacillus spreads from a carrier to a non-immune or susceptible individual. Throat infection with the bacillus may then result in the formation of a thick white membrane which swells and obstructs breathing, possibly causing suffocation.

On the skin, the bacillus can cause an ulcer known as 'Veldt sore'. This is seen most commonly in dry, semi-desert regions where washing facilities are scarce. More importantly, however, the bacillus produces a powerful toxin that may damage the nervous system, causing paralysis of the limbs or swallowing mechanism; the toxin can also affect the heart.

Penicillin is effective against the diphtheria bacillus, and an antitoxin is available to neutralize the toxin.

Infection is spread by direct skin contact with contaminated dust or by inhalation of infective droplets produced when a carrier coughs. Diphtheria of the skin can be prevented by daily washing, and by keeping the skin clean and dry.

Patterns of disease and immunity

The very low incidence of diphtheria in developed countries is due to the safe and reliable vaccine which is widely available and offered to all infants routinely.

Doctors working in developing countries have also reported a steady decline in serious disease, but for a different reason: diphtheria infection of the skin is now known to be widespread in hot, humid climates and this effectively immunizes the local population against the more dangerous forms of the disease.

More recently, however, severe disease has reappeared in tropical countries with an improving standard of hygiene—more frequent washing has meant a decline in the number of skin infections and therefore a fall in the number of people acquiring 'natural' immunity.

Diphtheria and the traveller

Travellers, especially to the tropics, are at risk from all forms of diphtheria unless they have been adequately immunized. Up to the mid-1970s nearly everyone in the developed countries received diphtheria immunization during childhood, so most adults are still adequately protected. Since then, however, attitudes to immunization have changed, mainly because of misinterpretation of risk statistics and irresponsible reporting by the press. In some countries, especially the UK, a substantial number of children have now never been immunized.

All travellers in doubt about their immune status should have this checked with a skin test (Schick test)—the full dose of vaccine may be harmful to those already immune—and should be immunized if they are found to be susceptible.

In the USA, a low dose of diphtheria vaccine is usually combined with tetanus toxoid as a routine procedure (Td), and skin testing before small booster doses is not necessary. A low-dose vaccine has also recently become available in the UK. (*Diphtheria Vaccine for Adults (Adsorbed)*: Regent Laboratories Ltd, Cunard Rd, London NW10 6PN Tel 01–965–3637.)

Cure is readily achieved if treatment is sought promptly when symptoms appear, but prevention is much easier, and clearly preferable.

Most adult travellers are adequately protected but many children remain at risk, and diphtheria will inevitably become a more important hazard to the next generation of travellers.

Meningitis

Meningitis is of little risk to travellers, even for those travelling through the 'meningitis belt' in Africa. Anyone who has had their spleen removed should take particular precautions.

Dr Christopher Ellis *is a Consultant Physician in the Department of Communicable and Tropical Diseases, East Birmingham Hospital, and spent part of his career working in Nigeria.*

The term meningitis means infection of the membrane lining the brain and spinal cord. Many different types of bacteria and viruses can cause meningitis; in general untreated bacterial infections can rapidly be fatal, whereas if a virus is responsible, the infection always subsides without treatment.

Whatever the cause, the patient suffers severe headache and neck stiffness which prevents bending the head forward, and usually prefers to remain in darkness because light is painful to the eyes.

Viral meningitis

All travellers should ensure that they are immune to one particular form of meningitis: that caused by the polio virus (see pp. 53–5). In polio, a form of meningitis usually precedes the paralysis. However, provided the traveller has been immunized as a child, with a booster when necessary before travelling to areas where the disease is still rife, there is no risk whatsoever from this infection.

Other forms of viral meningitis are also more common in areas with inadequate sanitation, since most of the causative viruses are carried from person to person by contaminated food and water. In practice, however, infections are usually not serious, and travellers are seldom affected by anything more than a severe headache in conjunction with a bout of stomach trouble.

Meningococcal meningitis

Meningitis caused by one species of bacterium, the meningococcus, is a particular hazard to travellers because it may occur in epidemics arising apparently out of the blue. Epidemics are especially likely to occur where people are crowded together, and infection is acquired by inhalation of bacteria in tiny droplets of mucus coughed or sneezed into the air—either by someone suffering from the disease, or more often by a healthy 'carrier'. Exposure to cigarette smoke is said to increase the risk. Between epidemics the bacterium survives in the throats of a tiny proportion of the population and only occasionally produces an isolated case of meningitis.

Even in hot countries the onset of cooler weather leads to people crowding together more than usual, so that 'winter' in such countries is often associated with a sharp increase in the number of (healthy) carriers, and sometimes with an outbreak of disease.

Symptoms and treatment

Meningococcal infection often causes a scattered blotchy rash which may precede the usual features of meningitis by a few hours. The disease may be rapidly fatal, death occurring within a few hours of the patient first feeling unwell, so treatment should be started immediately the diagnosis is made or strongly suspected.

Strictly speaking, the diagnosis can be proved only by growing the meningococcus from the fluid that circulates around the brain and spinal cord (the *cerebrospinal* fluid); but in practice, a doctor should be able to make the diagnosis with a fair degree of certainty when faced with a patient with fever and the characteristic rash, and with even more certainty if the features of meningitis are present. Naturally, if an epidemic was in progress a doctor would be particularly inclined to treat a patient, even if no means of proving the diagnosis was available.

Ideally, treatment consists of large doses of penicillin injected into a vein, but where this is impossible Penicillin G should be given intramuscularly in a dose of 2 mega units, 1 mega unit into each buttock. One mega unit should be repeated every eight hours till the temperature is normal. In people allergic to penicillin, chloramphenicol is an alternative and a single intramuscular dose of this antibiotic has produced complete cures. The same may well be true of a single dose of penicillin given intramuscularly but if more is available then it should be given as I have described.

The meningitis belt

The meningitis belt is a semi-desert region known as the Sahel which extends across Africa just to the south of the Sahara desert (between latitudes 10° and 15° North).

Outbreaks of meningococcal meningitis occur regularly in this region, with the onset of cooler weather. Every fifteen years or so epidemics occur on a large scale with great loss of life. Sudan, Ethiopia, and Chad have had recent outbreaks. The meningitis season coincides with European winter and ends with the start of the rains. It therefore coincides with the best time for overland crossing of the Sahara.

Outbreaks have also occurred in India, Nepal, and Saudi Arabia (see also p. 484).

Summary of advice for travellers

- The risk to visitors to any area where an epidemic of meningococcal meningitis is in progress is small, but someone intending to live in close contact with the local population during an epidemic should be immunized beforehand with meningococcal vaccine. The vaccine is not widely available, but in the UK a general practitioner can obtain it on application to the manufacturers (Merieux UK Ltd., Tel. 0628–785291; Smith Kline and French Ltd., Tel. 07073–25111); and it may also be available at specialist immunization centres. In the USA, the only licensed vaccine is manufactured by Connaught Laboratories, and is quadrivalent (active against four different subgroups of meningococci); in case of difficulty obtaining supplies, the manufacturers can be contacted by telephoning (800)–VACCINE.
- Travellers who have had their spleen surgically removed (e.g. after trauma to the abdomen) *should be immunized even if only passing through* the meningitis belt, as their chances of developing meningitis are much increased. They are also at increased risk of malaria, a fact that is not widely realized.
- People who have been in close contact with sufferers from meningococcal infection may be protected from infection by taking antibiotics by mouth for four days after contact, but I would emphasize that the vast majority of people in close contact with sufferers do not go down with meningitis even if they take no precautions of any kind.

Legionnaires' disease

Although legionnaires' disease occasionally hits the headlines, the risks to the traveller are in fact very small.

Dr Christopher Bartlett *has been involved in research on legionnaires' disease and related infections since 1977, and has investigated many outbreaks in the UK and abroad. He was a member of the WHO Working Group on Legionnaires' Disease.*

Legionnaires' disease is a newly recognized disease, so named after a dramatic outbreak of respiratory illness among delegates attending an American Legion convention in Philadelphia in 1976. Despite exhaustive investigation the cause remained a mystery for nearly six months, until eventually a small bacterium now called *Legionella pneumophila* was shown to be responsible. Subsequent studies showed that the disease was not in fact new, and cases dating back to 1947 have now been identified in retrospect.

The bacterium had escaped recognition because it does not grow on the conventional nutrients used to culture micro-organisms in diagnostic laboratories. *Legionella pneumophila* is found naturally in mud, lakes, rivers and streams. Surveys have shown that it commonly colonizes domestic hot and cold water systems and cooling towers used for air-conditioning and industrial purposes.

What is legionnaires' disease?

The principal feature of legionnaires' disease is pneumonia, with fever and cough and often shortness of breath and chest pain as the main symptoms. Diarrhoea or vomiting may also occur in the first few days, and confusion often develops at this stage; a small proportion of victims also develop difficulties with speech and balance.

Legionnaires' disease occurs both sporadically and in outbreaks, and it is the latter that have received the most attention in the media. Although legionnaires' disease is often described as a 'killer' disease, in reality the proportion of fatalities is less than that seen in many other types of pneumonia.

The infection does not appear to be spread from person to person but is acquired from environmental sources. The investigation of outbreaks has shown that hot water systems in public buildings are an important source of infection and, less commonly, the fine water mist generated by cooling towers has also been implicated. Inadequately treated whirlpools and spas have also recently been shown to serve as occasional sources of *Legionella* infections. The infection is thought to be acquired by the inhalation of fine water droplets carrying *Legionella pneumophila*. Drinking water containing bacteria is unlikely to cause the infection. Most people are probably in contact with low concentrations of the bacterium quite frequently at home, at work and elsewhere, but only rarely does this exposure lead to infection.

The diagnosis of legionnaires' disease is not straightforward, because although it is not too difficult to establish that an individual has pneumonia, identification of *Legionella pneumophila* as the cause (rather than any of the other organisms which might be responsible) presents technical problems. Special nutrient media for growing *Legionella pneumophila* from clinical specimens have been developed only recently and are not yet widely in use in diagnostic laboratories. Furthermore, the organism may be present only in very low concentrations in the patient's sputum and, consequently, may be difficult to detect.

The diagnosis can be confirmed by a blood test to detect the specific antibody produced by the patient to combat the infection. With this method, however, it is not possible to make the diagnosis at an early stage of the illness, because at least a week may elapse before measurable levels of antibody appear in the bloodstream. The test is widely available in the UK.

Several antibiotics, principally erythromycin, rifampicin, and some tetracyclines, have been shown to be effective in treating the infection. Many doctors now include one such antibiotic in the early treatment of any undiagnosed primary pneumonia to take account of the possibility of legionnaires' disease.

Legionnaires' disease and the traveller

Only about 3 per cent of all primary pneumonias are due to *Legionella pneumophila* and the majority of these are *not* associated with travel overseas. During the last five years, just over 350 cases of legionnaires' disease have been identified among British travellers—a very low frequency considering the many millions who went abroad during that period. Outbreaks have occurred among guests staying at several hotels in the UK and abroad; investigations revealed that the hotels' water systems were the source of infection in most cases, and have shown that, fortunately, growth of *Legionella pneumophila* can be controlled by continuous chlorination of the water or by raising the hot water temperatures to above 50°C.

So far there is no good evidence that any one country presents a greater risk of legionnaires' disease than any other. Many cases among British travellers have been associated with visits to the Mediterranean region, but this simply reflects the popularity of the region as a holiday destination.

Summary of advice for travellers

- Immunization is not available, but most people are probably not susceptible to *Legionella pneumophila*. The infection is readily treatable if the diagnosis is considered by the attending doctor, so if you should develop a chest infection it would be worth mentioning any recent travel to your doctor.

Creeping eruption (larva migrans and larva currens)

These rather alarming skin problems are caused by skin contact with soil or beaches contaminated with faeces. Treatment is easy and effective.

Dr Clinton Manson-Bahr *taught and practised in Africa and the Western Pacific for twenty-three years. He is a descendant of Sir Patrick Manson, the founder of modern Tropical Medicine, and is the editor of Manson's* Tropical Diseases*—the foremost medical textbook on the subject.*

Larva migrans

Hookworm larvae from dogs, cats, and various other animals occasionally burrow into human skin. Although they are unable to develop further in humans, they are still a nuisance because they migrate aimlessly under the skin, exciting an unpleasant skin reaction and causing slowly moving, itchy red lines. The red lines may sometimes be accompanied by considerable blistering, but any intensely irritant area—especially on the feet—should be suspected.

Larva migrans is contracted by walking in bare feet on sand or soil contaminated by dog or cat faeces. Sandy beaches, *above* the high-water mark, are often contaminated: the beaches of West, East and South Africa as well as Malaysia, Sri Lanka, and Thailand are all areas where this infection is common. It also occurs in North America (especially the Atlantic and Gulf coasts), South America, and the Caribbean. *Sand below the high-water line is safe*; exercise great care on beaches obviously fouled by dogs.

Areas underneath houses raised on stilts are also dangerous. Treatment is easy and very satisfactory. The drug used is thiabendazole (Mintezol), which can be taken by mouth or applied to the skin as an ointment (the ointment has to be prepared specially by a pharmacist from thiabendazole tablets: 0.5g thiabendazole crushed and mixed with 10g petroleum jelly—this has fewer side-effects than oral treatment). Cooling the skin with ethyl chloride also kills the larvae.

Prevention

Larva migrans can be prevented by wearing shoes or sandals at all times and by preventing children (who are most often affected) from running around barefoot on the beach. Use a beach mat or beach towel when sunbathing, and choose your beach carefully.

Larva currens

Larva currens is a similar condition to larva migrans, but is caused by the human worm *Strongyloides*. The eggs of this worm hatch in the bowel, and larvae are passed out of the faeces. However, the larvae sometimes penetrate the skin of the anus, causing a reinfection. This results in an irritating rash round the buttocks, extending up the back. The rash is composed of irritant red lines and weals which move quite quickly and may vanish within a few hours, appearing and disappearing repeatedly over a period of many years. (Many ex-prisoners from World War II who were held in the Far East still suffer forty years after infection.)

The infection is picked up from moist soil in villages and rural areas in Thailand, Malaysia, and Vietnam. Treatment with thiabendazole (Mintezol) is effective even after forty years.

There are also animal forms of *Strongyloides* which are especially common on mounds in tropical swamps. The worms move around under the skin, causing lesions similar to those of larva migrans.

Prevention

Avoid contact with moist soil under houses and wear shoes at all times. Do not sit on the ground with wet bathing suits or clothes since this will attract infective larvae. Avoid mounds in swamps, especially those fouled with faeces.

Summary of advice for travellers

- Walking around barefoot on soil or sandy beaches above the high water line is risky in many parts of the world—as the editor of this book discovered to his cost on a recent visit to Florida!

Leprosy

Leprosy poses a negligible hazard to the traveller, although many people still worry unduly about the risks.

Dr Stanley Browne *was a leprologist of international reputation. Past President of the Royal Society of Tropical Medicine, he advised on leprosy in sixty-eight countries.*

Holidaymakers and business travellers alike may well harbour important misconceptions about leprosy. Half-remembered stories from the Bible and from films like *Ben Hur*, pictures of horrible deformities and the spectre of frightful contagion—these are the sum total of most people's 'knowledge' of leprosy.

How then do you react to rumours: leprosy in Spain, in Malta, in Italy? It can't be true . . . . but it is. On visiting these countries, you will most probably never see a case; and even if you do, you probably won't recognize it.

If your travels take your further afield, say to Lagos or Madras, you may be accosted by beggars holding out their deformed and ulcerating hands. So this is leprosy. You shudder and turn away quickly, embarrassed and perhaps a little frightened. Will you catch leprosy? You are half-reassured by a dimly remembered phrase about 'prolonged and close contact' being necessary for infection to occur.

But what is leprosy? How much leprosy is there in countries advertised in glossy, inviting holiday brochures? What risk is there to the traveller, and are there any special precautions you should take?

What is leprosy?

The leprosy bacillus and its effects

Leprosy is caused by a tiny bacillus that can survive only in human tissues. It prefers to live in the skin and lining of the nose. It multiplies very slowly. The only symptoms of an early infection may be a non-itching rash and perhaps an occasional blood-stained discharge from the nose.

The potential seriousness of the disease derives not from the rash (which may disappear spontaneously), but from leprosy bacilli accumulating in the main nerves of the limbs and face. Dead bacilli inside nerves provoke inflammation which eventually destroys the nerve fibres, resulting in muscle paralysis and loss of feeling in hands and feet. This can lead to repeated injury—from handling objects that most people would find too hot to touch, or from walking carelessly over rough ground—resulting ultimately in scarring, ulceration, and deformity. The disease does *not* cause fingers and toes to drop off.

How infection is spread

Leprosy bacilli are spread in small droplets of nasal discharge from some patients with early, untreated, leprosy—who may look and feel healthy, with only slight signs in the skin and nose.

The disease is *not* particularly contagious or infectious, and chance contact is unlikely to lead to infection: most people exposed to living leprosy bacilli have some degree of built-in resistance to the disease, and will never develop signs of infection. Very few medical workers in daily contact with leprosy patients ever catch leprosy; they take no precautions beyond washing their hands, and perhaps wearing a face mask when examining patients' noses.

Ulceration of the hands and feet is *not* a sign of infectivity. Most beggars with overt signs of leprosy are *not* contagious.

Geographical occurrence

Leprosy is present in most countries, although the proportion of the population affected varies widely. As many as 15 million people may be affected worldwide: most of these live within the medico-geographical tropics. In Europe, most leprosy sufferers live in southern countries—Portugal, Spain, Italy, Greece, Turkey, the southern USSR, and the Mediterranean islands.

The leprosy problem worldwide is now probably stationary. Growing resistance of leprosy bacilli to the cheapest drug available for treatment—dapsone, which has been in use for over thirty years—is causing problems, as is the capacity of bacilli to lie dormant in the tissues, multiplying again years later and causing relapse.

In the UK, although some 1200 cases of leprosy have been

reported since 1951, these are all imported; nobody has caught the disease in the UK in the past fifty years, despite the fact that only a few patients are admitted to hospital at any one time. Most live normally in the community, receiving treatment from their family doctors, with the help of skin specialists where necessary. Modern drugs kill 99·8 per cent of leprosy bacteria within a few days of the first dose.

Summary of advice for travellers

- At present no vaccine is available to protect travellers from leprosy, and no preventive medicine is necessary.
- Due to the low infectivity of the disease, and most people's inbuilt resistance, the chances of a traveller catching leprosy *are virtually nil*—the only precaution necessary might be to avoid being sneezed at. Leprosy is a much less frightening disease than you may have imagined.

Anthrax

Although anthrax is most uncommon in travellers, certain handicrafts may be contaminated and should be avoided.

Dr Arnold F. Kaufmann *is Chief of Bacterial Zoonoses Activity, Centers for Disease Control, Atlanta, Georgia, USA, and specializes in public health control of anthrax and other infections acquired from animals.*

Anthrax is lethal bacterial disease of livestock that is occasionally transmitted to humans. A disease of considerable historic significance, anthrax occurs or has occurred in virtually every country of the world. It is currently a minor public health problem, even in developing countries, due to the wide use of animal anthrax vaccines. Lapses in local control programmes, however, can have serious consequences such as the recent epidemic of almost 10 000 human cases in Zimbabwe. The most frequent victims of this disease are persons closely associated with raising livestock or working in industries processing animal bones, hair, and hides.

How it is spread

Anthrax is caused by *Bacillus anthracis*, a bacterium normally present in various types of soil. The anthrax bacillus has a cyclic pattern of replication, growing rapidly when environmental conditions are optimal and then forming spores to survive adverse periods. These spores are resistant to disinfectants and can remain viable for many years. Animals become infected by grazing on soils where the anthrax bacillus is in its active growth phase.

Human anthrax results not from contact with the soil but from handling the tissues of infected animals.

When an animal dies of anthrax, the important control measure is either to bury or to burn the carcass. Poverty or failure to recognize the cause of death, however, frequently leads animal owners in developing countries to salvage anything of value. The meat may be eaten, and by-products such as bones, skin, and hair sold or used. Anthrax spore contamination of these by-products, which may be made into handicrafts or exported for industrial processing, can become a hazard to people far away.

Forms of anthrax

Human anthrax has three forms, namely cutaneous (skin), gastro-intestinal, and inhalation forms, and these directly reflect the route of the infection.

Cutaneous anthrax, the most common, results when the anthrax bacillus is introduced beneath the skin e.g. by a puncture, abrasion, or through a pre-existing break in the skin while handling contaminated materials. A red, raised area develops at the site of the infection—rather like an insect bite—and characteristically progresses to a large blister finally becoming an ulcer covered with a dark scab. This form of the disease is diagnosed easily and can be treated effectively with common antibiotics such as penicillin and tetracycline.

Gastrointestinal anthrax results from eating raw or undercooked meat from infected animals, and causes severe abdominal symptoms.

Inhalation anthrax is almost exclusively an occupational respiratory disease, associated with industrial processing of goat hair from western Asia. These two forms of the disease are difficult to diagnose and are often fatal; however, both are so rare as to be a negligible risk.

Summary of advice for travellers

- Although cutaneous anthrax may cause severe illness, the disease is only weakly contagious and presents little risk to the average traveller. Only one travel-associated case has occurred in a US citizen in the past forty years. This patient acquired her infection from a goat-skin handicraft purchased in Haiti.
- Subsequent studies revealed that Haitian handicrafts incorporating dried or poorly tanned goat skins were commonly contaminated with anthrax spores. As a result, rugs, drums, and other handicrafts containing goat skin with attached hair (the spores are found in the hair) are not permitted to be brought into the USA. Another case, not in a traveller, was traced to a coarse goat-hair yarn produced in Pakistan.
- Travellers should not buy any item made of coarse goat hair or goat skin with attached hair in any poor country.
- General commonsense precautions of eating only well-cooked meat and avoiding unnecessary handling of dead animals also apply. Otherwise, no special precautions or immunizations are necessary.

The dangerous viruses: Lassa, Marburg, and Ebola

Anxiety about these infections is misdirected: travellers are at little risk, and imported cases pose little or no threat to public health.

Dr Philip Welsby *has worked at the major referral unit for Lassa Fever suspects in London, and has also worked at the Hospital for Tropical Diseases.*

Infections with Lassa, Marburg, or Ebola are exceptionally serious because these viruses attack cells in all tissues and organs throughout the body. In contrast, most other viruses are rather more selective and tend to cause less widespread cell damage. The 'all-out' attack of Lassa, Marburg, and Ebola viruses accounts for the high death rate associated with these illnesses, although with Lassa fever there is now circumstantial evidence to suggest that trivial infections also occur.

Lassa fever

Suspected cases of imported Lassa fever periodically generate much publicity and public alarm in the UK. These anxieties are misdirected, because the general public is hardly at risk (more people in the UK are dying from imported malaria—which is both preventable and treatable). The main risk is to those responsible for looking after Lassa fever patients.

Geographical occurrence

Lassa fever is probably present in most bush areas of West Africa. Infection is transmitted to humans by the urine of a particular type of rat found only in bush areas and *not* in large towns. Only travellers who visit such areas might be at risk.

In parts of Liberia and Sierra Leone there is a steady flow of new cases of Lassa fever, and surveys have detected antibodies to Lassa fever in the blood of people living in Nigeria, Ivory Coast,

Mali, Central African Republic, Guinea, and eastern Senegal—confirming that infection is present in these countries. Some of these countries, doubtless feeling that the problems of Lassa fever have been rather exaggerated, deny the presence of infection.

How infection is spread

Human infection is probably acquired by inhaling aerosols of urine. This bizarre mechanism probably operates in travellers who enter bush huts in which rats have urinated into the thatch. Lassa virus might also be able to penetrate the abraded skin of people working in bush areas contaminated by bush rats.

Contrary to popular belief, it appears that in the early stages Lassa fever patients are not highly infectious to the general public unless the sufferer has marked respiratory tract symptoms. The hazard to medical and nursing staff arises because infection may easily be acquired from blood, urine, and other body fluids: thus hospital workers and paramedical personnel who deal with laboratory specimens from infected patients may also be at risk of infection.

The illness

After an incubation period of three to seventeen days illness begins gradually with fever, chills, headache, muscular and skeletal aches and pains, and profound malaise. A major clue to a diagnosis of Lassa fever is a sore throat with throat ulcers (which would be unusual in malaria or typhoid, two diseases with which Lassa fever might be confused).

In the first week vomiting and diarrhoea may occur and in the second week there may be deafness or ringing in the ears (the virus also attacks the ear tissues). In severe infections patients deteriorate rapidly during the second week, with signs of failure of many organ systems.

The death rate among hospitalized cases prior to 1975 was no less than 45 per cent. However, antibody studies in various bush areas of West Africa have shown that many people have evidence of previous infection, without having had an illness that was recognizable even in retrospect as Lassa fever. The true mortality rate is therefore uncertain, but figures of about 5 per cent have been suggested.

Imported cases

Only four cases of Lassa fever were imported into the UK between 1980 and 1988. When dealing with suspected cases, doctors are faced with the problem that Lassa fever is a non-specific feverish illness in its early stages, and so suspicions have to be based on circumstantial evidence such as whether or not the suspect visited bush areas, what happened there, and how symptoms developed.

In the UK, Lassa fever suspects are transferred to specially designated hospitals under conditions of strict isolation, which may include nursing them in negative pressure polythene isolation 'rooms' with special measures to ensure safe disposal of all waste material. Such draconian measures are designed primarily to protect the medical attendants rather than the general population. However, in West African bush hospitals only screens are used to separate suspected Lassa fever patients and, with the exception of one or two highly publicized episodes, there have been no dramatic outbreaks of Lassa fever. Similarly, it is not common for medical staff in these hospitals to catch Lassa fever.

Treatment and prevention

Treatment of Lassa fever is aimed at relieving the symptoms and treating complications. The possibility of malaria has always to be considered and tested for: most British Lassa fever suspects turn out to have malaria, and a large proportion of these have not taken anti-malarial tablets regularly.

Sufferers can be given antibodies from past patients who have recovered from the illness, or possibly the antiviral agent interferon (if this is available). There is no conclusive evidence to confirm that these measures are effective in humans, but an antiviral drug called ribavirin has recently been shown to be useful in treatment.

Apart from staying away from bush areas, no useful preventive measures can be employed.

Marburg and Ebola virus diseases

Marburg virus is better known as 'green monkey' disease after an outbreak of infection in 1967 in which about 24 per cent of sufferers died; the infection was traced to infected vervet (green) monkeys that had been exported from Uganda to Europe.

No one knows which animals usually harbour the infection in the wild—it is not vervet monkeys—and it appears that these monkeys, like humans, had been infected with a virus that presumably usually infects other animals. In 1975 two people were infected by a patient who had acquired his infection in Zimbabwe from an unknown source.

Ebola virus infection produces a similar illness to Marburg virus disease and is caused by a similar virus. An outbreak occurred in northern Zaire and southern Sudan in 1976 in which the death rate was about 65 per cent, and there was a second outbreak in the same area in 1979.

As part of the investigation of the first outbreak, specimens were sent to the UK for tests, and a laboratory worker accidentally jabbed himself with an infected needle and became seriously ill, yet he subsequently recovered. Although widely believed to have had green monkey disease, he in fact had Ebola virus disease!

The illness

In both Marburg and Ebola virus disease, there is a sudden onset of fever, headache, eye pain, backache, and severe malaise. A few days after the start of the illness vomiting, abdominal pain and diarrhoea commence. A rash develops around four to seven days after the illness begins and a bleeding tendency may occur.

Avoidance

With both Marburg and Ebola virus diseases, the natural reservoir of infection is unknown. In consequence, no rural bush area of Africa can be regarded as entirely risk-free, neither can precautions be issued for the traveller to follow. Future outbreaks will hopefully be notified rapidly so that travellers can be warned in advance to avoid such areas.

4

Diseases spread by insects

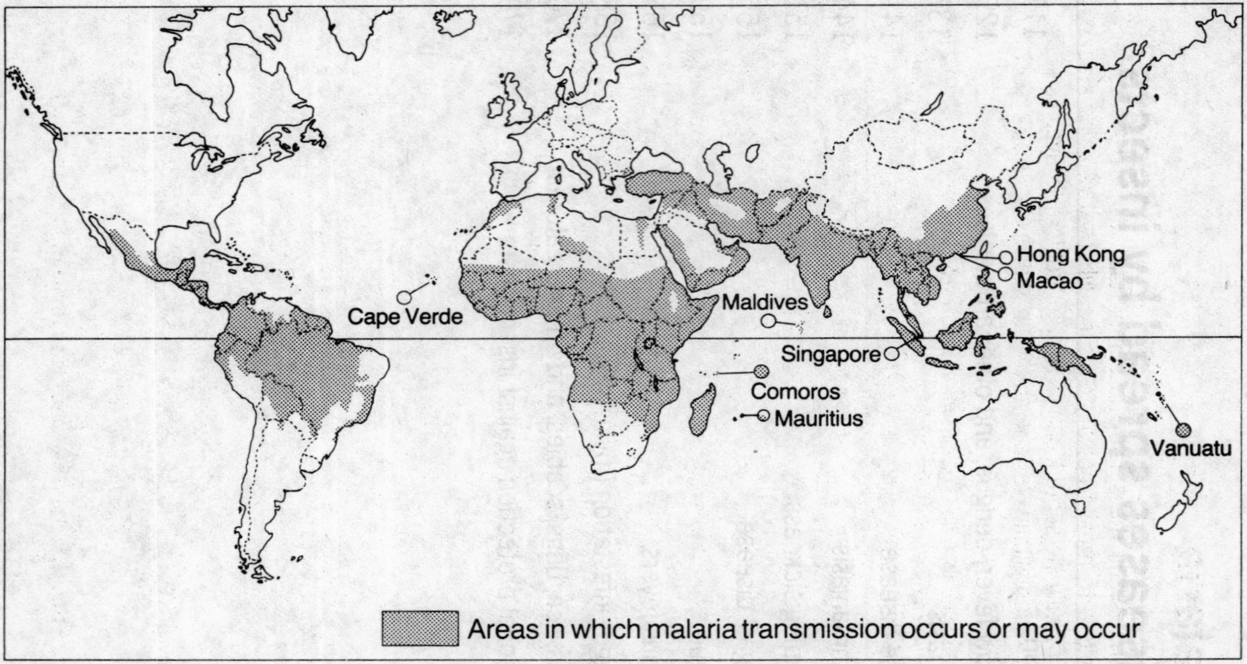

Map 4.1 Geographical distribution of malaria (1988). Note, however, that the exact distribution varies somewhat from time to time.

Malaria

Malaria is still the single most important disease hazard facing travellers to most tropical countries, where it remains a serious and usually neglected public health problem. Travellers have a clear responsibility to take adequate precautions to protect their health.

Dr Anthony Hall *has written numerous articles and medical papers about malaria. His patients with malaria have included US soldiers in Vietnam, rural Thais, and travellers from all over the world in London.*

Malaria is a parasitic disease spread by the bite of *Anopheles* mosquitoes (Figs. 4.1 and 4.2). Worldwide, at least 1600 million people are constantly at risk from malaria, and between 200 and 300 million people are affected by the disease each year. Each year, around one million infants and children die from malaria in Africa alone.

Travellers may acquire malaria from mosquitoes in about 105 countries (see Map 4.1 and Appendix 2) although many of these countries under-report their cases of malaria—perhaps so as not to harm their image or their tourist trade.

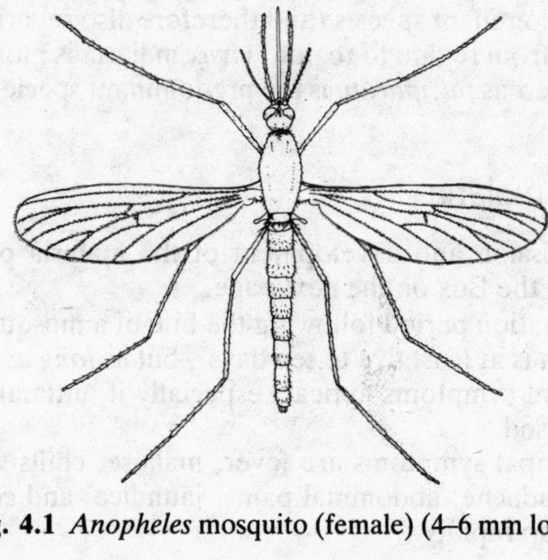

Fig. 4.1 *Anopheles* mosquito (female) (4–6 mm long).

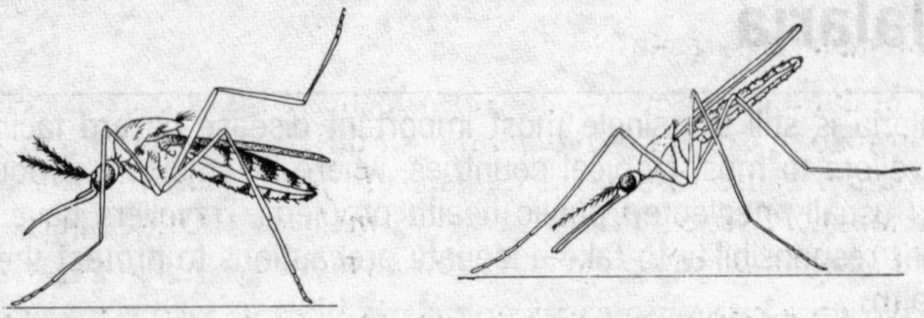

Fig. 4.2 Resting positions of mosquitos: *Culex* (left); *Anopheles* (right). Anopheles mosquitoes can be recognised by their characteristic posture.

The risks of contracting malaria vary greatly from country to country, and in particular, visitors to tropical Africa are at much greater risk than visitors to Latin America or South East Asia. For example, it would not be inconceivable for a traveller to acquire fatal (falciparum) malaria from the bite of a single mosquito during a brief airport stop-over in West Africa, whereas I have never yet known a tourist to get malaria in Thailand, despite the fuss that is often made about the problem of drug-resistant malaria there. (Among visitors to Thailand, malaria may occasionally occur in those working as missionaries or in refugee camps.)

There are four different types of malaria parasite (see below) and the predominant species (and therefore also severity of infection) varies from region to region: *vivax* malaria is more common in India, whereas *falciparum* is the predominant species in Africa.

Effects of malaria

The transmission and development of the malaria parasite are described in the Box on the next page.

The incubation period following the bite of a mosquito bearing the infection is at least five to ten days—but *as long as a year* may elapse before symptoms appear, especially if antimalarial drugs have been used.

The principal symptoms are fever, malaise, chills with sweating, and headache; abdominal pains, jaundice, and coma sometimes develop rapidly.

The malaria parasite

- Malaria is caused by parasites which consist of a single cell (protozoa), called *Plasmodium*. Four different species of *Plasmodium* cause disease in humans: *P. falciparum* (the most serious), *P. vivax*, *P. ovale*, and *P. malariae*. (Other species of *Plasmodium* cause malaria in birds, monkeys, and rodents.)
- When a mosquito carrying malaria bites its victim to suck blood, it first injects saliva to prevent the blood from coagulating and blocking its mouth parts. The saliva (which is also responsible for the unpleasant, itchy weal that may develop at the site of the bite) contains infective forms of the parasite (called *sporozoites*).
- After injection, the *sporozoites* pass into the blood, and then into the liver. They infect liver cells, in which they develop further over the next six to eleven days without causing symptoms. (At this stage they are now called liver *schizonts*.)
- When mature the schizonts burst, releasing numerous tiny parasites, called *merozoites*, into the bloodstream. These penetrate red blood cells, and now cause symptoms for the first time. The merozoites develop into ring-shaped *trophozoites*—the form of the parasite that is normally visible under the microscope to doctors trying to detect the disease.
- The trophozoites grow inside the red blood cells, into *schizonts*, which burst and release large numbers of *merozoites*, each able to infect a new red blood cell. Release of the merozoites coincides with fever; it takes two to three days for newly infected blood cells to release further numbers of merozoites, and this explains the intermittent character of the fever which is often seen with malaria. (In falciparum malaria, the infection is sometimes so severe that fever is continuous.)
- Some of the trophozoites also develop into forms called *gametocytes* which are capable of infecting mosquitoes. The gametocytes are sucked up during a blood meal, and develop within the mosquito's stomach. Between seven and twenty days later, infective *sporozoites* appear in the mosquito salivary glands, ready to infect a new victim.

In general, the severity of illness is related to the number of parasites in the blood. In vivax, ovale, and malariae malaria the number of parasites in the blood is relatively small: not more than 1 per cent of the red blood cells are parasitized, and death from these forms of malaria is unusual. In falciparum malaria, however, up to 80 per cent of the red blood cells may be parasitized; long-term residents in malarial areas usually develop some degree of immunity, but those with no immunity—visitors, in particular, and children—often develop severe or even fatal disease.

Features of severe falciparum malaria include liver and kidney failure, severe anaemia, convulsions, and coma (from cerebral malaria).

Unusual routes of spread

A bite from an infected mosquito in a hot country is not the only way of acquiring malaria. Occasionally mosquitoes hitch a ride in a plane, jump off somewhere like Paris, Rome, or Gatwick and bite someone who has never been to the tropics. If such a victim develops a fever, malaria is understandably not considered.

A person may develop malaria following the inoculation of infected blood. Many people have developed malaria and several have died following a blood transfusion from an infected donor who is usually free from the symptoms. For example, one elderly American died from fever after surgery. His blood transfusion had included a unit from an African student who had lived in the USA for three years and was free of symptoms.

Drug addicts occasionally transmit malaria when they share a syringe and needle.

Diagnosis

The early symptoms of malaria, of which fever is the most common, are non-specific. This is why—especially when symptoms do not appear until after the traveller has returned home—the possibility of malaria is not always considered and the diagnosis may be missed.

Table 4.1 Treatment of malaria[1]

Type of malaria	Treatment
Falciparum malaria	
Chloroquine-sensitive[2]	Chloroquine[3] 10–50 mg base per kg bodyweight, over one to five days. Usual course in adults: Day 1 600 mg dose 300 mg six hours later Day 2 300 mg Day 3 300 mg
Chloroquine-resistant[2]	*First attack:* Quinine 10 mg base per kg bodyweight (usually 650 mg quinine sulphate in adults) every 12 hours until fever resolves or longer (course three to seven days). Drug given by intravenous infusion if illness severe. Then single dose Fansidar (three tablets). *Mild first attack:* Mefloquine (Lariam). *Second attack (rare):* Quinine 10 mg base per kg bodyweight every 12 hours until fever resolves, then mefloquine.
Vivax malaria (or ovale or malariae)	Chloroquine as above, then primaquine 15 mg daily for 14 days (adult dose) to prevent relapses.

Notes
1. Treatment should preferably be carried out under medical supervision. Anyone with suspected malaria should seek medical help urgently.
2. For information on areas of chloroquine-resistant malaria, see Appendix 2.
3. One chloroquine tablet usually contains 200 mg chloroquine sulphate or 250 mg chloroquine phosphate, and both are equivalent to 150 mg chloroquine base. All doses in this book are expressed as chloroquine base.

If malaria is suspected a blood sample should be taken immediately, and examined under the microscope. Detection of parasites under the microscope confirms the diagnosis but requires experience and skill. Treatment is a matter of urgency, and should not be delayed if such skills are not available.

Treatment

The drug treatment of malaria is summarized in Table 4.1.

Resistance of the malarial parasites to chloroquine is common in Asia and parts of Latin America, and is increasing throughout Africa (see Appendix 2, pp. 525–6).

In the treatment of drug-resistant malaria, I prefer to give a course of quinine first; then to give 750 mg (3 tablets) of mefloquine (see pp. 125–6) at least 12 hours later, followed by another dose of 750 mg about 24 hours after the first. Nausea and dizziness may occur for a few days.

An increased dosage of chloroquine is necessary for people of above average weight.

An additional drug, primaquine, is given for treatment of vivax malaria, which otherwise may lie dormant in the liver and cause a relapse. This drug may have toxic effects in people of Mediterranean, African, or Asian descent, and a blood test (for G6PD deficiency) should be performed before it is given.

In severe falciparum infection, intravenous treatment with quinine is usually necessary.

An 'exchange' blood transfusion may occasionally be life-saving in severely ill patients with parasitaemias over 10 per cent.

Prevention

Public health measures

In many countries over several centuries, malaria has been controlled or eradicated by reducing the amount of stagnant water—which mosquitoes need in order to breed. Drainage of the pontine marshes around Rome and the more recent prohibition of stagnant water in Singapore were effective. Rice is the staple diet in most tropical countries, but mosquitoes often breed in rice fields. More plentiful rice but more mosquitoes is a cruel situation. Fortunately, the lining of water tunnels with concrete has reduced the numbers of mosquitoes. An important measure is the spraying of residual insecticide in houses and around buildings. (The insecticide is called residual because it remains effective for a long time.)

Unfortunately, however, mosquito resistance to the effects of insecticide remains a problem, and is only one of many reasons why malaria eradication schemes have been largely unsuccessful.

Personal protection

The most important way of reducing the number of mosquito bites (see pp. 178–86), in my opinion, is the application of insect repellent (containing diethyl toluamide or 'deet') to the skin, especially in the evening and, when out of doors, at night. Mosquito nets over the bed are a time-honoured way of avoiding bites at night and should be used. A wire mesh across the windows can also be helpful. Air-conditioners reduce the chances of being bitten but are often not available or out of order when they are needed most.

Antimalarial drugs for prophylaxis

The drugs at present available are not true prophylactics because they do not in fact prevent infection—they do not prevent the uptake of the parasites. Drugs such as proguanil (Paludrine), pyrimethamine (Daraprim), and primaquine may inhibit the development of parasites in the liver, but the main effect of prophylactic drugs is to suppress the development of the red blood cell forms of the parasite—which is why treatment has to be continued for so long after leaving the malarial area, if it is to be truly successful.

The following regimens which are also summarized in Table 4.2 (p. 124), may be helpful (adult doses given). The drugs should be started 1–2 weeks before entry to an endemic area (it is important to have a sufficient blood level of the drugs before exposure to malaria begins) and must be continued for at least four weeks (preferably six to eight weeks) afterwards.

For travel to areas with chloroquine-sensitive malaria:

• Proguanil (Paludrine) 200 mg daily is preferred for long-term prophylaxis because side-effects are minor and it is not used for treatment. Proguanil is less effective in areas where falciparum malaria is resistant to chloroquine and often pyrimethamine as well. Proguanil can cause mouth ulcers. It is not available in the USA, though it is recommended by many American authorities.

• Chloroquine (e.g. Nivaquine, Aralen, or Resochin—differences in tablet size are explained in Note 3, p. 121) 300 mg base once weekly following an initial dose of 600 mg is more suitable for short-term prophylaxis: a cumulative dose of over 100g may cause retinal damage and thus visual impairment. The French advise larger doses of chloroquine for prophylaxis, for example 100 mg daily rather than 300 mg weekly. Chloroquine is widely used for prophylaxis and is more effective than any other drug in the prevention (or treatment) of malaria due to *P. vivax*, *P. malariae*, or *P. ovale*. In most countries chloroquine is available as a syrup for children; in the USA and elsewhere this is not available, paediatric doses can be prepared in gelatine capsules. The side effects of chloroquine include itching, rashes, blurred vision, and dizziness.

Table 4.2 Drug prevention of malaria[1]

Adults

Areas where falciparum malaria is usually sensitive to chloroquine (i.e. Central America, Middle East, and W. Africa)[2]:

1. Proguanil (Paludrine) 200 mg (2 tablets) daily

and/or

2. Chloroquine 300 mg (2 tablets[3]) weekly (1st dose 600 mg)

Areas where falciparum malaria is often resistant to chloroquine (i.e. Asia, Central, East and South Africa, Oceania, and South America)[2]:

3. Proguanil and chloroquine as above

or in East Africa and Southeast Asia:

4. Chloroquine alone with Fansidar in reserve (see below)

   OR

5. Maloprim 1 tablet on Wednesdays *and* Chloroquine 300 mg on Sundays (see p. 125)

   OR

6. Doxycycline 100 mg (1 tablet) daily (not in pregnancy, or in children)

   OR

7. Mefloquine 250 mg (1 tablet) weekly in adults

Antimalarial drugs are safer than malaria in pregnancy.

Children

As above with doses calculated as follows:

Age less than one year	1/4 adult dose
Age one to five years	1/2 adult dose
Age six to 12 years	3/4 adult dose

Notes

1. Use of prophylactic antimalarial tablets should continue for at least four weeks (preferably six to eight weeks) after returning from a malarious area.
2. For further information on areas of chloroquine-resistant malaria, see Appendix 2.
3. See Note 3 p. 121 regarding chloroquine tablet size.

For travel to areas with chloroquine-resistant falciparum malaria:

A combination of proguanil, for example 200 mg daily for six days a week, and chloroquine once a week, can be taken by people who have developed malaria despite prophylaxis with one of the drugs alone, or who are travelling to areas where chloroquine-resistant falciparum malaria occurs.

• Chloroquine alone—along with a supply of Fansidar (three tablets to be taken as a single dose) in reserve, for prompt self-treatment at the earliest suspicion of malaria (if skilled care can not be obtained quickly)—is an approach currently favoured by many American doctors.

Amodiaquine (Camoquin) is a similar drug to chloroquine but may cause bone marrow failure (agranulocytosis), and should NOT be used for prophylaxis.

For travel to East Africa (where falciparum malaria is both drug-resistant and fatal in one in 10 000 visitors):

- Fansidar one tablet weekly (pyrimethamine 25 mg and sulfadoxine 500 mg) is no longer generally recommended because about one in 11 000 to one in 25 000 people who take the drug for prophylaxis develop a fatal skin condition (Stevens–Johnson syndrome) after taking between two and five doses. The problem is much more common if Fansidar and chloroquine have been taken together.

Although there is now understandable reluctance to prescribe or take Fansidar, this drug may still be worth considering in people who are not allergic to sulphonamides in circumstances where the risk of a chloroquine-resistant infection is high.

These problems with toxicity do not apply to the use of Fansidar in *treatment* of malaria.

- Maloprim one tablet weekly (pyrimethamine 12·5 mg and dapsone 100 mg) is rather less effective than Fansidar. It has been used especially by British and Australian travellers. A small number of patients have died of bone marrow failure after taking two tablets of Maloprim weekly, but toxic effects from taking one tablet weekly are rare. Again, where the risk of drug-resistant malaria is high, Maloprim, either alone or in combination with chloroquine should be considered. Maloprim, like primaquine, should not be used in G6PD deficiency.

- Doxycyline alone, 100 mg daily, is an alternative regimen for short-term travel to drug-resistant areas. Doxycycline is a tetracycline and may cause photosensitivity (an exaggerated sunburn reaction to strong sunlight). Tetracycline may cause vaginal candidiasis (thrush or yeast infection). Tetracycline should not be taken in pregnancy or by children.

- Mefloquine (Lariam) is a new antimalarial, chemically similar to quinine. It is effective against both chloroquine and Fansidar-resistant falciparum malaria.

For prophylaxis, one regimen is 250 mg mefloquine weekly. Mefloquine should not be taken by people taking beta blockers or other drugs which may alter cardiac conduction. Mefloquine should be used for prophylaxis only if at least one other regimen has failed.

Even if an antimalarial regimen is followed carefully, an attack of malaria may still occur, though it is much less likely to be fatal.

Prospects for a malaria vaccine

Three methods of vaccination against malaria are being tested in animals:

1. The first is to prevent infection by using a vaccine derived from sporozoites (the form of malaria parasite injected by mosquitoes under the skin).
2. The second is to alleviate clinical symptoms by using a vaccine made from merozoites or other blood stages.
3. The third is to prevent transmission by using a vaccine made from gametocytes (the forms of the parasite which infect the mosquito when sucked up in human blood).

There are many problems, and the prospect for a vaccine for humans still remains many years in the future.

Travellers at special risk

Malaria in pregnancy

Pregnant women should avoid travelling to malarious areas because no prophylactic regimen is completely effective. Malaria tends to be more severe in pregnancy and there is an increased risk of prematurity, abortion, and stillbirth.

Proguanil and chloroquine are the only drugs that should be used for prophylaxis in pregnancy because the other drugs are potentially hazardous to the fetus.

Women's resistance to malaria falls during pregnancy. The disease is more frequent and more severe, and both the mother and the fetus may suffer.

Table 4.3 Anti-malaria kit for travellers

	Drug	Quantity[1]
Prophylactic tablets[2]		
Choice depends on area to be visited and on possible resistance to chloroquine. For guidelines on choice and dosages see Table 4.2, p. 124. For areas of falciparum malaria resistance to chloroquine see Appendix 2, p. 525.	1. Chloroquine tablets 150 mg base[3]	at least 10 tablets per person per month abroad
	AND/OR	
	2. Proguanil (Paludrine) tablets	at least 70 tablets per person per month abroad
Treatment tablets		
Choice depends on type of malaria and on whether the malaria is sensitive or resistant to chloroquine. For guidelines on choice of treatment and dosages see Table 4.1, p. 121. Treatment should be taken under the supervision of a doctor, if at all possible.	3. Quinine sulphate 325 mg tablets	at least 28 tablets
	4. Chloroquine base 150 mg tablets[3]	at least 12 tablets in addition to those required for prophylaxis
	5. Fansidar tablets	at least 3 tablets
Insect repellent	Gel and liquid aerosol cans see p. 182	

Notes

1. It is wise to take and keep a duplicate, extra supply of tablets in a separate place from the main supply in case of loss of tablets by yourself or travelling companions, particularly if you are travelling to remote areas.
2. Prophylactic tablets should continue to be taken for at least four (preferably six to eight) weeks after returning from a malarious area.
3. See Note 3 p. 121 regarding chloroquine tablet size.

Malaria in pregnancy increases the rate of miscarriage and the likelihood of stillbirth. However, the malarial parasites do not usually cross the placenta, and only about one in 300 women who have malaria during pregnancy deliver an infected infant. But congenital malaria is more common in the non-immune (e.g. visitors) than in partially immune women (natives).

Former residents of endemic areas

People who migrate from malarial areas to countries where they are no longer exposed to malaria will quickly lose any immunity to infection that they may have built up. If they then return to their country of origin for a visit, they will be at high risk of serious illness unless they take adequate preventive measures.

Splenectomy

Malaria and other infections are a greater risk in people who have had their spleens removed (splenectomy).

Summary of advice for travellers

- Travellers should reduce the number of insect bites by applying insect repellent to the skin of the face, arms, and legs (if exposed) at least twice daily. It is sensible to avoid sunbathing when mosquitoes are about, and to be especially vigilant around dusk, when *Anopheles* mosquitoes prefer to bite—though it may not be too easy to notice insects while otherwise occupied on a tropical verandah.

- The contents of a suggested malaria kit are given in Table 4.3 on p. 127. Always travel with an adequate supply of tablets—you may have to give some to a friend, or a stranger in need.

- Check current recommendations before departure (see Appendix 6).

- The important point about drug prevention is *to take it*, whatever drug or combination of drugs you prefer. However, prevention is not perfect, and *even the most careful traveller or expatriate may develop malaria*.

- Please remember that falciparum malaria may not start with fever but just a feeling of being unwell. Headache, abdominal pain, and diarrhoea may occur. Of course, it can be difficult to differentiate malaria from other infectious diseases, including the common cold. Early treatment of most other infectious diseases is never so crucial. But if an attack of malaria is treated early, it is never fatal.

- If an attack of suspected malaria becomes severe, the victim should urgently ask for a blood test, if possible. Ideally, he or she should try to return home as soon as possible or at least to return to the closest city.

- Treatment: see Table 4.1, p. 121, and Table 8.2, p. 376.

Yellow fever, dengue, and other arboviruses

Arboviruses are a motley group of infections confined mainly to the tropics. Vaccination can be given against yellow fever; otherwise prevention depends mainly on avoiding insect bites.

Dr Philip Welsby *is Consultant Physician in Communicable Diseases at the City Hospital in Edinburgh.*

Arboviruses (*Ar*thropod-*Bo*rne-*Viruses*) are viral infections that mainly affect animals but are occasionally spread to humans. As their name implies, the infections are transmitted to humans by arthropods (insects and their close relatives), especially mosquitoes, ticks, and flies, which introduce the infection into the human bloodstream by their bites. The mosquito, in particular, is well suited to the transport and spread of infection, because it has to obtain blood to enable it to reproduce, and because mosquitoes have a wide distribution throughout the tropics. They also have the remarkable ability to fly backwards and upside down while avoiding rain drops!

Table 4.4 on p. 130 details a few of the eighty or so arboviruses currently known to infect humans.

Some general considerations

Risk of infection

Particular arbovirus infections are often given specific place names (Rift Valley fever, for example) which may help warn a traveller where the possibility of infection exists. Because certain arbovirus infections are prone to cause inflammation of brain tissue—an encephalitis—this attribute is often also included in the name of the disease (Japanese encephalitis, for example).

In areas at risk any large outbreak of infection will leave the local human population relatively immune from further infection, though they may be unknowingly surrounded by infection in the local wild animal population. Few human cases will then occur in local inhabitants, except in those with no previous

Table 4.4 Some arbovirus infections and their geographical distribution[1]

Virus name	Areas of distribution[1]
Chikungunya	South Africa, East Africa, Far East
O'nyong nyong	Africa
Kyasanur Forest disease	India
Eastern equine encephalitis	North America
Venezuelan equine encephalitis	North and South America
Western equine encephalitis	Belize, North and South America
Japanese encephalitis	Far East
Yellow fever	Africa, Americas, Caribbean
Crimean haemorrhagic fever	USSR, Bulgaria, Rumania
Tick-borne encephalitis	Forested areas of Eastern and Central Europe (see p. 483)
Rift Valley fever	UK
Louping ill[2]	UK

Notes
1. The geographical distribution of many of these diseases changes somewhat from time to time.
2. Louping ill is a rare occupational disease of shepherds, who acquire their infection from their sheep via tick bites. It is the only arbovirus infection native to the UK.

exposure to the infection i.e. young children and visitors to the infected area. *Thus travellers should not be reassured by statements that 'there have only been a few cases' in the areas they intend to visit.*

Arbovirus illnesses

The incubation period of arbovirus infections range from a few days to about two weeks. Most resulting illnesses tend to have two phases, the first when the virus is invading host cells, and the second a few days later when the body's immune system is fighting the infection. In the second phase of illness, virus and antibody produced by the body's immune system may be deposited in and cause damage to the blood vessels—this explains why arboviruses often cause bleeding.

Geographical occurrence

The incidence and geographical occurrences of most arbovirus infections are impossible to estimate as they vary considerably from time to time: the widespread presence of insects and other arthropods ensures that travellers to the tropics and subtropics will almost certainly be at risk of at least one kind of arbovirus infection. Fortunately not all arbovirus infections cause serious illness.

Treatment and prevention

With a few exceptions the treatment of arbovirus infections is of symptoms and complications, if any. Vaccination is available only for a few arbovirus infections, there are no specific antiviral drugs, and serum containing antibody from patients who have survived an infection is of limited use. As there is no cure, *prevention is essential*, which in practice means measures to avoid or deter insects including the use of mosquito netting at night, insecticides, insect repellents, and protective clothing (including pyjamas at night). See also pp. 178–86.

As with every febrile illness acquired in the tropics, the possibility of malaria will also need to be considered (see p. 117).

Yellow fever

Yellow fever is essentially a disease of monkeys living in tropical rain forests: humans are infected by rain forest mosquitoes, causing 'jungle yellow fever'. If an infected person then enters a densely populated area, infection may be spread from person to person by other types of mosquito, causing 'urban yellow fever'.

The world distribution of yellow fever—and also the distribution of mosquitoes capable of spreading the disease—is shown overleaf in Map 4.2. Interestingly, yellow fever is unknown in Asia despite the presence of mosquitoes capable of transmitting the virus.

The illness

Many infections are mild and thus go unrecognized, but severe life-threatening illness is not uncommon. After an incubation period of three to six days, fever, headache, abdominal pain, and vomiting develop. After a brief recovery period, shock, bleeding, and signs related to kidney and liver failure develop. Liver failure is associated with jaundice—hence the name yellow fever.

No specific drug is available to combat yellow fever virus directly, so treatment is aimed at relieving the symptoms and complications. Overall, about 5 per cent of patients may die, but in epidemics or in infections in non-vaccinated patients the mortality rate may rise to 50 per cent. Those who recover do so completely and are immune thereafter.

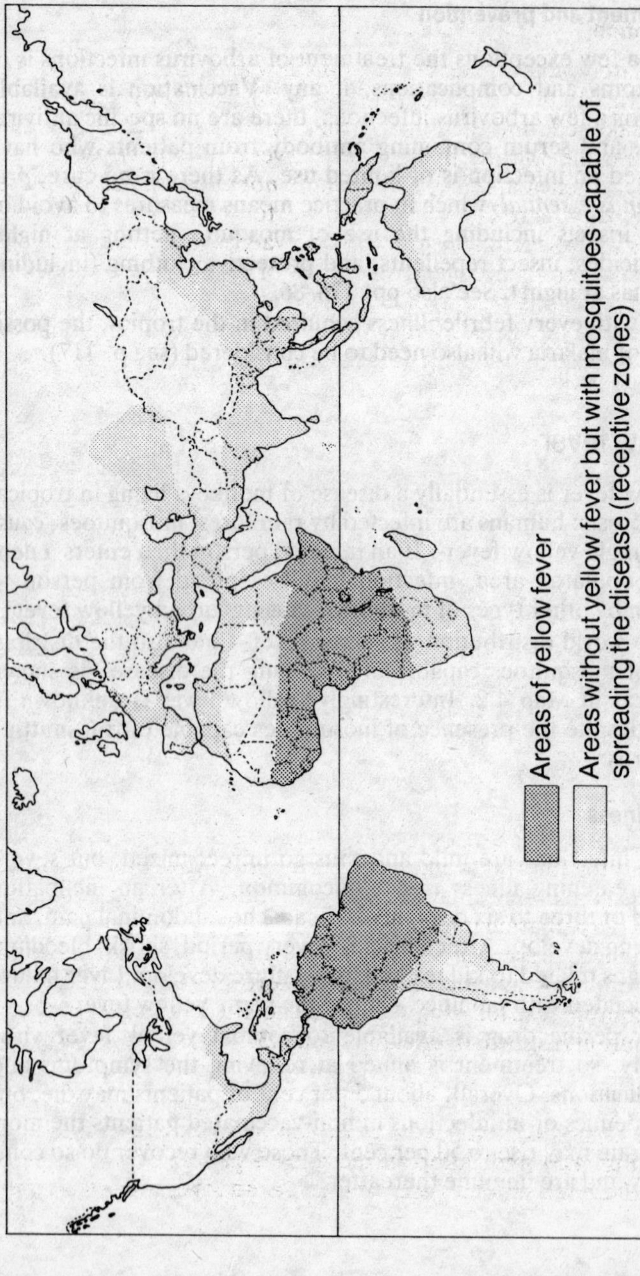

Map 4.2 Geographical distribution of yellow fever and of mosquitoes capable of spreading yellow fever.

Prevention

Fortunately yellow fever is one of the few arbovirus infections for which vaccination is available (see p. 478). A single injection of a live weakened (and therefore harmless) virus stimulates immune defences: the vaccine is highly effective and confers protection for at least ten years. *It is a vaccination not to be omitted for those visiting risk areas*. The vaccination has to be given at specialized centres where adequate storage of the vaccine is guaranteed.

Vaccination of pregnant women or of children less than nine months of age is best avoided unless areas of particularly high risk have to be visited. Other patients who should not be vaccinated include those with impaired defences against infections (patients with malignant tumours, for example) and those receiving medical treatment with certain drugs including corticosteroids.

Reactions to vaccination are rare and relatively trivial—redness or swelling at the site of injection, or headache. The International Certification of Vaccination becomes valid for ten years from ten days after vaccination, or immediately on revaccination within ten years. This certificate is required by many countries for entry of travellers coming from or through the yellow fever zones of Africa and South America, although precise requirements may vary from time to time according to which other countries currently have epidemics.

Dengue

Dengue probably causes as much illness as all the other arboviruses put together: it is an unusual arbovirus infection because no animals, other than humans and mosquitoes, play a significant part in perpetuating infection.

Dengue is present in South-East Asia, the Pacific area, Africa, the Caribbean, and the Americas where there have been dramatic outbreaks, for example in Puerto Rico. The geographical distribution is shown overleaf in Map 4.3.

The illness

Illness is spread from person to person by *Aedes aegypti* mosquitoes (Fig. 4.3) and, after an incubation period of five to eight days, there is a sudden onset of fever, headache, and severe joint

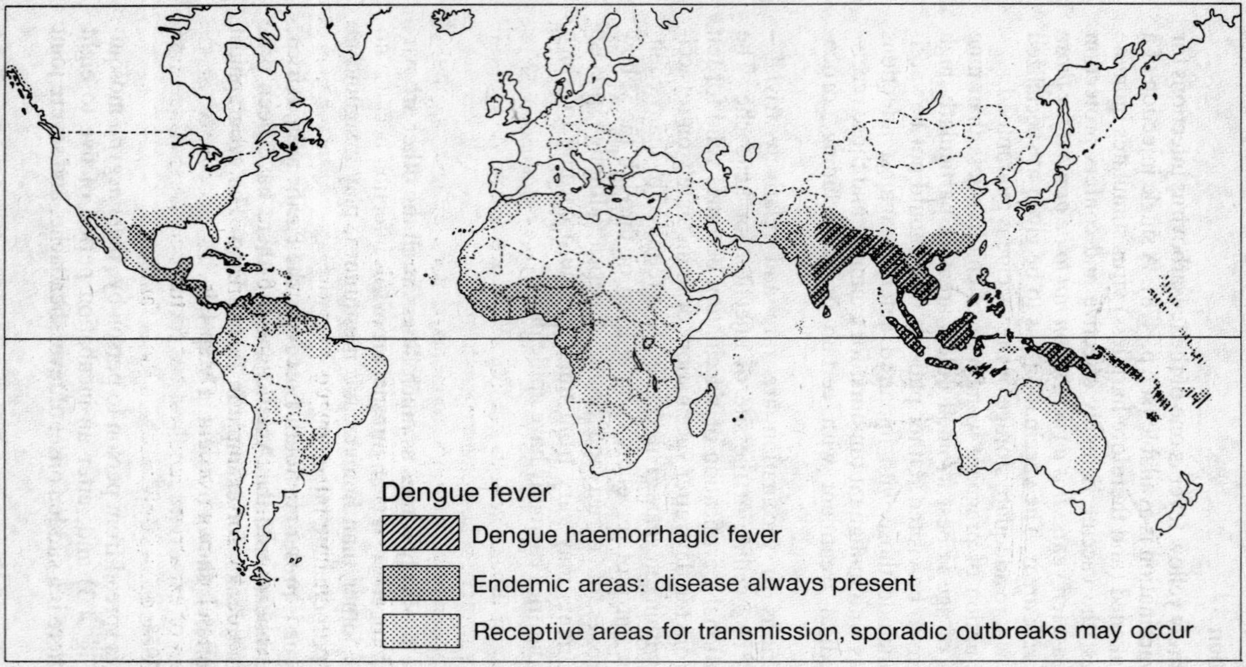

Map 4.3 Geographical distribution of dengue fever. Note, however, that the exact distribution can vary quite significantly from time to time. Sporadic outbreaks occur in the Pacific Islands. Reproduced, with slight modification, by kind permission of Dr C.J. Leake, Department of Medical Parasitology, London School of Hygiene and Tropical Medicine.

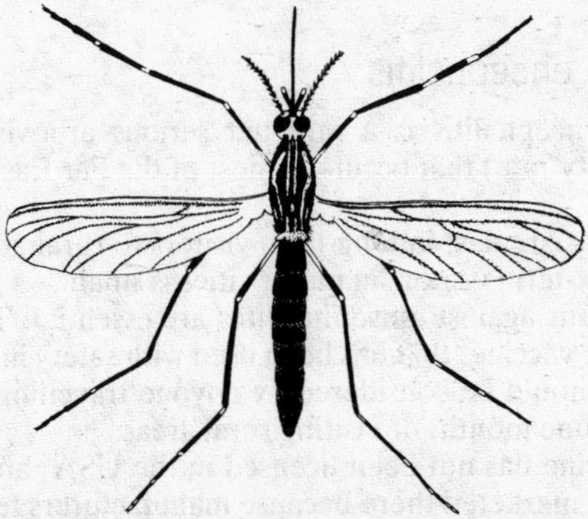

Fig. 4.3 *Aedes aegypti* mosquito (female) (4–6 mm long).

and muscle pains—the latter giving rise to the popular name of 'breakbone fever'. The initial bout of fever resolves only to recur, and a rash usually appears between the third and fifth days of the illness. The rash starts on the trunk and spreads to the limbs and face, and consists of small spots. Within a few days the fever subsides and recovery follows. Although undoubtedly an unpleasant illness, serious complications are uncommon, and in particular there is no persisting arthritis.

Unfortunately, immunity to infection does not last long and so second attacks, perhaps with a different strain of virus, are possible. There is no vaccine currently available.

Occasionally a more severe and life-threatening form of dengue may occur in children—dengue haemorrhagic fever—which is thought to be the result of a second infection in patients with some remaining immunity following a first attack. The second attack meets a vigorous immunological response in which severe blood-vessel damage occurs. Dengue is not uncommon in the children of expatriate families, but fortunately dengue haemorrhagic fever occurs only rarely in these families.

Prevention

Prevention of dengue, as with most arbovirus infections, and indeed many other tropical infections, involves measures to minimize contact with insects (see pp. 184–6).

Japanese encephalitis

Japanese encephalitis is a rare but serious arboviral infection (20% fatality rate) that occurs in most of the Far East and South-East Asia.

The risk is greatest in long-term visitors to rural areas, and the risk to short-term visitors in major cities is small.

Precautions against mosquito bites are essential. There is also an effective vaccine, that has been used with safety in many countries, and should be considered by anyone travelling to Asia for more than one month, or visiting rural areas.

The vaccine has not been licensed in the USA, and will probably not be marketed there because manufacturers fear litigation if adverse side-effects should ever appear. In Britain, the vaccine is available only on a named patient basis.

Filariasis

Filariasis encompasses a variety of worm infestations confined mainly to the tropics and spread from person to person by insects. Travellers have little to fear, but precautions must be taken against insect bites.

Dr David Haddock *was a Senior Lecturer in Tropical Medicine at the Liverpool School of Tropical Medicine. He also worked for long periods in Tanzania, Ghana, Nigeria, and Saudi Arabia, and was a WHO Consultant in Ghana and the Sudan.*
Dr George Wyatt *is a Senior Lecturer in Tropical Medicine at the Liverpool School of Tropical Medicine.*

Filariasis is caused by long, thread-like worms—up to 50 cm in length—which live in or under the skin and in lymphatic tissues. Several different types of human filarial infections are known: all are transmitted by biting insects, and occur only in warm climates, because the parasite needs high environmental temperatures to complete its development in insects.

Filarial worms may live for up to twenty years in humans, producing larvae that infect insects; but adult worms do not multiply in the body. Severity of disease depends largely on the number of adult worms present in the body, which in turn depends on the number of infective bites received: many people with few worms suffer little or no serious effects. Filariasis affects about 300 million people worldwide but produces significant disease only in some of these and rarely causes death. Drug treatment is effective if given before advanced disease is present.

Lymphatic filariasis

Lymphatic filariasis is caused by worms called *Wuchereria bancrofti* and *Brugia malayi* which live in the lymph glands and vessels. Over 200 million people living in Asia, Africa, South America, and Oceania are infected (see Map 4.4). Transmission is by many varieties of mosquito which become infected with larvae by biting infected people. Often, there may be no symptoms; sometimes, however, there may be recurrent, painful inflamma-

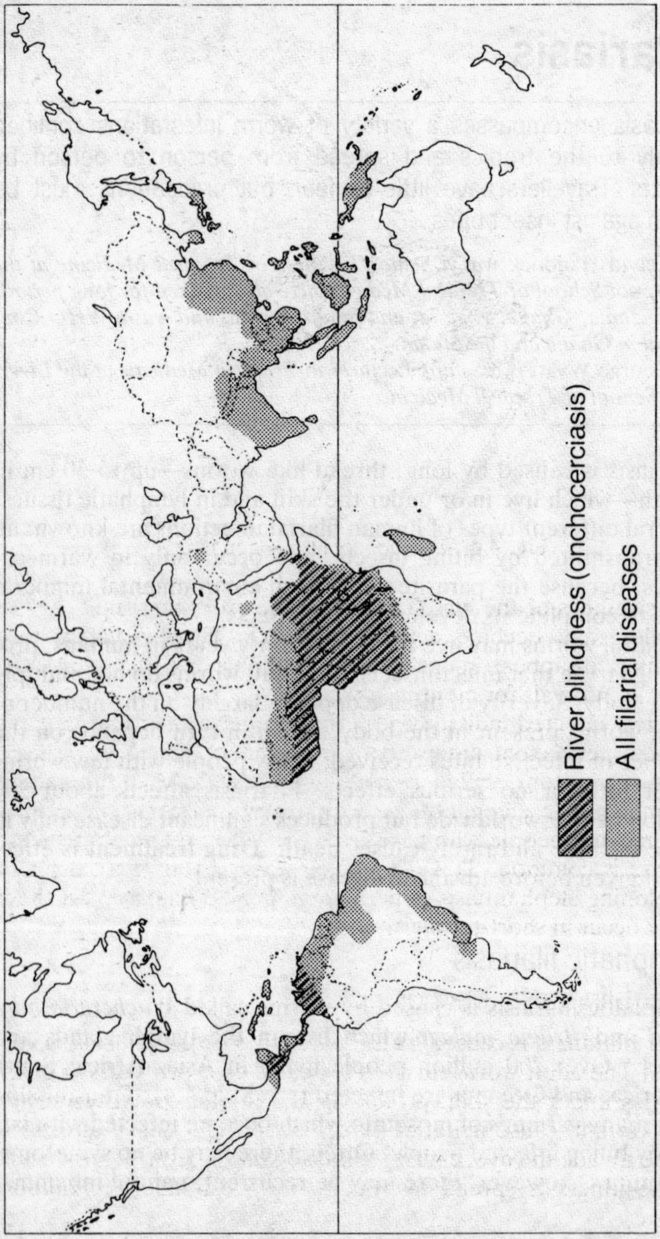

Map 4.4 Geographical distribution of filarial diseases.

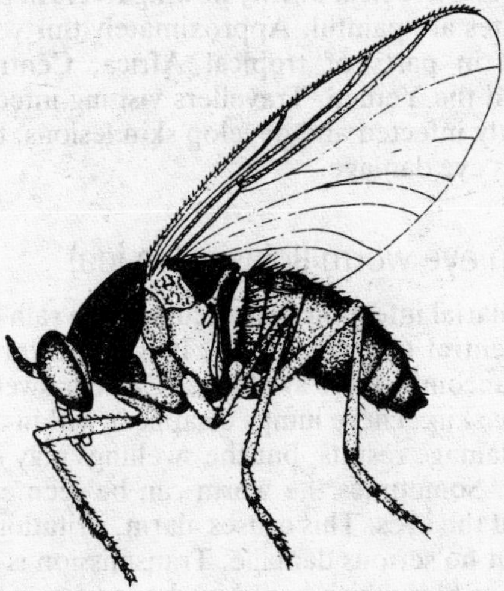

Fig. 4.4 *Simulium* fly (1.5–4 mm long).

tory swellings of the lymph glands in the groin or armpit, or the testicles may become acutely inflamed. These inflammatory swellings disappear spontaneously within a few days but may recur at intervals for months or years.

A few infected individuals (perhaps 5 per cent) develop more serious, permanent disease with incapacitating swelling of legs, arms or scrotum, called *elephantiasis* because of the resulting resemblance to elephant skin. Elephantiasis occurs only in heavily infected people who have lived for years in areas where the disease is common. Travellers often worry about the danger of developing elephantiasis or permanent genital damage, but these never occur in short-term visitors.

River blindness (onchocerciasis)

River blindness is caused by the parasitic worm *Onchocerca volvulus*. The adult worm survives for up to eighteen years in small nodules under the skin, producing larvae that spread widely in the skin and cause irritating skin reactions. In heavy infections larvae invade the eye, causing damage and sometimes blindness.

The illness is spread by small, biting blackflies (*Simulium*) which breed and live near swiftly flowing rivers in parts of the tropics; their bites are painful. Approximately thirty million people are affected in parts of tropical Africa, Central and South America, and the Yemen. Travellers visiting infected areas may become lightly infected and develop skin lesions, but they rarely suffer serious eye damage.

The African eye worm (loiasis, loa loa)

Loiasis is a filarial infection that occurs in the rain-forest areas of West and Central tropical Africa. It is characterized by recurrent, itchy, uncomfortable swellings (Calabar swellings) appearing under the skin. These lumps disappear within a few days. No permanent damage results, but the swellings may recur for up to fifteen years. Sometimes the worm can be seen crawling across the surface of the eyes. This causes alarm, irritation and watering of the eye but no serious damage. Transmission is by the bites of large *Chrysops* flies which breed in shaded forest pools and bite in daytime.

Summary of advice for travellers

- Travellers occasionally contract filariasis, but, practically always, the infections are only light and not serious. Diagnosis is made by examining blood or small pieces of skin under the microscope, and finding larvae. Most travellers' worries about filariasis are unjustified.

Prevention

- All types of filariasis are spread by insects that bite both at night and during the day. Protection against insect bites is important (see pp. 182–6). Screening of houses against insects and sleeping under mosquito nets helps. Wearing long trousers and sleeves and the application of insect repellents on the skin offers some protection. Loiasis can be prevented by taking diethylcarbamazine tablets (DEC, Banocide, Hetrazan) 200 mg daily for three consecutive days each month whilst in heavily infected areas, such as parts of Cameroon.

Lyme disease

Lyme disease occurs after tick bites that often have not been noticed, and is most commonly recognized by an expanding red rash at the site of the bite.

Dr George P. Schmid *is a physician specializing in infectious diseases at the Centers for Disease Control, and took part in some of the earliest studies investigating the cause and global distribution of Lyme disease.*

Lyme disease (*Lyme borreliosis*) is an infectious disease characterized initially by an expanding red skin rash (called *erythema chronicum migrans*, or ECM for short), often accompanied by headache, muscle, and joint aches, and a low-grade fever. The vast majority of cases occur during the summer and early autumn, and the causative bacterium, *Borrelia burgdorferi*, is transmitted to humans by the bite of certain ticks; ECM occurs at the site of the bite 3–32 days later. Early cases are successfully treated with oral tetracycline, but if the disease progresses to complications involving the joints, cardiac and nervous systems, antibiotic injections must be used.

Distribution

Lyme disease occurs in much of the United States, throughout Europe and the United Kingdom, and in selected coastal areas of Australia; cases have also been reported in China and Japan. Within these countries, the disease occurs only where the appropriate tick vectors are found, often in areas of forestation and brush. In the United States, the vectors are *Ixodes dammini* (the deer tick), *Ixodes pacificus*, and *Amblyomma americanum* (the Lone Star tick), and disease is concentrated in New England and coastal areas further south to North Carolina; and also in Minnesota and Wisconsin in the Midwest, Texas, and the Pacific Coast; at least 36 states have reported cases. In the United Kingdom and the rest of Europe, the vector is *Ixodes ricinus* (the sheep tick) and cases have been reported from nearly every country. Very few cases have been reported from Australia, China, or Japan, suggesting that the disease is rare in these countries.

One case of disease has occurred after a mosquito bite and other insects have been found to be infected, suggesting that additional arthropods or insects could be vectors.

The illness

Clinical illness begins 3–32 days following a tick bite, but only a minority of patients remember the initial bite. This is because the *Ixodes* ticks are quite small and bites are often not noticed. The first sign of disease is usually a red area at the site of the tick bite which, over a few days, expands in a circular fashion and may form a ring as its centre returns to a more normal appearance. This expansion occurs as the infecting organisms migrate outward in the skin.

The skin rash is usually accompanied by signs of general infection, as *B. burgdorferi* spreads to other areas of the body. These include a low-grade fever, muscle and joint pain (with spread to joints), headache and stiff neck (with spread to the cerebrospinal fluid of the brain), and an irregular heart beat (with spread to the heart). Additional neurological symptoms, in particular temporary paralysis of the muscles on one side of the face (Bell's palsy) and pain or weakness in specific nerves, may be prominent, although why these symptoms occur is still unknown.

Without treatment, ECM and the attendant symptoms will eventually resolve after several weeks in most patients. Many individuals, however, will have persistent or recurrent symptoms. The most common symptoms are recurrent attacks of arthritis lasting about a week, often accompanied by fatigue. Chronic neurological symptoms, such as persistent headache and stiff neck, mental changes, difficulties in thinking or concentrating, or numbness, weakness, or pain in specific nerves of the body may predominate. In a small number of patients, chronic arthritis, usually of the hip and resembling rheumatoid arthritis, may develop months or years following the initial illness.

It is important to note that Lyme disease is highly variable in the symptoms that it causes. Serological studies have shown that many people who have been infected have no prior recollection of illness. Some patients with the later symptoms of Lyme disease seek medical attention because of arthritis or neurological complaints, but likewise do not remember a skin rash. Other people have ECM and no other symptoms, while others have associated general symptoms but do not have or notice ECM. There are also geographic differences in disease, with neurological symptoms being more prominent in Lyme disease acquired in Europe and arthritis more prominent in disease acquired in the United States.

Treatment

The chance of developing Lyme disease after a tick bite appears to be very low, and prescription of antibiotics following a tick bite appears to be unwarranted. Patients with ECM and/or attendant symptoms should receive tetracycline tablets, 250–500 mg, four times a day for 10 days; this effectively treats the symptoms and prevents the development of subsequent complications in most patients. If symptoms have not significantly improved by the end of this period, a second course of tetracycline for 10 days is recommended. For patients who are unable to tolerate tetracycline, 500 mg of penicillin VK, four times a day for the same time period can be used but is less effective. There is reluctance to use tetracycline for children under the age of eight years and penicillin is most commonly recommended, although the greater effectiveness of tetracycline may outweigh the small chance of cosmetically apparent tooth staining.

For patients with established complications, such as meningitis or chronic arthritis, intravenous penicillin or ceftriaxone are recommended.

Summary of advice for travellers

- Tick repellents containing DEET (see p. 183) are effective. Individuals in outdoor areas where Lyme disease occurs should also tuck trouser legs into socks and examine each other at the end of each day for the presence of ticks.
- If an embedded tick is found, slowly pulling the tick out with tweezers is the best method of removal.
- If the symptoms of Lyme disease, particularly the appearance of a rash at the site of attachment, occur in the succeeding days or weeks, prompt medical attention should be sought.

Leishmaniasis

Leishmaniasis can be contracted in Mediterranean countries as well as in the tropics and subtropics, and may have serious disfiguring effects. Avoidance of sandfly bites is the main protective measure.

Dr Clinton Manson-Bahr *taught and practised in Africa and the Western Pacific for twenty-three years. He is a descendant of Sir Patrick Manson, the founder of modern Tropical Medicine, and is the editor of Manson's* Tropical Diseases*—the foremost medical textbook on the subject.*

Leishmaniasis is frequently underestimated as a health hazard to travellers, because it rarely causes serious illness. Its importance lies in the fact that when it does occur, doctors and health workers who are unfamiliar with the disease invariably fail to make the correct diagnosis.

Leishmaniasis remains an important public health problem in many parts of the world.

What is leishmaniasis?

Leishmania are tiny single-celled organisms, just smaller than red blood cells. They parasitize *macrophage* cells (part of the immune system) in the skin, spleen, liver, bone marrow, and lymph glands. Their life history involves certain types of sandfly (Fig. 4.5), which bite at night and become infected by sucking the blood of an infected individual. After a two to three-week period infective forms of leishmania appear in the biting parts of the insect, and infect a new host during each subsequent blood-meal.

Rodents, dogs, foxes, and jackals may also harbour the disease: leishmaniasis is therefore often referred to as a 'zoonosis'—an infection that passes between humans and animals. The existence of an 'animal reservoir' explains why the disease may be acquired in remote and uninhabited areas, and why it may suddenly occur out of the blue.

Cutaneous leishmaniasis

Cutaneous leishmaniasis (also known as Oriental sore, Baghdad boil, or Biskra button) occurs in much of the Middle East,

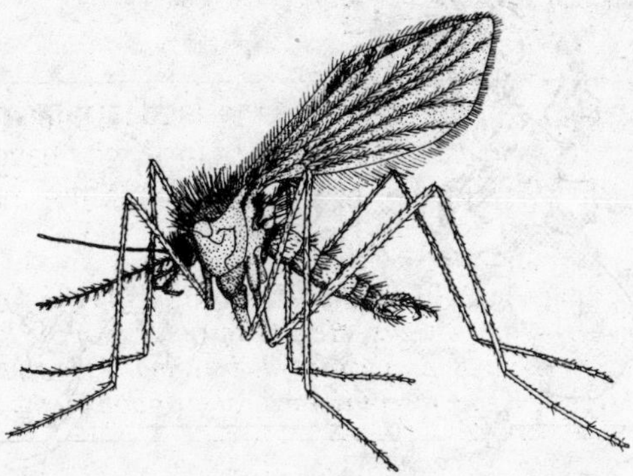

Fig. 4.5 *Phlebotomus* sandfly (2–5 mm long).

Asiatic Russia, North Africa (see Map 4.5, p. 146), and many areas of the tropics and sub-tropics. The observant traveller may have noticed that in many cities of the Middle East, nearly every inhabitant bears the unsightly scars that are the hallmark of the disease.

The infection is restricted to the skin at the site of the sandfly bite, and two patterns of disease occur—one in cities, and another in semi-desert areas.

The city form has a reservoir in dogs and is found in big cities such as Baghdad and Tehran; it is also found in the Costa del Sol, the island of Majorca and the Greek Islands, where it occasionally infects tourists. The reservoir for the rural form is a rodent (the giant gerbil) and travellers and picnickers in the semi-desert areas of Israel, Jordan, Libya, Iran, Iraq, and north-eastern areas of Saudi Arabia are at risk.

The infection shows itself as one or more chronic skin nodules which appear on the face or arms, and which may ulcerate. The disease is often self-limiting but may persist for up to a year, and can leave a disfiguring scar. Diagnosis is made by examining a smear from the cut edge of an ulcer, and treatment is with an antimony drug (see below).

Visceral leishmaniasis (kala azar)

Visceral leishmaniasis or 'kala azar' almost disappeared from India as a result of widespread use of insecticides during attempts

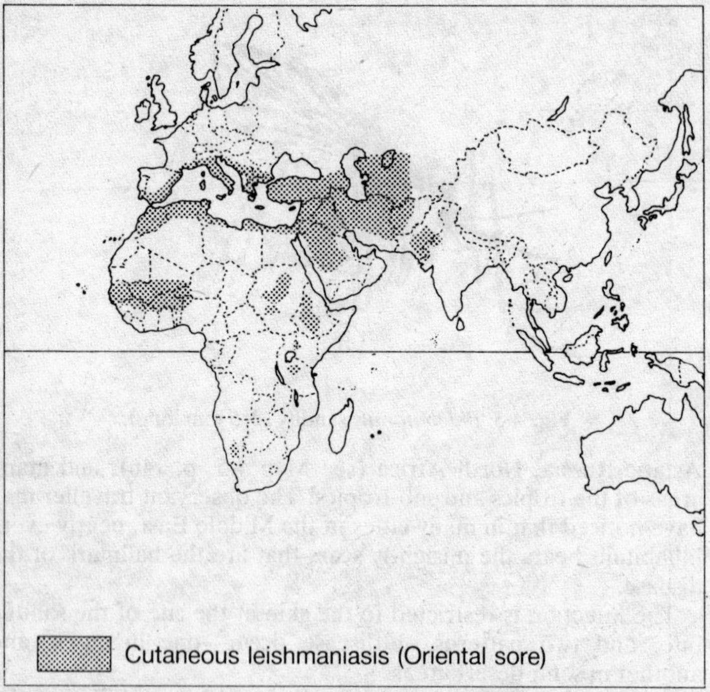

Map 4.5 Geographical distribution of cutaneous leishmaniasis (oriental sore and Ethiopian leishmaniasis).

to eradicate malaria. These efforts have lapsed, however, and it has now returned with a vengeance. The disease is widespread throughout large areas of India, has caused epidemics in Sudan and East Africa, and is found in many popular tourist destinations around the Mediterranean.

The parasites responsible for kala azar invade cells in the spleen, bone marrow, and liver causing serious illness and, if untreated, death. The disease is rare in travellers, but is an important infection among the inhabitants of eastern India, Africa south of the Sahara, and Brazil (Map 4.6). Tourists to North Africa and parts of southern Spain, France, mainland Greece (suburbs of Athens and Piraeus) can contract the disease. Although it is rare, travellers should always be aware of the

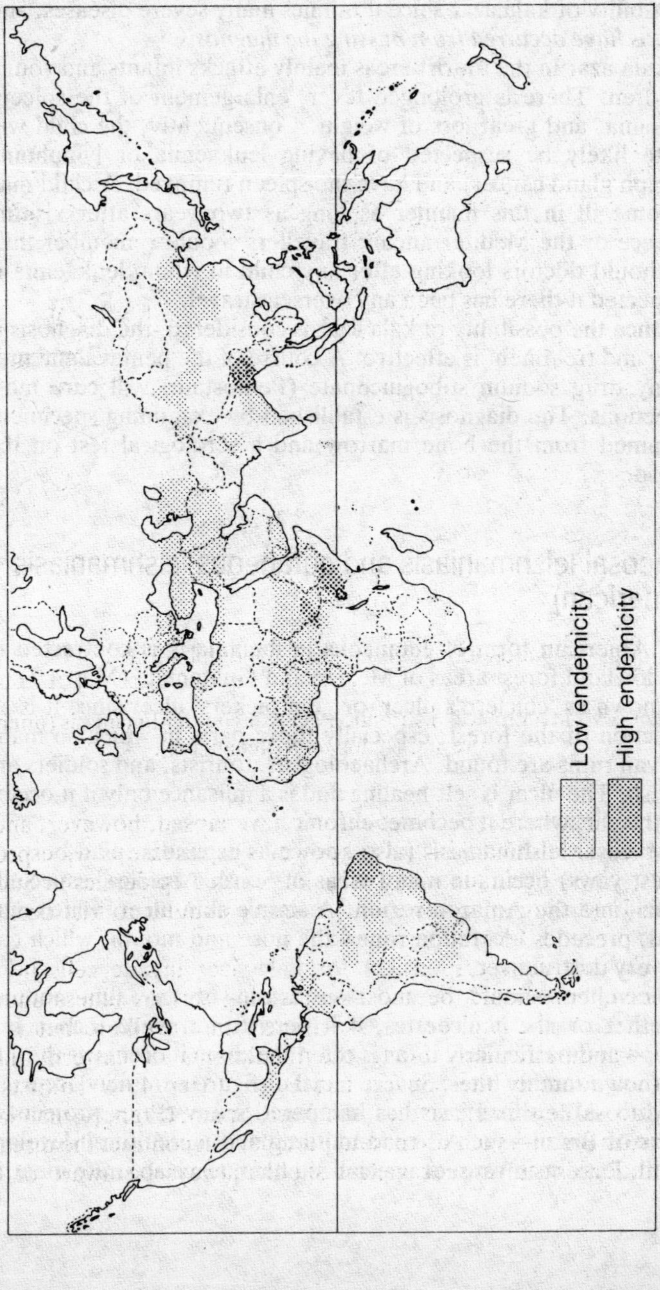

Map 4.6 Geographical distribution of visceral leishmaniasis (kala azar).

possibility of kala azar since it mimics many severe diseases, and *deaths have occurred from missing the diagnosis*.

Kala azar in the tourist areas mainly attacks infants and young children. There is prolonged fever, enlargement of the spleen, anaemia, and great loss of weight. Consequently, the child will quite likely be suspected of having leukaemia or lymphoma (lymph gland cancer) and have the spleen removed. A child may become ill in this manner as long as two years after visiting Greece or the Mediterranean; travellers should remember this, as should doctors looking after any child in whom leukaemia is suspected if there has been any overseas travel.

Once the possibility of kala azar is considered, the diagnosis is easy and treatment is effective. A course of the pentavalent antimony drug sodium stibogluconate (Pentostam) will cure most infections. The diagnosis is established by examining specimens obtained from the bone marrow and a serological test on the blood.

Mucosal leishmaniasis and cutaneous leishmaniasis (American)

An American form of cutaneous leishmaniasis is contracted in the lowland forest areas of Mexico and Guatemala (Map 4.7). It is known as 'chiclero's ulcer' or gum pickers' ulcer since it is an infection of the forest, especially those parts in which so many Mayan ruins are found. Archaeologists, tourists, and soldiers are at risk. The ulcer is self-healing and is a nuisance only if it occurs on the ear, where it becomes chronic.

Mucosal leishmaniasis (also known as espundia, pian bois, or forest yaws) occurs in many areas of South America, especially Brazil and the Amazon region. A simple skin ulcer, which may heal, precedes ulceration round the nose and mouth, which can be very destructive.

Travellers should be most suspicious of any skin nodule, whether or not it ulcerates, if it persists for more than a few days—and particularly if (as is often the case) it occurs at the site of known sandfly bites. Severe facial disfigurement may occur.

Mucosal leishmaniasis has hampered many major projects in parts of Brazil—such as road-building and agricultural development. Patients must seek specialized help, since accurate identifi-

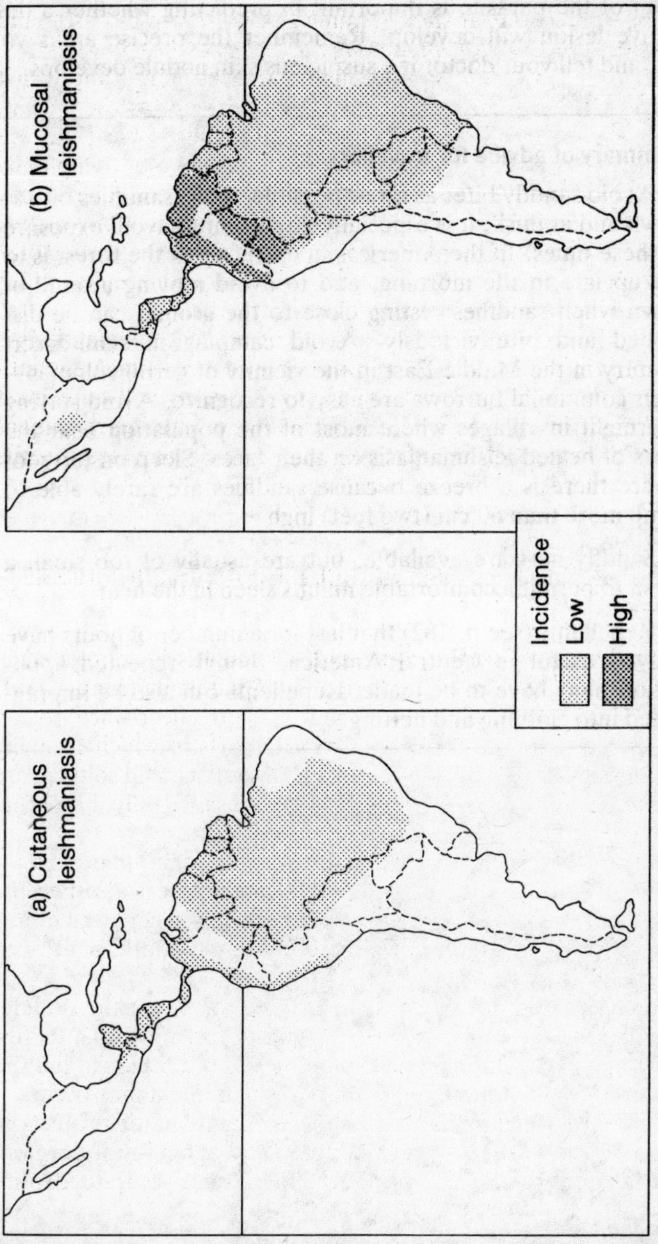

Map 4.7 Geographical distribution of American cutaneous and mucosal leishmaniasis.

cation of the parasite is important in predicting whether a destructive lesion will develop. Remember the precise areas you visit, and tell your doctor if a suspicious skin nodule develops.

Summary of advice for travellers

- Avoid sandfly bites as far as possible. Since sandflies bite at dawn and at dusk, it is especially important to avoid exposure at these times. In the Americas, a useful tip in the forest is to get up late in the morning, and to avoid moving around at dawn when sandflies resting close to the ground can be disturbed and bite viciously. Avoid camping in semi-desert country in the Middle East in the vicinity of gerbil colonies—their communal burrows are easy to recognize. Avoid staying overnight in villages where most of the population bear the scars of healed leishmaniasis on their faces. Sleep on the roof where there is a breeze because sandflies are rarely able to jump more than 60 cm (two feet) high.

- Sandfly nets are available, but are usually of too small a mesh to permit a comfortable night's sleep in the heat.

- Repellents (see p. 182) that last for a number of hours have proved useful in Central America, though repeated applications may have to be made. Repellents can also be impregnated into clothing and netting.

Sleeping sickness

Travellers to rural areas in tropical Africa may be at risk. Diagnosis and treatment are more difficult than prevention, so travellers should take care to avoid the bite of the tsetse fly.

Dr George Wyatt *is a Senior Lecturer in Tropical Medicine at the Liverpool School of Tropical Medicine.*

Sleeping sickness, also known as African trypanosomiasis, is an important disease of humans and animals in tropical Africa. It kills cattle readily, and is therefore of great economic concern in large areas of Africa. In humans, the disease is confined to certain rural areas, but within these areas it can be a serious problem, and from time to time major epidemics of sleeping sickness arise. Epidemics often follow social and political turmoil, when control measures break down and people migrate into endemic areas. There has been just such an epidemic in the Busoga area of Uganda since the late 1970s.

Sleeping sickness is not a familiar disease to doctors in developed countries, so infections in travellers may easily remain undiagnosed for some time. Some African countries play down the risks of sleeping sickness so as to avoid frightening away potential tourists.

How the disease is spread and its effects

The disease is caused by single-celled organisms called *trypanosomes*. The trypanosomes are spread by the bites of infected tsetse flies.

There are two varieties of sleeping sickness. In East Africa, the Rhodesian form of the disease is primarily an infection of wild animals such as the bushbuck; it is transmitted to people who live or travel near wild animals, by tsetse flies that breed in woodland or bush country.

In West and Central Africa a more slowly developing form of sleeping sickness, the Gambian form, is transmitted directly from person to person by the bites of tsetse flies that breed along the banks of rivers or streams.

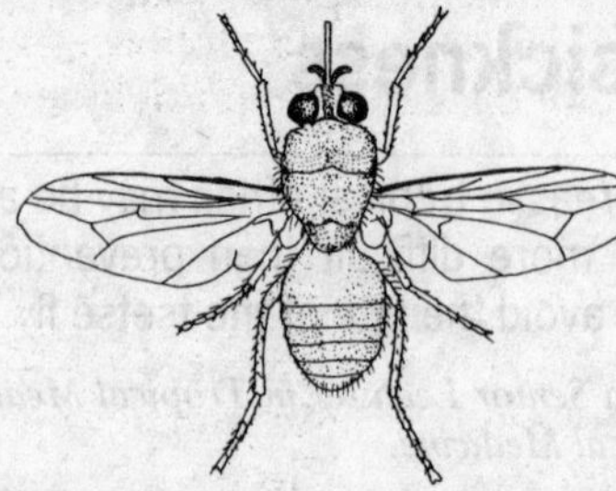

Fig. 4.6 Tsetse fly (female) (6–15 mm long).

The first sign of infection with trypanosomes may be a boil-like swelling which arises at the site of a tsetse bite, five or more days after the bite. Swellings that arise within a few hours of a bite are usually allergic in nature and not a sign of trypanosome infection. Fever (see p. 374) may begin within two or three weeks, and a severe illness may ensue which, unless adequately treated, often leads to infection of the central nervous system, and to the daytime drowsiness so characteristic of the disease.

Treatment

While the great majority of patients with sleeping sickness can be cured with proper drug treatment, the only drugs available are old-fashioned and hazardous to use, so that treatment should be given only by experienced doctors. Unfortunately there has been little research into new drugs for use against sleeping sickness: pharmaceutical companies see little profit in drugs that would mainly be required only by very poor people.

Sleeping sickness and the traveller

The chief group of travellers at risk from sleeping sickness are those who go on wild-life safaris in East Africa. Each year a handful of tourists among the many thousands who go on such safaris develop sleeping sickness; the risk is very low in the better-developed tourist areas.

Other travellers who visit remote rural areas in Africa or who work with wild animals may also be at risk.

African countries in which sleeping sickness occurs or has occurred in the recent past include the following, but note that only certain localities are dangerous and urban areas are free of risk:

Angola
Benin
Botswana
Burkina Faso
Burundi
Cameroon
Central African Republic
Chad
Congo
Gabon
Gambia
Ghana
Guinea
Guinea Bissau
Ethiopia
Ivory Coast
Kenya
Malawi
Mozambique
Niger
Nigeria
Rwanda
Senegal
Sierra Leone
Sudan
Tanzania
Togo
Uganda
Zaire
Zambia
Zimbabwe

Travellers who become ill following a safari holiday should make sure that their doctor knows which countries they have visited.

Summary of advice for travellers

- Unfortunately there is no vaccine against sleeping sickness, nor is there any liklihood of one being developed in the near future. This is because the trypanosomes are able to change their outer surface coat, thereby escaping the body's immune mechanisms.

- Although drugs are sometimes used as prophylactics against this disease, they cannot be advised for travellers since they do not always work, and when they fail they may mask infection until after the nervous system has been invaded.

- Prevention therefore depends largely upon avoiding the bites of tsetse flies. These flies are active during the daytime and are about the size of a common house-fly. They have a pointed 'proboscis' projecting forward from their head and at rest sit with their wings folded across their backs. Tsetse flies are attracted to large moving objects and to certain smells and colours such as dark blue (Table 4.7, p. 180).

- Flies soon follow any vehicle travelling through infested areas. It is therefore wise to keep car windows closed, and to kill any flies entering the vehicle with a 'knock-down' *pyrethrum* spray, to which they are highly susceptible.

- Tsetse flies are less attracted to people on foot, and if you ride a horse they are more likely to bite the horse than to attack you. Insect repellents such as diethyltoluamide (deet) are of some value against tsetse flies (p. 182) but are not always effective.

Chagas' disease

Chagas' disease is a potentially serious infection spread by a South American bug that lives in mud huts. Travellers to rural areas of Brazil are most at risk, but avoidance is reasonably straightforward.

Dr Clinton Manson-Bahr *taught and practised in Africa and the Western Pacific for twenty-three years. He is a descendant of Sir Patrick Manson, the founder of modern Tropical Medicine, and is the editor of Manson's* Tropical Diseases*—the foremost medical textbook on the subject.*

Chagas' disease is found only in South and Central America (see Map 4.8, overleaf). The disease is a major problem in Brazil, where it is present in most rural areas: poor peasants living in adobe (mud) huts are at greatest risk. True jungle areas such as the Amazon regions (with a mainly nomadic Amerindian population) tend to be free from the disease.

What is Chagas' disease?

Chagas' disease is caused by a small single-celled organism called *Trypanosoma cruzi*, which lives in the blood, and also in macrophage cells (part of the body's immune system) in the heart, intestines, and nervous system. The organism is similar in many ways to the trypanosomes which cause sleeping sickness.

How the disease is spread

The trypanosome is spread from one person to another by certain types of 'cone-nosed' bugs, also known as assassin bugs or kissing bugs (Fig. 4.7). (See p. 157 and Table 4.7, p. 180). The bugs become infected by feeding upon the blood of an individual who has the disease. They excrete infective trypanosomes in their faeces while biting a subsequent victim, and the trypanosomes enter through the bite wound.

The bugs live in the walls of mud huts and venture out only at night. They also feed on chickens, which are often kept in pens adjacent to the huts. Opossums and dogs also harbour the infection.

Map 4.8 Geographical distribution of Chagas' disease (South American trypanosomiasis) in South and Central America, 1988. Reproduced by kind permission of the Pan American Health Organization and Dr F.J. Lopez Antuñano.

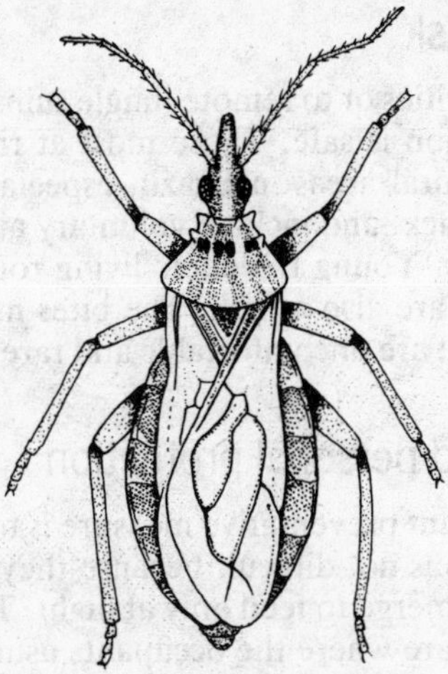

Fig. 4.7 *Rhodnius* 'cone-nosed' bug (1–4 cm long).

Symptoms

Although infection may be widespread among local inhabitants, only a proportion ever develop symptoms of disease. Early clues to a possible infection include local swelling around a bite, followed by swelling of the lymph glands or by a fever. At this stage it may be possible to detect trypanosomes with a blood test. The early symptoms soon settle.

The long-term complications of infection are serious: damage to the heart may lead to sudden death at a young age, and paralysis of the intestine and gullet causes severe constipation and difficulty swallowing (megacolon, megaoesophagus). A chance infection from a single exposure—such as on a short visit to an infected area—may pass undetected for years. It is not clear how often such infections lead to trouble.

Treatment

Treatment is difficult, because at present no drug is able to penetrate the macrophage cells and kill the parasite without harming the host; but parasites in the blood can be treated with a drug called nifurtimox (Lampit), although this should not be given lightly as its side-effects may also be serious.

Travellers at risk

Visitors to large cities or to remote jungle ruins are not at risk, and the Amazon region is safe. Those most at risk are travellers to well-populated rural areas in Brazil, especially to areas off the normal tourist track, and include voluntary aid workers or Peace Corps volunteers. Young travellers living rough and sleeping in local adobe huts are also at risk. The bites may be mistaken for bed-bug bites, but are uncomfortable and rarely escape attention.

Prevention and personal protection

The most important preventative measure is to avoid being bitten by the bugs. This is not difficult because they live in the walls of adobe huts and emerge to feed only at night. The most dangerous parts of the huts are where the occupants usually sleep, and near walls and adjoining the chicken pens. Adobe huts are best avoided altogether, and it is safer to camp some distance away. Always sleep under a mosquito net as this will keep the bugs out, but be careful to tuck the net in completely, all the way round. If it is impossible to avoid spending the night inside, sleep in the centre of the room, away from the walls; do not use old rugs, blankets, or sheets from the hut.

There is little or no prospect for a vaccine, and no preventative drug at present.

Check-up (see also Appendix 4)

The parasite is difficult to detect in the bloodstream once three weeks have elapsed following infection. However, if there is fever or local lymph gland enlargement the parasite can usually be found in the blood or in juice obtained from the lymph gland by needle puncture.

The best check test is a serum test (FAT fluorescent antibody test or ELISA test), which is now specific and accurate. Everyone who has travelled to rural areas of Brazil, or who has a blood transfusion in Brazil, should have these tests performed on their return home. If they are positive, a course of nifurtimox should be given until the tests return to normal.

Plague

Although plague is still present in several countries, the risk to travellers is very small indeed.

Dr Thomas J. Quan *is a Research Microbiologist with the Plague Branch, Centers for Disease Control, Fort Collins, Colorado, and has worked with plague for more than twenty-five years.*

Plague, a bacterial infection primarily of rodents, is one of the oldest diseases known. Periodically throughout recorded history, plague has spread to other parts of the world from what appears to be its ancestral home—the Yunnan Province of China. The first written description of the disease is perhaps that given in I Samuel v–vi, which reported an epidemic in about 1320 BC. Other major outbreaks include the 'Plague of Justinian' from 542 to 600 AD, the 'Black Death' of Europe during the fourteenth century, and the European epidemics of the fifteenth, sixteenth, and seventeenth centuries.

The current worldwide epidemic (pandemic) started in China in the mid-1800s and spread slowly to many other areas via both overland and marine mercantile trade routes. After its introduction in previously uninvolved areas (including the western USA, South America, and South Africa), the plague organism became established in native wild rodents and persists as a potential public health hazard.

Plague today

In 1977–86, nineteen countries in Africa, Asia, Asia Minor, and North and South America reported 7 631 human plague cases, including 570 deaths (Table 4.5). In 1987 to May 31, 1988, seven of these countries reported cases.

Disease reservoir and how it is spread

Human plague cases occur as the result of complex interactions involving four factors:

Table 4.5 Reported human plague 1977–86 (WHO statistics)

Country	Total No. cases (Reported)	Deaths	Cases reported 1987–88
Africa			
Angola	27	4	
Kenya	398	12	
Libya	19	6	
Madagascar	376	124	YES
Mozambique	109	14	
South Africa	19	1	
Tanzania	929	2122	YES
Uganda	493	30	YES
Zaire	6	4	YES
Zimbabwe	5	3	
Total	**2381**	**2320**	
Americas			
Bolivia	282	35	YES
Brazil	661	29	YES
Ecuador	91	4	
Peru	518	44	
USA	191	32	YES
Total	**1743**	**2124**	
Asia			
Burma	1170	42	
China	120	46	
Viet Nam	2182	236	
Total	**3472**	**2124**	
Asia Minor			
Saudi Arabia	35	2	
	35	**2**	
Grand Total	**7631**	**1570**	

1. The first is the agent—a bacterium called *Yersinia pestis*.
2. The second is an insect vector (transmitter—one or more of many types of flea (Fig. 4.8)).
3. The third is a rodent or other mammal 'host'.
4. The fourth is the human host.

The ebb and flow of evident plague activity is closely associated with the natural cycles of its hosts and their fleas and with the weather, climatic, and other ecological factors. Although

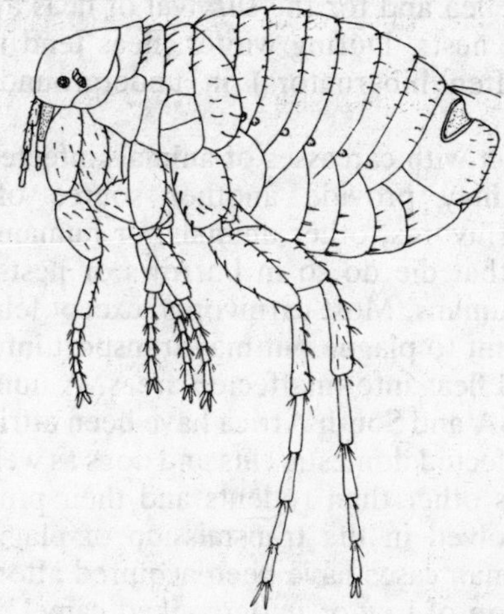

Fig. 4.8 *Pulex irritans* flea (male) (2–3 mm long).

human cases may occur at any time, most occur in warm (not hot) summer months.

Typically, plague bacteria circulate among rodent hosts which are relatively tolerant of the bacterium's harmful effects. Fleas become infected by feeding on infected rodents or other mammalian hosts. As long as the infection is transmitted only amongst moderately to highly resistant 'maintenance' rodent hosts, plague may remain undetected.

But infected fleas may transfer to and infect other, susceptible rodent species ('amplification' hosts); once the bacterium begins circulating among a sufficiently large population of susceptible rodents and appropriate kinds and numbers of fleas, a widespread die-off of the hosts may be initiated. Fleas then abandon their dead or dying hosts and migrate in active search of new hosts, including humans.

As more susceptible rodents die, progressively fewer are accessible to infected fleas, less contact occurs between infected and uninfected animals, and eventually the outbreak recedes. Even if the population of susceptible rodents is large, an outbreak may be interrupted or stopped by the advent of adverse weather. Long, hot, dry spells are unfavourable both to the bacteria in the flea and for the survival of fleas away from their hosts or hosts' nests. During winter, fleas tend to remain with their hosts (often hibernators) in underground burrows and nests.

Direct contact with carcasses of animals infected with or dead from plague may provide another source of infection to scavengers, carnivores, other animals, or humans. Fortunately, most animals that die do so in burrows or nests not generally accessible to humans. Most carnivores, except felines, appear to be fairly resistant to plague but may transport infected carcasses and/or infected fleas into unaffected areas. A number of human cases in the USA and South Africa have been attributed to direct contact with infected domestic cats and dogs as well as wild carnivores. Animals other than rodents and their predators are not commonly involved in the transmission of plague to humans. Occasional human cases have been acquired after direct contact with or ingestion of raw or undercooked camel, sheep, or goat meat in Libya, Afghanistan, and Saudi Arabia, and an infected antelope was the source of a recent human case in Montana, USA.

Symptoms

In human patients, the onset of *bubonic* plague symptoms is usually sudden, two to seven days after exposure (flea bite or direct contact). The chief symptoms include high fever, headache, muscular aches, shaking chills, and, commonly, pain in the groin or armpit.

The pain is due to the development of a *bubo*, an inflamed lymph node, which may or may not be enlarged until some time after onset of symptoms. Fully developed buboes are excruciatingly painful, and when in the groin may cause marked discomfort on walking. Buboes may also form in lymph nodes elsewhere in the body (in the neck, shoulder, knee, elbow, or deep in the chest or abdomen). In some patients, no buboes are evident: these cases are classified as *primary septicaemic* plague.

Untreated bubonic plague progresses rapidly, and bacteria spread via lymphatic and blood circulatory systems to other tissues and organs, including the lungs. When the lungs become involved an infectious pneumonia may develop, allowing person-to-person transmission via coughed-up, bacteria-laden airborne droplets. In the USA transmission by this route has been prevented by the isolation of plague patients, and contacts of patients are given preventive antibiotic treatment; in any case, person-to-person transmission probably requires very close or intimate contact. However, primary plague pneumonia cases have occurred in at least four people exposed to sick domestic pets in the USA.

Mortality and treatment

About 35 to 40 per cent of patients with untreated bubonic plague survive; however, patients with the more severe septicaemic and pneumonic forms of plague are unlikely to survive without early, specific antibiotic therapy. Diagnosed early, plague is readily curable. Effective antibiotics include streptomycin (the optimum choice), tetracycline, and chloramphenicol. If these antibiotics are not available certain sulphonamide drugs, especially sulphadiazine, are also effective.

Vaccination

Plague vaccines are available commercially, but vaccination for the general public or for casual visitors to plague areas is not practical. Vaccination is urged for persons who work with the organism regularly in the laboratory or those who are regularly exposed to hosts and/or transmitters of the organism in the field.

Prevention

The best defence against plague is to avoid fleas and rodents such as rats, rabbits, squirrels, and chipmunks (however attractive some species may be) in plague areas. Appropriate use of insecticides and rodenticides is recommended around permanent or semi-permanent dwellings. Regular use of suitable flea powders or dusts on domestic pet animals (dogs or cats) having access to both human and rodent habitats is strongly advised in plague areas. For short-term field excursions in plague areas, use of insect repellents, especially on legs and clothing, may effectively reduce flea infestation.

Summary of advice for travellers

- Fear of acquiring plague during routine sightseeing, hunting, on safari, or other tourist activities—even in active plague areas—should not prevent such activities or travel, provided that proper precautions are taken to minimize the risk.

- Reports of plague in travellers within or to the United States are uncommon; only ten out of the 300 cases that occurred in the United States from 1956 to 1987 were reported in persons who were exposed in one state but developed symptoms only after travel to another state. Intrastate travel by patients from the area of exposure to another area occurs more commonly. Only two cases of human plague have been reported in international travellers; one unconfirmed case was in a serviceman who became ill in Texas after exposure to plague in Vietnam. The second case was in a woman, exposed in Africa, who became ill in London while en route to Texas. Her illness was serologically confirmed as plague after her arrival in Texas.

- If you have been in a plague area and develop symptoms similar to those described above, professional medical help should be sought as soon as possible. An account of your travel itinerary and activities (especially of any possible exposure to infected animals or of flea bites) will alert the attending doctor and help the correct diagnosis to be made.

- If, and *only* if no such medical help is available within a reasonable time and the drugs are available, oral tetracycline (one 500 mg tablet four times daily for adults) for seven to 10 days can be taken. Professional medical help should be sought urgently, especially if the illness does not improve, or deteriorates.

Rodent hazard . . .

A Boeing 747 airliner in India was recently found to be unserviceable: rodents had nibbled cables in the upper deck area.

R.D.

Typhus fevers

Typhus may occasionally be a risk to travellers on walking holidays in certain tropical areas, or to those working with refugees.

Dr George Wyatt *is a Senior Lecturer in Tropical Medicine at the Liverpool School of Tropical Medicine.*

In the past, epidemic typhus has been one of the most feared diseases. Outbreaks killed many thousands of people during the world wars and under famine conditions both in Europe and in the tropics. At present, however, epidemic typhus is rare except among poor inhabitants of certain tropical highland areas. In recent years most of the world's cases have been reported from the highlands of Ethiopia, Rwanda, and Burundi, with smaller numbers from countries in South America. Epidemic typhus is spread by body lice, but other varieties of typhus spread by other insect transmitters are now much more common, worldwide.

All varieties of typhus cause fever (see p. 375), severe headache and a skin rash, but the severity of the illness varies greatly between different types of typhus. These infections respond rapidly to the correct antibiotic provided that it is given early enough in the illness.

Varieties of typhus

All varieties of typhus are caused by *rickettsiae*, which resemble very small bacteria.

Epidemic typhus

The rickettsiae causing epidemic typhus are spread from one person to another by the human body louse (Fig. 4.9); the organisms are passed in the louse faeces and cause infection if they are scratched through the skin, or sometimes if the faeces are inhaled with dust.

Other kinds of rickettsiae are principally infections of animals and their external parasites. People become infected by close contact with an infected animal or its parasites.

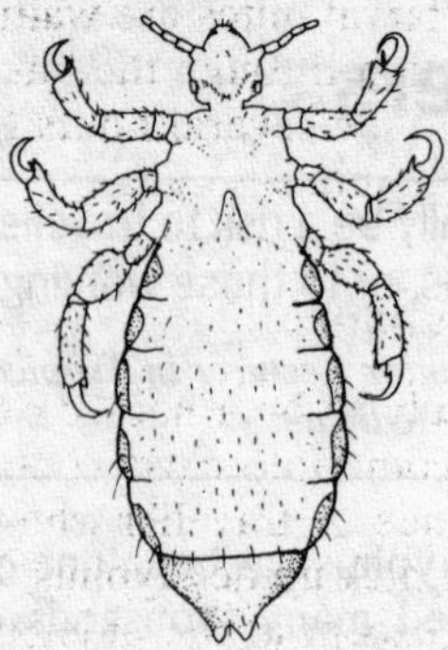

Fig. 4.9 *Pediculus humanus* the human body (or clothing) louse (2–3 mm long).

Endemic typhus

This is a disease very similar to epidemic typhus except that it is usually milder. The infection is transmitted in the faeces of infected rodent fleas (Fig. 4.8, p. 161). Sporadic human infections occur when people visit rat-infested buildings and are attacked by the rat fleas. Most kinds of typhus are rural infections but endemic typhus often occurs in towns, and occasionally there are sudden outbreaks, such as in Kuwait in 1978.

Tick typhus

Several kinds of typhus are spread to humans by the bites of hard ticks (Fig. 4.12, p. 173). In countries bordering the Mediterranean, dog ticks sometimes transmit tick typhus. In southern Africa, people who walk through the veldt may contract tick typhus from the ticks of cattle or of wild animals.

Scrub typhus

This is a disease of Asia and the Pacific islands. The reservoir for this infection is in the rodent population and in the mites that feed on these rodents. Once the mite population is infected, it may remain dangerous for many years because rickettsiae pass directly from one generation of mites to the next. Infected rodents and mites often live in quite small pockets or 'mite islands' in 'scrub' areas, also know as areas of 'secondary' or 'transitional' vegetation. People are infected by walking through an area where hungry larval mites are waiting for a blood meal. Rickettsiae cause infection through the bite of infected mite larvae, but infection may take several hours to be transmitted following attachment of the mite.

Typhus and the traveller

Epidemic typhus is likely to be a hazard only to people such as refugee workers who come into close contact with poor inhabitants of tropical highlands. A traveller who treks across the veldt in southern Africa may pick up tick typhus, but fortunately this is usually a mild disease except in the older traveller. People who hike in South-Eastern Asia are at risk from the more serious scrub typhus, especially if they travel through overgrown vegetation or old plantations. Typhus is very uncommon in the ordinary tourist or business traveller.

Summary of advice for travellers

- There are at present no commercially available vaccines against any variety of typhus.
- People who walk through tropical bush should inspect their skin carefully at the end of the day and remove any attached ticks (see p. 173). Repellents such as dimethyl phthalate, rubbed on to the skin every four hours, give useful protection against ticks and mites. Anyone intending to go walking in bush areas in South-Eastern Asia should also consider having boots and trousers impregnated with a mixture of benzyl benzoate and dibutyl phthalate.

Maggot infestation (myiasis)

Travellers to tropical Africa and South America may occasionally encounter this unpleasant affliction.

Dr Clinton Manson-Bahr *taught and practised in Africa and the Western Pacific for twenty-three years. He is a descendant of Sir Patrick Manson, the founder of modern Tropical Medicine, and is the editor of Manson's* Tropical Diseases—*the foremost medical textbook on the subject.*

The maggots or larvae of certain tropical flies are able to burrow into human skin, eyes, or the nasal passages, and are an occasional nuisance to visitors to the tropics. The resulting infestation is known as *myiasis*, and two types of larvae are of particular importance.

Tumbu fly

The tumbu fly is found in many parts of East and Central Africa. It lays its eggs on clothing—especially clothes that bear traces of urine or sweat. Clothes hanging outdoors on the washing line and clothes laid out on the ground to dry are the usual target.

The eggs hatch on contact with human skin. The larvae burrow into the skin and produce a characteristic boil, which contains not pus, but a developing maggot (Fig. 4.10). The boils are usually multiple and are found most often over the back, arms, scrotum, and around the waist.

The breathing apparatus of the maggots can usually be identified at the surface of the boil as a pair of black dots. A maggot can be removed by placing water or oil over its breathing apparatus, and gently squeezing it; the maggot will pop out. This is rather an unpleasant spectacle to witness.

Prevention

All clothes dried outdoors should be pressed with a good, hot iron to destroy any eggs that may be present. Clothes should otherwise be hung to dry indoors, in a fly-proof environment.

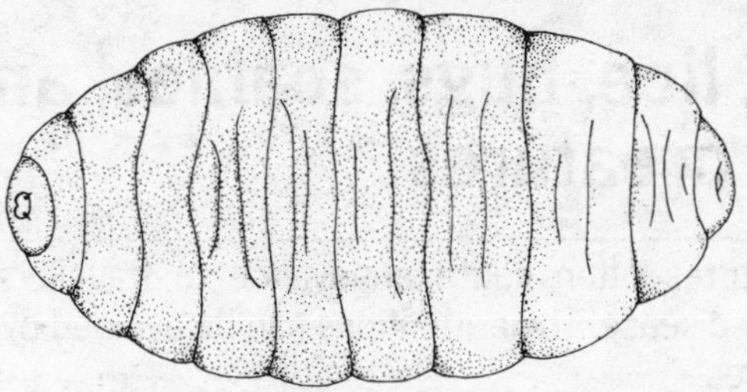

Fig. 4.10 Tumbu fly larva (11–15 mm long).

Macaw, or tropical warble fly

This tropical warble fly is found throughout South America. Its life history is complex, but the female lays its eggs directly on to mosquitoes' thoraces. When the mosquitoes bite, the eggs hatch, and larvae burrow into the victim's skin.

An inflamed swelling usually results, and this is especially dangerous when it occurs close to the eye; the maggot must then be extracted surgically.

Infection is uncommon, but travellers are at greatest risk on the forested eastern slopes of the Andes. General measure to avoid insect bites should always be followed (see pp. 182–6), but no specific precautions are possible. Attempts to wipe out the fly in certain areas have met with a degree of success.

Other forms of myiasis

Ordinary house-fly maggots may appear in the faeces when fly-contaminated food has been eaten. This is an alarming sight, but a dose of castor oil is all that is necessary to expel all of the larvae.

Bot flies, which usually lay their eggs in the skin of sheep or cattle, may occasionally attack man; the larvae can be found in the nasal cavity, and can be removed with ephedrine drops or by gargling with a strong salt solution. Infection is a hazard only in rural areas, under the most basic living conditions.

Fleas, lice, bugs, scabies, and other creatures

Such creatures often cause annoyance to travellers, but only rarely carry disease. Their attentions can be avoided by a few simple measures.

Rod Robinson *is an entomologist with training in Public Health, and has a special interest in lice.*

Humans provide many insects and other small creatures with both food and shelter from the elements (Table 4.7, p. 180). The intimacy of the association varies considerably: some parasites take up permanent residence, while others merely visit temporarily in search of food.

These creatures can be a particular nuisance to the traveller. Levels of infestation vary from country to country, but in general they are most common where standards of hygiene are low. The human flea is practically extinct in Europe, but our warm, dry homes are ideal for cat fleas. Infestations with lice, bed-bugs, and scabies are now comparatively rare in the UK, but are on the increase.

Fleas

Fleas are small (2–3 mm long) reddish-brown insects, compressed sideways; they lack wings, but have powerful hind legs for jumping (Fig. 4.8, p. 161). Their larvae are worm-like, and live on organic debris on the floor. Fleas breed wherever their hosts rest, jumping on to their victims to feed. Their larvae form pupae which remain dormant for several months, until vibrations from a passing victim provide a signal to come out and feed.

Fleas are able to transmit two important diseases—plague ('Black Death') (p. 159) and murine (endemic) typhus (p. 165)—but although fleas are widespread, disease is rare, and is confined to the poorest areas of urban squalor.

Otherwise, flea bites may be an uncomfortable nuisance, but are not dangerous.

Jigger fleas

The jigger flea is an unusual flea which lives outdoors in the sand in Central America and West Africa. The female penetrates the skin, usually around the toes, and swells up with eggs, causing inflammation and ulceration. If untreated, gangrene can set in. Local people can tell you which places to avoid, but if in doubt wear a good pair of jungle boots.

Lice

There are three types of human louse: the head louse, which lives on the scalp; the clothing louse (body louse), which infests clothing; and the crab louse (see also p. 395), which lives in coarse body hair (i.e. in the pubic region, armpits, in beards, etc.). All three types need to suck blood regularly, and if separated from the body for longer than a few days, they will die. Head and clothing lice are very similar in appearance, are 2–3 mm long, cream to brown in colour and lack wings (Fig. 4.9, p. 163). Crab lice are squatter and have prominent claws, giving a crablike appearance.

All three types of louse spread by direct contact between people, and in the case of the clothing louse by two people exchanging clothes. Their eggs are laid at the base of hairs or in seams of clothing, where body temperature enables them to hatch in seven to ten days.

Clothing lice can spread typhus, not by their bite but in their dried faeces, which can enter wounds or be accidentally inhaled. Like plague, typhus is restricted to the poorest areas, although it could break out wherever normal hygiene standards collapse.

Louse bites are otherwise merely a nuisance, although long-term infestation can lead to infections of the bites and allergic reactions to the louse saliva.

Bed-bugs

Bed-bugs are flat and oval, 6–10 mm long when fully grown, and reddish-brown in colour (Fig. 4.11). They live in bedrooms, in

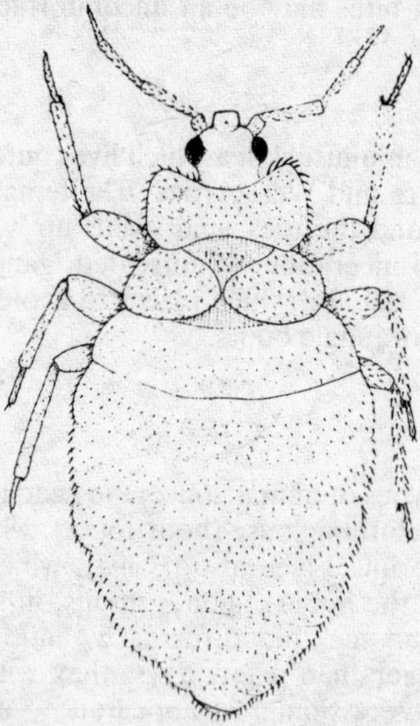

Fig. 4.11 *Cimex* bed-bug (male) (6–10 mm long).

the bedframe, in cracks in walls, and under wallpaper and carpets. They feed only at night, while their victims sleep.

They do not appear to carry any diseases, but their bites can be extremely uncomfortable.

Cone-nosed bugs

In South and Central America cone-nosed bugs (Fig. 4.7, p. 157) are common in rural areas where housing standards are low. They are relatively large creatures, 2–4 cm in length when fully grown, with a thin head and long mouthparts. They can carry Chagas' disease (South American trypanosomiasis, p. 155), and once again it is the faeces, not the bite that is infective.

Scabies

Scabies is caused by a small mite, which tunnels into the outer layers of the skin and causes a characteristic itch. Detecting the

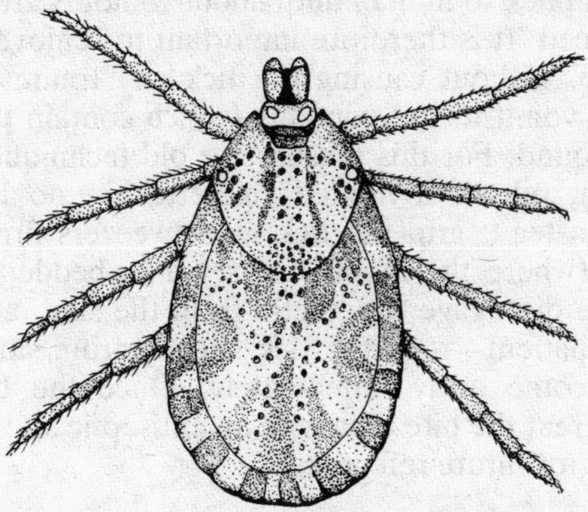

Fig. 4.12 Hard tick (about 3 mm long, but up to 20 mm when engorged with blood).

mite itself is difficult without a microscope, although with practice one can spot the meandering burrows. The itch itself can be almost unbearable, but the scabies mite does not carry any disease. (See also p. 395.)

Ticks and mites

Travellers walking through undergrowth or exploring caves may find ticks or mites attached to their skin (Fig. 4.12). Adult ticks can be alarmingly large when engorged, but they are relatively simple to remove with a pair of tweezers, or nimble fingers. Ticks can carry several diseases (see Table 4.7, p. 180). Rocky Mountain spotted fever occurs in parts of the United States, and so does Lyme disease.

Lyme Disease

This is a disease of deer and other animals which has recently (1976) been discovered to be capable of infecting man. It is caused by bacteria, and is spread by the bite of several tick species, found in woods, marshes, and grassland across mainland Europe, the UK, and the eastern USA. If untreated, it can lead to arthritis, heart problems, and nervous disorders. The disease is discussed in greater detail on p. 141.

There is some evidence to suggest that Lyme disease is rarely passed from tick to human until about 18 hours after the tick has begun to feed. It is therefore important to remove ticks as soon as possible, without causing the tick any trauma which might cause it to vomit its gut contents (which contain the bacterium) into the wound. For this reason, the old techniques of applying chloroform, oil, or a lighted cigarette are no longer recommended. Instead, grip the tick with tweezers firmly under the head end (where the mouth parts are embedded), push down carefully to disengage the 'teeth' from the skin, and gently pull away. Be patient—rock the tick slightly from side to side if it does not come away immediately. Once the tick has been removed, treat the bite area with an antiseptic and keep the tick, if possible, for future reference.

Mites

Mites can be dealt with in a similar manner, but in some species only the tiny mite *larvae* attack people, and they are difficult to spot. They attach themselves to the skin at the waist and ankles, leaving red weals. In South East Asia they can spread relapsing fever (a form of typhus).

Some hints on diagnosis

Flea bites tend to occur in groups, along clothing constrictions and around the ankles.

Bed-bugs bite on the face, arms and legs, where these protrude from the bedclothes.

Fleas and bugs often pass out undigested blood, leaving telltale bloodstains on the sheets. Pyrethroid flysprays, if available, can be sprayed into cracks and crevices and around bed-frames to check for bed-bugs; although the bugs are not killed by the spray, it irritates them enough to drive them from their hiding places.

Head lice bite only on the scalp, and crab lice on the body's hairy regions, whereas clothing lice may bite anywhere under the clothes. The best indicator of a louse infection is the discovery of white, empty eggshells, called nits, firmly glued to hairs or in the clothes.

In order to catch *scabies* it is necessary to be in close physical contact with an infected person for a prolonged time, and consequently the primary sites of infection are the hands, arms, legs, and sexual organs. The itch develops about six to eight weeks

Table 4.6 Treatment of personal parasites

Parasite	Preferred Treatment	Technique
Head lice	Malathion or Carbaryl-based lotion or shampoo, e.g. 'Prioderm', 'Derbac', 'Carylderm', 'Suleo'.	*Lotions:* apply the lotion liberally to the hair and rub in (avoid contact with eyes). Leave to air dry. Wash hair after at least eight hours with any shampoo. One treatment is usually sufficient. *Shampoos:* use the shampoo as an ordinary shampoo, except that it should be left on the head for at least four minutes. A course of at least three treatments, at three-day intervals, is recommended. *Neither treatment* will remove the eggs (nits) but these will be dead, and of no consequence.
Crab lice	As above	As above, except *all* hairy parts of the body should be treated, including beards, legs, chest, etc.
Clothing lice	Dry heat from tumble dryer, hot wash, or leave alone in plastic bag for two weeks minimum	Place clothes *dry* into tumble dryer for ten minutes at hottest setting. Alternatively, wash clothes in water hotter than 55°C (too hot to keep hands in). Clothes can otherwise just be left in a bag for at least two weeks, so lice starve to death. Rotate sets of clothing at one- to two-week intervals, thereafter. *No* treatment of the person is necessary, unless other parasites are found.
Scabies	γ BHC (lindane) based lotion, e.g. 'Quellada', 'Kwell'	Apply the lotion thoroughly over all the body from the neck down. Leave to air dry for 5–10 minutes. Wash off after 24 hours. Only one treatment is necessary, even when itching persists. Anti-histamine tablets may relieve the itch.
Ticks and larger mites	Tweezers or fingers	Hold the tick firmly by the head end. Push down the head to disengage the teeth, then pull away. If the tick does not come away immediately, try rocking it from side to side. This process may have to be repeated several times: patience is the key.

after infection, and is due to an allergic reaction. It is often worse at night, and often involves the sides of the body and between the legs, even though no mites are present there. A rash may also develop around the middle of the body.

Ticks and mites are often noticed by the traveller only after they have attached to the body. Travellers should take precautions against ticks by tucking trouser legs into thick socks, using a repellent, and wearing light coloured clothes if possible, which will make a better background to see ticks against. It is a good idea to get into a routine of examining your body for ticks and mites at a regular time, for example, just before getting into bed, when travelling in an area of high risk. Better still, get someone else to check you over and to look at your back.

• In medieval times travellers would take along pigs, which they would leave in their beds as soon as they arrived at an inn. By the time the traveller had dined, and was ready for bed, the fleas, bugs, and other insects in the room would—theoretically—have satisfied their appetite by feeding upon the unfortunate pig. Such measures are, I hope, not necessary today.

Treatment and prevention:

Summary of advice for travellers

• Treatment of the 'personal' parasites—lice and scabies—is the same, and consists of applying an insecticidal lotion to the affected areas (Table 4.6). In many parts of the world lice are resistant to organochlorine insecticides, so a lotion containing malathion, carbaryl, or pyrethroids should be used instead. With scabies, the itch will persist for a week or so, even after all the mites are dead, but can be alleviated somewhat with anti-histamine tablets (p. 349).

• Fleas and bugs can be controlled with insecticide sprays, which are best applied by experienced personnel. Flea bites may be prevented by tucking bedclothes into the mattress, because fleas can jump only six inches vertically at a time, and by discouraging fleas and bugs from climbing up bed legs by standing these in containers of water. If a vacuum cleaner is available it will be very useful in keeping down the flea population, and thorough cleaning will also help.

• If bed-bugs are also suspected, move the bed away from the wall and leave a light on in the room for the whole night because bed-bugs prefer to feed in the dark.

• Head lice can be discouraged simply by regular use of an ordinary pocket comb; washing hair, by itself, will only produce cleaner lice.

• Clothing lice are easily killed by putting the clothes *dry* into a tumble dryer for ten minutes, or else washing them in water that is hotter than 55°C (just too hot to keep hands in). Alternatively, the louse needs a period of two to three weeks to develop from egg to adult, so changing clothes once a week will prevent an infestation from becoming established.

• Crab lice and scabies may be detected on close inspection of prospective partners, although this may be difficult to accomplish discreetly!

• Ticks and mites can be discouraged from attaching by the use of repellents, as described in the next chapter. Dimethyl phthalate (DMP) is a more effective mite repellent than diethyl toluamide.

Personal protection against insect pests

Many serious diseases in the tropics and elsewhere are spread by insects. Personal protection against insects is thus an important health precaution for travellers.

Dr Christopher Curtis *qualified in genetics, and has worked for several years on the application of genetics to tsetse fly and mosquito control. He is now involved in developing 'appropriate technology' for mosquito control.*

Several types of insect—as well as related creatures like ticks and mites—obtain all their food by sucking blood from humans or animals, i.e. 'biting'. In certain other kinds of insects, including mosquitoes, the females require a blood meal in order to produce each batch of eggs. (See Fig. 4.13 for method of distinguishing male and female mosquitoes.)

Insect bites

The pain and discomfort that arises as a 'by-product' of insect bites is due to an allergic reaction to saliva introduced by the

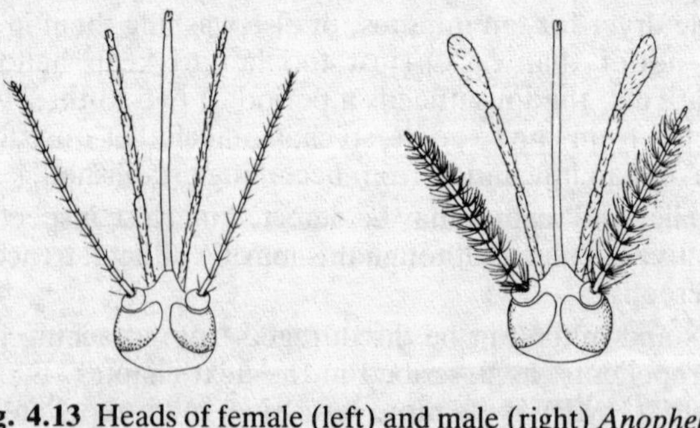

Fig. 4.13 Heads of female (left) and male (right) *Anopheles* mosquitoes. Unlike the females, male mosquitoes do not bite and can be recognized by their bushy antennas.

insect during blood-sucking. Such bites should be distinguished from the stings of bees, wasps, or ants which have a different biological function, namely to deter intruders from approaching their nests (see pp. 211–12). This distinction may appear somewhat academic to the unfortunate victim! The severity of skin reaction in different people to bites and stings varies greatly, and people also differ widely in their apparent 'allure' to biting insects. (Treatment—see p. 497.)

Diseases spread by insects

The nuisance of biting insects can be at least as great in the arctic summer as it is in the tropics. However, it is mainly only in the tropics that insect-borne diseases are still an important health hazard. The viruses, bacteria, protozoa, or worms responsible for these diseases take advantage of the biting habits of insects to enable themselves to be transported from the bloodstream of one victim to another.

Some insects hatch from their eggs already infected with viruses or somewhat larger organisms called *rickettsiae* (see pp. 165–7). which can cause human disease, but this is the exception rather than the rule. Most insects become infected when biting an infected individual and pass the disease on to someone else during a subsequent feed, or, with some diseases, by defecating on to the skin.

Table 4.7 gives a summary of the commoner biting insects and the diseases they may carry. The list of diseases may appear daunting, but the only ones commonly contracted by visitors to the tropics are malaria (see p. 117) and, in certain places, dengue (see p. 133), and cutaneous leishmaniasis (see p. 144). Of these, malaria presents by far the most serious risk. The other diseases need be considered only by travellers who will be living for considerable period in a tent, or in tropical villages, urban slums or refugee camps. In such cases it would be wise to take local advice about the particular risks and possible countermeasures.

Insects spread many diseases for which drug treatment is difficult, dangerous, or non-existent, and for which we do not yet have vaccines. **Prevention of insect bites is the single most sensible and effective precaution a traveller can take to avoid these diseases.**

Table 4.7 Insects, mites, and ticks that bite or burrow in the skin, and risk of disease transmission in different tropical and sub-tropical areas

Pest	Rough guide to identification of adult	Time and place of biting or burrowing	Disease	Risk of disease transmission (x=slight risk xx=moderate risk xxxx=high risk) Africa	Asia	Americas	Western Pacific
Mosquitoes							
Anopheles	head and body in straight line and at an angle to surface (Figs. 4.1, p. 117 and 4.2, p. 118)	night; indoors or out; mainly rural	malaria	xxxx	xx	x	xx
			filariasis	x			x
Culex	body parallel to surface, head bent down, whining flight; dull brown (Fig. 4.2, p. 118)	evening and night; indoors or out; urban or rural	filariasis	x	x	x	
			encephalitis		x	x	x
Aedes	body shape as for *Culex*; but tropical species are black and white (Fig. 4.3, p. 135)	day; indoors or out; urban or rural	dengue	x	xx	x	x
			yellow fever	x		x	
			filariasis				xx
Mansonia	as *Culex*; but patterned wings and legs	night; outdoors; rural	filariasis		x		
Tsetse flies	brown fly with proboscis projecting in front of head (Fig. 4.6, p. 152)	day; outdoors; rural; tropical Africa only	sleeping sickness	x			
Blackflies	1.5–4 mm, stout and black with humped body (Fig. 4.4, p. 139)	day; outdoors; rural	onchocerciasis	x		x	
Phlebotomine sandflies	tiny hairy flies (Fig. 4.5, p. 145)	evening; indoors or out; rural or urban	leishmaniasis	x	x	x	
			sandfly fever	x	x	x	
			bartonellosis			x	
Biting midges	tiny flies with spotted wings	evening; outdoors; rural	—				

Pest	Rough guide to identification of adult	Time and place of biting or burrowing	Disease	Risk of disease transmission (x=slight risk xx=moderate risk xxxx=high risk)			
				Africa	Asia	Americas	Western Pacific
Gadflies, horse-flies, stable-flies	as large or larger than house-fly; fast-flying	day; outdoors; rural	loiasis	x			
Ticks	attach tightly to skin and swell up with blood to pea size (Fig. 4.12, p. 173)	day or night; cling to long grass or hide on cave floors and attach to passers-by or sleepers	relapsing fever	x	x	x	
			typhus	x	x	x	
Bed-bugs	1 cm; brown beetle-like; but wingless (Fig. 4.11, p. 172)	night; in beds	? hepatitis B				
Triatomine bugs	1–4 cm; cone-like head; long legs (Fig. 4.7, p. 157)	night; in beds	Chagas' disease			x	
Fleas	2–3 mm; brown; flattened sideways; run and jump (Fig. 4.8, p. 161)	night or day; indoors	bubonic plague	x	x	x	
Lice	2–3 mm; cream or brown; claws often visible; flattened top to bottom; crawl (Fig. 4.9, p. 166)	night or day; on body hair or clothes for their whole life-cycle	typhus	x	x		
			relapsing fever			x	
Tumbu fly	9–12 mm; robust; yellow-brown; non-biting fly	larvae attach to clothing while it is being dried on the ground and burrow into skin (Fig. 4.10, p. 169)	myiasis	x			
Mites	tiny eight-legged creatures	climb on to skin from undergrowth or from other people and cling to or burrow in skin	typhus		x		x
			scabies	x	x	x	x

Protection from insect bites out of doors

Quite apart from the hazard of disease, insect bites themselves can be more than a trivial nuisance in some places—in Howrah, near Calcutta, 500 bites by *Culex* mosquitoes per person per night (about one a minute throughout the night) are usual—and in such situations few visitors would need encouragement to take measures for personal protection.

Repellents

A chemical repellent is the best, and perhaps only suitable personal protection against outdoor biting insects. As far as is known, repellents act by interfering with the sense organs with which insects locate their victims. Most of the commercially available insect repellent preparations contain diethyl toluamide (commonly known as 'deet' or DET), ethylhexanediol, or dimethyl phthalate (DMP). These preparations come as lotions, sticks, gels, creams, or aerosol sprays. In Australia, a mosquito repellent soap has recently been developed. This leaves a residue on the skin that can be washed off with water when no longer required.

Deet and DMP are harmful to some hard plastics and paint, cause a stinging sensation if they get into the eyes, and taste unpleasant: they should be applied with care. Conventional toxicity tests when deet first came on to the market in the 1950s were reassuring, and it has been used without harm by millions of people. More recently, however, occasional reports have appeared of serious reactions in a few individuals. Anyone who suspects an adverse reaction to deet should stop using it immediately and seek medical advice.

Deet is apparently effective against all free-flying biting insects, although the dose required may depend on the species of insect. When applied to the skin, deet remains effective for only a few hours. However, when impregnated into cotton (not synthetic) material it remains effective for several weeks, especially if the material is kept in a plastic bag or tin when not in use.

Clothes can be impregnated with an aerosol or, more economically, by making a suspension of concentrated deet in water and pouring it over the garment (1 ml deet and 8 ml water per 4g cotton or around 25 ml deet and 200 ml water for an average-sized shirt) and then hanging it up to dry. Concentrated deet can usually be obtained on special order from pharmacies*.

It is possible to impregnate ordinary clothing covering especially vulnerable areas such as the ankles, wrists, and neck; or an impregnated netting (approximately 1 cm mesh) overgarment may be preferred, which can be put on only when needed and minimizes skin contact with the chemical. Such a garment, with a hood, gives off sufficient deet vapour to protect the face from biting even in areas heavily infested with mosquitoes. Netting jackets may snag and tear if much used in dense undergrowth.

When one is sitting on a chair, most mosquito bites occur on the ankles or feet. Cotton anklets (ankle bands), 10 cm wide and each impregnated with 4ml deet, have been found to give 80–85 per cent reduction in biting by several species of tropical night-biting mosquitoes. One impregnation remains effective for several weeks if the anklets are kept sealed up when not in use.

Citronella oil is distilled from a tropical grass and is used as a soap perfume. It has long been sold as an insect repellent but does not remain effective for as long as deet. However some people prefer its lemony smell to the less agreeable smell of deet.

Buzzers

Electronic buzzers have been advertised widely to repel mosquitoes. Manufacturers claim that they simulate the sound of a male mosquito, and that such a sound is repellent to hungry mated females. There is no scientific evidence at all for this story, and in any case the buzzers are set at a far higher pitch than the beat of a male mosquito's wings. Some users believe that these devices work, but every time their effectiveness has been put to the test under controlled conditions, no difference has been found between the biting rate with the device on and with it off. At least twelve accounts of such experiments have been published, by entomologists from six different countries. All agree that the devices are completely useless.

* Concentrated deet is also available by mail order from Travelling Light, Morland House, Morland, Penrith, Cumbria CA10 3AZ, England, Tel. 09314–488 (Travelling Light also supplies vaporizing mats and a wide variety of other anti-insect products by mail order); and from MASTA (Appendix 6). High concentrations of deet are also found in 'Jungle Formula' products. In the USA, concentrated deet is sold as 'Repel 100', 'Cutter's', and Johnson's 'Off!' liquid.

Clothing

Long sleeves and long trousers have for many years been recommended to be worn after dark to minimize the risk of mosquito bites. Canvas mosquito boots can be purchased that make it impossible for mosquitoes to bite the ankles. Denim jeans are thick enough to be impenetrable to the probosces of blackflies, which prefer to attack the lower legs. Blue clothing is said to be very attractive to tsetse flies and should be avoided in the tsetse-infested areas of Africa.

Protection against insects biting indoors

In addition to the repellents already described, several other useful counter-measures can be employed when the 'target area' is confined to a house or hotel room.

Tight closure of well-fitting windows keeps out most mosquitoes but would be an uncomfortable proposition in a hot climate unless the room is air-conditioned. Ceiling fans help to distract the blood-seeking flight of insects, especially weak fliers such as phlebotomine sandflies.

Screens

Windows kept open for ventilation should be screened: fibreglass netting coated with PVC is more durable, more easily fitted, and less expensive than wire netting. The netting should have six or seven threads per centimetre width to keep out mosquitoes and should be closed before sunset, when *Culex* and *Anopheles* mosquitoes become active.

Similar netting should be used to keep mosquitoes from laying eggs in domestic water containers, in which their larvae could flourish. In cities such as Bombay the screening of roof water tanks, etc. is a strictly enforced legal requirement to prevent the breeding of the urban malaria mosquito *Anopheles stephensi* and the dengue-carrying mosquito *Aedes aegypti*. The screening of vent pipes and other apertures to cesspits, septic tanks, and pit latrines helps to prevent the mosquito *Culex quinquefasciatus* from breeding in these collections of polluted water, to which it is attracted.

A 2 cm thick floating layer of expanded polystyrene beads (as used in the manufacture of packing material) is highly effective against mosquito breeding and lasts for years in such sites.

Sprays, coils, and vaporizing mats

Screening windows is seldom completely effective in keeping mosquitoes out of rooms, so other lines of defence may also be needed. Aerosol spray cans of insecticide are available in many tropical countries. They usually contain pyrethroids, which are synthetic near-relations of the natural product pyrethrum and are very safe, although they should not be used over uncovered food. They do not harm pets or domestic animals.

Aerosols are good for clearing out mosquitoes that are lurking in a room before one goes to bed, but they have no residual effect on mosquitoes that enter later on during the night. The old-fashioned, but still effective, way of dealing with these insects is to light a slow-burning 'mosquito coil' which will smoke gently, giving off pyrethrum for 6–8 hours. These are available cheaply in many tropical countries. However, tests have shown that some fraudulent brands contain no pyrethrum. Local advice should be sought about good local brands, or some simple tests carried out for oneself.

A modern version of the same idea is a small mains-operated heating plate that slowly vaporizes a mat containing pyrethroids. They are more effective that mosquito coils, but a reliable electricity supply and a supply of the tablets may not be available in some parts of the tropics.

Vapona strips slowly give off vapour of the insecticide dichlorvos without any need for heating.

The vapour emitted by coils, vaporizing mats, or vapona strips kills mosquitoes in sealed rooms, but in comfortably ventilated rooms the vapours may do no more than repel or stun insects so that they do not bite. Care may be needed to achieve even this—for example, on a porch or verandah one should always place the source of vapour upwind of those to be protected and perhaps at floor level, to deter mosquitoes heading for the ankles.

Mosquito nets

The use of a mosquito bed net is strongly recommended wherever there is any risk of bites from *Anopheles* mosquitoes that carry malaria and bite at night, or the nuisance of *Culex* mosquitoes. It is well worth buying a good quality net, because slippage of the weave would allow mosquitoes to enter. Tears should be repaired or blocked with cotton wool and the net should be tucked in carefully under the mattress.

The net should be checked after getting into bed, using an electric torch to make sure that no gaps are left. Take care not to sleep with any part of the body resting against the net—mosquitoes feed through nets, and never miss an opportunity. Rectangular nets are safer in this respect than the 'tent' type. Increased security can be achieved by impregnating nets with permethrin (a pyrethroid) which is effective for several months in killing or repelling mosquitoes which contact it. A dose of 0.2 gm/m^2 is sufficient which can be achieved by dipping the net in a 1 per cent emulsion made by diluting an emulsifiable concentrate of permethrin* with water. The net is wrung out and laid to dry on a plastic sheet.

Many hotels in the tropics provide mosquito nets. If in doubt it may be worth taking your own, and if suitable anchorage points are not available you should ask the management to provide some.

Other measures

Ornamental ponds should be stocked with small fish to eat any mosquito larvae that may start to develop there. Other water containers around houses are likely to be rubbish and should be either carted away, flattened, and buried, or punctured so that they cannot hold water.

It almost goes without saying that residents should always co-operate with any community-wide insect control measures run by local authorities.

Control of domestic non-biting pests

Although they do not bite, house-flies, cockroaches, ants, and termites are often worrying pests in the tropics, and some may be a serious health hazard. Flies, for example, are able to carry more than 100 different types of harmful disease-producing organisms, and may transfer them directly from excreta to food and children's faces. In the kitchen, exposed food, unwashed plates, crumbs, and rubbish are an open invitation to flies, cockroaches, and ants. Very attractive foods such as sugar and jam should be kept in the refrigerator and others, such as breakfast cereals, biscuits, or bread, should be kept in screw-topped containers.

* In case of difficulty, this can be obtained from MASTA (Appendix 6), or direct from the Wellcome Foundation, Crewe Hall, Crewe, Cheshire, U.K. (tel: 0270–583151). In the USA, it is available as a 0.5 per cent spray (Permanone Tick Repellent) from Fairfield American, New Jersey.

Flies, ants, and cockroaches

House-flies breed in rotting rubbish, and if refuse is not regularly collected by the local authorities it should be buried under a thick layer of soil. Screening of the vent pipes of pit-latrines and cess-pits is a most effective measure against *Chrysomya* blowflies, because light attracts them into the pipes, and they are unable to escape. Mothballs on bathroom drain grilles discourage cockroaches from emerging from the drain. Ants' nests can often be located by following the trail of ants back to its source, and can then sometimes be destroyed with boiling water or, if the nest is in a small object such as a book, by placing it in an oven.

Old fashioned sticky fly paper can help to keep a fly infestation in check but, in the event of a persistent fly problem, periodic use of insecticide aerosol spray cans may be necessary. These pyrethroid insecticides may also be effective in irritating cockroaches and driving them out of the crevices in which they hide. Otherwise, the best insecticidal approach for a cockroach infestation is to scatter a carbamate insecticide such as 'Baygon' in powder form near crevices, drain-inspection covers, and in the bottoms of cupboards and closets.

Termites

In the many tropical areas where there is a serious termite problem, houses should be protected by pouring a persistent insecticide such as dieldrin into a trench around the foundations and impregnating timber with this insecticide (for further information see Overseas Building Notes No. 170, obtainable from Building Research Station, Garston, Watford WO2 7JR, UK). Before starting long-term occupation of a house, it is wise to enquire whether such precautions have been taken. For the short-term resident, termite infestation will be revealed by sinuous earth-covered tunnels adhering to the walls.

Termites can completely destroy books and other objects from within and before this happens, the trails should be followed to where they reach ground level and liquid 'Baygon' or a similar insecticide should be poured down any crevices. As an additional precaution, bookcases can be stood on bricks placed in basins of water covered in an oil film to reduce evaporation and prevent them becoming breeding places for *Aedes aegypti* mosquitoes.

5

Animal bites; rabies; venomous bites and stings

Animal bites; rabies; venomous bites and stings

Snakes and scorpions may spring most readily to mind as a fearsome zoological hazard to travellers, but in practice dog bite is a much more common problem: in many countries it carries a formidable risk of rabies, and in all cases requires prompt and careful management. Bathers and swimmers in the tropics should be aware of the various types of venomous marine animals, and individuals allergic to bee and wasp stings must also take special precautions.

Professor David A. Warrell *has treated animal bites and stings in five continents. He is Professor of Tropical Medicine and Infectious Diseases in the University of Oxford, Honorary Clinical Director of the Alistair Reid Venom Research Unit at the Liverpool School of Tropical Medicine, and a Consultant to WHO.*

Encounters with animals can produce the following medical problems, all of which are uncommon but potentially fatal: mechanical injury, poisoning, infection, infestation, and allergic reactions. Only the first three of these will be discussed in detail in this chapter.

Injuries: attacks by large animals

A wide range of animals are equipped with claws, teeth, tusks, horns, or spines capable of inflicting serious mechanical injuries which may prove fatal. With the one exception of bites by domestic dogs, these accidents are very rare and are easily avoided by treating all large animals with respect and avoiding unnecessarily close contact with them.

Most wild animals, unless they are ill or starving, avoid confrontation with humans. Visitors to game parks in the tropics, or to safari parks in the temperate zones should take local advice about where and when it is safe to walk. Strolls between dusk and dawn without a light invite attacks by large carnivores. It is usually safe to approach large carnivores in a hard-topped vehicle, but under some circumstances this may not be a safe place from which to view elephants or rhinoceroses (see also p. 369).

Animals in zoos or safari parks should not be assumed to be tamer and therefore safer. Three keepers have been killed by tigers and an elephant in a British safari park during the last few years, and in the last 15 years, tigers have killed 659 people in Sunderbans Reserve Forest, in West Bengal.

Other mammals known to have killed or severely mauled humans include lions, tigers, leopards, wild cats, and hyaenas, bears, elephants, hippopotamuses, buffaloes, wolves, and wild pigs.

Sharks claim about fifty lives each year out of 100 reported attacks, mostly between latitudes 30°N and 30°S. Much smaller fish may pose a greater threat to human life in some parts of the world. Garfish, for example (which have long spear-like snouts), have been known to leap out of the water and impale fishermen in parts of the Indo-Pacific Ocean. Moray and conger eels, groupers, barracudas, and stingrays can also produce severe mechanical injuries with their teeth or spines.

It is foolhardy to wade, bathe, or swim in rivers or lakes in the tropics unless they are known to be safe—not only from bilharzia (p. 90) but from crocodiles as well. Crocodiles continue to take a small toll of human life. Riverine populations in the Sudan, Central Africa, and South-East Asia are at risk. The annual mortality from the Nile crocodile in Africa may exceed 1000 and small numbers of accidents caused by the salt-water or estuarine crocodile continue to be reported from Indonesia, Sarawak, and Northern Australia.

The giant pythons (reticulated python of Indonesia, African rock python, and anaconda of South America) are certainly capable of killing a human and there are a few reliable reports of fatal attacks.

Travellers, however, are at far greater risk of receiving injury from a dog bite before leaving their home country than from a wild animal on their travels.

In the USA there are now more than a million dog bites each year requiring some sort of hospital attention; the number is increasing. In Liverpool and Sunderland, in the north of England, about 500 people per 100 000 population attend hospital each year because of dog bites. Reports of eleven deaths from dog bites were collected in a two-year period in the USA, and there have been several in the UK during the last few years. Domestic cattle (especially bulls), rams, pigs, cats, and even ferrets have also killed people.

Types of injury

Teeth and claws produce lacerating and destructive injuries to soft tissues. Tusks, horns, and antlers can tear and produce serious penetrating injuries resulting in blindness, pneumothorax, and haemothorax (leakage of air and blood into the lining of the lungs), perforation of the intestines, and bleeding from the liver and spleen. Even dog bites are capable of producing compound fractures (where the broken bone ends protrude through the skin).

All bites, gorings, and maulings carry a heavy risk of infection with bacteria, viruses, and other micro-organisms present in the animal's mouth or contaminating its claws, horns, etc. Large mammals may trample and kneel on the human victim, producing severe crush injuries.

First aid

A guide to the treatment of mammal bites, licks, and scratches is given in the Box on page 195. Mild superficial injuries should be cleaned thoroughly. Anyone who has suffered a serious attack should be taken to hospital for proper assessment. The use of antibiotics, anti-tetanus, and anti-rabies treatments may need to be considered.

Rabies

Rabies or 'hydrophobia' is a virus infection of mammals that can be transmitted to humans in a variety of ways, but usually as the result of a bite by a domestic dog.

Rabies probably causes at least 50 000 human deaths each year, although only a small fraction of these are reported to official bodies such as the WHO. In areas where rabies exists, the infection is usually established and circulates only in a few particular animal species. These may include domestic animals, particularly dogs, and/or wild animal species, for example, skunks, raccoons, foxes, and insectivorous bats in North America; foxes in the Arctic; mongooses and vampire bats in the Caribbean;

vampire bats in Central and South America; foxes, wolves, raccoon dogs, and insectivorous bats in Europe; and wolves, jackals and small carnivores such as mongooses and civets throughout most of Africa and Asia.

Humans may contract rabies from any rabid animal, domestic or wild, but because of the particularly close association between humans and dogs the most common cause of human rabies worldwide is the bite of a rabid domestic dog (which may itself have contracted the virus from another dog, cat, or from a rabid wild animal). In some countries such as the USA canine rabies has been largely eliminated through measures such as immunization, but there is still a risk to people who come in contact with rabies-affected wild animal populations—naturalists, animal trappers, and people on expeditions, for example. Thus a bite from a skunk in the mid-western USA or from a jackal in Africa could involve a very significant risk of rabies.

Geographical distribution

Rabies occurs in most parts of the world, in Greenland, Canada and North America, throughout the USSR, China, and New Territories of Hong Kong, as well as in the main tropical regions.

The following areas are free of rabies at present: Britain and Ireland, Norway, Sweden and Iceland, Malaysia, New Guinea, Borneo, Taiwan, Japan, Oceania, Antarctica, Australia and New Zealand. Human and animal rabies is most common in parts of South America, the Indian subcontinent, Thailand, and the Philippines.

How infection occurs

Rabies infection can occur when the normal protective barrier provided by healthy, unbroken skin is breached by a bite or scratch, and the wound is contaminated with the animal's saliva containing rabies virus. Rabies virus can penetrate unbroken mucous membranes such as those covering the eye and lining the mouth or nose. On a few occasions, rabies has developed after the virus had been inhaled—in the air of bat-infested caves—and as the result of a laboratory accident. On at least four occasions, recipients of corneal transplants from patients dying of unsuspected rabies have later developed rabies themselves.

After the virus has entered the body, one of three things may

Treatment of mammal bites, licks, and scratches

First aid

- Scrub with soap or detergent and running water for at least five minutes.
- Remove foreign material (e.g. dirt, broken teeth).
- Rinse with plain water.
- Irrigate with a virucidal agent, such as povidone iodine, 0·01 per cent aqueous iodine, or 40–70 per cent alcohol (gin and whisky contain 40 per cent). Note: hydrogen peroxide, mercurichrome and quaternary ammonium compounds—the brightly coloured antiseptic dyes still popular in some countries—are not suitable for this purpose.

At the hospital or dispensary

A medical attendant should:

- Check that first-aid measures (above) have been carried out.
- Explore and irrigate deep wounds (if necessary, under local or general anaesthesia). Dead tissue should be cut away, but wound excision is rarely necessary.
- Avoid suturing (stitches) and occlusive dressings.
- Consider tetanus risk and treat accordingly:

  [Booster dose of tetanus formol toxoid (0·5 ml by intramuscular injection) for those fully immunized in the past and boosted within the last ten years; human tetanus immunoglobulin (250 mg by intramuscular injection) for severe or grossly contaminated wounds that have been left untreated for more than four hours in a previously unimmunized person.]
- Consider risk of infection with other bacteria, viruses, and fungi particularly associated with mammal bites. Preventive antibiotic treatment is advisable for severely contaminated wounds, e.g. a broad spectrum antibiotic such as cephalexin (500 mg four times a day for five days).
- If the exposure occurred in a rabies-endemic area, consider post-exposure rabies vaccination.

happen. The virus may be killed by antiseptics used to clean the wound or by the person's own immune defence mechanisms. Unless this happens within a few days of the bite, the virus is likely to spread to the nerve endings in muscles and along the nerves which lead to the brain and spinal cord; it then multiplies and causes a severe infection of the central nervous system (called an encephalomyelitis) which is almost invariably fatal.

Rarely, it seems that the virus may become permanently or temporarily inactive after it has reached the nervous system; in the latter case the infection may flare up again, and progress months or even years after the initial bite, following some kind of stress. This may explain the occasional reports of very long incubation periods.

The incubation period—the time interval between the bite and the first symptoms of rabies—is usually two to three months but can vary from a few days to many years. The earliest symptom of rabies infection of the central nervous system is itching, irritation, tingling, or pain at the site of the healed bite wound. The disease advances rapidly, producing headache, fever, spreading paralysis, and episodes of confusion, aggression, hallucination and hydrophobia (literally fear of water). Attempts to drink water induce powerful contractions of the neck muscles and the muscles involved in swallowing and breathing in. These spasms are associated with indescribable terror. The patient dies in a few days.

Some species of animals such as mongooses, skunks, and vampire bats can recover from rabies encephalomyelitis, but in humans the infection is almost invariably fatal. During the last fifteen years, two patients with probable rabies and only one with proven rabies have recovered after prolonged intensive care.

The prospect of an agonizing death from this untreatable disease should encourage everyone to do everything possible to prevent rabies.

Pre-exposure vaccination

Pre-exposure vaccination against rabies should be considered in the case of travellers who run a particularly high risk. These include cave explorers, animal collectors, zoologists, botanists, hunters, and also those whose work involves walking and cycling in urban or rural areas. One of the safe, new tissue culture vaccines should be used, such as the Institut Merieux human diploid cell strain vaccine (HDCSV) and purified vero cell rabies vaccine (PVRV) or Behringwerke purified chicken embryo cell vaccine (PCEC) should be used (see Box, p. 198). Expense can be reduced by giving one tenth of the normally recommended dose by intradermal rather than intramuscular or subcutaneous injection.

Travellers within a rabies endemic area should avoid close contact with domestic or wild mammals. They should be particularly wary of wild animals that appear tame, for this change in behaviour is a common early sign of rabies in animals.

Action following a bite

Irrespective of the risk of rabies, all mammal bites, scratches, and licks on mucous membranes or broken skin should be cleaned immediately and vigorously (see Box, p. 195). Mammal bites (including human bites!) are usually contaminated by a variety of bacteria, some of which can cause serious infections.

In the case of deep penetrating or contaminated wounds, it is wise to take a prophylactic antibiotic (such as cephalexin 500 mg four times a day for five days—not to be taken by people with severe penicillin allergy). The risk of tetanus should always be considered: all travellers should be fully protected with a course of tetanus toxoid before starting their journey. An animal bite warrants a booster dose of tetanus toxoid (tetanus formol toxoid 0·5 ml) (see also p. 87).

Post-exposure vaccination

The aim of post-exposure vaccination is to neutralize the rabies virus introduced by the bite before it can enter the nervous system. Treatment should be started as soon as possible, but although the chances of preventing rabies decrease with delay, vaccination is still worthwhile even weeks or months after the bite. The decision about vaccination should be made by a doctor, who will need the following information:

1. When, where, and in which locality the bite occurred;
2. The severity and site of the bite;
3. The species, appearance, behaviour, and fate of the biting animal, and whether it had been vaccinated against rabies during the last year.

Rabies immunization schedules

Pre-exposure vaccination

Merieux human diploid cell strain vaccine (HDCSV)

0·1 ml by intradermal (*id*) injection on days 0, 7, and 28 + boosters of 0·1 ml by *id* injection every two years.

Post-exposure vaccination (Do not forget wound cleaning! See Box, p. 195).

A *For those who have been given pre-exposure vaccination*:
No passive immunization (human immune-globulin/equine antirabies serum) is needed.
HDCSV PVEV or PCEC 1 ml by intramuscular (*im*) injection on days 0, 10, 20, and 90.

B *For those not given pre-exposure vaccination*:
HDCSV PVEV or PCEC 1 ml by *im* injection on days 0, 3, 7, 14, and 30.*
and either

Passive immunization with human rabies immune-globulin 20 units/kg body weight *or* Equine antirabies serum 40 units/kg body weight	half infiltrated round the bite wound, half by *im* injection

This information should allow some assessment of the risk of exposure, but if there is any doubt it is safest to give a full course of vaccine with or without passive immunization (see Box, p. 198). The first dose of vaccine should be tripled and divided

* Two other regimens are considered effective and likely to be recommended in future:
1. 8-site intradermal regimen: 0·1ml HDCSV given at 8 sites (deltoids, suprascapular, abdominal, and thighs) on day 0, 4 sites on day 7, and single sites on days 28 and 90. This is economical and induces antibody rapidly.
2. 2-1-1 regimen: 2 x 1ml *im* injections on day 0, single 1ml injections on days 7 and 21. This is economical and requires only three vaccination sessions.

between several sites on the body if there has been more than 48 hours delay in starting vaccination, if passive immunization has been given more than 24 hours before vaccine, if the patient is elderly, malnourished or believed to be immunodeficient or immunosuppressed, and if passive immunization is not available.

Rabies prevention following exposure in a risk area

Minor exposure

including licks of the skin, scratches or abrasions, minor bites:

Treatment

- *Unprovoked attack by cat or dog*:

  Vaccine

  Stop treatment if animal remains healthy for five days.

  Stop treatment if brain fluorescent antibody test for animal proves negative.

  Administer serum on positive diagnosis and complete the course of vaccine.

- *Attack by wild animal or by domestic cat or dog unavailable for observation*:

Major exposure

including licks on mucosa or major bites (multiple or on face, head, fingers, or neck):

Treatment

- *Unprovoked attack by cat or dog or attack by wild animal, or domestic cat or dog unavailable for observation*:

  Serum and vaccine

  Stop treatment if domestic cat or dog remains healthy under observation for five days.

  Stop treatment if animal's brain fluorescent antibody test proves negative.

The newer tissue culture antirabies vaccines such as HDCSV carry no serious risk of reactions, unlike the older vaccines, which consisted of animal nervous tissue.

Passive immunization (see Box, p. 198) should never be omitted in cases of severe bites or high risk of exposure unless the patient has had pre-exposure vaccination. 'Ready-made' rabies-neutralizing antibody in the form of human rabies immunoglobulin (HRIG) or equine anti-rabies serum (EARS) is necessary to provide immediate activity against rabies virus during the interval of about seven days between vaccination and the first appearance of antibody produced by the body itself in response to the vaccine. HRIG is free from side-effects, but equine anti-rabies serum is complicated by allergic reactions such as serum sickness in up to 10 per cent of those treated.

Travellers who are exposed to the risk of rabies (mammal bites, licks, scratches, etc.) should seek immediate help at the time of the incident, and not wait for days (or even months) until they return home before considering post-exposure treatment.

Only orthodox/Western medical practitioners should be consulted about rabies, *not* herbalists, homeopaths, traditional practitioners, monks, priests, or other practitioners of 'fringe medicine'. In some countries even Western-style practitioners may not give adequate treatment. *No one exposed to rabies should allow themselves to be fobbed off with tablets or a single injection.*

In the UK, expert advice and materials for post-exposure treatment is available from the Central Public Health Laboratory, Colindale (Tel. 01–205 7041), and in the USA, from local or state health departments, or from the Division of Viral Diseases at the Centers for Disease Control, Tel. (404) 329–3095 during working hours, (404) 329–3095 nights, weekends and holidays.

Venomous animals

Many animals possess venoms that can be injected into the unfortunate traveller by a variety of mechanisms. The normal purpose of envenoming is to discourage enemies or to immobilize prey.

Some people become sensitized to venoms if they are stung or bitten repeatedly. In this case, the allergic reaction to the venom may prove far more dangerous than its toxic effects, and in some parts of the world, such as Europe and North America, there are more deaths from allergic (anaphylactic) reactions to bee and wasp stings than from lethal snake, scorpion, and spider venoms.

Tropical regions have the richest venomous fauna, and travellers to such regions often regard snake bite and scorpion sting as the two greatest medical hazards of their journey. However, it is nearly always the indigenous population, rather than the traveller, that falls victim to venomous animals.

Snake bite is a major cause of death among South American Indians who hunt barefooted in the jungle, and among rice farmers in South-East Asia who work barefooted and barehanded in the paddy fields. Travellers are usually less exposed and better protected, and there has been no report of a European traveller dying from a venomous bite or sting in recent years. However, a German tourist came close to death after being bitten by a cobra in central Bangkok, and several other Europeans have been severely envenomed in the jungles of South America and South-East Asia.

Anyone planning to travel off the beaten track in a tropical country should find out about the venomous fauna well before leaving home. An expedition to a particularly remote and snake-infested area may want to take its own supply of antivenom. Usually, this can be supplied only by a national centre of antivenom production; contact will have to be made with the centre well in advance. Many antivenoms available in Europe and in tropical countries are of dubious potency. Information supplied with commercial antivenoms (the 'package insert') may be misleading or even dangerous! It is also important to find out something about the quality of local medical services or referral centres in the larger cities.

Information and advice about venomous fauna and availability of antivenoms can be obtained from the centres listed at the end of this chapter.

Venomous snakes

Venomous snakes have one or more pairs of enlarged teeth, the fangs, in the upper jaw. Venom is conducted from the venom gland just behind the eye, through a duct to the base of the fang, and then through a channel to its tip.

Dangerous species

Important venomous snakes belong to four families:

The Colubridae, of which some members have small fangs at the back of their mouth. Effective bites in humans are very uncommon but a few species, notably the African boomslang has caused some fatalities.

The Elapidae, which include cobras, kraits, mambas and coral snakes, the South African ringhals and African and Asian spitting cobras can eject venom from the tips of their fangs as a defensive strategy.

The Hydrophiidae, which include sea-snakes and the Australian terrestrial venomous snakes.

The Viperidae, which are the largest and best-known family of venomous snakes and include the subfamilies *Viperinae*, the Old World vipers and adders; and *Crotalinae*, the New World rattlesnakes, moccasins and lance-headed vipers and Asian pit vipers.

Venomous snakes do not occur at high altitudes (more than 4000 metres or about 13 000 ft), in the Antarctic, nor in a number of islands such as Ireland, Iceland, Crete, New Zealand, Madagascar, and most Caribbean and Pacific islands (see Map 5.1).

The incidence and medical significance of snake bite has been underestimated because it is a problem of the rural tropics, often little known to academic centres in the capital cites even of countries where it is particularly common. As mentioned above, the incidence of snake bite is highest among native populations who are forced to live and work, relatively unprotected, within the snake's chosen environment.

Effects of snake venom

Snake venoms are complicated substances which contain a large number of harmful components. The main clinical effects of snake venoms are summarized below:

- *Local swelling, blistering, and necrosis (gangrene) of the bitten limb* are seen particularly with *Viperidae* and some cobras. Fluid and blood leaks into the tissues of the bitten limb. Swelling starts soon after the bite and may spread to involve the whole limb and adjoining area of the trunk.

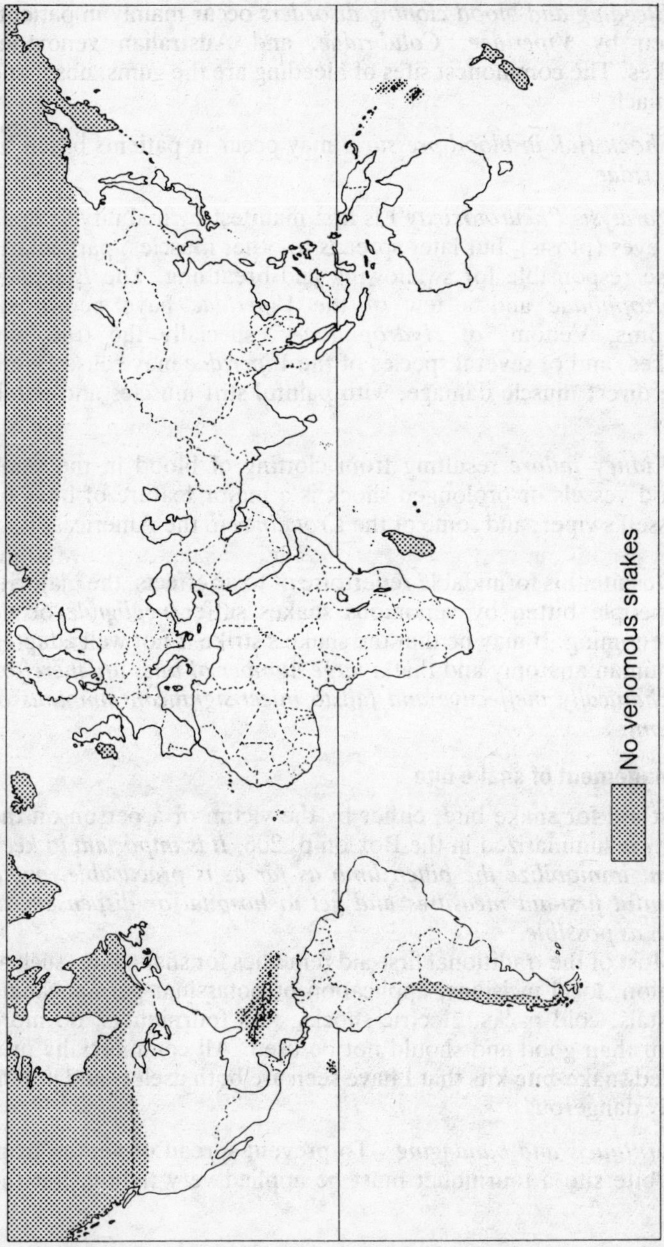

Map 5.1 Countries with no risk from venomous snakes.

- *Bleeding and blood-clotting disorders* occur mainly in patients bitten by *Viperidae*, *Colubridae*, and Australian venomous snakes. The commonest sites of bleeding are the gums, nose, and stomach.

- *Shock (fall in blood pressure)* may occur in patients bitten by *Viperidae*.

- *Paralysis ('neurotoxicity')* is first manifest by inability to open the eyes (ptosis), but later spreads to other muscles, particularly those responsible for swallowing and breathing. The *Elapidae*, *Hydrophiidae* and a few of the *Viperidae* have neurotoxic venoms. Venoms of *Hydrophiidae*, especially the true sea-snakes, and of several species of the *Viperidae* may cause extensive direct muscle damage, with painful stiff muscles and paralysis.

- *Kidney failure* resulting from clotting of blood in the small blood vessels or prolonged shock is a major feature of bites by Russell's viper, and some of the *Crotalinae* in the Americas.

Despite this formidable repertoire of toxic effects, the majority of people bitten by venomous snakes suffer *negligible* or *no* envenoming. It may be that the snake's strike is not well adapted to human anatomy and that *a large number of bites are therefore mechanically ineffective and fail to inject significant amounts of venom*.

Management of snake bite

First aid for snake bite, either by the victim or a person on the spot, is summarized in the Box on p. 206. *It is important to keep calm, immobilize the bitten limb as far as is practicable, avoid harmful first-aid measures and get to hospital or dispensary as soon as possible*.

Most of the traditional first-aid remedies for snake bite, such as suction, local incisions, application of potassium permanganate crystals, cold packs, electric shocks, and tourniquets, do more harm than good and should not be used. All commercially produced snake-bite kits that I have seen are both useless and potentially dangerous.

Tourniquets and bandaging To prevent spread of venom from the bite site a tourniquet must be applied very tightly, but the tighter the tourniquet the greater the risk of complications caused by local pressure and restriction of blood flow to the limb. The only circumstance where a tight tourniquet should be used is a definite bite by a dangerously neurotoxic elapid or hydrophiid such as some cobras, mambas, and Australian venomous snakes.

In such cases crepe (ace) bandaging and splinting of the whole bitten limb is more comfortable and possibly a more effective method than applying a pressure pad over the wound or a conventional tight (arterial) tourniquet round the upper arm or thigh. No tourniquet should be left in place for more than two hours. Ideally, a tight tourniquet used in these circumstances should not be released until medical help is available and antivenom treatment has been started.

Reassurance is a most important part of treatment. Most snake-bite victims are terrified, but only a minority of bites, even by dangerously venomous species, produce serious envenoming.

The speed of the lethal effects of snake venoms has been greatly exaggerated. To kill a man, lethal doses of venom usually take hours in the case of neurotoxic species such as cobras, mambas, and sea-snakes, or days in the case of vipers and rattlesnakes, not seconds or minutes as is commonly believed. This interval between bite and death is usually sufficiently long to allow effective treatment.

Pain If pain is a problem, a safe pain-killing drug for snake-bite victims is paracetamol (Panadol, Tylenol)—the dose is one or two 500 mg tablets for adults. Aspirin should never be used in snake-bite victims as it may cause stomach bleeding.

Medical treatment At the hospital or dispensary, medically trained staff should examine the patient and dead snake if brought, and decide about further treatment. The only specific remedy for snake bite is antivenom (also known as antivenin, antivenene, or anti-snakebite serum) which is made in animals, usually horses, by immunizing them with increasing doses of snake venom. Although most modern antivenoms are refined and purified, injection of 'foreign' protein (i.e. from another species of animal) always carries the risk of potentially serious reactions. To be optimally effective, antivenom must be given by a slow intravenous injection or infusion.

Not all people bitten by snakes require antivenom. Since the decision about antivenom treatment, the administration of anti-

Snake bite: First aid

1 Reassure the patient.

2 Immobilize the bitten limb with a splint or sling.

3 Move the patient to hospital or a dispensary as quickly as possible.

4 Avoid harmful measures such as incisions, suction, potassium permanganate crystals, electric shocks, and tourniquets (except as below).

5 If the patient has definitely been bitten by a dangerously neuro-toxic species (e.g. cobra, mamba, krait, coral snake, Australian snake, sea-snake) apply a tight tourniquet around upper arm or thigh *or* apply a pressure pad over the wound *or* firmly crepe-bandage and splint the bitten limb.

6 Use paracetamol *not* aspirin to treat pain.

7 If you have your own supply of antivenom, take it with you to hospital or dispensary.

8 If the snake has been killed take it along with you to hospital or dispensary, but do not handle it with your bare hands, even if it appears dead.

venom by the intravenous route and the treatment of antivenom reactions all require clinical skill, lay people should not undertake the medical treatment of snake bite except under most unusual conditions (for example a serious bite in a member of an expedition in a very remote area).

As a life-saving measure, antivenom may be given by intramuscular injection (the dose divided between the upper outer quadrants of both buttocks) followed by massage to promote absorption of the antivenom into the bloodstream. *However, this is certainly not recommended as a general rule!*

Patients who need antivenom are those in whom there is evidence that venom has been absorbed and is circulating throughout the body to produce severe general effects ('systemic envenoming'). The important signs are loss of consciousness, low blood pressure, failure of the blood to clot, bleeding from the nose or gums or vomiting blood, generalized pain and stiffness in the muscles, and paralysis.

The earliest sign of neurotoxic poisoning is an inability of the upper eyelids to retract when the bitten person tries to look up ('ptosis'). Slight bleeding from the site of the bite and mild local swelling and bruising are not normally regarded as justification for antivenom treatment, but massive local swelling involving more than half the bitten limb (for example above the knee and above the elbow in bites of the foot and hand respectively) indicate that significant amounts of venom have been injected and that antivenom is probably required, especially if the snake is known to have a venom that causes necrosis (gangrene).

Administration of antivenom by a medically-qualified person For intravenous injection, freeze-dried antivenom is reconstituted with sterile water for injection (usually 10 ml per ampoule) and liquid antivenom is given neat. The injection should be given slowly, at a rate not more than 2 ml per minute. A method that is easier to control, but requires more equipment, is to reconstitute or dilute antivenom with 'normal'/isotonic saline or 5 per cent dextrose solution, making up the volume to 200 ml. This is given through an intravenous giving set and is infused over about thirty minutes, starting slowly (30 drops per minute), then speeding up after about ten minutes if there is no reaction. The dose of antivenom varies with the manufacturer and the severity of envenoming. It is usually not less than five ampoules. The same dose should be given to children as to adults.

Antivenom should never be given, even by medically qualified staff, unless adrenaline (0·5 ml of a 1 mg/ml or 1 in 1000 solution by subcutaneous injection) is available to treat antivenom reactions.

The commonest symptoms of an antivenom reaction are itching, the appearance of a raised reddened rash (urticaria) and a throbbing headache. More serious symptoms include coughing, vomiting, wheezing, and fall in blood pressure leading to unconsciousness. At the first sign of a reaction, adrenaline should be given by subcutaneous injection.

Adrenaline is dangerous if given by other routes. An antihistamine drug should also be given, preferably chlorpheniramine maleate (Piriton) 10 mg by intravenous injection. Allergic patients (those suffering from asthma, hay fever, and eczema) are more likely to develop severe antivenom reactions than other people. Unfortunately there is no reliable way of predicting, by the use of a skin test, whether or not someone will develop a reaction.

Although I would strongly discourage lay people from giving antivenom themselves, it may be worth some expeditions taking a small supply (5–10 ampoules) of antivenom to be given by a local doctor or dispensary if the need arises. Unfortunately, the supply of antivenom to rural hospitals and health centres in the tropics is often very unreliable.

Infection There is a small but definite risk of tetanus and secondary bacterial infection following snake-bite. A booster dose of tetanus toxoid and a course of penicillin should therefore be given.

Prevention of snake bite

Fortunately, travellers can virtually exclude the risk of being bitten by a snake if they heed the following advice.

Snakes and snake-charmers should be avoided as far as possible. If you happen to see a snake, do not disturb, corner, or attack it, and never attempt to handle a snake even if it is said to be a harmless species or appears to be dead. Even a severed head can bite!

If you should happen to find yourself confronted with a snake at close quarters, try to keep absolutely still until it has slithered away: snakes strike only at moving objects.

Never walk in undergrowth or deep sand without boots, socks, and long trousers; and at night always carry a light. Unlit paths are particularly dangerous after rainstorms. Never collect firewood or move logs and boulders with your bare hands, and never push your hands or sticks, into burrows, holes, or crevices. Avoid climbing trees and rocks that are covered with thick foliage and never swim in overgrown rivers or lakes (there are a good many other reasons for not swimming in lakes and rivers in the tropics!).

If you are forced to sleep in the open or under canvas, try to raise your bed at least one foot off the ground or else use a sewn-in ground-sheet or mosquito net that can be zipped up or well tucked in. Snakes never attack man without provocation but will strike if grabbed, trodden on or even if someone rolls on to them in their sleep. Snakes are sometimes attracted to human dwellings in pursuit of their prey (domestic chicks, rats, mice, toads, and lizards). Sea-snakes bite only when they are picked out of fishing nets.

It has not proved possible, nor would it be desirable, to exterminate venomous snakes. The Burmese rice farmer may regard the Russell's viper as his enemy, but in fact the snake protects his livelihood, the rice crop, by controlling the rodent population.

Venomous fish

Fish sting by impaling their supposed aggressor on venomous spines which may form part of the dorsal and pectoral fins and gill covers or may be separate appendages situated in front of the dorsal fins or on the tail. Tropical coral reefs, especially of the Indo-Pacific region, harbour the greatest number and diversity of venomous fish. Fish stings can also occur in temperate waters such as along the coasts of the UK and Europe.

Dangerous species

Members of at least five families of fish have caused human deaths: sharks and dogfish, stingrays and mantas, catfish, weeverfish, scorpionfish, and stargazers.

Stingrays (Rajiformes) cause many stings in North America. Waders and bathers may tread on these fish as they lie in the mud or sand. The tail, armed with a formidable spine up to 30 cm long in some species, is lashed against the intrusive limb, causing severe mechanical trauma and releasing venom into the wound.

Weeverfish (Trachinidae) occur in temperate waters of the North Sea, Mediterranean, and north coast of Africa.

Scorpionfish (Scorpaenidae) include the very dangerous stonefish (which lies motionless and well camouflaged on the bottom, resembling a roughly textured lump of rock) and the attractive zebra or lionfish. They occur throughout the Indian and Pacific oceans.

Effects of fish venom

Fish stings can produce excruciating pain radiating from the wound, some local swelling, vomiting, diarrhoea, sweating, fall in blood pressure, and irregularities of the heartbeat.

Treatment To relieve the intense pain the stung limb, finger, or toe, should be immersed in water that is hot enough to be uncomfortable but not scalding (just under 50°C). Alternatively, a local anaesthetic such as procaine or lignocaine can be injected. The most effective way to deal with a stung finger or toe is to apply a 'ring block' of local anaesthetic—a simple procedure that any doctor should be able to perform. The stinging spine and membranes should be removed to prevent secondary infection of the wound. If the patient loses consciousness, stops breathing, and no arterial pulse can be felt, mouth-to-mouth respiration and external cardiac massage should be used.

Antivenoms for *Scorpaenidae* and *Trachinidae* are manufactured in Australia and Yugoslavia. Waders and bathers can avoid stepping on stinging fish by using a shuffling gait in sand or mud, and prodding in front of them with a stick. Footwear is protective, although not against stingray spines. Skindivers should be aware of the dangers of stinging fish, especially in the neighbourhood of coral reefs.

Food poisoning and marine animals: see pp. 66–70 (poisons and contaminants in food)

Venomous jellyfish and related animals

Jellyfish, sea wasps, Portuguese men-of-war, polyps, hydroids, sea anemones, sea nettles, and corals all belong to a group of animals called the *Coelenterates*. The tentacles of these often brightly coloured and beautiful animals are armed with myriads of stinging capsules (called nematocysts) which discharge when touched by a swimmer. In many cases the worst that can occur is an itchy skin rash, but some jellyfish can cause a severe sting. The most dangerous species is the box jellyfish (*Chironex fleckeri*) of the Indo-Pacific region. Severe stings produce violent shivering, vomiting and diarrhoea with fall in blood pressure, paralysis of breathing muscles, and fits.

Treatment

Fragments of tentacles must be removed from the skin as soon as possible without exciting a further discharge of stinging capsules. Commercial vinegar or dilute acetic acid effectively inactivates the capsules.

In the case of box jellyfish stings, a tight tourniquet should be applied in the hope of delaying absorption of the venom until the patient has reached hospital. Resuscitation (mouth-to-mouth respiration and cardiac massage) has proved effective in several cases as a first-aid measure, as the most severe effects of the toxins may be extremely transient. An antivenom for box jellyfish is manufactured in Australia.

Prevention

Coelenterate stings could be prevented if swimmers avoided the water during seasons when large numbers of jellyfish are washed inshore.

Other venomous marine animals

The venomous spines and grapples of echinoderms (starfish and sea urchins) can produce dangerous poisoning, and their spines can be a painful nuisance. All spines and grapples should be removed methodically from the wound after softening the skin with 2 per cent salicylic acid ointment.

A few molluscs (snails, slugs, sea-cones, and octopuses) are also venomous. Cone shells and the Australian blue-ringed octopus can produce fatal envenoming. No specific treatment is available but a tight tourniquet might delay absorption of venom until the patient reaches hospital.

Bees, wasps, and hornets

Stings by bees, wasps and their relatives are very common events throughout the world. Transient pain, local swelling, and redness are usually the only effects. People are occasionally attacked by swarms of bees. A rock-climber in Nigeria fell to his death when attacked by bees, and in Thailand one child died of kidney failure and another of swelling and blockage of the windpipe after being stung hundreds of times. In Zimbabwe, however, a man survived being stung 2243 times by an angry swarm.

Allergy

About one in 200 people develop an allergy to bee or wasp venom such that a single sting may produce a severe and even rapidly fatal effect. In the UK and USA, many more deaths occur from severe allergic reactions (anaphylactic reactions) to insect stings than from snake bites. Anyone who is allergic to bee or wasp venom may notice progressively severe responses to successive stings. Suggestive symptoms include tingling of the scalp, flushing, dizziness, fall in blood pressure, wheezing, and swelling of the lips, tongue and throat. The diagnosis of venom hypersensitivity can be confirmed by special skin tests.

Treatment

Embedded stings should be scraped out with a finger nail or knife blade, not grasped between the finger and thumb or tweezers (which may inject more venom into the skin). Aspirin is an effective pain-killer.

Insect sting anaphylaxis should be treated with adrenaline 1 mg/ml solution in a dose of 0·5–1 ml given by subcutaneous injection. People who know they are allergic to stings should carry an identifying tag such as provided by Medic-Alert Foundation International (UK address: 9 Hanover Street, London W1R 9HF Tel. 01–499 2261; USA: P.O. Box 1009, Turlock, Ca 95381 Tel. (209) 668 3333) in case they are found unconscious. They should always carry equipment for self-administration of adrenaline (systems are available from International Medications Systems (UK) Ltd, Tel. 03272–3231). Effective desensitization using purified specific venoms is now possible.

Venomous spiders

Almost all spiders have venom glands associated with a pair of small fangs near the mouth, but only about a hundred species are known to be capable of severe envenoming.

Dangerous species

The most important species from the medical point of view are the following:

Latrodectus tredecemguttatus, which occurs in Mediterranean countries and was known historically as tarantula.

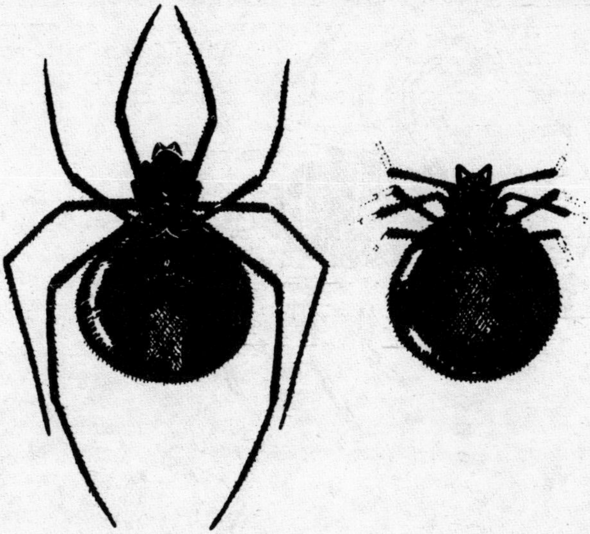

Fig. 5.1 *Latrodectus mactans*, the black widow spider of North America (female) (about 15 mm long) [Figs. 5.1–5.3 are drawn by S.N. McDermott and originally appeared in *Manual on Pest Control* (1984), ed. N.R.H. Burgess. They are reproduced by permission.]

Latrodectus mactans, the black widow spider of North America (Fig. 5.1).

Latrodectus hasselti, the Australian red-back spider.

Loxosceles reclusa, the brown recluse spider of North America.

Phoneutria nigriventer, the banana spider of South America.

Atrax robustus, the Sydney funnel web spider of Australia.

Spider venoms cause two groups of symptoms—neurotoxic, with painful muscle spasms and stimulation of the automatic nervous system (*Latrodectus, Phoneutria* and *Atrax*), or local necrosis (gangrene) and haemolysis (*Loxosceles*).

Treatment

Local infiltration of lignocaine (1–2 per cent) is effective for painful bites (e.g. *Phoneutria*).

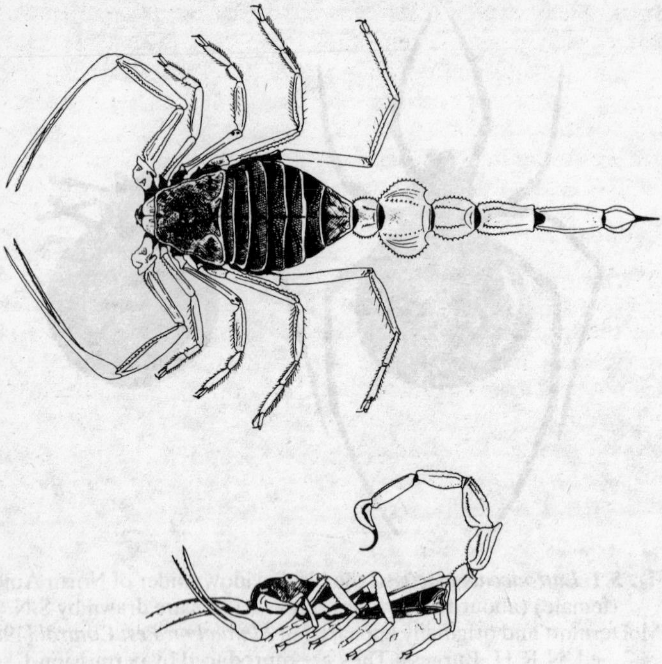

Fig. 5.2 *Apistobuthus pterycercus* scorpion. [Reproduced by permission—see Fig. 5.1.]

Neurotoxic symptoms may develop very rapidly in some cases, so a tight tourniquet or crepe bandage should be applied to delay spread of venom until the patient reaches hospital.

Spider antivenoms are manufactured in a number of countries. Calcium gluconate (10 ml of 10 per cent solution given by slow intravenous injection) is said to relieve painful muscle spasms dramatically in cases of *Latrodectus* bite.

Venomous scorpions

Dangerously venomous scorpions are found in South Africa, North Africa, Asia, North, Central and South America, and the Caribbean (Fig. 5.2). Scorpion stings are common in North

Africa, Mexico, South America, the Caribbean, and India. In Mexico, scorpions kill ten times more people than do snakes. Mortality is particularly high in young children. Scorpion venoms produce symptoms such as sweating, vomiting, and diarrhoea (due to the stimulation of the 'autonomic' nervous system). Damage to the heart muscle may cause a fall in blood pressure, irregular heartbeat, and development of heart failure.

Treatment

Local pain is very severe in all scorpion stings, even those that are not particularly dangerous. This is best treated with local anaesthetic given by a ring block in the case of stings on fingers or toes (p. 210). Emetine is effective but may cause necrosis. If this does not control the pain, a powerful analgesic such as pethidine (meperidine, Demerol in the USA) (50–100 mg by intramuscular injection for an adult) or even morphine may be needed. Antivenoms are made in the USA, South America, the Middle East, North Africa, and South Africa.

Millipedes and centipedes

Millipedes can secrete an irritant liquid which may produce blistering of the skin or more severe effects if it gets into the eyes. Centipedes can produce painful venomous bites but are rarely, if ever, dangerous.

Ants, beetles, and caterpillars

Ants, beetles, some hairy caterpillars, and a variety of other insects and their larvae can produce irritation of the skin and conjunctiva on contact, with pain, inflammation, and blistering. Serious effects caused by fibrinolytic venoms are common in some parts of Venezuela and Brazil. Haemolymph of blister beetles (family Meloidae) contains the vesicant substance cantharidin which is emitted in defence or if the insects are crushed. Beetles may be trapped inadvertently in body crevices and skin creases such as under the arm or in front of the elbow. Painful blisters are produced. The most famous species is *Lytta vesicatoria*, misleadingly known as 'Spanish fly'. Treatment of the blister with magnesium sulphate or methyl alcohol has been suggested.

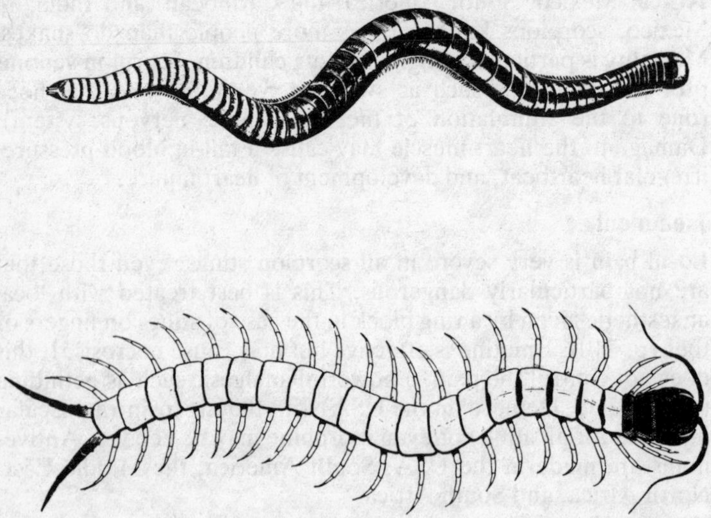

Fig. 5.3 *Spirostreptus* millipede (above) and *Scolopendra morsitans* centipede (below). [Reproduced by permission—see Fig. 5.1.]

Leeches

Leeches can be a severe nuisance to travellers, particularly in damp rain-forest regions of South-East Asia.

Land leeches wait in low vegetation near game tracks or paths until a large warm-blooded animal approaches. With incredible speed and efficiency they sense their victim and attach themselves. In humans they usually suck blood from the lower legs or ankles, easily penetrating long trousers, socks, and lace-up boots. An anticoagulant is secreted so that even after the leech has been removed or has fallen off, replete with blood, there is persistent bleeding.

Aquatic leeches attack swimmers and crawl into the mouth, nostrils, eyes, and other small openings into the body.

Treatment

Leeches are best removed by application of salt, alcohol, vinegar, or a lighted match or cigarette. If they are pulled off forcibly their mouth-parts sometimes remain in the wound, which may then become infected.

Prevention

Infestation with leeches can be prevented to some extent by smothering boots, socks, and trousers with ointment containing dibutylphthalate or *n,n*-diethylmetatoluamide (Deet, see p. 182). Coarse tobacco rolled into the top of the socks and kept soaked is also effective. Aquatic leeches are best avoided by refraining from swimming or bathing in forest streams and pools.

Useful addresses

Liverpool School of Tropical Medicine	Pembroke Place, Liverpool L3 5QA, UK Tel. 051 708 9393
Poisondex Rocky Mountain Poisons Center	 645 Bannock Street, Denver, Colorado 80204, USA Tel. 303–629–1123
Arizona Poison Control & Antivenin Index	University of Arizona, Tucson, AZ 85721, USA Tel. 602–626–6016

6

Air and sea travel

Air travel

Most health problems in air travellers are minor, and can usually be anticipated. All travellers should know about the possible effects of reduced cabin pressure.

Squadron Leader Richard Harding *is the co-author of the book* Aviation Medicine, *published by the British Medical Association. His research interests include respiratory physiology during flight.*

Air travel is remarkably safe: it is a tribute to the technological and practical skills of aircraft designers, airlines, and air-traffic controllers that of more than 1100 million people who travelled on scheduled passenger flights during 1988, only 633 were involved in just 15 fatal accidents (excluding deaths due to deliberate acts of destruction: a cause which accounted for the loss of a further 578 lives). This level of safety has been the norm for many years and, although 1985 was a particularly bad year for aircraft accidents, 1984 was the safest year for air travel since the earliest days of flight.

Preparation for the journey

Immunizations and medicines

Even the seasoned air traveller should double-check requirements and recommendations for immunization and malaria prevention—not just for the ultimate destination, but also for any stop-over points *en route* (see pp. 473–88, and Appendixes 1 and 2). Don't forget to carry any medical supplies you may need for the trip in hand luggage at all times, and it may also be sensible to take along a prescription or certificate, signed by your doctor, confirming the details of your medical treatment. Passengers taking regular medication (such as those with diabetes mellitus or epilepsy) should remain on 'home time' during a long journey, and readjust timings only after arrival.

Fear of flying

Flying is an exciting and exhilarating experience but some people may also be anxious and, occasionally, frightened by it. This is particularly likely in inexperienced passengers, although fears usually abate very quickly once they are airborne.

For the habitually fearful passenger, mild sedation may be advisable for a few days before and during the flight. Such treatment can be discussed and prescribed on a pre-trip visit to your doctor, and minimizes the personal misery that can surround an impending air journey. Remember that sedatives enhance the effects of alcohol, so avoid alcohol when taking these drugs.

Once at the airport, the hustle and bustle increase tension for many people, particularly the elderly, and if at all possible a 'dummy run' to the airport some weeks before flying is one way to reduce this. So too is arrival in good time on the day of travel, and prompt transfer to the departure lounge, where the surroundings are usually much calmer.

Pacemakers

The security devices through which passengers must pass in most international airports work by detecting changes in an electromagnetic field made by metal objects passing through it. The intensity of the field is set, in the UK, the USA, and other western countries at a level which will not induce changes in the electrical components of pacemakers, but machines used in other countries may not be so innocent. People fitted with pacemakers should mention the fact to security officials: this will enable a personal body check instead, and remove any possibility of interaction.

Fitness to fly

The presence of a pacemaker and indeed of *any* other serious medical condition should be notified to the airline at the time of booking. This useful precaution is as much for the benefit of the passenger as for the airline and, if in doubt about whether or not to notify a condition, ask your family doctor to contact the airline's medical department for advice.

Patients may well be advised not to fly when suffering from a disease or condition that will be affected by the environmental changes produced by ascent to altitude. Ascent carries with it certain physiological problems, the most important of which is a *fall in atmospheric pressure* from 760 mm mercury (mm Hg) at sea level to about 600 mm Hg at 6000 feet (a realistic cabin 'alti-

> **Airport radiation risk**
>
> A delegate at a travel medicine conference reported the recent case of a young Eskimo mother who had never flown before, travelling with an infant swaddled to a cradle-board. Airport security staff insisted on passing the unfamiliar bundle through their X-ray machine . . .
>
> R.D.

tude' for a civil aircraft, maintained by the pressurization system regardless of the actual height of the aircraft).

The fall in *total* pressure may cause problems for passengers because it allows gases in body cavities to expand. But the associated fall in pressure of each constituent gas in the air, and in particular the reduced oxygen pressure, is also highly important.

At sea level, the *partial* pressure of oxygen contained in the lungs is about 103 mm Hg and this pressure allows healthy individuals to function normally. At 10 000 feet, however, the partial pressure of oxygen falls to only 60 mm Hg. In fact, because of the peculiar way in which oxygen is bound to blood, healthy people are virtually unaffected by this reduction, but the health of people who have any difficulty obtaining sufficient oxygen at sea level will be further compromised by the fall in pressure, and they may develop symptoms of *hypoxia* (lack of oxygen).

Aircraft designers build in a safety margin which ensures that cabin altitude is held well below 10 000 feet and, as mentioned above, typically at 6000 feet, where the partial pressure of oxygen in the lungs is a 'safer' 74 mm Hg. If the cabin was not pressurized in this way, passengers would be obliged to breathe oxygen from face masks whenever the aircraft altitude exceeded 10 000 feet. In addition, they would be unable to enjoy any freedom of movement within the cabin. Cabin pressurization systems also allow the cabin temperature to be controlled.

Medical conditions unsuited to flying

Table 6.1 on page 224 lists many of the pre-existing medical conditions that may be affected by hypoxia and/or pressure changes associated with even the modest climb to 6000 feet. It also lists

Table 6.1 Pre-existing medical conditions unsuited to or requiring special consideration for air travel

Condition	Reason	Comments
Conditions made worse by hypoxia (lack of oxygen)	lower partial pressure of oxygen at altitude compromises already impaired oxygenation	
Respiratory disorders e.g. chronic bronchitis, emphysema, bronchiectasis causing breathlessness at rest		may fly if able to walk about 150 feet and climb 10–12 stairs without symptoms
Severe anaemias of any sort		
Cardiovascular disorders e.g. severe heart failure, severe angina		
heart attack		should not fly within 2 weeks
Neurological disorders e.g. stroke		risk improves with time but wait at least 21 days
hardening of the arteries in the elderly, causing confusion at night		should be accompanied
epilepsy		drug dose may need to be increased
Conditions made worse by pressure changes		
Recent ear surgery		
inner (e.g. stapedectomy)	risk of severe damage	wait at least 2 weeks, ideally two months
middle		wait until eardrum healed
Recent abdominal surgery	gas expansion may cause disruption of the wound	wait at least 10 days
Recent gastrointestinal bleeding	re-bleeding may occur	wait at least 21 days
Recent chest surgery	trapped gas may expand and reduce lung function	wait at least 21 days
Collapsed lung (pneumothorax)	trapped gas may expand and reduce lung function	wait until lung re-expanded
Recent cranial procedures	trapped gas may expand and compress brain tissue	wait at least 7 days
Fractured skull (with air entry)	trapped gas may expand and compress brain tissue	wait at least 7 days

Condition	Reason	Comments
Plaster casts	trapped air in plaster may expand and compress limb	consider splitting plaster for long journeys
Other conditions requiring special consideration		
People with colostomies/ileostomies	increased gas venting may occur	carry extra bags and dressings
Psychiatric disorders	novelty of airport and flight environments may exacerbate conditions	trained escort needed
Diabetes mellitus	problems with control may occur, possibly complicated by motion sickness	remain on home time during flight; consider anti-nauseant treatment; see p. 440.
Facial surgery	at risk of asphyxia if jaws are wired and vomiting occurs	should be accompanied by a person trained to release wires quickly
Pregnancy	aircraft are not ideal delivery suites	no flying after 34–35 weeks of pregnancy on international routes and after 36 weeks on domestic routes
Newborn infants	at risk from hypoxia if lungs not fully expanded	should not fly until over 48 hours old
Terminally ill	death in-flight is distressing to other passengers and is legally most complex	may be allowed to fly on humanitarian grounds or for urgent treatment but not if likely to die on board
Infectious diseases and disease characterized by offensive features such as vomiting, diarrhoea, copious sputum, or severe skin disfigurement	Cabin staff have neither the training nor the time to act as nursing attendants; they also have to handle food	

certain other conditions that should be discussed with a doctor before a flight is contemplated *and* about which the airline's medical department would wish to know.

Such prior notification enables the airline to support needy passengers during embarkation/disembarkation procedures, and to provide wheelchairs and escorts if appropriate. Extra seats and special arrangements may be required for those wearing large plaster casts or with orthopaedic problems, or for whom a stretcher is needed. The cabin staff will also wish to know of any passengers who might need oxygen during the flight. The airlines normally make no additional charge for such supporting services, but passengers are expected to pay for any extra seats occupied.

Physiological effects of flight

Fortunately, the vast majority of passengers do not have a serious pre-existing illness and are fit to withstand the rigours of air travel. They are not, however, immune from certain other risks.

Hypoxia

Hypoxia may affect those who are heavy smokers, because carbon monoxide in cigarette smoke reduces the oxygen-carrying capacity of the blood; it may also affect drinkers (because alcohol enhances and mimics the effects of hypoxia) as well as those who are fatigued or have minor illnesses such as acute head colds. The last group should avoid or delay flying if at all possible, while heavy smokers and drinkers should avoid these vices, at least while airborne! The effects, such as acute irritation of the respiratory tract, and the effects of 'secondary smoking' on non-smoking passengers, are minimized by both segregation of smokers and by efficient cabin air conditioning. By mid-1987, however, many regulating bodies (including those in Australia, Canada, and the USA) had gone further and prohibited smoking on most internal flights: a move which has met with widespread approval.

The symptoms and signs of mild hypoxia are subtle and insidious, and resemble the early stages of alcoholic intoxication: personality change, euphoria, impaired judgement, mental and muscular incoordination, and memory impairment may all be features, along with blueness of the lips, ear lobes, and nail beds.

The treatment is administration of oxygen, and this should be given by the cabin staff whenever hypoxia is suspected.

Hyperventilation

A more common, but happily less sinister, problem is hyperventilation, which may best be described as inappropriate overbreathing. The symptoms and signs of this condition are similar to those of hypoxia and, indeed, hypoxia can cause hyperventilation. But the commonest cause is emotional stress, and the picture is usually one of an obviously anxious passenger who becomes increasingly agitated, breathes rapidly, and then complains of light-headedness, feelings of unreality and anxiety (which reinforce the condition), pins and needles, and visual disturbances.

All of these features are the result of an excessive loss of carbon dioxide by overbreathing and, since carbon dioxide controls the acidity of the body, this loss leads to increasing alkalinity of the tissues.

The treatment is to re-breathe the expired air (traditionally from a brown paper bag!), which will minimize the loss of carbon dioxide. Reassurance, explanation, and firm instructions to breathe more slowly should also be given. Habitual hyperventilators may require mild sedation during the flight.

Gas expansion

Gas expansion on ascent may manifest itself in healthy individuals by a tighter than normal waistband, particularly if much alcohol or carbonated (fizzy) drink is consumed or if gas-producing foods such as beans, brassica vegetables e.g. cabbage, turnips, etc. and curries are eaten. Moderation in drinking and gastronomic habits is therefore advisable, and comfortable, loosely fitting clothes are recommended. (Women who are susceptible to cystitis should in any case not wear tightly fitting trousers for long flights.)

Dehydration

Continuous plying with drinks is partly a legitimate attempt by the cabin staff to counteract dehydration caused by the dry circulating cabin air. Water or juices are the preferred means of fluid replacement because of the problems with alcohol and fizzy drinks. The dryness of cabin air may also affect wearers of contact lenses and such passengers should be aware of accelerated drying of both soft and hard lenses (see p. 363). Dehydration increases the risk of thrombosis, considered below (p. 229).

Ears and sinuses

During ascent, gas expansion will also take place in the middle-ear cavities and the sinuses, and some gas must escape to the outside; the middle-ear cavities vent gas via the eustachian tubes, which open into the back of the throat, and the sinuses vent via tiny holes, called *ostia,* into the back of the nose. Such venting during ascent is entirely normal, and will be noticed when the ears 'pop': it should be neither unpleasant nor painful and does not require the help of sweets or other manoeuvres.

Unfortunately, the same cannot be said of the pressure changes that take place in these cavities as the aircraft descends. The volume of a gas decreases as the pressure increases, so that there is a 'contraction' of gas inside the middle-ear cavities and sinuses on descent. If the eustachian tubes and ostia are reasonably clear, air passes freely into the cavities, and the pressure inside rises to equal the pressure outside. If, however, the tubes and ostia are closed or are only partially clear—because, for example, they are inflamed and swollen as the result of a cold—air cannot enter the cavities and a *pressure differential* develops.

In the case of the middle-ear cavity, this differential is across the eardrum, which is pushed inwards: slight deafness and feelings of fullness are followed by discomfort and increasingly severe pain. Similarly, if the ostia are blocked, severe pain develops in the sinuses above the eyes or in the cheeks. Such *barotrauma* (trauma due to pressure) may happen to anybody, but is clearly more likely in those with a severe head cold.

Prevention of this kind of problem is one of the principal reasons for the slow rates of descent adopted by passenger aircraft. Sinus involvement is uncommon, but middle-ear barotrauma is a relatively frequent event.

Fortunately, the ability to 'clear the ears' by forcible opening of the eustachian tubes relieves the pressure differential, and correct use of manoeuvres for achieving this will prevent much airborne misery. Helpful manoeuvres include pinching the nose and, with the mouth shut, blowing out hard or swallowing; pinching the nose and drinking; moving the lower jaw from side to side; yawning, or simply opening the mouth wide. Such techniques should be repeated during descent at regular intervals when pressure on the eardrum is felt, and it is therefore advisable not to be asleep during this time.

Nasal decongestant sprays or drops may help keep both the eustachian tubes and ostia clear, but there is no voluntary means of opening the latter. Babies and small children are less affected by barotrauma because of the anatomy of the ostia and eustachian tubes, but crying or sucking will also help!

Airsickness

Many people worry about motion sickness, but only a small number of passengers suffer symptoms.

Prevention with medication is a realistic approach, and motion sickness is discussed further on p. 233.

Immobility

It is advisable to take frequent walks about the cabin during long flights. This is because prolonged sitting encourages swelling of the feet and legs (*postural oedema*) which in turn is responsible for the familiar sight of people struggling to replace footwear at the end of a flight.

Walkabouts prevent this problem, but also have another much more important role: postural oedema and stasis or stagnation of blood flow in the legs predispose to development of deep vein thrombosis (DVT)—painful clotting of blood in the deep veins of the calves—especially in those with a past history of such problems. This may, on rare occasion, lead to pulmonary embolism (caused by movement of the clot from the leg to the lungs), which is a very serious and potentially fatal condition (see also p. 420).

Emergencies in the air

Accidents (see also p. 251)

When in your seat, it is always as well to keep the lap strap loosely fastened: this not only prevents injury should the aircraft suddenly encounter turbulence, but also prevents any likelihood of being sucked out of the aircraft should it decompress rapidly!

Airborne emergencies are very rare, but do occur occasionally. So pay attention to safety briefings given by cabin staff before take-off, and take careful note of the description of the emergency oxygen system (some masks deliver oxygen only after they have been firmly pulled on to the face), the location of emergency exits, and to any other advice offered. You should also be aware of the danger of fires on board caused by illegal smoking in the lavatories.

In the unfortunate event of an in-flight emergency, passengers can do little more than follow instructions carefully, stay calm, and help one another. Should a crash landing be announced, pay particular attention to crash posture since survival will depend upon being fully conscious and mobile immediately after landing; most crash landings are survivable, but deaths have commonly occurred because of toxic fumes generated by post-crash fires. Again, in the aftermath of several 'survivable' tragedies of this nature, the regulating bodies have acted to insist upon the use of fire-blocking and less toxic materials for cabin furnishings, and upon the assessment of other aids to survival and escape (e.g. fire extinguishers, exit route lighting, smokehoods, etc.). Speedy and panic-free evacuation is of the greatest importance, however. Once at the foot of the escape slide, move quickly out of the way of following passengers in order to avoid the risk of a collision injury.

Illness during a flight

The statistics available are difficult to interpret, but the 'attack rate' for illness in passengers during a flight is of the *order* of one in 13 000—increasing to one in 350 for passengers who have a previously notified disability. This means around one medical emergency in every four or five flights.

The most common problems are associated with the central nervous system, including stress and anxiety, the alimentary system, the cardiovascular system, and the respiratory system. Of these, the cardiovascular disorders are the most serious and include angina, heart attacks, and heart failure.

The chances of a doctor being on board any flight have been variously estimated at 40 per cent on domestic routes to 90 per cent on international flights. The all-important decision, after any necessary or possible first aid has been administered, is whether or not to divert the aircraft if help can possibly be obtained sooner than at the intended destination: an expensive and inconvenient course to take! The decision is ultimately that of the aircraft captain, but he will naturally take advice from any available professional source.

Decompression sickness following aqualung diving

An unusual form of in-flight medical emergency, normally only a risk to aqualung divers, is decompression sickness (often known as the 'bends'), which is caused by the release of nitrogen bubbles in body tissues as pressure is reduced. Decompression sickness does not occur in healthy individuals at altitudes below 18 000 feet and is very rare below 25 000 feet. Passengers within a pressurized aircraft are not, therefore, at risk *unless* they have been aqualung diving shortly before undertaking a journey by air.

Diving allows compression of more nitrogen than normal into the body tissues, some but not all of which will evolve on return to the surface; the rest may evolve during ascent in an aircraft. Symptoms and signs include joint pains, itching, and rashes (see also pp. 311 and 314–15).

Subaqua enthusiasts should avoid any dive requiring a decompression 'stop' in the twenty-four hours preceding their flight and should not dive at all during the two to three hours preceding their flight. Most divers will or should be aware of these precautions and what constitutes a dive requiring 'stops', but if in any doubt, a fool-proof rule is to avoid diving to a depth greater than 9 m (30 feet) in the twenty-four hours before the flight.

The risk of decompression sickness affecting passengers after a failure of cabin pressurization is also remote, since the aircraft will rapidly be flown to a safe altitude.

Jet lag

Finally, modern air travel can cause disruption of desynchronization of many physiological and psychological rhythms. These circadian rhythms are governed or entrained in part by environmental cues—clock hour, temperature, day and night. Rapid passage across several time zones outstrips the ability of environmental factors to readjust these rhythms: desynchronization occurs and 'jet lag' develops.

Jet lag is discussed in further detail on p. 237, and simple methods to minimize its effects include sleeping on the aircraft, with or without the effect of a short-acting hypnotic (but remember the interaction with alcohol) (see also p. 496), avoiding heavy meals and excessive alcohol, avoiding important commitments for at least twenty-four hours after arrival, and generally being aware of the inevitable reduction in performance for a few days. Sensible behaviour along these lines will help make your trip a successful one.

Motion sickness and jet lag

Motion sickness and jet lag are two common problems related to travel itself, and it is helpful for travellers to understand the underlying mechanisms.

Dr Alan Benson *is a Senior Medical Officer* (*Research*) and Group Captain Tony Nicholson *is a Consultant in Aviation Medicine at the Royal Air Force Institute of Aviation Medicine, Farnborough, UK.* Alan Benson *has had a long interest in vestibular and allied problems in aviation, and more recently, space medicine*, and Tony Nicholson *has for many years been involved in the problems of sleep disturbance in aircrew.*

Motion sickness

Motion sickness is characterized by nausea, vomiting, pallor, and cold sweating, and occurs when we are exposed to unfamiliar motion stimuli, real or apparent. There are many types, including sea sickness, air sickness, car sickness, swing sickness, flight simulator sickness, and space sickness. Despite the diversity of possible causal environments, however, the provocative stimuli have essential characteristics in common, and so have our responses to them.

'Motion sickness' is really a misnomer, as symptoms can be evoked as much by the absence of an expected motion as by the presence of an unexpected motion. This can be seen with flight simulators and with 'Cinerama sickness'. Furthermore, motion sickness is quite a normal response for a healthy individual exposed for a sufficient length of time to unfamiliar motion of sufficient severity. Indeed, severe stimulus conditions, in the absence, rather than the presence of symptoms, can indicate a poorly functioning vestibular system (the balance mechanism of the ear). It would be more appropriate to label the condition as the 'motion maladaption syndrome'.

The development of motion sickness follows an orderly sequence with the time scale determined by the intensity of the stimulus and the susceptibility of the individual. The initial symptom is usually discomfort around the upper abdomen, and if the provocative motion continues, well-being can deteriorate quite quickly with nausea of increasing severity. At the same time, the face, or the area around the mouth, becomes pale and the individual begins to sweat. With the rapid worsening of symptoms, the so-called 'avalanche phenomenon', there may be increased salivation, feelings of bodily warmth, a lightness of the head, and, not infrequently, depression and apathy. Vomiting is then not long delayed, though some people can remain severely nauseated for long periods and do not obtain the transitory relief that many report once vomiting has occurred.

Apart from pallor, sweating, nausea, and vomiting, other signs and symptoms are frequent, though more variably reported. Increased salivation, belching, and flatulence are commonly associated with the development of nausea. Hyperventilation (p. 227) sometimes occurs, and alternation of sighing and yawning occasionally precedes the 'avalanche phenomenon'. Headache is another variable initial symptom, usually affecting the front of the head, and complaints of tightness around the forehead or of a 'buzzing' sensation are not uncommon.

Drowsiness is an important, yet often ignored symptom, even if not necessarily an integral part of the motion sickness syndrome. Feelings of lethargy and somnolence may persist for many hours after the provocative stimulus has been withdrawn and nausea has abated. In certain circumstances a desire to sleep may be the only symptom evoked by exposure to motion, especially when the intensity of the stimulus is such that adaptation occurs without significant malaise.

Incidence

The incidence of sickness in a particular environment is influenced by several factors. They are the physical characteristics of the stimulus (frequency, intensity, duration, and direction), the natural susceptibility of the individual, the nature of the task performed, and environmental factors such as odour. The incidence of air sickness ranges from a fraction of 1 per cent in large civil transport aircraft (that usually fly above the worst turbulence) to 100 per cent during 'hurricane penetration flights' in those who had no previous experience of such severe turbulence; 90 per cent of those who have flown in such conditions before may experience the problem again.

The considerable variability between people in their response to provocative motion is an important aspect. However, susceptibility appears to be a relatively stable and enduring individual characteristic, for there is evidence that those who are sensitive to one type of motion are likely to succumb when exposed to another. Motion sickness is rare below the age of 2 years, but susceptibility increases rapidly to reach a peak between the ages of 3 and 12 years. Over the next decade there is a progressive increase in tolerance that continues, albeit more slowly, with increasing age. This reduction in susceptibility with age has been recorded for both sea sickness and air sickness, though the elderly are not immune. About a fifth of those suffering from sea sickness on a Channel Island ferry were aged 60 years or more.

Females are more susceptible to motion sickness than males of the same age, and a higher incidence of vomiting and malaise is reported by female than by male passengers on ferries. The difference in susceptibility between men and women is in the ratio of about 1 to 1.7. The reason for this, which applies both to children and to adults, is not clear. It may be that females are more ready to admit to having symptoms. Hormonal factors may also play a part as susceptibility is highest during menstruation and is increased in pregnancy.

Prevention

Passengers in an aircraft can minimize the problem by restriction of head movement, by pressing the head firmly against the seat or other available support, preferably in a reclined position. If space permits, they should lie down on their backs, as this posture has been shown to reduce the incidence by approximately a fifth. Symptoms are decreased by closing the eyes, unless the passenger has a clear view of the horizon or other stable reference outside the aircraft. Attempting to read a book, while a desirable means of occupying the mind and diverting attention from a lack of well-being, more often accentuates the conflicting sensory information reaching the brain.

The most useful treatment, at least in the long term, is to adapt to the motion. This is 'nature's own cure' and is the preferred method of preventing sickness, particularly for aircrew. The approach is to be gradually introduced to the provocative motions of the flight environment, and that adaptation, once achieved, is maintained by regular and repeated exposures to the stimuli.

Over the years, many medicinal remedies have been proposed,

Table 6.2 Adult dose regimen for anti-motionsickness drugs

Drug	Dose (mg)	Time of onset (h) (approx)	Duration of action (h) (approx)
Hyoscine hydrobromide* (Kwells, and many other popular remedies)	0.3–0.6	0.5–1.0	4–6
Cyclizine hydrochloride (Valoid, Marezine)	50	1–2	4–6
Dimenhydrinate (Dramamine)	50–100	1–2	6–8
Cinnarizine (Stugeron)	30	1.5–2.0	6–8
Promethazine hydrochloride (Phenergan, Sominex) *Promethazine theoclate* (Avomine)	25	1.5–2.0	24–30

but relatively few are effective, (Table 6.2 lists doses and brand names) and none completely prevents signs and symptoms in everyone in all environments. When the motion is relatively mild hyoscine is very useful, but when the motion is of some severity and duration even a large dose of hyoscine (1.0 mg) may still leave 1 in 10 of the population unprotected. In life-rafts, sickness rates approaching 100 per cent have been reported, so it is not surprising that a significant proportion of the occupants will still suffer from sea sickness even when the dose of drug given is sufficient to cause side-effects.

None of the drugs of proven efficacy in the prevention of motion sickness is entirely specific in its action, and all have side-effects. Some anti-histaminics, such as promethazine and dimenhydrinate, and the anti-cholinergic, hyoscine, are depressants and can cause impairment of performance. Hyoscine adversely affects tasks requiring continuous attention and memory, and at doses greater than 0.8 mg interferes with psychomotor skills. Promethazine (25 mg) also impairs psychological reactions and co-ordination. Hyoscine may also lead to blurred vision,

* Hyoscine is called scopolamine in the USA. It is available in the form of a skin patch (Scopoderm TTS) applied behind the ear 5–6 hr before exposure to provocative motion and left in place for 24–72 hours, allowing slow absorption of the drug throughout this period. Although the patches are becoming increasingly available without prescription (e.g. Transderm Scōp, USA) it is always recommended that they be used under medical supervision. It is inadvisable to drink alcohol while wearing the patch. On short sea crossings, they should be used with caution: drowsiness may persist for several hours after removing the device, making it dangerous to drive a car. Elderly people should only use this product under medical supervision.

sedation, dizziness, and dry mouth, as well as urinary retention in older men.

The choice of a preventive drug depends, in part, upon the expected duration of exposure and susceptibility of the individual. In practice, if one drug is not effective or not well-tolerated, then another drug or combination of drugs may be tried. Where the objective is to provide short-term protection, oral l-hyoscine hydrobromide (0.3–0.6 mg) is the drug of choice. This acts within 30 minutes and provides protection for about 4 hours. However, side effects can be troublesome particularly with repeated administration (at 4–6 hourly intervals). With the development of trans-dermal drug-transport techniques it is now possible to provide a loading dose of 200 μg hyoscine with controlled release at 10 μg/h for up to 60 hours. The protection is reported to be comparable with that achieved by oral hyoscine, but there does appear to be some variability between individuals. When hyoscine is administered transdermally, peak blood levels are not reached until 8–12 hours after application of the patch, so it is necessary to anticipate the requirement for prevention.

The antihistamines promethazine and meclozine, when taken by mouth, are absorbed more slowly than hyoscine and are not effective until about 2 hours after administration, though they provide protection for at least 12 hours. Other drugs in the same group, such as cyclizine, dimenhydrinate, and cinnarizine, are absorbed at about the same rate though their duration of action is shorter—about 6 hours.

D-amphetamine increases tolerance and enhances the potency of hyoscine and antihistamines, while decreasing sedation. However, ephedrine is almost as effective as amphetamine in this respect and should be used in preference to amphetamine. Essentially, the combination of l-hyoscine hydrobromide (0.3 mg) with ephedrine sulphate (25 mg) is most effective for short-term (4 hours) protection, but for longer periods promethazine hydrochloride (25 mg) with either ephedrine sulphate (25 mg) or d-amphetamine sulphate (5 mg) is recommended.

Jet lag

Present day aircraft operating round northern and southern latitudes cross time zones almost at the same rate as the earth rotates. Journeys between Europe and North America can be completed within a few hours, and a shift of the day or night is experienced. After a westward flight when it is 8 o'clock in the evening in London, it is only 3 o'clock in the afternoon on arrival in New York, and the day will appear to have been lengthened. On the other hand, after eastward flights, which occur mostly overnight, it is 8 o'clock in the morning on arrival in London, but only 3 o'clock in the morning in New York. The night will appear to have been shortened, and several hours' rest will have been lost. It is clearly in the interest of the intercontinental traveller to plan to avoid or minimize disturbance of sleep during the journey, and the most useful approach, if airline schedules permit, is to travel during the day and arrive in time for bed. However, nearly all eastward flights to Europe from North America are overnight, and in these circumstances sleep loss may be inevitable.

If sleep loss can be avoided during the journey, as with daytime flights, there is still the problem of adapting to the new time zone. After *transmeridian* flights the individual may have difficulty in falling asleep when it is local time for rest, and there may be spontaneous awakenings during the night as well as early awakening in the morning. Adjustment needs time. There may also be some impairment of alertness or well-being during the day either due to poor sleep overnight or to the displacement of the sleep-wakefulness rhythm from the pattern of rest and activity of the new time zone.

A period of rest is therefore appropriate before one is ready again to make decisions. Many journeys from north to south are without a time zone change, and only require a period of rest if the flight occurs during the normal sleep period; but recovery after a transmeridian flight can be delayed and the delay depends on many factors including the duration of the flight, number of time zones crossed, direction, and time of departure.

We will now consider the effects of transmeridian flights, in particular on circadian rhythmicity and on sleep-wakefulness, and will discuss the usefulness of sleeping medication in alleviating the adverse effects on sleep.

Circadian rhythms

The reason why there may be difficulty with sleep and possibly impaired alertness for several days after a transmeridian flight is that our functions vary with time in a periodic and regular manner, and are normally synchronized with the solar day. Conflict of circadian rhythmicity with that of the environment arises therefore after transmeridian flights. Transmeridian flights produce rapid and often large time zone changes, and the sudden shift disengages the environmental and biological rhythms. Subjectively, most people complain of tiredness, impaired appetite, and a general loss of well-being, while sleepiness is experienced at inconvenient times of the day. Performance may be impaired in the late afternoon and evening of at least the first day after a flight in a westwardly direction, and in the morning and early afternoon after travelling eastwards.

Re-entrainment of rhythms to a new time zone occurs gradually. In man, social cues and timing of meals are important and adopting local times for meals accelerates the phase shift. Nevertheless, individuals differ in the ease and speed of their adaptation. Resynchronization takes between 2 and 6 days after westward flights and between 3 and 11 days after eastbound flights, though in some subjects eastbound travel may require even longer for complete adjustment to be attained.

Disturbed sleep

After a westward flight, one falls asleep relatively easily: the traveller is going to bed later than usual, the day of the journey has been lengthened, and the night time rest period has been delayed.

After an eastward flight, there can be more persistent sleep disturbances. For many days, it can be more difficult to fall asleep: the traveller goes to bed earlier than usual. However, if he or she has not slept during the journey, the loss of sleep may overcome difficulty in falling asleep on the first night at the new destination.

There are also subtle changes in the normal phases of sleep, such as rapid eye movement (REM) sleep and slow wave sleep. Reduction in REM sleep occurs after eastward flights, and this is presumably due to the displacement of sleep to earlier in the natural rhythm of sleep and wakefulness. On the other hand, with westward flights, there is an increase in the amount of REM sleep, and the normal temporal pattern is re-established within a day or two. Slow wave sleep may also be reduced for several days after an eastward flight, but with a westward flight the only change appears to be an increase of slow wave sleep during the first night due to the delay to sleep.

Wakefulness during sleep is clearly increased during the adaptation to a new time zone. This is seen during the first night after a westward flight; and after an eastward flight, an increase in wakefulness and number of awakenings is seen for several days, and sleep efficiency declines. It would appear that eastward flights may lead to relatively persistent impairment of sleep, whereas the alterations after a similar westward flight are far less marked, and probably do not persist for more than a day or two.

Sleeping medication

The use of sleeping medication is an important question for the frequent intercontinental traveller. Medication is likely to be of help during long flights, particularly when there are suitable seats or a sleeperette and also during post-flight adaptation. However, it must be realized that even transatlantic journeys are unlikely to provide a rest period of more than five hours, and the dose of any medication used must reflect the duration of the journey. The *lowest* dose of the normal therapeutic range should be used if the flight is unlikely to provide rest of more than five hours, though with longer flights a higher dose may be appropriate. If sleeping medication is to be used during the flight, it should be tried beforehand to ensure the most appropriate response. In this context temazepam (Normison, Restoril), 10–20 mg, and brotizolam, (Lendormin, *Boehringer Ingelheim*) 0.125–0.25 mg are useful sedatives.*

However, the most relevant issue for the intercontinental traveller is adapting to the new time zone with the drive for sleep and wakefulness coinciding slowly with the local pattern of rest and activity. The most disturbing effect may be the inability to stay asleep, and so there is need to sustain sleep during the night. In this context, sleeping medication may be useful for the first night or so after flying westward and for several nights after an eastward flight. What is needed is medication that is likely to sustain sleep without residual effects or 'hangover' and that is free of accumulation on daily use. Brotizolam (0.25 mg) is ideal, and zopiclone, 3.75–7.5 mg, (Zimovane, *Rhone-Poulenc*, and *May & Baker*) is likely to be equally useful.

* Brotizolam is currently available only in Germany, Belgium, the Netherlands, Luxemburg, Portugal, Ireland, Japan, Mexico, Argentina, and Italy.

Recent studies support the potential of such drugs as brotizolam to sustain sleep, though, in addition it has been shown that, in appropriate doses, they are free of residual effects on performance, and of accumulation with daily use. Certainly, studies on the sleep of individuals flying between the United Kingdom and North America have shown that brotizolam reduces wakefulness during the first night after a westward flight and alleviates the persistent sleep disturbance after an eastward flight.

Such medication can be very helpful after intercontinental flights, though there is no evidence that they quicken the alignment of sleep and wakefulness with the rest and activity pattern of the new time zone.

Health at sea

Cruise liners are generally very healthy places, but travellers may need to take precautions against motionsickness, and certain pre-existing medical conditions are best not taken to sea.

Dr Peter Oliver *is the Medical Director of the Cunard Shipping Company, and is responsible for the medical services on board all Cunard passenger vessels. He has acted as principal medical officer on the QE2 from time to time, and has travelled widely.*

Despite the passing of the great passenger liners, cruising has become an increasingly popular form of holiday and is no longer the exclusive privilege of the rich and famous: an estimated 100 000 passengers now travel by sea each year from the UK. Of course, long sea voyages are less common nowadays, and most holiday cruises are of just one or two weeks' duration, although longer world cruises lasting ten to twelve weeks are still popular.

A cruise on a modern liner can offer many health advantages compared with a land-based holiday abroad—for example, the assurance of hygienic food and water on board and the immediate availability of medical facilities.

Avoidance of currency problems and political upheaval is conducive to relaxation. Modern liners are fully air-conditioned, fitted with stabilizers to reduce the ship's movement in rough weather and have lifts to all decks; separate toilet and shower or bath are usually also available. These advantages apply, at least, to cruises run by reputable shipping companies on modern liners.

Some cheap package cruises may not offer all the facilities listed above, and conditions and standards of hygiene aboard 'flags of convenience' vessels may be questionable. Obviously, careful enquiry is essential in choosing a cruise to suit your individual requirements. As a general rule, you get what you pay for: paying a little more may well be worthwhile to secure peace of mind and a comfortable and safe holiday.

Remember that many cruise holidays operate on a fly-cruise basis, which may involve a long and fatiguing journey by air before reaching one's port of embarkation. For elderly people or those with debilitating medical conditions, a cruise starting nearer to home may well be preferable—special facilities for such passengers such as wheelchairs and assistance at embarkation can usually be provided on request.

Sea travel is one of the safest modes of transport: for example, no serious disaster had occurred to a British passenger vessel since the loss of the *Titanic* in 1912, a record marred only by the loss of the *Herald of Free Enterprise* off Zeebrugge, Belgium, on 6th March 1987, with the loss of 188 passengers. All passenger vessels have stringent safety regulations regarding the number of life-boats, safety rafts, and life-jackets, and routine life-boat drills are carried out on every voyage. Delays may occasionally occur as a result of rough weather or navigational problems, but at least you are still being well looked after while on board.

Travel on short sea crossings, for example from the UK to the Continent, usually presents few problems, apart from occasional sea-sickness. Bear in mind, however, that no medical facilities exist on board such vessels, so take with you anything you require.

Preparation for the voyage

Selecting suitable accommodation for your needs can be most important. An outboard cabin is generally preferable to an inboard one especially if you suffer from claustrophobia, and provided your finances allow. The centre of the ship, called amidships in seamen's parlance, is more stable and less subject to vibration and movement in bad weather.

Immunization

The medical services of most passenger cruise lines can normally provide up-to-date information, and can administer any necessary inoculations on board should you have failed to take the necessary precautions before joining the ship (see pp. 473–88). It is more sensible, however, to arrange for immunization to be completed well in advance—and I would suggest that you aim to complete any immunization schedule at least two weeks prior to departure. Although vaccine reactions are uncommon, they occasionally do occur and may spoil the first few days of holiday, which is always a disappointment.

Fitness to travel

Many shipping companies require a certificate of fitness for travel from your own doctor if you are over seventy-five years of age. If you are under treatment from your doctor it is essential that you have sufficient medication with you for your cruise. You would be surprised at the number of passengers who, on joining of a ship, have forgotten or lost their regular medication, sometimes with serious consequences. Those with a medical condition that may cause complications should bring a full medical report from their doctor. This is invaluable to the ship's doctor should any treatment be necessary. If in doubt about your health, have a check-up with your doctor prior to embarkation.

Most British passenger lines have comprehensive medical services ashore from whom advice can be obtained and special facilities arranged for invalids and the infirm, such as special diets, wheelchair assistance, and medical care on board.

The QE2, for example, provides full dental and physiotherapy services on its longer cruises, as well as a supportive cardiac unit.

Seasickness

With the widespread introduction of ship's stabilizers, which largely control the movement of the ship in rough weather, motion sickness is nowadays much less common. However, smaller vessels, such as cross-channel ferries, may not be so equipped and you may therefore be affected.

Prevention is better than cure. Try to avoid that farewell party and the undue fatigue of overnight travel. Smoking may aggravate the condition. When necessary, and where possible, lie down and avoid moving the head from side to side.

A wide variety of tablets are beneficial in preventing motion sickness. All these should be taken some hours in advance of the onset of symptoms wherever possible. They are discussed in detail on p. 235.

Once vomiting has occurred I find oral medication next to useless and, in these circumstances, would recommend promethazine hydrochloride (Phenergan) by injection, or if preferred by rectal suppository. This drug is highly effective and its failure rate minimal.

With correct and well-chosen medication seasickness should not nowadays be a problem.

Pre-existing medical conditions

Generally, cruising presents no special problems to travellers with pre-existing medical conditions, provided proper precautions are taken beforehand and that your doctor has approved the vacation you have in mind. Sophisticated radio satellite communications systems now make it possible for passengers to talk directly with their own personal physician, if necessary, and make it possible to seek expert medical advice without difficulty.

Gastrointestinal illness

Patients suffering from active stomach ulceration should not undertake a sea voyage of more than twenty-four hours' duration as the risk of stomach perforation or haemorrhage is too great, especially in circumstances where expert facilities and blood transfusion are not available. Well-controlled cases, with appropriate medication and diet, are no problem. Patients with a subacute or 'grumbling' appendix should also never contemplate a sea voyage.

Changes in normal eating habits and the consumption of unfamiliar food and drink, often associated with an alteration in social pattern, may cause considerable upset to colostomy patients, unless well controlled. Remember that cabin accommodation is often shared, so it may be necessary to make special arrangements to ensure privacy.

There is a high risk of diarrhoea from eating ashore in certain countries—such as Mexico, for example. It is important to pay constant attention to the food hygiene precautions outlined elsewhere in this book.

Cardiovascular disorders

With the ever-increasing number of older passengers taking the opportunity of a holiday cruise, the incidence of heart and circulatory disease is high. Most large passenger vessels provide facilities in the form of electrocardiography, cardiac monitoring, and resuscitation to deal with cardiac emergencies should they occur. Passengers whose pre-existing heart condition is well controlled by medication and who have adopted a sensible lifestyle present no problem.

Respiratory diseases

Upper respiratory infections (coughs and colds) are all too

common in the enclosed confines of an air-conditioned ship, where the opportunity for the spread of infection is high. Nevertheless, the risk to individuals who suffer from pre-existing lung disease, such as bronchitis or emphysema, is minimal as appropriate antibiotics and medical support at an early stage of the infection is highly effective. Chest X-ray facilities will usually be available on board should complications develop.

Asthmatics prone to severe bronchospasm may run into serious difficulty at sea. Poor air-conditioning in some vessels, combined with a sense of claustrophobia in tourist-class cabins, may aggravate an attack. Oxygen therapy and expert medical treatment may not be available in all cases. Well-equipped ships' hospitals providing steroid therapy can deal effectively with such emergencies, but beware of flags of convenience vessels that operate low-cost package holidays and have minimal medical facilities. Severe, uncontrolled asthmatics should not travel by sea.

Mental illness

Although a sea cruise can provide an enjoyable and relaxing break from the daily rat-race, ships are poor places to suffer from a psychiatric disorder. Contrary to popular belief, depressed people do very badly at sea: the anticipated improvement from escaping the anxieties of life ashore does not occur. Individuals suffering from severe depression should never travel by sea, where the risk of suicide from jumping overboard is too great.

Epilepsy

Attacks present no special danger provided skilled medical help is available on board if needed. Occasionally, the disruption of the normal daily routine and the fatigue of travel may exacerbate the frequency of attacks.

Drink problems

The convivial life at sea, freely available cheap alcohol, and no worries about getting home after an evening's drinking can pose problems to people who have difficulty in controlling their alcohol intake or have a past history of drink problems. The complications of mental disorder and even delirium tremens are not uncommon. If you have had any problems with drink, long sea voyages are best avoided.

Pregnancy

Normal pregnancy presents no particular difficulty at sea. Most companies do not accept passengers in an advanced stage of pregnancy, and usually such passengers should not embark if they will be more than thirty-six weeks pregnant on the day of disembarkation. Women with histories of repeated miscarriages, especially in the first few months of pregnancy, are best advised not to travel. Bear in mind that blood transfusion on board can be a complicated and risky procedure. (See also pp. 417–22.)

Keeping fit

Keeping fit on a long sea voyage is an ever-present problem, owing to the lack of exercise and possible overindulgence in food and alcohol. Fortunately most cruise liners provide gymnasium facilities and swimming-pools, and many run organized fitness programmes.

Debilitating illness or infirmity

Sea travel need not present undue concern to those convalescing from a debilitating illness, nor to the aged or infirm. Special facilities can normally be arranged, including wheelchairs for the disabled, and assistance at embarkation or at ports of call, although this is not always possible at every port; it is important to confirm this in advance. Disabled passengers should normally be accompanied by an escort. The shipping company should be given plenty of notice to enable arrangements to be made. Only occasionally, where complications are likely, may travel be refused.

Insurance

Most well-run shipboard medical services will endeavour to treat you on board ship and avoid disembarkation to hospital ashore—where there may be problems such as language difficulties, non-availability of drugs, the expense of treatment, and possibly questionable standards of care. Be prepared, however, and never travel overseas unless you have taken out adequate health insurance protection, not only for all medical expenses but for your repatriation should this prove necessary. A minimum cover of £5000 is essential, and cover for up to £500 000 may be advisable if you are travelling to the USA (see pp. 467–71).

Summary of advice for travellers

• Medical hazards at sea are relatively uncommon and do not differ significantly from those ashore. Should you have the misfortune to fall ill, what better place to be than a modern luxury liner! Most major shipping companies provide comprehensive medical services which are concerned not only with treating of illness and injury on board but also with maintaining high standards of hygiene and safety throughout the ship. Good luck and *bon voyage*!

7

Environmental and recreational hazards

Explorers and speleologists, beware . . .

- Histoplasmosis is caused by inhalation of spores of the fungus *Histoplasma capsulatum*. Symptoms are a 'flu-like illness with fever, headache, and a dry cough; the illness usually lasts 3–7 days, and almost always gets better without treatment.
- Spores are found in bird and bat droppings, and in the soil. Cases have occurred in travellers to Central America and the USA, and are particularly associated with inhalation of dust from bat-infested caves during dry weather, which should be avoided.

Accidents

Accidents abroad are an underestimated hazard. More travellers die from accidents than any other cause, and most accidents are avoidable.

Dr Richard Fairhurst *is the Chief Medical Officer of The Travellers' Medical Services, the Chairman of the British Aeromedical Practitioners Association, and was formerly the Chief Medical Officer of Europ Assistance. He has supervised the medical assistance rendered to more than 60 000 ill or injured travellers abroad, and has logged 5000 flying hours repatriating some of them..*

Many travellers will regard exotic infections as the biggest danger to their health abroad, but in fact these represent only a small proportion of medical problems involving travellers. Half of all medical incidents notified to travel insurance companies are accidental injuries, and 60 per cent of these result from road traffic accidents. Such figures are hardly surprising when one considers that, in the UK, accidents are the main cause of death between the ages of two and forty-five.

Infectious diseases are important, of course. They are preventable, and a proper programme of vaccination as well as the general precautions described elsewhere in this book are vital. However, travellers should also employ a number of other strategies to protect themselves.

Risk and the traveller

Travellers fall into different categories of risk: many have paid out a great deal of money in the expectation of enjoyment for themselves and their families, and are under pressure to have a good time regardless of inconvenient safety rules and common sense. Others, alone perhaps, and travelling on business, are under pressure to complete the business deal at any cost, to press on regardless with itineraries, and to use dangerous short cuts to achieve results.

Because of these pressures, and the absence of the usual constraints of home, family and work, many people behave in a quite reckless, uncharacteristic manner while abroad—exposing themselves to risks they would never dream of taking at home. Of course, a certain amount of risk-taking is all part of the excitement and enjoyment of being on holiday—but if you are to avoid accident and injury, you must examine the hazards to which you are exposing yourself and decide whether these are really justified.

Everyday risks

First of all, travellers should realize that they face at least the same risk of everyday accidents abroad as they do at home. Travel does not suddenly remove these dangers; on the contrary, the enjoyment and carefree attitude that travel engenders can increase the hazards.

As a general rule, *you should continue to apply your usual safety standards even if the legal requirements in the country you are visiting are lax*. For example, most motorists in the UK comply with the seat-belt law in the knowledge that this markedly reduces the risk of serious injury; to stop wearing seat-belts abroad, just because there is no legal requirement to do so, is inviting trouble. The same applies to wearing helmets on motorcycles and mopeds and observing traffic regulations. If you believe that driving at more than 70 m.p.h. is dangerous (and UK accident statistics suggest that it is), then you should stick to 70 m.p.h. abroad, even in countries where there are no speed limits.

The same approach extends to safety in the home. In the UK in 1986 there were 5700 deaths and two million injuries in the home, from causes such as falls, misuse of electrical appliances, and domestic poisoning.

These dangers are no less common abroad. A room with an antiquated electric lighting system will require special precautions. Gas installations should also be treated with great respect—recent tragedies with gas water-heaters in Portugal were due to poor ventilation. Be alert and apply a strict safety code to any device you may use. This applies particularly in working environments where the temptation to cut corners is ever-present.

The possibility of robbery and assault is another danger that travellers all too easily forget. Tourists are prime targets for muggers, yet people who will not walk through their own city centre for fear of attack are often happy to stroll unaccompanied through the more dangerous areas of New York, Miami, or Bangkok. Again, these risks are under your own control.

Transport risks

All forms of transport pose some danger to the traveller—with road transport at the top of the list. However, most hazards can be minimized with a little forethought and attention to detail.

Road transport

Motoring is by far the most dangerous form of transport. In the UK in 1987, 5125 people died as a result of road traffic accidents, and there were 64 300 serious injuries and 311 500 minor ones. On venturing abroad, motorists may find it difficult to keep their chances of injury down even to this appallingly high level.

The wisdom of wearing a seat-belt and observing reasonable speed limits has already been mentioned. Other obvious precautions are to avoid driving when you are tired, and above all not to drink and drive.

Air transport

The risk of injury on a scheduled airline is very small. In 1987 there were no passenger deaths on British Airlines, either scheduled or charter. In 1988, however, 270 people died in a single incident, the sabotage of a Pan American Boeing 747 over Scotland. And in the first week of 1989, 46 people died when a British Midland Airways Boeing 737 crash landed on the M1 motorway after both its engines failed—though remarkably there were more than eighty survivors. Of course, certain airlines and airports have much worse safety records than others. 'Flight International' regularly publishes data on these risks and a little attention to such information can lead to a potentially safer routing for your trip (see also p. 221).

Airlines are required by their regulating bodies to provide safety briefings on every flight. Listen carefully to the briefing, and read the safety instruction card. Even though you may have travelled by air hundreds of times before, this particular airliner might have a different configuration and different safety equipment. For example, not all oxygen masks fall out of the cabin roof on depressurization: on DC10 aircraft they are in the head rest of the seat in front of you. On flights with only short over-water sectors the crew may not brief you on the location of life-vests; make sure you know where they are.

Other more subtle strategies may also be important: a seat near the tail of the aircraft may give you a statistically greater likelihood of survival in a crash. Unfortunately airlines have the strange habit of making the rear of their cabins the smoking section, so you have to balance the risks of being exposed to other people's cigarette smoke against the chance of surviving in an accident!

Turbulence occasionally causes injury, so move around the cabin as carefully as possible, and keep your seat-belt fastened at all times. Be particularly careful when hot drinks and meals are being served, because sudden movement can spill scalding fluid into your lap.

Baggage poses an additional hazard—both on and off the plane. Avoid travelling with more baggage than you can carry comfortably and beware of other travellers who cannot keep their luggage trolleys under control—this is a frequent cause of injury.

On boarding the plane, try to restrict your hand luggage to one small item: the more the cabin is cluttered, the greater the risk in an accident. Overhead racks are getting larger and larger, but resist the temptation to put heavy items on these racks; in an accident they may fall on top of you and may even prevent your escape.

Duty-free alcohol is a particular problem. A fully laden Boeing 747 may be carrying up to 350 litres of inflammable alcohol in its cabin: this not only creates an obstruction but also constitutes a considerable fire risk. The sooner Customs Authorities around the world rationalize the system and allow passengers to buy duty-free goods at the port of entry, the safer everyone will be.

Smoking on board aircraft is potentially hazardous—not only to your own health, but also to the safety of the aircraft. If you must smoke during a flight, be very careful to extinguish cigarettes and matches properly. Use only the ashtrays provided. Above all, do not smoke when moving around on the aircraft and never smoke in the washrooms. There is a recent example of a serious cabin fire caused by an unextinguished cigarette left in a washroom.

Hijacking is still a problem, so co-operate with security procedures. If it happens to you stay calm, do not do anything to single yourself out as a specially useful hostage, and try to form a bond of friendship with your captors.

Once out of the realm of commercial airlines, the risks of accidents increase greatly. If you are thinking of travelling in a private aircraft, try to form an impression of whether the operation is being run professionally; if it is not, it is probably dangerous, and you should make excuses and find another way of getting to your destination.

Sea transport (see also p. 242)

Accidents and injuries at sea to passengers on commercial carriers are extremely unusual; for instance, on British ships in 1986, only 15 accidental deaths occurred. However, the tragic loss of a passenger ferryboat, the *Herald of Free Enterprise* in 1987, highlighted the crucial importance of observing simple safety measures. Make sure you know how all the safety devices work, and where they are located. Where is your life-jacket? Where is your muster station for the life-boats? Where are the emergency exits, and what signals will be used in case of an emergency? Does someone at home know of your travel plans?

The risks of injury are greater from rough seas than from the vessel foundering. Remain seated, make sure you are clear of any loose fittings that may crash around, and if possible lie on your bunk. If you have to move around, be very careful of wet floors and in particular of steep stairways. Do as any professional sailor would do and use both hands.

Finally we cannot leave the subject of sea travel without mentioning the possibility of piracy. In many areas of the world this is still commonplace. In general, pirates are interested in robbery and not in murder. If you are unfortunate enough to be the victim of piracy, remain calm, obey instructions, give up your possessions as required and do not provoke an argument or a fight.

Rail travel

Rail travel is remarkably safe; in the UK only 8 passenger deaths occurred in 1986, these all being one accident at the Lockington Level Crossing. In 1988, however, 36 people died in a multiple rail crash in South London following a signal failure; many of those killed had survived the initial impact, and were hit by a train on an adjoining track. Most injuries are the result of being hit by an open carriage door or falling under the train on getting off. So keep well away from your train as it approaches the station and, at the end of your journey, refrain from opening the door and stepping off until the train has stopped.

Risks at your destination

Road hazards

The heavy toll of road accidents has already been mentioned. The risks of driving abroad may be compounded by bad roads with ill-maintained surfaces, and local traffic laws which are not enforced or are even dangerous. (Cities where traffic laws are generally ignored can be recognized by the constant sound of car horns—so familiar to many travellers—the last resort of drivers struggling to make their presence known.)

Unfamiliarity with road signs, local customs and driving habits, and especially driving on the 'wrong side' of the road, are a hazard to drivers and pedestrians alike—most travellers are potentially at risk and should take particular care. (See also p. 461.)

Greece has a particular problem with moped accidents, which are very common in holidaymakers, and moped accidents are also a serious problem in many other island holiday destinations, such as Bermuda, the Caribbean, and Bali. The problems are made worse by the fact that most people who rent mopeds abroad do not wear crash helmets or protective clothing, and that skilled medical care is often not available to treat the injuries incurred.

One recent survey of motorcycle and moped accidents abroad found that 60 per cent were simply due to loss of control, and 20 per cent involved collision with an animal. Other vehicles were involved in only 20 per cent.

Political and cultural risks

Insurance policies exclude war risks and riots but unfortunately civil disturbances, bombings, or even invasion are liable to occur virtually anywhere nowadays. Politically unstable areas (which vary from time to time) are obviously best avoided, although this may not be possible for the business traveller.

Foreign ministries—the Foreign Office in the UK and the Department of State in the USA—will generally advise intending visitors to trouble spots on request. If you are unfortunate enough to be caught up in a riot, *coup d'état*, or invasion, keep in contact with your own country's consular or diplomatic representatives.

At a more personal level, most difficulties with the local population or authorities can be avoided by finding out how you are expected to behave at your destination. As a general rule avoid political discussions of any type, and avoid making political statements even in private. Don't use cameras or binoculars in aircraft, airports, government installations, or ports, however great the temptation to photograph an interesting item of local flora. In some societies women still have a very sheltered status; visitors to such countries are well advised to comply strictly with local customs.

Theft

The risk of theft while shopping can be reduced by being discreet with large amounts of cash, and shopping only in areas which are known to be safe for visitors. If a bag, briefcase, or handbag is snatched, particularly by a motorcyclist, let it go. More people are seriously injured by being pulled over in this situation than from any other type of robbery.

Hotel safety

Fires Hotel fires are unfortunately all too common and smoke, reduced visibility, and panic are the most serious hazards. Some basic precautions include finding out where the fire escape is as soon as you arrive at a hotel, following it down to see exactly where it emerges, and if possible finding out what the fire alarms actually sound like. Keep a torch or flashlight handy in your hotel room in case of an alarm at night, and in the event of a fire try above all to stay calm. Remember that smoke rises, and that it is safest to crawl on the floor in a smoke-filled room. In the ski resort hotel fire in Bulgaria in 1988, there were no burn or smoke injuries; all the casualties sustained broken limbs, while jumping out of windows to escape from the smoke.

Lifts Hotels lifts are a potential source of danger. If the lift looks unsafe, it probably is; use the stairs instead. Lift cages with only three sides (the fourth side being the wall of the lift shaft) are common in Europe and pose a particular danger. Do not under any circumstances lean against the wall of the lift shaft as it slides by; sadly, people have lost limbs when their clothes were trapped between the lift cage and the shaft wall.

Balconies Finally, remember that hotel balconies and their balustrades are often designed to look nice rather than to be safe. Make sure the fixing of the balustrade is secure, and that the height of the balustrade is sufficient to stop you over-balancing and falling. Europ Assistance, on average, deals with five deaths from falls from hotel balconies each year.

Camp-sites

Camp-sites in all countries pose particular risks: lack of security, leading to robbery and assault; and vulnerability to natural disasters such as fires, floods, sandstorms, and avalanches. In some countries there is also the risk of being attacked by dangerous animals or bitten all over by insects. Tents should be in groups, with someone always on the watch. If you choose to camp alone in a remote area then you must accept that you are taking a serious risk.

Sports, hobbies, and special pursuits

Most sports and special pursuits involve a risk factor, which is often an important component of the sport's enjoyment and attraction. When accidents do occur, they can usually be traced to entirely avoidable factors—such as poorly maintained equipment, lack of training or an inadequate level of fitness—rather than any intrinsic danger of the sport itself. Most serious skiing accidents, for example, are due either to inadequate mental and physical preparation or to badly adjusted ski bindings (see p. 319).

As a traveller intent on cramming the maximum amount of enjoyment into the time available, you may be tempted to cut corners, but this is unwise. Always make sure that the equipment you use is maintained to the highest standards—as the experts do—and if the sport you are interested in involves a high level of exertion, avoid 'overdoing things' until you have built up an appropriate level of fitness and stamina.

Certain pursuits—for example scuba-diving (p. 311) and hang-gliding—can be carried out safely only after a fairly long period of graduated instruction and training, including training in the avoidance of the specific risks involved. While abroad you may be offered an opportunity to indulge in such pursuits with only a minimal degree of instruction and supervision: offers of this type are best declined until you have undergone a proper training, and preferably obtained a certificate of competence.

If your pursuit carries you far away from human habitation, make sure that a responsible person knows where you are going and when you expect to return to base. When you are injured on a crevasse on a mountain, or marooned in a boat at sea, nobody can help you unless they know where you are!

In our experience, however, it is not the esoteric pursuits on holiday that carry the biggest risk, but the simple ones. Fathers, unaccustomed to exercise, seem particularly prone to ligament and bone injuries, or even heart attacks from playing cricket or football on the beach. Every year, there is a terrible toll from diving into shallow water, with serious neck and spinal injury in young men leading to paralysis for life. This accounts for approximately one tenth of all spinal cord injuries. *Do not under any circumstances dive into water of uncertain depth, or take running dives into the sea from a sloping beach.*

Alcohol

Travellers may use alcohol as an adjunct to enjoyment or in consolation for loneliness; it increases all other risks of injury and should be treated with great care. Alcohol and swimming make a particularly bad mix: almost half of all drownings are associated with alcohol consumption (p. 309).

A recent study has shown that in road traffic accidents involving pedestrians, the pedestrian is more likely to be intoxicated with alcohol than the driver of the car which hits him. Unfortunately, travellers are under great pressure to consume alcohol in excess, most of all on the airlines, where it is given out with reckless abandon particularly in the first-class cabin.

Consequences of injury abroad

The consequences of any injury abroad are often more serious than they would be if the same injury were sustained at home. In many areas of the world no organized emergency medical services are available to provide care at the site of an accident, or even an ambulance service to take the casualty to hospital. The more 'unspoilt' and picturesque the location, the greater the probability of the local 'hospital' being unworthy of such a title.

No medical help may be available at all. Small islands are always a risk. Usually, it requires a population of about a quarter of a million people to support a comprehensive medical service, and an island with a population smaller than this may well not have one (although better facilities may be available within reasonable range). If the island is many miles from the nearest mainland, even the simplest injury can cause problems. Similar risks apply to travellers, visiting small, isolated communities anywhere—desert oases, for example.

If you or any of your companions has suffered injury, and you cannot speak the local language, you may not be able to summon help even when it is available. Find out how the local system works, and what the emergency telephone number is. Remember that however good the local emergency services, you have problems if you cannot contact them.

Summary of advice for travellers

- All life's activities involve a balance between risk and benefit: we take risks in order to obtain benefit. Travellers who wish to avoid injury must examine the risks they run and decide whether they are justified. Everyone should have a strategy for safety, and wherever they are, whatever they are doing, should know very clearly what their escape route will be and how to behave in an emergency. Above all, no one should expose themselves to avoidable risks that they would never take in their normal environment.

Personal security and safety

Careful precautions to avoid disease are not enough; awareness of other hazards to safety is an important factor in staying healthy abroad.

Dr Peter Janke *is Director of Research at Control Risks Information Services Ltd, London, which publishes an online Travel Security Guide.*

Most children are taught an awareness of danger. As adults we assume that we know the dangers in our environment: we are accustomed to the risks, they are topics of conversation with neighbours and friends, and radio, television, and newspapers bring them to our attention daily. But when travelling abroad we move outside our usual environment, where, to a greater or lesser extent, we are ignorant of prevailing conditions. Furthermore, we are intent upon business or pleasure: our natural awareness of our own security and safety is diminished. The foreigner is always at greater risk than the native. If we remain conscious of only this one factor, we significantly reduce the likelihood of falling into danger.

Important background considerations

Cultural and religious factors

At home, we are not normally especially conscious of our own race, colour, religion, class, sex, nationality, occupation, or dress, nor do we think of such elements in terms of the reaction they may produce from others, or any offence that they may give. But any or all of these factors can put us at risk abroad. For example, where racial antagonism and hostility exist, it is important to be well-informed about prevailing attitudes.

It is not true that a white man is necessarily in danger in Africa, but because of specific temporary tensions, arising sometimes from minor, local incidents, he may encounter a dangerous environment on account of his colour. And the same is true for a black man, an Arab or an Asian, in visiting certain North American or European cities and neighbourhoods.

A Christian must be aware of Islamic values in Islamic countries, and behave in an appropriate manner, having regard not merely for what is illegal, such as alcohol, but for what may be considered rude or abusive, such as smoking, crossing one's legs, or kissing or holding hands in public. A woman cannot expect the same treatment in Islamic countries that she receives in the cosmopolitan executive or official circles of Paris, London, or New York; nor should she expect to wear the same clothes. 'Modesty' in dress and comportment is essential for safety.

Political factors

Many travellers take little or no interest in politics, and yet the interplay of governments seeking their national advantages on the international scene often engenders antagonisms that can occasionally lead to the detention of foreigners on trumped-up charges. The European and North American media frequently comment upon anti-American, anti-South African, anti-Israeli, and anti-Arab sentiments, but there are other and less well known prejudices for which it is wise to prepare.

Business factors

Before setting out few business travellers consider whether the purpose of their visit is at variance with the interests of others. Action may be taken generally, if not specifically, to impede a business traveller's plans. Nuclear power, defence sales, pharmaceutical and chemical manufacturing activities, and the sale of certain foods are all controversial in some countries from time to time.

Environmental scanning is therefore relevant for safety, as well as for business success. Popular demonstrations against such activities may be spontaneous or planned: direct action against companies or industrial sectors by militant groups can also put unsuspecting business travellers at risk.

Unwelcome tourism

Nor is the tourist always welcome. Tourism can hurt and antagonize some sectors of the local population to the extent that foreigners may encounter verbal abuse which can lead to physical assault. At the very least, tourists are obvious targets for criminals and tricksters intent on stripping them of valuables and money, using violence if necessary.

Country risk assessment

After considering how he or she may be personally at risk, travellers would do well to consider whether the country they are visiting is risky.

Country risk grading is a professional activity. It requires daily monitoring of events which have an impact on stability of government, and the ability to judge whether the government is handling events successfully. That way, the possibility of a military coup can be assessed, and whether or not it is likely to be a bloody affair. A judgment can be made as to whether demonstrations are likely to involve bloodshed or not. Civil war or insurgency are watched, and dangers in specific provinces and cities constantly reviewed, so that a judgment can be made as to the course political violence will take in the immediate future. The threat to travellers from kidnap, assassination, bomb explosions, road-blocks, hijack, illegal detention, and assault is thereby assessed.

The extent of this kind of problem comes as a surprise to the non-politically-minded traveller. More than 20 countries have continuing wars or insurgencies that require the traveller's special attention. These include Afghanistan, Angola, Burma, Cambodia, Colombia, El Salvador, Ethiopia, Guatemala, India, Iran, Iraq, Lebanon, Mozambique, Namibia, Nicaragua, Peru, Philippines, Sri Lanka, Sudan, Uganda, and Zimbabwe. War and insurgency do not necessarily imply that it is unsafe to go to a country, but that precautions should be taken. Conditions constantly change, and with them, the risk factors. It is important to seek advice from reliable sources before embarking on travel to troubled areas. Addresses and telephone numbers for the Foreign Office (Britain) and Department of State (USA) are listed in Appendix 6.

In other countries certain provinces suffer from terrorist campaigns that impinge from time to time on travellers' schedules and could put them at risk. Among these are the United Kingdom, France, Spain, and Israel. Still others have groups that operate from time to time against specific targets; these include the Federal Republic of Germany, Italy, Greece, Cyprus, Japan, Korea, and Turkey.

Some of these groups operate abroad and stage international incidents which may particularly affect airports and airlines.

Security risks and the traveller

A selection of security risks facing travellers will now be considered briefly. The extent to which some of these risks apply obviously largely depends on individual circumstances.

Kidnap

The risk of kidnap should not be exaggerated, particularly for travellers. However, the opportunist abduction of construction engineers, oil technicians, and aid workers in remote areas of the Third World occurs where insurgency is long-standing. Seek advice on prevailing circumstances from the foreign ministry and from professional security consultants. If you are at risk, your company may be willing to insure against it.

Attacks on tourists

Tourists are sometimes also attacked under such conditions. Before booking adventure holidays that involve trekking over little known overland routes, inform yourself and ensure that the travel company provides guides who are knowledgeable, experienced, and, above all, up to date. Premeditated assassination of travellers is extremely rare and only possible with a publicly known schedule, though incidental killing and opportunist murder sometimes occur when travellers are found in violent or lonely places. Should they be there at all?

Hijacking

Hijacking also is relatively infrequent. There are, none the less, risks in the choice of carrier, risks at the airport and on arrival, and in the selection of, and route to, the hotel. There are risks in public places, and during travel to and from the place of work or leisure.

Airline security

In choosing an airline most people have only their timetable in mind, and then possibly comfort and service. Some may consider an airline's safety record, though this is not readily to hand; few will consider whether an airline is a target for a hostile insurgent or terrorist group.

By and large, a major western airline is a safer bet than one from the Third World, in the same way that standards of airport security are generally higher in countries with a colder climate and where laws regarding alcohol consumption, general discipline, and standards of hygiene are stricter. It is not true that an airline under threat, such as El Al, is necessarily less safe, for so much depends upon the level of security that the airline and the country provide and are able to put into effect. On long-haul flights, consideration should be given to the safety of stop-over airports, where security may be lax, and local political conditions unstable.

Hotel security

Even if the traveller himself is not at risk for any reason, the nationality of a hotel chain or the fact that a hotel is known locally as a meeting-place for an unpopular group of expatriates could, in some trouble spots, involve unnecessary risk. It may then be as well to seek professional advice regarding the local standing of particular hotels, and to enquire into hotel security.

In general, the larger international chains provide better security, but it is often possible to choose one that is away from buildings likely to attract the attention of demonstrators or rioters. It may be worth considering a hotel out of town or one at a discreet location in the centre.

The larger hotels have limousine services to and from airports, otherwise it is important to select only properly registered taxis, and to enquire beforehand if there is any possibility of being met locally. In the latter event it is never wise for the traveller to display his name or that of his company, any more than it is to travel with obviously identifiable and ostentatious luggage or clothes. Again, discretion and anonymity are worth much in terms of security. Once inside the hotel, use its safe facilities, double-lock your room, and leave on the light and radio when you are out. Keep the keys on you, rather than leaving them at reception. When answering the phone, establish the identity of the caller before revealing your own name, and if receiving visitors, ensure you identify them before opening the door. Be as unpredictable in your routine as is practicable.

Safety at night

Going out at night presents special problems in a foreign environment. It is invariably safer to be accompanied by a resident who knows and understands the local scene. Failing that, proper advice should be sought from the hotel management, and great care taken in following the directives. No one is more at risk than when relaxing in the evening. Travellers are normally most at risk from muggers or gangs of youths seeking thrills from intimidation. In both cases it is extremely unwise to resist: the best course by far is to ensure in advance that private transport is on hand for the return as well as the outward journey.

Keeping a low profile

Never consult a map in the street or in the car—do so before leaving the hotel, office, or restaurant, and make all enquiries before setting off, taking time fully to understand the directions. Drive with windows and doors locked, and choose busy, well-lit routes. Only pull over if you are hailed by recognizable police. Above all, do not pick up anyone waiting for a lift.

If you have to use public transport ensure you understand the metro, subway, underground, rail, or bus system for boarding, alighting, payment, and routes before setting out. Travel in daylight or in well-lit conditions, and with other passengers. Try to ensure your connections do not involve lengthy waits, and do not appear ignorant or nervous—always remain alert. Carry as little cash as is reasonable and do not display jewellery or expensive personal effects.

If you find yourself unexpectedly on the fringes of a demonstration move quickly and purposefully away; if you are caught up in it as an innocent bystander the police will not distinguish you from the crowd—get away as fast as you can.

Some final precautions

When travelling with family, keep together, and ensure that all members know how to return to the hotel and to contact emergency services such as police and consulates by telephone. If it is necessary to split up, pre-arrange times and places for contact and for the return schedule, and for procedures to be followed in the event of a change of schedule. Your own schedule should be known only by those with a need to know, and care should be taken not to reveal it.

Summary of advice to travellers

- Remember the foreigner is always at greater risk than the native.
- Think how your nationality, race, colour, religion, class, sex, or occupation might put you at risk in the country to which you are travelling.
- Inform yourself of prevailing cultural and political circumstances, and consider what risk they present to you or to your visit. If in doubt consider changing your plans; if this is impossible, seek advice.
- Take advice on the safest route, carrier, and hotel.
- Travel as inconspicuously as possible.
- Inform only those who need to know of your itinerary and plans.
- Be as unpredictable in your routine as is practicable.

High altitude

Mountain sickness is a serious, but largely preventable illness, and travellers who are well informed and take sensible precautions should have little reason to fear it.

Dr John Dickinson *was Medical Superintendent of Patan Hospital, Kathmandu. After serving as a Christian missionary in Nepal for 17 years he is now a consultant physician with the Royal Army Medical Corps.*

The traveller who feels the effects of altitude follows in a long tradition. Plutarch refers to mountain sickness in his account of the crossing of Alexander's army into India in 326 BC, and ancient Chinese sources refer to the dangers of the 'Headache Mountains' of the Karakoram. The Inca civilization of the Andes (1100–1532 AD) suffered from 'soroche', a word still used today for mountain sickness in South America.

Mountain sickness is still found in the Andes, where road, rail, and air routes can take the traveller quickly to 13 000 feet (3950 m) or more, the Himalaya, which in Nepal draws about 43 000 trekkers a year, Mount Kenya and Mount Kilimanjaro in East Africa, and the Rockies of Canada and the USA, where climbers, skiers, and even residents are frequently affected.

Although the first autopsy on a victim of mountain sickness was performed in France on a climber from Mont Blanc, severe mountain sickness is rare in the Alps because most climbers sleep at the relatively low altitudes of the villages and mountain huts.

How high is high altitude?

Where does the risk of mountain sickness begin? This is a hard question to answer, because people vary so much in their susceptibility. The disease is well known in skiers at 8000 ft (2450 m) in the USA and fatalities have occurred below 10 000 ft (3050 m). I have seen a typical sufferer who insisted that he had not been above 7000 ft (2150 m). Generally, however, in Nepal most of our patients have become ill between 12 000 and 14 000 ft (3650–4250 m). That is not to say that we do not see cases from even higher: my 'record' case was from 23 000 ft (7000 m). Since

Some altitudes

Place	*(feet)*	*(metres)*
Mt Everest	29 028	8 848
Everest base camp	18 000	5 500
Mt Kilimanjaro	19 340	5 895
Mt Kenya	17 058	5 199
Mont Blanc	15 771	4 807
Mt Cameroon	13 353	4 070
Potosi, Bolivia	13 045	3 976
Lhasa, Tibet, China	12 002	3 658
La Paz, Bolivia	11 736	3 577
Cuzco, Peru	11 152	3 399
Aspen, Colorado	7 908 to 11 212	2 410 to 3 417
Quito, Ecuador	9 249	2 819
South Pole Station (USA)	9 186	2 800
Sucre, Bolivia	9 154	2 790
Val d'Isère	6 609 to 11 480	1 850 to 3 499
Zermatt	5 315 to 12 533	1 620 to 3 820
Toluca, Mexico	8 793	2 680
Bogota, Colombia	8 393	2 644
St Moritz	6 089 to 10 837	1 856 to 3 303
Cochabamaba, Bolivia	8 393	2 558
Pachuca de Soto, Mexico	7 960	2 426
Addis Ababa, Ethiopia	7 900	2 408
Asmara, Ethiopia	7 789	2 374
Arequipa, Peru	7 559	2 304
Mexico City, Mexico	7 546	2 300
Netzahualcoyotl, Mexico	7 474	2 278
Darjeeling, India	7 431	2 265
Sining, Tsinghai, China	7 363	2 244
Sana'a, North Yemen	7 260	2 242
Simla, India	7 225	2 202
Puebla, Mexico	7 094	2 162
Manizales, Colombia	7 021	2 140
Santa Fe, USA	6 996	2 132
Guanajuato, Mexico	6 726	2 050

Everest Base Camp at 18 000 ft (5500 m) can be reached by simple (though strenuous) walking, it should be obvious that the high altitude trekker is as much at risk as the mountaineer.

Who is at risk?

Mountaineering groups seem relatively less likely to be troubled by mountain sickness than trekkers because they are generally better-informed and plan ascents to allow sufficient time for acclimatization. The greater risk seems to be not the altitude reached, but the *speed of ascent*.

Those who drive, ride, or fly to a high altitude are more at risk than those who walk, and those who climb rapidly are more at risk than those who take their time. At least partly because they climb more slowly, older people do better than the young. There seems to be no significant difference in risk between males and females.

Thus the risks of developing mountain sickness are to a large extent under the traveller's own control: mountain sickness is a preventable illness.

Altitude and the human body

The important feature of high altitude, as far as the human body is concerned, is reduced atmospheric pressure which causes an oxygen lack. The proportion of oxygen remains the same, anywhere in the atmosphere, but the pressure of the atmosphere falls as we ascend from the surface of the earth. Atmospheric pressure at Everest Base Camp, for example, is about half that at sea level. It is *pressure* that drives oxygen from the atmosphere into our blood across the vast gas-exchanging surface of our lungs. Reduced pressure means less oxygen available to the tissues, a condition called *hypoxia* (see pp. 222, 226, and 311).

Of course our bodies adapt to compensate for low oxygen pressure. Breathing and the work of the heart increase. One effect of increased breathing, though, is to drive off more of the waste gas, carbon dioxide. This is not entirely a good thing because it causes the body to become more alkaline. Compensation for this can be carried out by the kidneys, but this takes a few days, and meanwhile increased alkalinity has a braking effect on the ability of the body to increase breathing to compensate for oxygen lack. This is one aspect of the process of acclimatization.

Acclimatization also involves changes in the oxygen carrying capacity of the blood and in the ability of the tissues to extract oxygen from the blood. There are also probably mechanisms that increase the efficiency of oxygen use at cell level.

Nitrogen is an inert atmospheric gas which is normally dissolved in blood and tissues to a small extent at sea level. On ascent to levels of lower pressure it is released from the tissues and may form small bubbles in the blood. This is similar to what happens when divers ascend from the depths (p. 314). Although we do not develop 'the bends' at altitude as incautious divers may, it is possible that these bubbles cause other problems such as increased coagulability of the blood.

Both cold and exercise have effects on the body that may summate with the effect of hypoxia and contribute to mountain sickness.

Types of mountain sickness

Acute mountain sickness (AMS) is used here to refer to all the interrelated types of mountain sickness that occur after exposure to altitude, commonly within 2–4 days. In rare cases, AMS may be delayed by as long as three weeks. Chronic mountain sickness is seen mainly in long term residents at high altitude in the Andes and is not of importance to travellers.

Benign AMS

Benign acute mountain sickness is called just 'AMS' by some specialists. Sufferers experience loss of appetite, headache, nausea, vomiting, sleeplessness, and a sense of 'fullness' in the chest, or some combination of these symptoms. As far as it goes, the condition is fairly harmless, but it may progress to a more serious form. It is therefore not only a nuisance, but also an *important warning* and should not be ignored.

Malignant AMS

Malignant acute mountain sickness is so called because it may be fatal, and therefore must be handled correctly when it threatens. It may develop from benign AMS or it may begin with little or no warning.

There are two types of malignant AMS, which may occur independently, but the commonest pattern in Nepal is for both to occur together:

Pulmonary acute mountain sickness (high altitude pulmonary oedema) Fluid builds up in the lungs. This 'waterlogging', together with other changes, leads to breathlessness which persists even at rest, cough, white sputum, and often blueness of the lips (cyanosis).

Cerebral acute mountain sickness (high altitude cerebral oedema) Sufferers develop headache, drowsiness, unsteadiness on the feet, abnormal behaviour, impaired consciousness, and often coma. If the onset is gradual, the 'drunken' walk and inability to sit upright may give clues to what is happening, but commonly the patient passes rapidly into coma, often overnight so that he or she 'wakes up unconscious' the next day.

Causes

It would be nice to be able to give a neat, convincing explanation of how AMS is caused. Unfortunately, although there are plenty of theories, there is no general agreement. We do know that patchy high blood flow and increased permeability of the small blood vessels to water are involved in causing oedema in the lungs and similar mechanisms may operate in the brain where fragile capillary vessels may be deprived of their usual protection from surges of blood pressure.

Small and even large blood clots are often found in the blood vessels of those who have died from AMS. These may be the result of the nitrogen bubbles discussed earlier, and they may affect the permeability of the capillaries to water. Hormone changes may also play a part, though there is no definite evidence that the menstrual cycle alters women's susceptibility to AMS or that the use of oral contraceptives is harmful. Another factor may be that low levels of oxygen in the brain interfere with the ability of nerve cells to communicate with each other, a situation that must clearly alter brain function.

Treatment

For practical purposes, drugs and oxygen have only a minor part to play in the emergency management of AMS, so that *a well-informed layman can be as effective as a doctor*.

Benign AMS

In the event of benign AMS, the rule is to remain at the same altitude until you have recovered. This often takes only one or two days, and you can then ascend cautiously if you wish. If you do not seem to be able to recover in 3–4 days, or if things get worse, you should go down. Some doctors believe that drugs such as dexamethasone or acetazolamide can speed recovery, but this is not recommended routinely.

Malignant AMS

Malignant AMS sufferers are often in no condition to make decisions for themselves. Their judgment may be impaired as well as their physical capacity. *They should be brought down as a matter of urgency*. Sometimes they can walk, or stagger down; most sufferers will need to be carried by a porter, yak, or horse. Descent should not be delayed while a helicopter is summoned and it should start even at night if this is possible. An American doctor once saved the life of his wife: he heard her groaning at about midnight and could not awaken her. Recognizing cerebral AMS, he insisted that his Sherpa guide arrange for her to be carried down at once. She eventually recovered, but it was touch and go; if he had delayed till morning, she would certainly have died.

When evacuating a cerebral AMS victim, it is important to prevent obstruction to breathing. Patients lying on a stretcher should be turned to one side. Pulmonary AMS patients are often more comfortable in the sitting position and may be brought down sitting on a yak or in a basket on a porter's back; the head should always be kept forward. If oxygen is available, give it, but this is much less important than descent. No drugs are known to be helpful for malignant AMS.

Patients with pulmonary AMS often improve rapidly after a descent of 2000–3000 feet. However patients with cerebral or mixed AMS may not regain consciousness for days or even weeks, though recovery, when it occurs, is usually complete.

Prevention

I have said enough to make it clear that gradual ascent is the key to prevention. The schedule for any given journey has to depend on local details, but it is essential to avoid rapid ascents and to allow time to acclimatize above 8000 feet.

Those who fly to high-altitude airfields must be prepared to spend time acclimatizing on arrival. In addition, I recommend 'rest days' every 3000 feet above 9000 feet. On the Everest trek, for example, it is advisable to stay two nights in the region of Namche Bazaar (11 300 feet, 3450 m) and another two at Pheriche (14 000 feet, 4250 m). During these 'rest days', you can actually climb as high as you like, provided you return to sleep at the same altitude as the previous night. 'Climb high, sleep low' is a useful motto. The Himalayan Rescue Association in Kathmandu provides advice on safe schedules for Nepal.

Drugs such as acetazolamide (Diamox), spironolactone, and

dexamethasone have been recommended for the prevention of AMS. They can prevent the symptoms of benign AMS but severe and even fatal AMS has occurred in people taking these drugs. They may have an *adverse* effect by hiding the warning symptoms. Though they may be necessary for rescue parties, I do not recommend them for travellers. It is much safer to rely on good planning and gradual ascent.

It is always good to be physically fit for a walk or climb, but unfortunately this does not prevent AMS. In fact, some of the fittest have become victims for the obvious reason; they go up too fast.

It is not yet possible to identify the type of person who is most at risk, but those who have previously suffered from AMS should ascend particularly cautiously. One experienced Alpine guide, unused to Himalayan altitudes, was evacuated with malignant AMS in two successive seasons. Many others have had multiple attacks, but some seem never to be affected.

Other problems at altitude

Some people develop swelling of the body at high altitude (high altitude subcutaneous oedema). Many of these are otherwise well, although some may show the features of benign AMS. The swelling should probably be regarded as a warning sign.

Bleeding at the back of the eye (high altitude retinal haemorrhage) occurs in many people but most are not aware of it unless a doctor examines their eyes with an ophthalmoscope. Only rarely may vision be affected, and then usually only temporarily.

If you have significant disease of the heart, lungs, or blood, you will probably find it difficult to tolerate the extra strain placed on the body by high altitude, especially if you are planning to walk or climb. It is extremely important that you consult your doctor for advice about going to high altitude.

Epilepsy and migraine are conditions that occur in attacks, and there may be more risk of an attack at high altitude. Many asthmatics, on the other hand, do not have attacks at altitude, unless precipitated by exertion or cold.

People with sickle cell disease or trait (which only affects black people) usually know that they have the condition but may not be aware that they may get 'crises' at high altitude. These are painful and may be dangerous.

Conclusion

For many of us, there are few satisfactions greater than reaching the high and lonely places of the world. There is no reason for this to be spoilt by illness if we are aware of the risks and take simple precautions.

Trekking safety

A survey of 148 000 trekkers in Nepal over a three and a half year period found that 23 people died, and 111 had to be rescued. Falls were the commonest cause of death, followed by illness and acute mountain sickness. Trekking is reasonably safe, concluded its authors.

R.D.

Effects of climatic extremes

Throughout history, sailors and soldiers, pioneers and prospectors, traders and trappers have travelled, worked and fought in all climates. Men and women of every race and all ages have explored for the sake of adventure or personal gain; some braved the elements in search of peace of mind, and others sought respite from persecution. Not all survived.

Colonel James M. Adam *was a Consultant Physiologist with the British Army for nearly thirty years, responsible mainly for problems of maintaining combat effectiveness of British soldiers in all extremes. He served in Antarctica, Korea, Malaysia, and the deserts of the Middle East, and left the Army to help set up the Institute of Environmental and Offshore Medicine, Faculty of Medicine, University of Aberdeen.*

It is perhaps a sad reflection on human nature how often advances in the technology of living and surviving have followed fast on the heels of warfare: and this applies particularly to research into the problems of heat and cold. Cyrus the Great, for example, was worried about the possibility of heat illness in his troops when he was reorganizing the armies of the Medes and Persians in 539 BC—so he ordained that they be taken into the desert every day to work until they sweated. In similar vein, the potentially lethal effects of cold-water immersion seem to have first been noted during the naval wars between the Greeks and Persians in the fifth century BC. Such lessons have had to be relearned again and again up to the intensive research that followed World War II.

The ease of high-speed air travel to distant climes, whether for business or leisure, has occasioned risks to many travellers. The fatigue of such flights, especially those with a large easterly or westerly component (causing the greatest 'jet lag') will upset particularly the unfit person, the ill, the infirm, and the ageing. On arrival, a hostile climatic environment may compound the stress.

Some general considerations

Heat transfer

Physicists have long since determined the rules that govern the exchange of heat from one object to another; the fundamental principles of such heat exchanges are of great relevance to an understanding of the effects on the human body of climatic extremes.

Net flow of heat energy is always from hotter to colder objects. Such heat flow can occur in three main ways:

Radiation All objects radiate heat energy in the form of electromagnetic waves of various wavelengths; the hotter an object, the more heat it radiates. Radiant energy can be absorbed by another, distant object, the amount absorbed depending on such factors as the colour and texture of the receptive object's surface (light-coloured surfaces tend to absorb less than dark-coloured surfaces). Heat can pass by radiation even across a vacuum, as when the sun heats the earth, across space.

Convection is the term given to the transport of heat by the motion of warmed fluid (or gases). A small amount of the fluid is in contact with the heat source and is heated by conduction (see below). As its temperature rises the fluid expands, becomes lighter and so it rises away from the heat source. Further fluid replaces that which has floated away, is heated in turn, and so on. As the heated fluid cools elsewhere it contracts, becomes denser, and sinks. In this way a convection current is set up.

Conduction is the transfer of heat from a heat source to a cooler object by direct contact and without demonstrable motion of the parts of the object such as described above in 'convection current'. Metals conduct heat away most readily, while still air is the most effective barrier to heat lost by this route.

Body temperature and its control

The upper limit of the average normal temperature of the human body at rest is 36·9°C (98·4°F), although patients inactive in bed may register a normal value of 36·4°C (97·5°F). In very hot or very cold climates accurate temperature measurements cannot be made by means of a thermometer in the mouth, and instead the thermometer must be placed in the rectum.

The human body exchanges heat with its surroundings by the avenues mentioned above. Heat is gained by the body by the absorption of radiation from distant hot objects (such as the sun) and also by conduction and convection from the surrounding air or water if these are at a higher temperature than the body. Conversely, heat can be lost by radiation to distant cooler objects and also by conduction and convection to the surrounding air or water if these are at a lower temperature than the body.

In addition, two other processes have an important influence on the body's heat balance. First, the body is always *gaining* heat produced during the digestion of food and from working muscles. Second, heat is *lost* by the evaporation of sweat from the surface of the skin. Heat loss by sweat evaporation is at the rate of 1464 kilojoules per litre of sweat (350 kilocalories per pint), which is a considerable but at times very necessary heat loss. In experiments with fit paratroopers working under severe desert conditions, I have measured sweat losses of more than 10 litres (17·5 pints) daily providing a heat loss of about 25 000 kilojoules (6000 kilocalories) just to keep body temperature constant.

Our bodies function efficiently by means of a myriad of chemical changes that occur almost simultaneously. These have an optimum temperature of reaction for continued health of 36·9°C (98·4°F), with the slight variations described above.

Many of the vast number of reactions are centred in the main organs of the body, and of these, the brain is the most sensitive to temperature change. Indeed, a departure of just over 0·5°C above or below the normal 36·9°C central body (core) temperature, as measured in the rectum, can be demonstrated to produce malfunction of this organ and of the parts of the body that it governs. The further the departure from normal, the greater the degree of malfunction, so that a rise of core temperature of 2°C to 38·9°C (102·0°F) is accompanied by signs and symptoms of definite illness. Equally, a fall of the same magnitude to 34·9°C (94·8°F) takes the person into the realms of hypothermia, which is defined as a core temperature of 35·0°C (95·0°F) or less.

All evidence available points to the existence of a heat-regulating centre in the hypothalamus (an important area of the brain). The control mechanism is influenced not only by the temperature of the blood reaching the brain, but also be nerve impulses arising in the skin. The mechanisms by which the hypothalamus controls the body temperature are very complex and cannot be considered in detail here. Suffice it to state that in the fineness and speed of its control, the hypothalamus is a better thermostat than most of those available commercially.

Categories of climatic extreme

A better understanding of the possible ills which may result from climatic variations requires a redefinition of some basic variable factors. Consideration of the extremes of temperature and humidity give four main climatic categories:

Hot/wet describes the environment of the rain forest, the jungle and secondary jungle in which the air or shade temperature is rarely above 38·0°C (100°F) in daytime and is more commonly 33–34°C. The combination of abundant moisture, tree canopy, and frequent cloud cover serves to maintain the temperature at a fairly constant level all the year round, with little variation between day and night. The humidity is high, varying between about 65 per cent by day and 100 per cent by night; air speeds are generally low.

Hot/dry describes the climate of the tropical and subtropical desert and semi-arid tracts of land. The tropical deserts have low humidity, scarce or absent vegetation, cloudless skies, intense sunshine, airspeeds varying from low to violent with dust and sand-storms, and scanty and erratic rainfall. At night, the clear skies permit rapid heat loss to space by radiation and convection, so there may be heavy dew and occasional frost. There is thus a high day-to-night variation in air (shade) temperature from as high as 55°C by day (the record is 58·05°C) to as low as −5·6°C in the Western Sahara or −42°C in the winter-time Gobi desert at night.

Cold/wet describes the climate of large areas of the world, including most of western Europe north of the latitude of the Pyrenees. The term 'temperate zone' is often applied to such regions, but is something of a misnomer since it may lead people to underestimate the speed with which changes in the climate can occur, as well as its hazards and severity. The air temperature ranges between about 10°C and −2°C (50°F and 28°F), with rain, hail, sleet, mud, puddles, and high winds as possible accompaniments.

Cold/dry is the environment in which the air (shade) temperature rarely if every rises above the freezing point of water (0·0°C or 32°F) at any time of the day. The terrain is frozen, and there is no free still water (as in puddles and ponds). Snow and ice cover may be total, skies are often clear of clouds, and sunshine may be brilliant, especially in the absence of wind. However, movement and navigation can sometimes be hampered by 'white-out' conditions, snow precipitation, and blizzards.

Hot climates

Acclimatization

An oft-repeated statement is 'Man is a tropical animal' but, one would suggest, the tense of the verb is wrong and should be 'was', especially in the case of the European dweller who is heading for the tropics for the first time.

The body possesses the mechanism necessary to survive in hostile, hot climates, but time is required to evoke them. The adaptive process takes one, two or three weeks depending on the severity of the hot climate. Briefly, the strain on the body is shown by a high pulse rate and body temperature, and the condition will progress to one or other of the heat illnesses (see below) unless the stress is lessened or muscular activity reduced.

With graded exposure and gently increasing activity, the sweat glands are trained to produce more, start more quickly, continue longer without sweat-gland fatigue and to retain more salt in the body. The circulatory system (heart and arteries) learns to absorb water in much larger quantities from the stomach and intestines, and to transport it to the sweat glands in the skin, whence it emerges to be evaporated for cooling the body.

In circumstances where the air temperature is higher than body temperature, the body can no longer cool itself through radiation, convection, or conduction and must rely *solely* on the evaporation of sweat for continuing health. On first exposure to the stressful conditions there is a great deal of discomfort, which varies according to the amount of muscular activity. As adaptation or acclimatization progresses, this discomfort gradually diminishes and disappears after about two weeks.

Acclimatization is generally more difficult in the jungle climates than in hot/dry or desert environments. Two main reasons can be given for this:

1. The high humidity of the hot/wet environment is maintained by day and by night, and the higher this relative humidity the more difficult it becomes for sweat to evaporate from the body and cool it.

2. Nights in the desert vary from cool to cold, so the body's sweating mechanism has some rest. This is not so in the jungle.

A state of acclimatization to the jungle may be transferred to the desert without ill effect, but the reverse is more difficult, for the reasons already mentioned.

Heat acclimatization can be achieved to a considerable degree in the privacy of one's own home. Commencing three weeks before the intended journey, devote one hour daily to fitness training, and one-and-a-half hours to lying in a bath with the water kept as hot as possible (42°C, 108°F). Staying in the bath for this long may be difficult for the first two days or so, but persevere. As much of the body should be immersed as possible, eyes, nose, and ears only out of the water. This is one of the simplest methods of 'artificial acclimatization', but it should only be attempted if you are physically fit.

Age and build

Children adapt to hot environments very quickly and happily, especially thin, wiry, active children who have a large surface area/weight ratio, which facilitates evaporative cooling. The same build is an advantage to adults, but the rule again is 'the younger and fitter, the faster'. Unfit, plump, podgy, and obese persons represent an increasing order of risk. The elderly and anyone with known heart or circulatory disorders such as high blood pressure and hardening of the arteries should either be dissuaded from facing the stress of a hot climate or, with medical advice, should take special precautions—absence of exertion, travel by sea rather than by air, and as much air-conditioning as possible.

Thirst, salt, and water

The human thirst sensation is defective where water requirements are concerned. It seems, in general, to account for only about 75 per cent of the body's actual needs in the tropics. Despite a high degree of training in these matters, the British Army has had four times as many cases of kidney or urinary stones directly attributable to inadequate water consumption in the Middle and Far East as in home stations. The message for the newcomer is to drink water or watery drinks (beware alcohol, which dehydrates) *beyond* the point of thirst-quenching. *Alternatively, ensure enough intake by drinking sufficient water to produce urine that is consistently pale in colour*: dark urine or a low urine output are both signs of developing dehydration.

Loss of salt from the body in the sweat has been mentioned above, and this chemical must be replaced if bodily function is to continue. Salt tablets are often used but can cause vomiting and stomach upsets. The author has put entire regiments on to pre-salted water with excellent effect, by treating all tea, coffee, cocoa, soup, lemonade (from crystals) as well as all water used in cooking. The required salt concentration is one quarter of a level teaspoonful (about one gram) per pint or two level teaspoonfuls to each gallon. This concentration is below the taste threshold and must be accompanied by a mixed diet.

Clothing and shelter

The jungle Nudity is the ideal state for the jungle environment, as even the thinnest material can interfere with the required loss of heat by radiation and convection. But sweat can be evaporated from the clothes instead of the skin with the same amount of cooling by either route.

Clothing is usually required, however, not only to satisfy local customs and religions, but also to protect against thorns, cutting plants, and the onslaughts of biting insects. Protective leg and footwear is essential for jungle trekking for these reasons as well as for protection against snake bite and parasitic diseases such as hookworm.

The desert The intensity of sun in the desert necessitates head and body protection to prevent sunburn, which apart from being extremely painful may hinder the function of sweat glands, thus causing serious illness. Again, the materials used must be the lightest possible, not only in weight but also in colour. While colour is not important for jungle clothing, in the desert a light or white colour will aid the body's heat balance by reflecting radiant heat away.

Desert clothing comprises loose-fitting long-sleeved upper garments, preferably cotton, with long trousers, to minimize the skin's exposure to intense solar radiation—until a good tan has developed after strictly graded sunbathing. Here the head requires a broad-brimmed floppy hat to protect forehead and neck before 'tanning'. The Arab head-dress, the khaffieh (a one-metre square of muslin) is very useful in a variety of ways: it can be wrapped around the face for protection in sand-storms or used as a neckerchief to prevent sunburn under the chin in the vicinity of water (which reflects ultraviolet solar radiation upwards). (See also the next chapter—Sun and the traveller).

Footwear Footwear can be as diverse as there are people to have opinions. The author's preference has been quite simple—boots and puttees for trekking in the jungle and 'flip-flops' for rest periods to allow skin and footwear to dry out. The heavy tread of boots provides warning to jungle denizens such as snakes, who hopefully will 'slope off'.

Desert boots with thick crepe rubber soles and uppers mostly of reversed calf leather, but sometimes of canvas, are preferable to almost any other form of footwear for the desert. A word of caution, however, if you intend to clamber around the very sharp rocks characteristic of some deserts: these require much stouter boots. As in the jungle, desert footwear requires 'time off' to dry out.

Shelter Shelter in the jungle environment, from the single-person poncho or bivouac to permanent buildings, requires a waterproof roof and little else, to take advantage of every slight breeze. Tents and houses should be surrounded by deep run-off systems for the frequent heavy downpours that occur. Sleeping platforms, well above ground level, must be surrounded by mosquito nets. Temporary or permanent shelter in the desert climate should preferably have a double roof (and no corrugated iron sheets, please) to minimize heating of the interior by direct solar radiation.

Air-conditioning Sweat-soaked clothing will chill the wearer rapidly on entering air-conditioned habitation. Carry either a complete change or extra items for such eventualities. Air-conditioned offices are a mixed blessing for many, especially for newcomers to the Far East in Singapore, Bangkok, Hong Kong, and the like. They find that they can work intensively during the day but, on leaving the cool, fairly dry conditions, for the 'outside world' they are quite exhausted by early evening. Reliance on alcoholic refreshment is an unwise habit to develop in these circumstances.

Heat illnesses

Heat hyperpyrexia (heat stroke)

Hyperpyrexia means 'high fever' and some specialists regard it, or rather the condition it describes, as the first stage in the development of heat stroke, while others use the terms as alternatives. 'Sunstroke' is a misnomer as the illness may occur without direct exposure to the sun.

This serious condition begins with impairment of the heat-regulating mechanisms of the body, although how this occurs is not yet fully understood. Sweating diminishes and the body temperature rises—a sufferer who is still sufficiently alert will complain that he or she is feeling peculiar and is not sweating very much. The body temperature will be in the region of 39°C to 41°C (102–106°F), and the higher it rises, the worse the likely outcome: *this condition can result in death within two to four hours* of the first symptoms.

In the areas where sweating has ceased, the skin becomes flushed and red. Headache develops and soon becomes severe, often described as dull and pounding. Walking soon changes to staggering, and signs of mental confusion and perhaps unusual aggression appear. Unable to stand, the sufferer becomes delirious, develops stertorous breathing, and may convulse.

In the total absence of sweating, the temperature continues to rise until death occurs at about 43°C to 44°C (109–111°F). The only treatment is immediate cooling once the illness is recognized or suspected. Under shelter from the sun, remove all clothing and cover the patient with a wetted bedsheet, towel, or other lightweight material and start fanning to promote cooling by evaporation. Keep the coverings wet, and fanning and wetting must continue all the way to hospital, where electrical fans and needle-spraying of cooled water will hopefully be available.

Definitive prevention of the condition is difficult because the cause of the failure of the body's regulatory system is not yet fully understood. Factors that play a part in its occurrence are these:

1. Continuous heat stress, day and night.
2. A lack of fitness, overindulgence in alcohol, or excessively strenuous exercise.
3. A premature return to activity after a previous episode of heat exhaustion, particularly in an unacclimatized person.

4. Any of the above in a person whose sweating ability is seriously impaired by a skin complaint or disorder.

Do not forget that the patient may have a fever-producing illness in addition, which may not have been recognized. It is essential to treat hyperpyrexial patients for *cerebral malaria* as well as cooling them, if there is a danger of malaria in the area (see also pp. 121 and 376).

Heat exhaustion

Heat exhaustion may be one of the three types, namely water-deficiency, salt-deficiency, or anhidrotic heat exhaustion (anhidrotic = absent sweat). Each is serious and the first and third can go on to heat stroke because of the implied interference with cooling by evaporation of sweat.

Water-deficiency heat exhaustion occurs when there is a restriction of water intake in a heat-stress situation. Extreme examples occur in people stranded in a desert or adrift in tropical seas without water. Remember that water requirements in a hot climate may be very high (10 litres or 17·5 pints a day in the example cited above). The potential victim is thirsty and complains of vague discomforts, then lack of appetite, giddiness, restlessness, and tingling sensations. Any urine passed is in small quantity and deeply coloured. Lips, mouth, and tongue become so dry that speaking is hardly possible. The temperature rises steadily, the pulse rate increases, breathing becomes faster, and the lips are blue. Hollow cheeks and sunken eyes complete the picture before the victim sinks into a coma and, if not treated, death.

The comatose patient requires cooling and fluids supplied intravenously, if possible, with medical assistance. The patient who can still understand and walk is quickly restored in cool surroundings with the following regime: 0·5 litres (nearly 1 pint) of water of any flavour to be drunk every 15 minutes for two hours or until a large quantity of pale urine is passed. Thereafter keep him cool for two days and advise on drinking past the point of thirst-quenching.

Salt-deficiency heat exhaustion commonly occurs in the inexperienced newcomer, after two or three days of heavy sweating and work, with plenty to drink but no salt replacement because of lack of appetite. Quite frequently, vomiting and/or diarrhoea have hastened the onset. The body's salt 'reserves' have vanished and the cells and tissues that require it are malfunctioning. Increasing fatigue is soon followed by lethargy, headache, giddiness, and extremely severe muscle cramps. Pallor of the face and around the lips is very typical as the patient collapses, still soaked with sweat.

Do not allow the casualty to sit up or move as this may precipitate a fatal collapse. Urgent treatment with bed-rest in cool surroundings, and a high intake of salted drinks—one level teaspoonful of salt per half litre (nearly 1 pint) given hourly for six hours will supply some 15 g of the daily requirement of 20 g of salt (see also p. 33). Thereafter, return to the pre-salted water regime mentioned above—had this been observed in the first place, the condition might not have occurred! The pre-salted water replaces one half of the salt lost in unacclimatized sweat, and the rest should come from the diet. Be prepared, however, to supervise your patient's eating habits and to insist on empty plates. A return to work should be gradual.

Anhidrotic heat exhaustion arises as a disorder of sweating in people who have been in a hot climate for several months. It may be defined as a state of exhaustion and heat intolerance. The skin, mainly of the trunk and upper arms, shows a rash of little vesicles (called *miliaria profunda*) and there is little or no sweat in these parts when all around are sweating freely. Fairly rare, it is worst in the heat of the day—symptoms include fatigue, unpleasant sensations of warmth, giddiness on standing up, frightening palpitations, and rapid, sometimes gasping breathing. The face sweats profusely, and there is a frequent and insistent urge to pass urine, sometimes in larger quantities than usual. The disorder is often preceded by an attack of prickly heat (see below). These seriously heat-intolerant individuals should be removed to a cool environment for one month's rest, and then be supervised carefully on return, because another attack may lead to heat stroke.

Other conditions caused by heat

Prickly heat or miliaria rubra (literally red millet seeds) consists of a vast number of vesicles or tiny blisters set in red, mildly inflamed skin, worst around the waist, upper trunk, armpits, front of the elbows, and even on the scalp. The rash is accompanied by intensely aggravating prickling sensations. The cause is not yet clear, but an important factor is the constant wetting of the skin by unevaporated sweat as occurs at times of high humidity in hot/wet climes. The skin becomes unhealthy and waterlogged, sweat ducts are blocked with debris and infection starts, causing a large number of pimples. Sleep is almost always upset and is delayed until the coolest period of the night, around 4 to 5 a.m. As a result, bad temper and irritability are usual, with a diminution in working efficiency. The prickling can be relieved by taking a cool shower, gentle dab-drying of the skin to prevent further damage, then calamine lotion and zinc oxide dusting powder. The clothing should be starch-free and of loose fit. (See also p. 346.)

Heat oedema (heat swelling) of the ankles used to be called 'deck ankles' and appeared in passengers when the ships first entered tropical waters. Now it is indistinguishable from the swollen ankles of long air journeys (p. 229), and is found to last for a few days in the unacclimatized newcomer to extreme heat. The condition requires no treatment and will disappear as acclimatization progresses.

Heat cramps may occur without the signs and symptoms of salt-deficiency heat exhaustion described above, and are due to the same problem—salt lack—from whatever cause. They are excruciatingly painful, and occur at random intervals in whichever muscle groups are used most. The treatment is the same as for salt-deficiency heat exhaustion.

Heat syncope (fainting) occurs typically in the unacclimatized on first exposure to the heat. Due to circulatory instability during the early days, it occurs after prolonged standing or on sudden change of posture. The 'head-low' or lying position will return the blood to the brain. An hour or two of rest and graded exercise will soon banish the condition.

Cold climates

'Cold', as far as the human body is concerned has a number of possible interpretations. In this context, it simply denotes an immediate environment that is below body temperature and is likely to cause the body temperature to fall.

Hypothermia

As stated earlier, heat always flows from a hot source to one that is lower in temperature, and the human body can lose heat through the avenues of conduction, convection, and radiation.

The requirement for a stable central or core temperature within ± 0·5°C of 36·9°C has already been stressed. If this temperature falls by a generalized chilling of the body to 35·0°C (95·0°F), the resulting condition is called hypothermia (deficient heat). A special low-reading clinical thermometer is necessary to record such low body temperatures. Hypothermia leads to deterioration of the function of organs and cells, and if not controlled and corrected, ultimately to death. The brain tolerates hypothermia badly, and the manifestations of its malfunction are virtually identical to those which occur under conditions of excessive heat—a point that has received little or no attention—possibly because few investigators have had the opportunity to study both.

Cold injury

Central or core temperature is maintained in two ways: first, and of greatest importance when the body is at rest, heat is generated by the use of the body's fuel reserves of fat and carbohydrates; second, any muscular activity generates further heat. In a fit person, muscular activity may increase heat production by a factor of 10 or 15. Heat is conveyed from the core of the body to the skin and extremities by the circulating blood. Heat is then lost to the environment, and the cooled blood returns, tending to lower the core temperature. In cold conditions, therefore, the body's heat can be lost through inadequate insulation of the skin and extremities in generalized chilling. If there is severe localized chilling, cold injury can occur even if the core temperature is not substantially altered—and such injury can be sufficiently serious to require hospital treatment.

Different forms of cold injury include the non-freezing type called 'immersion foot' ('trench foot' of World War I) from long exposure to cold, damp conditions, and frostbite, which follows freezing of the tissues of the extremities, especially the nose, cheeks, chin, ears, fingers, and feet in cold dry environments. Less serious injuries—though often annoying ones—include chapped skin of the lips, nose and hands in cold windy weather;

and sunburn (pp. 300–8) and windburn which, with snow-blindness (p. 361), typically occur in cold dry climates.

Acclimatization

The human body has no mechanism for acclimatizing to cold which corresponds to the way it adapts to hot climates. Instead it must rely on insulation, provided not only by our layers of body fat, but also by modern clothing and shelter technology. Travellers generally have to rely on trapped still dry air in clothing and housing to keep them warm, and this remains the best insulant known.

Prevention of the effects of cold thus depends upon the maintenance of body heat by an adequate supply of energy (food and drink) for internal energy production; on blocking avenues of heat loss; and finally upon preservation of an insulating shell of still dry air.

It is pertinent at this point to discuss a source of possible confusion in terminology. The World Health Organization has decreed that hypothermia in this context should be known as 'accidental hypothermia'. Terms such as exposure, mountain hypothermia, and immersion hypothermia are no longer recognized.

Wind: an additional risk

Wind speed has an important effect on human heat balance in both cold/wet and cold/dry conditions. Much of the important research on this subject was carried out by the late Paul Siple and his colleague C.F. Passel, who in 1945 published a method of assessing the effects of wind, which has stood the test of time and is known as the Wind Chill Factor. A slight modification of the original is reproduced here (Figure 7·1, p. 292) as the Wind Chill Index. By measuring or assessing the present and possible trend of temperature and wind speed, the traveller can allocate the prevailing conditions to one of the zones A–G on the graph, and then decide whether it is safe to stray away from shelter.

When using this method, I recommend deeming the air temperature to be 6°C (11°F) *lower* than actual temperature if the clothing is soaked through with water. This adjustment is necessary because of the extra heat loss by conduction through waterlogged apparel.

Use of the method obviously requires some means of measuring air temperature and wind speed. Air temperature is simple to

Table 7.1 A guide to estimating wind speed (Beaufort scale of wind force)

Wind speed (miles per hour)	Beaufort scale	Wind force	Effects
1	0	calm	smoke rises vertically
1–3	1	light air	wind direction shown by smoke; wind vane does not move
4–7	2	slight breeze	wind felt on face; leaves rustle; wind vane moves
8–12	3	gentle breeze	leaves and small twigs in constant motion; light flag lifts
13–18	4	moderate breeze	dust and loose paper raised; small branches move; snow begins to drift
19–24	5	fresh breeze	small trees begin to sway; wave-lets created on inland waterways
25–31	6	strong breeze	large branches in motion; umbrellas difficult to use; high snow-drifts
32–38	7	high wind	whole trees in motion; visibility obscured by drifting snow
39–46	8	gale	twigs break off trees; walking increasingly difficult
47–54	9	strong gale	slight structural damage to buildings
55–63	10	whole gale	inland trees uprooted
64–72	11	storm	rare; widespread damage
73–82	12	hurricane	very rare; widespread severe damage

measure using inexpensive equipment such as the sling or whirling psychrometer. As the name implies, this apparatus is rotated rapidly like a (British!) football rattle for a minimum of thirty seconds and the reading taken. Of great use in cold and hot climates, the instrument can be small enough to slip into the pocket.

If very cold conditions are expected, a thermometer containing coloured alcohol that will not freeze is required. Measurement of wind speed requires an anemometer, which is generally a rather delicate and expensive instrument. The Beaufort table of wind-speed, shown in Table 7.1 above, supplies an alternative to the use of an instrument, but does require some practice in its use.

Cold effects and injuries (see also p. 321)

The most important harmful effect of cold is that already referred to as accidental hypothermia, defined as a result of the generalized chilling of a person such that he or she has a core temperature of 35°C (95·0°F) or less.

In the field, the measurement of temperature in the mouth, armpit or ear is useless. Placing the thermometer in the stream of urine as it is passed is reliable, but requires a full bladder, or a minimum of 200 ml of urine. Usually the only reliable method with simple apparatus is to place the thermometer in the rectum.

In practice, the onset of the condition may be fast or slow, and this is a convenient approach to its description as acute or chronic.

Acute accidental hypothermia

This is most commonly due to immersion in cold water. Falling into water colder than 5°C (41°F) is a grave emergency with almost immediate effects. The victim gasps, shivers violently, curls up, inhales water, and is dead from drowning in about five to fifteen minutes. It is doubtful whether even onlookers experienced in the first aid of drowning can act quickly enough. If the subject is wearing plenty of clothing which retards the loss of body heat, a life-jacket that keeps the head out of the water, has face protection to prevent cold water from splashing on it (which stops the breathing, slows or stops the heart, and predisposes to drowning), and has been well enough trained to know to keep *perfectly still* in the water, he or she has well-established average chances of survival from the immersion. These expectations are: about fifty minutes in freezing water; around three hours in water at 10°C (50°F), some six hours at 15°C (59°F), and very many more hours at 20°C (70°F) and above.

Other factors that influence the onset of hypothermia in water are increasing age; lack of fitness; liability to panic; lack of recent food intake for internal heat production; and the recent drinking of alcohol, which without food causes a severe fall in blood sugar, with immediate confusion and clumsiness.

Any insulating material will protect against hypothermia. The protective influence of fat under the skin as an insulant against heat loss in the water led Professor Keatinge of the London Hospital to bring an old adage up to date by suggesting that, instead of 'women and children first', it should read 'thin boys and men first', and then 'plump girls and women'.

If the casualty is known to have collapsed in the water after some five to fifteen minutes' immersion, then drowning is the

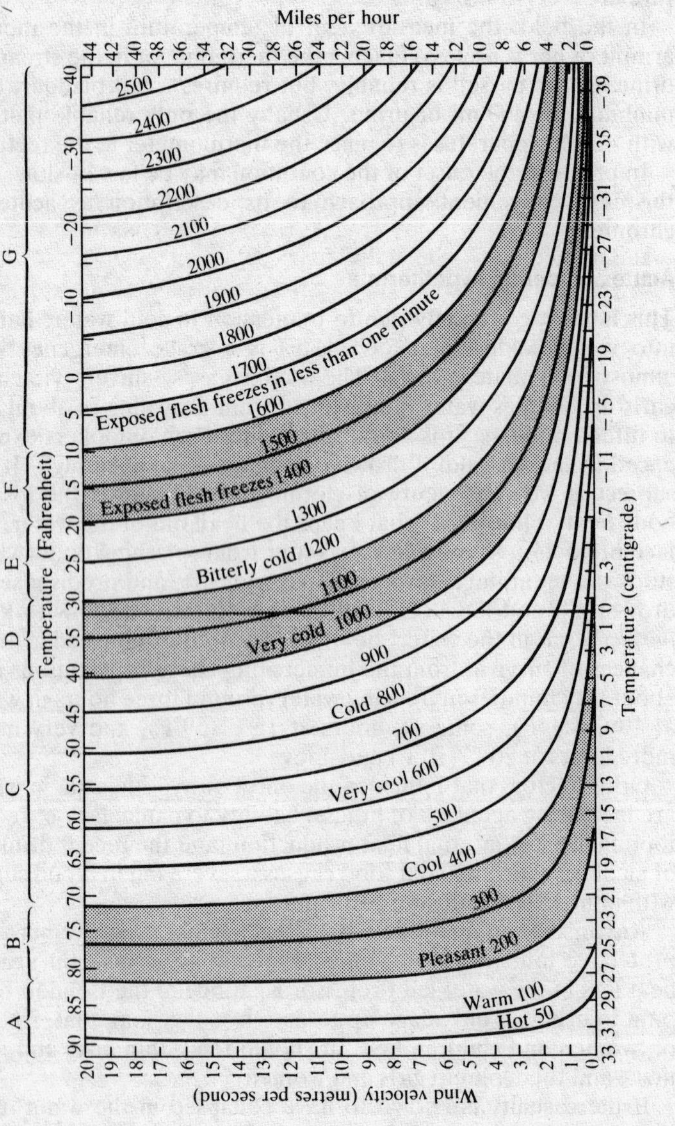
Miles per hour
Temperature (Fahrenheit)
Temperature (centigrade)
Wind velocity (metres per second)
A
B
C
D
E
F
G
2500
2400
2300
2200
2100
2000
1900
1800
1700
Exposed flesh freezes in less than one minute
1600
1500
Exposed flesh freezes 1400
1300
Bitterly cold 1200
1100
Very cold 1000
900
Cold 800
700
Very cool 600
500
Cool 400
300
Pleasant 200
Warm 100
Hot 50

most likely explanation. If he or she is conscious, can talk only clumsily, or is incoherent and cannot answer questions, then hypothermia is the diagnosis.

Do not constrict the chest with any harness or allow the victim to make any movement, especially climbing nets to board a ship or to clamber into a small boat—there have been many surprising deaths after rescue that are now thought to be due to sudden stress on a heart already grievously affected by the cold.

Ideally, the patient should be placed in the horizontal position, with the head slightly down, protected from further heat loss and taken immediately to a facility for rapid rewarming. Try to ascertain if water has been inhaled in however small a quantity, because hospital investigation is then urgent. In the meantime commence rapid re-warming in a bath (showers are not of any use) in which the water is kept at 42°C or as hot as the *bare elbow* can tolerate.

If the rectal temperature is being monitored during this treatment, it will be found that it continues to fall for the first fifteen minutes or so—the notorious 'after-drop', the significance of which is not yet completely understood. Resuscitation facilities should ideally be available—collapse may occur at any time until the patient is out of danger. If rapid (bath) re-warming is not available the victim must be allowed to 'come round' from his or her own internal heat production in a bed with duvet, 'space

---

Fig. 7.1 Wind chill index. (Modified from: Adam, J.M. (1969). *Community Health* 1, 39–46.)

The Wind Chill Index is indicated by the point at which the air temperature (vertical axis) and wind velocity (horizontal axis) cross; record it at hourly intervals to monitor deteriorating conditions.

Zone A No danger. *Zone B* Little danger when wearing light clothing provided meals are regular and overexertion avoided. Beware of a sudden deterioration in the weather. *Zone C* Requires full clothing protection, waterproof shelter, hot food and drink, prevention of overexertion. In the UK, most deaths from hypothermia occur in this zone. *Zone D* Travel becomes dangerous on overcast days—sudden rain, sleet, hail, or snow can be hazardous. *Zone E* Temporary shelter is dangerous to live in, travel should be contemplated only in heated vehicles. *Zone F* Exposed flesh starts to freeze. *Zone G* Exposed flesh freezes in less than one minute, and survival efforts are required.

blanket', or light blanket insulation only. The supply of external heat by electric lamp cradles, electric blankets, and the like requires a hospital environment, with intravenous fluids, oxygen, and injectable drug supplies ready to hand.

Chronic accidental hypothermia

This is defined here as being much longer in its onset than the foregoing, (which may require 20–30 minutes only, if the water is cold enough). The very young and the elderly are generally the most susceptible to hypothermia, but the accent here is on the middle age groups engaged in exploring, biological surveys and observations, hill-walking, mountaineering, or stranded in a cold and hostile environment. Commonest in the cold/wet climate, it is usually the product of soaked garments and a wind chill factor in zone C or above in Figure 7.1. It is often complicated by over-exertion, especially in those who are unprepared for sudden weather changes, who become lost and also have no reserve food or clothing, tent or sleeping bag. Mist, rain, sleet, hail, snow, and white-out may occur suddenly, and absence of map and compass, torch and whistle help to compound the situation.

Early recognition of the condition is of the greatest importance, and this requires one or more companions in a group (beware the lone ranger) who know each other well and can adopt the 'buddy system' to watch one another. Warning signs include complaints of feeling cold, tired, or listless; inability to keep the pace, progressing to stumbling and then repeated falls; unexpected, unreasonable, or uncharacteristic behaviour with unusual aggression; and failure to understand or respond to repeated questions or commands.

Uncontrollable bouts of shivering, which then cease, and disturbances of vision herald collapse and unconsciousness with dilated pupils. The victim's pulse at wrist or neck will be irregular. In the unlikely event that temperature measurement has been possible, it will have been about 35°C (95°F) at the start of the above list of signs and symptoms, and about 32°C (90°F) by the time the shivering is diminishing. The risk to life is now increasing and death may occur suddenly below 28°C (82°F), with disturbance of the heart rhythm and eventual cardiac arrest. The sooner the following action starts, the better the outcome:

1. *Stop* activity.

2. *Protect* from wind, rain, etc. by rigging a tent, poncho, or other bivouac or shelter, laying the victim in the 'head-down' position if he is conscious, or the coma position if not, on a groundsheet, 'space blanket', or in a large polythene bag.
3. *Insulate* him, having stripped the wet clothing if possible, with sleeping bag(s) covering head and face as well.
4. *Re-warm* him if unconscious by the body warmth of a companion—stripped and in bed beside him. If conscious, a quick 'brew-up' of hot sugary tea followed later by hot food will hasten recovery.
5. *Observe* for cessation of breathing or pulse when mouth-to-mouth resuscitation and/or external cardiac massage must start.
6. *Send* two people for help, but first give them tea and food in case they too are affected by the cold conditions.
7. *Treat* the patient as a stretcher case, no matter what may be said to the contrary. If he is injured, of course there will be no argument, and transport must be organized.

Frostbite

Local severe chilling of exposed or poorly insulated tissues—nose, cheeks, chin, ears, hands, and feet—can occasion freezing with or without the general chilling of hypothermia. The time required for the 'frost' to 'bite' depends on how cold it is, the degree of wind chill and the amount of tissue at risk. The last comprises either the area of skin exposed, or a tissue to which the blood supply has been restricted (i.e. by tight boots and matted socks where feet or toes are concerned). One patient of mine was a young soldier driving a Euclid earth-mover in winter-time Korea. His engine broke down as night was falling, so he curled up in the cab and fell asleep. The temperature dropped during the night, and the blood supply to his right foot was sufficiently impeded by his awkward posture to cause frostbite and eventual loss of the foot.

The initial warning of impending frostbite is intense pain in the part at risk, and at this stage the part must be re-warmed. The victim, however, may not be aware of the pain—from intense preoccupation, exhaustion, having suffered an injury, or from profound lethargy—and it eventually disappears. The part becomes numb, white and hard to the touch because it is frostbitten. 'Buddies' watch each other's faces for this.

Prevention of frostbite consists of being aware of the risk, keeping an eye on the wind chill index and discussing the conditions with local inhabitants, and wearing adequate protective clothing (see below).

Treatment At the painful stage of impending frostbite, the treatment follows the sequence set out above—stop, protect, insulate and re-warm the part. Cover nose, cheeks, or ears until shelter is erected and warm; hands and fingers are slipped under the clothes to the opposite armpit or between the thighs. Feet require the heroic test of friendship—through the clothing on to the belly of a companion! Pain will disappear and normal colour and sensation will indicate when danger is over. Take the opportunity to correct any other factors that may predispose to frostbite by changing wet clothing, producing a hot meal, or reminding one's companions of other dangers such as the touching of bare metal with bare hands—this can cause instantaneous freezing, as can slopping petrol on to bare skin.

Established frostbite is a serious problem, particularly when it involves fingers and hands, or feet and toes, when lasting damage may affect the victim's earning capacity in later life. A speedy but gentle journey to hospital is essential. Once frostbitten tissue has thawed, up to 3 month's of skilled medical attention may be necessary; moreover, if tissue once thawed is even slightly chilled again, it is liable to much more extensive damage. In an emergency involving a frozen foot (the worst) far from any hospital, there are three options:

- If the journey must be completed and no patient transport is available, remember that it is possible to walk on a frozen foot, though most certainly not on one that has thawed. Ideally hot food and drink are necessary, together with correction of any clothing defects. Give a pain-killer such as two tablets of paracetamol, with an oral antibiotic such as a penicillin or tetracycline in capsule or tablet form, dosage 250 mg every five to six hours day and night to combat any infection.
- If a stretcher with men to carry it, or alternatively a man or dog-drawn sledge is available, treat the victim in warm shelter as above, not omitting the pain-killers and antibiotics. Remove the

boot and sock as carefully as possible, cover the foot lightly with gauze, pad it with cotton wool, and wrap it up loosely. Make him or her comfortable and warm and immobilize the foot gently before setting off.

• If the patient is at a static base with medical advice available and the possibility of eventual evacuation, then the patient should stay put. Keep him or her in a room, where a high temperature can be maintained (about 21°C or 70°F). Elevate the part on a pillow with sterile precautions if available. Expose the foot to the warm air, wash it gently with an antiseptic solution such as warm 1 per cent cetrimide, dab it dry, inspect carefully and report the findings by radio for medical advice. This is likely to include the administration of a course of antibiotics and pain-killers as above.

If the fingers and/or hand are frostbitten, clean the skin area with the cetrimide solution and dab dry very gently. Separate the fingers with cotton wool after winding a sterile bandage around each, and place a thick sterile pad in the palm of the hand so that the fingers are in a 'glass-holding' position. Bandage the whole lightly and elevate the forearm in a sling. Commence a course of antibiotics and pain-killers as already outlined. Reassurance and gentle treatment are of the essence until the patient arrives at hospital.

Never rub frostbite with snow or anything else, because the delicate tissues will suffer more damage.

Immersion foot

Immersion foot occurs when the lower limbs and feet have been kept in cold conditions for hours or days, as happened in the trenches of World War I and in the life-boats after shipwreck during World War II. After the first sensation of cold passes off, the feet feel numb, and this continues for the long period of immobility and restriction of blood that is a prerequisite of the disorder. The patient may be unable to walk, or walks with difficulty, complaining that it feels like walking on cotton wool. Inadequate food, general chilling, lack of sleep, and exhaustion complete the typical picture.

On examination, the skin is blotchy-white, the ankles are swollen and marked deeply with pressure ridges from boots, etc. As the patient becomes warm, and the affected area is dried gently, the feet become hot, red and more swollen, and there is intense pain. The victim must be taken to hospital, and if this is likely to take time, should be treated with pain-killers and antibiotics as for frostbite. The legs must be elevated, protected from further damage and exposed in a warm room. Blisters may form on the feet in the first two days or so, and must be kept scrupulously (but gently) clean. It may be many months before an established case is able to return to work.

Chilblains

Chilblains are the mildest form of cold injury and are due to alternate exposure to wet/cold conditions and rapid re-warming. The disorder occurs frequently in the UK, where 50 per cent of the inhabitants are said to have suffered from it at one time or another. Prevention is by keeping the extremities warm, heating the house, eradicating draughts, and avoiding long periods of standing without moving (see also p. 345).

Clothing for cold conditions

Clothing should be well fitting and built up on the 'layer' principle from the innermost air-trapping layers to the outermost windproof and/or waterproof coverings. Each layer must be larger than the one beneath it to prevent constrictions and to preserve the insulating air. Neck and wrist openings are recommended as they permit ventilation by 'bellows action' so that water vapour from sweat can escape when one is working hard. Thus the inner layers do not become wet with condensed sweat, whence chilling could occur. Layers, too, may need to be donned and doffed for that same reason, as the work load dictates. I do not favour polo-necked sweaters because they cannot be ventilated.

Special requirements include the protection of the head which, in still air at 0°C, can lose one quarter of the entire body's heat production per hour; and this rate increases with lower air temperatures and higher wind chill. The peculiar shape of the feet and ankles make their insulation a problem, and great care should be exercised in the selection and fitting of socks and boots. Socks that are worn for too long become a double hazard by becoming matted or developing holes so that they lose insulation value, and by shrinking so that the blood supply to the toes and feet is impeded. Ensure a good overlap of sleeves with the gloves or mittens, because a strip of frostbite on the inner side of the wrist is extremely painful.

Summary of advice for travellers

Hot climates

- Full acclimatization takes about 3 weeks.
- Thirst sensation is a poor guide to your true water requirements in a hot climate—always drink more than you think you need.
- Salt requirements are also high—you may need to consider adding salt to drinking water, as described on p. 33.
- Guidelines for preventing and treating heat stroke and heat exhaustion are given on p. 286.

Cold climates

- No acclimatization is possible, so it is vital to be adequately prepared for cold conditions, with suitable clothing and equipment.
- Cold injuries and emergencies are described on p. 287.

Sun and the traveller

A suntan may be attractive and socially desirable, but obtaining one can have harmful effects both in the short and long term. Understanding the circumstances likely to lead to sunburn—and avoiding them—can help improve your trip.

Dr John Hawk *is a Consultant Dermatologist at St. John's Hospital, London, and Honorary Senior Lecturer in Photobiology at the Institute of Dermatology. His main research interests include the effects of sun upon the skin, and skin disorders that follow exposure to sunlight.*

The sun's rays have been this planet's energy source for the past 4500 million years. They have initiated and maintained life, both by providing warmth and light, and by fuelling specific important biological processes such as photosynthesis in plants, and the manufacture of vitamin D in human skin. Sunshine improves the quality of life, and has also been claimed to improve a person's overall work performance.

Unfortunately, not all solar energy is put to constructive use by living matter, and in many circumstances it may damage exposed substances: well recognized examples include effects on human skin such as sunburning, tanning, ageing, and cancer, and cataracts of the human eye.

Abnormal skin reactions also occasionally occur. As many as ten per cent of people develop an irritating, spotty rash within a few hours of sun exposure lasting for up to a week. This is not prickly heat, which it is sometimes mistakenly called, but polymorphic light eruption, a harmless condition usually kept in check by high protection factor sunscreens and avoidance of strong sunlight. Other abnormal reactions include excessive sunburning caused by photosensitivity to certain perfumes, cosmetics, sunbarrier creams, and medications taken by mouth or applied to the skin.

During man's evolution, protective responses have developed against these phenomena, in the form of tanning and thickening reactions of exposed skin. These occur however only as a result of sun damage and not before: thus although a brown skin may give good protection against further exposure, its acquisition through sun exposure rather than inheritance is always associated with skin injury.

If a tan however is still considered a social necessity, then it should be acquired gradually and carefully to minimize damage and its unpleasant consequences, both short term (sunburn) and long term (skin ageing and cancer).

Sun effects on the skin

The harmful rays

The damaging rays in sunlight are called ultraviolet radiation (UVR). Short-wavelength UVR, or UV-C, is most damaging to living cells, but is completely absorbed by oxygen and ozone in the atmosphere. If ozone layer depletion continues however, as a result of its destruction by chlorofluorocarbons from aerosols and other sources, UVC radiation will penetrate the atmosphere and lead to increased sunburning and skin cancer, and perhaps more important, death of much unicellular life with disruption of important ecosystems. Middle-wavelength UVR (called UV-B), also emitted by sunlamps, also has a marked tendency to produce sunburn. This is generally followed by tanning in susceptible people, and by skin ageing and cancer after long repeated exposures.

Long-wavelength UVR (called UV-A) also burns, but at much higher radiation doses than for UV-B and UV-C, and tanning usually occurs before burning. Chronic repeated exposure to UV-A also causes marked skin ageing, and accelerates or induces skin cancer. UV-A rays are the main component of UVR in sunlight and in sunbed radiation.

Circumstances leading to damage

The stronger the UVR in sunlight, the worse the skin damage following exposure. The amount of damage thus depends on the time, locality, and circumstances of the exposure.

UVR in sunlight is strongest when the sun is high in the middle of the day in summer. This intensity further increases near the equator and with increasing altitude. If there are also adjacent reflecting surfaces such as snow, metal, white materials, or rippling water, reflected UVR will further increase exposure. Sunburning is therefore particularly likely on beaches, at sea, in desert, and on ski slopes. Cool winds, haze, and light cloud do not much alter UVR intensity.

Sunburning does not occur only through direct exposure to the sun's rays, and shade may provide only a small amount of protection: much UVR can be scattered from a blue sky. Furthermore, UVR readily penetrates water, so that swimming gives little protection. Thin, close-fitting, or loose-weave clothing may also be of only moderate help.

Susceptibility to skin damage

The damage caused by sunlight at times of high UVR intensity also depends on the type of exposed skin. Black-skinned people are well protected against all the effects of the sun, and brown and yellow-skinned people are several times better off than white people, though they do burn if outdoors for long enough. Most white people burn relatively easily, particularly those with red hair and freckles. Others tan readily, sometimes with a little burning.

Most people know from experience how they react in sunlight with high UVR intensity, and should protect themselves accordingly. If their skin is completely unable to tan, as in albinos, or unable in patches, as in the disease vitiligo, great care is needed—although some protection still develops from superficial skin thickening.

While the early effects of sunlight are mainly a problem for sunbathers, watersports, or skiing enthusiasts, chronic effects such as ageing or cancer of the skin occur may occur in any outdoor enthusiast or tropical dweller, particularly if fair-skinned.

Harmful and helpful effects of UVR exposure

UVR penetrates the skin surface well, often better when the skin is wet or oily, and damages the nuclei and membranes of cells. Irritating chemicals released as a result cause damage to the surrounding tissues, leading to early and late visible changes:

Early: 1 Sunburn, i.e. redness, soreness, pinkness, or sometimes in severe cases swelling, blistering, or weeping of sun-exposed skin.

2 Tanning, i.e. formation of brown melanin pigmentation in the skin.

3 Hyperplasia, i.e. thickening of all skin layers, but particularly of the superficial dead horny layer.

Late: 1 Ageing, i.e. degenerative changes of chronically exposed skin, apparent as loss of substance, dryness, coarseness, yellowing, wrinkling, and laxity, with large blackheads, whiteheads, and spidery dilated blood vessels.

2 Precancers and cancers, i.e. persistent rough patches or irregular slowly growing lumps or sores coloured brownish, reddish, or dark.

All these changes are responses to injury, but the tanning and hyperplasia are also useful protective responses against further damage that work by partly absorbing subsequent radiation before it reaches vulnerable targets. However, acquisition and maintenance of tanning and hyperplasia always results in a degree of permanent injury never fully repaired.

The only potentially beneficial result of skin UV exposure is the production of vitamin D in the skin, but since adequate amounts are available in the normal diet, UV exposure for this reason alone is not necessary. It has also been claimed that UV exposure from sunlight improves mood and work rate, but any such improvement seems unlikely to result from the UV content of sunlight, and rather from the visible portion acting through the eye; skin exposure for this purpose is therefore inappropriate.

The only other sought-after effect of UV exposure is the purely cosmetic, subjective, and psychological one of having a tan. It should be understood however that this has no direct health-giving effect whatsoever!

Preparation for a sunny holiday

You need do very little, apart from obtaining a few tubes of sun-barrier cream from your pharmacist. Although courses of sun-lamp and sunbed treatment have been advocated to give a preliminary tan and consequent protection against later sun exposure, the advantages of this are extremely questionable.

Effects of sunlamps and sunbeds

Sunlamps, which are no longer very readily available, emit mostly UV-B and may well cause burning as well as tanning, and this with the associated hyperplasia may give some protection from later exposure. However, sunlamps are usually too small to obtain a tan over enough skin to be useful.

Sunbeds emit mostly UV-A and may induce good tanning without burning in people who tan well, but there is usually so little hyperplasia that overall protection from such a tan will be minimal, and other protection will still be necessary.

The only real reason for using sunlamps or sunbeds is thus essentially a cosmetic one and, like sunlight UV exposure, their use is not a healthy pastime: a small amount of skin damage always inevitably occurs. Often there are also other annoying side effects such as itching, dryness, redness, freckling, and occasionally drug rash, polymorphic light eruption, and a tendency to lessened skin resistance to minor injury. If you must use sunbeds, go to a reliable operator, such as, for example in the UK one belonging to the Association of Suntanning Operators, who will try to ensure that you are a relatively suitable candidate for treatment. If you are not, you may well end up with one of the side effects mentioned above, or you may not tan at all, so you could well be wasting your money.

If you are still desperate for a pre-holiday tan, exposure three times weekly (e.g. Monday, Wednesday, Friday) for two to three weeks until the holiday with either sunlamp or sunbed should give some colour, but regular use of a sunscreen when you arrive at your destination would be a better policy.

On holiday

Your intention on holiday should be to take full advantage of the enjoyable aspects of sun exposure while avoiding the harmful ones. So if you don't care about a tan, cover up, and wear loose-fitting but tightly woven airy clothes, best in cotton: and apply a highly protective sun-barrier cream (see below) to any remaining exposed areas every hour or so when you are outside.

If you insist on a tan, you should start by exposing unacclimatized skin for no more than about twenty minutes per day,when UVR intensity is high, for the first day or two; and apply a highly protective sun-barrier cream every hour or so, particularly after swimming or exercise. Over the next few days, gradually increase your exposure if you want to, and if your skin feels comfortable, apply the sunscreen a little less frequently or change to a preparation with a somewhat lower protection factor. At the end of a day in the sun, it is worth using a moisturizing cream from time to time to help minimize skin dryness and irritation.

If you tan readily, you should be fairly brown after about a week to ten days, although increasing tanning may gradually continue over a few more weeks. If you burn easily on any particular areas of the body such as the nose, lips, or particularly white patches, you will have to be especially careful. Conventional high protection sunscreens are effective, but zinc oxide or titanium dioxide-containing creams and pastes are particularly good for such areas, although cosmetically unsuitable for widespread use on the skin because of their white or brown colour.

If you decide to wear very little or to go topless, you will need to be very careful with the pale areas of skin, especially when the UVR intensity of the sunlight is high, and use a particularly high protection factor cream, as well as covering up sooner. If you ever start feeling uncomfortable and weatherbeaten, cover up.

In general, with a little thought and care, and with today's strong sun-barrier preparations, you should have no problems, and you should get your tan as well. However, carelessness and overdoing it on the first few days, will cause painful burning, swelling, blistering, and peeling, will result in a poor or patchy tan, and will leave you with a legacy of permanently damaged skin to increase your chances of later wrinkling and even skin cancer.

Sunscreens and tanning lotions

Use of sun-barrier preparations (also known as sunscreens, suncreams, and suntan oils or lotions) is a very effective way of protecting against much of the effect of UVR in sunlight, and some high protection factor preparations have recently been developed. There are two main types of these preparations: absorbent and reflectant.

Absorbent sunscreens are the well-known, conspicuously packaged, and pleasantly perfumed oils, creams, and lotions available in pharmacists as the indispensable adjunct to a wonderful holiday. They act by absorbing many of the potentially harmful UV rays before they reach the skin surface and then dissipating them as relatively innocuous heat. The advantages of the absorbent sunscreens are their cosmetic acceptability and their efficacy in protecting against UV-B. Their disadvantages are the ease with which they dry or wash off (most people need repeated applications), their tendency to produce an allergic rash on occasion, their tendency to irritate the skin immediately after application, and their relative inefficiency against UV-A rays.

Reflectant sunscreens, usually containing zinc oxide or titanium dioxide, are reserved mainly for occasional medical use, but may be applied thickly to limited areas such as lips and nose which are particularly liable to sunburning.

The efficacy of sunscreens can be gauged to a large extent from their experimentally estimated sun protection factor (SPF), a rough guide to the amount of protection they can give. The SPF tells how much longer you may stay in the sun if you apply the product regularly every hour or so during the day. For example, a product with an SPF 12 means you can stay exposed for about twelve times longer before you burn.

SPF values are approximate, so do not assume that a preparation of SPF 10 is necessarily much different from one of SPF 9 or 11. Cost is no guide whatsoever, so choose the cheapest product that suits you. If you find a sunscreen causes you unpleasant effects, change it. If you burn easily, you should start with a preparation of SPF 15–25. If you burn initially but later tan a little, look for an SPF 10–15. If you burn a little and tan well, choose an SPF of 5–10. If you do not burn, you need only an emollient or a cream of SPF less than 5. However, there is never any harm in choosing a higher SPF than you need.

Water-resistant sunscreens can be especially useful in children.

You may also want a lip-salve, or if your lips and nose burn easily, you may be better off with the white zinc oxide compound paste or similar coloured preparations now available. Cold sores are discussed on p. 360.

Buttocks and breasts need a higher SPF product than elsewhere. After a few days, when these areas start to tan, move to a lower SPF preparation or use the one you started with, but less often.

Tablets to protect against the sun have never been shown to work effectively, and the added possibility of adverse side-effects means you would best avoid them.

Pretanning agents are virtually useless, although artificial or fake tanning preparations, which stain the skin brownish for a few days, are harmless and do often provide a reasonable colour.

If you get a spotty red, itchy rash when using your sunscreen, it is usually not because of the sunscreen but because of polymorphic light eruption, the annoying but harmless condition mentioned earlier. Use a higher SPF sunscreen and cover up, but if the trouble persists, see a doctor.

Treatment

Too much sun exposure is harmful. It causes pain, redness, swelling, blistering, generalized redness, and occasionally scarring of the skin, as well as fever, coma, or even death in the short term, dryness, thinning, yellowing, wrinkling, coarseness, looseness, freckling, spidery vessels, or cancers of the skin in the long term.

The delayed effects cannot be reversed, except perhaps a little by plastic surgical techniques and to a lesser extent by use of moisturizers. The short-term effects can be only partially reversed as well, although of course they resolve spontaneously within hours or days.

Calamine cream or lotion soothes burnt areas, and mild analgesics such as aspirin and paracetamol relieve pain and inflammation. Indomethacin 25 mg tablets taken three times a day have been shown to provide a little help if taken soon enough after exposure, as may a lotion containing 0.25 per cent indomethacin in ethanol, propylene glycol, and dimethylacetamide (mixed in the proportion 19: 19: 2 by volume); this can be obtained from a doctor, although it is not regularly prescribed, and should be applied as soon as possible after sun exposure. Steroid creams (obtainable only on doctors' prescription) may also be slightly helpful.

However, none of these preparations reduces or averts the long-term effects of sun exposure, even if they may seem to help symptoms a little in the short term.

Treat severe sunburn in the same way as an ordinary heat burn, by protecting the area and keeping it clean to avoid infection.

For widespread severe sunburn, fluids and bed-rest with painkillers, steroid tablets and antibiotics may be necessary. Do not sunbathe the day after any bad burn, but allow healing to take place for a day or so.

Summary of advice for travellers

- Excessive sun exposure causes skin damage.
- Acute episodes of sunburn increase the risk of certain kinds of skin cancer.
- The best way of minimizing problems is to avoid excessive sun exposure in the first place rather than trying to treat the symptoms once they have occurred.
- Understanding the circumstances that lead to high UVR exposure, plus the use of suitable clothing and appropriate sunscreens where necessary should enable you to have a pleasant burn-free tanning holiday.

Water and watersports

Holidaymakers should prescribe for themselves a large dose of caution during their sea and lakeside adventures—and ensure some adequate training beforehand for more complex activities such as scuba diving.

Surgeon Lieutenant Commander Simon Ridout *is a medical officer in the Undersea Medicine Department at the Institute of Naval Medicine, Alverstoke, Gosport, UK. He has been diving for the Royal Navy and for sport for more than 10 years.*

Many people consider water and watersports an essential part of their holiday, but unfortunately most activities involving water—from swimming to snorkelling, scuba diving, sailing, windsurfing, and water-skiing—also involve some element of risk. Water in any form, from hotel swimming-pool to river, lake, lagoon or open sea, demands respect.

The old adage not to swim with a full stomach is correct, and alcohol is its most dangerous filling: half of all UK drownings in the 20 to 30-year-old age group take place after drinking. As a group, holidaymakers have a higher than average alcohol intake and would do well to remember that mixing alcohol with watersports all too often results in tragedy.

Swimming

Swimming-pools, fresh-water or sea-water, require filtration and cleansing unless the water is frequently changed. If this is not done conjunctivitis (infection of the eye) and ear infections are a hazard.

If the general cleanliness and hygiene standards of a hotel are satisfactory, its swimming-pool is likely to be safe.

Weil's disease (leptospirosis) occurs following exposure to water contaminated with infected rat urine. A few cases occur every year in people who swim in contaminated water, or are exposed through activities such as canoeing, rafting, and caving. Symptoms include a 'flu-like illness, fever, muscle pains, conjunctivitis and jaundice. Prompt antibiotic treatment is necessary.

Fresh-water lakes, dams, and slow-flowing rivers are all infected in countries where schistosomiasis (bilharzia) is endemic (p. 90). Do not be influenced by the attitude of local kids. They frequently have a low-grade chronic infection which gives rise to a partial immunity.

Sea water is safe from schistosomiasis. Other aspects of sea water and disease are discussed on p. 458. The open sea does pose the danger of tidal streams and currents: local advice should be sought if in doubt as to the strength of the tide. Few can swim against a current of one knot (nautical mile per hour) and even the strongest swimmer cannot swim against half a knot for very long. Swimming along the shore rather than out to sea is always safer, and reduces the danger of overestimating how far one can swim.

Sharks, sea-snakes, and other dangerous marine animals are another reason for caution. Local advice and custom should be sought: for example, some areas are safe by day but not by night. (See section on animal bites and stings, p. 191.)

Snorkelling

Snorkelling is an easy, cheap, and pleasant method of bridging the gap between the sea surface and its floor. It enables the swimmer to see the underwater world of fish and coral reefs. Snorkelling is safe provided a few simple rules are obeyed.

First, the right sort of equipment should be used. A mask is essential because, unlike fish, our eyes are not designed for use underwater: we require air in contact with the eyes in order to see clearly. As well as the eyes, the mask *must cover the nose*: during descent, the increasing pressure pushes the mask painfully against the face, but this can be counteracted by blowing some air through the nose into the interior of the mask. Snorkellers who use goggles without a nosepiece are liable to end up with black or bloodshot eyes: goggles should therefore be avoided.

The snorkel should be a simple J- or L-shaped tube about 2 cm in diameter and 35 cm long. Too long or too narrow a snorkel should be avoided as it will increase breathing resistance.

Do not take more than one deep breath prior to a dive. The urge to surface for another breath derives from the build-up of waste carbon dioxide in the blood rather than from the falling level of oxygen. Taking several deep breaths, or 'hyperventilating' before a dive delays the build-up of carbon dioxide, so that the snorkeller may use up all his oxygen and lose consciousness before the urge to surface and breathe again is felt. Hyperventilating prior to a dive in an attempt to stay underwater longer has led to many deaths by drowning.

Scuba diving

Scuba diving is an acronym for Self-Contained Underwater Breathing Apparatus—also known as an aqualung. Scuba or aqualung diving can be a fascinating pastime, but it is also potentially dangerous unless carried out with proper training beforehand and an appreciation of the risks involved and methods of avoidance. Some of the main medical and physiological hazards are described below, but newcomers to the sport should realize that these are not the *only* hazards (or necessarily the most common ones) and would be well advised to undergo a full training course before attempting even a supervised dive in open water on page 259.

Medical fitness

Anyone intending to take up aqualung diving should have a medical check-up first. Most diving clubs in the UK and dive centres in other countries will not allow you to use aqualung equipment unless you can produce a medical certificate—and obtaining a certificate abroad can be difficult and expensive.

A medical history of chronic ear and sinus disease, severe head injury or cranial surgery, asthma, bronchitis, pneumothorax, heart disease, or chest surgery is sufficient to make you unfit to dive, as your body will be unable to cope with the stresses imposed underwater. A history of epilepsy means a complete ban on diving, and diabetics should not dive because of the risk of hypoglycaemia and a probable increased tendency to decompression sickness (the 'bends').

The medical check-up should include a chest X-ray to look for signs of chest disease that are not detected by the physical examination.

Effects of pressure

On land, our bodies are subject to atmospheric pressure—the pressure exerted by the column of air that extends for ten miles

Scuba diving abroad

- A basic aqualung training course should include instruction and practice in the use of diving equipment (including buoyancy control and life-jackets); safety and emergency procedures including life-saving; lectures on the theory and practice of diving, the various hazards involved and their avoidance; and the supervised acquisition of experience, beginning in a swimming-pool or shallow water and gradually progressing to deeper dives in open water. A full-time course covering the above could be expected to take two to three weeks.
- In addition to physiological hazards caused by pressure changes, divers have to learn to deal with all sorts of other stresses, which range from mask-flooding to air-supply failure, from buoyancy problems to zero underwater visibility. While a trained diver will be able to cope with such eventualities, a succession of such mishaps can rapidly reduce the novice to a state of helplessness or panic, with disastrous results.
- Travellers thinking of taking up diving on holiday should undergo some basic training—for example via a local branch of the British Sub-Aqua Club (BSAC) or in the USA at any dive school run by instructors certified by the Professional Association of Diving Instructors (PADI) or National Association of Underwater Instructors (NAUI). Alternatively, a number of dive centres abroad offer formal instruction on courses lasting two to three weeks.
- Most diving centres abroad apply stringent safety procedures and will not hire out equipment or organize dives except for those who can produce a recognized certificate of competence (such as the BSAC 'sports diver' qualification) or have undergone the centre's own training course. In some places however, a beginner may be offered a 'try-out' dive with little or no instruction or supervision, while at the same time being asked to sign an insurance disclaimer absolving the dive centre of any responsibility in the event of an accident. *This arrangement is best avoided unless you are unconcerned about your safety*: beginners should insist on several hours' instruction in the basic techniques, and on their first few dives, the accompaniment and *undivided attention* of an experienced instructor.

or so above our heads. Underwater, pressure increases rapidly: in fact, with every ten metres of depth, the pressure increases by an additional one atmosphere (also called one bar). Thus at ten metres depth, the total pressure is two bars or twice the surface pressure, and at thirty metres it is four times the surface pressure.

Fluid-filled parts of the body are not affected by the increase in pressure but air-filled parts, such as lungs, ears, and sinuses, are noticeably affected. Unless the pressures inside and outside the body are equalized, the higher pressure squeezes the lower pressure and causes tissue damage and pain.

Lungs

Charged aqualung cylinders contain air at high pressure (up to 200–250 bars); the aqualung regulator (which delivers the air to the diver's mouth) is designed to reduce this pressure and supply air to the diver at the same pressure as that being exerted externally on his chest, irrespective of his depth. Thus at ten metres, air is supplied to the diver at a pressure of two bars, and at thirty metres at a pressure of four bars. In this way, the pressure of air in the diver's mouth is equalized to the external pressure, and breathing is just as easy as at the surface, apart from a slight resistance to the air-flow caused by the regulator. During ascent, however, the air in the lungs expands as the external pressure drops *and if the diver makes the mistake of holding his or her breath, the lungs will overinflate with the risk of a 'burst lung'* (see below).

Ears and sinuses

During descent, some discomfort or pain is usually experienced in the region of the eardrums and less obviously over the forehead, due to the difference between the external pressure of air in the ears and the sinuses. This discomfort is easily relieved by pinching the nose and (by means of a little expiratory effort as though you were sneezing) forcing some additional air up into the sinuses and middle ear, via natural passages connecting these structures to the back of the nose (see p. 228).

During ascent, this additional air escapes back out again without any action on the part of the diver. Problems are rarely encountered except when injury or illness has caused damage to the air passages, or during a heavy cold when the passages may be blocked by mucus: diving with a heavy or even moderate cold is inadvisable.

Diving illnesses

Decompression sickness, also known as the 'bends', can always be avoided by diving within the rules of well-tried diving tables. Under pressure, more nitrogen is dissolved in the body tissues. The amount dissolved depends upon the depth (pressure) and time spent under pressure. If the pressure is released quickly, bubbles of nitrogen come out of solution into the body tissues (just like gas bubbles appearing in a bottle of lemonade when the top is released) and cause the symptoms of decompression sickness.

The symptoms depend upon where the bubbles are released. Joint pains are the most common, but more serious symptoms are caused if the bubbles affect either the spinal cord or the brain. Weakness or numbness of the limbs, difficulty in passing urine, disturbance of vision or balance are all symptoms of decompression sickness. Decompression sickness symptoms usually appear within three hours of a dive but may be delayed for up to twenty-four hours.

Treatment of decompression sickness requires recompression of the diver in a recompression chamber (commonly but mistakenly called a decompression chamber) to force the offending bubbles of nitrogen back into solution. Oxygen is also breathed to speed the elimination of nitrogen from the body. The chamber operator then follows a schedule, called a therapeutic table, for bringing the recompressed diver safely back to the surface pressure.

In the absence of a recompression chamber the diver should be given oxygen to breathe while transport is arranged to the nearest chamber, if necessary by low-level flight in an aircraft or helicopter. (Water and aspirin are also a useful emergency treatment to reduce blood viscosity.) Never try to treat decompression sickness by diving again. This will make the diver worse rather than better.

Decompression sickness can be avoided by always ascending slowly from a dive (no faster than 15 m/min) and diving within the rules of a set of diving tables. These indicate what 'stops', if any, the diver should carry out during the ascent to release the nitrogen safely from the body tissues.

Any aqualung training course should include instruction in the use of diving tables, which cannot be described in detail here. Remember always to err on the side of safety when calculating safe dive times, depths, and decompression stops.

Decompression computers have recently become available in the UK and other diving areas. They appear attractive because divers are given greater time under water when diving a variable depth profile in which there is gradual ascent throughout the dive, compared to traditional dive tables which assume a rectangular dive profile. However diving computers should be used with great caution because they give data based on mathematical predictions which have not been tested during extensive immersion in water diving trials. Traditional diving tables, for example Royal Naval or US Naval tables, have been extensively tested. The introduction of diving computers into the UK has been associated with a marked increase in the prevalence of decompression sickness. It is at present too early to state if this is because the computer calculations are based on incorrect data, or because the computers are being misused.

Burst lung While ascending from a dive, the air in the lungs expands as the pressure reduces. Normal breathing allows this excess air to be dispersed. If, however, divers either hold their breath, or have a pre-existing lung disease that causes air to be trapped in the lungs, problems can occur. As trapped air expands it can cause the lung to burst. The medical term for this is pulmonary barotrauma. The air escapes from the lungs, may enter the bloodstream, and may reach the brain via the heart. A bubble of air in the brain can cause a blockage of blood flow and dramatic symptoms. This is known as arterial gas embolism.

The symptoms of pulmonary barotrauma and arterial gas embolism always occur either on surfacing or within the first ten minutes after surfacing. The symptoms include coughing up blood, chest pain, shortness of breath, confusion, visual disturbances, weakness or paralysis, convulsions, or unconsciousness. The need for treatment is urgent—recompression in a chamber is required.

Burst lung is unlikely with correct training, which teaches divers to avoid holding their breath while ascending, and thorough medical screening, which prevents those with past or present chest disease from diving.

Nitrogen narcosis

A further important physiological hazard of diving is nitrogen narcosis. Although also caused by the presence of nitrogen in the body, this is quite different from decompression sickness in that the symptoms appear at *depth* rather than during or after the ascent.

Below a depth of around 30–40 metres, nitrogen builds up in the bloodstream to a level at which it may have toxic effects on the brain quite similar to the effects of alcohol or drug intoxication. Although nitrogen narcosis has been described as 'rapture of the depths', the symptoms are not necessarily pleasant, with a feeling of detachment from reality, possibly fear or apprehension, and most dangerously a loss of concentration and slowing of thought processes. The symptoms become more acute the deeper the diver descends below forty metres. Fortunately, nitrogen narcosis is fairly easily dealt with by ascending 5–10 metres, when the symptoms will clear.

Fifty metres should be considered as the absolute maximum depth for sports diving, below which it becomes unacceptably dangerous. This is for three reasons. First, mental co-ordination and thought processes are slowed due to nitrogen narcosis, limiting the diver's ability to act correctly in an emergency. Secondly, the high density of the air that is being breathed under pressure increases the diver's work of breathing, limiting physical performance. And finally, decompression tables have not been well tested and are less reliable below this depth.

Other diving problems

Other problems are more minor but far more frequent. The ears are the most usual cause of trouble. In either polluted or warm tropical water infection of the outer ear canal (*otitis externa*) may occur. This leads to a painful ear. It is easily prevented by showering in fresh water after the dive and drying the ear canal by shaking the head. Do not try to dry the ear canal with a towel, cotton wool or a finger. In practice, I have not found *otitis externa* to be a problem when these simple rules are applied. Infection of the middle ear (*otitis media*) is caused by bacteria from the nose or throat entering the ear while diving. This is another reason for not diving with a cold, sore throat, or chest infection.

Cuts and grazes sustained while diving in tropical waters may take up to three months to heal if nematocysts (p. 210) or other micro-organisms have entered the wound. Wounds are easily prevented by wearing either a wetsuit or a pair of overalls if the water is very warm. Underwater photographers are particularly at risk, as they concentrate on looking through their camera viewfinders and miss seeing a coral outcrop.

Diving and air travel

Finally, at the end of a diving holiday, it is not safe to fly home immediately after a dive. The decreased pressure, even in a pressurized aircraft, can bring on an attack of the bends. No dive requiring decompression stops (or for complete safety, no dive to a depth greater than nine metres) should be undertaken in the twenty-four hours prior to a flight (p. 231).

Sailing, windsurfing

Sailing and windsurfing pose few medical problems. A sense of balance is needed for windsurfing. Always sail upwind first, not downwind, or along a coast rather than out to sea. This lessens the dangers if the wind strength increases while sailing. Windsurfers can quickly tire in a strong wind and become exhausted, particularly in cold water. There are many types of protective clothing available. These are either wetsuits or drysuits both of which if correctly fitted will retain body heat without causing overheating during strenuous activity. Do not overestimate your abilities and sail into dangerous waters. Wearing a life-jacket or other buoyancy device is always advisable, however experienced you are.

Water-skiing

Water-skiing is quickly learnt by anyone with a sense of balance and timing. Unless high-speed or competition water-skiing is tried, the risks are few. Always wear a life-jacket in case you are stunned when falling into the water. Women should prevent a high-speed vaginal douche by wearing an adequate bikini or swimsuit which provides protection. For competition or high-speed water-skiing, a wetsuit should be used to help cushion the blow when falling on to water at high speed.

Skiing

Most ski injuries can be prevented by preparation, instruction, care on the slopes, and awareness of potential hazards.

Mr Basil Helal *is a Consultant Orthopaedic Surgeon at the London Hospital and the Royal National Orthopaedic Hospital. He is a medical adviser to the British Olympic Association.*

Skiing is an exhilarating pastime providing exercise, often in a majestic environment. It is one of the fastest growing sports, and between half and three-quarters of a million British skiers now take ski holidays abroad each year.

There are three main forms: downhill skiing; Nordic (cross country) skiing; and ski mountaineering. 'Hot-dogging' is a form of acrobatics on skis, and ski jumping or 'flying' is for the few who dare. 'Figling' is done on boot length Figl skiis and generally used to ski over fresh avalanched snow. For the very expert, there is also the monoski, with platforms for both feet, and the surfboard.

Each has its advocates. Perhaps ski mountaineering provides the purist with the most attractive elements that this form of sport can offer.

However, unless skiers are aware of the possible hazards they face, and take careful steps to protect themselves, skiing can also be a most dangerous pastime.

Preparation

Selection of ski garments

Clothing should be warm, waterproof, and windproof. The outer garment—anorak and salopet—should in addition be easily visible against the snow and should not be so smooth as to allow frictionless descent down a mountain after a fall.

Hats and helmets Around 20 per cent of body heat loss can take place through the head—so an adequate, warm, waterproof head covering which will also protect the ears is mandatory. Children can easily damage the skull in falls and collisions; a child's skull is not as strong as an adult's and crash helmets are strongly advised.

A facemask to protect from high wind and driving snow is also a valuable asset.

Goggles or glasses should either have photosensitive lenses or should have exchangeable lenses for varying conditions. They should protect against driving snow and high wind, and against strong sunlight. They should also provide side cover for the eyes, and this is especially important for ski mountaineering.

Mittens are warmer than gloves. A thin pair of warm gloves, cotton or silk, worn inside the mitten allows one to handle metal bindings without getting a 'cold burn' in very low temperatures.

Socks The 'tube' type are very good. A dry spare pair is always worth carrying especially if ski mountaineering or touring are envisaged.

Ski gaiters should be worn by anyone planning to ski in deep snow, to prevent snow from entering the boots.

Undergarments should be light and allow freedom of movement. Two thin layers provide more insulation than one thick layer.

A small backpack or knapsack does not interfere with skiing and can be used to carry clothes that are not needed—weather conditions change rapidly and in any case it is much cooler towards the end of the day—as well as any extra items such as bandages and a screwdriver that may prove useful.

Selection of skis, boots, bindings, and poles

Ski boots should be comfortable and allow some toe movement. Boots that are adjustable for heel grip and midfoot grip as well as for ankle grip are preferred.

A different, softer boot is required for climbing on skis, and for Nordic skiing a special shoe with a toe extension is necessary.

Bindings anchor the boot to the ski and are designed to release if an undue force is applied in a rotational or forward pitch direction. They should be adjusted according to the weight, bone thickness, and strength of the subject, and this is best done by an expert. The bindings require some momentum to release easily, so the most dangerous fall is a 'slow' one.

Special bindings which allow the heel to rise when climbing but anchor for skiing are necessary for the ski mountaineer, and quite different bindings, which provide only a toe grip, are used in Nordic or cross country skiing.

Skis should be selected with care. They should not be too long, as this makes turning more difficult. The short, wide 'Scorpian' ski is ideal for the beginner, who can graduate to longer skis with an increase in expertise. Longer skis increase leverage on the leg in a fall (see below).

Ski poles These should be of correct length, and the loops should break away on a strong tug.

General fitness

A high degree of general fitness is desirable, for skiing is an energetic pastime and is carried out at altitudes where the pressure of oxygen may be lower than that to which most skiers are accustomed in their home environment; exercise is an essential part of preparation.

Running is most suitable for those who are accustomed to it, but can cause stress injuries in those who take it up suddenly and intensively in a last minute attempt to get fit for a skiing holiday. It should preferably be carried out on grass or forest floor rather than on concrete or asphalt.

Cycling is much less traumatic and besides improving fitness, will also serve to strengthen the muscles that are used in skiing.

Leg strength Exercise specifically intended to strengthen the quadriceps muscles should be dynamic and not static; otherwise patellar chondromalacia (softening of the articular surfaces of the knee cap) may ensue.

Practising ski skills on dry slopes Dry slopes are sensible places for beginners to become familiar with ski equipment and basic skills, but dry slope skiing carries its own hazards. Most artificial ski surfaces consist of nylon brush squares; falls can be abrasive, and if the thumb is caught in this surface its ligaments are easily torn.

Special equipment

Ski mountaineers need other special equipment, such as avalanche detectors, harnesses (e.g. Whillan's) and rope, and extra protection such as a cagool (a light windproof overcoat).

Environmental hazards

Altitude (see also pp. 268–75)

Skiing generally involves ascent to altitudes of 10–12 000 feet or over, where the atmospheric pressure is lower and the air is drier. Oxygen transfer to the lungs is less easy.

Altitude or mountain sickness can be very dangerous, and can cause both pulmonary and cerebral oedema; diuretic treatment and oxygen may be of some help, but descent to a higher pressure zone is the safest answer if there is no response to other forms of treatment. An early diuresis (passage of a large volume of urine) on ascent seems to indicate good adaptation to altitude. Minor symptoms are relatively common, especially at some of the higher ski resorts.

More evaporation occurs at altitude, and the nasal passages dry more easily, especially during sleep when this is often exacerbated by central heating. It is best to increase fluid intake—have an extra drink of water before you go to bed, even if you don't feel especially thirsty. Try also to keep the humidity in the bedroom high—a bowl of water or wet towels on the radiators can be very helpful in preventing a dry sore throat.

Cold (see also pp. 290–8)

Skiing requires snow—except on artificial surfaces, of course—and alas sometimes there is ice and water too. Unless you're unlucky with conditions, you are likely to be skiing at temperatures around 0°C or lower.

Skiing also requires muscular effort and this is optimal at body temperature or slightly above (40°C). Getting yourself chilled is at best uncomfortable and at worst can be fatal, so it is wise to be prepared.

Insulation Several layers of clothing will trap air at body temperature efficiently (p. 298). Generally speaking, clothes made from cellular materials, especially natural fibres, are best, and animal fur is the warmest. As mentioned previously the outermost layer should be windproof and not too slippery.

Wind The chill factor in wind can lower the effective air temperature rapidly and substantially. Thus with a wind speed of 20 m/sec, 0°C will feel the same as −50°C on a windless day (p. 292).

Damp Insulation is rapidly degraded if clothing becomes wet. Wise skiers therefore carry a dry pair of woollen socks in a plastic bag, for feet can easily get wet when skiing in deep powder snow.

Heat conservation If cooled, the body tries to preserve its central core temperature. Heat loss is reduced by reflex constriction of the skin blood vessels. Heat is produced by muscle activity and this is the reason for the shivering reaction. Anything that reduces activity such as being stranded on a chair lift or on a drag lift can result in a rapid fall in temperature, and it is best to try to maintain some movement of the limbs under these circumstances. Similarly, concussion or any injury which results in immobilization will cause a rapid fall in temperature.

Alcohol Heat loss is increased by dilatation of the blood vessels of the skin; alcohol is a vasodilator—so beware. (Like drinking and driving, drinking and skiing do not mix; drinking increases the risk of an accident on the slopes.)

Cold injury The skin itself is at risk from injury, and the skier should carry a face mask to protect the nose and cheeks, and warm headgear which can come over the ears. The lips are also vulnerable. Frost 'nips'—white patches on the skin which are numb—should have external warmth applied rapidly. Rubbing is dangerous, however, and can further damage the skin. Frostbite involves freezing of the deeper tissues and starts at the tips of the fingers and toes. Rapid and careful rewarming is essential.

Hand protection In practice the hands are better protected by a mitten than a glove for this allows better movement of the fingers. Remember that for handling of metal portions of equipment at very low temperatures a light cotton glove worn inside the mitten will protect against a cold burn. On no account should metal at temperatures below −10°C be handled even with warm hands as skin will blister or adhere to the metal.

Children Children are particularly susceptible to cold injury and even frost nipped hands and feet can suffer permanent damage with subsequent distortion of or stunting of growth. Make sure that children stay warm, and inspect them repeatedly if they are playing in snow, snowballing, etc.

Cigarettes Among the many harmful effects of cigarettes is vasoconstriction, or clamping down of blood vessels at the extremities. This has been well established by thermographic and doppler tests. So please do not give injured skiers a 'steadying' smoke—it may quite literally result in loss of their fingertips and toes.

Cold collapse is a response to a falling core temperature and to a reduction in the blood sugar level. Brain function fails if the core temperature falls below 35°C (95°F). Early signs include weakness with frequent falls, followed by a stage of aggressive behaviour which goes on to apathy, and then collapse and loss of consciousness.

Rewarming Rapid warming is essential and a fit person's body heat is perhaps the best emergency solution. If both victim and rescuer huddle together in a thermal blanket (which is made of light foil, can fold to the size of a handkerchief and can be carried in a skier's pocket) or a sleeping bag if one is available, there is an excellent chance of raising core temperature to a safe level—particularly if the partner is of the opposite sex!

If the limbs are frostbitten do not thaw them if there is a likelihood of refreezing and do not rub the frozen part as this will further damage the skin.

Back in civilization the accepted method of restoring the core temperature is by immersion in a warm bath (40–44°C) until flushing of digital pulps (fingertips) occurs. Blisters should be kept intact if possible and antibiotics given to prevent infection of any damaged tissue; use open dressings to allow easy inspection.

Survival in the cold

Failing visibility, perhaps due to mist or fog, may cause a delayed return. At nightfall, there is usually a marked drop in temperature. If there is no hope of reaching shelter or even some doubt, construct an igloo or a substantial snow hole and huddle if there are a number of you or curl up tight to reduce the surface area from which heat loss can occur if you are alone. This will give you the best chance of survival.

People with certain medical conditions should take particular care to avoid chilling or placing themselves at this risk: they include sufferers from previous heart attacks, chronic bronchitics, people with poor circulation, and some people in whom low temperature causes their red blood cells to break down (this is a form of allergy to cold).

Sun

Sunburn is a real hazard in the clear mountain atmosphere and barrier creams should always be worn, particularly by the fair skinned (see p. 305).

Reflected glare from expanses of white snow can cause severe eye damage—conjunctival burns and even *uveitis* leading to so called snowblindness (see also p. 361). This is best prevented by wearing adequate sunglasses, possibly with side protectors.

Visibility

Conditions may change very rapidly and in certain flat light conditions it is impossible to identify hollows, drops, and rises; skiing 'blind' is very difficult and can be most dangerous.

Even worse are conditions of heavy mist or driving blizzards. Often under such circumstances it is better to ski where there are trees as these provide light contrast and visibility is much improved.

Terrain

Cliffs are especially dangerous in poor visibility. Crevasses are fissures in the earth that are often concealed by a bridge of snow. Some are large and deep, and there is danger of injury or death from the fall. Others are narrower and a skier may be trapped a few feet down, be unable to move and die from hypothermia if rescue is not rapidly to hand.

Collision can produce serious injury; obstacles include trees, buried rocks, and other skiers. If a skier wishes to stop he or she should do so off the piste or track, and away from the bottom of a run.

Avalanche

Avalanches normally occur on steep slopes where there is

already a substantial depth of snow, and the risk is greatest usually when the weather changes and there is a sudden rise in temperature.

They can be triggered by noise or by skiers, and also occur spontaneously.

In most ski resorts automatic devices are placed to set them off before they can cause harm; they are precipitated by small grenade explosions.

There are two types of avalanche—the soft snow avalanche which forms a wave, or the slab avalanche in which heavy blocks of snow and ice come away.

Two types of injury occur—crushing and drowning.

Avalanche survival

If an avalanche starts above you, try to ski away from its line of fall. If you have time, take off your skis, and hyperventilate so as to be able to hold your breath for as long as possible if you are covered. Curl up and protect your head, and hang on to your ski poles.

Once covered, try to create an air space. Do not panic, but push the ski poles up to see if you can create a breathing hole, then gradually move snow down from the roof to the floor of your hole, packing it below as you go.

If you are caught high up by the avalanche, spreadeagle, and try to ride the surface and swim as you would surf-ride a wave.

Hazards from lift equipment

Cable cars Cable cars have been known to crash from a height, but such accidents are exceptionally uncommon.

Chair lifts Poor co-ordination when joining or leaving a chair lift can result in injury. The chair can give the unwary skier a sharp knock. People have also been injured by falling out of chairs and by having articles of their clothing hooked or trapped by the chair as they alight. Failure of the lift system, leaving the unfortunate skier trapped, suspended, and very cold, can provide a powerful temptation to try and jump off. Don't—even mild frostbite is preferable to severe injury or death.

Drag lifts T-bars and tow bars can entangle with clothing, or if released at the wrong moment can recoil against other skiers and cause injury.

Acclimatization and orientation

On arrival at the ski resort, allow yourself time to acclimatize. The higher the resort, the longer this may take.

Check that your clothes and equipment are suitable and in good order. Obtain a map of the ski area and select runs that are appropriate for your experience and ability.

It is important to obtain adequate insurance for yourself and your equipment as well as third party insurance (see pp. 256–7). In isolated mountain resorts, medical costs are high and facilities and standards are sometimes poor; medical insurance should be sufficient to cover the cost of bringing you home by air ambulance, if necessary.

Ski injuries

The average overall injury rate is 4 per 1000 'skier days'.

In a recent survey, 58 per cent of injuries were in beginners, with 36 per cent in intermediate skiers, and 6 per cent in expert skiers.

Not surprisingly, leg injuries are most common—and in another survey, accounted for 86 per cent of all injuries. Of these, 45 per cent were knee injuries, and 43 per cent were tibial (shin) fractures. Eight per cent of injuries involved the arms—mainly wrist fractures—and four per cent were shoulder dislocations.

Equipment factors

There are three important ways that the ski itself can produce injury. Firstly, it acts as a lever on the leg; a torque of as little as seven kilograms at the tip of a ski can produce a fracture of the tibia (shin bone). Modern rigid ski boots protect the foot, ankle and lower tibia from this kind of injury, but in doing so inevitably transfer stress to the knee, making ligamentous injuries at the knee joint an increasingly common hazard.

Secondly, if the bindings release a ski during a fall, and the ski is tethered to the ankle by a safety strap, the tethered ski may recoil against its owner; ski edges are sharp, and can produce severe lacerations. 'Ski stoppers'—a pair of prongs which project below the under-surface of the ski when the boot has been released from the binding are preferable to safety straps. (Some skiers reduce the risk of losing skis without safety straps in deep snow by trailing ribbons from their bindings when skiing in deep powder).

Thirdly, a 'rogue' ski—released during a fall—can become a dangerous projectile if it accelerates unchecked down a slope. It may strike or impale other skiers in its path. Ski stoppers reduce the likelihood of this occurrence.

Check that your bindings release under reasonable force. They should have been adjusted professionally according to the size of your bones, your general muscularity, and experience, but you should always test them yourself. Do not handle the bindings or any other metal with your bare hands when temperatures are below freezing, or a cold burn will result.

Boots must be comfortable and hold the foot firmly so that movement is transmitted instantly to the ski, thereby protecting the ankle from injury.

Ski poles can cause injury, especially to the thumb; the strap and ski pole handle should never be held in such a way that the thumb may become trapped.

You should always be able to see both hands in front of you when you are skiing. Holding the poles close in to one's side can be dangerous, especially upon reaching the bottom of a slope, where a sudden rise uphill can drive the pole handle up and into the eye; I have seen an eye enucleated by this form of accident. One other important point about the ski pole is that its loop should break loose with a strong tug. If its basket catches, on trees or brush, for instance, a severe injury to the shoulder can occur if the loop does not release. Such an injury can commonly result in a dislocation of the shoulder, but can also cause a less common but more serious injury—a traction injury on the *brachial plexus*, damaging the main nerves that enter the arm from the neck to supply the muscles and sensation of the upper limb; permanent paralysis may ensue.

Other contributory factors

Many important factors that contribute to the risk of injury are under a considerable degree of individual control:

- *Fatigue* The majority of ski injuries occur on the first day of a ski holiday, especially towards the end of the morning or afternoon session. Make sure you stop skiing well before the stage when you are feeling tired and your legs ache.

- *Inexperience* There is no substitute for skilled, *professional* ski instruction, so don't try to get by without lessons.
- *Poor technique* Having attained a basic level of proficiency, don't become complacent about the need to improve your technique further. Lessons are not just for beginners.
- *Excessive speed*, especially dangerous on crowded slopes, often causes collisions with other skiers accounting for up to 10 per cent of accidents.
- *Poor surface and conditions:* avoid them.

If you need to rest, do this off a run. The worst possible places to stop are near the bottom of a run and in the middle of the piste. This invites a collision.

Ligaments

Whilst skiing, the body's weight is borne by one or other leg unless one is travelling directly downhill. Unlike the straight knee, the *flexed* knee permits a degree of rotation without damage to ligaments. An important principle to remember is that in an unstable or uncontrolled situation, totally unloading the inactive ski (usually the uphill one) and further flexing the knee bearing your weight will protect the ligaments from damage; sitting down may be undignified on skis, but ignominy is preferable to any sort of injury.

First aid management

In the event of an injury, first aid treatment is most important in order to avoid compounding any damage that may have occurred. No skier who feels even moderate pain or the least instability on standing should ever attempt to continue skiing. A further fall may result in a much more serious injury. Any doubt about the integrity of joints, ligaments, or bone must be treated seriously and the part protected by splintage until such time as an expert opinion can be obtained. The vast majority of doctors practising in ski resorts are very experienced and generally give wise counsel. Local orthopaedic surgeons usually give an extremely good service. There is, however, in some places a tendency to resort to surgery when perhaps a conservative line of treatment would suffice. A patient can always request immobilization and return home for treatment by a surgeon of his or her choice.

Conclusion

Despite its many hazards skiing is an enjoyable pastime. If the advice and precautions mentioned are observed then the small risk of injury can be reduced even further.

'Apres ski' activity has its pleasures and its hazards, but that is another story.

Psychotropic drugs

The use and acceptability of mind-altering drugs varies from one country to another. Travellers who hazard the consumption of such drugs do so at their own risk, but should realize that locally-produced substances may have unexpectedly potent and possibly dangerous effects and that the penalties for illegal possession are frequently severe.

Dr Martin Mitcheson *is the Clinical Director of the South West Regional Drug Advisory Service and the Avon Drug Problem Team, UK.*
Roger Lewis *is a research specialist in international drug traffic and is the author of a number of studies of illicit drug makers in Britain, Italy, and elsewhere.*

In almost every society in the world, mind-altering or *psychotropic* substances are used for recreational, ritual, and medical purposes. Just as different nations favour different pharmaceutical, homoeopathic, and folk preparations, they also display preferences for different types of social and recreational drug use. These preferences are influenced by such factors as the plant life indigenous to the region, traditional familiarity with particular drug effects, the impact of aggressive colonial marketing, and the solace and oblivion that some drugs may provide for individuals suffering from boredom, poverty, and privation or ethnic groups threatened with extinction or assimilation.

Patterns of psychotropic drug use worldwide

Tobacco and alcohol

Tobacco and alcohol are, broadly speaking, available throughout the world, although some Islamic countries such as Saudi Arabia impose severe penalties upon individuals who consume, or traffic in, the latter.

Cannabis

Cannabis, known in its various preparations as hashish, ganja, marijuana, bush, grass, and countless other names, grows or can be cultivated in most parts of the world. Since the 1960s one of the attractions of countries such as India, Pakistan, and (until recently) Afghanistan to young European travellers has been the quality and quantity of cannabis preparations readily available to them. In Africa and the Americas the drug usually comes in herbal form and, despite the denials of many governments who view alcohol as 'civilized' and cannabis as 'primitive', cannabis is consumed in a controlled and considered fashion by large sections of the world's population.

The opium poppy

The opium poppy, from which morphine and heroin are derived, grows within a geographical band running from Vietnam's Gulf of Tonkin to Turkey's Anatolian plain. Some tribal peoples have successfully integrated the poppy into their daily lives, although addiction has emerged as a problem in Iran, Pakistan, and parts of South-East Asia.

Once refined and converted into heroin, opiates present a particular threat to the young, semi-Westernized populations of Bangkok, Karachi, Tehran, and Singapore—as well as an increasing problem of addiction, with associated severe physical and psychological difficulty, among young people in developed countries.

Cocaine

Cocaine is derived from the coca leaf, which originates in Latin America. The Indian peoples of Colombia, Bolivia, and Peru chew the leaf or drink an infusion as a source of nutrition and energy for work and relaxation. Problems have arisen associated with 'gringo' entrepreneurs intent on profiting from the sale of the plant's chemical derivative, cocaine, to North America and Europe. Like 'crack' in North America, cocaine base smoking has become an increasing problem in South America.

Other drugs

Apart from the major psychotropics, travellers may come across other drugs that may create legal, medical, and psychological problems. The peyote cactus, for example, may be found in the south-western USA and northern Mexico, the psilocybin mushroom in western Europe and North and Central America, and 'fly-agaric', the white-spotted mushroom of fairy-tale, in North America, northern Europe, and northern Africa. They all have strong hallucinogenic properties and are treated with respect by those folk cultures that employ them for such properties.

Drug problems involving travellers

Travellers may experience unforeseen physical problems from the consumption of psychotropic drugs abroad; and legal problems with the possibility of arrest and imprisonment, as a result of illegal possession (including inadvertent possession).

Physical problems

If drugs are used in situations where there is uncertainty about the strength of preparations, and if drugs are injected when sterile equipment is not available, the potential hazards of drug taking are increased considerably.

Problems include: overdose of drugs, either accidental or deliberate; intoxication produced by sedative tranquillizers; panic reactions resulting from consumption of a variety of drugs, including potent preparations of cannabis and psychedelic drugs such as lysergide or mescaline; and acute paranoid states from cocaine and amphetamines. Regular daily consumption of drugs of the sedative tranquillizer group, or of the opioid group, followed by abrupt cessation, can produce an unpleasant and potentially dangerous withdrawal illness, particularly when coinciding with physical illness of the type that may easily occur abroad. Physical complications may arise as a result of the mode of administration, particularly injection, or where a drug-centred existence leads to the neglect of nutrition and personal hygiene.

Overdose The distinction between overdose and other acute reactions is part dependent on the type of drug consumed and partly on the relative dose level. Broadly, opioids and sedative tranquillizers depress cerebral function and decrease the sensitivity of the brain's respiratory centre. When sedation is profound, reflexes that normally protect the airway by coughing when foreign material is present, are suppressed. A sedated person may be lying in a position where simple mechanical obstruction to an airway can occur.

When someone is believed to have taken an overdose of this kind of drug, hospital treatment is always recommended; while waiting for assistance, turn the affected person into the semiprone position. This is achieved by laying them on their side, with the upper leg bent, their face at an angle towards the floor, and their neck gently extended, with the lower jaw pulled forward to maintain an airway. In this position, regurgitated food from the stomach is much less likely to be inhaled into the lungs. If breathing is so depressed that mouth-to-mouth ventilation is necessary, it is important to remember to clean any food debris from the mouth before inflating the lungs. These techniques are clearly explained and demonstrated in first aid books. The specific medical antidote for opioid overdose is an injection of the pure antagonist, nalorphine.

Other acute reactions Acute anxiety or fleeting hallucinatory experiences, can occur under the influence of alcohol, other sedative tranquillizers and volatile inhalants, as well as psychedelic drugs. Acute panic reactions, popularly referred to as 'bad trips', occur most frequently amongst novice consumers, those taking the drug in anxiety-provoking situations, older people experimenting with an unusual experience, and any consumer who unexpectedly encounters an unaccustomedly large dose. These factors are more likely to occur in a foreign country.

Adverse reactions are uncommon from the relatively weak psychedelic drug cannabis, particularly when this is consumed with some care by inhalation; but they are more likely to occur when cannabis is consumed by mouth with less control over the dose. The predominant symptom and sign of an adverse reaction is acute anxiety which may be related to subjective perceptual disturbance, or to external anxiety-provoking events. In a severe reaction, true hallucinations may be experienced. These perceptions may lead the sufferer to believe they are experiencing a severe psychiatric illness and a simultaneous increased heart rate may lead to fears of imminent death. The management of these acute reactions is reassurance, which will need to be repeated often since short term memory is usually also affected. A companion should endeavour to relate the sufferer's current experience to the fact that they have consumed a drug. The use of tranquillizers plays a small part in the management of acute reactions. Admission to a psychiatric institution is generally counterproductive.

Persecutory delusions (paranoia) are the principle serious adverse reaction to both amphetamines and cocaine. Individual dose response can vary widely. The acute episode is indistinguishable from acute schizophrenia. Disorder is generally self-limiting within a period of two or three days if the person ceases drug use. Administration of major (phenothiazine) tranquillizers may confuse the diagnosis.

Drug withdrawal reactions

Withdrawal from the sedative tranquillizer group of drugs is potentially medically hazardous since epileptic convulsions and a confused state with hallucinations can occur (the syndrome known as delirium tremens—DT's—in alcohol withdrawal). The immediate management of severe withdrawals is to administer any convenient drug of this group such as alcohol, phenobarbitone, or benzodiazepines such as diazepam (Valium). It is highly probable that the alcohol withdrawal syndrome is exacerbated by poor nutrition, which is common in chronic alcoholics, and it is important to ensure adequate vitamin supplements, particularly B6, to avoid the risk of permanent brain damage.

Disease in drug users

Hepatitis occurs commonly amongst heavy drug users and is broadly of two types: hepatitis A, otherwise known as infectious hepatitis, occurs in association with poor hygiene, and is common where food products may be contaminated by excreta used as fertilizer or infection carried by flies from latrines to food preparation areas. The onset usually occurs within four weeks following infection. Hepatitis B, also known as serum hepatitis commonly caused by the hepatitis B virus, but also by other viruses, usually occurs as a result of using a contaminated needle or syringe. It should be noted that it is extremely difficult to adequately resterilize the disposable syringes now almost invariably used in industrialized societies. The relative poverty of medical services in the Third World often results in this equipment being reused with a high risk of infection as a result of any injection. Serum hepatitis has a longer incubation period of the order of two to three months from the time of infection.

HIV, though less contagious then hepatitis B, is similarly transmitted and is particularly common in Central and East Africa and areas where intravenous drug use is common or which are frequented for commercialized sex. It should be noted that in some areas blood transfusion is one means by which impoverished people can raise money and therefore blood transfusion products are more likely to be a source of infection.

Any form of hepatitis can be a debilitating and potentially serious illness requiring medical care and in severe cases medical repatriation is needed. Active immunization is available to protect against hepatitis B; but not to confer protection against non-A/non-B hepatitis nor against HIV infection. Hepatitis is discussed in greater detail on p. 56 and HIV on p. 396.

Legal problems

Young travellers in particular may be quite frequently offered psychotropic drugs in foreign countries. Such drugs may be widely used by the local population, but are formally illegal. Some countries like Turkey and Thailand conduct the specific policy of applying the full force of their laws against foreign nationals, who are highly visible as well as being more vulnerable. This particularly applies to countries that have reputations as centres of illicit traffic and have attracted the censure of importing countries.

It always pays to do one's homework about the countries one intends to visit. Travellers in sunny places tend to forget that things are rarely as easy-going as they seem. A single cannabis cigarette in Greece means prison for one year plus one day, minimum. In some countries second-class passengers often ask first-class passengers to assist with their luggage allowance. There may be no ulterior motive to such a request, but even inadvertent smuggling still means severe penalties.

If taken into custody, never sign anything unless it can be read and understood. Remember this even under intense physical and psychological pressure. The only friend left in such circumstances may be your Consul. Consular officials may not be able to do a great deal but should be able to recommend a local English-speaking lawyer (fellow-prisoners may also have some ideas). Different countries have different regulations regarding legal aid, if it exists at all. It makes sense to discover the details as soon as possible.

Your Consulate will inform your family about your situation unless you wish otherwise. Generally, the Consul is expected to visit you as soon as possible after your arrest, to ensure you are legally represented and to make sure that your treatment is *no worse* than that of the local population. UK consular officials are not obliged to visit more than once a year but most do more than this.

Prescribed drugs

Many drugs such as heroin and other opioids, cocaine and cannabis, are subject to international treaty agreements governing the international trade in these substances. At present the majority of stimulants and sedative tranquillizers, including barbiturates, are not so strictly controlled but may be restricted under local regulations. In many countries the importation of any potential drug of abuse may be regarded as a criminal offence.

Patients who need to take regular medication for the treatment of physical or psychological disease should of course have consulted their usual medical adviser before undertaking foreign travel. Because of the laws regarding importation of psychoactive drugs, anyone requiring a continued supply should arrange with their doctor to receive a local legal prescription from a doctor in the country they intend to visit.

Note that an open letter to 'any doctor whom it might concern' will usually be insufficient to obtain immediate treatment because (a) any drug mentioned in the letter may not be legally available in the destination country and (b) even if it is, many doctors are not prepared to take on patients at short notice, nor are they prepared to take on nationals of another country.

On the other hand, specialists working in the field of drug dependence often do have knowledge of similar colleagues in other countries and may be able to organize medical care by prior arrangement, particularly if it is only to cover a short visit or to attend to family affairs, and in particular, bereavements. These particular precautions refer primarily to opiate drugs and amphetamines.

Minor tranquillizers and barbiturate sedatives prescribed in small amounts should be declared to customs officials and may or may not be accepted for importation. Major tranquillizers (phenothiazines such as chlorpromazine) and tricyclic antidepressants are almost always permitted, although problems could arise if a customs official was uncertain of the status or content of the tablets: in some cases, tablets may be confiscated for analysis.

Summary of information for travellers

- Consumption of psychotropic drugs in a situation without the support of friends or in unfamiliar surroundings is more likely to result in an anxiety reaction.
- The strength of preparations available in producing countries is likely to be greater than that of preparations which are available at home, where the product may have been diluted to increase the seller's profit margin and where the active principle may have been reduced in potency due to the time taken in transit.
- The consumption of unaccustomed powerful drugs increases the risk of adverse reactions.
- The risk of physical complications from self injection of drugs is considerably higher in countries where injecting equipment is expensive and imported.

[illegible] summary of information on the [illegible]

[illegible]

[illegible]

[illegible]

[illegible]

8

Some common troubles

Skin problems in travellers

A few simple precautions can save the traveller from the irritation or embarrassment of a skin problem.

Dr John H. S. Pettit *is a Consultant Dermatologist who has worked in Asia since 1959. His* Manual of Practical Dermatology *was published in the UK in 1983 and another,* Manual of Tropical Dermatology, *was published in New York in 1984.*

Around the world, skin diseases make up about one in seven of all new illnesses seen by doctors: travellers are no less prone to these problems than those who stay safely at home. Different diseases are more common in different regions, of course, and more affluent travellers staying in first-class hotels are less likely to encounter certain problems than those 'roughing it' or on a restricted budget. Younger adventurers, scantily clothed and slightly shod, and often dependent on local hospitality, are liable to acquire any disease around.

Most acquired diseases are infective in nature, but many skin disorders that appear in travellers for the first time—eczema, psoriasis, skin cancer, lupus erythematosus, and others with long unpronounceable names—are not necessarily the consequence of travelling; their appearance during a holiday may be entirely fortuitous.

Some ubiquitous problems

Overexposure to sunlight

Exposure to strong sunlight (see pp. 300–9), or exposure to sunlight for longer periods than you are accustomed to, can result in sunburn so severe that painful swelling of the skin can ruin the rest of your holiday. Sunburn is not confined to beach holidaymakers in hot countries: the amount of harmful solar radiation reaching the skin increases with altitude and by reflection off sea or snow, so mountaineering, skiing, watersports and in fact most prolonged outdoor activities also present a serious risk. Fair-skinned holidaymakers in particular should be careful to take precautions—i.e. protective clothing, use of sunscreens.

Blisters

One of the surest ways to ruin an active holiday is by using inappropriate footwear; climbers, high-mountain walkers, golfers, and members of the armed forces all need to use sturdy boots or walking shoes, and an unwise choice can seriously interfere with enjoyment of the journey.

Boots, shoes, or even sandals, should have soft upper parts, and the inside of the sole should be well-adapted to the shape and needs of the wearer's feet. They should be worn in gradually and with care. Footwear that is new and rigid, or that contains penetrating nails or rucked inner soles, may cause local friction. If sustained, the layers of the skin may separate, and a blister will form. These may be up to several centimetres in diameter, and may tear leaving painful, raw tissues dangerously exposed to secondary infection. Such blisters may also arise from footwear that is too loose, allowing much movement between the back of the shoe and the back of the foot.

Prevention Always travel with at least one pair of comfortable, well worn-in shoes—a spare pair is a sensible precaution. New boots should be worn for up to two or three hours daily, over several weeks, before they can be considered truly suitable partners for a climbing holiday. It is also wise to ensure that all foot-wear is reasonably waterproof. Soaking them in water before the daily breaking-in process, will help to make the leather or canvas uppers well-fitting and suitably supple.

Treatment Blisters that are still intact should not be de-roofed, since this will leave a painful, raw area, open to infection. The roof of the intact blister should be pierced with a sterile needle. After puncture, a soft gauze pad should be applied to the whole blister and be strapped on by a flexible adhesive dressing. The affected foot should not go back into the shoe that caused the trouble—if it was too tight before it will certainly be too tight afterwards!

If the roof of the blister has already rubbed off, the raw surface should be carefully washed with warm water and soap and a suitable antiseptic cream applied. It should be covered with a sterile non-adhesive dressing before bandaging. Different foot-wear should be worn until the skin has healed. The guilty boot should be suitably treated before it is put back to work.

Other blisters Blisters may appear on the palms or fingers, from carrying unsuitably heavy luggage; always divide heavy luggage into two equally balanced smaller bags. Such blisters are usually less troublesome than those on the feet. Blisters may also appear on the shoulders, under the rigid straps supporting backpacks, rucksacks, etc. These respond to commonsense treatment, and should be protected from further friction.

Blisters may also follow other types of skin trouble; sunburn, insect bites, jellyfish stings may all have a blistering element, while some sensitizing plants may cause a streak of blisters after contact in gardens, parks or jungles. Recognition of the cause of such blisters is usually not a problem.

Urticaria

One of the commonest skin troubles to affect holidaymakers is an attack of hives or nettle-rash (urticaria) which can follow the eating of contaminated food. A sudden outbreak of itchy red or white weals, occurring either on its own or with diarrhoea and vomiting, should point to the probability of some dietary indiscretion. Most attacks do not last long, but if the weals continue to appear for longer than three days it is wise to seek medical advice. Prolonged attacks are unlikely to be due to food-poisoning and more frequently result from sensitivity to intestinal parasites (hookworms, roundworms, etc) or to a food allergy, infection or drug reaction.

Antihistamines in small doses may be useful (see p. 497) but avoid promethazine (Phenergan), which has been known to make patients sensitive to sunlight and should never be prescribed for use in the daytime.

Bedbugs and insects

Bed-bugs lie in wait for all types of traveller, who may be awakened in the middle of the night by itchy little red bumps that should always lead to a search for the blood-gorged culprits (see pp. 171–2). Some individuals are abnormally sensitive to these bites and may develop nasty swollen reactions lasting for several days; usually the itching subsides within thirty-six hours. If bedbugs are suspected, the bed should be dusted with DDT powder. Many people also react badly to the stings of mosquitoes and other flying insects. They should use an insect repellent (see p. 182), of which the best usually contain dimethyl phthalate or diethyl toluamide. (Diethyl toluamide is not readily available in some parts of Asia.)

Fungal infections

Keratin—the more or less impermeable material that forms the outer layer of the skin—unfortunately provides a suitable home for various types of fungi. Moisture and sweat tend to encourage invasion and spread of the fungi through the keratin layer, and the result is an annoying and often itchy rash. Athlete's foot, ringworm, and dhobi itch are all examples of fungal infections, which in general are a common problem in travellers.

Ringworm infection of the scalp Fungi that affect hair produce circular patches of red, scaly hair loss on the scalp. This occurs only in children and takes several weeks to develop; it is not often seen in holidaymakers, but children may acquire these infections from local playmates or pets (cats or dogs with mangy skins should be carefully avoided). Treatment (tablets) should only be prescribed by a doctor.

Ringworm of the groin Other fungi cause ringworm of the groin—itchy, red scaly patches that spread outwards while clearing in the centre. The advancing edge consists of small blisters that develop as a reaction to invasion by the fungus. Fortunately, ringworm of the body rarely affects the scalp, and vice versa. Treatment with ointments applied to the affected area is usually successful; creams containing econazole, miconazole, or clotrimazole can be used.

Athlete's foot Several sorts of keratin-inhabiting fungus prefer to take up residence between and underneath the toes; these sites are also popular with various yeasts, especially the *Candida* variety which causes thrush. Individuals whose feet remain wet for long periods—with water from a swimming pool, the sea, rivers, or in floods—will find that soaking the skin encourages invasion by these organisms, and an itch that starts between the fourth and fifth toes is followed by scaling and splitting of the skin that slowly spreads to other toe webs and other parts of the foot.

People wearing woollen socks and sneakers in the tropics will almost always develop trouble sooner or later. In many of these cases more than one organism is present at the same time, so most antifungals are only partly helpful, but creams containing ketoconazole are usually able to control fungal, candidal, or combined infections.

People who live in deserts rarely get athlete's foot as their feet are as dry as their climate; even in humid equatorial areas, the use of open footwear with no socks usually ensures that toe webs are adequately ventilated, and prevents the condition.

Thrush The *Candida* group of organisms are yeast-like fungi that proliferate in any moist area of skin. They are the cause of oral 'thrush' in babies' mouths, exacerbate athlete's foot, and also frequently cause a shiny red soreness in the folds of the groins. A colourful paint, Castellani's paint, will usually clear this latter condition in a few days. Nystatin (Nystan) or miconazole (Daktarin) cream are also useful and frequently more acceptable to the sufferer. Affected individuals, especially those who are overweight or wear nylon 'jockey' underwear, may suffer frequent reinfection in the groin. (See also p. 371.)

Problems associated with cold climates

Even when the temperature remains below freezing point all day long, the traveller who dresses carefully and follows the example of local residents should encounter few problems.

Frostbite

Gloves, earmuffs, suitable headgear, clothes, and footwear are all necessary to prevent frostbite (see also p. 295), which results from freezing of the skin, and most often affects the fingers and toes, the nose, and the ears. Unfortunately the frozen waxy flesh is not usually painful, and foolish newcomers to such conditions often fail to take the problem seriously. Affected areas should be immersed in water at about 40°C for up to fifteen minutes—rubbing with snow or ice is not helpful and only makes matters worse. If the skin goes black, gangrene threatens, and urgent hospital admission should be sought.

Chilblains

People usually know if they have a tendency to chilblains and try to prevent further itchy, painful swellings by keeping their hands and feet warm and dry. Symptomatic treatment with calamine lotion is all that is needed to stay comfortable while the chilblains get better. Warming a chilblain will make it more painful: travellers to the tropics may find that the sudden rise in temperature on arrival can make chilblains almost intolerably uncomfortable.

Fungal infections

The most common skin problem affecting travellers to cold countries is an attack of athlete's foot or ringworm of the groin—usually in people with just a slight itch before they left home. The heavy, warm clothing needed in cold climates exacerbates any tendency to sweat—particularly between the toes and in the groin—and so encourages the fungus to spread. It is wise to use an antifungal dusting powder regularly as a preventative.

Problems associated with desert and tropical climates

Most skin conditions that occur elsewhere also occur in warm climates—including sunburn, of course, and fungal infections. Certain conditions, however, such as prickly heat and some parasitic skin infections, are much more common in tropical climates.

Prickly heat

Prickly heat is a very common condition in warm, sunny environments and is due to plugging of sweat ducts; if the mouth of the duct is blocked, tiny shiny vesicles appear which may quickly dry up. Deeper blockage results in the small, irritant red papules which form the rash called prickly heat, and which break out on the trunk and around the neck. Sufferers should avoid washing too frequently, and simple application of calamine lotion or Nivea cream will relieve discomfort. The condition disappears as the traveller becomes acclimatized (see also pp. 286–7 and 434).

Bacterial infections

If bacteria called pyococci penetrate the skin following damage, the itchy, crusty, or blistering condition known as *impetigo* may develop. This is best prevented by washing grazes twice daily with warm water and soap—more frequent washing is unwise since removal of protective greases from the surface will only make it easier for bacteria to penetrate undamaged skin. Some people still believe that penicillin or sulpha ointments are useful for scratches and cuts, but so many patients react badly to such preparations that these should not be used. A simple cetrimide cream is safer, and creams containing tetracyclines, gentamicin, sodium fusidate, or nitrofurantoin may also be helpful.

Fungal infections

Fungal infections such as athlete's foot, thrush, and ringworm are very liable to occur in warm climates: prevention and treatment are as discussed above.

Pityriasis versicolor One yeast infection that is much more common in tropical countries is *Pityriasis versicolor*. This is relatively rare in Europe and has no common name in English, but its frequency elsewhere is such that in many tropical countries it has been dignified with a local title. The condition appears as small, superficially scaly, red or brown skin patches which are initially circular, but as they extend or coalesce, produce a scalloped appearance. In darker races the patches are usually paler than normal skin, but in lighter-skinned people the patches are often darker. The condition does not usually itch and is a problem mainly because of its cosmetic unacceptability. Travellers would do well to put up with the disease until they return to a cooler country where treatment is more likely to be permanently effective. Tropical residents may buy a 4 oz bottle of Selsun shampoo and, using half of the contents each time, apply the liquid all over the body except the face and leave it there for four hours on two occasions with a three day interval.

Parasitic infections

All kinds of parasites may enter and infest the skin, and are common in many parts of the world; they are a particular problem in hot climates.

Leishmaniasis The unpleasant organisms known as *Leishmania* are injected into the skin by the bite of an infected sandfly. A few weeks later, a boil develops; this ulcerates after two to three months and does not disappear for about a year (see pp. 144–50).

Worm infestations River blindness is a worm infestation transmitted by the bites of blood-sucking blackflies (see p. 139). Drinking infected water may cause dracunculiasis, in which Guinea worms live in the body and produce large soft swellings on the ankles which burst on contact with cold water (p. 71); other worms cause elephantiasis and loa-loa (p. 140), and schistosomiasis (see p. 90).

Holidaymakers on short visits to infected areas are much less likely to be affected, but people who spend time sharing their living conditions with the indigenous people may at a later date produce signs and symptoms that will probably be recognized only by a specialist in tropical medicine. Chronic ill health associated with lumps in or under the skin are signs that should be taken seriously by people who have lived for a long time in Africa, Asia, or the equatorial parts of South America.

Creeping eruption A number of parasitic worms that live in the intestines of humans or dogs produce soil-dwelling larvae that penetrate the skin of the feet or ankles of people walking without shoes or socks. Children playing on tropical beaches or in sandpits are particularly at risk. The larvae wander aimlessly through the skin, producing a pinkish line that itches and extends by a few centimetres each day. The larvae eventually die off, and most attacks can be left untreated except with calamine lotion and mild antihistamine tablets. Patients with extensive infection need medical treatment (see pp. 47 and 103–4).

Sexually transmitted diseases

Increasingly large numbers of travellers seek the sexual favours of fellow-travellers or of less affluent inhabitants of their host country.

Gonorrhoea (which is often more difficult to cure than the variety found at home), syphilis (still putting up a valiant struggle against extermination), herpes genitalis (increasingly feared though possibly no more common than before and other less famous sexually transmitted diseases (see p. 381) may produce a discharge from, or ulceration of, the sexual organs. These are often painless and short-lived, but the disappearance of the signs does not mean that the disease is not alive and well and spreading through the body.

'Tokyo Rose' is the name said to have been invented by American soldiers in the Far East to describe the acquisition of several sexually transmitted diseases at the same time.

Always seek specialist treatment as soon as possible.

Pre-existing skin problems

Acne

Acne is improved by sunlight, but patients taking tetracyline regularly for it may find that their nails become loose after sunbathing. Skin sometimes becomes greasier in the tropics, and if this happens acne may get worse or even break out for the first time. Do not wash yourself more often than usual: simply carry a small towel and wipe your face frequently.

Eczema (atopic)

This unpleasant family disease, usually associated with hay fever and asthma, will probably get worse in humid countries, and travel to such places is best avoided.

Psoriasis

Psoriasis is often improved by sunlight. If you have severe psoriasis why not spend your holiday in a psoriasis treatment centre such as have been established on the coast of Bulgaria or by the Dead Sea in Israel? Your skin will probably get a lot better. Your dermatologist can give you details.

Skin care items for your medical kit

1. A small tube of cetrimide cream, tetracycline ointment, gentamicin cream, sodium fusidate, or nitrofurazone should always be carried and applied to any scratch, graze, bite, or broken blister.
2. Many antihistamines, including chlorpheniramine maleate (Piriton, Chlor-Trimeton) make patients feel sleepy, but terfenadine (Seldane, Teldane, Triludan) or astemizole (Hismanal) tablets do not. They will not only help an attack of urticaria but will damp down prickly heat or itching caused by insect bites, and are becoming more widely available. See pp. 497–8.
3. People who react badly to bites should use an insect repellent.Those containing dimethyl phthalate or diethyl toluamide are useful (p. 182).
4. If you are visiting a humid area, an antifungal dusting powder should be used every day between the toes and in the groin. Do not forget to apply this powder before a long plane journey.

Summary of advice for travellers

- Always use footwear—far too many infections penetrate the unprotected skin of the foot. Beware rubber sneakers in hot countries.
- Wash damaged skin twice daily with warm water and non-medicated soap.
- Never continue to treat yourself for a condition that has got worse steadily for four days: seek skilled care.
- Never sit in the sun without protection (clothes or barrier cream). Remember that the shade of a palm tree does not protect you from the sun rays reflected from nearby sea and sand.
- If you need to visit a doctor when you get home don't forget to say where you have been, and what you did there.

Dental problems and the traveller

A check-up prior to departure, and adequate arrangements to cover the possible expense of emergency treatment are the main precautions to consider.

Professor Gordon Seward *is Head of the Department of Oral and Maxillo-Facial Surgery at the London Hospital Medical College. His profession has taken him to Europe, Africa, Australia, and the USA, and he has acted as an Examiner in Nigeria, Malaysia, and Singapore.*
Andrew Dawood *is a dentist in private practice in Central London and also at Guy's Hospital. He shares a family passion for travel, and has worked in South America and in Asia.*

Dental problems arising while travelling abroad are, in general, given little thought and consideration both by prospective travellers and by those responsible for emergency treatment. If a dental emergency occurs, the traveller may experience more difficulty obtaining help and is more likely to have to pay for it out of his or her own pocket than if he or she has a medical problem.

Before departure

Travellers on short visits or holidays abroad are unlikely to face a dental emergency (other than an accidental one) if they have had a careful examination by their own dentist, including 'bitewing' radiographs, within a few months of their journey, and any necessary treatment has been completed. However the examination is not a guessing game, and the dentist should be told about current symptoms or problems. Furthermore, the initial appointment should be booked a sufficient time before departure to permit treatment to be completed without haste. People with heavily restored mouths, or large complex restorations should seek advice on how to cope with any particular problems that might arise.

Travellers intending to spend a long time abroad should consider treatment for any conditions likely to cause trouble in the future—for example currently symptomless impacted teeth or the replacement of a just adequate but ancient denture. Dental problems in long term expatriates are surprisingly common. In American Peace Corps Volunteers (who each spend two years overseas), they consistently represent the third or fourth most frequently reported of all health problems.

The cost of specialist care abroad can be considerable. Unlike repairs to the family car or a household appliance, the majority of UK citizens are largely unaware of the current costs of medical and dental care in real terms.

Dental problems associated with travel

Few dental problems are directly a hazard of travelling. Seasick passengers, if they vomit over the side of the ship, may lose their dentures! Swimmers also may lose dentures or orthodontic plates. Ex-aircrew members from World War II may recall that pressure changes could produce pain in filled teeth, but as modern aircraft are fully pressurized, this does not happen to civilian passengers. Some people suffer pain and locking of the jaw joints, and an awkward posture on a long flight that induces lateral pressure on the jaw has been known to exacerbate this complaint. An unaccustomed indulgence in alcoholic drinks can precipitate an attack of 'periodic facial migraine' (Horton's syndrome), an uncommon cause of a recurrent severe throbbing pain in one cheek. For various reasons some people may drink more wine and spirits than usual on a flight, and sufferers may come to associate such attacks with flying.

Dental emergencies

Emergencies tend to fall into three categories: pain; lost or broken fillings and other restorations; and more serious emergencies (infection or traumatic injury).

Toothache

A relatively trivial dental problem can give rise to a totally disproportionate amount of pain, and make life quite miserable. Extreme sensitivity to hot and cold may be the first sign of trouble; if treated at this stage, the tooth may settle down. If left untreated, the pain may become spontaneous and long lasting;

the nerve in the tooth may eventually die, and act as a focus for infection and abscess formation.

A dental abscess can cause severe persistent pain, exacerbated by pressure on the tooth. In all cases, a swollen face should be taken seriously; it is wise to seek treatment early as there is a small but significant risk of life-threatening spread of infection if this is neglected.

The usual treatment for an abscessed tooth in many countries would be extraction; however if the abscess is caused by death of the nerve, it is often possible to perform root canal treatment to save the tooth—the nerve chamber is opened with a drill, and the infection drained. Later, the nerve chamber is filled with an inert or antiseptic material. Where a high standard of dental treatment is available, baby teeth may be treated in a similar fashion; otherwise it may well be more sensible to accept loss of a milk tooth, rather than risk a spreading infection.

If treatment is unavailable antibiotics should be taken, although every effort must be made to see a dentist as soon as possible. Treatment should be sought early for another reason; in few countries outside the UK is a general anaesthetic readily available for the extraction of an abscessed tooth. Once an abscess develops, extraction with a local anaesthetic may prove more difficult, and the patient may have to take antibiotics for some days in the hope that the infection may subside sufficiently for the extraction to be performed.

Another type of abscess may develop where teeth are badly affected by gum disease. Such an abscess may sometimes be treated by deep cleaning of the tooth to remove infected deposits under the gum. However once again, the only treatment offered in some countries may be extraction of the tooth. A similar abscess may develop around the crown of an impacted tooth, usually a lower wisdom tooth, and this is quite common in young adults. Extraction of the impacted tooth will eventually be necessary, although antibiotics, hot saline mouth washes, and good tooth brushing may help control the infection until the traveller returns home.

It is sensible for individuals who have heavily restored dentitions, or who have suffered any kind of dental abscess in the past, to discuss the management of such problems with their own dentist, who may well recommend travelling with a supply of antibiotics.

Occasionally, two to three days after a tooth has been extracted, the clot may liquefy and be lost from the socket exposing bone. This allows food debris to accumulate in the socket, which may become infected. Warm water pumped by the cheeks in and out of the socket may be sufficient to keep it clean and relieve pain, but in more severe cases expert irrigation and a medicated dressing may be needed.

Fillings, crowns, bridges, and dentures

Though often a source of great inconvenience, the loss or breakage of a dental restoration cannot be considered to be a true emergency; the freshly exposed tooth surface is often sensitive to hot or cold, and jagged edges may irritate the soft tissues of the mouth. It is not, however, absolutely essential to seek immediate treatment unless there is considerable discomfort. The survival and fate of a tooth are unlikely to be affected by a delay even of a few weeks; this means that it is almost always possible to wait until you can see your own dentist, or can find a dentist on personal recommendation.

If extreme sensitivity or a toothless smile necessitate treatment in the absence of adequate facilities, it is wise to seek provisional treatment only. It is often a simple matter for a dentist to insert a temporary filling, or temporarily recement a crown or bridge, but in many countries even the most basic dental materials may prove to be unobtainable. 'Do-it-your-self' repairs and repair kits are not to be recommended without advice from your own dentist as there is a risk that restorations may be inhaled or swallowed if they become loose in the mouth during sleep; once a restoration has become decemented it should be removed.

More serious emergencies

Fractured jaws and spreading infections need hospital dental treatment by an appropriate dentist (an oral and maxillo-facial surgeon). Standards of skill in treating jaw and facial bone fractures probably vary more from country to country than for any other injury. If it becomes clear that skilled treatment is not available locally, and if after emergency care the patient is deemed fit enough to travel and is not at risk from obstruction of the airway, it may be best to return home for further treatment.

A front tooth that has been broken as a result of a blow—particularly in a child—may not always seem to need urgent care: in fact, expert treatment within a matter of hours may make all the difference between conserving the tooth or losing it.

If a child's permanent front tooth is knocked out, it may be possible to reimplant it. The roots of some reimplanted teeth are subsequently eaten away by the body, like those of baby teeth, and the tooth is lost again; but others survive and give good service. If there is to be a chance of success, the tooth must be reasonably clean when picked up and it must be washed in cold water or milk. Hold the tooth only by the crown, and do not touch, rub, or scrub the root. The root must be kept moist, so put the tooth in a clean container, in cold drinking water to which salt has been added (one teaspoon to a glass), or some milk. If the tooth has been thoroughly washed it may be pushed back fully into its socket, straight away. Be sure that the crown is the right way round! The procedure will not be too painful. The patient should bite on a handkerchief to retain the tooth in place, and get to a dentist as soon as possible. Milk teeth should not be reimplanted.

The dentist should splint the reimplanted tooth in place, give antibiotics, and arrange for a tetanus booster injection. If a dentist is not immediately available a temporary splint may be improvised using softened chewing gum (preferably sugar free), pressed around the tooth and its neighbours, and covered with aluminium foil. It is best not to reimplant a tooth that has fallen on to pasture grazed by animals, because of the increased risk of tetanus infection.

Teeth successfully replaced within half an hour are most likely to reattach normally. If the tooth is kept moist there is a reasonable chance of success for up to two hours. Beyond two hours the results are poor. The splint should normally remain in place for about 2 weeks. In all cases the tooth should be checked by a dentist upon returning home, and subsequently at regular intervals.

Choosing a dentist abroad

Non-sterile instruments and needles may be a source of hepatitis B (see pp. 60–5 and 334–5) and you should satisfy yourself that any dentist you consult uses instruments that have been adequately sterilized. 'Cartridge' syringes are the safest for giving local anaesthetic. These are made of metal, and a fresh glass vial, closed with a bung at each end and filled with sterile local anaesthetic solution by the manufacturer, slides into the barrel for each patient. A fresh needle from an intact plastic tube should be used for each patient. The syringe should be sterilized between patients—autoclaving is preferable, but boiling the metal part is acceptable. Absolute sterility is less critical than with syringes in which the solution has to be drawn up into the barrel itself.

Needles and plastic syringes should come from intact original packages, and should be discarded after each patient. Beware of needles re-sterilized by soaking in antiseptic or by boiling. Beware also of plastic syringes that have been 're-sterilized' by soaking in antiseptic. Be wary also of bottles of solution from which doses for other patients have been withdrawn. Needles that have been used on patients can easily contaminate the contents.

Bear in mind that high-speed drills use water as a coolant, and this water (and any other water used in your mouth) is likely to be only as clean as the local supply.

Personal recommendation is usually the best basis for choosing a dentist.

Important points to mention

If you have had rheumatic fever, St Vitus's dance (chorea), have a heart valve defect or disease, or a hole in the heart, a heart murmur or have had heart valve surgery, then you should have antibiotic cover for any extraction and should make this plain to any dentist you see. Antibiotic cover is also advisable for extractions if you have an artificial joint or a heart pacemaker.

You should also tell the dentist about any steroid treatment that you have had, even many months before, as it may be necessary for you to have additional steroid treatment at the time of a tooth extraction or similar surgery.

Patients who are taking anticoagulant drugs or who have had trouble with excessive bleeding from cuts etc. or who suffer from haemophilia should make sure that the dentist understands the situation.

Naturally you should tell the dentist about any serious illnesses you have had and any medicines, injections, or tablets that you take as a routine. If you are allergic to any drugs, (e.g. penicillin or aspirin), or dressings, it is essential that the dentist or pharmacist knows about this. Language problems may make this difficult.

Remember also that not all cultures attach a great deal of importance to saving teeth. You must make your own feelings on this subject quite clear!

Financial matters

A few travel insurance policies include a specific section on emergency dental treatment, either as part of the package or as an optional extra. Many do not. If there is such a section, enquire beforehand about what it covers. While a spreading dental infection may need urgent hospital admission, insurance companies may not consider this to be included under the heading of emergency hospital treatment (perhaps because treatment is given by a dental specialist). Travellers at special risk of accidental injury (e.g. on skiing holidays) are advised to ensure that they are fully covered by appropriate insurance.

The cost of such emergency treatment may be very high; and so will be the cost of any crown, bridge, or denture work.

Reciprocal arrangements for British travellers

There are reciprocal agreements for emergency medical treatment with a number of countries, particularly within the EEC. In many countries, however, emergency *dental* care is *not* included, or may be obtained only from certain clinics or hospitals. Leaflet T1 (see p. 471) gives details of entitlement as well as the application form for certificate E111, which you will need in EEC countries (see p. 471). In many countries you will need your passport, and in some (e.g. Bulgaria, Poland, Romania, and Hong Kong) you will need your NHS medical card as well; in others, your driving licence in addition to your passport will do.

In broad terms, in Italy, Poland, Romania, the USSR, East Germany, West Germany, and Yugoslavia, treatment is free; in Bulgaria, hospital dental treatment is free and emergency treatment is free in Alderney and Guernsey. It is also free for children in Sweden and for those aged under sixteen years in New Zealand and between six and fifteen in Iceland. Free emergency treatment is available from public health dentists in the Irish Republic and Government Clinics in Hong Kong.

In Belgium, France, and Luxembourg you must pay, but you should apply for a partial refund before leaving the country. In Denmark a dentist registered with the Danish Public Health Service will give free treatment, or if there is a charge, a refund can be claimed if a receipt is presented at the appropriate office. In Norway, emergency extractions are free, but in Gibraltar you will have to pay except for emergency extractions during normal working hours at St Bernard's Hospital. In all other countries, you will need to pay.

Looking after your teeth

When travelling in a hot country, it is sometimes tempting, and often necessary—when safe drinking water is unobtainable—to drink large amounts of canned or bottled soft drinks. In some countries it may also be customary to serve guests with heavily sweetened tea or coffee. Frequent consumption of sugary food or drink is especially damaging to the teeth. It may take only a few months for early decay to develop in a previously unaffected tooth; small quiescent or reversing lesions may become active and irreversible.

Tooth cleaning becomes even more important when sugar consumption is high. Using dental floss or an interdental brush every day will help to prevent decay on otherwise inaccessible surfaces. Dental floss has been found to be a versatile and indispensable travelling companion by one of the authors, who has had cause to use it on occasion as a clothes line, for repairing a tent, and for hanging a hammock. The possibilities are limitless!

Fluoride and living abroad

A small amount of fluoride (one part per million in temperate climates) in drinking water undoubtedly reduces the likelihood of tooth decay, particularly in children; however an excessive fluoride intake (greater than two parts per million in a temperate climate), can lead to mottling and discolouration of developing teeth. In countries that have a well-developed mains drinking supply, the fluoride content is carefully controlled to the proper level. Not only is the appropriate small amount added where it is required, but a natural excess of fluoride is removed.

Unless it is known for certain that fluoride is absent from the

Cold sores

The herpes virus that causes cold sores predominantly affects the inside of the mouth, lips, and the areas of skin around the mouth, nose, and eyes. Initial infection usually passes unnoticed, though it can occasionally cause malaise, sore throat, enlarged lymph glands, and widespread ulceration of the mouth—the whole of the oral mucosa may be bright red and sore; this is most commonly seen in children, and is called herpetic stomatitis. A slow recovery takes place over a period of about 10 days. However the virus is not completely eliminated from the body, and remains in a latent form which, when reactivated, is responsible for the production of cold sores.

Cold sores are caused by a complex reaction involving herpes simplex virus Type I, and the body's own defence system. Some individuals find that the condition may be triggered by exposure of the face to strong sunlight, although other factors such as cold temperatures, stress, menstruation, and any debilitating condition may also be important. The most common location for a cold sore is on the lip.

If an association between sunlight and cold sores has been observed, then the most sensible precaution is to keep out of the sun, and to wear a hat or sun shade; sun-blocking preparations on the lips and face will also help.

Typically, arrival of the lesion is preceded by a period of itching and irritation over the affected area. Within a few hours, blisters appear and these then burst and form a scab. Healing then takes place over a period of about 10 days.

Be particularly careful not to touch the cold sore with the fingers and then rub the eyes. An infection of the finger end around the nails is possible, or worse, a serious infection of the surface of the eye. Do not kiss while you have a cold sore and especially avoid kissing children who may as a result develop herpetic stomatitis (see above).

Frequent sufferers should consider obtaining a prescription for the anti-viral agent acyclovir (Zovirax) to take away with them. The cream should be applied to the affected area, and can shorten the duration of an outbreak considerably, especially when used immediately the first symptoms are recognized.

local water supply or is present only in a very low concentration (much less than one part per million), the use of fluoride supplements for children is unwise. In any case, supplements should be used only when prescribed by a knowledgeable local dentist or doctor. Where fluoride levels are high, it may be wise to use alternative sources of drinking water for babies and small children, bearing in mind that water intake and thus total fluoride intake is higher in hot countries.

Young children often swallow a significant amount of toothpaste when they brush their teeth. If the toothpaste contains fluoride, and fluoride levels in the drinking water are already on the high side, this may result in an excessive total fluoride intake. Only under these circumstances is it better for babies and young children to use a fluoride-free toothpaste.

Eye problems in travellers

Exposure to strong sunlight, dust, and infection, with limited access to skilled care if problems occur, are the main difficulties facing the traveller. Simple precautions will prevent most problems.

Mr Peter Fison *is an Ophthalmologist at Sutton Hospital in South London. A traveller himself, his own memories of sunstroke and snowblindness, coupled with clinical experience in the Casualty Department at Moorfields Eye Hospital and St Thomas's Hospital, London, have convinced him that eyes, though sensitive, are pretty resilient.*

Classical writers described the eye as the window of the soul, and even today we tend to treat our eyes with exaggerated respect. But our eyes are tough and resilient organs, well designed to put up with a variety of physical insults, and during the course of evolution we have developed good protective reflexes to maintain perfect vision. When our eyes are damaged or inflamed we soon know about it, because the many nerve endings around the eye respond to any painful and noxious stimuli.

Because we rely constantly on our eyesight to orientate ourselves in our surroundings, as travellers we should take particular care of our eyes. We take our eyesight so much for granted that it is only when our eyes go wrong that we realize quite how much we depend on them. Fortunately, serious eye injuries are unusual. A little common sense and some simple precautions will ensure that most damage to the eyes can be anticipated and avoided.

Sunlight

Anyone who has been skiing or sailing in bright sunlight knows that their eyes can easily become sore, red, and inflamed. Because ultra-violet rays (which also cause sunburn) are reflected off the surface of snow and water, the eyes get a double dose of damaging radiation (see p. 301).

The eyebrows and eyelashes throw a shadow across our eyes, filtering the light, and a reflex action usually makes us screw up our eyes in strong sunlight. This reduces the amount of light reaching the two particularly sensitive areas, the cornea and the retina. Over-exposure to ultra-violet radiation can damage the cornea directly, causing the cells on the surface to swell up. This produces intense irritation and severe pain, forcing the eye to water profusely and to close, because this part of the eye is exquisitely sensitive (which is why welders wear protective masks to avoid the aptly named 'arc eye').

The discomfort often starts several hours after exposure to sunlight, and may waken you from sleep. Travellers in bright sunlight should always wear sunglasses to avoid this reaction: most of the better brands filter out the harmful ultra-violet radiation. The damaging light rays are at their peak concentration during the middle of the day when the sun is at its highest, so a hat with a brim may be another useful precaution. The choice of style is of course entirely up to you!

While sunglasses are effective under most conditions, skiers and mountaineers will know from bitter experience that goggles are often necessary. At higher altitudes the concentration of ultra-violet light is greater, because it has not been filtered out by the atmosphere. Goggles are also helpful if weather conditions change, since they help prevent the reflex watering of the eyes induced by cold wind and snow that may blur your vision and endanger your safety. Remember too that harmful ultra-violet rays can penetrate apparently dense cloud cover at high altitude.

The combined effects of heat, dust, and wind may cause dryness of the eyes in desert conditions. Continuous exposure to these stimuli over many months may lead to the development of permanent changes in the eye, which can themselves cause further irritation. Fair-skinned people are more likely to develop a pterygium if their eyes are not adequately protected from the sun under these conditions. A pterygium is an extension of the conjunctiva across the cornea, which progresses slowly over several years with repeated exposure to sun and wind, frequently causing discomfort. If a pterygium extends to the edge of the pupil, it needs to be excised surgically. Appropriate use of good quality sunglasses will help prevent this unsightly condition.

Infection

Conjunctivitis Eye infections occur more frequently in hot climates. Conjunctivitis is the commonest infection, producing a sticky discharge which is likely to gum your eyelids together when you sleep. The affected eye is red, and feels as if you have sand under the lids. Most conjunctivitis is caused by bacterial infection, and usually responds within a few days to treatment with chloramphenicol or neomycin eye drops every two hours, both of which are safe to use. Avoid using antibiotic preparations which also contain steroids, since these may harm your eyes in the presence of a virus infection, which has identical symptoms.

Trachoma One infection that gives rise to particular anxiety is trachoma. In hot, dry countries where this disease is endemic, it can lead to progressive blindness. However, travellers who contract trachoma conjunctivitis experience only mild symptoms of redness and irritation, with a sticky but rather watery discharge from the eyes. Blindness occurs only with recurrent infections over many years among people who are already debilitated through chronic malnutrition, primitive sanitary conditions, and overcrowding. The infective agent is spread by close contact with infected individuals, their fingers and their clothes, and by flies. Trachoma of the eye is caused by the same organism as the sexually transmitted disease chlamydia (see p. 394), and it is possible to have both infections at the same time. If you think you have trachomatous conjunctivitis, a three-week course of tetracycline eyedrops, with ointment at night, will cure the condition. Antibiotics (tetracycline or erythromycin) should also be taken by mouth to ensure complete eradication of the infection. If you remain in an area where trachoma is endemic, reinfection may occur, and a further course of treatment would then be necessary.

Contact lenses

Everyone who wears contact lenses knows that their eyes can tolerate so much and no more. Hard lens wearers who have worn them too long know how intensely painful this mistake can be. Soft lens wearers can develop irritable eyes with infection or allergy from cleaning, soaking, and rinsing solutions.

Discuss your trip with your contact lens practitioner before you leave. Travellers who normally wear contact lenses should never leave home without an up-to-date pair of eyeglasses as well, just in case of trouble, and should also take a pair of sunglasses for protection from dust, wind, and sunlight. At the earliest sign of irritation or discomfort, leave the lenses out for at least twenty-four hours. The commonest problems for hard lens wearers are overwear, and dust particles trapped under the lens. Remind yourself to keep blinking to renew the tear film under the lens. The cells on the surface of the cornea depend on this tear film for their oxygen supply, and when this runs short they tend to swell up. Exquisite discomfort then occurs, similar to that experienced after overexposure to ultra-violet light. Treatment involves removing the lens, and resting with your eyes closed—there may be too much discomfort to do anything else! Mild pain-killing tablets will help a little.

A scratch on the cornea from a dust particle trapped under the contact lens may feel much the same. A gritty sensation when you blink, and excessive watering, will usually make you keep your eyes closed. After removing the lens, a soft pad fixed by adhesive tape will rest the eye; but keep the eye closed under the pad. If you keep both eyes closed they move less, allowing the scratch on the cornea to heal more quickly.

An additional problem on long flights is that contact lenses tend to dry out. Humidity aboard an aircraft is less than 2 per cent, because the air supply is drawn from the rarefied outside air by compressors in the engine and circulates continuously. Always keep a lens case and lens solutions with you when you fly.

Aerosol insecticide sprays are sometimes used on board aircraft, in accordance with international regulations, to clear the cabin of unwelcome stray insects. In a confined space, these aerosols may be absorbed by soft contact lenses and irritate the eyes, so it is sensible to keep your eyes closed during spraying and for a minute or so afterwards.

Recent reports have highlighted the painful condition of keratitis, which is an infection of the cornea. Keratitis caused by bacteria (usually staphylococci) and viruses (either *Herpes simplex*, which also causes cold sores, or Adenovirus, responsible for the common cold) is not uncommon, whether you wear contact lenses or not. This sort of keratitis is treated either with antibiotic drops (chloramphenicol or neomycin) or anti-viral ointment (acyclovir).

Particular interest has centred on a rare but serious cause of keratitis called *Acanthamoeba*, which most frequently occurs in contact lens wearers, though it has also been found in corneal ulcers following minor trauma. *Acanthamoeba* is a protozoal organism which lives freely in the soil and in water, and does not normally cause infections in man. Because contact lenses cause a slight amount of damage to the surface of the cornea, the organism can gain access to the corneal substance and establish a colony. All contact lens wearers should therefore be particularly careful to remove their lenses before bathing in swimming pools, hot tubs, and even in fresh water, and they should never moisten their contact lenses by licking them, since *Acanthamoeba* has even been isolated from normal saliva. It has also been found in contact lens solutions that have been left open for a while, but not in unopened bottles of sterile distilled water.

If you should develop an intensely painful red eye, with blurred vision and acute sensitivity to light, the chances are that you may well have a form of keratitis. If the degree of pain is out of all proportion to the apparent inflammation, particularly if you are a contact lens wearer, it is just possible that you may have this rather unusual corneal ulcer caused by *Acanthamoeba*. Whatever the cause, once you have removed the lens, you may safely treat the eye with Brolene drops (0.1 per cent propamidine isethionate), until you can seek expert ophthalmic advice. Brolene is a non-prescription eyedrop which has a specific effect against *Acanthamoeba*, although a prolonged course of treatment under medical supervision is necessary to achieve a complete cure.

Lens wearers should not rely on being able to obtain supplies of their usual cleaning, rinsing, and soaking solutions at their destination, and should take an ample supply with them. Be sure only to use unopened sterilized distilled water when making up solutions yourself, and follow manufacturers' instructions carefully. A number of cases of *Acanthamoeba* have occurred with home-made solutions, so do not attempt to concoct your own. Do not depend on heat sterilization of lenses when you travel, since adequate facilities may not always be available.

Disposable contact lenses have recently become available, and these—although inevitably more expensive—might help you to avoid some of the difficulties described above.

Dust particles under the eyelid

In dusty conditions, whether you wear contact lenses or not, particles of grit may get stuck under the top eyelid. There are some fairly obvious ways to avoid this. Do not put your head out of the window while travelling, particularly on a steam train. Keep your eyes closed in dust storms. Wear protective goggles whenever necessary.

Removing a dust particle from under someone else's upper eyelid is a simple procedure, and gives immediate relief from severe discomfort. Sit down in front of the affected person (who should also be seated), and ask him or her to look down, and keep looking down. Gently pull the eyelid away from the eye by holding the lashes firmly between the index finger and thumb of your left hand. While your patient continues to look down (this relaxes the muscles of the lid), gently press the centre of the eyelid about 5 mm from the lid margin, where you can see a shallow groove in the skin. Press downwards and slightly backwards, using a cotton bud, a paper clip, the tip of a key, or a blunt pencil. This gentle pressure will flip the lid inside out, and if you adjust your pull on the eyelashes slightly upwards, the eyelid will remain everted. Now wipe the inside of the eyelid gently with a clean tissue or the tip of a cotton bud to remove the offending piece of grit, which is often so small that you cannot see it. Finally, pull the eyelashes gently outwards and down so that the lid returns to its normal position.

Although it sounds complicated, this manoeuvre is actually quite simple, provided that both you and the affected person stay relaxed and avoid sudden movements, and that you perform each step without force. A pad to protect the eye for twenty-four hours will usually heal any scratch on the corneal surface.

Eyeglasses

If you wear glasses, always take along a spare pair and a note of your prescription. Do not leave glasses lying around: in some parts of the world they are a surprisingly popular prize for thieves. If you are going abroad for a long time, have a check-up before you leave.

Working abroad

Safety standards may be different abroad. If you intend to work abroad, or to take part in any activity involving a risk of injury to your eyes, make sure that you take along any protective or other safety equipment that may be needed—and be sure to use it.

For your medicine kit

An eye-bath, with a proprietary eye lotion, may help to relieve inflamed eyes. A teaspoonful of ordinary salt dissolved in a pint of tepid water is an effective alternative, but always boil the water first, and allow it to cool down before application. Proprietary lubricant eyedrops may also help to relieve tired and aching eyes. Antibiotic drops should be used if there is a sticky discharge associated with grittiness of the eye: chloramphenicol or neomycin drops are safe, effective, cheap, and widely available.

Note that in countries with no restrictions on the sale of medicines to the public you may be offered eyedrops and ointment containing steroids; these may be dangerous and should only be used on specialist advice.

First aid

If in doubt about the cause of a problem, it is always safe to close the eye and apply a pad to the worst affected eye: take a couple of pain-killing tablets and rest the eyes overnight. Folded paper tissues or a clean handkerchief may be used instead of an eye pad. Clear adhesive tape is better than sticking plaster to secure the patch, as it is easier to remove the next day. If the discomfort is no better, then specific treatment may be required and it may be necessary to obtain skilled medical advice.

Gynaecological problems

Gynaecological problems are common in women travellers. Most problems are not serious, but even a supposedly minor problem can ruin a trip.

Dr John Naponick *is a public health physician with specialist training in gynaecology, obstetrics, and tropical medicine. He has worked in the USA, Canada, Cameroon, Malaysia, Bangladesh, Thailand, and Burma and is currently Medical Adviser to the US AID mission to El Salvador.* Ellen Poage *is a registered nurse and a health educator. She has travelled and worked in Central America, Africa, Africa, and Asia, and now lives in El Salvador.*

Women travellers who plan a long trip abroad, or who plan to live in a country where good medical facilities may not be easily accessible, are well advised to have a gynaecological check-up before they leave home—preferably six weeks or so before departure; it is always a good idea to begin a trip with a clean bill of health. Those with previous gynaecological problems should have a clear understanding of their medical history, or should carry a written note of any problems.

Menstrual problems

Personal supplies

Women should make a careful estimate of their likely requirements for personal hygiene. Although women throughout the world menstruate, not all of them take the same approach to feminine hygiene. So if the traveller to a remote area is not sufficiently adventurous as to experiment with the only facilities available locally—such as balls of cotton wool, cloths and towels tied on with strings, or even handfuls of leaves—she should be certain to ensure an uninterrupted supply of her own preferred variety of tampon, sanitary napkin, or pad.

In developing countries locally made menstrual supplies are usually available in most major cities, although the standard varies. In relatively more advanced countries such as Thailand and Malaysia they may be of high quality. In poorer countries such as Bangladesh, napkins are beginning to replace the more traditional towel and string methods in the wealthier section of the community; those make locally, however, tend to look (and feel) more like a mattress than the kind of slim-line product with which most women living in developed countries are familiar.

Menstruation

Some women travellers prefer not to have periods at all while travelling; this can be accomplished by taking the Pill continuously, without a break between packets (p. 406).

Women who travel to game parks should consider this option or should avoid close proximity to predatory animals (bears, lions, tigers etc.) while menstruating. There have been a number of reported attacks on menstruating women. Likewise, if they swim or dive in shark-infested waters, they are at increased risk of attack by sharks.

In some parts of South-East Asia, such as Indonesia, women may be asked not to enter local temples if they are menstruating.

Irregular bleeding

Periods may stop completely in travellers. Often, the cause of this proves to be pregnancy. However, an irregular cycle is usually the result of the hormonal changes that follow any disruption of normal routines, and may even be partly psychological in origin. One example of this phenomenon has been studied extensively: nursing students who leave home and move into shared accommodation almost always experience some disturbance of menstruation: after a while, a normal cycle returns, with the girls menstruating in unison.

Heavy bleeding

A detailed discussion of causes of heavy vaginal bleeding is outside the scope of this book. Suffice it to say that certain types of frequent bleeding may be due to a serious underlying condition requiring surgical treatment, and expert medical advice should always be obtained.

In many cases, this kind of irregular bleeding may be due to a hormonal disturbance, and will respond to hormonal treatment. If you are bleeding heavily, and are in a remote area where no skilled medical advice can be obtained, it is worth trying the following treatment *provided that* you have had a recent check-up, you are otherwise healthy, and you *are certain that you are not pregnant.*

Take one combined oral contraceptive pill, for example Norinyl 1 or Eugynon 30, four times a day for five days. These pills contain standard doses of progesterone and oestrogen hormones, and are readily available worldwide.

I call this a medical or hormonal curettage. Bleeding should stop during treatment, and you should have a period by the seventh day after the last day of treatment. If bleeding does not stop during treatment, the problem will require a skilled assessment, and probably surgery or curettage. If you do not have a period within five to seven days of stopping treatment, you may be pregnant.

Remember that even if this treatment is successful, there may still be an underlying problem, so specialist advice should be obtained at the earliest opportunity.

Unintended pregnancy

Some women become pregnant while travelling, and others begin their trip in the earliest stages of pregnancy. Those who choose not to allow the pregnancy to continue are advised to be very careful. A termination of pregnancy in a developed country, where technical facilities and specialist skills are widely available, is generally a safe procedure; a termination of pregnancy performed without these facilities, and under unhygienic conditions, can cause life-threatening complications and may have serious implications for the mother's future health and fertility. Remember that it is your responsibility to ensure that the facilities you choose are clean and safe—even if this means travelling on to a country where better facilities are available, or returning home.

Also remember that in most cases, time is on your side. Up to six weeks from the last menstrual period, a simple menstrual regulation procedure can be performed. Up to twelve weeks from the last period the termination procedure is safe, although you should definitely avoid delaying any further than this (see p. 412). In exceptional circumstances, action can be taken at up to twenty or twenty-four weeks, depending upon local laws (see Map 9.2, p. 413).

Those who are happy to continue with their pregnancy should

make sure that they have access to adequate medical care (p. 417).

Genital and urinary tract infection

Thrush

Thrush or vaginal candidiasis is one of the most common gynaecological problems encountered by travellers in hot, humid, tropical conditions. Thrush is caused by overgrowth of a yeast normally found in the female genital area. Several factors promote growth of this organism: heat, humidity, the oral contraceptive pill, certain antibiotics, and diabetes. The best way to prevent the problem is to keep the genital area dry and cool; cotton underwear which absorbs perspiration is strongly recommended, and synthetic fabrics should be avoided.

A yeast infection is characterized by a red rash, itching, and a thick, white 'cottage cheese' vaginal discharge.

Treatment Daily vinegar douches (one tablespoon vinegar per quart of water—or roughly 30 ml per litre) may be sufficient to relieve the itching, and return the vagina to its correct pH (acidity). If nothing else is available, yoghurt may also provide relief. When stronger treatment is required, clotrimazole (Canesten) 100 mg intravaginally, daily for seven days, or nystatin (Nystan) 100 000 units intravaginally for fourteen days may be used. An effective single dose treatment has recently become available in some countries, fluconazole 150 mg (Diflucan 150) by mouth. Despite treatment, the condition may recur if the predisposing factors mentioned above have not been rectified.

Cystitis

Cystitis, also called urinary tract infection or the 'urethral syndrome', is a common condition in women and may be a particularly distressing and inconvenient problem in travellers. It often follows an unaccustomed increase in sexual activity. Symptoms usually consist of frequent urination. The infection is usually due to contamination of the urinary passage with bacteria from the patient's own anal area, but may occasionally be the result of a sexually transmitted disease. If laboratory facilities are available, cultures should be performed.

Pain on urination without frequency may be due to vaginal infection, or to genital herpes. A thorough examination should be obtained.

Treatment If symptoms of cystitis appear, drink plenty of fluids. Women from the USA often prefer cranberry juice because it alters the acidity of the urine and may provide some symptomatic relief; cranberry juice is rarely available outside the USA, and citrus fruit juices are an acceptable substitute.

Self-treatment with antibiotics is usually inadvisable. If there is no prospect of skilled medical care, and if symptoms persist, tetracycline 500 mg by mouth four times a day for seven days (total dose 14 g) or doxycyline 100 mg by mouth twice daily for seven days may be taken; these drugs will cover the important possible causes of urinary symptoms, including gonorrhoea, which has always to be considered. It is essential to complete the full course, and this treatment should not be used in pregnancy; milk products interfere with absorption of these drugs.

Only if there is no possibility of a sexually transmitted disease would I advise using more conventional antibiotic treatment for a urinary infection—such as co-trimoxazole (Septrin, Bactrim, etc), two tablets twelve-hourly, for five days—without a laboratory diagnosis.

Self-treatment should be resorted to only in an emergency, and advice from a qualified medical practitioner should be obtained at the earliest opportunity.

Choosing a doctor abroad

Unfortunately, it is not safe to assume that the high standard of medical ethics and professional behaviour you may be accustomed to in your home country will automatically apply to all doctors in every country you visit. For obvious reasons, when dealing with gynaecological problems in a strange country it is important to choose your doctor with care. Your embassy or consulate (or staff who speak your language from another embassy or consulate), expatriates, and local residents may be able to recommend a suitable physician; often, the most reliable recommendations are those from satisfied patients. If you can find a female doctor so much the better.

Always insist on a chaperone when being examined; use your

common sense, but be prepared to refuse if you are asked to submit to what seems to you to be an unreasonable procedure.

Other hazards

Female travellers appear to be at slightly *less* risk of malaria infection than male travellers; one possible explanation is that they take greater care to observe the necessary precautions!

Living abroad

Screening procedures normally taken for granted at home may not be offered as a routine to long-term residents abroad. All women should request screening for cervical cancer, and be familiar with the technique of breast self-examination. The American Cancer Society advises mammography (to detect breast cancer at an early stage) every one to two years in women over forty and annually in those over fifty. Abroad, good quality tests of this type are not always readily available.

On return home

A gynaecological examination on return home is a sensible precaution; be sure to tell your doctor where you have been.

Fever

Many fevers are harmless, but in the tropics the possibility of malaria has always to be considered.

As a physician at the Hospital for Tropical Diseases in London, Dr Anthony Hall *has treated travellers for malaria, amoebic dysentery, typhoid, syphilis, and many other diseases acquired outside the UK.*

Fever has a variety of possible causes (see Table 8.1 below). Most fevers are caused by viruses, such as those responsible for

Table 8.1 Some possible causes of travellers' fever*

Protozoa	
	malaria
	trypanosomiasis (sleeping sickness)
	visceral leishmaniasis (kala-azar)
	amoebiasis (especially amoebic liver abscess)
Bacteria	
	typhoid
	shigellosis (bacillary dysentery)
	meningitis
	brucellosis
	leptospirosis
	tuberculosis
Rickettsiae	
	typhus
Viruses	
	influenza
	viral hepatitis
	arbovirus
	polio
Localized diseases	
	pneumonia
	urinary tract infection
	salpingitis
	appendicitis
	abscess (e.g. dental)
Other	
	heatstroke (see p. 284)

*Note: This list is not comprehensive

the common cold and influenza, and cannot be treated directly. But malaria is the most important cause of fever in the tropics and *a delay in treatment can result in death.*

Important possible causes of fever: some clues

• Fever, chills, and headache are the commonest symptoms of *malaria* (see pp. 119–21) but cough, abdominal pain, diarrhoea, and jaundice may also occur, and may misleadingly suggest that other diseases might be responsible. The fever is often intermittent.

• Fever, nausea, and vomiting, right upper abdominal pain or tenderness, jaundice and dark urine occur in *viral hepatitis* (see pp. 56–65).

• An *amoebic abscess* of the liver may cause fever, with pain in the right upper part of the abdomen.

• *Typhoid* is a common cause of persistent fever. Constipation often occurs early and bloody diarrhoea may develop later (see p. 36).

• *Meningitis* causes fever with headache, neck stiffness, intolerance of bright light, and sometimes a rash (see p. 98).

• *Trypanosomiasis* (sleeping sickness) (see p. 151) is a potentially fatal disease acquired from the bite of a tsetse fly (fresh, perhaps, from having bitten an animal which the traveller has stopped to photograph). It also causes fever.

• *Typhus* also causes fever: the disease is heralded by a red rash on the trunk, which is often faint. At the site of the insect bite, a sore with a black scar called an 'eschar' develops (see p. 165).

• The feverish traveller may, of course be suffering from a 'global' disease rather than one which is more common in or even exclusive to the tropics. For example, pneumonia is a common cause of fever (best revealed by a chest X-ray). A urinary tract infection may cause frequency and burning on urination. Pain in the right lower abdomen may be caused by appendicitis. Pelvic pain in a women may be caused by infection in the fallopian tubes (salpingitis). Fever with a painful tooth may be due to a dental abscess (see p. 350).

Table 8.2 Guidelines for treatment of travellers' fever (if no medical care is available)

Additional symptoms	**Possible diagnosis**	**Suggested treatment**
+ headache in Africa, South East Asia and Latin America	falciparum malaria	quinine 650 mg (two tabs) twice daily for seven days (See also Table 4.1, p. 121)
+ headache in India	vivax malaria	chloroquine base 300 mg (two tabs) twice daily for three days
+ headache and no response to anti-malarial	typhoid	co-trimoxazole (sulphamethoxazole with trimethoprim) (Septrin, Bactrim etc.) two tabs twice daily for two weeks
+ bloody diarrhoea	? bacillary dysentery	co-trimoxazole (sulphamethoxazole with trimethoprim) as above, for five days
+ tender liver (underneath rib cage on right)	? amoebic liver abscess	metronidazole (Flagyl, Zadstat) 800 mg three times daily for 10 days

A tender lump anywhere in the body may be caused by an abscess, which may need surgical treatment.

Treatment

Ideally, a sick traveller should consult a doctor for examination, tests and treatment. However, efficient medical care may not be available.

Most fevers are due to a temporary illness, usually viral, which does not need treatment. Aspirin can be taken to relieve the symptoms of a mild fever.

But if a traveller becomes feverish in tropical Africa, South-East Asia, or Latin America, falciparum malaria is the most likely cause and fever in travellers should always be taken seriously. So I recommend treatment with two tablets of quinine twice daily for seven days (see Table 8.2 above). If fever and headache develop in India, vivax malaria may be the cause, and suitable treatment would be chloroquine 300 mg twice daily for three days. (Further treatment, with primaquine, will be necessary to prevent a subsequent relapse—see p. 122.)

If antimalarial drugs do not cure a fever, then a course of sulphamethoxazole with trimethoprim, also called co-trimoxazole

(Bactrim, Septrin, etc.) may be tried for the presumptive diagnosis of typhoid. Fever plus bloody diarrhoea may be caused by bacillary dysentery, and co-trimoxazole may be helpful (see Table 2.2 p. 36).

Fever and a tender liver (pain in the right, upper abdomen) may be caused by an amoebic liver abscess and a ten day course of metronidazole (Flagyl, Zadstat) may provide relief.

Getting home: aeromedical evacuation

People who are ill and want to fly on a commercial airline are supposed to submit a 'Medical certificate of fitness for air travel', completed and signed by a physician. Airlines regard several diseases as unacceptable in their passengers (see Table 6.1 p. 224), including infectious diseases during the infectious phase. Thus a traveller with a condition such as typhoid or diarrhoea should, strictly, not fly on a plane.

This exclusion could prove fatal to an unfortunate victim, trapped in any one of 100 or so countries with poor medical facilities and a shortage of drugs.

As far as the individual traveller is concerned, the priority is simple: to get home as quickly as possible. Doctors sometimes feel a divided responsibility—to the individual, and to the airline and its other passengers. However, no doctor who cares about the welfare of travellers can fail to sympathize with anyone who is seriously ill, and goes to extraordinary lengths to get on to the next flight out, regardless of airline regulations.

If you do find yourself on board an aircraft, and suspect that you may have an infectious disease, take sensible precautions to minimize the risk to others. Take a seat near the toilet, and keep all physical or verbal contact with the crew or other passengers to a minimum. On arrival at your destination, take a taxi, or if absolutely necessary an ambulance, to the nearest major hospital, preferably one that specializes in infectious diseases (see Appendix 6).

9

Sex and contraception abroad

Sexually transmitted diseases

Travellers are at increased risk of acquiring sexually transmitted diseases. All travellers should know how to reduce the risks if they do not intend to avoid them.

Dr John Naponick *is a public health physician with specialist training in gynaecology, obstetrics, and tropical medicine. He has worked in the USA, Canada, Cameroon, Bangladesh, Thailand, and Burma and is currently Medical Adviser to the US AID mission to El Salvador.*

When Christopher Columbus returned from his voyage of discovery to the New World, an epidemic of syphilis swept Europe. Ever since, historians have debated whether or not Columbus and his sailors were to blame. One thing that *is* certain, however, is that today's traveller is at as great a risk as ever of acquiring a sexually transmitted disease.

Sexually transmitted disease (STD), still popularly known as VD (venereal disease), has reached epidemic proportions in many countries and is a major problem worldwide, encompassing a wide range of infections. Everyone has heard of gonorrhoea and syphilis, but more recently recognized diseases such as chlamydia infection—often harder to document—may be twice as common. Herpes, recently the subject of much public interest, has now been eclipsed by the spectre of AIDS; Although AIDS may be transmitted by contaminated needles, blood products, and from mother to fetus, and is discussed in greater detail on p. 396, it is still above all else a sexually transmitted disease. Changing attitudes to sexual behaviour, as well as promiscuity, prostitution, and homosexual practices, have each contributed to the present pattern of sexually transmitted disease.

As far as the individual traveller is concerned, however, the public health aspects of sexually transmitted infections are less important than their immediate implications.

Risk factors

All STD risk factors depend on individual behaviour. If you do not intend to place yourself at risk, you do not need to read this chapter. The only absolute ways of avoiding STD are abstinence, or sexual intercourse with a partner who is known to be disease free and is completely faithful. Any other type of behaviour will place you at risk of infection. Risk factors include:

• *Travel* People behave differently when they travel. Tourists travel to seek adventure and new experiences, and to make new friends. Sex is certainly part of the attraction. Sex is sometimes even the sole purpose of travel, as evidenced by the growth of the 'sex tourism' industry to certain parts of Asia. The usual norms of the home environment no longer control behaviour. Travellers separated from their families, for example business travellers, the military, seafarers, and immigrants, are all at particular risk.

• *Number of sexual partners* The more sexual partners a person has, the greater the risk of acquiring—and passing on—an STD. Rates of infection are very high in promiscuous homosexuals. Prostitutes in some Asian cities have infection rates reaching 100 per cent. In 1987, 90 per cent of Kenyan prostitutes were found to be HIV positive. Even if you have only one contact with a prostitute you are at high risk of contacting an STD.

• *Frequency of sexual contact* The greater the frequency of sexual contact, the greater the risk of acquiring an STD. For example, men have a 20 to 35 per cent chance of acquiring gonorrhoea from each contact with an infected partner. Two exposures would obviously increase the risk.

• *Age* The highest incidence of STD is found in the fifteen to thirty year-old age group. The incidence declines as age increases. Theoretically one could reduce the risk by choosing a more mature partner.

• *Choice of partner* Certain groups of people are known to be at high risk. They include intravenous drug users, homosexuals, prostitutes, young people with multiple sex partners, and bisexual men; special categories of high risk groups for AIDS include people who have received multiple blood transfusions, haemophiliacs, people who have resided in Haiti or central Africa, or anyone who has had regular sexual intercourse with individuals in the above categories.

In addition to an increased risk of acquiring an STD, travellers face many other difficulties. They may be going from an area of modern medical care to an area with less sophisticated medical facilities. The medical professionals may or may not be as well trained, and the laboratory back-up services may be non-existent. Language barriers may pose an obstacle to communication.

Diseases

A wide variety of diseases can be transmitted sexually, and some are considered in Table 9.1 overleaf. It is beyond the scope of this book to give exhaustive information about each disease; medical texts and lay publications are available for that purpose.

Bacteria, viruses, protozoa, and arthropods may all be transmitted by sexual contact. Sexual intercourse is the usual mode of transmission, but any close contact that allows transfer of infected materials or secretions can transmit disease. The disease can establish itself wherever it finds a suitable environment—usually those areas of the body that are warm, moist, dark, and lined with a mucous membrane, such as the genital area, the mouth, the rectum, etc.

The spectrum of diseases that can be contracted is immense and there is no limit to the number with which one may be afflicted at any one time. Furthermore there is no such thing as immunity towards most of these diseases, so reinfection is likely unless precautions are taken.

Some sexually transmitted infections, such as crab lice, are merely a nuisance. Herpes may recur, may be particularly troublesome, and is possibly linked to cancer of the cervix. Gonorrhoea and chlamydia can cause infertility and painful, incapacitating pelvic infection. Lymphogranuloma venereum can result in genital deformity. Syphilis can lead to insanity and damage to the nervous system, the heart and major blood vessels. AIDS is spreading fast, is no longer just a 'gay plague', and is a hazard that every sexually active male or female traveller must take seriously; AIDS kills. These complications are presented not to scare you, but merely to make you aware of the far-reaching consequences that these diseases have.

Geographical distribution

It is unfortunately not possible to construct a world map showing

Table 9.1 Sexually transmitted diseases

Disease	Causal agent	Occurrence	Incubation	Likely symptoms	Complications
Gonorrhoea	*Neïsseria gonorrhoeae*	worldwide (250 million people affected at any one time)	2–7 days	burning on urination, penile and vaginal discharge	infertility; arthritis; pelvic abscess
Chlamydia	*Chlamydia trachomatis*	worldwide	5–7 days	same as gonorrhoea but may be milder	infertility
Syphilis	*Treponema pallidum*	worldwide (50 million cases each year)	10 days–10 weeks	painless ulcer, rash	occur late; cardio-vascular problems or mental changes
Chancroid	*Haemophilus ducreyi*	subtropical and tropical	3–14 days	painful necrotizing ulcers, painful swelling of lymph nodes	localized
Lymphogranuloma venereum	*Chlamydia trachomatis*	subtropical and tropical	3–30 days	small painless ulcer	stricture of rectum; genital elephantiasis
Herpes	*Herpes simplex* virus	worldwide	2–12 days	painful multiple ulcers	recurrence; cancer of cervix (possible)
Trichomoniasis	*Trichomonas vaginalis,* (a protozoan)	worldwide	4–20 days	vaginal discharge and irritation	local only
Non-specific vaginitis	*Gardnerella vaginalis*	worldwide	7 days	odoriferous vaginal discharge	local only
Anogenital warts	human wart virus	worldwide	1–20 months	cauliflower-like growths	localized
Scabies	*Sarcoptes scabiei* (a mite)	worldwide	2–6 weeks	itching, skin eruptions	local infection
Pubic lice	*Phthirus pubis,* (the crab louse)	worldwide	1–2 weeks	itching	local infection
Intestinal infections	*Campylobacter jejuni* *Shigella* species non-typhoidal salmonella *Entamoeba histolytica* (amoebic dysentery) *Giardia lamblia* (giardiasis)	worldwide in those who practise anal–oral sex as well as by non-venereal transmission	varies	diarrhoea jaundice etc	depend on disease
Others: AIDS	HIV	probably worldwide	2 weeks–5 years (or more)	fever, weight loss etc.	opportunistic infection, death
Hepatitis B	Hepatitis B virus	worldwide	2–6 months	jaundice	carrier state; chronic liver disease

global distribution of risk. While some places certainly have a higher incidence of STD than others, it is important to bear in mind that risk depends on behaviour, not geography.

AIDS has been reported from almost all countries. The highest incidence is in the USA (New York and California), the central African countries of Zaire, Rwanda, Burundi, Central African Republic, Congo, Zambia, Tanzania and Uganda, and Haiti. In the USA, it is mainly a disease of homosexual and bisexual men, but introduction into the heterosexual population has begun. In Africa, AIDS is transmitted heterosexually as well as by contaminated needles, blood products, and from mother to fetus.

Lymphogranuloma venereum (LGV) and granuloma inguinale (GI) are diseases of the tropics and subtropics. LGV is found in West Africa, Asia, the southern USA, South America, Singapore, and major seaports; GI is found in India, the Pacific Islands, Papua New Guinea, West Africa, the West Indies, South America, and the southern USA; chancroid also occurs mainly in the tropics and sub-tropics, but small outbreaks do occur elsewhere.

Most other STD's occur worldwide, gonorrhoea and syphilis in particular are found more often in urban settings, seaports and trading centres; the young (fifteen to thirty-five years) are most often infected; males outnumber females; male homosexuals are at great risk. Heterosexual transmission of AIDS appears to be most common in central Africa, but is growing worldwide.

While it would be nice to give a 'top ten' country-by-country guide to STD, I think it safer to look warily upon easy sex as the greatest risk: sexually transmitted diseases are a worldwide problem.

Prevention

Public health measures

China is the only country in the world that claims to have eradicated syphilis and possibly also gonorrhoea. Its campaign involved eliminating prostitution, providing health education and treatment on a large scale, exerting pressure on health workers and the general public to identify cases, and actively discouraging premarital and extra-marital sex. The success of such measures has few immediately obvious benefits for the traveller: finding a consort may be difficult in countries where the risk of contracting an STD is low!

Personal protection

The only sure way to avoid STD is to avoid sexual contact altogether, or to keep to a mutually faithful relationship with one partner known to be disease free. Anyone not willing or able to do either should know how to minimize the risks and maximize protection.

Marsha Blachman of U C San Francisco says that dealing with AIDS by deciding to be celibate is like trying to deal with being overweight by fasting, it may work for a while, but eventually you get so hungry you eat anything you can find . . .

It is important to acknowledge the risk factors already described, and to avoid sexual contact with individuals at highest risk. In the USA the usual advice on avoiding AIDS includes limiting the number of partners, using condoms, and avoiding anal intercourse; choice of partner is the most important factor and this applies to all STDs.

Clearly prostitutes constitute a high-risk category, and in many Asian countries up to 90 per cent of all sexually transmitted infections result from contact with prostitutes. Brothels, massage parlours, and singles bars offer a high probability of infection.

While it is worth trying to examine a prospective partner for sores, ulcers, pus, or other signs of disease, remember that patients with wide variety of infectious conditions, including AIDS, often look and feel healthy. It is more important to try to find out about their sexual history.

Safe sex STD's (including AIDS) are transmitted by body fluids such as blood, semen, vaginal secretions, urine, and saliva. The term safe sex is used to describe sexual acts that do not allow exchange of body fluids. Examples of safe sex are mutual or simultaneous masturbation, and consistent and correct condom use from start to finish of sexual contact (vaginal, anal, or oral). This approach should be the rule in all casual encounters.

Contraceptive measures

The condom (sheath) is particularly valuable in helping to prevent infection and is also safe, cheap, effective, and widely available. AIDS virus will not pass through an intact condom. If used correctly—throughout sexual contact—a condom appears to reduce the risk to men of acquiring syphilis or gonorrhoea by a factor of 10. Risks to women are also reduced; so when necessary, women should insist that their male partner wears a condom.

Even with a condom, anal intercourse between an infected individual and an uninfected partner poses a risk of transmitting HIV and other infections because condoms may break.

The following recommendations for proper use of condoms to reduce the transmission of STD are based on current advice provided by the CDC, Atlanta:

- Latex condoms should be used because they offer greater protection against viral STD than natural membrane condoms.
- Condoms should be stored in a cool, dry place out of direct sunlight.
- Condoms in damaged packages or those that show obvious signs of age (e.g. those that are brittle, sticky, or discoloured) should not be used. They cannot be relied upon to prevent infection.
- Condoms should be handled with care to prevent puncture.
- The condom should be put on before any genital contact to prevent exposure to fluids that may contain infectious agents. Hold the tip of the condom and unroll it onto the erect penis, leaving space at the tip to collect semen, yet assuring that no air is trapped in the tip of the condom.
- Adequate lubrication should be used. If exogenous lubrication is needed, only water-based lubricants should be used. Petroleum- or oil-based lubricants (such as petroleum jelly, cooking oils, shortening, and lotions) should not be used since they weaken the latex.
- Pessaries, suppositories, and vaginal or rectal preparations that are oil-based, are likely to damage condoms and contraceptive diaphragms made from latex rubber, reducing their contraceptive efficacy as well as reducing protection from STDs.
- Use of condoms containing spermicides may provide some additional protection against STD. However, vaginal use of

spermicides along with condoms is likely to provide greater protection.

• If a condom breaks, it should be replaced immediately. If ejaculation occurs after condom breakage, the immediate use of spermicide has been suggested. However, the protective value of post-ejaculation application of spermicide in reducing the risk of STD transmission is unknown.

• After ejaculation, care should be taken so that the condom does not slip off the penis before withdrawal; the base of the condom should be held while withdrawing. The penis should be withdrawn while still erect.

• Condoms should never be reused.

A diaphragm (cap) can also provide a mechanical barrier to infection, as well as a chemical barrier if used, as recommended, in conjunction with a spermicide. Women who use a diaphragm or whose partners use a condom contract gonorrhoea only one fifth as often as users of oral contraceptives or IUDs. Spermicides will kill most organisms that can cause STD, including the AIDS virus.

Oral contraceptives (the Pill or progestogen-only Pill) do not protect women from STD. However, oral contraceptives do have one protective effect in that they cause thickened cervical mucus. This thick mucus may protect against pelvic inflammatory disease (PID) as it inhibits the spread of STD infections up the cervical passage to the uterus. PID is the consequence of an STD infection spreading up to the fallopian tubes and ovaries and producing fever, abdominal pain and eventual fibrosis, adhesions and scarring. Scar formation may be the cause of later infertility.

One survey showed that women who use an oral contraceptive for twelve months or longer can halve their risk of PID.

Long acting progestogens (p. 408) in the form of implants or injections (Depo-Provera or Noristerat) may also help to prevent PID. The lack of menstruation and thickened cervical mucus may be factors.

IUDs on the other hand, increase the risk of PID by a factor of almost four especially if there is exposure to STD.

Other, time-honoured methods of STD prevention include washing the genital area and urinating immediately after the sex act. These are sensible measures, although keeping a full bladder during the sex act is a prerequisite for the latter, and is not always comfortable or possible; but avoiding transfer of body fluids is much more reliable.

When consulting your doctor prior to travel for advice on the most suitable contraceptive method (pp. 405–13), it is worth taking into account the possible need for protection against STD.

In case of infection

If you think you have caught an STD, or even if you just suspect you have been exposed, you should seek examination by a fully qualified medical practitioner. Early prompt treatment is essential if the disease process is to be arrested and permanent complications are to be avoided. Incorrect, inadequate, or inappropriate treatment may mask the symptoms and allow the disease process to advance. Some diseases, such as syphilis, disappear for long periods of time after the initial symptoms, as if cured, only to reappear again in a more serious form at a later date. There is no effective treatment for AIDS.

Travellers sometimes face a problem in obtaining correct diagnosis and treatment. Some sexually transmitted infections take weeks to appear, and by then the traveller may have moved on to a different country, where the disease may be unfamiliar: several infections favour hot climates, but unfortunately many physicians know only about locally occurring diseases. It is always advisable to tell the physician exactly when and where exposure took place.

You should try to locate the best possible medical facilities: expatriates, diplomats, medical associations, and local businesses may be helpful in directing you to qualified practitioners. In areas where STDs are common, STD clinics can be found more easily. You should not be reluctant to attend a clinic if you think you have a disease: we all think it will never happen to us, but it can.

Diagnosis

Some diagnoses can be made on simple inspection, some require microscopes and cultures and some a serological examination (blood test). The more reliably a diagnosis can be documented, the greater the likelihood that treatment will be effective. I would recommend keeping detailed records of any symptoms you have had, any diagnoses that have been made, any laboratory examinations done, and all treatment. This information may be valuable to your physician upon your return home should you fail to get better.

Dangers of self-diagnosis and treatment

I would discourage you from attempting either self-diagnosis, or self-treatment. If you found yourself alone on a desert island you would have to decide for yourself what to do in those circumstances, but such situations are rare, and you should usually be able to obtain some sort of medical advice. Drugs are available in some countries without prescription, but you may do yourself much harm by making the wrong diagnosis and giving yourself the wrong treatment.

There are several reasons for this. First, there is no one drug that will treat all sexually transmitted infections, and use of the wrong drug may not cure the infection or may not completely cure it.

Second, no drug is free from side-effects, and if you use the wrong drug you may expose yourself to undesirable effects without obtaining any benefits.

Third, there is the problem of *resistance* to certain antibiotics and other drugs. Diseases unfortunately appear capable of keeping one step ahead of medical science. When penicillin first became available in the 1940s, small doses of the drug were capable of killing a wide range of microbes. Since then, certain strains of organism have become resistant to penicillin—i.e. they are able to escape the lethal effects of the antibiotics. This has happened to some strains of gonorrhoea, and *especially those found in many parts of Asia*.

Indiscriminate, inappropriate or incorrect use of a drug against bacteria that have developed resistance to that drug may mean that (i) the infection is not cured (at least using normal doses) and (ii) drug resistance is further encouraged, thus increasing the public health problem. Few buttocks are large enough to receive injections of penicillin in the doses which would now be required to treat infection with penicillin-resistant gonorrhoea.

Once a drug becomes useless, doctors have to switch to using another drug, but unfortunately bacteria that have developed resistance to one antibiotic have a tendency to develop resistance to others as well—for example, some strains of gonorrhoea have become resistant not only to penicillin, but possibly also to tetracycline and to spectinomycin. Ultimately, more expensive, more potent drugs—with more side-effects—have to be used.

A fourth reason for avoiding self-diagnosis and treatment is that you may give yourself a false sense of security that your disease has been cured when in fact is has subsided, only to reappear at a future time in a more dangerous form.

Prophylactic treatment For similar reasons, you should also avoid the prophylactic use of antibiotics or other drugs in an attempt to prevent infection: the drug you choose may well not be effective against any infection you pick up; it will give you a false sense of security, probably increasing the risk of infection: and its indiscriminate use will encourage the development of drug resistance.

Correct treatment

When prescribed a treatment, the most important thing is to take it in the correct amount for the correct time. Taking a drug for shorter than advised may not effect a cure and may encourage drug resistance.

It is usual during treatment to have the symptoms subside after 24 to 48 hours, so it is often tempting to stop the treatment then rather than complete the full course—especially if the medicine you are taking is one that makes you feel lousy.

The standard treatment schedules of the Centers for Disease Control, USA, and the World Health Organization are listed in Table 9.2 on pp. 394–5. I have provided these *not* so that you can treat yourself, but rather to enable you to compare them with any treatment you are offered abroad. If you are diagnosed as having STD and are offered treatment which appears to be substantially different, request an explanation.

Anyone given treatment for an STD should always return to a clinic for a follow-up examination—to confirm that treatment has been successful.

Sexual activity should be avoided during treatment, both to prevent further spread of disease and to avoid confusion: it is rather easier to distinguish recurrence from reinfection if one remains celibate during treatment.

Contacts

In some countries, it is the law that all sexual contacts of individuals who have contracted an STD be named, traced, and treated. This is good practice, as it is the only way to stop the spread of the diseases. Even where it is not the law, mere concern for others should prompt anyone who is being treated for an STD to tell their contacts so that they can seek medical advice in turn. Although this may be embarrassing, it is to be highly recommended.

End of journey

I strongly advise travellers with any possibility of exposure to STD to take the precaution of seeking a physical and laboratory examination on their return home—to protect subsequent, unsuspecting sexual partners from unwelcome gifts from abroad.

Conclusion

Scare tactics have never yet been successful in campaigns to stop promiscuous behaviour, though the AIDS epidemic may change this. The only protection against sexually transmitted diseases is education, and a common-sense approach to prevention combined with prompt treatment of both partners if treatable disease occurs.

If you have difficulty resisting temptation abroad, perhaps you should consider travelling with your usual partner whenever possible.

What to do in an emergency

- In the unusual situation of a traveller developing symptoms of a sexually transmitted disease in a remote place, where no medical advice can be obtained, no laboratory facilities are available, but there is access to a supply of medicines, I advise the following approach—bearing in mind the warnings given in the text regarding self-treatment:

- *Penile discharge in males* The most likely causes of this are gonorrhoea and chlamydia. One antibiotic treatment that could cure both is tetracycline hydrochloride, 500 mg by mouth, four times a day for at least seven days. This treatment would give you a period of seven days to seek medical advice. Even if treatment succeeds, I strongly recommend a check-up after your travels. You might have contracted syphilis at the same time, and this treatment would not have eradicated it.

- *Vaginal discharge in females* I would advise the same treatment as given above for males, for the same reason. If this treatment fails I would then give 2 g metronidazole (Flagyl) by mouth, in a single dose to treat trichomonas. If that failed, I would then give treatment for vaginal thrush (see page 494). If this also fails then medical advice must be sought, even if this means changing your plans.

- *Genital ulcers* In addition to penile and vaginal discharge, the other major manifestation of STD is genital ulceration. There are several diseases that can produce genital ulcers. A good treatment to start with would be tetracycline hydrochloride, 500 mg by mouth, four times a day for 15 days. This would treat syphilis and lymphogranuloma venereum. If this treatment failed you could take a treatment for chancroid: erythromycin 500 mg, by mouth, four times a day until the ulcer has healed. These treatment schedules should give you enough time to find medical assistance.

- Finally, I would caution you once again to seek medical assistance if at all possible, and not to attempt to diagnose and treat yourself unless there is no alternative. There are side-effects to all medicines. These treatments may not be suitable in your particular case, and tetracycline is unsuitable for use in pregnant women.

Table 9.2 Recommended treatment schedules for various sexually transmitted diseases

Disease	Recommended treatment
Chlamydia	tetracycline hydrochloride[1]: 500 mg by mouth, four times a day for at least seven days or doxycycline[1]: 100 mg, by mouth, twice a day for at least seven days or erythromycin: 500 mg, by mouth, four times a day, for at least seven days
Gonococcal infections	tetracycline hydrochloride[1]: 500 mg, by mouth, four times a day for at least seven days or doxycycline[1]: 100 mg, by mouth, twice a day for at least seven days or amoxycillin[2]: 3 g with 1 g probenecid by mouth in one dose or ampicillin[2]: 3·5 g with 1 g probenecid by mouth in one dose or aqueous procaine penicillin G: 4·8 million units injected intramuscularly at two sites with 1 g of probenecid by mouth
Resistant gonococcal infections	ceftriaxone: 250 mg im, plus doxycycline: 100 mg orally twice daily for seven days or tetracycline hydrochloride: 500 mg orally four times a day for seven days
Nongonococcal urethritis	tetracycline hydrochloride[1]: 500 mg, by mouth, four times a day for at least seven days or doxycycline: 100 mg[1], by mouth, twice daily, for at least seven days or erythromycin: 500 mg, by mouth, four times a day, for at least seven days
Gardnerella vaginalis infection	metronidazole: 500 mg, by mouth, twice daily for seven days or ampicillin[2]: 500 mg, by mouth, four times a day for seven days
Trichomoniasis	metronidazole: 2 g, by mouth in a single dose
Syphilis	benzathine penicillin G: 2.4 million units total, injected intramuscularly in a single dose or tetracycline hydrochloride[1]: 500 mg, by mouth, four times a day for 15 days

Table 9.2—*continued*

Disease	Recommended treatment
Chancroid	erythromycin: 500 mg, by mouth, four times a day or sulphamethoxazole with trimethoprim (co-trimoxazole) (Septrin, Bactrim, etc.): one double strength tablet (160/800 mg) by mouth, twice daily for at least 10 days and until ulcers and/or lymph nodes have healed
Lymphogranuloma venereum	tetracycline hydrochloride[1]: 500 mg, by mouth, four times a day for at least seven days or doxycycline[1]: 100 mg, by mouth, twice daily for at least two weeks or erythromycin: 500 mg, by mouth, four times a day for at least two weeks or sulphamethoxazole: 1 g, by mouth, twice daily for two weeks
Scabies (see also p. 172)	lindane[3] (one per cent) lotion or cream: one ounce (30 g) applied thinly for eight hours; wash off thoroughly or crotamiton (10 per cent): apply thinly overnight for two nights, wash off thoroughly 24 hours after second application or sulphur (6 per cent) petrolatum: apply sparingly for three consecutive nights, washing thoroughly 24 hours after the third application
Pubic lice (crab lice) (see also p. 174)	lindane[3] (one per cent) lotion or cream: as for scabies above or lindane[3] (one per cent) shampoo: apply for four minutes and wash off or pyrethrins and piperonyl butoxide: apply to infected area and wash off after 10 minutes

Notes
1. Tetracycline and doxycycline should not be used in pregnancy.
2. Drugs such as ampicillin and amoxycillin are related to penicillin and so should not be taken by anyone who is allergic to penicillin.
3. Lindane is also known as γ BHC.

Acquired immunodeficiency syndrome (AIDS) and its cause: human immunodeficiency virus (HIV)

AIDS has attracted much publicity because it is still relatively new, it is serious and it mainly affects young adults. So far, most AIDS cases have been reported from the United States, but the number of cases reported from other countries is rising rapidly. Risks to travellers depend more upon their own behaviour than upon their choice of destination.

Dr D. Peter Drotman *has been a medical epidemiologist with the Centers for Disease Control, Atlanta, since 1979. He has been working exclusively with AIDS since 1982.*
Thomas A. Leonard *is a senior public health advisor at CDC. He has worked with AIDS since 1983 in the United States and Africa.*

Acquired immunodeficiency syndrome (AIDS) is the name given to a group of health problems first recognized in the United States in 1981. By early 1989, more than 85 000 cases had been reported to the Centers for Disease Control (CDC) from all over the United States. That total is expected to exceed 350 000 by the end of 1992. In 1981, the World Health Organization (WHO) received reports of AIDS cases from eight nations. By late 1988, that figure had risen to 140 countries, 18 of which had reported more than 1000 cases (Table 9.3).

People with AIDS have developed a specific defect in their natural immune (defence) system, which has left them vulnerable to illnesses that would not otherwise be a threat. These illnesses are referred to as 'opportunistic' diseases. The cause of the defect is an infection with a virus called human immunodeficiency virus (HIV).

Who is at risk?

In Europe, the Americas, and Australia, nearly all reported

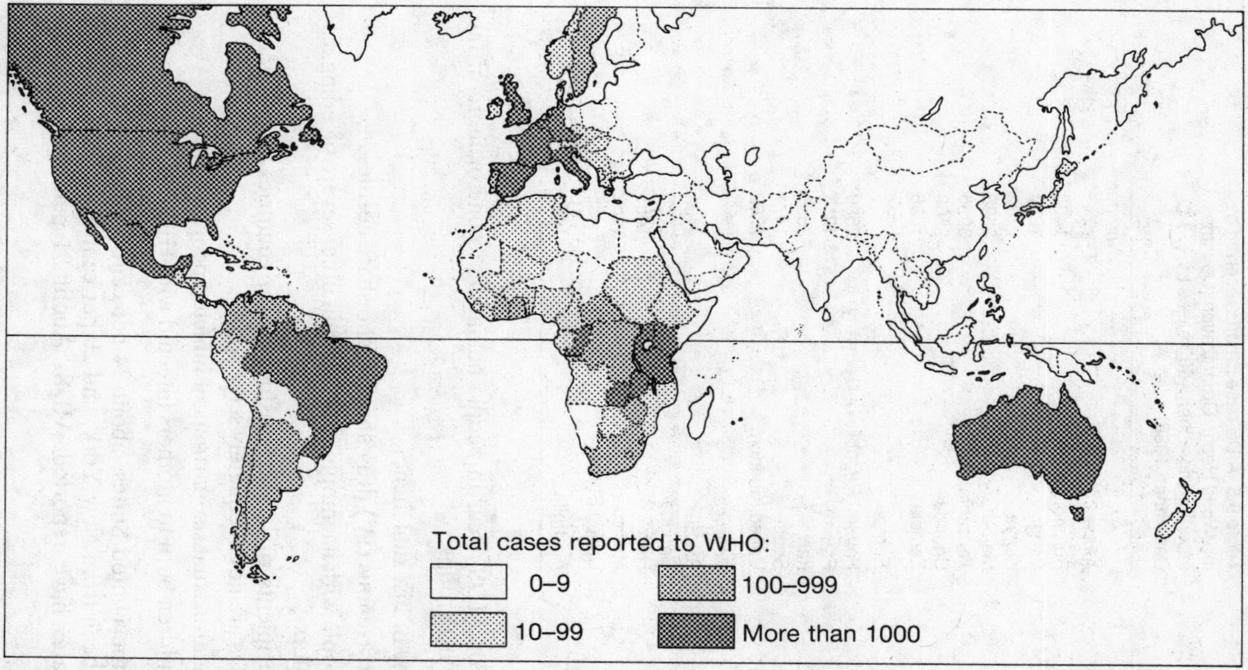

Map 9.1 Global distribution of officially reported AIDS cases (December 1988). Note: case reporting is unreliable in many parts of the world, and may underestimate the true number of cases by as much as 90 per cent. Reproduced by courtesy of the WHO Global Programme on AIDS.

Table 9.3 AIDS case reports received by the World Health Organization (Countries reporting more than 1000 cases by December, 1988).

	Number
Africa:	
Burundi	1408
Congo	1250
Kenya	2732
Malawi	2586
Tanzania	3055
Uganda	5508
Zambia	1056
Europe:	
Federal Republic of Germany	2580
France	4211
Italy	2556
Spain	1471
United Kingdom	1862
Americas:	
Brazil	4436
Canada	2156
Haiti	1455
Mexico	1562
United States	78 485
Australia	1079

cases of AIDS occur in people belonging to one or more of the following groups:

1. Gay or bisexual men;
2. Intravenous (IV) drug abusers who share needles;
3. People with haemophilia (or certain other severe bleeding disorders);
4. Recipients of blood transfusions (in countries where donations are not adequately screened);
5. Heterosexual sex partners of infected people;
6. Children born to mothers infected with HIV.

In the United States, about 24 per cent of all cases reported have been from New York, and 20 per cent from California; all 50 states have reported AIDS. About 91 per cent of AIDS patients investigated so far have been male; and about 75 per cent of these have been gay or bisexual. The age of those affected ranges primarily from 25–44 years. All races and ethnic groups have been affected.

In Africa, men and women are affected in about equal numbers, and transmission via heterosexual contact and unscreened blood transfusion seems more common, along with transmission to newborn babies from infected women during pregnancy. The precise magnitude of the AIDS problem in Africa is poorly documented, but accumulating evidence indicates it is certainly substantial. WHO estimates that only about 10 per cent of cases are actually officially reported.

Although the number of cases reported from Asia has so far been small, the potential for sexual transmission is considerable if effective preventive measures are not implemented. The role of transmission through IV drug abuse and needle-sharing in Asia is being investigated. In Thailand in 1985, 2–3 per cent of IV drug abusers were HIV positive. By 1988, that figure had risen to 30 per cent.

The problem in South America is growing rapidly. Brazil is second only to the United States in number of reported cases in the Americas.

In summary, AIDS and HIV infection are global problems and are increasing. The World Health Organization estimated that between 5 and 10 million people worldwide were infected with HIV in 1988, of whom approximately 1 million were in the USA. Sexual and drug-using behaviour, rather than geography, determine the risk that most travellers face.

How is HIV transmitted?

Epidemiological and laboratory evidence clearly show that HIV is transmitted from one person to another sexually (between gay men, and heterosexually both from women to men and from men to women). It is also transmitted through exposure to blood or blood components; and before, during, and shortly after childbirth, when infected women may transmit the virus across the placenta to the fetus or to the infant at the time of birth and possibly through breast-feeding. The most important behavioural risk factors for contracting HIV infection include having multiple sexual partners and needle sharing among intravenous drug abusers. In countries where disposable medical equipment is not available, reuse of needles, syringes, or other blood-contaminated items presents a potential route of transmission. Moreover, in many of the same countries, safe alternatives to breast-feeding may not be available, and this contributes further to the local problem.

HIV is not transmitted via casual contact. Several studies of the families and communities of AIDS patients, and of medical personnel involved in AIDS patient care, show no virus transmission via casual contact, household contact (including sharing kitchens, utensils, toilets, and baths), or other means such as mosquito bites. Animals, food, water, air, the environment, schools, the workplace, public areas, coughing and sneezing, and swimming pools have not been associated with HIV transmission.

To what illnesses are AIDS patients prone?

Various 'opportunistic' diseases may affect patients with AIDS. About 70 per cent of patients studied have had one or both of two opportunistic diseases: a type of cancer known as Kaposi's sarcoma, and *Pneumocystis carinii* pneumonia, a parasitic infection of the lungs.

Other opportunistic infections seen in AIDS include unusually severe infections with mycobacteria, candida (yeast), cytomegalovirus, herpes simplex virus, and toxoplasma. Milder infections with these organisms do not suggest immunodeficiency and are not considered opportunistic.

Kaposi's sarcoma The opportunistic diseases that characterize AIDS are not new. Kaposi's sarcoma was first described over 100 years ago. Before 1980 in Europe and North America, it primarily affected elderly men and was seldom fatal, even five or ten years after diagnosis. It was also seen in children and young adults in some parts of equatorial Africa and in a few other locations.

Kaposi's sarcoma usually occurs anywhere on the surface of the skin or in the mouth. In the early stages, it may look like a bruise or blue-violet or brownish spot. The lesions grow larger and may ulcerate. It may spread to other organs, including lymph nodes, causing them to enlarge. Some AIDS patients with Kaposi's sarcoma have responded to a newly licensed treatment, interferon.

Pneumocystis carinii pneumonia (PCP) affected a few hundred adults and children in the United States each year before its increase was noted in 1978–79, but usually it was seen only in patients with a severe underlying illness (such as leukaemia) or in patients receiving therapy with drugs known to suppress the immune system (such as the drugs used in kidney transplant patients to prevent organ rejection). In fact, an increase in cases of PCP without such underlying predisposing factors was one of the first clues that the epidemic of AIDS was beginning.

Pneumocystis carinii pneumonia has symptoms similar to any other form of severe pneumonia, especially fever, cough, and difficulty in breathing. Specific antibiotic treatments for this pneumonia are available, such as trimethoprim/sulfamethoxazole, pentamidine, and several experimental drugs, but the case fatality rate is still high and *Pneumocystis carinii* pneumonia remains the leading cause of death in AIDS patients in most countries. Some AIDS patients have had Kaposi's sarcoma and *Pneumocystis carinii* pneumonia at the same time.

How serious is AIDS?

AIDS has a very high fatality rate, and investigators at CDC do not know of any patient with AIDS who has regained lost immunity. There is no cure for AIDS or HIV infection as yet, but experimental trials are under way with drugs that interrupt the replication of HIV. One such drug is zidovudine (often called AZT), which appears to prolong the lives of some AIDS patients. It is now licensed in some countries, including the United States and the United Kingdom. It is expensive, has toxic side effects, and patients must take it indefinitely.

Symptoms and diagnosis

Infection with HIV typically begins with a flu-like illness that resolves spontaneously. The infected person is then symptomless for up to 10 years or more in some cases. However, an infected person can transmit HIV to sex partners and needle-sharers during this long asymptomatic period. There are no clear-cut symptoms that indicate the loss of immunity, but many patients who have developed AIDS experienced fever, loss of appetite and weight, extreme fatigue, and enlargement of lymph nodes. These early symptoms often occur over a period of months. In some cases, they are severe enough to result in hospitalization or disability. In parts of Africa (mainly East Africa), this condition is sometimes called 'slim disease' because of the characteristic weight loss. Some patients develop associated diseases—such as Kaposi's sarcoma and *Pneumocystis carinii* pneumonia, and are then classified as having AIDS.

HIV can also infect the central nervous system directly and produce various disorders including dementia, encephalopathy, sensory-motor deficits, and other problems.

Tests

No single specific test is available for diagnosing AIDS. In many patients the number and function of certain white blood cells decreases. Although this can be measured, these tests are not generally available, nor perfectly sensitive and specific. They are expensive, and are usually done in major research centres. However, other tests may also help the physician to establish the diagnosis of AIDS and its associated diseases.

A test to detect antibodies to the virus that causes AIDS became available in 1985. This test does not indicate the presence of the virus directly, but a repeatedly reactive antibody test does provide evidence of infection. This test is used to screen donors of organs, blood, plasma, and other tissues for transfusion, transplantation, or manufacture of clotting factor concentrates for people with haemophilia, and for other blood products. It is also used as an adjunct to diagnosis, and to assist in prevention-oriented counselling of sexually active men and women at risk for HIV, women contemplating pregnancy, intravenous drug abusers, and others.

Some countries require HIV antibody testing before granting certain classes of visas (usually longer term resident, work, or student visas). The World Health Organization does not endorse or approve of this practice, and travellers should check testing requirements of nations on their itinerary with appropriate consular authorities.

Prevention

The US Public Health Service has made the following recommendations for prevention:

- A mutually faithful sexual relationship with a non-infected person is a safe way to avoid HIV infection.
- Do not have sexual intercourse with people who have or might be suspected of having AIDS or HIV infection.
- Do not use intravenous drugs, or have sexual intercourse with people who abuse them.
- Be aware that having multiple sexual partners increases the chance of contracting AIDS or HIV infection.
- People whose behaviour puts them at risk for HIV infection should not donate blood or plasma or organs for transplantation.
- Blood transfusions (see p. 501) should be given only when medically essential and should be screened.
- Use extreme care when handling hypodermic needles. Do not recap, bend, or clip needles. Dispose of them into impervious containers.

Advice for travellers is summarized overleaf.

Summary advice for travellers

- Travellers are normally at no special risk for HIV infection or AIDS unless they engage in sexual or drug-taking behaviour that puts them in contact with people who might be infected with the virus that causes AIDS.
- Gay men and sexually active heterosexual men and women should take particular note of the recommendations of the US Public Health Service above. Engaging only in safer sexual practices and using condoms for all sexual intercourse (vaginal, anal, or oral) can reduce the risk of infection with HIV and other sexually transmitted organisms. Spermicides containing nonoxynol-9 or other active agents have been recommended as adjuncts to using condoms. Even though laboratory evidence shows that these spermicides inactivate HIV rapidly, they should not be used without condoms.
- Intravenous drug-abusers risk multiple health problems outside the scope of this chapter. Suffice it to note that needle sharing is very dangerous.
- When living or travelling in countries where reuse of medical equipment is common, it is important to make sure that medical staff who look after you are trained in and practice good infection control techniques, such as sterilizing needles, syringes, and surgical equipment before reuse. Blood transfusion abroad is discussed further on p. 501.
- Unless you are certain that new or sterile equipment is being used, skin piercing procedures such as tattooing, ear piercing, acupuncture, or electrolysis should always be avoided.
- Gammaglobulin (injection for prevention of hepatitis A) is screened and treated to remove the risk of viral infection. It is safe from HIV if manufactured according to the recommendations of health authorities in industrialized nations.
- An epidemic of HIV infection precedes an epidemic of AIDS by several years. HIV infection is usually not clinically obvious; travellers should not assume that AIDS is an insignificant risk in countries that may have reported only a small number of cases, and should always take appropriate precautions.

Contraception and travel

Contraception is a neglected aspect of health care for travellers, but can make all the difference between an enjoyable trip and a miserable one. Not all methods of contraception are equally problem-free in travellers, and an appropriate method should be chosen carefully before departure.

Dr Elphis Christopher *has been involved in Family Planning for over twenty years. She lectures to medical students and has made numerous radio and TV appearances to discuss sex education, family planning, and related topics.*

Glossy holiday brochures use covert promises of sexual adventure to sell holidays. Away from everyday stresses and routines, and far from the influence of anyone who might disapprove, holidays and travel bring relaxation of inhibitions, a sense of freedom and are undoubtedly a time of increased sexual activity both for couples and those travelling on their own.

Too many travellers leave home unprepared. Single people—particularly women, who are most at risk from the consequences—may be unwilling to anticipate a holiday sexual adventure on the grounds that 'I am not that kind of girl'; they may find it difficult to believe that pregnancy can begin on holiday, or that contraceptive precautions may be necessary in advance of a romantic attachment. Others, men and women, simply don't bother.

Avoiding an unwanted pregnancy, an unintended souvenir of an otherwise enjoyable holiday, is not merely a question of chance; travelling prepared must not be confused with promiscuity, and it is always better to be safe than sorry.

If you are sexually active and settled on a particular contraceptive method, all you may need to do is visit your own doctor or family planning clinic for a check-up and obtain any contraceptive supplies you will need while away—and also confirm that the method you are using is appropriate for the length and nature of your trip. Family planning clinics in the UK are usually sympathetic about providing extra supplies without charge, but for prolonged periods abroad it is worth finding out what is available in the country or countries you intend to visit before you leave. The International Planned Parenthood Federation (IPPF) can provide information on this*.

Travelling may reduce the effectiveness of contraceptive precautions which are otherwise perfectly adequate at home, and the specific problems that arise for each method are discussed below. Normally these problems are not serious enough to warrant changing from your established method, but you should be aware of them, and perhaps travel prepared to switch to an alternative method in an emergency.

Once you have decided upon a method, or if you plan to switch to a new method, it is worth getting used to it well in advance of your trip, to enable any side-effects or problems to reveal themselves in time to be sorted out. This is a particularly important consideration with the Pill—nausea and tiredness and slight spotting (breakthrough bleeding) are common when taking it for the first time, but usually settle by the third packet—and with the coil (IUD).

The various methods available are discussed below along with their advantages and disadvantages, although travellers may well need to consult their doctor or family planning clinic so as to make the most suitable choice for their own circumstances.

It may be advisable to travel with *two* methods to ensure against failure of one of these methods.

The combined oral contraceptive: 'the Pill'

The Pill is a popular method of contraception, familiar and convenient to use; with correct use its reliability is 93–99 per cent. If you are on the Pill be sure to travel with an adequate supply, because further supplies of your particular brand may not necessarily be easy to obtain—especially in remote areas. Make allowances for delays and any unexpected extension of your trip.

If you run out, keep an empty pack so that a doctor or a pharmacist can identify your brand—brand names of the same variety of the Pill usually differ from country to country. Thus a widely prescribed variety like Microgynon 30 occurs under no fewer

* addresses: UK: Regent's College, Inner Circle, Regent's Park, London NW1 4NS Tel. 01 486 0741.
USA: 105 Madison Avenue, New York, NY Tel. (212) 679 2230.

than twenty other brand names around the world. If exactly the same Pill cannot be obtained and a different one is prescribed, do not leave a seven-day gap between packets, but go straight on to the new Pill regardless of any bleeding. Other contraceptive precautions will not then be necessary.

Stomach upsets and diarrhoea affect most travellers at some time or another. *Stomach upsets and severe diarrhoea reduce absorption of the Pill, and may leave the traveller without protection.* All travellers on the Pill should be aware of this, and should be prepared to use an alternative method when necessary.

A barrier method (see below) should be used to protect intercourse over the duration of the stomach upset and for seven days after it has ended. If vomiting occurs within three hours of taking a pill, an additional pill should be taken. If vomiting continues another method of contraception will have to be used.

Antibiotics such as tetracycline or ampicillin also reduce the absorption and effectiveness of the Pill, and another method of contraception should be used during a course of antibiotics and for seven days afterwards.

In both instances, if the seven days coincides with the seven pill-free days, do not take a break of seven days but carry straight on with another packet of pills. Do not worry if there is no withdrawal bleeding.

Time zones cause another potential hazard to travellers on the Pill. When time zones are crossed, make sure that you take a pill every twenty-four hours, and continue to do so every day at the same time. If that means having to wake up in the middle of the night to take a pill, take it *earlier* before going to sleep rather than later; no more than twenty-four hours should elapse between doses—particularly with newer varieties of the low-dose Pill—both for protection against pregnancy and to prevent breakthrough bleeding or spotting.

Air hostesses who are continually travelling may find it useful to have two wristwatches, and to keep one of them on 'home time' for this purpose.

Travel can interfere with periods, even when a woman is on the Pill; so a missed period does not necessarily mean that she is pregnant (p. 368)—provided of course that the daily doses have been taken regularly. Women who prefer not to have periods at all while travelling can take the Pill continuously, without a seven-day break in between packets; *but remember to take extra packets to allow for this*. This is not advisable with the biphasic or triphasic Pills because the dose in the first seven pills is too low to prevent possible breakthrough bleeding; triphasic brands are probably best avoided for long journeys which cross time zones, since the margin of error is less with this type and the risk of pregnancy increases if they are not taken regularly.

High altitude, dehydration, and extreme cold stress, are all associated with changes in blood viscosity. Although as yet there is no clear evidence of an increased thrombosis risk among women taking the Pill at high altitude, it would seem wise not to do so.

The progestogen-only Pill (POP)

The progestogen-only Pill, or POP, is sometimes used by women who cannot take the combined Pill, although the same considerations apply. It is *not* 100 per cent effective (only 96–98 per cent) and it *must* be taken at a fixed time each day in order to remain effective. For this reason it is not suitable for women going on long journeys or crossing time zones. If a pill is forgotten, take one as soon as it is remembered, but use an additional method for 48 hours. Antibiotics do not affect the progestogen-only Pill.

The coil or intrauterine device (IUD)

Women who already have a coil should have it checked before going abroad. If it is a copper-bearing device such as a Copper 7 or Copper T, make sure that it is not due for a change. These coils are effective only for three years, although newer copper-bearing devices—such as Nova T or Novagard—remain effective for five years. All-plastic devices such as the Lippes Loop can remain in the womb for many years provided that there are no problems.

The coil is only 98 per cent effective, but has the advantage that it is not affected by stomach upsets or time zones. It can, however, be expelled by the womb, so it is a sensible precaution to check after each period that the threads can still be felt. If a 'hard bit' (part of the coil itself) can be felt as well as the threads, the coil may be coming out and will need to be checked by a doctor. An examination is not necessary once the coil has come out;

obviously protection ceases immediately, and another method must be used.

The coil is not suitable for women with heavy or prolonged periods—it may make these worse. A newly fitted coil may also cause irregular and sometimes heavy bleeding in the first couple of months—hardly ideal if you are just off on a beach holiday in a new bikini! Heavy or continuous bleeding may make you feel tired and ruin your holiday. It is therefore a good idea to have the coil fitted well in advance, so that any problems can be sorted out before you travel. A coil may also increase the risks of sexually transmitted disease (see p. 388). The coil is most suitable for older women who have had children, since side-effects such as heavy, painful periods are less common, and there is less chance of the coil being expelled.

In the USA, many IUD manufacturers have withdrawn their products from the market, on account of fear of litigation. These products are still available in other countries.

Barrier methods

The sheath (condom)

This male method is about 85–98 per cent effective when used correctly. Although it interferes with the sex act it provides some protection against sexually transmitted disease including HIV (see p. 387), and is particularly useful for a man travelling alone.

It is also valuable for women or couples who want to take along a reliable alternative, in case of problems with the Pill, or in case the coil is expelled. The sheath is a good method for the chance sexual encounter, and travels well. In the UK sheaths are available free of charge from family planning clinics (though not from GPs).

The cap (diaphragm)

The cap is another useful method, with about the same effectiveness as the sheath. It needs to be fitted by a doctor, and the woman must be taught how to use if correctly. A cap lasts for about six months to one year, so on a long trip it may be advisable to take along a spare.

The cap must be used with spermicidal cream or jelly. Creams may become more messy in hot climates but do not lose their effectiveness. Foams in aerosol containers can be a useful alternative. In addition, pessaries should be inserted if a second act of intercourse takes place soon after the first. Pessaries are designed to melt at body temperature, and this can be an obvious problem in hot countries; pessaries wrapped individually with silver foil travel best, and should be kept in a cool place.

Foaming tablets also travel well, although if conditions are humid the lid of their container should always be firmly closed: moisture will make the tablets dissolve. Foaming tablets are unfortunately no longer available in the UK, although they can often be obtained in other countries. The cap provides some protection from sexually transmitted diseases (see p. 387).

The contraceptive sponge

This is an attractive-sounding method that is convenient and easy to use. Unfortunately it is not very effective, but it is certainly better than using nothing.

The sponge, which is impregnated with spermicide, is inserted into the vagina and fits over the neck of the womb (cervix). It provides protection for up to twenty-four hours, and during this time, intercourse may be repeated without need for further measures. It should not be left in for longer than this, and is discarded after use.

It does not require a doctor's prescription, and is sold at most pharmacies (in packets of three). It is relatively expensive.

It is unsuitable for young, fertile women who need 100 per cent protection—it is 20 times *less* effective than the Pill; it is most suitable for women over 45 in whom the risk of pregnancy is in any case small, or for women who do not particularly mind when their next pregnancy occurs.

Injectable contraceptives

Injectable contraceptives (Depo-Provera and Noristerat) are virtually 100 per cent effective and work in a similar way to the progestogen-only pill.

Depo-Provera is given by injection into the muscle of the buttock or upper arm and remains effective for three months. It is useful for women going on long trips, and crossing time zones frequently. It is not affected by stomach upsets or antibiotics. Side-effects often occur, such as irregular and occasionally heavy bleeding, especially with the first injection. With subsequent injections, the periods may stop altogether. This is how the injection *should* work, which makes it an ideal method for the woman who does not want regular periods. If Depo-Provera is chosen, the woman needs to be settled on it before she travels. It is available in many countries.

A second injectable contraceptive, Noristerat, has similar properties (and side-effects) to Depo-Provera and is equally effective. Noristerat is also available in many countries, including some where Depo-Provera is unavailable. Neither is available in the USA.

Using contraception for the first time

The Pill is probably the most sensible method for a couple going on honeymoon, who have not had sex before and who do not want a pregnancy straight away. Although honeymoons are often pictured to be idyllic and carefree, in reality they can be a time of great anxiety and stress, with both partners worrying whether sex will be all right.

Sexual adjustment to each other may take time, and methods that directly interfere with the sex act—such as the sheath or cap—may interrupt love play and can make that adjustment more complicated. If you choose the Pill, begin taking it well in advance, so that any problems can be dealt with before you leave.

The 'morning after' Pill, or postcoital contraception

This method of birth control may be used in an emergency. It works by preventing implantation of the fertilized egg in the womb. It is preferable to abortion but should not be used on a regular basis. It is useful on those occasions when a sheath bursts or the coil is expelled, or for the woman who has had unprotected intercourse.

Two tablets of the combined Pill, Eugynon 50 or PC4 (norgestrel 500 μg, ethinyloestradiol 50 μg) or Ovran (levonorgestrel 250 μg, ethinyloestradiol 50 μg), must be taken within 72 hours of an unprotected act of sexual intercourse and then another two tablets 12 hours later. The tablets often cause nausea, and if vomiting occurs within three hours of the tablets another two tablets should be taken. The next period may arrive slightly earlier than expected.

The 'morning after' Pill can be obtained from family planning clinics or general practitioners.

Abortion

Travellers who become pregnant abroad and want an abortion may find this difficult to arrange. At the last count 60 out of 128 countries listed by the IPPF prohibit abortion except in extreme circumstances—rape, or life-threatening illness. Skilled medical care may be very expensive, or almost impossible to obtain (see p. 370). Map 9.2 (opposite) gives an indication of the legal position in most countries; further information can be obtained from the IPPF (address on p. 406) which also publishes a list of family planning offices in different countries.

RU 486 (the abortion pill)

RU 486 (Mifepristone) is a synthetic steroid which counteracts the hormone progesterone. Progesterone is produced naturally in the body and is essential to maintain a pregnancy. By blocking the action of progesterone RU 486 induces a miscarriage. It is more effective when used with another drug, prostaglandin. RU 486 is given as a single dose (three 200 mg tablets) by mouth, and a pessary of prostaglandin is inserted into the vagina 48 hours later. The abortion or miscarriage happens spontaneously about 6 hours later. This treatment can be given to women who are up to 8 weeks pregnant and is effective in 95 per cent of cases. Side effects include period pains and prolonged bleeding. Less than 10 per cent of women have severe pain lasting about an hour. This responds to a strong pain-killer.

RU 486 is only licensed for use under medical supervision in France and China.

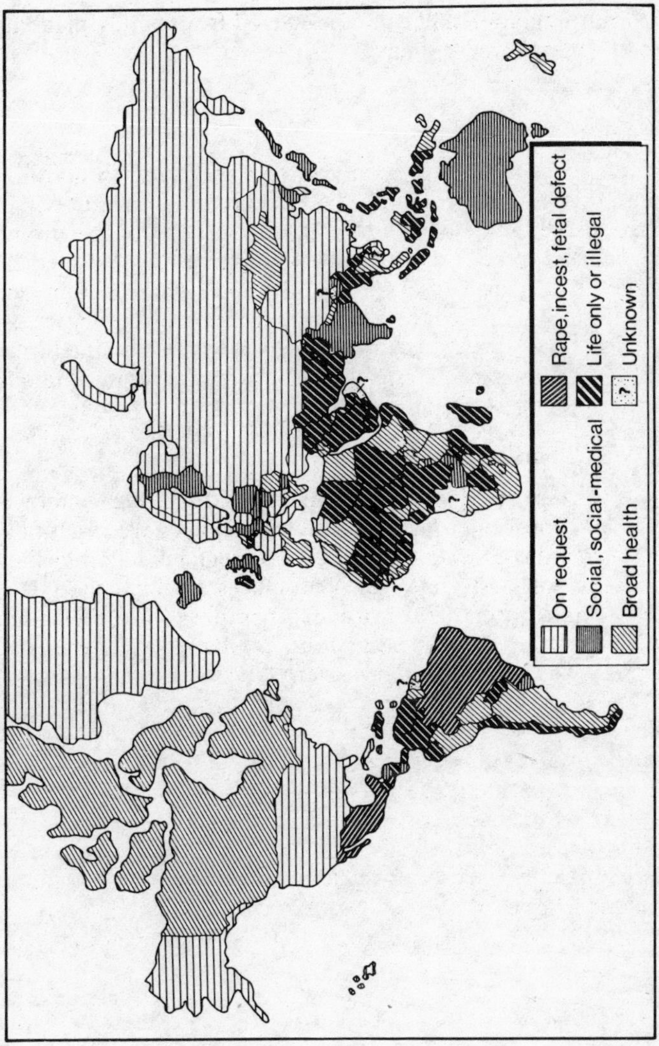

Map 9.2 Abortion: Legal status in different countries. (From *Induced abortion, a world review*, Tieze, C. and Hawan, S. K., The Alan Guttmacher Institute, New York 1986. Reproduced by permission.)

10

Travellers with special needs

Travel in pregnancy

No woman can be realistically assured in advance that her pregnancy will be trouble-free, and for travel, some extra precautions are necessary.

Professor Herbert Brant *is Professor of Clinical Obstetrics and Gynaecology at University College Hospital, London.*

We take travel increasingly for granted, but its implications for women who are pregnant or may become pregnant whilst away are worth a little thought. Large numbers of women do travel in pregnancy, and they sometimes travel long distances; most have no real problems, but an unlucky few regret having ventured forth. The widely varying standard of medical care and its availability in different countries is more important than the direct effects of travel on pregnancy. But at least being aware of the problems may help you to minimize their effects.

Possible problems

Why should pregnant women be more concerned about travel? The likelihood of a problem needing medical attention arising is greater during pregnancy. On statistical grounds alone, women should hesitate before travelling to any area where medical services will be of doubtful quality or where misunderstandings due to language or cultural problems are going to make communication and therefore diagnosis and treatment more difficult.

No woman can be realistically assured in advance that she will have a trouble-free pregnancy. Although it is not always a popular concept, it is worth remembering that pregnancy is normal only when viewed in retrospect—that is, *after* no problems have occurred.

Routine tests in early pregnancy

Don't miss out on important tests that should be completed in the first half of pregnancy—postpone your trip, if necessary. Serious blood conditions of the fetus such as thalassaemia (in those of Mediterranean or Asian origin) or sickle cell anaemia (in those of

African origin) can be detected early in pregnancy—in time for a pregnancy to be terminated if the fetus is affected. The blood test for spina bifida (AFP) is carried out at 16–18 weeks, and the amniocentesis test for Down's syndrome in older women at about 16 weeks. (In many countries, amniocentesis is likely to be largely replaced by the new chorion biopsy test, which is carried out between 9 and 11 weeks). It is now quite common to have an ultrasound examination at some time in the first 24 weeks (but usually at 18 weeks) to confirm the age of the fetus in case of problems later in pregnancy, and also to detect abnormalities that might have arisen during development of fetal organs.

Miscarriage

Spontaneous abortion (miscarriage) is the commonest problem of early pregnancy. It usually occurs during the first three months. If it merely threatens, as evidenced by vaginal bleeding, the eventual outcome will *not* be altered because the woman travels.

Miscarriages in the early months are due to the inevitable errors of a biological system—errors in cell division during the early stages of development of the fetus or the placenta, and errors concerned with the attachment of the placenta to the wall of the uterus. Travel won't cause miscarriage other than *indirectly*, through the effect of, say, high fever associated with infection, or severe dehydration associated with diarrhoea.

Of more pressing concern are the immediate complications of miscarriage, which include the occasional life-threatening haemorrhage, the occasional serious infection or the problems of inept medical treatment employed to cope with them.

Miscarriage, although uncommon at a later stage of pregnancy, can occur at any time though once the fetus is able to survive, it is termed premature labour; the above complications are more common with later miscarriages. Any pregnant woman who has had a previous late miscarriage, or has any condition predisposing to miscarriage, is ill-advised to travel in mid-pregnancy.

Premature labour

If labour starts early but at a time when the resulting baby could live (any time after 24 weeks) then the whole future of the baby can depend on the availability of expert care. Without this, the baby is likely to be seriously mentally or physically handicapped for life—if he or she survives. If expert care is available it can be extremely expensive, especially if prolonged intensive care is necessary. Where good obstetric care is available, treatment can sometimes be given to stop or delay premature labour.

Other complications

In late pregnancy, other possible problems are haemorrhage from a normally situated placenta or from a placenta growing near the cervix (placenta praevia); so-called toxaemia of pregnancy which is usually heralded by a rising blood pressure; and premature rupture of the membranes. Such complications threaten both mother and fetus, and ready availability of expert care reduces the risks.

Before you go

Women who are pregnant or are contemplating pregnancy should find out as much as possible about medical services at their destination before travelling to foreign parts or deciding to become pregnant during a prolonged stay abroad.

Insurance

Be sure to check that any travel or sickness insurance covers medical care for the consequences of pregnancy; such additional cover will usually need to be arranged separately (p. 469).

You may need to make advance arrangements to have finance on call, as most insurance will be in the form of a refund. If you are British and travelling to an EEC country, obtain the pamphlet T1 and apply for certificate E111 from your local National Insurance (Department of Health and Social Security) Office (p. 471).

Immunization

Vaccinations that involve a live virus or are likely to lead to a high temperature should be avoided during pregnancy. A medical certificate can circumvent the vaccination requirements for travel.

Poliomyelitis, measles, rubella, and yellow fever vaccines all involve live viruses (and so did smallpox). Vaccination against rubella and poliomyelitis should have been carried out *before* pregnancy. Diphtheria and typhoid vaccines may cause high temperature and should be avoided. BCG (against tuberculosis) can affect the fetus, and is therefore also not given. (See also p. 485.)

Antimalarial tablets

If you are pregnant and are travelling to an area where there is a risk of contracting malaria, it is strongly advisable to take the appropriate tablets to prevent infection (p. 124). In some areas malaria is resistant to certain drugs, so seek expert advice on what to take for the area you intend to visit. Chloroquine (Avloclor, Nivaquine) and proguanil (Paludrine) are generally agreed to be quite safe in pregnancy. There has been some reluctance to recommend the combined antimalarial drugs Maloprim (pyrimethamine+dapsone) and Fansidar (pyrimethamine+sulfadoxine) in pregnancy on theoretical grounds (unrelated to the toxic effects discussed on p. 126), and expert advice should be sought before using them.

Travel

Air

Provided that the cabin is pressurized, reduced pressure on board an airliner (p. 223) should have no adverse effect upon healthy women with a normal pregnancy. If a significant problem with the function of the placenta is suspected, however, air travel should be avoided because the slightly reduced oxygen level may harm the fetus.

Most airlines will not accept you for travel after 32 weeks of pregnancy, but will sometimes stretch this to 36 weeks if you can produce a medical certificate stating that all is well. Policy varies between airlines and also depends on the length of the flight. It is obviously difficult to obtain medical assistance in the air if labour begins unexpectedly!

Pregnant women and those in the first month after delivery have a small but definitely increased risk of developing a blood clot in the deep veins of the legs (deep-vein thrombosis). These clots occasionally travel to the lungs via the bloodstream and can prove fatal. When travelling by air do not sit in a cramped position for a long period, because pressure from the seat and from the fetus slows the circulation in the legs (see p. 229). Tense up the legs and wriggle the toes from time to time; and stand up and walk about the airplane at least every hour.

Other forms of travel

Sitting in a cramped position in a car, bus, or train has the same effect of impairing blood circulation in the legs. Stand up and walk about every hour or so; if you are travelling by road, stop the car every hour, get out and take a walk.

During pregnancy, women should drive with more care and more slowly, as pregnancy sometimes affects concentration and reaction time in an emergency. Pregnant women should wear seat-belts, because in a crash injuries are more serious without them.

Nausea and vomiting

The tendency to nausea and vomiting in early pregnancy is likely to be aggravated by travel. All travel sickness tablets cause some unwanted effects, such as drowsiness, altered reaction time, dry mouth, and blurred vision, and so should be used only when symptoms warrant (and not at all when driving). Drugs based on hyoscine (e.g. Kwells) and antihistamine preparations such as promethazine (Phenergan, Avomine) are safe for use in pregnancy.

At your destination

Food and drink

Dehydration Try to avoid dehydration during air travel or in a hot climate—this aggravates the tendency to thrombosis and also the problem of constipation, which is common in pregnancy. Drink plenty of fluids—preferably in the form of plain water—bottled or boiled if the local supply isn't safe (see pp. 73–80).

Take an extra supply of natural bran and increase your intake of fruit and vegetables to counteract the constipation which often goes with changed daily routines and possibly a more refined diet than you are used to at home.

Avoid alcohol, not only because of its dehydrating properties but also for its possible harmful effects on the fetus. *Severe* dehydration—such as may follow prolonged diarrhoea—increases the risk of miscarriage.

Toxoplasmosis Don't eat undercooked meat—the condition toxoplasmosis may result. It causes only mild illness in adults but occasionally has serious effects on the fetus. You could be checked to see whether you are immune, but it is a difficult test, not generally available.

Listeriosis This infection is acquired from contaminated food—particularly poultry which is either fresh or frozen and then *incompletely* cooked. It also occurs in cows' and goats' milk and is not always eliminated by pasteurization. Soft, ripened cheeses often contain the bacteria in high numbers and pre-prepared salads are not safe, as the bacteria can survive in the refrigerator. All these points should be borne in mind by the pregnant traveller, as the infection has little effect on most healthy adults but can cause serious effects in the fetus. If a 'flu-like illness develops in pregnancy, then it is probably wise to have antibiotic treatment (such as ampicillin), just in case.

Drug treatment abroad

Prescribing habits vary considerably from country to country, and awareness of potential hazards from drug treatment in pregnancy is far from universal. One group of drugs that may possibly be prescribed for you, but which should be avoided in pregnancy, are the tetracycline group of antibiotics.

Summary of advice for travellers

- You will probably have gathered that I am rather against travelling to remote spots at any time in pregnancy, but if a time for a break has to be selected, between 18 and 24 weeks is probably the best. This is after the risk of nausea and miscarriage—and after the necessary tests should have been completed—but before the problems of premature labour loom. You should be back at base for late pregnancy, just in case!

Children abroad

Problems of travelling with children vary according to where you intend to go, how you will be getting there, and how long you will be away. Whether you are moving abroad to live or are merely off on a short trip, careful preparation will be amply rewarded.

Dr Tony Waterston *is a paediatrician who has worked for several years as a doctor and teacher in Zambia and Zimbabwe and has spent shorter periods in several other parts of Africa. His wife (a doctor too) and three children have also contributed to this chapter.*

Parents travelling abroad often anticipate all sorts of problems with their children, some concerned with the journey itself, others with what will happen at the destination. Will the change of environment be good for the children or bad? Will the food be suitable? Will it be safe for them to play outside? What dreadful diseases will they get? How will the baby take the heat?

Fortunately, the reality of travelling with children is usually much better than you might expect and is generally a formative and valuable experience for the whole family. In this chapter, I hope to answer some of the most common questions about children's health abroad and help you prepare for your trip, whether it be a package tour to the Mediterranean or a long-term posting to some faraway destination in a developing country.

I will discuss three aspects of the trip with respect to children. First, what preparations to make, and the journey itself; second, health hazards encountered while living abroad; and third, some points about children's diet, and baby care.

Before you go

Plenty of time spent finding out as much as you can about the country you plan to visit will be amply repaid; and if you are going to live abroad, this includes attending any special courses that may be laid on for you before you leave. The longer you intend to stay away, the more preparation will be needed, and you should try to find out all you can (from friends, employees, or through your embassy) about the following:

The local health system

Is insurance necessary (see pp. 467–72)? If it is, will all your family be automatically included and will the cost of return travel home be paid in case of major illness? What are the facilities available for treating sick children? Wherever you are, a child may get appendicitis, a fracture or a severe infection and need specialized care. This might be available only at a major centre and could be a factor in deciding where you are to live.

Can medicines be obtained easily? You will quite likely need antimalarials and may need antibiotics. A small supply of over-the-counter remedies will come in useful for minor illnesses and should be bought in advance. If you have a baby and are going for more than a few weeks, find out where and how routine immunizations can be carried out (see below for schedule). There should not be any difficulty in obtaining immunization in any country you visit.

In many developing countries, the emphasis in the medical system will be on *primary health care*. This means basic care concentrating on common ailments and on prevention, delivered by workers with a short training. Do not therefore be surprised if you do not see a doctor at a clinic—the health worker you see should be trained to recognize and treat the common childhood complaints.

Be sure to avoid all treatment by injection unless it is absolutely essential, and unless you are certain that the needle has been sterilized (see page 501).

Dental care

Dental care abroad is often expensive or nonexistent. The whole family should have a dental check and receive essential treatment before going (see p. 351).

The main diseases

In Europe, North America, and Australia, the diseases are very similar to those encountered in the UK, whereas the developing countries of Africa, Asia, and South America share a wide spectrum of infectious diseases, which are discussed elsewhere in this book.

Find out what the main problems are in the country you intend to visit and what specific precautions you should take (e.g. in Asia most malaria is resistant to chloroquine, whereas it is more often sensitive in Africa). Do not feel that it would be unsafe to take children to a country where tropical diseases such as malaria and bilharzia are common: simple precautions will protect against these diseases, and it is often more trivial complaints such as cuts, bites, and diarrhoea and respiratory infections that become important when you are there. These problems are dealt with below, but you would be wise also to take with you one of the many child care books which deal with the management of minor illnesses at home.

Water and food

Find out whether the local water supply is drinkable—if not, you should pay careful attention to the information in this book about water purification (pp. 73–80). Clean water is essential for young children, as stomach upsets are the commonest disorders encountered. It always pays to be careful about water quality when travelling—even bottled carbonated drinks are not necessarily always safe. It may be wise to stick to tea when in doubt.

What are the major local foods? If they are not of a kind you feel up to preparing (such as maize meal, sweet potato, plantain, yam) you will need to depend on imported foods. Is there always a constant supply of these?

Foreign exchange is scarce in many countries, and Weetabix or even wheat may not be at the top of the list of priorities. Can you bake bread? Sacks of flour can sometimes be obtained and will allow you to live through temporary bread or flour shortages. You could arrange to have limited stocks of food sent out, but this will prove expensive and it is sensible to try to 'live off the land'.

Is the milk drinkable and if not, is powdered milk available? This is something you could quite easily take and may need to if you have a formula-fed baby (see notes below under baby care).

In most cases it is quite easy to provide a balanced diet for children, but it will pay if you learn something about the nutritional content of the foods you will encounter abroad.

Immunization

Children should have had the normal schedule of immunization set out below, before travelling abroad—and the same schedule should be used for babies living abroad (but see note on p. 501 about injections abroad).

3 months:	(usually given at 2 months in USA)	first dose of diphtheria/pertussis/ tetanus + oral polio
5 months:	(usually given at 4 months in USA)	second dose of diphtheria/pertussis/ tetanus + oral polio
9–11 months:	(usually given at 6 months in USA)	third dose of diphtheria/pertussis/ tetanus + oral polio
12–15 months:		measles, mumps, and rubella (MMR)
5 years:		booster: diphtheria/tenanus/polio + MMR if not already given
12 years:		rubella (German measles)—given to girls only, in the UK.

In the UK, tuberculin or 'Heaf' testing is also normally carried out at twelve years and BCG vaccine given to protect against tuberculosis for those who are not already immune (see pp. 83–6). However, this can be carried out at any age from infancy for children going to a country with a high prevalence of tuberculosis. BCG should be given at birth to babies born in countries where tuberculosis is common. It should always be given intradermally in the left upper arm.

Boosters against tetanus (unless immunized within the last five years) and polio should be given before departure.

In addition, yellow fever and cholera immunization may be mandatory for the country you are to visit. Protection can optionally be obtained against typhoid, hepatitis A (see below) and rabies. All these additional vaccines may be safely given to children of six months and over, but not earlier. Malaria prevention is dealt with separately below.

The domestic situation and education abroad

Find out in advance what kind of house you will have and whether you will be put first in a hotel or small flat. If so, and you have several children, it may be better for them to follow once the house has been obtained. How well equipped will the house be? For a family, a refrigerator is essential, and you may need to take this out yourself.

If you do not intend to employ domestic help, then a washing machine should also be considered and in a developing country it will be much cheaper to take it with you than to buy there.

If you have school-age children, find out something about the schools, whether there is a choice and whether the teaching is what you are used to. If not, and you intend to return them to their original schools later, seek advice from their teachers on whether books should be taken with you to help bridge the gap. For pre-school children, you should take out plenty of books, toys, and playgroup materials and obtain addresses of mail order firms who will send things out (for example Nursery 345, Mothercare, Bookworm).

If both parents are to be working, then care arrangements will be needed for pre-school children. Home helps are generally child-minders rather than educators and this should be borne in mind: nursery schools of the quality available at home may not be easy to find. You may find it necessary to organize your own playgroup.

If you have a baby, it may be wise to take several sets of baby clothes to expand into as he or she grows. Cotton clothes are preferable to those made of stretch nylon, and plastic pants should be avoided. A hat or sunshade is a must. Further aspects of baby care are dealt with below.

The journey

Travelling long distances with children can be stressful. Some tips are given below on how to reduce the stress:

- *If you have a baby,* breast-feeding on the move is far easier than formula feeding, especially if you are not inhibited about feeding in public. If you are flying, ask for a 'sky cot' well in advance (and check again before travelling) otherwise you will be balancing the baby on your knee all the way. Disposable nappies are a boon for the journey, even if you normally despise them, and often they will be supplied by the air hostess on the aircraft. If you bottle-feed, prepacked milk is very useful for the journey.

- *Suitable books and toys or games* should be kept handy, as bored children sitting in an enclosed space for a long period will not stay happy. 'Looking at the view' may be fun for parents but not for a two-, or even a six-year-old.

- *A small supply of food and drink* should be taken, for example some sandwiches, biscuits, and a bottle of water, as the meals available *en route* may be neither palatable nor healthy, if you can get them at all.

- *Travel sickness* should be prevented in advance if your children are prone to it. Kwells (containing hyoscine) is a suitable medication. Avoid overdosage, which leads to sleepiness, dry mouth, and irritability.

- *A light sedative* may help children get through an especially long journey, and may provide some respite for parents, though most medication tends to have side-effects. A suitable choice is promethazine (Phenergan), in a dose of 5–15 mg for one to five-year olds, and 10–25 mg for over-fives. It is available as tablets or elixir (prescription not required in the UK).

Health hazards at your destination

Malaria

Malaria is fully covered in another chapter (see pp. 117–28), and the manifestations, treatment, and the choice of antimalarial tablets will not be discussed again here, although you should note these points:

- A baby is at risk of malaria from birth, so in a malarial area, protective measures should be taken from then on.
- The main antimalarial drugs are safe for children, in reduced dosages.
- In malarial areas, taking the tablets or medicine should become a routine, like brushing the teeth.
- As with adults, children should commence taking antimalarials one week before departure and continue for at least four weeks after returning.
- Keep the tablets or syrups in a safe, secure place—even the most trustworthy toddler may swallow a bottleful.

As well as the use of antimalarial tablets or syrups, other control measures should also be used to reduce the likelihood of mosquitoes biting (see pp. 182–6). Netting is valuable, though hot to sleep under. If the windows are netted, an individual cover will not be necessary—but check for holes in old window netting. Infants should always be covered with a separate net. It may be wise to take nets with you for use when travelling outside urban areas.

Mosquito control consists of ensuring that there is no standing water near the house to act as a breeding ground, and spraying the bedroom at night.

AIDS

The risk to children is mainly from contaminated injections or blood transfusions. Check needle sterility before allowing your child to receive an injection; if necessary take a small supply of needles and syringes with you when travelling to a high risk country (see p. 397). It is worth knowing your child's blood group, and your own; if they are compatible, you may be able to act as a donor in an emergency.

Fever

Fever is a much more worrying complaint in children overseas than at home, because of the fear of exotic tropical infections. Although malaria is an ever-present worry (even in the child on antimalarial tablets or syrup), the vast majority of fevers in children have the same causes anywhere, namely, viral nose and throat infections (coughs, colds, tonsillitis, and the like). The symptoms of these will usually include cough and a runny nose, with perhaps a sore throat or earache and general malaise with loss of appetite, and sometimes vomiting due to swallowed phlegm. Warning signs of another cause would be these:

1. If a child has a very high fever (40°C, 104°F) with headache (? malaria)
2. If a child suffers from a severe headache and vomiting with neck stiffness (? meningitis)
3. If a child appears jaundiced (with yellow eyes) (? hepatitis or malaria)
4. If a child has blood in stools or severe diarrhoea (? dysentery)
5. If a child feels burning on passing urine, or must visit the toilet frequently (? urinary infection)
6. If a baby refuses to feed (? blood infection)
7. If a child has a severe cough with breathing difficulty (? pneumonia)
8. If a child suffers persistent abdominal pain (? appendicitis)

If these signs are not present but cold symptoms are, then it is quite reasonable to give the child paracetamol and extra fluids, keep him or her cool and carry on as normally as possible (an antibiotic does not help most throat and nose infections, which are usually caused by a virus, but may be needed for severe sore throats or earache). If one of the above features is present, if the fever is in a baby under a year, or if it lasts over two days without improvement and fever is the only symptom, then medical help should be sought.

Should a fever in a malarious area be routinely treated with chloroquine, just in case it is malaria? This is difficult to answer (see p. 374). Certainly a supply of chloroquine should be kept in the house and you should know how much to give. If medical aid is not readily available, the child has been exposed to mosquitoes, and the features are not typical of a cold, then a chloroquine course should be given *unless* you are in an area of chloroquine resistance, in which case medical assistance must be sought first.

However, a *blood test should, if practicable, always be taken for malaria* before giving the chloroquine—only a few drops of blood on a slide are needed for this. Otherwise it will be hard to decide later whether it was malaria or not. The local hospital or clinic may show you how to take the test yourself.

Respiratory infections

These seem to be worse in children living in the tropics, perhaps because of more frequent swimming leading to ear infections, or perhaps because of exposure to a new set of infective agents.

The commonest serious infections are *tonsillitis* (throat infection) and *otitis media* (middle-ear infection), both of which may need antibiotic treatment. Penicillin, ampicillin, or co-trimoxazole (Septrin or Bactrim) are the most effective antibiotics used for these conditions and they are available worldwide. If your child is penicillin-sensitive make sure that this is clear to anyone giving treatment.

Diarrhoea

Diarrhoea is extremely common in children when travelling or in another country (see pp. 21–42). 'Gastroenteritis' is simply the technical name for a stomach or intestinal infection leading to diarrhoea and is not necessarily severe or life-threatening. The seriousness of diarrhoea depends on how much fluid is lost from

Table 10.1 Some causes of children's diarrhoea in the tropics*

Cause	Symptoms
Rotavirus (commonest cause)	mild fever, watery diarrhoea, vomiting
Salmonella (food poisoning)	diarrhoea and vomiting, abdominal pain, fever, malaise
Shigellosis (bacillary dysentery)	bloody diarrhoea, high fever
Cholera	profuse watery diarrhoea (leading rapidly to dehydration)
Typhoid	diarrhoea or constipation, fever, headache, rash, persistent weakness
Giardiasis	offensive stools, recurrent diarrhoea, malaise, abdominal pains (this is a more chronic or lasting condition)

*Note: For a fuller account of possible causes, see the section on diarrhoea pp. 21–42.

the body: because a child's total fluid volume is greater in proportion to body weight than an adult's, the effect is greater the younger the child. A baby can become dehydrated (dried out) within a few hours of the onset of severe diarrhoea.

Diarrhoeal disease is usually contracted by contact with infected food or fluid, but also from hands that have touched infected material. Faeces of an infected person are highly contagious, and therefore very careful hand-washing is essential after using the toilet. These diseases spread more easily in the tropics and also certain causative agents are commoner—the features of some of these are given in Table 10.1 above.

Suspect one of the causes in Table 10.1 if the diarrhoea is bloody, very profuse and watery, or associated with a high fever. If one of these symptoms is present, or if the diarrhoea goes on for longer than 3 days (one day in a baby), medical help should be sought. However, in most cases a rotavirus or similar infection will be the cause, and the natural course is only two to three days.

Replacement of fluid loss is the most important part of treatment. Drugs are quite ineffective in the vast majority of cases. A suitable fluid replacement solution may be made with a finger pinch of salt and a teaspoon of sugar added to 250 ml (about one mugful) of boiled water, with a squeeze of orange juice to provide flavour (and a token amount of potassium). The concentration is very important as the sugar helps aid the absorption of the salt, but too much of either is harmful. Taste the solution before giving to your child, and if it tastes saltier than tears, discard it and start again (see also p. 33).

Special packets of powder (e.g. Dioralyte, Rehidrat) for adding to water may be obtained from your doctor or at a pharmacy before you go and are valuable for journeys. Give one cupful of mixture for each loose stool. Seek medical help if the child vomits or appears drowsy, has fast breathing or is dehydrated (eyes become sunken, tongue is dry, skin loses elasticity). Profuse diarrhoea in a baby is also a reason for seeking assistance early.

Diet Feeding should be continued during diarrhoea if the child feels like eating—especially high-calorie, low-residue foods. Bananas, cereals, bread and margarine or butter, biscuits, eggs, and milk are all suitable—concentrate on the foods the child likes most. Starving a child suffering from diarrhoea is now thought undesirable, although appetite is often reduced.

Drug treatment is necessary only for some of the specific types of diarrhoea mentioned in Table 10.1, such as severe dysentery, typhoid, cholera, and giardiasis—all of which are much less likely than a viral cause. Antidiarrhoeal agents such as kaolin, codeine, diphenoxylate (Lomotil), and over-the-counter mixtures should be avoided. Lomotil in particular has toxic side-effects (depression of the respiratory system) and should not be used in young children, nor should preventive drugs such as clioquinol (Entero-Vioform). For the older child (over 5 years), loperamide (Imodium, Arret) is the most acceptable drug if parents feel that symptomatic treatment is absolutely necessary.

Prevention The likelihood of diarrhoea can be minimized by observing these tips:

- Pay close attention to household hygiene—particularly hand-washing before meals and after using the toilet.
- Maintain good hygiene in the kitchen by washing hands before food preparation; keeping stored food in the fridge (especially meat) covering all food left out in the open, even for short periods; cooking meat thoroughly; boiling water if there is any doubt about its purity (then keeping it in the fridge—it will taste

better); washing fresh fruit and vegetables thoroughly before eating; and not permitting flies in the kitchen.

- Avoid the use of pre-cooked foods bought in the streets; milk and milk products (especially ice-cream) unless you are quite sure they are manufactured hygienically; salads and other uncooked foods, and cold meat eaten in hotels and restaurants.

Viral hepatitis

Hepatitis comes in two main forms—named A and B. Of these, hepatitis A or 'infectious hepatitis' is more common in children: it is usually spread by the 'faecal-oral' route and resembles diarrhoea in its origins. It is not usually a serious disease in children, and indeed may sometimes not be noticed ('subclinical') but is nevertheless best avoided. The features of the illness and how to deal with it are covered in another chapter (pp. 56–65).

Prevention depends mainly on food hygiene and avoiding dubious foods, as discussed under diarrhoea. 'Passive' immunization is available for hepatitis and is given in the form of an intramuscular injection of gamma-globulin obtained from patients who have recovered from the disease. Immunity lasts only for six months, but the injection is recommended for children aged six months and over. A simple antibody test performed first will show if the individual is already immune, and if so gamma-globulin will not be needed (p. 481). A new vaccine is available against hepatitis B, for those at special risk.

Swimming hazards

Bilharzia is present in most rivers and lakes in Africa, the Middle East and Asia, and some parts of South and Central America and prohibits swimming with only a few exceptions (see pp. 90–4). Some areas are treated against snails (which infect the water), but be sure you have a reliable local source of information on this. The infective risk of a single brief exposure is not great and may be reduced by showering in clean water immediately afterwards, but it is better to be safe than sorry.

Before swimming in pools, check that the chlorine supply has not run out—a common problem in developing countries.

Ear infections occur quite frequently in hot countries and swimming should be avoided until well after recovery from an episode.

Babies may be encouraged to swim from a very early age quite safely as long as the water is safe, and you are careful to avoid sunburn. See also p. 309.

Other hazards

Sunburn is an obvious environmental hazard, particularly in high or mountainous countries where the tropical sun burns very quickly (see p. 300). Also, beware of burning even when it is cloudy. The usual advice of big hats and covering the arms and legs should be followed rigorously until all the children are mahogany-coloured. Children's hair usually bleaches pale blond, but will darken on returning to cooler climates. Sunscreens, preferably water resistant, are advisable when at the swimming-pool or seaside.

Sunburn should be treated by puncturing blisters and draining the fluid. Clean the burned area and paint with calamine lotion. Protect against contact and further exposure to the sun.

Prickly heat is common in hot climates and particularly in humid countries, and can be very troublesome. It is caused by sweating, with blockage of the sweat ducts leading to itching red spots and tiny blisters, usually on the neck, back, and chest.

Treat by washing the area with an antiseptic soap, then dry and powder with talc. Calamine lotion may also be used.

Prevent prickly heat by avoiding sweating as much as possible, by frequent bathing, by wearing loose clothing (p. 287), and by drying the skin whenever it becomes wet.

Walking barefoot should be avoided, outside your garden or land you know well. Snakes are more afraid of people than we of them, but if stood upon will bite defensively (p. 208).

A more common hazard for the barefoot is *hookworm*, acquired from soil contaminated with human faeces (see p. 46). The worm passes through the skin of the feet and circulates through the lymphatics and lungs before eventually settling in the small intestine, where chronic bleeding leads to severe anaemia.

Tumbu fly (also known as 'Putsi' in some areas) is another infestation commonly picked up from soil in which eggs of the fly have been laid (see p. 168). It does not depend on faecal spread and may occur even where sanitation is perfect (e.g. your garden). Larvae may enter the skin directly from the soil or from eggs laid in clothes left hanging in the shade or laid on the ground to dry.

Lesions resembling boils develop under the skin and may be very painful. The main preventive measure is to iron all clothes and sheets which have been left out to dry, so as to kill the eggs.

Cuts, sores, and insect bites are common in hot countries but heal more slowly than at home, probably because of greater sweating. Treat them meticulously in the early stages by cleaning, disinfecting, and covering. Gentian violet is a good standby for disinfection despite its messiness—the tropical bathroom should preferably be painted purple so that the stains don't show up. Gentian violet is also useful for mouth ulcers, but don't use in the mouth for more than three days as it can become an irritant.

For itchy skin lesions and bites, calamine lotion is effective.

Pets If you keep a dog, ensure that rabies vaccine is given at the right time and that the dog is dewormed. Also be on the lookout for ticks and remove them immediately (drop into meths or paraffin). They can cause *tickbite fever* in animals and humans.

Dogs and cats may be a source of *toxoplasmosis* which causes a glandular fever-type illness. An infected pregnant woman may transmit the disease to the fetus causing congenital deformities, although this condition is rare (p. 422). Spread may take place through contamination of food by cat and dog faeces, so again good hygiene is the best prevention.

Remember that if you bring a pet back to the UK, there is a six-month quarantine period at the point of entry.

Stray animals should be avoided and children warned carefully of their risks. Animals in the street should never be petted because of the risk of rabies and other diseases.

Childrens's diet abroad

Children tend to eat less in a hot climate, so it is all the more important to ensure a balanced intake of nutrients. Foods obtainable will generally be healthier (few junk foods and sweets) and vegetables and fruit will be abundant and fresh (but always wash them thoroughly if eaten raw). Remember that too many mangoes/guavas/pawpaws may cause intestinal upsets. Here are some tips:

- *Meat* should be thoroughly cooked, particularly beef which may carry tapeworms.

- *Eggs* are likely to be readily available (see p. 24).
- *Milk and milk products* (particularly cream and ice-cream) should be viewed with caution, and milk boiled unless you are sure it has been hygienically prepared.
- A reasonable *salt* intake is necessary but usually this may be obtained by adding extra to food, without the need for salt tablets.
- *Vitamins* should be readily available from the following sources:

vitamin A	carrots, highly coloured or dark green vegetables/fruit (e.g. mango, guava, pawpaw, spinach)
vitamin B	nuts, cereals, milk, eggs, meat
vitamin C	oranges, lemons, guavas, potatoes
vitamin D	margarine, eggs, fish, sunlight
folic acid	green leafy vegetables

- *Fluoride* is valuable in preventing dental caries but water supplies overseas are rarely fluoridated. Fluoride supplements are quite safe but best obtained before departure: they are recommended from infancy to twelve years of age *if the local water supply is deficient*. Drops are available for babies. A prescription is not needed in the UK, but is necessary in the USA (see also p. 358).

Baby care abroad

In general, the care of babies in hot countries does not differ from anywhere else, but a few tips may be helpful.

Breast-feeding

Breast-feeding should be carried out if possible in preference to bottle, not just because it is better for the baby, but because of the example the expatriate mother sets to the local community. Bottle-feeding is a major cause of death among babies in poor countries because of the difficulty mothers face in boiling water, keeping bottles clean, and just buying milk powder. One reason why the local mother may turn to bottle-feeding is because it carries 'prestige'—since expatriate mothers do it.

Extra water is not needed routinely by the breast-fed baby, even in hot climates, unless he or she is feverish or suffering from diarrhoea. But the mother must be sure to maintain a high fluid intake herself.

Infant foods

For the same reason, it is preferable to use natural foods rather than commercial tins or jars for weaning the baby—it is also cheaper and probably healthier, as some proprietary foods have a high concentration of salt and other additives. The first food will probably still remain a proprietary cereal but when mixed feeding is commenced, then liquidized vegetables, fruit, meat, cheese, and eggs may all be used quite safely (this will usually be over the age of six months).

Malaria prevention in babies

Malaria prophylaxis in babies should be started immediately after birth. Even if you are breast-feeding and taking a drug yourself, an insufficient amount will reach the baby to be effective. Use nets carefully to avoid mosquito bites.

Cots

A basket is a better place for a baby to sleep than a carry-cot, as it will be cooler. Often you will find that special baskets can be made locally.

Children with special problems

If you have a child with diabetes (see next chapter), cystic fibrosis, coeliac disease, or another chronic disorder, you will need special advice before travelling abroad. Obtain this early from your usual specialist or one of the support organizations, as a lot more advance planning will be required.

Conclusion

• Do not let the above list of exotic diseases and problems overwhelm you with horror. Most can be prevented by simple precautions, and on the positive side, there will be the outdoor life, the absence of junk foods and TV, and the exposure to quite different cultures and traditions. You and your children should come back with a much deeper understanding of people of other races and cultures, and of the nature of the problems facing developing countries. It will be worth it.

The diabetic traveller

Provided that a few basic guidelines are followed carefully, travel poses few problems to the majority of diabetics.

Dr Peter Watkins *is a Consultant Physician at King's College Hospital, London, and is an authority on diabetes.*

Diabetes mellitus is a very common disorder. In developed countries, 1–2 per cent of the population have diabetes, so that in the UK, for example, there are about 750 000 diabetics. Since diabetes is commonest in middle age, there are always a great many diabetic travellers!

Types of diabetes

There are two main types of diabetes—insulin-dependent diabetes and non-insulin-dependent diabetes. Common to both forms, and the main cause of symptoms in each, is an above-normal level of sugar (glucose) in the blood—a condition called 'hyperglycaemia'.

Glucose arrives in the blood from the gut after absorption from food and is also made in large amounts by the liver. Normally, the hormone insulin then facilitates use of the glucose as an energy source by various parts of the body: in this way insulin keeps the blood-sugar level under control. Insulin-dependent diabetics are unfortunately unable to make their own insulin, so need daily insulin injections throughout their lives. Without these injections their blood-sugar level would rise uncontrollably, leading to coma and eventually to death.

With non-insulin-dependent diabetes, the cause of the raised blood-sugar level is more complex: insulin deficiency is responsible in some cases, but other factors such as obesity may also play a role. Whatever the cause, the blood-sugar level can be kept in check without resort to insulin injections.

Symptoms are the same with both forms of the disorder: patients describe thirst or dry mouth, pass large amounts of dilute urine, lose weight, and feel tired. Sometimes itching of the genital organs occurs because of thrush, and a few people experience blurring of vision.

Treatment is aimed at restoring health by lowering blood sugar to as near normal a level as possible. Dieting is a key part of treatment for both types of diabetes and at the very least, apart from other dietary measures, all simple sugars must be eliminated.

Insulin-dependent diabetics must inject insulin under the skin between one and three times each day. Non-insulin-dependent diabetics may just need a special diet, sometimes supplemented by tablets which help to lower the blood-sugar level. These tablets will not work in diabetics who require insulin injections. Most diabetics monitor their 'control' by performing either their own blood-sugar tests after pricking a finger to obtain a small sample of blood, or by testing urine specimens for sugar.

Travel

Travelling generally presents few real problems to diabetics provided that they follow the simple guidelines presented below. It is obviously more difficult for those taking insulin, especially when major time changes occur when travelling long distances by air. No country need be out of bounds, although places very remote from medical services might not be ideal for those lacking confidence. Those who wish to work abroad can generally do so, but diabetics on insulin ought to remain within reach of medical services, and some remote areas may not be appropriate for long spells. Many of the comments that follow apply only to insulin-dependent diabetics.

Before you go

Immunization

Diabetics should be immunized in exactly the same way as non-diabetics (see pp. 473–88). There are only a few reasons for not undertaking immunization and they apply equally to non-diabetics.

Supplies

Ensure that ample supplies of tablets or insulin, syringes, needles and urine- or blood-testing equipment are carried. It is best to keep some supplies in at least two separate items of luggage in case of loss. Insulin should not be put in luggage that will travel in the luggage hold of an aircraft, where it may freeze.

Storage of insulin is not generally a problem. Refrigeration is not necessary during the journey and in temperate climates insulin will keep for some months at room temperature. Refrigeration (*not* deep freezing) is recommended for long-term storage, especially in the tropics.

Insurance

For travel in EEC countries, all British travellers should arrange health cover by completing form E111 (see p. 471). Holiday insurance premiums may be quoted at higher rates than normal, but adequate insurance cover is always essential (see p. 467). In Britain, the British Diabetic Association (10 Queen Anne Street, London W1M OBS, Tel. 01–323 1531) will offer advice on the best 'buy'. The address of the American Diabetes Association is 2 Park Avenue, New York, NY 10016 USA, Tel. 212 683 7444. Other addresses include the Canadian Diabetes Association, 78 Bond Street, Toronto, Ontario M5B 2J8, Tel. 1–416/362–4440; the Australia Diabetes Foundation, GPO Box 944, Civic Square, Canberra ACT 2608, Tel. 062/41565, Fax 62–573140; and the Diabetic Association of New Zealand, PO Box 54, Oamaru, Tel. 64/48–100.

Motion sickness

Diabetics can use the same anti-motionsickness tablets as non-diabetics (see p. 244). These tablets do not affect diabetic control. Don't forget that many preparations cause drowsiness, and it is best not to drive while under their influence. If vomiting should occur, the method of managing the diabetes is described below.

Identification

Some form of identification is most valuable in case of problems. All diabetics should carry with them at all times a clear statement that they are diabetic with details of their treatment, indicating their usual doctor or clinic. *Medic-Alert Foundation International* (see addresses on p. 212) offers a valuable service in this regard, and their bracelet is widely known. Identification will also help if there are any problems with regard to customs officials (syringes and needles may be confused with the paraphernalia of drug addicts). You should not under any circumstances hand in your equipment to any official.

Travelling companions

Insulin-dependent diabetics travelling to remote parts of the world should ideally be accompanied, so that immediate help is available, especially in the event of a low blood-sugar level (hypoglycaemia—see below).

The journey

Time changes during long-distance air travel

This will cause minor temporary upset of diabetic control in insulin-treated diabetics.

Flying west

The time between injections can, with little problem, be lengthened by two to three hours twice daily. Regular tests should be performed and if they are very 'sugary' a little extra soluble insulin (perhaps 4–8 units) can be given. If the time gap between injections is lengthened still further, a small supplementary injection of soluble insulin (4–8 units) is given between the usual injections.

Flying east

The time between injections will need to be shortened by two to three hours each time, which could result in rather low blood sugars. Careful testing should be performed, and if required each dose can be reduced by a small amount (4–8 units on average). Regular meals should be taken as normal. Many airlines will make special provision for diabetics if notified in advance.

Abroad

While on holiday, the chief problems are these:

1. Vomiting, either from motion sickness or stomach upsets
2. Other illnesses affecting diabetic control, e.g. infections
3. Hypoglycaemia (a low blood sugar)

Table 10.2 Items containing 10 grams carbohydrate

Item	Amount
Milk	one third of a pint
Coca-cola	90 ml (six tablespoonfuls)
Sugar	two teaspoonfuls
Sugar lumps	three small lumps
Lucozade	60 ml (four tablespoonfuls)
Ribena	15 ml (one tablespoonful)
Dextrosol	three tablets

4. Alterations of diabetic control due to major changes in diet or activity

Vomiting and other illness

The blood sugar tends to increase during any illness, even if little food is being taken, and quite often the insulin dose needs to be increased. At the very least, *insulin should never be stopped*, otherwise deterioration of diabetes is inevitable, leading to diabetic ketoacidosis (pre-coma) and hospital admission.

Take the following steps:

- Monitor sugar levels carefully (urine or blood-sugar tests) at least four times daily. If the results are poor (urine sugars persistently 2 per cent, or blood sugars greater than 15 mmol/l) then extra insulin is needed. This can be done either at the normal times by increasing the soluble insulin by about 10 per cent (normally 4–8 units) or as additional doses of soluble insulin at noon or bedtime if tests remain poor then.
- Carbohydrate should be maintained if possible by taking the normal quantity in fluid form. Table 10.2 shows the amounts of various fluids and simple sugar preparations containing 10 grams of sugar (i.e. one carbohydrate 'portion').
- If vomiting persists, or if the general condition deteriorates, it is best not to delay seeing a doctor or attending hospital.

Hypoglycaemia

A low blood sugar develops if too much insulin is taken, too little food is eaten, or if there is a marked increase in physical activity. The symptoms fall into three phases: early warning, when the person may shake or tremble, sweat and note 'pins and needles' in the lips and tongue, palpitations or headache; a more advanced phase, with double vision, slurring of speech, difficulty of concentration or even confusion and odd behaviour; and eventually, without treatment, the person may become unconscious.

All diabetics taking insulin should be aware of the possibility of hypoglycaemia, and all are supposed to carry with them, at all times, some form of sugar, usually as sugar lumps, sweets or dextrose tablets (see Table 10.2). About 10–20 grams of sugar should be taken at the first warning of hypoglycaemia; if a diabetic becomes confused, his or her companions should compel the person to take a dextrosol tablet or sugar lump.

To help those who are seriously prone to troublesome hypoglycaemia with unconsciousness, an injection of glucagon (1 mg intramuscularly) can easily be given by a companion. Glucagon causes a rapid increase of the blood sugar. Glucagon is supplied in a small kit: it must be prescribed by a doctor, and those carrying glucagon must learn how to use it before the emergency arises.

Alteration of diabetic control

Lifestyle and routine during travelling are likely to be very different from those at home, and this change may alter diabetic control.

If physical activity is much greater than usual (hiking or swimming, for example), hypoglycaemia is more likely to occur. Food intake needs to be increased, or a small decrease in insulin dose will be required. Most diabetics know that extra carbohydrate is needed *before* considerable physical exertion in order to avoid hypoglycaemia.

If the level of activity on holiday is much less than usual, then blood sugar tends to increase. This needs to be monitored and, if necessary, a little more insulin given.

Keeping to a diet abroad can be difficult. However, even with foreign foods it should still be possible to keep to the usual amount of carbohydrate. Do you best not to exceed your normal amount.

Non-insulin-dependent diabetes

There are few problems for those not taking insulin but diabetes should not be neglected, and regular tests should be conducted as if at home. Above all, diabetics should not overeat as this will very probably lead to poor control. If any illness occurs, control must be monitored with special care, and attention from a doctor may be necessary. Remember that with this type of diabetes, insulin may occasionally be needed temporarily during an illness, especially if there is an infection.

Summary of advice for diabetic travellers

- If careful preparations are made and proper precautions followed, travelling should not present any problems for diabetics. The major hazard, as at other times, is hypoglycaemia—*remember to carry sugar* and make sure someone else knows how to help you if hypoglycaemia occurs.

The handicapped traveller

Since travel has become a necessity of modern life, rather than a luxury, people have begun to realize that physical handicaps are not the insurmountable barriers that they once seemed. As in golf, even with some strokes against you, you're still in the game.

Louise Weiss *is a travel writer and author of* Access to the world: A travel guide for the handicapped. *She lives in New York.*

Which areas of the world are best equipped to accommodate the needs of travellers with any sort of handicap? This is easy to answer; just imagine a globe: draw a horizontal line under the United States and Canada, over to the British Isles and northern Europe, curve it down around South Africa, then over to Israel, take in Hong Kong and Singapore, Australia, New Zealand, and the islands that comprise the state of Hawaii. As far as the rest of the world is concerned, leisure travellers would be well advised to consider whether they wish to spend their money attempting to cope with situations completely inimical to their particular handicap. This is in no way to imply that the countries mentioned above are completely barrier-free. They do indeed have fewer barriers, but of no less importance is the fact that they are psychologically more attuned to accepting the handicapped into the mainstream of society.

In the United States alone, government agencies have estimated the handicapped population to be between 35 and 50 million. This may seem mind-boggling until one realizes that handicapping conditions fall into two categories; visible and invisible. Among the most visible, of course, are conditions requiring a wheelchair. Blindness is too, but deafness less so. Diabetes, heart conditions, kidney disease, and respiratory ailments are not visible to the casual observer, but each presents specific problems for the traveller.

There are differences too, between what has been defined by the Air Traffic Conference of America as 'static' and 'non-static' ambulatory and non-ambulatory conditions.

- A static ambulatory condition would be blindness or deafness.

- A non-static ambulatory condition describes someone who has recently undergone surgery or had a heart attack but is capable of walking short distances.
- Non-static, non-ambulatory would describe all stretcher cases as well as seriously ill people who require a wheelchair.
- Static non-ambulatory applies to paraplegia, quadriplegia, or any other condition that confines an otherwise healthy person to a wheelchair because of inability to walk.

Wheelchairs

Being confined to a wheelchair is like travelling with a large piece of furniture strapped to one's back. Unless one is simply too tall or heavy, it is best to use a lightweight folding chair, usually called a 'junior' model. Battery-operated chairs are heavy and unwieldy and easily damaged in baggage compartments. If such a chair is absolutely necessary, it is imperative to check with the airlines about their rules concerning carriage of batteries. In the United States, wet cell batteries may now be transported on aircraft if they conform to Federal regulations. A device called a 'wheelchair tightener' is invaluable for squeezing out that last half-inch or so that will get the chair through a door. Carrying a few basic tools for making simple repairs is advisable.

Blindness

Logistically, blindness presents fewer difficulties than one might suppose. No furniture problem here. Restaurants are beginning to offer Braille menus, hotels to provide safety instructions in Braille. If flight attendants do not volunteer the information, they should be asked the number of rows to the nearest exit. On United States airlines, blind passengers are allowed to keep their long canes at their seats if they wish. Guide dogs are permitted in passenger cabins on United States domestic flights (except to Hawaii), but whether they can be carried internationally depends upon the destination. The lengthy quarantines imposed by Australia, Hawaii, Hong Kong, Ireland, New Zealand, and the United Kingdom, make transporting a guide dog impractical for the vacationer. Bermuda, Denmark, Norway, and Sweden require medical certificates for dogs. It is essential to check with the embassy or consulate of the destination country well in advance of travel. Do not rely on airlines for complete information.

Deafness

The hearing population tends to be unaware of how much information is conveyed through the ear rather than the eye. Announcements of departures and delays, meals and bar service or the lack thereof, fire alarms, 'abandon ship' signals, train and bus stops—these are but some of the bits of information that may swirl unheeded around the hearing-impaired traveller. Transportation and hotel staff should be informed about the handicap and asked to make sure that emergency warnings are delivered visually or in person. Many hotels have installed fire and smoke detectors with flashing lights as well as sirens. Hearing guide dogs trained to alert their masters to specific situations, such as a crying child, are becoming more common. The same precautions about travelling with them should be taken as with dogs for the blind, with the caveat that officialdom may need more convincing that these are indeed legitimate guide dogs. In some countries, TTY and TDD telecommunication reservation systems for the hearing- and speech-impaired are available for several hotel chains, railways, and travel agencies.

Diabetes

Major requirements are refrigeration facilities for insulin and 24 hour a day access to food. It is best to carry small snacks at all times, since meals in transit may be delayed or even skipped. Daily exercise is also important, a point to be remembered on long coach tours. Foot care should be meticulous, since extended periods of sitting as well as more walking than usual impose added burdens on fragile feet.

Heart conditions

These should not preclude travelling, unless constant medical supervision is necessary, but it is important to take sensible precautions. Avoid high altitudes and extremely cold weather, keep schedules flexible enough to avoid stress and use luggage with wheels or a collapsible luggage carrier. If you prefer the convenience of an organized tour, but want to avoid the often frenetic pace, consider going with a tour for the handicapped. This can be an excellent choice for heart patients or the elderly who are not mobility-impaired but require a slower pace. Cruises, too, provide an especially low-key mode of travel, but be sure that all decks of the ship are served with lifts.

Kidney patients

With their physician's approval, kidney patients can travel abroad and maintain their dialysis routine at hospitals and renal centres that accept transients. Reservations should be made well in advance. A physician's summary and recommendations for treatment are required, as well as a recent result of a hepatitis B antibody test. If travel plans are delayed or cancelled, the host unit should be notified immediately because a 'no show' would disrupt scheduling and inconvenience regular patients. An international directory of dialysis facilities is available for people who wish to travel*.

Respiratory ailments

The medical aspects of flying with respiratory problems are covered on page 226. This section considers some of the practical aspects. If you use an oxygen-powered respirator, you must make special arrangements with airlines and shipping companies. Most ships, but not all, permit passengers to bring their own oxygen abroad. Airlines require 24 to 48 hours' notice and must abide by strict safety regulations, so it is best to consult as far in advance of travel as possible. Often, only airline-supplied oxygen may be used, for which there may or may not be an additional charge. Dry-cell battery respirators are permissible on aircraft. If your respirator needs a domestic electrical supply, you must be able to manage without it for the length of your air journey, plus a couple of hours leeway in case of delay in takeoff or landing. While most of the world operates on 220-volt electric current, Canada and the United States use 110-volts.

* *The list of transient dialysis centers* is published by Creative Age Publications, 7628 Densmore Avenue, Van Nuys, California 91406–2088; Tel. (818) 782–7328. Price $4.00 (US currency bank draft only).

A converter is necessary to use a respirator on incompatible current, plus adapters for differently shaped plugs even with similar current.

Planning ahead

Successful travel depends upon careful planning, and planning depends upon correct information. Ask questions that are sufficiently detailed, for instance:

Airplanes Is there a ramp or sleeve for boarding? A wheelchair accessible lavatory? An aisle chair for moving handicapped passengers to their seats? Does any leg of the journey involve a small airline which may not be able to accommodate a collapsible wheelchair? What are the oxygen regulations? Is a companion necessary?

Buses Is there a mechanical wheelchair lift? Are employees permitted to lift passengers manually? On group tours, are buses available in which passengers can remain in their wheelchairs, and can these be safely secured to the floor? Do rest stops have accessible lavatories and restaurants?

Ships How wide are the cabin doors, the bathroom doors, and the lift doors? Is there turn-around space for a wheelchair to get into the bathroom? Can wheelchairs fit at restaurant tables? Are there ramps over door sills? If not, are portable ramps available? Are wheelchairs allowed on tenders when ships cannot moor at docks? Is there accessible transportation for sightseeing in port?

Trains Are there accessible lavatories? Where are they located? Can food be brought to the passenger? Is there a difference in height between the platform and the train? Do the stations have accessible lavatories? Are porters available?

Summary

The population of industrialized countries is getting older, and medical and technological advances have increased the abilities of people who might once have been totally incapacitated by congenital defect, illness, or accident. Rising expectations increase pressure on society to accommodate the needs of those who are less than physically perfect. While not everyone can do everything, more and more travel experiences are opening up to people with a wide range of handicaps.

Useful addresses*

1. *UK*

RADAR (Royal Association for Disability and Rehabilitation)	25 Mortimer St, London WIN 8AB
Holiday Care Service	2 Old Bank Chambers, Station Rd, Horley, Surrey RH6 9HW
The Disability Press, Ltd	60 Greenhayes Avenue, Banstead, Surrey SM7 2JQ

2. *USA*

Accent on Information	P O Box 700 Bloomington, Illinois 61702 (computerized information service for the handicapped)
Mobility International USA	P O Box 3511 Eugene, Oregon 97403

3. *AUSTRALIA*

Australian Council for Rehabilitation of Disabled	P O Box 60 Curtin ACT 2605

* Further information sources for the handicapped are listed in *Access to the World* (see Further Reading, p. 559).

11

Living abroad

Living abroad

A positive attitude and awareness of the possible pitfalls hold the key to staying healthy while living abroad.

Dr Anthony Hall *was the Chief Physician at a US Army hospital in Vietnam, spent three years in Thailand conducting research on malaria, and lived in the USA for six years.*

The usual reason for living abroad is to work or to accompany a working spouse or parent. Living and working in a foreign country presents a challenge to be met with energy, creativity and diplomacy. Most countries—in the tropics and elsewhere—offer a multitude of diversions, such as beautiful countryside, sailing and other sports, food and drink, but my own advice is to avoid being sidetracked too much from the task in hand; many non-working spouses and other expatriates, however, face a contrasting problem—not having enough to do.

Living conditions vary considerably from one country to another, and in some countries an adverse climate, poor social and economic conditions, and increased health risks can pose a significant degree of hardship for the European or American expatriate. It is difficult to define hardship or to quantify it for any particular country, but statistics such as the bonus payments paid by the US government to its employees in various countries can give a guide. These bonus payments range from zero for countries considered the most desirable, rising to 25 per cent for countries where significant hardship might be anticipated (Table 11.1). Note that bonuses vary between cities within certain countries, as well as between countries. Other organizations and countries doubtless have different rates and approaches to the problem of compensation, but the US table is a useful guideline.

Psychological health

For the expatriate, staying mentally healthy is often a bigger problem than avoiding physical illness: the climatic and social stresses of living in a poor, tropical country can prove intolerable for some people. Heat, humidity, dirt, insects and frequent insect

Table 11.1 Hardship bonuses paid to US Government employees on foreign service[1]

25 per cent	20 per cent	15 per cent	10 per cent	0 per cent[2]
Afghanistan*	Central African Republic	Algeria	Brazil—Brasilia	Barbados
Bangladesh	China—Peking, Shanghai	Bahrain	Brunei	Brazil—Rio de Janeiro
Benin	Cuba	Cameroon	Bulgaria	Kenya—Nairobi
Bolivia	Egypt	Colombia*	Cyprus	Malaysia—Penang
Burkina Faso	Haiti	Ecuador	Japan—Okinawa	Mexico—Mexico City
Burma	India—Bombay, Madras	El Salvador*	Kenya—Mombasa	Singapore
Chad	Indonesia—Medan, Surabaya	Fiji	Malaysia—Kuala Lumpur	
Ethiopia	Nepal—Kathmandu	Gabon—Libreville	Paraguay	
Ghana	Oman	Guatemala	Philippines—Manila	
India—Calcutta	Pakistan	India—Delhi	Romania	
Iraq	Peru	Indonesia—Jakarta	Thailand—Bangkok	
Kuwait*	Saudi Arabia—Jeddah, Riyadh	Ivory Coast	Trinidad	
Laos	Seychelles	Jordan	Tunisia	
Lebanon*	Sri Lanka	Martinique	Turkey	
Liberia	Syria	Philippines—Cebu	UAE—Dubai	
Madagascar	Thailand—Udorn	Poland	Zimbabwe—Harare	
Mali	Togo	Qatar—Doha		
Mauritania	USSR	Senegal		
Mozambique	Zaire—Kinshasa	Thailand—Chiang Mai		
Nicaragua		UAE—Abu Dhabi		
Niger		UK—Belfast		
Nigeria		Zambia		
Papua New Guinea				
Sudan*				
Tanzania—Dar es Salaam				
Thailand—Songkhla				
Uganda				
Zaire—Lubumbashi				

Notes
1. This is not a comprehensive list, and unless otherwise stated, refers to posting in the capital city.
2. Most European countries are also zero-rated.
* Employees in these countries receive an additional 25% danger pay

bites can all be psychologically stressful. Many things do not work as well or as efficiently as at home. Power failures, poor roads, traffic congestion, unfamiliar food, and language can each contribute to frustration, high blood pressure and frayed tempers.

Some expatriates, particularly non-working spouses (see below) may find it difficult to make new friends and social contacts or may simply lack things to do in their spare time. Failure of a project or financial problems can add to the stresses on an individual or family, as can worries about employment upon returning home.

Such factors add up to a high incidence of anxiety, depression, alcoholism, and other problems while abroad. There are no easy answers, although employers should make every effort to give their staff as much support as possible.

Some possible tips for contentment abroad include these:

- Expatriates must accept that life abroad cannot be the same as at home. You must try to adapt yourself to the society you are living in; attempts to accomplish the reverse are doomed to failure.
- Exercise will keep you physically fit and reduce the psychological stress.
- A radio link with home can do much to sustain your sanity, whether you prefer listening to music, sports commentaries, or the ten o'clock news. I advise long-term travellers to take a powerful mains/battery operated-radio, capable of receiving the BBC Overseas Service anywhere in the world. Do not rely on a television to keep you amused—unless you take your own video equipment and pre-recorded tapes—with few exceptions, television in most countries is not worth watching.
- If you play a musical instrument, take it and play it, for your own enjoyment and the entertainment of others.
- Spare-time interests are important. Various possibilities are considered below under 'Problems of non-working spouses', and some may apply equally to working individuals.

Problems of non-working spouses

Non-working spouses of expatriates—in practice usually wives—may experience particular difficulty in adapting satisfactorily to a foreign country. Male expatriates generally have their jobs and colleagues, and children their school and classmates. But non-working wives—away from family and friends and with the housework often taken out of their hands by servants—can all too easily become isolated, frustrated, and bored. With a little imagination and determination, however, alternative activities can be found that would make a year or two in the tropics both fun and rewarding.

Learning the language and customs Language lessons can give the new expatriate a goal, fill spare time, offer the chance to meet others in similar circumstances, and help create a favourable impression with local people.

Voluntary work Some people dedicate their whole life to the service of others; for most of us, only a part is so channelled. Difficulties with work permits prohibit many wives from finding paid employment, but most tropical countries have little social welfare, and your services would almost certainly be welcome in orphanages, schools, and hospitals. Local churches, missionary organizations, or your embassy should be able to provide further information about where help is needed.

Cultural activities History, archaeology, art, crafts, and other aspects of the local culture can be absorbing and fascinating—though not in *all* tropical countries.

Travel If the country in which you reside is safe enough, take the opportunity of travelling outside urban areas to see what life is like for the majority of local people. It could be an eye-opening experience.

Academic You may be able to enrol on a degree course at a local university.

Hobbies Pastimes of any sort can be taken up or developed. Any activity outside the home will keep you from worrying about the domestic minutiae and will provide social contact with others.

As an example of a successful, non-working spouse abroad, I would cite my wife: during a three-year spell in Thailand she learned to speak Thai, was an active member of a museum group, led field visits to native craft centres, taught blind Thai children to swim, played a great deal of tennis, and during the second year studied assiduously for (and obtained) a master's degree in education and had a baby!

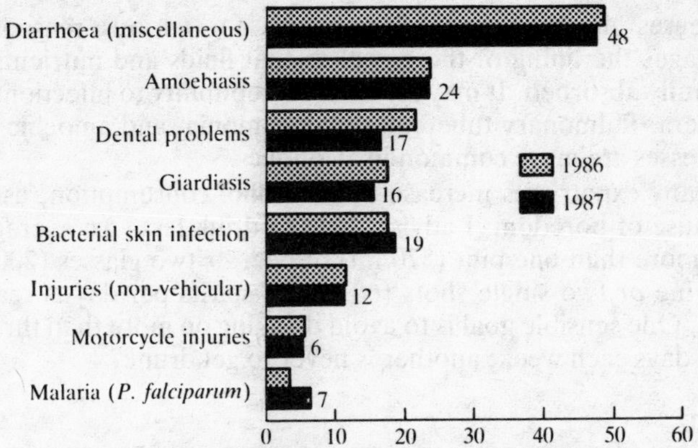

1. Figures represent numbers of cases requiring skilled medical treatment per hundred Peace Corps Volunteers per year.
2. Figures underestimate the rates of minor illnesses, since not all volunteers have easy access to medical cases.

Fig. 11.1 Health problems in Peace Corps Volunteers. Reproduced by courtesy of Dr Kenneth W. Bernard, Centers for Disease Control, Atlanta.

Physical health

Examples of results from studies of health and illness among travellers are given on p. 14.

The incidence of illness (for a given period abroad) is rather less in long-term visitors than in short-term tourists. The results from one important survey of illness in long-term visitors are shown in Fig. 11.1 above, which gives data from a study of 5500 Peace Corps Volunteers living in 62 countries.

Most specific health hazards—such as the risks of water-borne and insect-borne disease—and their avoidance are considered in detail in the first few sections of this book. I would like to stress some particularly important general aspects of healthy living for the long-term visitor.

Alcohol consumption

Apart from the psychological and social problems associated with alcohol dependence, excessive alcohol consumption has various deleterious effects on physical health. A high alcohol intake increases the incidence of both infectious diseases and diarrhoea—of particular relevance to residents in the tropics. Alcohol increases the incidence of diarrhoea for various reasons. It damages the lining of the bowel so that fluids and nutrients are not fully absorbed. It may increase susceptibility to infection with cholera. Pulmonary tuberculosis, pneumonia, and amoebic liver abscesses are more common in alcoholics.

Many expatriates increase their alcohol consumption, usually because of boredom; I advise them to drink less. An average of not more than one pint (570 ml) of beer *or* two glasses (200 ml) of wine *or* two single shots (60 ml) of spirits per day is reasonable. One sensible goal is to avoid drinking on more than three or four days each week; another is never to get drunk.

Food

Food hygiene in hot weather is a major problem. The essential rule is to avoid storing foods such as cooked meat, poultry, seafoods, and rice at temperatures at which bacteria proliferate. Food must, therefore, be served shortly after cooking or else cooled rapidly and stored in a refrigerator to 4°C within about an hour.

In many countries, raw salads and shellfish should be avoided because they often carry typhoid, cholera, and viruses that can cause hepatitis (p. 23). Even well-cooked shellfish should be avoided.

Some guidance on diet can be gained by considering the religious dietary rules of some peoples living in warm countries. For example, Jews and Muslims are forbidden to eat pork and thus won't develop *cysticercosis* (see p. 50) from the larval cysts of the pork tapeworm and are less likely to develop *trichinosis*. Orthodox Jews avoid eating shellfish and thus are much less likely to get infectious diarrhoea. Strict Muslims and Seventh-Day Adventists have a tremendous health advantage in that they don't drink alcohol.

Swimming

A doctor was once quoted as saying 'it isn't what you eat in Spain that does most of the damage, it's what you swallow when you swim'. Polluted water drunk while swimming may cause illness, and the Mediterranean Sea contains a high concentration of faecal bacteria: it has a coastal population of 120 million that almost doubles in the summer, and Greece, for example, treats only 3 per cent of its sewage. (Even Britain dumps 5 millions tons of raw sewage into the sea, every year, with one in three bathing beaches officially designated as dirty and unsafe.) Surveys show that beaches in many parts of Europe fall well below EEC safety standards.

A study on the Costa Brava showed that 15 per cent of swimmers in the sea had stomach upsets, compared with 3 per cent of non-swimmers. Doctors in the South of France confirm that half the patients who see them in the summer have got sick through either eating seafood or swimming.

Swimming should be restricted to chlorinated swimming-pools or safe areas in the sea. (Do not swim or paddle in fresh-water lakes or rivers in the tropics, unless there is known to be no risk of contracting schistosomiasis—p. 93).

Clothing

The best clothes for hot weather are made from cotton or silk, which allow the skin to breathe. Keep your clothes loose. Even walking in the heat, a wet handkerchief tied around the neck can be refreshing. Dark glasses help to reduce the glare. Paradoxically, a sweater is needed in certain countries where the air-conditioning may be too efficient.

Children should be dressed for coolness and in cotton. Little girls usually wear sleeveless, pinafore-style dresses. Cotton skirts and blouses are useful for older schoolgirls. A generous supply of underwear should be taken. In planning a good basic supply of clothes for children, take into account the abuse clothes will receive from frequent washing and sun-drying over and above the wear that children normally give them.

Sex and frustration

For many people and religions, sex with one's spouse is the only type acceptable. In practical terms, however, many people working abroad are unaccompanied by their spouse or other sexual partner and may be in need of an alternative sexual outlet. Similar considerations apply to single people.

Masturbation is the safest sexual outlet for those wishing to avoid emotional complications or any possibility of sexually transmitted disease. However, a relationship with someone else is likely to be more interesting and rewarding.

Friendship is the best basis for a sexual relationship whether inside or outside marriage. Some of my patients have developed close friendships and satisfactory sexual relationships with local people abroad. Regular sex is healthier than alcoholism.

Prostitutes in many tropical countries are attractive and skilful—particularly those working as masseuses in massage parlours. But there are risks: some prostitutes carry guns and may have a pimp who will extort money while the victim has his pants down. The chances of contracting a sexually transmitted disease are also high (see p. 381), and the growing risk of AIDS makes abstinence altogether a much less hazardous alternative.

Crime

Crime against the visitor

Visitors to some foreign countries run a significant risk of being robbed, raped, or even murdered, and there are numerous recent examples of violent crimes against tourists and travellers in all parts of the world.

Homes in the tropics are often robbed, sometimes violently—although the victims are usually wealthy natives rather than foreigners.

Vehicles may be stopped by criminals and their occupants robbed or even murdered. Criminals may dress up as police or soldiers, while in some places they *are* the local police or militia. Sometimes, a large bribe has to be paid to escape unscathed.

On the other hand, some countries—for example some Islamic states—have an exceptionally low crime rate.

Some partial solutions can be suggested

- Avoid carrying large amounts of money or valuables on your person. Any money you must carry, and also your passport, should be kept in a body belt or in a buttoned-down inside pocket. Avoid carrying anything more than small amounts of money in a bag.
- Dress and behave in a quiet and unobtrusive manner.
- If you travel by road, choose a modest car, and have an escort, if possible, who understands the language.
- Ensure adequate security at your residence.

Local laws

It is as well to find out and observe the laws of the host country. The laws that visitors seem most prone to fall foul of relate to alcohol and drugs. In Saudi Arabia, for example, it is a crime to brew, sell, and even to drink alcohol; selling usually has the most serious repercussions.

One British worker in Saudi Arabia was jailed and received 300 lashes for brewing and selling beer. Incarceration was in Riyadh's Malaz jail, in a circular room accompanied by 600 other prisoners. Prisoners slept with their heads to the wall, each allocated eighteen inches' head space. This was the privileged position reached after four months. He escaped. In 1984, Europeans were forbidden to celebrate Christmas in Saudi Arabia.

Remember that in most countries, imprisonment is the punishment for use or possession of 'recreational' drugs such as cannabis, cocaine, and heroin (see p. 330). Visitors are well advised to steer clear of the use, selling, or transport of such drugs. Even innocuous substances such as antimalarial tablets can be viewed with suspicion by customs officials and others; prescriptions and medical reports should be carried so as to verify the legitimate use of such drugs.

Any type of insulting behaviour should be carefully avoided. In 1978, an Englishman in Thailand made a remark about a photograph of the Thai Queen. The shopkeeper claimed he had insulted her, handed him over to the police, and he was jailed.

Road and motoring hazards

Road traffic accidents are more common in the tropics (see p. 256). Many roads are poorly surfaced and maintained; and motorists drive too fast, frequently overtaking on blind corners or hills. In some Third World cities, such as Cairo, normal rules of the road are largely ignored and replaced by a cacophony of horns; in others, such as Lagos, the continuous traffic congestion can make driving extremely frustrating. Among European countries, Greece is possibly the most dangerous place to drive; in 1979, the number of deaths per 100 000 cars was 195 in Greece compared with 90 in France, 58 in Italy and 46 in the UK.

Expatriates in the tropics are often expected to be driven by a local man, but this usually increases the chances of an accident. If possible, you should drive the vehicle yourself with the local driver or colleague sitting beside you to interpret in case of an accident. Vehicles should always be driven reasonably slowly, although efforts should be made to fit in with the flow of traffic. Driving at night should be avoided if at all possible. Avoid drinking alcohol whether you are a driver or passenger—not only for safety but also so that you can think and talk lucidly in the event of an accident.

Longer journeys should be planned carefully. The journey should be started early so that it can be completed by dusk. Good-quality dark glasses should be worn to reduce glare. Breaks should be taken every hour or two and drinks taken under the shade—non-alcoholic for the driver. Meals should be light so that driver and passengers do not fall asleep.

Fuel is often difficult to obtain in rural areas (and even in some cities), so fuel stops should be planned carefully, and if necessary a reserve supply kept in a jerrycan in the boot. Naturally, the vehicle should be regularly serviced and thoroughly checked before any journey. All five tyres should have a thick tread, and wheel-changing should be practised between journeys. A comprehensive kit of spare parts should be carried.

In an accident that results in injury to anyone else, prison custody for the driver is the rule in many countries, until the case is eventually heard. This is at present the situation in Turkey, currently a popular holiday destination for travellers from the UK and Europe. Always make sure that you are adequately insured for driving abroad. Car insurance, and insurance for rented cars, should cover bail bonds, fines, and legal costs. It can be difficult to raise the money for such expenses at short notice from the inside of a prison cell. The risk of illness in prison may also be high.

In many countries, including Saudi Arabia, compensation may be demanded if a local person is killed in an accident, even if the local was at fault. In some African countries, such as Angola, motorists who accidently kill pedestrians may be stoned to death if they stop the car to tend the victim. Sometimes, people deliberately run in front of the car to facilitate a robbery or car theft. The cardinal rule in such countries must be to drive on, even if someone has been knocked down, and to ask questions later.

Adequate insurance coverage for luggage in cars is especially important in Italy, where thieves often steal from cars and may smash windows or slash tyres in the process.

Parasitophobia and anxiety about health

Many people worry excessively about the risks of catching exotic or wormy diseases in the tropics. The precautions necessary to stay healthy are simple ones, and illness abroad is rare in fit people who behave sensibly. An understanding of the risks should dispel excessive fears.

12

Preparations for travel

Health insurance for international travel

Costs of health care abroad can be very high. Make sure that all your requirements are adequately covered before you travel.

Dr Richard Fairhurst *is the Chief Medical Officer of The Travellers' Medical Service, and was formerly the Chief Medical Officer of Europ Assistance, London.*

Health insurance is an important part of health care for travellers. It is becoming an increasingly complex field, so travellers need to think about and specify exactly what they require. Remember that health insurance provides money after the event and *not* medical care.

It is very important that the amount of money provided by the policy is adequate for any likely need. There has been a growing tendency to increase the amount of medical cover provided—indeed, some policies now provide unlimited medical cover—but, in my experience, £500 000 is perfectly adequate even in the USA, provided repatriation expenses are covered separately in another section of the policy.

Medical assistance for travellers

Traditionally, health-care insurance benefits are paid out against a completed claim form, filled in after an episode of illness is over and the patient is back at home.

This begs a number of questions. Will the amount of money insured be adequate to reimburse the costs of treatment abroad? How easy will it be to obtain money in an emergency to pay for treatment? Not all hospital authorities and doctors abroad necessarily accept travel insurance documents as evidence that they will eventually be paid, although when prolonged treatment abroad is necessary it is often possible to make arrangements for insurance companies to pay the costs directly.

UK and European Community nationals are entitled to free or reduced cost medical treatment in certain countries (see p. 471), but additional insurance is still necessary to cover the costs of repatriation and any other expenses.

However much money is available, will adequate facilities for treatment exist at the site of the incident?

These problems resulted in the development of combined Health Insurance and Assistance services, which endeavour to provide on-the-spot help, together with repatriation for further treatment if necessary. In practical terms, this demands expertise in obtaining air ambulance facilities at short notice, medical and logistic support, and the ability to judge which circumstances justify evacuation—and to where. Remember that it is not necessarily appropriate to repatriate every single case of illness abroad by air ambulance, and in many countries poor communications and lack of airport facilities may make this impossible anyway.

The risks

So what are the risks that an international traveller runs? From insurance company records, we know that one in 600 travellers will call with a medical problem, one in 10 000 will require repatriation by air ambulance for medical reasons; and eight in 100 000 will die abroad.

Pre-existing illness

The basis of all insurance is that a contract is taken against a risk, before that risk occurs. This is summed up neatly by the saying that it is impossible to insure a house that is already on fire. When this principle is applied to medical risks, certain problems become clear.

Many policies exclude cover for pre-existing illness, or 'risks which could be reasonably foreseen by the client', or 'travelling against the advice of a medical practitioner'. If anyone has any type of pre-existing medical condition, it is very important that they should notify the company with which they are proposing to insure, and obtain confirmation in writing that the problem *will* be covered in the event of a claim.

There is of course a moral issue here. Is it reasonable for insurance companies or doctors to encourage people who have a pre-existing illness to travel abroad on holiday? Often a person who is ill perceives the holiday as being a valuable part of convalescence, and looks forward to the benefits it will bring.

No less often, however, neither the patient nor his doctor gives adequate consideration to what will happen if the patient becomes ill again outside his home environment. Even in countries with good medical facilities, being ill in a hospital where the doctors do not speak your own language and cannot refer to your previous records can be a dangerous and unpleasant experience. In countries where medical facilities are poor, what was conceived as a period of convalescence and relaxation can be transformed all too readily into a nightmare.

People with a pre-existing illness (and their doctors) should therefore satisfy themselves that adequate facilities for treatment really will be available if the condition recurs or deteriorates, and should think carefully about whether or not the risks are justified.

The young, the old, and the pregnant

These special groups are worthy of particular comment. In general, children and young people are accepted on the same terms and the same premium as adults. A small number of companies offer a discount for children. The elderly obviously have an increased chance of making a claim under a health insurance policy and are more likely to have pre-existing medical conditions which should, as mentioned before, be notified specifically to the insurance company. Disabled people in general are no more likely to become ill than anyone else, though disabilities can cause problems with repatriation from time to time, and it is therefore prudent for disabled people to notify insurance companies of their disability in advance.

Pregnancy poses a great problem. Some companies completely exclude cover in pregnancy. Others say that pregnancy is not a medical illness and therefore include only abnormalities of pregnancy. In any event it is very difficult to arrange insurance cover for the result of a pregnancy—the newborn child (see p. 418). Remember that if a pregnancy ends unexpectedly early and produces a premature baby, the baby's medical care in a neonatal intensive care unit could be very expensive. Many insurers take the view that a child who does not exist at the time the contract is taken can never be covered by a contract, though others would be prepared to write special (and very expensive) contracts to cover this possibility.

Check that you are covered

Other problems occur with insurance contracts, which should be foreseen before difficulties arise. Contracts for holiday insurance almost always exclude manual labour and work, and anyone who is going abroad to do any sort of manual work should check carefully that they are covered.

Similarly many policies do not cover mountaineering, scuba diving, parascending, or motorcycle riding. All these activities are becoming increasingly common, particularly with holidaymakers. If you intend to indulge in any of these activities it is vital to make sure that the risks are covered. Some policies also do not cover driving, or driving rented cars (see p. 462).

It may be necessary to 'shop around' to find an insurance company that will cover you for the particular sport you are interested in. Medical insurance policies often also cover baggage, cancellation, and curtailment of the trip, and indeed almost half the claims under such policies are in these sections. Make sure the sums insured under each section are appropriate for your needs, remembering that personal belongings may already be covered under other policies that you may have. Most policies include some sort of death benefit following accident: note that this is not life cover and covers only *accidental* death; it should not be confused with life assurance.

Annual insurance

Traditionally, health insurance has been bought on a trip basis, in other words you purchase fixed-term insurance to cover the duration of a single trip. More recently there has been a trend towards providing annual policies, albeit with a limit to the duration of any one trip. These annual policies are particularly attractive to frequent travellers, especially because they do not require prior notification of trips, and are always in force.

Expatriates

Expatriates need a form of permanent health insurance that will provide for their normal health-care needs wherever they are

UK Nationals: Reciprocal arrangements for free or reduced cost medical care abroad

Eligible nationals and residents of the UK and European Community countries are entitled to emergency medical treatment either free or at reduced cost, when visiting other Community countries.

Travellers from the UK will need *Certificate E111* in order to obtain treatment. Leaflet T1, 'The Traveller's Guide to Health', is available free from DHSS Leaflet Unit, Stanmore, Middlesex, and contains an application form. Certificate E111 gives entitlement to treatment in the following countries:

Belgium
Denmark
France
Germany
Gibraltar
Greece
Irish Republic (only proof of entitlement is necessary)
Italy
Luxembourg
Netherlands
Portugal
Spain

There are also reciprocal arrangements between the UK and the following countries for free or reduced-cost emergency medical care:

Anguilla
Australia
British Virgin Islands
Bulgaria
Channel Islands
Czechoslovakia
Falkland Islands
Finland
East Germany
Hong Kong
Hungary
Iceland
Malta
Montserrat
New Zealand
Norway
Poland
Romania
St Helena
Sweden
Turks & Caicos Islands
USSR
Yugoslavia

living. This usually includes some form of repatriation cover, which may be limited to repatriation to the nearest place of medical excellence rather than all the way to their home country. The policies are usually taken out by their employer, rather than on an individual basis. Employees are best advised to demand such policies as a condition of employment.

Summary of advice for travellers

In conclusion, a wide range of health insurance contracts is available. Each individual traveller should define his or her needs and then study the full insurance proposal or contract in order to make sure it meets these needs exactly. If there are any queries, these should be raised in writing with the insurer before going abroad.

Immunization

Large numbers of travellers are exposed to the risks of infectious diseases abroad. Immunization is an effective measure against some important diseases, and all travellers should ensure that they receive the available protection.

Dr Gil Lea *joined the airline medical service more than 15 years ago, and as Senior Medical Officer at the British Airways Immunization unit in London has supervised the administration of over one million doses of vaccine to travellers.*

International travel is increasing, and so are opportunities for more adventurous holidays in more exotic places. Relaxation of immunization regulations has made it easier—though no less hazardous—for travellers to visit risk areas without first having to seek specialist advice.

Mandatory and non-mandatory immunization

Travellers should understand that there are now very few *mandatory* immunization requirements for travel—vaccination against yellow fever is now virtually the only example, and even then is required only for travel to or through certain parts of Africa and South America. Most are non-mandatory, but one or more such vaccinations are nevertheless still *strongly advised* for most destinations—the only exception being for direct travel to countries in northern Europe, the USA, Canada, Australia, and New Zealand. In terms of health protection, these non-mandatory vaccinations are often far more important.

Unfortunately, many travel agents and embassy officials mention only the mandatory immunization requirements for a particular country (i.e. those for which a certificate is required), omitting to mention other advisable precautions. In consequence, travellers may gain the impression that no vaccinations are necessary for destinations such as India or Thailand simply because there are no mandatory requirements. In fact, several immunizations should be considered, and advice about malaria prevention (see p. 117) is also important.

Travel companies cannot reasonably be expected to provide detailed information about optional vaccinations and the choice of antimalarial tablets, but should certainly inform travellers of any mandatory requirements and remind them to consult a doctor or an immunization centre. An outline of the current position is given below and in Appendix 1, but all travellers should check their individual needs several weeks before departure (see Appendix 6). A full immunization schedule may take two months or more to complete, but if less time is available valuable protection can still be gained.

About vaccines

Strictly, the word 'vaccination' refers only to that given (in the past) against smallpox. However, International Regulations refer to other immunizations by the same term, and the words 'vaccination' and 'immunization' have come to be used interchangeably.

Vaccines stimulate the body's defence systems by the introduction of a small amount of the bacteria or virus concerned into the tissues. Some vaccines contain the killed or inactivated germ organism or its toxin; others contain a related live organism selected as safe for inoculation. The vaccine stimulates the production of antibodies, which are then ready to act once the real infection is encountered.

The number of doses required and the spacing between them depends on whether it is a 'live' or 'killed' vaccine and on previous protection received. Once the initial courses of polio, tetanus, and typhoid vaccines have been completed, single 'booster' doses every few years are all that is required to maintain protection. The period of protection conferred by a vaccine varies from six months (cholera) to ten years (yellow fever).

It is important to realize that few vaccines provide 100 per cent protection, and other precautions such as care with food, drink, and personal hygiene are still necessary even when you have been vaccinated.

The only travel injection that is not a vaccine is gamma-globulin, used to protect against hepatitis. Instead of stimulating the body's defences, gamma-globulin is ready-made antibody. It does not last long in the body after injection, so it is given close to departure and after the other injections.

Not every vaccine is suitable for every person, for reasons such as allergy, pregnancy, age, or because of certain medical conditions; these problems are considered below.

Obtaining immunization

Where?

Immunization centres can provide accurate and up-to-date advice on both mandatory immunization requirements and non-mandatory recommendations and can also give the vaccines themselves. Their staff are specialists, and will usually be able to provide a quick service. Alternatively you can go to your own doctor, who can obtain and give all vaccines except yellow fever, and will usually be closer to home.

Some centres provide only yellow fever vaccination, and these centres are usually found in large towns. Centres providing a complete range of travel immunizations tend to exist only in main cities with a large population of potential travellers, and some of the main centres are listed in Appendix 6. In the USA there tend to be fewer centres providing a fully comprehensive service.

When?

It is wise, but not always possible, to inquire about immunization some two to three months ahead of departure, especially for longer trips. But even with only 10 days or so left before departure, a first dose of typhoid or polio vaccine is still worthwhile; and a single dose of any vaccine of which a course has been completed previously, will usually boost protection and can be taken at even shorter notice if necessary.

Common reasons for vaccination requests at the last minute are unexpected business trips, sudden outbreaks of disease (such as the typhoid scare in the Greek island of Kos in 1983 or the meningitis outbreak in the Middle East in the later summer of 1987), and failure to find out in advance that protection is recommended for an intended destination. Business travellers and others who may be called upon to travel at short notice can avoid most problems by keeping their typhoid, tetanus, and polio protection up to date by means of booster doses every few years.

The dates for booster injections are not critical to the exact week and can be taken at any convenient time. Anyone who may have to travel at short notice to tropical Africa or South America should also ensure that they have an up-to-date yellow fever vaccination certificate—the certificate is not valid until ten days after injection but then remains valid for ten years. The only injections that it is sensible to leave close to departure are cholera and gamma-globulin, should they be required.

Those who regularly take holidays abroad should ideally follow a similar strategy—and thus avoid getting caught in a sudden rush for vaccine at the time of an outbreak. The 1983 typhoid scare in Kos reminded numerous travellers that, in future, it might be wise to plan precautions in advance.

If only one dose of a course of vaccine has been taken due to shortage of time, the course can be completed after the holiday to ensure that the same problem does not occur next time.

Immunization schedules

Different schedules for immunization are used by different centres. Some typical examples of schedules for different circumstances are shown in Table 12.1, but schedules generally need to be planned on an individual basis for each traveller.

If time is relatively short, two visits spaced four to six weeks apart will allow administration of most commonly needed vaccinations—but a third visit six weeks later will be needed for a traveller taking a first-ever course of polio vaccine. Yellow fever and rabies vaccinations, if required, can be fitted into a two-visit schedule, but an extra visit to allow fewer injections at the same time would be preferable.

Where many vaccines are required, it is probably easier to go to an immunization centre if there is one in a convenient location.

The injections

A surprising number of people are frightened by the thought of an injection. Young adults may not have had one since childhood and it may still loom large in their memory. Nowadays, disposable needles are very small and sharp, and anyone who is well practised can give these injections almost painlessly. Smaller amounts of purer vaccines are often used which result in fewer adverse reactions.

Most travel vaccines are given into different layers of the skin, and the outer part of the upper arm is a convenient site. (Preferences vary: the French often give travel injections into the back,

Table 12.1 Examples of immunization schedules. (These should be planned individually for each traveller)

A	**Overland trip through Africa, with six weeks before departure:**	
	First attendance:	yellow fever typhoid (first dose) tetanus (booster) [rabies (first dose)]
	Second attendance: (four weeks later)	typhoid (second dose) polio (booster) [rabies (second dose)]
	Third attendance: (a few days before departure)	cholera gamma-globulin
B	**Rushed schedule, with only one attendance possible:**	
	For Africa:	typhoid* tetanus* cholera polio* gamma-globulin yellow fever
	For Asia:	typhoid* tetanus* cholera polio* gamma-globulin
	For South America:	typhoid* tetanus* polio* gamma-globulin yellow fever

*These typhoid, tetanus, and polio immunizations should be booster doses, if not, courses should be completed *en route*, but only if hygienic medical facilities can be found (see note on p. 501 regarding injections abroad).

just below the shoulder blade.) The thigh could be used but often aches more than the arm afterwards. At the British Airways Immunization Centre, the only injection given into the buttock is gamma-globulin, which contains more fluid and is more comfortable given into a large muscle.

Those attending for injections (and especially anyone who is prone to feeling faint) should eat normally beforehand, and ensure that some breakfast has been taken prior to a morning appointment. In general, there are no special rules regarding alcohol before or after an injection. However, if several injections are given in one day it is advisable to avoid strenuous exercise or alcohol for several hours, but each individual should be guided by how he or she feels.

The doctor or nurse giving the injections should advise about malaria protection without being asked, but it is sensible for the traveller to check on this should it not be mentioned.

Individual vaccines

Smallpox

Smallpox has been eradicated worldwide (see pp. 511–14)—an achievement entirely due to the effectiveness of the smallpox vaccine. At first it was hard to believe that there was not a village somewhere that had been missed in the vaccination campaign; but after more than a decade of following up reports of suspected cases, no evidence of the disease has been found.

Smallpox vaccine sometimes produces harmful side-effects, and there is now no reason for receiving it. After several years of uncertainty about which visa departments and which port health authorities still required a smallpox vaccination certificate, no country now officially requires one. Occasionally visa forms are issued that demand a certificate, but any such request should be circumvented by a medical certificate of exemption, signed by a doctor and giving details of the reasons for not vaccinating.

Yellow fever (see pp. 131–3)

Most of the remaining international certificate requirements relate to yellow fever vaccination (the rest relate to cholera). The vaccine provides virtually 100 per cent protection for at least the ten years that the certificate lasts, so it is understandable that many countries maintain their yellow fever regulations, although a traveller visiting only the capital city of a country reporting the disease may not be at risk.

There are some common misconceptions about the yellow fever regulations, and travellers often ask for yellow fever vaccination when they do not need it. On the other hand, a television reporter following the Royal Tour of Kenya and the Indian subcontinent in November 1983 was quarantined on trying to enter India because she had not been vaccinated. The regulations may seem complicated at first, but are in fact quite reasonable.

Yellow fever exists only in two endemic zones, one across Central Africa and the other in the northern part of South America (see Map 4.2, p. 132). Not all these countries report the disease all the time, but when planning to travel through these areas, it is wise to inquire from a yellow fever centre whether the vaccination should be given and a certificate obtained. Some countries require a certificate from all travellers; the rest may not require a certificate from those on direct flights from the UK or USA, but may do so for travel from one country to another within the zone; in addition it may be worth taking the vaccine for personal protection even if a certificate is not required.

The section of the regulations most commonly misunderstood is based on there being 'yellow fever receptive' areas outside the zones. These are countries that have similar climates (and mosquitoes) to the countries where yellow fever is endemic, and naturally wish to prevent introduction of the disease. Some, such as the West Indies and South Africa, are close to the existing zones while others are in tropical parts of Asia.

As yellow fever does not exist in Asia, yellow fever vaccination is quite unnecessary for travel to Asian countries, *provided* travel is by the usual direct routes from the UK or USA. However, for travel via Kenya to India, for example, as on the Queen's Commonwealth Tour, the certificate is required, as India wishes to avoid the introduction of the disease from Africa. Yet a traveller seeking information from the Indian High Commission in London might easily be told that no certificate is necessary: it would be assumed that the enquiry related to travel direct from London.

Staff at several London embassies have on many occasions appeared to know the regulations only for direct travel to their countries, and it is therefore important, when inquiring about vaccination from a yellow fever centre, to mention all the countries to be visited.

Cholera (see pp. 30–1 and 40–1)

In 1973 the World Health Organization (WHO) recommended that cholera certificates should no longer be required for entry to any country, as vaccination does not prevent the international spread of the disease. Since then, countries have gradually reduced their requirements and since August 1985 no country has required a certificate from all travellers, although several countries require one for travel via cholera-infected areas. The cholera certificate may also be checked when leaving India if onward travel is to a country that demands one.

In view of this, the fact that the vaccine is less effective than others, and the fact that most travellers are anyway at very low risk from cholera (only 12 cases of cholera occurred in European travellers in 1987), the vaccine is now less commonly recommended. However, it does provide a degree of personal protection and may still be advised for some countries in Africa and Asia, especially for travel to rural areas.

Only a single dose is required to obtain a certificate (valid for 6 months starting 6 days after vaccination); this may still be necessary for travel that will involve crossing several international boundaries within cholera endemic zones. No country requires a certificate for direct entry from Europe or USA.

All the vaccines mentioned below are optional, except that typhoid vaccination is required on some Nepal visa forms.

Typhoid and tetanus

Until a few years ago, protection against typhoid (pp. 30, 37) was usually given by means of the infamous TAB vaccine: this contained vaccine against paratyphoid A and B as well as typhoid. It is now thought that protection against paratyphoid was not effective and was responsible for unpleasant reactions, so typhoid vaccine is now given on its own, which is a considerable improvement. An oral vaccine is used in parts of Europe and trials are being conducted on its effectiveness.

TAB used to be combined with cholera vaccine as TAB/Cho and with tetanus toxoid as TABT. As cholera vaccination lasts for only six months, some frequent travellers were being given TAB/Cho every six months and were getting more typhoid vaccine than they needed. I have never considered it a useful vaccine and its recent withdrawal from availability was timely. TABT was more useful as a way of giving tetanus protection at the same time as travel vaccines.

As tetanus can follow an injury (p. 87), everyone should be protected whether they travel or not. Certain kinds of travel—camping trips, for example—carry an increased risk of injury; and good medical facilities following injury may not always be easily available. Tetanus is now given to adults as a separate vaccine (though in the USA it is often combined with diphtheria).

Typhoid vaccine provides a reasonable level of protection, but as with cholera vaccine, it should be used only as an adjunct to hygiene precautions.

Tetanus is contained in the children's triple vaccine, and so long as the routine course has been followed correctly it need not be given to children before they travel.

Polio (see pp. 54–5)

Oral (Sabin) polio vaccine, taken on a sugar lump or as drops on the tongue, is also included with the childhood vaccines, usually starting at three months of age. Any child who has not completed the course should do so prior to travel, and unprotected adults should consider taking the vaccine for everywhere beyond Europe except North America, Australia, and New Zealand.

There are three types of polio virus and three doses in the initial course of vaccine. Each dose contains all three viruses and one of them has an opportunity to 'take' each time. This provides a high level of protection, although sometimes not all types have taken, so booster doses are recommended every five to ten years for travel.

An injected (killed) polio vaccine is also available: this is an up-to-date version of the Salk vaccine used before the oral (live) vaccine was developed. The modern injected vaccine is used by choice in a few countries, but only small amounts are available in the UK for those for whom the live vaccine is unsuitable. The disadvantage is that the injected vaccine may take longer to confer protection.

Hepatitis (see pp. 57–65)

Gamma-globulin is an injection of antibody that could be expected to provide protection against a number of diseases, but for the purposes of travel is useful only against hepatitis A, the common type caught from infected food and water in places where sanitation is poor, or from contact with an infected person.

Protection is particularly important for overlanders and travellers to rural areas, but an increasing number of travellers prefer to take gamma-globulin even for short trips rather than risk a protracted period of illness after return.

There is no doubt that the injection provides a useful level of protection against hepatitis A, but it is still necessary to take care with food and water hygiene as there are other diseases, including another less common type of hepatitis (enteric non-A, non-B hepatitis) also spread by this route.

Gamma-globulin does not normally cause much in the way of reaction apart from slight local soreness. (The injection is given higher up on the buttock than the part which is sat upon!)

Frequent travellers, or those going to live or work abroad, who would otherwise need repeated injections of gamma globulin, may be interested in the blood test for hepatitis A antibody. This test is becoming more easily available and shows whether or not the individual already has protection against this type of hepatitis. Young adults without a previous history of the disease are not very likely to have a positive result, but the incidence increases with age and in those who have lived in the tropics. Of course if the test is negative, the gamma globulin injection will still be necessary.

No *vaccine* is available against hepatitis A but there is a new vaccine against hepatitis B. Hepatitis B is transmitted in rather similar ways as AIDS; via blood serum, non-sterile needles, and sexual contact with those living in highly endemic areas. The vaccine against hepatitis B, although now a little cheaper is often thought to be too expensive for most travellers, but should be taken by those in high risk groups, and should be considered by frequent or long term travellers. It is discussed in detail on p. 62.

Rabies (see pp. 193–200)

Until recently the only rabies vaccine available was so unpleasant that it was not used until after the bite, when the patient was faced with the imminent threat of rabies. The French human diploid cell vaccine is effective and safe and produces very few reactions (though a small percentage of people seem to be allergic to it and should not continue the course). This vaccine makes immunization prior to possible exposure to rabies feasible for the first time.

It does not preclude the need for treatment after a bite but will reduce the amount of treatment necessary (fewer doses of vaccine and no serum injection) and can be expected to be effective even if there is a short delay before the treatment booster doses of vaccine are obtained. The vaccine is particularly valuable for those leaving the beaten track, more than a day's journey from good medical care.

One disadvantage of this vaccine is that it is expensive. In 1979 the British Airways Immunization Unit started giving smaller doses of vaccine at a once-weekly session, bringing the price within reach of the overland traveller. Numbers have gradually increased to the point that daily vaccination sessions can now be held at our main (Regent St, London) centre. Experimental results from this small-dose technique are nearly as good as those obtained with the larger dose, but anyone at high risk (such as vets handling sick animals abroad) should take the full dose. It has been suggested that choroquine may inhibit the vaccine and those currently on that antimalarial tablet may prefer the large dose. The small dose method can be used only where there are many people needing it concurrently, and by staff skilled in its execution. Where this is not available, the large dose can usually be obtained.

Pre-exposure administration of the vaccine reduces the hazard of rabies for those travelling through areas where dogs can be infected; but it is still important that there should be no unnecessary delay in starting treatment after a bite.

The vaccine is not at present recommended for travel to France or other European and North American countries that have rabies only in wild animals such as foxes and skunks, and where excellent treatment should be rapidly available.

Plague and East European tick encephalitis

These two vaccines are occasionally obtained specifically for particular types of travel. Plague (see p. 159) is transmitted by rodent fleas and the vaccine may be given to relief workers in disaster areas or for other work in plague endemic areas where avoiding contact with rats might be difficult. East European tick encephalitis is an arbovirus infection that occurs especially in early summer in warm forests of central Europe and is mainly of concern to foresters, although campers and hikers in such areas could also be at risk.

Meningococcal meningitis and Japanese encephalitis

Until recently these vaccines were only rarely given. Usage of both has now increased, though neither is usually given for short, package-type holidays unless there is an outbreak which has been reported in the locality.

Meningococcal meningitis exists worldwide. There is no vaccine yet in use against the B strain that caused widely publicized outbreaks in England in 1988; but there is a vaccine against type C; and against type A, which produces outbreaks outside the UK and the USA.

In the last few years, Nepal, India, and Pakistan have reported meningitis outbreaks, while Brazil has had several epidemics; there is also an endemic zone that stretches right across Africa (see p. 99). A serious outbreak occurred in Khartoum in 1988.

In view of the increase in reports of meningitis in the home countries of Muslim pilgrims travelling to Mecca, and the fact that there had been a number of cases in the Middle East the previous year, the health authorities in Saudi Arabia took the unprecedented step of making vaccination against meningococcal meningitis, and a vaccination certificate, mandatory for those joining the Haj pilgrimage in 1988.

Meningitis is not a disease for which an International Certificate of Vaccination is provided under World Health Organization regulations, and this example illustrates how countries may, from time to time, impose their own restrictions on visas, making them conditional upon additional health certificates and requirements.

Despite this, travellers from the UK and USA rarely contract the disease, and in general, the vaccine is only advised for those going to areas with outbreaks in progress, or staying in endemic zones during the dry season. (See note on p. 99 regarding protection of travellers who have had their spleens removed.)

Japanese encephalitis

This disease is endemic across Asia, affecting many countries from India to Japan. It is seasonal in the temperate zones affected, but may be all year-round in the tropics.

The virus is transmitted to man by mosquitoes which have bitten farm animals or birds, so that prolonged travel through agricultural regions constitutes the highest risk. The disease can be serious or fatal, but it has fortunately only been reported in a tiny number of western travellers, and as the vaccine has to be imported from Japan in small amounts, a course tends to be rather expensive.

Travellers intending to visit rural parts of Asia for any length of time should enquire about the likely risk before they travel.

Diphtheria, BCG and measles

All children going overseas who have not completed their routine childhood immunization course, including measles vaccine, should do so.

Diphtheria vaccine is included in this schedule, but any adults who will be in close contact with children in developing areas, for example nurses and teachers, should have their immunity checked by Schick test and be vaccinated if necessary. (A vaccine, already available in the USA, has recently become available in the UK which removes the need for Schick testing.)

BCG vaccination (against tuberculosis—see pp. 84–6) is usually given in the UK at 11–13 years but can be given from birth in those going to live in higher-risk areas. Adults going to work in similar areas and who may be unprotected can be tested and vaccinated if necessary. The public health approach to TB in the USA is different, and American travellers are not generally encouraged to have BCG (pp. 84–6).

Measles immunization is recommended for travellers from the USA born after 1957 who have not previously been immunized or had the disease, and American travellers should consult their physician for advice about this prior to departure.

When not to be vaccinated

Each case should be considered individually, but there are some general guidelines.

Vaccines to which the recipient has a known allergy are not normally given, nor are vaccines given during acute illness. Otherwise, there are no particular circumstances when killed vaccines (cholera, typhoid, tetanus, rabies) should be avoided—with the exception of the injected polio vaccine, which contains trace quantities of penicillin and several rare antibiotics.

In practice, by far the most common problem is a history of penicillin allergy (which anyway may not be true allergy). There is no other way of protecting against polio (both types of vaccine now contain traces of penicillin), and unless penicillin allergy is known to have caused collapse in the past, the oral vaccine is often given with no ill effect.

Other specific cautions are allergy to eggs for yellow fever and measles, and to several rare antibiotics for both vaccines and polio.

Immune disorders

People with an impaired immune system, whether due to serious disease, cortisone-type or anticancer drugs, or deep X-ray treatment, should not usually take live vaccines (yellow fever, oral polio).

Gut infections at the time of vaccination may inhibit the polio vaccine from 'taking'.

Pregnancy

During pregnancy (see pp. 417–22) live vaccines are generally avoided, but on certain occasions they may still be advised. There is no evidence that yellow fever vaccine has ever been harmful, and where there is a real threat from the disease (not just a certificate requirement), it may be given. Where urgent polio protection is vital, oral vaccine has been used, but the killed vaccine is preferable during pregnancy.

Other killed vaccines (cholera, typhoid, tetanus) have been used for many years without any known ill effect, although anything causing a high temperature is undesirable, so cholera and typhoid could be given by a small-dose method or even omitted completely in those prone to reactions.

Small children

Cholera and typhoid vaccines are not usually given under one year of age, and yellow fever not below nine months old. Routine childhood vaccines will not be discussed in detail here (see section on children abroad, p. 423).

Exemption

Where a certificate would normally be required, a medical certificate of exemption signed by a doctor is usually acceptable to the authorities. Those who cannot be vaccinated on medical grounds have to consider the risks of travel without protection.

Reactions to vaccines—what to expect

Yellow fever, oral polio, and modern rabies vaccines usually produce virtually no reaction. Cholera, typhoid, tetanus, and injected polio may do the same, but often produce some local

Table 12.2 Dose intervals for travel vaccines

VACCINE OR IMMUNOGLOBULIN	*PRIMARY COURSE*			*BOOSTER INTERVALS*
	No. of doses	Interval between 1st & 2nd dose	Interval between 2nd & 3rd dose	
Yellow fever	1			10 years
Cholera	2	7–28 days		6 months
Typhoid	2	4–6 weeks		3 years
Tetanus	3	6–12 weeks	6–12 months	5–10 years
Polio	3	At least 6 weeks	At least 6 weeks	5–10 years
Rabies (pre-exposure)				
UK	3	4–6 weeks	6–12 months	2 years
USA	3	7 days	21 days	2 years
Meningitis (meningococcal)	1			3 years
Japanese encephalitis	3	1–2 weeks	2–3 weeks	1–4 years
Tick encephalitis (East European)	3	1–3 months	9–12 months	3 years
Plague	3	1–3 months	3–6 months	6 months
Gamma globulin (hepatitis A)	1			2–6 months according to size of dose
Hepatitis B	3	1 month	5 months	2–5 years

Note: Recommended regimens vary slightly between vaccine manufacturers and countries. Intervals can in some cases be shortened or lengthened to suit travel requirements.

soreness of the arm. Rubbing the arm may increase the irritation and should be avoided. A general off-colour feeling, sometimes accompanied by a raised temperature, may follow cholera and typhoid vaccines and lasts for up to 36 hours.

Should treatment be necessary, rest, plenty of fluids, paracetamol tablets (elixir or Calpol for children) or soluble aspirin for adults (unless there is a past history of stomach ulcers) should be adequate. Red marks often appear at the injection sites and may disappear quickly or fade slowly, but they are not permanent scars. A few people fear injections because they have a tendency to faint, but this can be prevented by taking them while lying down.

Side-effects

Isolated cases of more serious side-effects have been recorded *but are extremely rare*. Oral polio vaccine has been known to produce polio-like symptoms in some recipients or their close contacts on very, very few occasions (about three per 5 million doses). It is recommended that unprotected parents take the vaccine at the same time as their babies.

Summary of advice for travellers

- Travel vaccinations have changed in the last few years. The days when a large ship could be delayed because one passenger had forgotten a smallpox certificate, and when a traveller could be forcibly vaccinated in non-sterile conditions at a foreign airport, have virtually, but not entirely, disappeared.
- The few regulations that remain should not be ignored and an immunization course should be planned individually for each traveller, to provide the best possible protection in the time available.
- An increased range of vaccines is now available, and it is important for anyone travelling to a warm country, or intending to live abroad, to seek advice from an immunization centre.

Medicines and medical supplies for travel; injections and blood transfusions abroad

What medical supplies should one travel with? Individual needs vary widely, and will of course depend upon precise travel plans: the destination, nature, and duration of one's trip, and whether or not skilled medical care, medicines, and medical supplies are likely to be available locally.

Dr Richard Dawood *devised this project and is the editor of this book. He has travelled in almost 70 countries around the world—and has survived.*

In this chapter, a number of common problems are considered briefly, and so are the kinds of remedies that might be worth taking along for them.

Some general points

Safety

All drugs known to have any useful effect may also be potentially harmful, especially if taken inappropriately or in excess. No drug is suitable for everyone: if at all possible, you should seek advice from your own doctor about any medication you intend to use abroad. Read manufacturers' instructions carefully, and take notice of them.

Don't forget to keep all drugs and medicines out of reach of children.

Do check the 'expiry date' of any medicines you purchase abroad. 'Out-of-date' medicines can be harmful or ineffective, especially if they have not been stored correctly.

Counterfeit drugs and vaccines are a growing problem in developing countries; some products are ineffective, and others are actually dangerous. There have been a number of recent reports of cases involving a variety of well-known brand names particularly in Africa and the Far East, where drug counterfeiting is believed to occur on a large scale. In early 1989, a large quantity of fake Zantac tablets (an anti-ulcer treatment) was found to have been illegally imported into Britain, probably from Greece—the first known case of counterfeit drugs penetrating the British market. It is better to take along anything you know you might need, rather than to rely on being able to buy supplies locally. Inspect all packaging carefully. And bear this problem in mind, if locally purchased medication fails to produce the desired effect.

Dosage

Keep strictly to recommended doses—twice as much is not necessarily twice as effective!

Always complete a full course of treatment if you are taking antibiotics (usually five to seven days), but discontinue any drug you suspect of causing adverse effects.

Drug names

Most drugs have two names—a *generic*, or scientific name, which is usually the same or similar in most countries, and a *trade* or *brand* name which may vary from one country to another (some drugs are sold under several different brand names even in the same country). For example, in the UK there is a popular motion sickness remedy called *Kwells*; a British traveller asking for this brand name at an American pharmacy might easily be given a bottle or two of *Kwell*, lotion for killing lice, and American travellers reading this book will probably be surprised to see it listed as a motion sickness remedy. (It is called Quellada in the UK.) Make sure that you get what you *want* at a pharmacy abroad, not just what you have asked for.

Throughout this book, the *generic* name appears first; any names following in brackets are *brand* names, but where there are a large number of different brands, these are not listed or only the better known brand names are given.

Pre-existing medical problems

Travellers with any pre-existing medical condition requiring drug treatment, besides taking with them an adequate supply of their usual medication, should also carry a prescription or written record of their medication giving its *generic* name in case further supplies are needed in an emergency.

In the UK, medicines intended for use abroad cannot normally be obtained through the National Health Service.

Prescriptions

Medicines marked * are available in the UK only on a doctor's prescription, and the same applies in the USA to medicines marked #.

In many countries, however, they can be purchased at any pharmacy or dispensary without restriction.

When travelling with medicines, the risk of customs difficulties can be reduced by making sure that they are all clearly labelled and in their original container, and that a prescription is carried whenever possible.

Diarrhoea

The advantages and disadvantages of the use of antidiarrhoeal agents for symptomatic treatment of diarrhoea are discussed in detail on p. 37. One of the following should suffice (see also Table 2.3, p. 38):

1. *Loperamide* (Arret, Imodium)
2. *Diphenoxylate with atropine* (Lomotil) * #
3. *Codeine phosphate* * #

Of these, loperamide, is generally preferable, since it is the fastest–acting and has fewest side-effects. It acts locally on the intestine, without entering the blood system. It is the only effective anti-diarrhoeal medication suitable for use by athletes, since it does not influence the results of drug tests.

The theoretical place of these drugs has been the subject of debate, but most doctors seem to use them without much hesitation when they themselves have troublesome symptoms.

Bismuth subsalicylate (Pepto-Bismol) may also be of value (30 ml or 2 tablets, 4-hourly), though it generally takes 6–24 hours to become effective. It should not be used on children.

See below for antibiotic treatment/prevention, and treatment of dehydration.

Intestinal infections

Treatment

Treatment of diarrhoea with antibiotics is discussed at length on p. 34. *Metronidazole* * # (e.g. Flagyl, Zadstat) and *sulphamethoxazole/trimethoprim* * # (e.g. Septrin, Bactrim) are useful drugs, and it is probably worth travelling with a course of each if you are likely to be staying in a remote area for long. Instructions for use are given in Table 2.2, on p. 36.

Prevention

Prevention of travellers' diarrhoea with antibiotics is a controversial subject, and is discussed on p. 34. The following drugs are sometimes advocated, and there is evidence that they will prevent as many as 50 per cent of attacks, but they should not be used for longer than two weeks:

1. *Sulphamethoxazole/trimethoprim* * #
2. *Doxycycline* (Vibramycin) * #
3. *Streptotriad* * (not available in the USA).

Dehydration

Severe diarrhoea causes rapid loss of fluid and salts, which can be particularly dangerous in small children, but can also cause symptoms in adults. Glucose promotes intestinal absorption of salts and water, and an understanding of this mechanism led to the formulation of special oral rehydration solutions. These solutions are easy to prepare, and instructions for making one's own are given on p. 33. A double-ended plastic spoon for measuring the correct amounts of sugar and salt can be obtained free from TALC, P.O. Box 49, St Albans, Herts, England (send a stamped, addressed envelope, and if possible a donation to support their excellent health educational work in developing countries). They are an effective remedy.

Oral rehydration powders such as Dioralyte, Rehidrat, or Sodium Chloride and Glucose Oral Power BNF, provide all the necessary ingredients in convenient sachets, which can simply be added to water, and should be carried in high risk zones, especially when travelling with children. They are not readily available in the USA. In the UK, Dioralyte is also available as effervescent tablets.

Salt losses increase under tropical conditions and salt replacement may be necessary. Depending on the nature of your trip, it may be worth travelling with a small supply of ordinary table salt in a small, waterproof container.

Constipation

This can sometimes be a problem with travellers. Dehydration, readjustment of bowel habits after crossing time zones, dietary changes, and initial reluctance to use dirty toilets may each contribute to the problem. A high fluid intake and a high fibre diet are preferable to medication; it may be worth travelling with a small supply of natural bran (also available in tablet form).

Heartburn, indigestion

This is a common complaint at home and abroad, and can be exacerbated by unfamiliar foods and over-indulgence in alcohol. There is little to choose between the various antacid preparations; select one that is to your taste and not too bulky to carry (e.g. Bisodol).

Gastric acid has a slight protective effect against several intestinal infections, so antacids should not be used unless symptoms warrant—nor should drugs that prevent acid secretion, like cimetidine (Tagamet) and ranitidine (Zantac).

Vomiting

Specific treatment of vomiting in food poisoning is not generally advised or considered necessary unless symptoms are sufficiently severe as to require skilled medical treatment.

Once vomiting has begun, treatment with tablets is unlikely to afford relief.

Metoclopramide * # tablets (Maxolon, Primperan, Reglan) 10 mg are occasionally useful to treat nausea unrelated to motion sickness.

Motion sickness

Motion sickness is, by definition, almost exclusively a complaint of travellers, although individuals vary considerably in their susceptibility. It is discussed in greater detail on p. 233.

Since different anti-motionsickness drugs appear to suit different people, susceptible individuals may need to try several different pills on successive occasions until they find an effective remedy or regime—and then keep to it. Both hyoscine-containing pills such as Kwells and antihistamine-containing remedies such as promethazine (Avomine, Phenergan) # and dimenhydrinate (Dramamine) can have unwanted side-effects; in particular, do not drive after taking them, as they may cause drowsiness (see also p. 236).

Hyoscine is called scopolamine in the USA. It is becoming more widely available in the form of an adhesive patch that allows absorption of the drug through the skin, that remains effective for up to three days (see p. 236). These should not be used in children or the elderly, and may also cause drowsiness.

Remember that anti-motionsickness pills are of little use once vomiting has started—so make a point of taking the pills some hours before your journey begins.

Urinary tract infections

Symptoms of 'cystitis' are common in women and troublesome when they occur during a trip. Sufferers from cystitis should discuss the problem with their own doctor before leaving home, and take along a course of a suitable antibiotic or other remedy.

Sulphamethoxazole/trimethoprim * # (e.g. Septrin, Bactrim) in a dose of two tablets (i.e. 800 mg sulphamethoxazole, 160 mg trimethoprim) twice daily for five days, is likely to be effective for most urinary tract infections, but will not treat gonorrhoea, which is a possible cause of urinary symptoms in travellers. Dr Naponick's comments about this on p. 390 are worth noting.

Vaginal infections (candidiasis, thrush, yeast)

Like cystitis, this can be a particularly annoying problem when it occurs abroad. Treatment is discussed on p. 371, and it is well worth travelling with a suitable remedy, especially if you are prone to it. An effective single dose treatment, fluconazole* (Diflucan 150), has recently become available in the UK.

Other infections

Causes of fever in travellers are discussed on p. 374; do not rely upon antibiotics to treat a fever without seeking medical advice unless the cause of the fever is obvious—such as a dental abscess or an infected wound. It is probably worth travelling with a course of a 'broad spectrum' antibiotic in the case of skin, sinus, or throat infections, and sulphamethoxazole/trimethoprim is a sensible choice (dosage as in 'urinary tract infections', above).

Pain

Headache, toothache, sunburn, minor injuries, and other causes of mild to moderate pain respond well to aspirin and paracetamol, which are probably the only two mild painkillers the traveller need consider taking.

Painkillers

Aspirin: water-soluble preparations reduce the chance of gastric symptoms, and are absorbed more rapidly. Preparations that dissolve in the mouth, without water, are now also available (e.g. Solmin) and may be more practical for travellers. Aspirin also reduces temperature in a fever. It should be avoided by sufferers from stomach ulceration, and should not be given to children.

Paracetamol (Panadol, Tylenol) has a comparable pain relieving effect to aspirin, and causes no gastric symptoms. It also reduces temperature in fever. (It is called acetaminophen in the USA).

Codeine phosphate * # is often used by travellers to relieve diarrhoea, as a constipating agent; in a dose of 30–60 mg, four-hourly, it is also a valuable remedy for moderate pain, and is especially effective when given simultaneously with aspirin.

Buprenorphine (Temgesic) * # is often recommended to travellers in case of moderate to severe pain, because although it is a powerful drug, it may be prescribed without the kind of restrictions that apply to drugs like morphine, and is therefore unlikely to cause problems with customs officials.

The tablets each contain 0.2 mg and should not be swallowed

but allowed to dissolve under the tongue. The recommended dosage is 1–2 tablets 6–8 hourly or as required. It must not be used in children, and is not readily available in many countries, including the USA.

Pentazocine (Fortral, Talwin) * # can be used as an alternative, in a dosage of 25–100 mg every three or four hours. It is less satisfactory, however, because of its tendency to cause mental symptoms, and should not be used unless absolutely necessary.

Jet lag

No specific treatment has ever been conclusively proven to be of value. A short-acting sedative/hypnotic such as temazepam (see below) may be helpful for the journey, and during re-adjustment of sleep patterns. (See also p. 237.)

Sleep

Sleeping tablets can be useful on especially long and tiring journeys—particularly across time zones, or overnight journeys in noisy surroundings. However a small alcoholic drink may be sufficient for many people. They may also facilitate readjustment of sleep patterns in a new time zone, when used for the first night or two after arrival.

Adults:

Temazepam * # (e.g. Euhypnos, Normison, Restoril) in a dose of 10–30 mg (5–15 mg in elderly people) is effective, short-acting, and rapidly eliminated from the body. It causes little or no hangover effect. It should not be taken with alcohol, which enhances its effects. Do not drive a car until the effects have fully worn off.

Triazolam * # (Halcion) 0.25mg (0.125mg in elderly people) is similar and is more commonly prescribed in the USA.

This group of drugs may cause amnesia for subsequent events, if taken in excess of the recommended dose or in conjunction with alcohol.

Brotizolam and *zopiclone* are probably more appropriate for travel, when these can be obtained (see p. 240).

Children:

Promethazine (Phenergan) # in a dose of 5–10 mg for children aged six to twelve months; 15–20 mg for children aged one to five years; and 20–25 mg for children aged six to ten years, may be useful occasionally.

Malarial prophylaxis and treatment

A detailed discussion of the choice and dosage of antimalarial drugs can be found on p. 121 and the contents of a suggested 'malaria kit' for travellers appear on p. 127.

Side-effects

As chloroquine-resistant malaria has become more common, large numbers of travellers have had to resort to alternative drugs. Side-effects from these less familiar drugs were previously thought to be extremely rare, but their use on a larger scale has now revealed occasional serious effects. These now limit the routine use of both Fansidar and amodiaquine for prophylaxis, and make it essential to seek confirmation that any proposed regimen is both appropriate and safe before travel (Appendix 6).

Insect bites

Treatment

Crotamiton (Eurax) cream or lotion is often sufficient to relieve local irritation, and is probably more effective than calamine lotion.

Antihistamines may be required if bites are widespread, with persistent, itchy weals. Antihistamine creams and ointments should be avoided—sensitivity to them can occur following exposure to light. Chlorpheniramine maleate (Piriton, Chlor-Trimeton) tablets in a dose of 4–16 mg daily are often helpful, but cause drowsiness. Terfenadine # (Seldane, Teldane, Triludan) one 60 mg tablet twice daily; astemizole * # (Hismanal) one 10 mg tablet daily; and ceritizine* (Zirtek) 10 mg once daily, are effective new antihistamines that do not cause drowsiness.

Steroid creams such as betamethasone (Betnovate, Beta-Val) * # are advised for those who develop severe reactions to bites—provided there is no evidence of infection and the skin is unbroken.

Antibiotic treatment is occasionally necessary when bites are scratched and become infected. Sulphamethoxazole/trimethoprim would be effective in most circumstances (dosage as in 'urinary tract infections' above). Such bites also need careful local treatment, to prevent formation of a skin ulcer that may take many weeks to heal.

Prevention

Insect repellents are a most sensible precaution, and are an essential part of any medical kit for travel to a hot country—see p. 182.

Allergies

Treatment of bee-sting allergy is discussed on p. 212. Travellers who have had a serious allergic reaction of any kind in the past are strongly advised to travel with all they may need in an emergency. If necessary, this includes adrenaline in pre-loaded syringes, or an inhaler.

Chlorpheniramine tablets (Piriton, Chlor-Trimeton) in a dose of 4–16 mg daily are often useful to treat allergic skin reactions, and steroid creams may also be useful (see 'insect bites' above).

Sunburn

Prevention is the most sensible strategy. Sunscreens (see also p. 182) should be applied liberally. Water-resistant sunscreens are now widely available and are especially recommended for children. Apart from protection factor and cosmetic acceptability, there is little to choose from the wide range available.

Indomethacin (Indocid, Indocin) * # tablets (25 mg three times a day) or indomethacin lotion may also be of value if used soon after exposure to strong sunlight. This is discussed further on p. 307. *Calamine lotion* may be helpful for treatment of mild cases. *Aspirin* or *paracetamol* are useful for pain relief (see 'painkillers' above).

Conjunctivitis

Eye irritation following excessive exposure to sun and dust, and minor eye infections, are common in travellers.

Chloramphenicol eye ointment * # and *drops* are probably worth taking if medical supplies are not likely to be available *en route*, especially if you wear contact lenses.

Colds/sinusitis

Air travellers liable to colds or sinusitis should travel with a decongestant spray (e.g. Sinex) to avoid discomfort from pressure changes during flight.

Cold sores, herpes blisters

Strong sunlight, cold, and wind, can trigger cold sores. Anyone who is prone to cold sores should use a high protection factor sun screen on the lips. The duration and severity of attacks can be reduced by applying acyclovir cream # * (Zovirax) at an early stage; this is not widely available abroad. Lip salve may also be helpful.

Cuts, grazes, and animal bites

Prompt cleansing of any wound—with running water, or better still, with an antiseptic solution—is the most important step in treatment. Subsequently, keeping a wound clean and dry under arduous travelling and living conditions in a tropical environment can be difficult, but is of great importance.

Treatment

Local people sometimes ask travellers to remote areas to treat minor wounds, and it is worth carrying extra supplies of an antiseptic.

Iodine is a valuable antiseptic agent. A dry powder povidone iodine spray is now available in a small container (Savlon Dry, or Betadine Aerosol Spray) which does not sting, and removes the need to touch damaged skin.

Cetrimide cream (e.g. Savlon) is also a useful antiseptic.

Steristrips, and similar adhesive tapes, are useful for holding together the edges of a clean, gaping wound if medical care cannot be obtained.

Band-aids and other wound dressings must be changed frequently; wounds should always be kept clean and dry. A plastic spray dressing can also be useful.

Antibiotic treatment may occasionally be necessary if infection is more than trivial (see p. 191 for treatment of animal bites).

Fungal skin infections

Antifungal cream and dusting powder is useful for treatment of athlete's foot and other fungal skin infections. See also p. 344.

Some other things to take

1. *Water purification supplies* are discussed in detail on pp. 73–80. I usually take along a small plastic dropping bottle of 2 per cent tincture of iodine—one drop will purify a cup of water—which doubles as a useful antiseptic for minor cuts.
2. *Contact lens solution* Take ample supplies, and do not rely upon being able to obtain your preferred brand abroad. Bottles of sterile intravenous saline can usually be obtained cheaply from pharmacies in most countries, and are useful if other supplies run out. Keep solutions with you on long flights.
3. *Contraceptive needs* are discussed on pp. 405–13.
4. *Feminine hygiene* Take all your likely needs with you, unless you *know* that acceptable supplies will be available locally (p. 368).
5. *First aid items* A crepe (ace) bandage may provide relief following a joint injury. Non-adherent dressings (e.g. Melolin) may be difficult to obtain abroad, and may be useful, but other bandages, dressings, and slings can usually be improvised, and are probably not worth taking.
6. *Thermometer* If required, a thermometer should be carried in a protective container, and kept away from excessive heat. An

ordinary clinical thermometer is not suitable for detecting or monitoring hypothermia (see p. 288); a special, low-reading thermometer should also be taken if likely to be needed.

7. *Toilet paper* Away from the beaten track, seasoned travellers take their own. In many parts of the world, toilet paper is not used, or is not readily available.

8. *Injection swabs*—alcohol soaked wipes in small sachets—are also useful for cleaning minor wounds, and at a pinch can be used on suspicious-looking plates and cutlery.

Injections abroad

• Hepatitis and AIDS are important hazards that have been covered in detail elsewhere in this book. Hepatitis B has occurred in numerous travellers who have received injections with contaminated needles and syringes, and the AIDS risk from this route of infection is also high. Disposable pre-sterilized needles and syringes are not widely available in many poor countries. If you are going abroad to live in one, or expect that you will need any other medication by injection (including dental anaesthesia) while you are away, you should *either* satisfy yourself that any needle or syringe used has been adequately sterilized (i.e. boiled for at least ten minutes) *or* you should take your own supply. Remember that if you have an accident when driving abroad, a blood test for alcohol may be compulsory—in Turkey, for example.

• In the UK, needles and syringes are available without prescription at the discretion of a pharmacist. They are also available in kits that include other medical items, from MASTA Ltd (see Appendix 6); and from SAFA, 59 Hill St, Liverpool L8 5SA Tel: 051–708–0397. In the USA and most other countries, a prescription is necessary. And a prescription should *always* be carried when travelling.

Blood transfusion abroad

• The AIDS risks have received much publicity, but are not the only hazard of blood transfusion abroad. Other risks include hepatitis A, hepatitis B, non-A non-B hepatitis, cytomegalovirus, syphilis, and malaria. There are also important non-infective hazards: transfusion with badly matched blood causes severe reactions and can be fatal, and has important long term consequences in girls or women of childbearing potential, leading to serious antibody reactions between mother and fetus in a subsequent pregnancy; allergic reactions and febrile reactions may also occur, and the risk of these is greater when storage conditions are poor.

• In most of western Europe, North America, Japan, and Australasia, all donated blood is now screened for HIV antibodies, and prospective blood donors are questioned carefully about their lifestyle and risk factors for AIDS.

• Elsewhere adequate facilities for screening donated blood and selecting donors are the exception rather than the rule, and at least two thirds of blood donations are thought to be unscreened. In 1987 1 per cent of donated Kenyan blood was found to be HIV positive. Building up a pool of blood donors requires a motivated and well-educated local population, and a well-organized infrastructure. It also requires skills and resources that poor countries do not have. Most developing countries have only the most rudimentary blood transfusion services, accessible perhaps only in capital cities. The risks from blood transfusion in such circumstances are high. The World Health Organization is working to improve blood transfusion services in all developing countries, but it will be many years before safe facilities are widely available.

• Blood transfusion should be given only when medically essential. The risks from an unscreened blood transfusion must, however, be put in perspective, and balanced against the more immediate risks of NOT having a transfusion when there has been serious blood loss and there is a clear medical need. It is foolhardy to risk death from blood loss by refusing transfusion; most travellers who need transfusion in an emergency may find they in fact have little choice in the matter.

• Pregnancy, and medical conditions such as duodenal ulceration, may lead to haemorrhage. Anyone with such a condition should do everything possible to avoid travelling to destinations where good medical facilities will not be available.

• Accidents are the commonest reason for travellers to need a blood transfusion, and after an accident, other medical facilities of a good standard may also be lacking. Most accidents are preventable, however, and travellers should be constantly alert to ways of reducing the risk (see pp. 251–60). Avoiding accidents is the most effective measure that any traveller can take to avoid needing a blood transfusion.

- It is possible to travel with plasma substitutes and intravenous fluids for use in an emergency, though such products require skill to use, and an adequate supply is bulky and heavy. In an emergency, supplies can sometimes be obtained from embassies. Likewise, sterile equipment to administer transfusions (giving sets and cannulae) may be scarce; such items are sometimes included in first aid kits for travel (above). Large expeditions with trained medical officers may find it valuable to travel with such resources, but these are impractical for the majority of travellers.
- Knowing your blood group in advance may make it easier to find a blood donor in an emergency—the embassy of your country may keep a record of screened donors who are willing to help.
- Blood transfusion is in fact only one of many possible hazards of medical treatment abroad which is why the *preventive* information in this book is so important.

Fitness for working abroad

Choose an overseas assignment with care, and make sure that you are in peak mental and physical condition before you go.

Dr Anthony Hall *is the medical adviser to a number of companies and accompanied the England cricket team which reached the final of the World Cup in Pakistan and India in 1987.*

The success or failure of an overseas assignment often depends on the ability of the individual to remain physically and mentally healthy under difficult circumstances.

Some people cope better than others: think about your fitness and suitability for your assignment well in advance; the wrong decision has far-reaching consequences for your own career and for your employer.

Desirable attributes

The apposite biblical quotation for foreign service is 'many are called but few are chosen'. Positive attributes for successful overseas service include birth or previous residence in the tropics and a family history of stability and successful accomplishment, especially abroad; a personal record of success in work and play and a happy marriage.

Your reasons for going are important: a desire for new challenges and interest in your work are better harbingers of success than a desire for money or a need to escape—from a broken marriage, job failure, or after an abortion.

Psychological stability

Those who work in the tropics have to adapt to a variety of psychologically adverse stimuli, including heat, humidity, bright light, poor diet, noise, road traffic accidents, boredom, language difficulties, racial tension, and the risk of being assaulted and robbed. Coping with these factors demands a high degree of mental toughness and emotional flexibility. If you are considering working abroad and are not sure whether you possess these attributes, it is probably worth thinking again.

Unfortunately, many companies and other organizations regard the Third World as somewhere to send their misfits, so as to get rid of them. Employees may be given inadequate information about a foreign country, the job and the problems they are likely to face (in fact these may be deliberately concealed), and back-up facilities are often poor. Companies who employ such a policy in the selection and treatment of their overseas personnel are likely to meet with disaster—especially in the face of strong competition for the provision of goods and services.

Physical fitness

Everyone is at greater risk of illness in the tropics. In my opinion—based on examining several thousand people before employment abroad—the three most important avoidable risk factors are: a high alcohol consumption, obesity, and cigarette smoking.

Alcohol

A high alcohol consumption frequently leads to a deterioration in work performance. Individual responses and tolerance to alcohol are variable but a consumption of more than 20 grams of alcohol daily (contained in about 1 pint of beer *or* 2 glasses of wine *or* 2 single measures of spirits) is often related to an increased incidence of disease (see also p. 457).

Psychological stress, less expensive alcohol, and boredom may induce people living in the tropics to increase their alcohol consumption. Individuals with an existing high alcohol intake (i.e. higher than quoted above) who intend to work abroad are at significant risk of jeopardizing their health and may need seriously to reconsider their decision. Companies should avoid appointing heavy drinkers for work in tropical countries.

I advise expatriates to attempt to reduce rather than increase their alcohol intake.

Obesity

Excess fat is a greater hazard in hot than in cold climates. Apart from the higher risk of sudden death due to a heart attack, fat people have a higher incidence of sore rashes in the groin, heat intolerance, and other symptoms that may reduce the capacity for hard sustained work under conditions of heat and humidity.

Measurements of the circumference of the waist and hips are a useful guide to obesity. Most men have excessive body fat if their waist measurements are over 81 cm (32 inches) and women if their buttock (hip) size is over 91 cm (36 inches). The body mass index (BMI) is another useful guide.

The BMI is the weight in kilograms divided by the height in metres squared. In my opinion a BMI as near as possible to 20 (around 140 lb or 64 kg for a 5 ft 10 in (1.78 m) man or around 126 lb or 57 kg for a 5 ft 6 in (1.68 m) woman) is desirable for a tropical climate.

A BMI over 25 indicates obesity, except in some very muscular young athletes.

Smoking

People who use tobacco have a higher incidence of disease including heart trouble, peptic ulcer, lung cancer, and respiratory infections; stopping smoking is likely to improve your health wherever you are living, and going abroad presents a timely opportunity to give up smoking.

In rough terms, an alcoholic has at least twice the chance of becoming ill as a non-alcoholic, and obesity and smoking carry similar two fold penalties. So an alcoholic obese smoker has 8 times the chance of becoming ill as a fit person. Of course, many companies would not be able to fill all their foreign vacancies if they employed only slim, fit, teetotal non-smokers. The sort of people who are willing to work on an oil rig or in a remote mining camp are the sort of people who like to drink, smoke and over-eat. Nevertheless, such problems as high blood pressure, irritability and diarrhoea may all lessen if some excess fat is dieted off and if alcohol intake and smoking are halved.

Pre-tropical check-up

A thorough medical check-up is advisable before undertaking any long-term overseas assignment. Spouses and children should also be examined, and women should not go to the tropics when pregnant because malaria increases the risks of stillbirth or miscarriage, and obstetric care is often inferior (see pp. 417–22).

Doctors carrying out pre-tropical examinations should not skimp on giving appropriate, and if necessary strict, advice to intending overseas workers or their employers, nor should such advice be ignored, even if it is not what the individual wants to hear. It is surprising how often the wrong advice is given, and the most unlikely people are passed 'fit' for blatantly unsuitable assignments; setting off for the tropics in anything less than optimal physical and mental condition may all too easily result in an enforced early return home, either alive or in a box.

13

A special achievement

Smallpox

Smallpox is no longer a hazard to travellers, and no country now requires smallpox vaccination as a condition of entry. Eradication of smallpox was a unique achievement in human history.

Andrew N Agle *was directly involved in the eradication of smallpox from large areas of West Africa, the Indian subcontinent, and Afghanistan.*

Responsible for deaths in hundreds of thousands through the ages—including the deaths of Queen Mary II of England and France's King Louis XV—smallpox has often affected the course of history. During the Franco-Prussian War, for example, 200 000 troops were infected, of whom 25 000 died, while in Paris 18 000 civilians died. In his *History of England*, Lord Macaulay called smallpox 'one of the most terrible of all ministers of death'.

Smallpox no longer exists. The last naturally acquired case was in Somalia in 1977. The final two cases in the world resulted from a laboratory accident in the UK in 1978.

Smallpox—the disease

A viral disease spread from person to person, usually via the respiratory tract, smallpox was characterized by sudden onset of illness with fever, headache, backache, and prostration, following an incubation period of about two weeks. After two to four days of fever, the temperature fell and a rash appeared, first on the face, then the trunk and extremities. The rash would progress through stages of spots, blisters, pustules, and finally scabs which would fall off at the end of three to four weeks.

Two types of smallpox occurred: *variola major* (classical smallpox and *variola minor* (alastrim). Although indistinguishable in appearance, the two differed greatly in outcome: 20–40 per cent of *variola major* cases were fatal, but for *variola minor*, mortality was 1 per cent or less.

Vaccination, as first introduced by Edward Jenner as long ago as 1796, was effective in preventing both types of smallpox. Once smallpox was contracted, however, there was no effective treatment for it.

Smallpox eradication

The elimination of smallpox was the result of an organized international effort co-ordinated by the World Health Organization (WHO). The Smallpox Eradication Programme was launched in 1967 as a ten year campaign to rid the world of smallpox.

Some thirteen years later, after close scrutiny for a prescribed two-year period following the last reported case of smallpox, a Global Commission certified that the disease was no more. In Geneva, the following declaration was made:

Declaration of global eradication of smallpox

- The Thirty-third World Health Assembly, on this the eighth day of May, 1980;
- Having considered the development and results of the global programme on smallpox eradication initiated by WHO in 1958 and intensified since 1967;

1. Declared solemnly that the World and all its peoples have won freedom from smallpox, which was a most devastating disease sweeping in epidemic form through many countries since earliest times, leaving death, blindness, and disfigurement in its wake and which only a decade ago was rampant in Africa, Asia, and South America;
2. Expresses its deep gratitude to all nations and individuals who contributed to the success of this noble and historic endeavour;
3. Calls this unprecedented achievement in the history of public health to the attention of all nations, which by their collective action have freed mankind of this ancient scourge and, in so doing, have demonstrated how nations working together in a common cause may further human progress.

For the first time in human history, a disease had been eradicated. WHO estimated the total cost of the eradication programme to have been just over $300 million—considerably less than the *annual* cost to the nations of the world of preventing and controlling the disease.

Implications for eradication of other diseases

Success with eradicating smallpox encourages the hope and expectation that eradication programmes for other diseases will also succeed. The lessons learned from the smallpox campaign have already been applied to other disease-control activities, and have led to many improvements.

However, smallpox possessed a unique set of characteristics which facilitated eradication:

1. An effective vaccine was available (heat-stable and easily administered).
2. There was no non-human reservoir (e.g animals or insects).
3. The disease was easily recognized and diagnosed.
4. Victims were infectious to others for only a relatively brief period of time (during which they were usually immobilized by the illness).
5. The disease was universally feared.

A few other diseases share some of these characteristics. Measles, for example, is often mentioned as a candidate for eradication; its complications are especially harmful to children in developing countries. Measles vaccine, however, although very effective when properly handled and administered, is still heat-sensitive and difficult to maintain in tropical areas. Measles is also highly contagious and, in many communities, strikes at a very young age—thus making *early* vaccination (before twelve months of age) an essential element of control. Measles eradication is technically feasible but logistically, operationally, and economically poses a challenging problem.

Smallpox today and in the future

Like eradication itself, management of the post-eradication period is a new human experience. The Thirty-third World Health Assembly called upon WHO to maintain vigilance: specifically, to investigate smallpox rumours; to maintain smallpox vaccine reserves; and to continue surveillance of human monkeypox.

WHO reports that all subsequent smallpox rumours have been investigated (approximately twenty per year), and that all have proven to be chickenpox or some other non-smallpox disease. WHO maintains two refrigerated storage depots for smallpox vaccine with a quantity sufficient to vaccinate more than 200 million people. Many countries also have their own vaccine stocks in reserve.

The variola virus, which causes smallpox, is still maintained at two laboratories: the Centers for Disease Control, Atlanta, USA, and the Research Institute for Viral Preparations, Moscow, USSR. Both are WHO Collaborating Centres with maximum containment facilities, and provide laboratory support for the post-eradication surveillance and research programme. They are periodically inspected by WHO.

Some nations continue to vaccinate military personnel.

The Smallpox Eradication Unit of the WHO was formally disbanded on 1st January 1988, adding the final punctuation mark to the end of the smallpox era.

Summary of advice for travellers

• International Certificates of Smallpox Vaccination are no longer required from travellers to any country. WHO encourages all countries to discontinue smallpox vaccination, other than to protect laboratory workers exposed to orthopox viruses.

Appendixes

Appendix 1

Vaccination requirements and recommendations for international travel

Notes

1. Chart shows vaccination requirements *for direct entry from the UK, North America, or Australasia*—if visiting several countries there may be additional yellow fever or cholera regulations (see also chapter on 'immunization', pp. 473–88).
2. *Where hepatitis protection is listed* take into account length of stay, whether visiting rural areas etc. The injection may not be necessary for short visits staying in good hotels, especially in areas marked (A).
3. *Check before you travel*, as regulations occasionally change and additional advice may be given at times of outbreaks (see Appendix 6).
4. *Children* should have completed their routine immunizations (pp. 425–6).
5. *Cholera* Opinions vary on the value of cholera immunization (see pp. 40–1 and 479–80).
6. *Tetanus* is not included here, but everyone should be protected (see pp. 480–1).
7. *Hepatitis B* (pp. 62–3), *Rabies* (pp. 196–9 and pp. 482–3), *meningitis* (p. 97) and *Japanese encephalitis* (p. 483) are not included here.
8. *Chart based on* WHO & DHSS information (1989).

Key
C = certificate required
A = advised
(A) = advised except for short visits staying in good hotels

Country	Yellow fever	Cholera	Typhoid	Polio	Hepatitis A (gamma-globulin)
Afghanistan	—	A	A	A	A
Albania	—	—	(A)	—	(A)
Algeria	—	—	A	A	A
American Samoa	—	—	A	A	A
Angola	A	A	A	A	A

continued

Country	Yellow fever	Cholera	Typhoid	Polio	Hepatitis A (gamma-globulin)
Antigua & Barbuda	—	—	A	A	(A)
Argentina	—	—	A	A	(A)
Australia	—	—	—	—	—
Austria	—	—	—	—	—
Azores	—	—	(A)	—	(A)
Bahamas	—	—	A	A	(A)
Bahrain	—	—	A	A	(A)
Bangladesh	—	A	A	A	A
Barbados	—	—	A	A	(A)
Belgium	—	—	—	—	—
Belize	—	—	A	A	A
Benin	C—except under one year of age	A	A	A	A
Bermuda	—	—	—	—	—
Bhutan	—	A	A	A	A
Bolivia	A	—	A	A	A
Botswana	—	A	A	A	A
Brazil	A—except under one year of age	—	A	A	A
Brunei	—	A	A	A	A
Bulgaria	—	—	(A)	—	(A)
Burkina Faso	C—except under one year of age	A	A	A	A
Burma	—	A	A	A	A
Burundi	A—except under one year of age	A	A	A	A
Cameroon	C—except under one year of age	A	A	A	A
Canada	—	—	—	—	—
Canary Is.	—	—	(A)	—	(A)
Cape Verde Is.	—	—	(A)	A	(A)
Cayman Is.	—	—	A	A	(A)

continued

Country	Yellow fever	Cholera	Typhoid	Polio	Hepatitis A (gamma-globulin)
Central African Republic	C—except under one year of age	A	A	A	A
Chad	A—except under one year of age	A	A	A	A
Chile	—	—	A	A	(A)
China	—	—	A	A	A
Colombia	A—except under one year of age	—	A	A	A
Comoros	—	—	A	A	A
Congo	C—except under one year of age	A	A	A	A
Cook Is.	—	—	A	A	A
Costa Rica	—	—	A	A	A
Côte d'Ivoire	C—except under one year of age	A	A	A	A
Cuba	—	—	A	A	A
Cyprus	—	—	(A)	—	(A)
Czechoslovakia	—	—	—	—	—
Denmark	—	—	—	—	—
Djibouti	—	A	A	A	A
Dominica	—	—	A	A	(A)
Dominican Rep.	—	—	A	A	A
Ecuador	A—except under one year of age	—	A	A	A
Egypt	—	A	A	A	A
El Salvador	—	—	A	A	A
Equatorial Guinea	A—except under one year of age	A	A	A	A
Ethiopia	A—except under one year of age	A	A	A	A
Falkland Is.	—	—	A	A	(A)
Fiji	—	—	A	A	(A)
Finland	—	—	—	—	—

continued

Country	Yellow fever	Cholera	Typhoid	Polio	Hepatitis A (gamma-globulin)
France	—	—	(A)—South Coast only	—	—
French Guiana	C—except under one year of age	—	A	A	A
French Polynesia	—	—	A	A	A
Gabon	C—except under one year of age	A	A	A	A
Gambia	A	A	A	A	A
German Dem. Republic	—	—	—	—	—
German Fed. Republic	—	—	—	—	—
Ghana	C	A	A	A	A
Gibraltar	—	—	(A)	—	(A)
Greece	—	—	(A)	—	(A)
Greenland	—	—	—	—	—
Grenada	—	—	A	A	(A)
Guam	—	—	A	A	A
Guadeloupe	—	—	A	A	(A)
Guatemala	—	—	A	A	A
Guinea	A—except under one year of age	A	A	A	A
Guinea Bissau	A—except under one year of age	A	A	A	A
Guyana	A—except under one year of age	—	A	A	A
Haiti	—	—	A	A	A
Honduras	—	—	A	A	A
Hong Kong	—	—	A	A	(A)
Hungary	—	—	A	—	—
Iceland	—	—	—	—	—
India	—	A	A	A	A
Indonesia	—	A	A	A	A
Iran	—	—	A	A	A
Iraq	—	—	A	A	A

continued

Country	Yellow fever	Cholera	Typhoid	Polio	Hepatitis A (gamma-globulin)
Irish Republic	—	—	—	—	—
Israel	—	—	A	A	(A)
Italy	—	—	(A)	—	(A)
Jamaica	—	—	A	A	(A)
Japan	—	—	A	A	(A)
Jordan	—	—	A	A	A
Kampuchea	—	A	A	A	A
Kenya	A—except under one year of age	A	A	A	A
Kiribati	—	—	A	A	A
Korea N.&S.	—	A	A	A	A
Kuwait	—	—	A	A	(A)
Laos	—	A	A	A	A
Lebanon	—	—	A	A	A
Lesotho	—	A	A	A	A
Liberia	C—except under one year of age	A	A	A	A
Libya	—	—	A	A	A
Luxembourg	—	—	—	—	—
Madagascar	C—if coming (or transit) from YF area	A	A	A	A
Madeira	—	—	(A)	—	(A)
Malawi	—	A	A	A	A
Malaysia	—	A	A	A	(A)
Maldives	—	A	A	A	A
Mali	C—except stay under two weeks	A	A	A	A
Malta	—	—	(A)	—	(A)
Martinique	—	—	A	A	(A)
Mauritania	C—except stay under two weeks or under one year of age	A	A	A	A
Mauritius	—	A	A	A	A
Mexico	—	—	A	A	A
Monaco	—	—	(A)	—	(A)

continued

Country	Yellow fever	Cholera	Typhoid	Polio	Hepatitis A (gamma-globulin)
Mongolia	—	—	A	A	A
Montserrat	—	—	A	A	(A)
Morocco	—	—	A	A	A
Mozambique	—	A	A	A	A
Namibia	—	A	A	A	A
Nauru	—	—	A	A	A
Nepal	—	A	A	A	A
Netherlands	—	—	—	—	—
Neth. Antilles	—	—	A	A	A
New Caledonia	—	—	A	A	A
New Zealand	—	—	—	—	—
Nicaragua	—	—	A	A	A
Niger	C—except under one year of age	A	A	A	A
Nigeria	A—except under one year of age	A	A	A	A
Niue	—	—	A	A	A
Norway	—	—	—	—	—
Oman	—	—	A	A	A
Pakistan	—	A	A	A	A
Panama	A	—	A	A	A
Papua New Guinea	—	A	A	A	A
Paraguay	—	—	A	A	(A)
Peru	A—except under one year of age	—	A	A	A
Philippines	—	A	A	A	A
Pitcairn	—	—	A	A	A
Poland	—	—	—	—	—
Portugal	—	—	(A)	—	(A)
Puerto Rico	—	—	A	A	A
Qatar	—	A	A	A	(A)
Reunion	—	A	A	A	A
Romania	—	—	(A)	—	(A)
Rwanda	C—except under one year of age	A	A	A	A

continued

Country	Yellow fever	Cholera	Typhoid	Polio	Hepatitis A (gamma-globulin)
St Helena	—	—	A	A	A
St Kitts/Nevis	—	—	A	A	(A)
St Lucia	—	—	A	A	(A)
St Vincent & Grenadines	—	—	A	A	(A)
Samoa	—	—	A	A	A
Sao Tome & Principe	C—except stay under two weeks or under one year of age	A	A	A	A
Saudi Arabia	—	—	A	A	(A)
Senegal	C—except under one year of age	A	A	A	A
Seychelles	—	—	A	A	(A)
Sierre Leone	A—except under one year of age	A	A	A	A
Singapore	—	—	A	A	(A)
Solomon Is.	—	—	A	A	A
Somalia	A—except under one year of age	A	A	A	A
South Africa	—	A	A	A	(A)
Spain	—	—	(A)	—	(A)
Sri Lanka	—	A	A	A	A
Sudan	A—except under one year. C may be required leaving	A	A	A	A
Surinam	A—except under one year of age	—	A	A	A
Swaziland	—	A	A	A	A
Sweden	—	—	—	—	—
Switzerland	—	—	—	—	—
Syria	—	—	A	A	A
Taiwan	—	A	A	A	A

continued

Country	Yellow fever	Cholera	Typhoid	Polio	Hepatitis A (gamma-globulin)
Tanzania	A—except under one year of age	A	A	A	A
Thailand	—	A	A	A	A
Togo	C—except under one year of age	A	A	A	A
Trinidad & Tobago	—	—	A	A	(A)
Tunisia	—	—	A	A	(A)
Turkey	—	—	A	A	A
Tuvalu	—	—	A	A	A
Uganda	A—except under one year of age	A	A	A	A
United Arab Emirates	—	—	A	A	(A)
UK	—	—	—	—	—
USA	—	—	—	—	—
USSR	—	A-Asian part only	A	A-Asian part only	A-Asian part only
Uruguay	—	—	A	A	(A)
Vanuatu	—	—	A	A	A
Venezuela	A—except under one year of age	—	A	A	A
Vietnam	—	A	A	A	A
Virgin Is.	—	—	A	A	(A)
Yemen N.&S.	—	—	A	A	A
Yugoslavia	—	—	(A)	—	(A)
Zaire	A—except under one year of age	A	A	A	A
Zambia	A—except under one year of age	A	A	A	A
Zimbabwe	—	A	A	A	A

Appendix 2

Malaria—risk areas for disease and drug resistance

Countries where malaria occurs

Afghanistan
Algeria
Angola
Argentina
Bangladesh
Belize
Benin
Bhutan
Bolivia
Botswana
Brazil
Burkina Faso
Burma
Burundi
Cameroon
Central African Republic
Chad
China
Colombia
Comoros
Congo
Costa Rica
Djibouti
Dominican Republic
East Timor
Ecuador
Egypt
El Salvador
Equatorial Guinea
Ethiopia
French Guiana
Gabon
Gambia
Ghana
Guatemala
Guinea
Guinea-Bissau
Guyana
Haiti
Honduras
India
Indonesia
Iran
Iraq
Ivory Coast
Kampuchea
Kenya
Laos
Liberia
Libya
Madagascar
Malawi
Malaysia
Maldives
Mali
Mauritania
Mauritius
Mexico
Morocco
Mozambique
Namibia
Nepal
Nicaragua
Niger
Nigeria
Oman
Pakistan
Panama
Papua New Guinea
Paraguay
Peru
Philippines
Rwanda
Sao Tome & Principe
Saudi Arabia
Senegal
Sierra Leone
Solomon Islands
Somalia
South Africa
Sri Lanka
Sudan
Surinam
Swaziland
Syria
Tanzania
Thailand
Togo
Turkey
Uganda
United Arab Emirates
Vanuatu
(formerly New Hebrides)
Venezuela
Vietnam
Yemen
Yemen, Democratic
Zaire
Zambia
Zimbabwe

Areas where chloroquine-resistant falciparum malaria occurs

Central and South America
Bolivia, Brazil, Colombia, Ecuador, French Guiana, Guyana, Panama, Peru, Surinam, Venezuela

Asia
Bangladesh, Bhutan, Burma, China, India, Indonesia, Kampuchea, Laos, Malaysia, Nepal, Pakistan, Philippines, Sri Lanka, Thailand, Vietnam

Oceania
Papua New Guinea, Solomon Islands, Vanuatu

Africa
Angola, Benin, Burkina Faso, Burundi, Cameroon, Comoros, Congo, Equatorial Guinea, Ethiopia, Gabon, Gambia, Ghana, Guinea-Bissau, Kenya, Madagascar, Malawi, Mozambique, Namibia, Nigeria, Rwanda, Senegal, Somalia, South Africa, Sudan (part), Swaziland, Tanzania, Togo, Uganda, Zaire, Zambia, Zimbabwe

Chloroquine-resistant falciparum malaria may occur in any country in sub-Saharan Africa.

Note: malaria distribution may vary significantly within countries and from time to time. Use the addresses in Appendix 6 to obtain up-to-date information, and if necessary refer to the WHO publications listed under 'Further reading' (p. 559). Malaria prophylaxis is much safer than malaria, so if in doubt it is safest to take it.

World Health Organization

Malaria Action Programme, World Health Organization, 1121 Geneva, 27–Switzerland, Tel. 91 21 11, Telex 27821 OMS.

Appendix 3

M.R. Barer and R.M. Dawood

Geographical distribution of disease

One of the most basic and obvious questions that a book like this could be expected to answer is also the most complex: what diseases occur where?

In one sense, the answer ought not really to matter. Travellers who want to stay healthy should adopt healthy habits wherever they go, and not throw caution to the wind when the risk of any particular disease decreases.

Statistics that filter back to the World Health Organization in Geneva depend upon:

1. An accurate medical diagnosis in the first place, which in turn usually needs doctors and perhaps laboratory facilities for confirmation;
2. A public health bureaucratic infrastructure, with sufficient resources and enthusiasm at every level to accumulate the figures and pass them on;
3. Governments' and authorities' willingness to permit disclosure of such information.

Reliable information about the distribution of disease is therefore most lacking from the countries of greatest interest to readers of this book, countries with plenty of disease, but scarce medical resources; and where official figures do exist, they tend to underestimate the true scale.

The tables that follow are a compromise that takes account of the fact that travellers nonetheless need access to this kind of information. They are based on WHO figures and a combination of other sources, with modifications when these are unconvincing or inadequate. Where official figures are absent, estimates have been sought from doctors working in the countries concerned or with specialist knowledge of particular diseases.

The figures given here do not correspond directly with risk to individual travellers: they give a ROUGH INDICATION of the occurrence of particular diseases in the local population. There is often considerable variation in the distribution of disease WITHIN any one country, and all of the figures listed here are based on generalizations that cannot take account of this, or of differences in disease patterns between rural and urban areas. It is virtually impossible to make any meaningful generalization, for example, about a non-uniform land mass the size of the USSR (which we have omitted from the tables), and the same probably applies to China, India, Brazil, and the Sudan.

The tables are far from flawless, and should be used with caution. In particular, they should NOT be used as a basis for important decisions, such as whether or not medical treatment should be sought after a dog bite.

We would like to acknowledge our gratitude to colleagues in some sixty countries (mostly Fellows of the Royal Society of Tropical Medicine & Hygiene) who kindly gave us the benefit of their opinion and local experience in amending the tables. We are most anxious to receive further amendments to whatever inaccuracies inevitably remain.

Key

S: Similar or smaller number of cases per million population to those occurring in the UK, France, or West Germany (Western Europe); or no cases at all.

L: 3–10 times number of cases relative to Western Europe.

Or

Less than 10 cases per million population (where disease does not occur in Western Europe).

M: 11–100 times number of cases relative to Western Europe.

Or

11–100 cases per million (where disease does not occur in Western Europe).

H: Greater than 100 times number of cases relative to Western Europe.

Or

More than 100 cases per million population (where disease does not occur in Western Europe).

Africa (North)	Cholera	Typhoid	Shigellosis	Amoebiasis	TB	Plague	Brucellosis	Diphtheria	Meningococcal infection	Polio	Yellow Fever	Dengue or other arboviruses	Viral hepatitis (A + B)	Rabies	Typhus	Malaria	Leishmaniasis	Trypanosomiasis	Syphilis	Gonorrhoea	Schistosomiasis	Liver flukes	Hydatid disease	Tapeworms	Filariasis	Hookworm	Other intestinal worms
Algeria	H	H	L	M	H	S	M	L	S	M	S	S	M	H	S	L	M	S	S	S	L	S	H	L	S	L	L
Egypt	S	M	L	L	M	S	L	M	S	M	S	L	L	L	L	L	M	L	L	L	H	L	H	L	L	L	L
Libyan Arab Jamahiriya	L	L	M	L	M	M	S	M	S	M	S	S	M	H	L	H	L	L	S	S	M	L	M	L	L	S	L
Mauritania	L	M	L	M	H	S	S	M	S	L	S	S	M	M	L	H	L	L	L	S	L	S	L	L	M	L	L
Morocco	M	L	M	M	M	S	S	M	S	M	S	S	M	H	L	L	M	S	L	L	H	S	M	L	S	S	L
Tunisia	M	M	L	M	M	S	S	L	S	M	S	S	L	H	L	S	M	S	S	L	L	L	M	L	S	L	L

Africa (Western)	Cholera	Typhoid	Shigellosis	Amoebiasis	TB	Plague	Brucellosis	Diphtheria	Meningococcal infection	Polio	Yellow Fever	Dengue or other arboviruses	Viral hepatitis (A + B)	Rabies	Typhus	Malaria	Leishmaniasis	Trypanosomiasis	Syphilis	Gonorrhoea	Schistosomiasis	Liver flukes	Hydatid disease	Tapeworms	Filariasis	Hookworm	Other intestinal worms
Benin	L	L	H	H	M	S	M	L	M	H	S	S	M	M	L	H	S	L	S	L	H	L	L	M	L	M	M
Burkina Faso	L	M	M	H	L	S	M	M	M	L	S	S	M	H	L	H	L	M	L	L	L	S	L	L	L	L	M
Cameroon	L	L	L	M	L	S	L	M	M	M	S	S	M	M	L	H	S	M	L	H	M	L	M	L	M	M	M
Cape Verde	L	L	L	L	M	S	L	L	H	M	S	S	L	M	H	H	S	L	H	H	H	L	M	M	L	M	H
Chad	L	H	M	H	M	S	M	M	M	L	M	M	M	L	M	H	L	M	L	S	L	L	L	L	M	L	L
Gambia	L	L	M	M	M	S	L	L	H	L	M	M	H	M	L	H	S	L	H	H	H	L	L	M	L	M	L
Ghana	M	H	M	H	M	S	L	S	M	H	M	M	H	M	S	H	S	L	S	H	H	S	L	L	M	H	H
Guinea	L	M	M	M	M	S	M	M	L	M	S	M	M	L	L	H	S	L	S	M	H	L	L	L	H	M	M
Guinea-Bissau	L	M	M	M	L	S	S	M	L	L	S	L	M	L	L	H	S	L	L	L	L	L	L	L	M	M	M
Ivory Coast	L	M	M	M	L	S	L	M	L	L	L	L	L	M	L	H	S	M	S	S	M	S	L	M	L	M	L
Liberia	L	M	M	M	L	S	L	M	L	M	L	L	L	M	L	H	S	L	S	M	L	L	L	L	M	L	M
Mali	M	M	L	M	L	S	L	M	L	H	S	S	L	H	L	H	L	L	M	L	M	L	L	L	H	L	M
Niger	L	L	L	M	L	S	L	M	M	H	M	M	L	H	L	H	S	M	M	M	H	L	L	L	H	L	L
Nigeria	L	L	H	H	L	S	M	L	M	M	L	L	L	H	L	H	S	M	S	M	H	L	L	L	H	L	M
Sao Tome and Principe	S	L	L	H	L	S	M	M	S	H	S	S	M	M	L	H	S	M	S	L	L	L	L	L	H	L	L
Senegal	M	M	L	H	M	S	L	H	L	H	M	M	M	M	L	H	S	L	M	S	L	L	M	L	L	L	M
Sierra Leone	H	M	M	M	H	S	L	S	L	M	L	L	M	M	L	H	S	L	S	H	H	S	S	L	H	M	M
Togo	L	L	L	H	L	S	L	L	M	H	S	S	M	H	L	H	S	M	S	S	H	L	L	L	H	M	M

Africa (Central and East)	Cholera	Typhoid	Shigellosis	Amoebiasis	TB	Plague	Brucellosis	Diphtheria	Meningococcal infection	Polio	Yellow Fever	Dengue or other arboviruses	Viral hepatitis (A + B)	Rabies	Typhus	Malaria	Leishmaniasis	Trypanosomiasis	Syphilis	Gonorrhoea	Schistosomiasis	Liver flukes	Hydatid disease	Tapeworms	Filariasis	Hookworm	Other intestinal worms
Burundi	S	M	M	H	L	S	M	L	L	M	M	M	L	L	H	M	S	M	S	S	L	L	L	L	L	S	L
Central African Republic	L	M	M	H	L	S	L	M	M	M	M	M	L	M	L	H	L	M	S	L	L	L	L	M	L	S	L
Congo	L	N	M	M	L	S	M	M	L	L	M	M	M	M	M	H	S	M	L	L	M	L	L	L	M	M	L
Djibouti	M	M	H	H	L	S	S	M	L	H	L	L	L	M	L	H	L	L	S	L	L	L	L	L	L	M	L
Equatorial Guinea	L	M	M	M	L	S	S	M	L	M	M	M	L	M	L	H	S	M	L	S	L	S	L	L	L	L	L
Ethiopia	H	M	M	H	M	S	M	M	L	M	S	S	M	M	M	M	M	L	S	L	L	L	H	H	L	L	L
Gabon	L	M	L	M	L	S	L	L	L	M	S	S	L	M	L	H	S	M	S	S	L	L	L	L	L	L	L
Kenya	L	L	L	L	L	L	L	M	L	M	S	S	L	L	M	M	M	M	S	S	L	L	L	H	M	L	L
Malawi	M	M	M	L	M	S	L	L	L	L	S	S	M	M	L	H	S	M	S	L	H	L	L	L	M	H	M
Rwanda	M	M	H	H	L	S	L	L	M	H	S	S	L	M	L	L	S	M	M	L	M	S	L	L	M	L	L
Seychelles	S	S	S	L	L	S	S	M	L	M	M	H	L	L	L	M	S	M	M	L	L	L	L	L	M	L	L
Somalia	M	M	L	H	H	S	L	L	L	M	S	S	L	M	L	H	S	M	L	L	L	L	M	L	M	L	L
Sudan	H	M	M	L	M	S	L	H	M	H	S	S	M	M	L	H	H	M	M	L	H	L	M	M	M	M	M
Tanzania	L	L	L	M	L	L	L	L	L	L	S	S	M	H	L	H	S	M	S	S	M	L	L	L	L	L	L
Uganda	M	M	M	M	H	L	L	M	M	M	L	L	H	H	L	H	L	M	S	S	H	L	L	M	M	H	H
Zaire	M	M	M	M	L	L	L	M	L	L	L	L	L	M	H	H	S	M	L	S	L	L	L	L	H	L	L

Africa (Southern)	Cholera	Typhoid	Shigellosis	Amoebiasis	TB	Plague	Brucellosis	Diphtheria	Meningococcal infection	Polio	Yellow Fever	Dengue or other arboviruses	Viral hepatitis (A + B)	Rabies	Typhus	Malaria	Leishmaniasis	Trypanosomiasis	Syphilis	Gonorrhoea	Schistosomiasis	Liver flukes	Hydatid disease	Tapeworms	Filariasis	Hookworm	Other intestinal worms
Angola	L	M	M	M	M	M	M	L	S	M	L	L	M	M	L	H	S	M	S	L	H	L	L	L	H	H	L
Botswana	L	L	L	M	L	S	L	L	L	L	S	S	M	M	L	M	S	M	L	S	L	L	M	H	M	L	H
Lesotho	S	M	L	S	H	L	S	L	L	L	S	L	M	M	L	S	S	S	M	M	S	S	S	H	S	S	H
Madagascar	L	L	M	L	L	L	S	M	S	M	S	S	M	M	L	H	S	S	S	S	L	L	L	L	L	L	H
Mauritius	S	M	L	L	S	S	S	L	S	M	S	S	L	S	L	M	S	S	S	S	H	L	L	L	L	L	L
Mozambique	M	S	L	M	L	L	M	L	S	M	S	M	L	M	L	H	S	M	S	S	M	L	L	M	M	H	H
Namibia	L	M	M	L	M	L	L	L	L	L	S	L	L	H	L	H	S	M	S	S	L	L	L	M	L	L	H
Reunion	S	M	L	H	L	S	L	M	S	L	S	S	L	M	L	M	S	L	M	S	L	L	L	M	L	S	L
South Africa	M	L	L	M	H	L	M	M	L	L	S	M	L	M	L	H	S	S	M	M	H	L	M	H	S	M	H
Swaziland	M	M	M	M	M	S	M	L	L	L	S	M	M	M	S	H	S	S	M	M	H	S	S	H	S	M	H
Zambia	S	L	M	M	L	S	L	M	L	M	S	S	L	H	L	H	S	H	M	L	M	L	L	M	M	M	H
Zimbabwe	S	L	L	L	L	L	L	L	L	L	S	S	M	L	L	H	S	L	M	M	H	L	S	M	L	M	H

Key S: Similar or fewer cases relative to Western Europe

Asia: Near and Middle East	Cholera	Typhoid	Shigellosis	Amoebiasis	TB	Plague	Brucellosis	Diphtheria	Meningococcal infection	Polio	Yellow Fever	Dengue or other arboviruses	Viral hepatitis (A + B)	Rabies	Typhus	Malaria	Leishmaniasis	Trypanosomiasis	Syphilis	Gonorrhoes	Schistosomiasis	Liver flukes	Hydatid disease	Tapeworms	Filariasis	Hookworm	Other intestinal worms
Afghanistan	S	M	M	M	M	S	H	M	S	L	S	S	H	M	M	L	M	S	S	S	L	S	M	L	L	H	H
Bahrain	L	H	M	H	L	S	L	L	S	H	S	S	M	H	M	H	M	S	S	L	L	S	L	L	L	L	M
Iran	M	H	H	M	L	S	H	L	S	L	S	S	M	L	S	H	H	S	S	S	M	S	M	M	S	M	H
Iraq	S	M	S	M	L	S	L	H	L	H	S	S	M	M	M	H	H	S	S	S	M	S	M	L	L	L	M
Israel	S	M	H	S	S	S	S	L	S	M	S	S	M	L	M	S	M	S	S	S	S	S	S	L	S	S	S
Jordan	L	M	M	M	L	S	S	L	S	L	S	S	M	S	S	L	L	S	S	S	L	S	M	M	S	M	M
Kuwait	S	H	M	M	M	S	H	L	M	L	S	S	H	S	L	S	M	S	S	S	S	S	M	L	S	S	L
Lebanon	H	M	L	L	L	S	L	L	L	M	S	S	M	L	L	S	L	S	S	S	L	L	M	S	S	L	L
Oman	L	M	S	L	M	S	L	H	L	H	S	S	H	M	M	H	M	S	S	L	M	S	L	L	L	L	L
Qatar	L	H	S	S	M	S	H	M	S	M	S	S	M	L	L	S	S	S	L	S	M	S	L	L	L	L	L
Saudi Arabia	L	M	L	M	L	S	M	M	H	L	S	S	H	S	L	M	M	S	S	S	M	S	L	M	L	L	M
Syrian Arab Republic	L	M	S	M	S	S	S	H	L	M	S	S	M	M	M	H	M	S	L	L	M	S	M	L	L	L	L
Turkey	L	M	M	M	L	S	L	M	L	M	S	S	M	M	M	H	L	S	S	S	L	L	H	M	L	S	H
United Arab Emirates	L	H	H	M	H	S	S	M	S	L	S	S	H	H	L	H	L	S	S	S	M	S	L	L	L	M	M
Yemen	L	M	S	M	H	S	S	H	M	L	S	S	M	H	M	H	M	S	S	S	H	L	M	L	M	S	H
Yemen (South)	M	M	H	M	M	S	M	H	M	H	S	S	M	M	M	H	M	S	S	S	M	S	L	L	L	L	L

Asia: Central and S. East	Cholera	Typhoid	Shigellosis	Amoebiasis	TB	Plague	Brucellosis	Diphtheria	Meningococcal infection	Polio	Yellow Fever	Dengue or other arboviruses	Viral hepatitis (A + B)	Rabies	Typhus	Malaria	Leishmaniasis	Trypanosomiasis	Syphilis	Gonorrhoea	Schistosomiasis	Liver flukes	Hydatid disease	Tapeworms	Filariasis	Hookworm	Other intestinal worms
Bangladesh	H	M	H	H	M	S	S	M	M	L	S	M	H	H	M	H	L	S	S	L	S	S	L	L	M	M	H
Brunei	S	L	L	L	M	S	S	S	S	S	S	L	L	S	M	S	S	S	S	S	L	S	S	L	L	M	M
Burma	M	M	M	M	M	L	M	L	S	S	S	M	H	H	L	H	L	S	S	S	S	S	M	L	M	M	H
India	M	H	H	H	H	S	H	H	H	M	S	L	M	H	M	H	M	S	S	S	S	M	M	M	M	H	H
Indonesia	L	M	M	M	M	S	L	M	L	M	S	H	M	H	M	H	S	S	L	L	L	S	S	L	M	H	H
Malaysia	M	M	M	L	M	S	M	M	S	S	S	M	M	S	L	H	S	S	S	S	L	L	S	L	M	H	H
Mongolia	S	L	S	S	L	L	M	M	L	S	S	L	L	L	L	S	L	S	S	S	L	S	L	S	L	L	L
Nepal	S	M	L	M	M	S	S	M	H	S	S	L	M	M	L	L	L	S	S	S	L	L	L	L	L	H	H
Pakistan	M	H	M	H	M	S	H	H	L	M	S	M	H	H	M	H	M	S	S	S	S	L	M	M	M	H	H
Singapore	M	M	L	L	M	S	S	L	S	S	S	M	L	S	L	S	S	S	L	L	S	S	S	L	L	L	L
Sri Lanka	L	M	L	M	M	S	L	L	L	M	S	M	M	M	L	H	S	S	H	H	S	S	S	S	M	H	H
Thailand	M	M	H	M	M	S	M	H	S	M	S	M	M	M	L	H	M	S	S	M	M	M	M	M	L	H	H

L: 'Low' M: 'Medium' H: 'High'

Asia: Far East	Cholera	Typhoid	Shigellosis	Amoebiasis	TB	Plague	Brucellosis	Diphtheria	Meningococcal infection	Polio	Yellow Fever	Dengue or other arboviruses	Viral hepatitis (A + B)	Rabies	Typhus	Malaria	Leishmaniasis	Trypanosomiasis	Syphilis	Gonorrhoea	Schistosomiasis	Liver flukes	Hydatid disease	Tapeworms	Filariasis	Hookworm	Other intestinal worms
China	S	L	M	L	M	L	L	M	L	L	S	L	M	M	L	H	L	S	S	S	M	L	L	L	M	M	M
Hong Kong	L	L	M	L	H	S	L	L	S	L	S	L	H	M	L	S	L	S	L	M	L	M	L	L	L	L	L
Japan	L	S	L	L	L	S	L	L	S	L	S	L	L	S	L	S	L	S	S	S	L	L	L	L	L	L	L
Kampuchea	L	M	M	M	L	L	M	H	M	H	S	M	M	M	M	H	L	S	S	S	L	L	M	M	L	M	M
Korea (North)	L	L	S	L	L	S	M	M	L	L	S	L	L	L	M	S	L	S	S	S	L	M	M	L	L	L	L
Korea (South)	L	L	S	L	M	L	M	M	L	L	S	L	L	L	L	S	L	S	S	L	L	L	L	L	M	L	L
Lao People's Dem Rep	L	L	L	M	M	S	M	H	L	L	S	M	M	M	L	M	L	S	L	L	L	L	L	L	L	L	L
Macau	L	L	M	S	H	L	L	L	L	L	S	L	H	L	L	S	L	S	L	M	L	M	L	L	L	L	M
Philippines	M	M	H	H	M	L	M	H	L	M	S	L	M	H	S	H	L	S	S	L	M	M	M	M	L	M	H
Taiwan	L	M	L	M	L	L	L	L	L	L	S	L	M	S	L	S	L	S	S	L	L	L	L	M	L	L	L
Vietnam	L	M	M	H	M	H	M	H	S	M	S	H	M	M	L	H	M	S	L	L	L	M	M	M	M	L	M

America (North and Central)	Cholera	Typhoid	Shigellosis	Amoebiasis	TB	Plague	Brucellosis	Diphtheria	Meningococcal infection	Polio	Yellow Fever	Dengue or other arboviruses	Viral hepatitis (A + B)	Rabies	Typhus	Malaria	Leishmaniasis	Trypanosomiasis	Syphilis	Gonorrhoea	Schistosomiasis	Liver flukes	Hydatid disease	Tapeworms	Filariasis	Hookworm	Other intestinal worms
Belize	S	L	L	M	L	S	L	M	S	L	S	M	L	H	L	M	M	M	S	L	L	L	L	L	M	M	M
Canada	S	S	L	S	S	S	S	S	S	L	S	S	S	L	L	S	S	S	S	S	S	S	S	S	S	S	L
Costa Rica	S	L	S	H	S	S	L	M	S	L	S	L	L	M	L	H	H	L	L	M	L	L	M	M	M	M	H
El Salvador	S	M	M	H	L	S	L	M	S	L	S	L	L	H	L	M	L	L	L	L	L	L	L	L	L	M	M
Guatemala	S	M	H	M	M	S	L	M	S	M	S	L	L	M	L	H	M	L	L	S	L	L	L	M	M	M	M
Honduras	S	M	M	M	M	S	L	L	S	M	S	H	L	H	L	H	M	M	L	L	L	L	L	M	L	M	H
Mexico	S	M	M	H	S	S	S	L	S	M	S	M	L	H	L	H	L	L	S	S	L	S	M	M	L	M	H
Nicaragua	S	H	M	M	M	S	S	M	S	M	S	H	M	H	L	H	H	L	L	L	L	L	L	M	L	M	H
Panama	S	M	M	H	L	S	S	M	S	L	L	M	M	H	L	H	M	M	M	M	L	L	L	M	M	M	H
USA	S	S	M	L	S	L	S	L	S	S	S	S	M	L	L	S	S	S	L	M	S	S	L	S	S	L	L

Key S: Similar or fewer cases relative to Western Europe

L: 'Low' M: 'Medium' H: 'High'

Americas: Caribbean	Cholera	Typhoid	Shigellosis	Amoebiasis	TB	Plague	Brucellosis	Diphtheria	Meningococcal infection	Polio	Yellow Fever	Dengue / arboviruses	Viral hepatitis (A + B)	Rabies	Typhus	Malaria	Leishmaniasis	Trypanosomiasis	Syphilis	Gonorrhoea	Schistosomiasis	Liver flukes	Hydatid disease	Tapeworms	Filariasis	Hookworm	Other intestinal worms
Antigua and Barbuda	S	L	L	L	S	S	S	S	S	S	S	M	L	S	S	S	S	S	L	L	M	L	L	L	L	M	M
Bahamas	S	S	M	L	S	S	S	S	S	S	S	M	L	S	S	S	S	S	M	M	S	S	L	L	L	L	M
Barbados	S	S	M	L	S	S	S	S	S	S	S	H	L	S	S	S	S	S	L	L	S	S	S	S	S	L	L
Bermuda	S	L	L	L	S	S	S	S	S	S	S	L	L	S	S	S	S	S	L	H	S	L	L	L	L	L	M
British Virgin Island	S	S	S	M	L	S	S	S	S	S	S	M	L	S	S	S	S	S	L	H	L	L	S	L	L	L	L
Cuba	S	S	M	H	S	S	L	M	S	S	S	H	M	M	S	S	S	S	L	L	L	M	S	L	L	M	M
Dominica	S	M	M	L	S	S	S	S	S	S	S	L	M	S	S	S	S	S	L	L	S	L	S	L	L	M	M
Dominican Rep	S	M	L	H	S	S	L	H	L	L	S	H	L	M	S	M	S	S	M	M	L	L	L	L	L	M	M
Grenada	S	L	L	L	L	S	S	S	S	S	S	L	L	L	S	S	S	S	L	L	S	L	L	L	L	M	M
Guadeloupe	S	L	L	L	L	S	S	L	S	S	S	L	L	S	S	S	S	S	L	L	S	L	S	L	L	M	M
Haiti	S	M	M	H	L	S	L	M	S	M	S	H	M	L	S	H	L	S	L	M	S	L	L	L	L	M	M
Jamaica	S	S	S	M	S	S	L	L	S	S	S	M	L	S	S	S	L	S	L	M	L	L	L	L	L	M	M
Martinique	S	L	L	L	L	S	S	L	S	S	S	L	L	S	S	S	S	S	L	L	S	L	L	L	L	M	M
Montserrat	S	S	S	M	S	S	S	S	S	S	S	M	M	S	S	S	S	S	H	H	M	L	L	L	L	M	M
Puerto Rico	S	S	M	L	S	S	S	S	S	S	S	H	L	L	S	S	S	S	L	L	L	L	L	L	L	L	M
St. Kitts and Nevis	S	S	S	L	S	S	S	S	S	S	S	M	L	S	S	S	S	S	L	M	M	L	L	L	L	M	M
St. Lucia	S	S	L	L	S	S	S	S	S	S	S	M	L	S	S	S	S	S	M	M	H	L	S	L	L	M	M
St. Vincent	S	L	L	L	S	S	S	S	S	S	S	L	L	S	S	S	S	S	L	L	S	L	S	L	L	M	M
Trinidad and Tobago	S	S	L	L	S	S	S	S	S	S	S	M	L	L	S	S	S	S	L	M	L	L	L	L	L	M	M

America (South)	Cholera	Typhoid	Shigellosis	Amoebiasis	TB	Plague	Brucellosis	Diphtheria	Meningococcal infection	Polio	Yellow Fever	Dengue / arboviruses	Viral hepatitis (A + B)	Rabies	Typhus	Malaria	Leishmaniasis	Trypanosomiasis	Syphilis	Gonorrhoea	Schistosomiasis	Liver flukes	Hydatid disease	Tapeworms	Filariasis	Hookworm	Other intestinal worms
Argentina	S	L	S	M	L	S	L	M	L	L	S	S	M	M	L	L	L	H	L	L	L	L	M	L	L	H	M
Bolivia	S	L	L	M	L	L	L	M	S	L	M	S	M	M	L	L	M	M	S	S	L	L	M	M	L	M	M
Brazil	S	M	L	H	H	M	L	M	L	L	L	L	H	L	S	H	M	H	M	M	H	L	L	M	L	H	H
Chile	S	M	L	L	S	S	S	M	S	L	S	S	L	S	L	S	L	L	S	L	L	L	M	M	S	M	M
Colombia	S	H	H	H	M	S	S	M	S	L	H	H	M	H	L	H	H	M	L	L	S	L	S	M	M	H	H
Ecuador	S	H	L	H	L	L	S	M	S	L	L	L	L	M	L	H	M	L	S	S	M	L	M	S	M	M	M
Falkland Islands	S	S	S	S	L	S	S	S	S	S	S	S	S	L	L	S	S	S	M	M	S	L	H	L	S	L	L
French Guiana	S	M	M	M	H	S	S	S	S	S	S	M	L	S	S	H	H	L	M	H	S	S	S	L	L	H	H
Guyana	S	M	M	L	M	S	S	L	S	S	L	L	L	M	L	H	M	M	S	S	M	M	L	M	M	H	H
Paraguay	S	L	M	M	L	S	S	M	L	L	S	S	L	M	L	M	M	L	L	S	M	L	M	M	L	H	M
Peru	S	L	H	M	L	M	S	M	S	L	L	L	L	M	L	H	M	L	S	S	L	M	L	M	L	S	H
Surinam	S	M	M	H	M	S	L	L	S	S	L	M	L	S	L	H	M	H	L	L	H	L	M	L	M	H	H
Uruguay	S	L	L	M	L	S	L	M	L	L	S	S	M	S	L	S	L	M	L	L	L	L	M	M	L	H	M
Venezuela	S	L	L	L	L	S	L	M	S	L	L	L	M	M	L	H	M	H	M	H	M	L	S	L	M	H	M

Oceania	Cholera	Typhoid	Shigellosis	Amoebiasis	TB	Plague	Brucellosis	Diphtheria	Meningococcal infection	Polio	Yellow Fever	Dengue or other arboviruses	Viral hepatitis (A + B)	Rabies	Typhus	Malaria	Leishmaniasis	Trypanosomiasis	Syphilis	Gonorrhoea	Schistosomiasis	Liver flukes	Hydatid disease	Tapeworms	Filariasis	Hookworm	Other intestinal worms
American Samoa	S	M	H	L	S	S	L	L	S	L	S	S	M	S	S	S	L	S	L	L	S	S	S	S	L	M	L
Australia	S	S	M	L	S	S	S	S	S	S	S	S	S	S	S	S	S	S	S	S	S	L	L	S	S	L	S
Cook Islands	S	S	S	S	H	S	L	S	M	L	S	S	L	S	S	S	L	S	L	M	S	S	S	S	L	L	L
Fiji	S	S	M	M	L	S	S	S	S	L	S	H	L	S	S	S	L	S	L	L	S	S	L	S	M	L	L
French Polynesia	S	M	M	M	M	S	S	S	L	L	S	H	M	S	S	S	L	S	M	L	S	S	S	S	M	M	H
Guam	S	S	L	M	M	S	S	L	L	L	S	M	M	S	S	S	M	S	L	M	S	S	S	S	M	M	M
Kiribati	S	L	L	M	H	S	S	L	S	L	S	S	M	S	S	S	L	S	L	S	S	S	S	S	M	M	M
New Caledonia	S	M	M	H	L	S	S	S	S	S	S	L	M	S	S	S	S	S	M	M	S	S	S	S	M	M	M
New Zealand	S	S	M	L	S	S	S	S	S	S	S	S	M	S	S	S	L	S	S	S	S	S	S	S	S	S	S
Pacific Islands	S	L	L	H	L	S	S	S	S	L	S	M	M	S	S	S	L	S	L	M	S	S	S	S	H	M	M
Papua New Guinea	S	M	M	H	H	S	S	S	S	L	S	H	H	S	S	H	S	S	L	L	S	S	S	S	H	H	H
Samoa	S	M	L	L	M	S	S	L	L	L	S	H	M	S	S	S	S	S	L	S	S	S	S	S	M	H	M
Solomon Islands	S	L	L	L	H	S	S	S	L	S	S	M	M	S	S	H	S	S	L	S	S	S	S	S	M	H	M
Tonga	S	H	M	M	H	S	S	L	S	S	S	H	M	S	S	S	L	S	L	S	S	S	S	S	M	M	M
Vanuatu	S	L	L	L	M	S	S	L	L	S	S	M	M	S	S	H	L	S	S	S	S	S	S	S	M	M	M
Wallis and Futuna Islands	S	L	L	H	M	S	S	S	S	S	S	H	M	S	S	S	L	S	L	S	S	S	S	S	H	H	H

Europe (selected countries)	Cholera	Typhoid	Shigellosis	Amoebiasis	TB	Plague	Brucellosis	Diphtheria	Meningococcal infection	Polio	Yellow Fever	Dengue or other arboviruses	Viral hepatitis (A + B)	Rabies	Typhus	Malaria	Leishmaniasis	Trypanosomiasis	Syphilis	Gonorrhoea	Schistosomiasis	Liver flukes	Hydatid disease	Tapeworms	Filariasis	Hookworm	Other intestinal worms
Bulgaria	S	S	H	L	S	S	L	S	S	S	S	S	M	S	L	S	S	S	S	S	S	S	L	S	S	S	S
Cyprus	S	L	S	S	S	S	M	L	L	S	S	S	L	S	M	S	L	S	L	L	S	S	L	S	S	S	L
Czechoslovakia	S	S	H	L	S	S	S	L	S	S	S	S	M	S	S	S	S	S	S	S	S	S	S	S	S	S	M
Denmark	S	S	L	M	S	S	S	S	S	S	S	S	S	S	S	S	S	S	S	L	S	S	M	L	S	S	S
Finland	S	S	M	M	S	S	S	S	S	S	S	S	S	S	S	S	S	S	S	L	S	S	S	L	S	S	S
Greece	S	M	S	L	L	S	M	S	S	S	S	S	L	S	L	S	M	S	S	S	S	L	H	S	L	L	S
Hungary	S	S	H	L	S	S	S	S	S	S	S	S	L	S	S	S	S	S	S	L	S	S	L	S	S	S	S
Iceland	S	S	S	S	S	S	S	S	L	S	S	S	S	S	S	S	S	S	S	L	S	L	L	S	S	S	S
Norway	S	S	S	S	S	S	S	S	M	S	S	S	S	S	S	S	S	S	S	S	S	S	L	S	S	S	S
Portugal	L	M	S	S	L	S	L	M	S	S	S	S	L	S	S	S	L	S	S	S	S	S	S	S	S	S	S
Romania	L	S	H	S	L	S	S	S	S	M	S	S	S	M	S	S	S	S	S	S	S	S	L	S	S	S	S
Spain	L	M	M	S	S	S	M	L	L	S	S	S	S	S	S	S	L	S	S	S	S	L	S	L	S	L	S
Sweden	S	S	L	S	S	S	S	S	S	S	S	S	S	S	S	S	S	S	S	L	S	S	S	S	S	S	S
Yugoslavia	S	L	H	S	L	S	L	L	S	S	S	S	M	L	L	S	L	S	S	S	S	L	L	M	S	S	S

Key: S: 'Similar' L: 'Low' M: 'Medium' H: 'High'

Appendix 4
Post-tropical check-up

The need for a medical examination on returning from the tropics depends largely upon what you have been doing while abroad; some people find it reassuring, and it may occasionally reveal an unsuspected problem.

Dr Anthony Hall *has performed thousands of check-ups on people who have returned from the tropics, and has detected many ordinary, as well as exotic, diseases.*

Opinions vary on the value of check-ups, post-tropical or otherwise, in people without symptoms. However, a medical examination, preferably within one week of leaving the tropics, may reveal treatable disease.

A check-up is obviously more valuable in people with symptoms, and in those who have been close to earth, water, and the local population, or who have lived abroad for a long time. Where you go is usually less important than what you have been doing there—so, for example, an accountant in Harare is less likely to pick up schistosomiasis than a water engineer in rural Zimbabwe.

Check-ups are more important in people who have returned from tropical Africa or Asia.

Symptoms

The symptoms of tropical diseases are many and varied. Diarrhoea (possibly containing blood), fever, a rash, an itch, spots, or skin swellings require prompt, skilled attention.

However, symptoms of many important conditions are vague and non-specific: unexplained symptoms are often due to malaria, and delay in diagnosis may result in death. Patients think they have influenza, and don't bother to go to a doctor; and even if they do, the doctor may also fail to recognize the symptoms. Fever, chills, and headache are the cardinal symptoms of malaria but others include diarrhoea, vomiting, cough, abdominal pain, and jaundice.

Viral hepatitis is also common in travellers, and can cause

vague symptoms initially, including tiredness and loss of appetite.

Examination

A number of diseases may be detected on physical examination. The physician may feel an enlarged spleen due to malaria, hepatitis, or leishmaniasis; an enlarged liver due to malaria, an amoebic liver abscess, or even alcoholism; enlarged lymph nodes in the groin due to syphilis or lymphogranuloma venereum; or may see a rash due to syphilis, scabies, typhus, or cutaneous larva migrans.

Tests

The following screening tests are often useful:

Blood tests

- White blood cell count: a count of the number of *eosinophils* (a type of white blood cell) in the blood is, in my opinion, the most useful screening test for a worm infestation, and the doctor will need to examine a faecal specimen for parasites if the eosinophil count is raised.
- Blood films: for malaria; trypanosomiasis; and filariasis.
- Liver function tests: for hepatitis, or alcoholic liver damage.
- Serological tests (antibody tests): for syphilis; schistosomiasis; filariasis and HIV.

Stool

Microscopic examination may be carried out, for detection of parasites or their eggs.

Urine

Microscopic examination of the urine may detect eggs in schistosomiasis (see p. 92).

Advice

The doctor will probably use this opportunity to remind you to keep taking antimalarial tablets for at least four (preferably six to eight) weeks after leaving a malarious area. Make sure that your doctor knows which places you visited, when, and for how long—such information will be valuable if you develop an illness later, and are not in a fit state to recount the details of your trip.

Where to go

The major centres specializing in tropical diseases are listed in Appendix 6. To receive a check-up under the National Health Service in the UK, you will need to bring a letter from your General Practitioner.

And finally . . .

After leaving the tropics, many people celebrate their return home by overeating, and by drinking too much alcohol. Remember, however, that many diseases, including malaria, typhoid, and hepatitis may become apparent during that period for the first time. So, I advise a convalescent period of at least four weeks, during which alcohol consumption should be kept to a minimum—to reduce the effect on the liver of any disease that may be incubating. Rich food (with a high fat content) should also be avoided during this period—especially by those who have been used to a simple, mainly vegetarian diet.

Appendix 5

Some hints on eating abroad under extreme conditions of bad hygiene

1. **Choice of food**

- If possible, choose food that *must* have been freshly cooked—e.g. omelette, chips.
- Freshly boiled food is always safe—e.g. rice, sweetcorn.
- Eat fruit or vegetables that you can peel or cut open yourself—e.g. bananas, citrus fruits, melon, papaya.
- Eat food from sealed packs or cans.
- Choose acceptably prepared local dishes rather than incompetently prepared imitation western-style food.
- Regard all cooked food as only safe when served hot.
- Be prepared to send food back and to complain, when appropriate.

Whenever possible, prepare your food yourself, or watch it being cooked.

2. **Don't eat**

- Salads
- Food that you do not *know* to have been freshly cooked, including hotel buffet food left out in warm temperatures
- Food on which flies have settled or may have settled
- Shellfish and prawns
- Intricate dishes that have required much handling in preparation
- Unwashed (clean water) or unpeelable fruit or vegetables
- Ice cream and ices
- Dairy products made from unpasteurized milk. In some countries, not all 'pasteurized' milk has really been pasteurized
- Sauces and relishes, left out on the table ('hot' chilli sauces, however spicy, are not self-sterilizing!)

Where there is no alternative to unsafe food, smaller quantities are safer. Consider missing a meal; many western travellers can afford to lose a little weight, and it is safer to do so by choice than from illness.

3. **Plates and cutlery**
need to be washed with detergent, rinsed with clean water, and protected from flies.
When this has not or cannot be done, and you suspect that they are contaminated, the risk can be reduced by rinsing with hot weak tea, a small amount of whisky, or by cleaning with an injection swab. Cutlery can be flamed with a candle or a cigarette lighter.
Otherwise, don't eat the bottom layer of food on the plate—easy when food is served on a bed of rice. Alternatively, use paper plates and your own cutlery.

4. **Hands and fingers**
should be washed at every opportunity. Only eat food that you have handled if your hands are scrupulously clean; otherwise, use a clean tissue, the inside of a clean plastic bag, or a piece of bread to handle food; or use your fingers, but discard any part of the food that you have handled.

5. **Drinking water**
should be sterilized with iodine, or boiled. Don't use ice.

6. **Cups and glasses**
that may be contaminated can be swilled out with hot tea or boiling water before use. Flies often settle on rims—pour away a little tea to rinse the rim of a teacup. Otherwise, use your own cup or water bottle, or drink bottled drinks directly from their bottle.

Local delicacies on offer to athletes and spectators at the 1988 Olympiad in Korea included dried fish heads, roasted locusts, sea slugs, toasted silkworms, snake and dog meat. No matter what food you are offered, you should always apply the same principles of food hygiene.

Appendix 6

Immunization units, specialist centres, and government departments: sources of up-to-the-minute information and advice ‡

United Kingdom

Main yellow fever vaccination centres †

(centres marked * give other vaccinations too).

ENGLAND AND WALES

Barnsley
The Medical Services Clinic, New Street, Barnsley, South Yorkshire Tel. 0226 83221

Basingstoke
Basingstoke District Hospital
Park Prewet, Basingstoke, Hants Tel. 0256 3208 Ext 3640

Birmingham
* Immunization Section, 90 Lancaster Street, Birmingham B4 7AR Tel. 021 235 3428

Blackburn
Larkhill Health Centre, Mount Pleasant, Blackburn BB1 5BJ Tel. 0254 63611 Ext. 231

Bournemouth
Averbury Child Health Clinic, Maderia Road, Bournemouth. (Wed. at 2 p.m. by appointment only) Tel. 0202 25253

Bradford
Community Health Services, Joseph Brennan House, Sunbridge Road, Bradford BD1 2SY Tel. 0274 724575 Ext. 44

Brighton
School Clinic, Morley Street, Brighton BN2 2RH Tel. 0273 693600 Ext. 271

Bristol
* Central Health Clinic GPO Box No 201, Tower Hill, Bristol BS2 OJD Tel. 0272 291010 Ext. 277

Cambridge
Yellow Fever Clinic, Clinic 10, Addenbrooke's Hospital, Hills Road, Cambridge (For appointments: Community Health Services, Tel. 0223 245151 Ext. 7538)

‡ Organizations wishing to be listed in this section, in future editions of this book, are invited to write to the editor, c/o Oxford University Press.

† Immunization against yellow fever takes place at specially licensed centres because the vaccine used for many years required special storage conditions. A heat-stable vaccine is now widely used, and it is likely that regulations will eventually change to allow GPs to administer it.

Cardiff

Riverside Health Centre, Wellington Street, Canton, Cardiff Tel. 0222 398623 Ext. 31

Carlisle

The Central Clinic, Victoria Place, Carlisle CA1 1HN Tel. 0228 36451

Chelmsford

The Health Suite, Ground Floor, Block A, County Hall Extension, Chelmsford CM1 1LX Tel. 0245 67222 Ext. 2756

Coventry

Gulson Road Child Health Clinic, Gulson Road, Coventry (Appointments should be made at: Communicable Disease Control, Spire House, New Union Street, Coventry CV1 2PT Tel. 0203 24055 Ext. 6035/6)

Derby

Cathedral Road Clinic, Derby (For appointments: Community Health Services Tel. 0332 45934)

Doncaster

Health Clinic, Chequer Road, Doncaster DN1 2AD Tel. 0302 67051/6

Exeter

Exeter Yellow Fever Vaccination Centre, Dean Clarke House, Southernhay East, Exeter EX1 1PQ Tel. 0392 52211 Ext. 212

Gloucester

Gloucestershire Royal Hospital, Great Western Road, Gloucester GL1 3NN Tel. 0452 28555 Ext. 4210

Great Missenden

Chiltern Hospital, Great Missenden, Bucks Tel. 02406 6565

Grimsby

The Clinic, 34 Dudley Street, Grimsby, South Humberside DN31 1QQ Tel. 0472 53771 (mornings only)

Gwynedd

The Clinic, Ffordd Argyle, Llandudno, Gwynedd Tel. 0492 78787

Haverfordwest

Pembrokeshire Health Authority, Merlins Hill, Haverfordwest, Dyfed SA61 1PG Tel. 0437 3345 Ext. 38

Kingston upon Hull

The Central Clinic, 74 Beverley Road, Kingston upon Hull HU3 1YD Tel. 0482 28888 (For appointments: Victoria House, Park Street, Hull Tel. 0482 223191 Ext. 30)

Lancaster

Ashton Road Clinic, Lancaster Tel. 0524 2558

Leeds

* Immunization Centre, Chapeltown Health Centre, Spencer Place, Leeds LS7 4BB Tel. 0532 486351

Leicester

Princess House, 20 Princess Road West, Leicester Tel. 0533 549969 Ext. 206/7/8

Lincoln

Community Health Services, St Mark's House, St Mark's Station Yard, Tel. 0522 27196

Liverpool

* Vaccination Clinic, 26 Hatton Garden, Liverpool L3 2AW Tel. 051 227 3911 Ext. 69

* School of Tropical Medicine, Pembroke Place, Liverpool L3 5QA Tel. 051 709 2298 or 051 708 9393

London

* Immunization Service, British Airways, 75 Regent Street, London W1 Tel. 01 439 9584/5

* Thomas Cook Ltd., 45 Berkeley Street, London W1 Tel. 01 499 4000

* Yellow Fever Vaccination Service, Hospital for Tropical Diseases, 4 St Pancreas Way, London NW1 OPE Tel. 01 387 4411 Ext. 136/6

The Health Centre, 3 The Manor Drive, Worcester Park, Surrey Tel. 01 337 0246

* Yellow Fever Vaccination Service, Medical Department, Unilever House, Blackfriars, London EC4P 4BQ Tel. 01 822 6017

* Yellow Fever Vaccination Service, 53 Great Cumberland Place, London W1H 7LH Tel. 01 262 6456

Kings Road Clinic, Kings Road, Richmond, Surrey TW10 6EF Tel. 01 940 9879

Maidstone

Maidstone Health Authority, Springfield, Sanding Road, Maidstone Tel. 0622 671411 Ext. 4034

Manchester

* Basement Clinic, Town Hall Extension, Manchester M60 2JB Tel. 061 236 3377 Ext. 2554/6

Middlesbrough

Occupational Health Clinic, West Lane Hospital, Acklam Road, Middlesbrough, Cleveland, Tel. 0624 813144 Ext. 265

Newcastle upon Tyne

Shieldfield Health and Social Services Centre, 4 Clarence Walk, (off Stoddart St) Newcastle upon Tyne NE2 1AL Tel. 0632 738811 Ext. 575

Newport

Clytha Clinic, 26 Clytha Park Road, Newport (Vaccination by appointment; enquiries and requests for appointment should be made to: Community Health Sector, St Cadoc's Hospital Grounds, Lodge Road, Newport NP6 1XS Tel. 0633 422644)

Northampton

Northampton Yellow Fever Vaccination Centre, 67 St Giles Street, Northampton Tel. 0604 30030 (Appointments should be made at: Northampton District Community Services, Sunneyside, Cliftonville, Northampton NN1 5BE Tel. 0604 21155 Ext. 267)

Norwich

The Health Centre, West Pottergate (Appointments should be made at: Community Health Services, Norfolk Tower, Surrey Street, Norwich NR1 3SX Tel. 06036 611911 Ext. 56)

Nottingham

Meadow Health Centre, 1 Bridgeway Centre, The Meadows, Nottingham NG2 2JG (For appointment: Personal Health Services, Tel. 0602 580551)

Oxford
Brown Waiting Area, Outpatients Department, John Radcliffe Hospital, Headley Way, Headington, Oxford (By appointment only: ring Community Sector Offices, Radcliffe Infirmary, Oxford OX2 6HE Tel. 0865 249891 Ext. 567)

Penzance
Health Clinic Bellair, Alverton, Penzance Tel. 0736 2321

Plymouth
Community Health Dept, Longfield House, Greenbank Road, Plymouth Tel. 0752 834598

Sheffield
Central Health Clinic, Mulberry Street, Sheffield S1 2PJ Tel. 0742 731661

Shrewsbury
Area Health Office, 2nd Floor, North Block, Shirehall, Abbey Foregate, Shrewsbury Tel. 0743 222524

Southampton
Central Health Clinic, East Park Terrace, Southampton Tel. 0703 34321

Southend-on-Sea
Health Centre, PO Box 26, Queensway House, Essex Street, Southend-on-Sea Tel. 0702 616322

Swansea
Swansea Central Clinic, 21 Orchard Street, Swansea SA1 5BE Tel. 0792 51501

Taunton
Tower Lane Clinic, Taunton (Appointments to be made with: Somerset Health Authority, County Hall, Taunton TA1 4EJ Tel. 0823 73491 Ext. 255)

Truro
* Health Area Office, The Leats, Truro Tel. 0872 2202

York
Health Services Centre, 31 Monkgate, York Tel. 0904 30351

SCOTLAND

Aberdeen
View Terrace Clinic, 1 View Terrace, Aberdeen AB2 4RS Tel. 0224 631633

Dundee
King's Cross Hospital, Clepington Road, Dundee DD3 8EA Tel. 0382 816116

Edinburgh
Central Vaccination Clinic, 9 Johnston Terrace, Edinburgh EH1 2PP Tel. 031 225 8474 Ext. 33

Glasgow
Vaccination Clinic, 20 Cochrane Street, Glasgow G1 1JA Tel. 041 221 9600 Ext. 2411

Orkney
Health Centre, New Scapa Road, Kirkwall, Orkney Tel. 0856 2763

NORTHERN IRELAND

Balleymena
* Yellow Fever Vaccination Centre, 51 Castle Street, Ballymena Tel. 0366 6324 or 2108

Belfast

* Yellow Fever Vaccination Centre, Lincoln Avenue Clinic, Antrim Road, Belfast BE14 6AZ Tel. 0232 241771 Ext. 2432

Omagh

* Yellow Fever Vaccination Centre, The Health Centre, Mountjoy Road, Omagh Tel. 0662 3532 Ext. 264

DHSS offices

For up-to-date information about vaccination requirements, contact one of the following UK Government Health Departments

England

International Relations Division, Department of Health and Social Security, Alexander Fleming House, Elephant & Castle, London SE1 6BY Tel. 01 407 5522 Ext. 6749

Scotland

Scottish Home & Health Department, St Andrew's House, Edinburgh EH1 3DE Tel. 031 556 8501 Ext. 2438

Wales

Welsh Office, Cathays Park, Cardiff CF1 3NQ Tel. 0222 825111 Ext. 3395

Northern Ireland

Department of Health & Social Security, Dundonald House, Upper Newtownards Road, Belfast BT4 3SF Tel. 0233 63939 Ext. 2593

or see page 50063 on PRESTEL. (There is free access to this service at most UK public libraries.)

Major UK centres specializing in tropical diseases

Hospital for Tropical Diseases, 4 St Pancras Way, London NW1 OPE Tel. 01 387 4411

Liverpool School of Tropical Medicine, Pembroke Place, Liverpool L3 5QA Tel. 051 708 9393

Department of Communicable and Tropical Diseases, East Birmingham Hospital, Bordesley Green Road, Birmingham, B9 5ST Tel. 021 772 4311

Communicable Diseases (Scotland) Unit, Ruchill Hospital, Glasgow G20 9NB Tel. 041 946 7120

Other sources of information

Recorded information from the Hospital for Tropical Diseases Tel. 0898 345081

The Malaria Reference Laboratory, at the London School of Hygiene & Tropical Medicine, Keppel St, London WC1E 7BR Tel. 01 636 7921, provides free specialist advice about antimalarial precautions for indivdiual countries, in the form of a recorded telephone message; it can also advise in cases of particular difficulty.

Medical Advisory Services for Travellers Abroad Ltd (MASTA) is based at the London School of Hygiene & Tropical Medicine, Keppel St, London WC1E 7BR Tel. 01 631 4408. They provide computerized health print-outs tailored to individual requirements.

The Foreign & Commonwealth Office, King Charles Street, London SW1 Tel. 01 270 3000, provides information about political risks abroad, and should be consulted if you intend to visit a part of the world where there is currently unrest or instability.

AIDS Hotlines and Government information numbers: Tel. 0800 555777; 01 981 2717; 01 980 7222; and 0345 581151.

United States of America

State Departments of Health in the United States

In the USA, city, county, and state departments of health provide information for the public about immunization for travel.

Alabama
Alabama Department of Public Health, 515 W. Jeff Davis Avenue, Montgomery, AL 36104 Tel. 205 263-6671

Alaska
Juneau Health Center, 320 Willoughby, Suite 202, AK 99801 Tel. 907 586 3736

Arizona
Bureau of Disease Control, PO Box 2111, Phoenix, AZ 85001 Tel. 602 258 6381

Arkansas
Arkansas Department of Health, 4815 W. Markham, Little Rock, AR 72201 Tel. 501 661 2000

California
Department of Health, 2921 Stockton Blvd, Sacramento, CA 95817 Tel. 916 732 3770

Colorado
Colorado Department of Health, 4210 East 11th Avenue, Denver, CO 80220 Tel. 303 331 8331

Connecticut
State of Connecticut Department of Health Services, 150 Washington Street, Hartford, CT 06106 Tel. 203 566 5657

Delaware
Division of Public Health, Capitol Square, Dover, DE 19901 Tel. 302 736 4745

District of Columbia
DC Department of Human Services, 1875 Connecticut Avenue, Rm 815, Washington DC 20017 Tel. 202 673 6715

Florida
Public Health Unit, PO Box 2745, Tallahassee, FL 32316 Tel. 904 487 3186

Georgia
Department of Human Resources, Immunization Program, 878 Peach Tree Street, Rm 211, Atlanta, GA 30309 Tel. 404 894 6598

Guam
Department of Public Health & Social Services, PO Box 2816, Government of Guam, Agana, Guam 96910 Tel. 671 734 2951

Hawaii
State Department of Health, PO Box 3378, Honolulu, HI 96801 Tel. 808 548 5987

Idaho
Department of Health and Welfare, Statehouse, Boise, ID 83720 Tel. 208 334 5930

Illinois
Illinois Department of Public Health, 525 West Jefferson, Springfield, IL 62761 Tel. 217 782 2016

Indiana
Indiana State Board of Health, 1330 West Michigan Street, PO Box 1964 Indianapolis, IN 46206 Tel. 317 633 8583

Iowa
State Department of Health, Lucas State Office Building, 3rd Floor, Des Moines, IA 50319 Tel. 515 281 5424

Kansas
Kansas Department of Health and Environment, Forbes Field, Building 321, Topeka, KS 66620 Tel. 913 296 1500

Kentucky
Department of Human Resources, 275 E. Main Street, Frankfort, KY 40601 Tel. 502 564 6620

Louisiana
State Health Dept, Epidemiology Section, 325 Loyola Avenue, PO Box 60630, New Orleans, LA 70160 Tel. 504 568 5005

Maine
Department of Human Services, Bureau of Health, State House, Station #11, Augusta, ME 04333 Tel. 207 289 3201

Maryland
Maryland Department of Health, 201 West Preston Street, Baltimore, MD 21201 Tel. 301 225 6677

Massachusetts
Massachusetts Department of Public Health, Room 562, 305 South St, Jamaica Plain, MA 02130 Tel. 617 722 2686

Michigan
Michigan Department of Public Health, 3500 North Logan, PO Box 30035, Lansing, MI 48909 Tel. 517 335 8163

Minnesota
Minnesota Department of Health, 717 Delaware Street, SE, Minneapolis, MN 55440 Tel. 612 623 5588

Mississippi
Board of Health, 420 East Woodrow Wilson, Jackson, MS 39215 Tel. 601 362 4401

Missouri
Missouri Division of Health, PO Box 570, Jefferson City, MO 65102 Tel. 314751 6133

Montana
Montana Department of Health & Environmental Sciences, Cogswell Building, Helena, MT 59620 Tel. 406 444 4740

Nebraska
State of Nebrasksa Department of Health, 301 Centennial Mall South, PO Box 95007, Lincoln, NE 68509–5007 Tel. 402 471 2937

Nevada
Department of Human Resources, Room 200, Kinhead Building, 505 E. King Street, Carson City, NV 89710 Tel. 702 885 4800

New Hampshire
New Hampshire Division of Public Health, Health and Welfare Building, Hazen Drive, Concord, NH 03301 Tel. 603 271 4482

New Jersey
New Jersey Department of Health, CN 360, Trenton, NJ 08625 Tel. 609 588 7512

New Mexico
Health & Environmental Department, PO Box 968, Sante Fe, New Mexico 87504–0968 Tel. 505 827 0006

New York
New York State Health Department, Tower Building, Room 1084, Empire State Plaza, Albany, NY 12237 Tel. 518 474 4284

North Carolina
Department of Health, PO Box 949, Raleigh, NC 27602 Tel. 919 755 0761

North Dakota
State Health Department, Division of Disease Control, Capitol Building, Bismarck, ND 58505 Tel. 701 224 2378

Ohio
Ohio Department of Health, 246 North High Street, Columbus, OH 43266–0588 Tel. 614 466 4643

Oklahoma
Oklahoma Department of Health, N. E. 10th and Stonewall, Oklahoma City, OK 73152 Tel. 405 271 4073

Oregon
Oregon State Health Division, Immunization Section, Rm 507, 1400 SW 5th Avenue, Portland, OR 97201 Tel. 503 229 5534

Pennsylvania
Pennsylvania Department of Health, PO Box 90, Harrisburg, PA 17108 Tel. 717 787 5681

Puerto Rico
Puerto Rico Department of Health, San Juan, PR 00936 Tel. 809 766 1616

Rhode Island
Rhode Island Department of Health, 103 Cannon Building, 75 Davis Street, Providence, RI 02908 Tel. 401 277 2362

South Carolina
Health Department, 1305 Harden St, Columbia SC 29204 Tel. 803 748 4980

South Dakota
State of South Dakota Health Department, 523 E. Capitol, Pierre, SD 57501 Tel. 605 773 3357

Tennessee
Department of Health, 311 23rd Avenue North, Nashville, TN 37203 Tel. 615 327 9313

Texas

Texas Department of Health, Bureau of Epidemiology, 1100 West 49th Street, Austin, TX 78756 Tel. 512 458 7328

Utah

Utah Department of Health, PO Box 1660, Salt Lake City, UT 84116–0660 Tel. 801 538 6191

Vermont

State Health Department, 60 Main Street, Burlington, VT 05401 Tel. 802 863 7240

Virginia

Virginia State Health Department, Room 703, 109 Governor Street, Richmond, VA 23219 Tel. 804 786 6246

Virgin Islands

Virgin Islands Department of Health, PO Box 7309, St Thomas, US VI 00801 Tel. 809 776 8311

Washington

US Public Health Service, Seattle-Tacoma International Airport, Room S 212, Seattle, WA 98158 Tel 206 442 4519

West Virginia

West Virginia Department of Health, 515 11th Avenue, Charleston, WV 25303 Tel. 304 348 2188

Wisconsin

State Health Department, PO Box 309, Madison, WI 53702 Tel. 608 266 2346

Wyoming

Department of Health and Social Services, Preventive Medicine Services, Hathaway Building, 4th Floor, Cheyenne, WY 82002 Tel. 307 777 6004

Major travellers' clinics and US centres specializing in tropical medicine*

Arizona

Travelers' Clinic, University of Arizona Health Sciences Center, (Department of Family and Community Medicine), Tucson AZ 85724 Tel. 602 626 7900

California

Travel Clinic, UCSD Medical Center, (Department of Family Medicine), 200 South Annex, San Diego, CA 92130 Tel. 619 543 6222 or 619 543 5787

Overseas Medical Center, 10 Calaifornia Street, San Francisco, CA 94111 Tel. 415 982 8380

Department of International Health, University of California, San Francisco CA 94143 Tel. 415 666 1872

* I am grateful to Dr Leonard Marcus and the American Society of Tropical Medicine and Hygiene for assistance in obtaining some of these addresses.

RMD

Colorado

Infectious Disease Division, University of Colorado Health Science Center, 4200 East 9th Avenue, Denver CO 80262 Tel. 303 320 7277

Connecticut

International Travelers' Medical Service, University of Connecticut Health Center, Farmington CT 06032 Tel. 203 674 3245 or 203 674 3553

Tropical Medicine and International Travelers' Clinic, Yale University School of Medicine, 20 York St, New Haven, CT 06504 Tel. 203 785 2476 (Emergencies: 203 785 2471)

District of Columbia

Travelers' Clinic, George Washington University Medical Center, 2150 Pennsylvania Avenue NW, Washington DC 20037 Tel. 202 676 5558 or 676 8466

Travelers' Medical Service, 2141 K Street NW, Washington DC 20037 Tel. 202 466 8109 or 331 0287

Department of Geographic Medicine, Howard University Hospital, 2041 Georgia Avenue NW, Washington DC 20060 Tel. 202 745 6641

Florida

Institute of Tropical Medicine, 1780 NE 168th St, North Miami Beach, FL 33162 Tel. 305 947 1722

Hawaii

Straub Clinic & Hospital, 888 South King Street, Honolulu, HA 96813 Tel. 808 523 2311

Illinois

Travel Clinic, University of Chicago Hospitals & Clinics, 5841 South Maryland, Chicago, IL 60637 Tel. 312 962 6112

Kansas

International Medicine & Infectious Disease Consultants, 631 Horne, Suite 420, Topeka, KA 66606 Tel. 913 234 8405

Louisiana

Department of Tropical Medicine, Tulane Medical Center, 1430 Tulane Avenue, New Orleans LA 70112 Tel. 504 588 5199

Massachusetts

Division of Geographic Medicine and Infectious Diseases, New England Medical Center Hospitals, 750 Washington St, Boston, MA 02111 Tel. 617 956 7621 or 617 956 7009

Travelers' Advice and Immunization Center, Massachusetts General Hospital, Boston, MA 02114 Tel. 617 726 2478

Travelers' Health and Immunization Services, 148 Highland Avenue, Newton, MA 02160 Tel. 617 527 4003 or 366 0060

Travel Clinic, Mount Auburn Hospital, 330 Mount Auburn St, Cambridge, MA 02238 Tel. 617 499 5026

Maryland

Travelers' Clinic, University of Maryland Hospital, 22 South Green St, Baltimore MD 21201 Tel. 301 328 5196

Travel Clinic, Johns Hopkins University, Hampton House, 624 North Broadway, Baltimore MD 21205 Tel. 301 955 8931

Michigan

Travel Health Clinic, Henry Ford Hospital, 2799 West Grand Boulevard, Detroit, MI 48202 Tel. 313 876 2561

Missouri

Infectious Diseases Division, Washington University Medical Center, 216 South Kings Highway, St Louis, MO 63110 Tel. 314 454 7782

New York

International Health Care Services, Cornell Medical College–New York Hospital, 440 East 69th Street, New York, NY 10021 Tel. 212 472 4284

International Health Clinic, Albert Einstein College of Medicine, 1300 Morris Park Avenue, Bronx, New York, NY 10461 Tel. 212 430 2059

Ohio

Travelers' Clinic, Department of Medicine, University Hospitals, Cleveland OH 44106 Tel. 216 844 3295

Pennsylvania

International Travel & Infectious Disease Service, Montefiore Hospital, 3459 Fifth Avenue, Pittsburgh, PA 15213 Tel. 412 648 6410

Pittsburgh Infectious Diseases, 1400 Locust Street, Pittsburgh PA 15219 Tel. 412 232 7398 (24-hour coverage)

Travelers' Clinic, Milton S. Hershey Medical Center, Pennsylvania State University, Hershey, PA 17033 Tel. 717 531 8161

Travellers' Health Center, Medical College of Pennsylvania, 3300 Henry Avenue, Philadelphia PA 19129 Tel. 215 842 6465

Texas

Department of Geographic Medicine, University of Texas Health Service Center, 6431 Fannin, Houston, TX 77025 Tel. 713 792 2121

Utah

Center for Infectious Diseases, Microbiology & Immunology, University of Utah School of Medicine, Salt Lake City, UT 84132 Tel. 801 581 8811

Washington

Travelers' Medical and Immunization Clinic of Seattle, 525 First Avenue W, Seattle, WA 98119 Tel. 296 281 1610

Travelers' Clinic, Pacific Medical Center, 1200 12th Avenue S, Seattle, WA 98144 Tel. 206 745 6641

Travel and Tropical Medicine Clinic, University of Washington School of Medicine, University Hospital RC–02 1959 NE Pacific, Seattle WA 98195 Tel. 206 548 4000 or 548 4226

Wisconsin

International Travelers' Clinic, St Luke's Hospital, 2900 West Oklahoma, Milwaukee, WI 53212 Tel. 414 649 6664

West Virginia

Travelers' Clinic, Marshall University School of Medicine, 1801 Sixth Avenue, Huntington, WV 25701 Tel. 304 526 0630

Other sources of information

The Centers for Disease Control (CDC), Atlanta, Georgia 30333 Tel. 404 639 3311. Publishes *Health information for international travel* (see Further reading), and is able to provide expert advice on infectious hazards of travel in cases of special difficulty.

US State Department Overseas Emergency Center, Tel. 202 647 5225; provides information about political and other risks abroad, and should be consulted if you intend to visit a part the world where there is currently unrest or instability; also provides advice for travellers in distress. Using a touch-tone phone, you can select pre-recorded advisory information for any country; or you can speak directly with a State Department employee.

Immunization Alert, P.O. Box 406, Storrs, CT 06268; provides computerized health briefings, tailored to individual requirements and itineraries (prices from approximately $40).

World Status Map. Monthly summary of advisories and alerts (mainly political), available on subscription. Box 466, Merrifield, VA 22116 Tel. 301 564 8473

Canada

Department of National Health and Welfare Travel Information Offices

Newfoundland

St. John's
Health and Welfare Canada, Room 410, Sir Humphrey Gilbert Building, Duckworth Street, PO Box 5759, A1C 5X3 Tel. 709 772 5571

Gander
Health and Welfare Canada, PO Box 368, Gander International Airport, A1B 1W7 Tel. 709 256 3035

Nova Scotia

Halifax
Health and Welfare Canada, 3129 Kempt Road, B3K 5N6 Tel. 902 426 3998

Sydney
Health and Welfare Canada, 63 Charlotte Street, B1P 1B8 Tel. 902 564 7290

New Brunswick

Saint John
Health and Welfare Canada, 89 Canterbury Street, Room 513, E2L 2C7 Tel. 506 648 4862

Quebec

Montreal
Services Médicaux, Santé et Bien-être social Canada, Le Complex Guy-Favreau, 200, Dorchester ouest, H2Z 1X4 Tel. 514 283 4880

Ontario

Toronto
Health and Welfare Canada, 3rd Floor, 55 St. Clair Avenue East, M4T 1M2 Tel. 416 966 6245

Thunder Bay
Health and Welfare Canada, 33 South Court Street, Room 350, P7B 2W6 Tel. 807 345 1443

Ottawa
Medical Services, Health and Welfare Canada, 301 Elgin Street, K1A 0L3 Tel. 613 990 0641

Manitoba

Winnipeg
Health and Welfare Canada, Room 500, 303 Main Street, R3C 0H4 Tel. 204 949 3616

Saskatchewan

Regina
Health and Welfare Canada, 1855 Smith Street, S4P 2N5 Tel. 306 359 5413

Alberta

Edmonton
Health and Welfare Canada, 401 Toronto Dominion Tower, Edmonton Centre, T5J 2Z1 Tel. 403 420 2697

British Columbia

Victoria
Health and Welfare Canada, 5th Floor, 2130 Government Street, V8W 1Y3 Tel. 604 566 3387

Prince Rupert
Health and Welfare Canada, 581–309 2nd Avenue West, V8J 3T1 Tel. 604 627 1381

Vancouver
Health and Welfare Canada, 7th Floor, 1133 Medville Street, V6E 4E5 Tel. 605 666 6196

Prince George
Health and Welfare Canada, 1294 — 3rd Avenue,V2L 3L4 Tel. 604 562 6675

Yellow fever vaccination centres for Canada

Newfoundland

St. John's
Medical Officer of Health, St. John's and District Health Unit, Public Service Building, Forest Road, A1C 5T7 Tel. 709 737 3435

Nova Scotia

Halifax
Medical Officer-in-Charge, Medical Services, Health and Welfare Canada, 3129 Kempt Road, B3K 5N6 Tel. 902 426 3998

Sydney
Physician-in-Charge, Cape Breton Health Unit, Provincial Building, Prince Street, B1P 5L1 Tel. 902 564 4447 or 564 4448

New Brunswick

Saint John
District Medical Health Officer, Public Health Services — Region II, 157 Duke Street, E2L 3XI Tel. 506 658 2455

Prince Edward Island

Charlottetown

Division of Nursing, Department of Health and Social Services, Sullivan Building, 1st Floor, 16 Fitzroy Street, PO Box 2000, C1A 7N8 Tel. 902 892 5471

Quebec

Iontréal

Département de santé communautaire, Clinique Santé-Voyage, 1001, rue St-Denis, 2e étage, H2X 3H9 Tel. 514 285 6304

Clinique médicale du Chemin de fer C.N., 935, rue Lagauchetière ouest 2e étage, H3C 3N4 Tel. 514 877 5690

Quebéc

Département de santé communautaire, Hôpital du Saint-Sacrement, 1050, Chemin Ste-Foy, G1S 4L8 Tel. 418 688 3670

Chicoutimi

Département de santé communautaire. Clinique de vaccination des voyageurs, 479, boul. Talbot, G7H 4A3 Tel. 418 543 0761

Ontario

Sherbrooke

Clinique du voyageur international, Boutique Santé 2000, Carrefour de l'Estrie, 3050, boul. Portland, J1L 1K1 Tel. 819 564 1010

Rimouski

Centre local de services communautaires de l'Estuaire, 165, des Gouverneurs, G5L 7R2 Tel. 418 7247204

Dorval

Services médicaux d'Air Canada, Aéroport Dorval, H4Y 1C2 Tel. 514 636 2973

Ontario

Toronto

Zone Director, Medical Services, Health and Welfare Canada, 3rd Floor, 55 St. Clair Avenue East, M4T 2M5 Tel. 416 966 6245

Toronton General Hospital, Travel and Inoculation Clinic, 200 Elizabeth Street M5G 1L7 Tel. 416 595 3670 No appointment necessary.

Canadian National Railways Medical Department, 97 Front Street West, Suite 257, Union Station, RRB Box 133, M5J 1E5 Tel. 416 860 2711

Air Canada Medical Services, Box 6002, Toronto AMF, L5P 1B4 Tel. 416 6762 400

London

University Hospital Immunization Clinic, 339 Windermere Road, N6A 5A5
Tel. 519 663 3395

Ottawa

Regional Director, Overseas and National Capital Region, Medical Services, Health and Welfare Canada, 301 Elgin Street, K1A 0L3 Tel. 613 990 0641

Thunder Bay

Lake Superior Health Centre, Medical Services, Health and Welfare Canada, 33 South Court Street, Room 350, P7B 2W6 Tel. 807 345 1443

Kingston
Base Hospital, Canadian Forces Base Kingston, K7L 2Z2 Appointment: Tel. 613 545 5508

Sudbury
Medical Officer of Health, Sudbury and District Health Unit, 1300 Paris Crescent, P3E 3A3 Appointment: Tel. 705 522 9200

Astra
Base Surgeon, Canadian Forces Base Trenton, K0K 1B0 Appointment: Tel. 613 392 2811 Ext. 3432

Midhurst
Simcoe County District Health Unit, County Administration Centre, L0L 1X0 Appointment: Tel. 705 726 0100

Hamilton
Operating Division, McMaster University, 1200 Main Street West, L8N 3Z5 Tel. 416 521 2100 Ext. 6307

Peterborough
Medical Officer of Health, Peterborough County City Health Unit, 835 Weller Street, K9J 4Y1 Tel. 705 743 1160

Petawawa
Base Surgeon, Canadian Forces Base Petawawa, K8H 2X3 Tel. 613 687 5511 Ext. 381

Timmins
Medical Officer of Health, Porcupine Health Unit, 169 Pine Street South, P4N 8B7 Tel. 795 267 1181

Manitoba

Winnipeg
Director, Special Services, Medical Services, Health and Welfare Canada, Room 500 303 Main Street, R3C 0H4 Tel. (204) 949 4194

Saskatchewan

Regina
Medical Officer of Health, City Health Department, 1910 McIntyre, S4P 2R3 Tel. 306 522 3621

Saskatoon
Medical Health Officer, Saskatoon Community Health Unit, 350 — 3rd Avenue North, S7K 6G7 Tel. 306 664 9627

Alberta

Edmonton
Central Health Clinic, 10005 — 103 A Avenue, T5J 0K1 Tel. 403 428 3444

Calgary
International Travel Immunization Clinic, Health Services Centre, 3330 Hospital Drive N.W., T2N 4N1 Tel. 403 220 4274

Medley
Canadian Forces Hospital, Canadian Forces Base Cold Lake, T0A 2M0 Tel. 403 594 8750.

British Columbia

Victoria
Director, Vancouver Island Zone, Medical Services, Health and Welfare Canada, Room 510 — 1230 Government Street, V8W 3G7 Tel. 604 388 3565

Lazo
Base Hospital, Canadian Forces Base Comox, V0R 2K0 Tel. 604 339 2211 Ext. 2267

Vancouver
Zone Director, Medical Services, Health and Welfare Canada, 7th Floor, 1133 Melville Street, V6E 4E5 Tel. 604 666 3331

Prince George
Northern Interior Health Unit, 1444 Edmonton Street, V2M 6W5 Appointment: Tel. 604 565 7311

Vernon
North Okanagan Health Unit, 1277 — 15 Street, V1T 8S7 Tel. 604 545 0651

Immunization: a guide for international travellers is published by Health and Welfare Canada; this leaflet is available free from its offices, and lists additional information sources, as well as immunization recommendations. It is updated annually.

There are tropical disease units at:
Toronto General Hospital, Toronto, Ontario, M5G 1L7 Tel. 416 595 3671

Vancouver General Hospital, Vancouver, BC V5Z 1M9 Tel. 604 875 4148

Information about AIDS
National AIDS Centre, Health Protection Building, Tunney's Pasture, Ottawa, Ontario K1A OL2 Tel. 613 957 1774

Public Education Panel on AIDS 15 Overlea Blvd., Toronto, Ontario M4H 1A9 Tel. 416 965 2168

Other sources of information

The Tropical Traveller, Hobbit Software Inc, P.O. Box 308, Victoria Station, Montreal, Quebec H3Z 2VB. Personalized computer health briefings, in English or French.

Australia

Most information about immunization recommendations and requirements is available from GPs.

Further information can be obtained from Regional Offices of the Commonwealth Department of Health, listed below.

Regional Offices

New South Wales
Commonwealth Department of Health, Commonwealth Government Centre, Chifley Square, Corner Phillip and Hunter Streets, Sydney, NSW 2000 Tel. 239 3000

Victoria
Commonwealth Department of Health, Commonwealth Centre, Corner Spring and LaTrobe Streets, Melbourne, Vic. 3000 Tel. 662 2999

Queensland
Commonwealth Department of Health, Australian Government Offices, Anzac Square, Adelaide St, Brisbane, Qld 4000 Tel. 225 0122

South Australia
Commonwealth Department of Health, I.M.F.C. House, 33–39 King William Street, Adelaide, S.A. 5001 Tel. 2163911

Western Australia
Commonwealth Department of Health, Victoria Centre, 2–6 St George's Terrace, Perth, W.A. 6000 Tel. 323 5711

Tasmania
Commonwealth Department of Health, Kirksway House, 6 Kirksway Place, Hobart, Tas 7000 Tel. 20 5011

Northern Territory
Commonwealth Department of Health, M.L.C. Building, Smith Street, Darwin, N.T. 5794 Tel. 80 2911

Australian Capital Territory
C.T.H.C. Building, Corner Moore and Alinga Sts, Canberra City, A.C.T. 2601 Tel. 454111

Central Office

The Secretary, Commonwealth Department of Health, PO Box 100, Woden, ACT 2606

There is a specialist infectious diseases unit at:
Commonwealth Institute of Health A27, University of Sydney, NSW 2006, Tel. 660 9292

AIDS telephone information hotlines
Alice Springs: Tel. 089 502639

Canberra: Tel. 062 454401

Darwin: Tel. 089 812951

Melbourne: Tel. 03 347 5650

Tasmania: Tel. 008 005188

Western Australia: Tel. 09 11642

New Zealand

Up-to-date advice on requirements and recommendations, and information about yellow fever vaccination centres are available from general practitioners and district offices of the Department of Health, addresses below. The Department of Health also publishes a booklet entitled *Health information for travellers*, available from Government Print Offices or on application to the Department of Health, PO Box 5013, Wellington, New Zealand.

There is an infectious disease unit at Auckland Hospital.

District offices: addresses and phone numbers

Auckland
Bledisole State Building, Civic Square, Auckland, Tel. 774 494

Christchurch
Reserve Bank Building, 158 Hereford Street, Christchurch, Tel. 799 480

Dunedin
State Insurance Building, Princess, Dunedin Tel. 770 213

Gisborne
Government Life Building, Gladstone Road, Gisborne Tel. 89 039

Hamilton
Rural Bank of Finance Corporation, Bryce Street, Hamilton Tel. 82 569

Hutt
Andrews Avenue, Lower Hutt Tel. 660 764

Invercargill
7th Floor, State Insurance Building, Don Street, Invercargill Tel. 87 242

Napier
Tennyson Street, Napier, Tel. 53 139

Nelson
50 Halifax Street, Nelson Tel. 88 389

New Plymouth
4th Floor, T and G Building, Liardet Street, New Plymouth Tel. 85 203

Palmerston North
1st and 2nd Floors, AMP Building, Broadway Ave, Palmerston North Tel. 81 055

Rotorua
Departmental Building, Haupapa Street, Rotorua Tel. 83 089

South Auckland
Leyton House, Leyton Way, Manukau City Centre, Wiri Tel. 2785024

Takapuna
Karaka House, Huron Street, Takapuna, Auckland Tel. 449 166

Timaru
Government Life Building, George Street, Timaru Tel. 44 064

Wanganui
State Insurance Building, Victoria Avenue, Wanganui Tel. 55 526

Wellington
Education House, 178–182 Willis Street, Wellington Tel. 858 769

Information about AIDS
Nationwide toll-free hotline: Tel. 09 395560

Further reading

Publications marked * are primarily written for doctors.

Adler, M.W. *ABC of sexually transmitted diseases*. British Medical Association, 1984. *

American Medical Association. *Family medical guide*. Random House, 1987.

American Red Cross. *Standard first aid and personal safety* and *Advanced first aid and emergency care*, both 1979.

Auerbach, P.S. *Medicine for the outdoors*. Little, Brown, 1986.

Auerbach, P.S. and Geehr, E.C. *Management of wilderness and environmental emergencies*. Collier Macmillan, 1983. [Everything from plant and wildlife hazards to lightning, forest fires, and drowning.] *

Bell, D.R. *Lecture notes on tropical medicine*. Blackwell Scientific Publications, 1985. [A good introduction to the subject.] *

Benson, A.J. Motion sickness. In *Vertigo* (ed. M.R. Dix and J.D.Hood), pp. 391–426. Chichester, J. Wiley & Sons 1984.

Bolz, F. *How to be a hostage and live*. Lyle Stewart, New Jersey, 1987.

Brand, J.J. and Perry, W.L.M. Drugs used in motion sickness. *Pharmacological Review*, **18**, 895–924, 1966.

Bruce-Chwatt, L.J. *Essential malariology*. 2nd edn. Heinemann Medical Books, 1985. [A fascinating account of the world's most important disease.] *

Bennett, P.B. and Elliot, D.H. *The physiology and medicine of diving*. Balliere Tindall, 1982.*

Bezruchka, S. *A guide to trekking in Nepal*. Diadem, 1985, [How to do it safely.]

Blashford-Snell, J. and Ballantyne, A. *Expeditions the expert's way*. Faber & Faber, 1977.

British Medical Association. *Living with risk*. Wiley, 1987.

Centers for Disease Control, Atlanta Ga., USA. *Health information for international travel*—Supplement to Morbidity & Mortality Weekly Report. Published annually, in August. Available from the Superintendent of Documents, US Govt. Printing Office, Washington DC 20402. [The official US publication for doctors.] *

Chippaux, J.P. and Goyfon, M. Producers of antivenomous sera. *Toxicon* **21** (6) 739–52, 1983.

Cohen, M.M. *Dr. Cohen's healthy sailor book*. International Marine Publishing Co, Maine, 1983.

Collins, P. *Living in troubled lands*. Paladin Press, Boulder, Colorado

DeHart, R.L. *Fundamentals of aerospace medicine.** Lea & Feabiger, Philadelphia 1985.

Department of Health and Social Security (UK). *The Traveller's Guide to Health* (T1) (includes E111 application). Published annually, free. Available by mail from DHSS Leaflet Unit, Stanmore, Middlesex HA7 1AY. Can be ordered by phone: 0800 555 777. *Immunization against infectious disease.* HMSO, London, 1990. A practical guide for doctors.*

Department of Trade, UK. *The ship captain's medical guide.* HMSO, London, 1983.

Diabetic traveller. PO Box 8223 RW, Stamford, CT 06905, USA. Quarterly newsletter.

Disabled travellers' international phrase book. Disability Press [Available from RADAR, 25 Mortimer Street, London WIN 8AB.]

Editorial. Jet lag and its pharmacology, *Lancet*, 30 August, 1986. 493–4.

Edmonds, C. *Dangerous marine animals of the Indo-Pacific region.* Wedneil Publications, Newport, Australia, 1975.*

Fit to fly: a medical handbook for pilots. British Airline Pilots Association Medical Study Group, Granada, 1988.

Flight international. Business Press International, U.K. [Air transport industry information, statistics and news in a weekly journal.]

Gifford, N. *Expeditions and exploration.* Macmillan, 1983.

Grossman, S. *Have kids, will travel.* Christopher Helm, 1987.

A guide to the accessibility of airport terminals, Access Travel. Available from Airport Operators International, 1700 K Street NW, Washington DC 20006, USA. [For disabled travellers.]

Guillebaud, J. *Contraception: your questions answered.* Pitman Publishing, 1985.

Harding, R.M. and Mills, F. *Aviation medicine.* British Medical Association, 1988.*

Heath, D. and Williams, D.R. *Man at high altitude.* Churchill Livingstone, 1981.*

Holidays for disabled people. RADAR, 1985. [Available from RADAR, 25 Mortimer Street, London WIN 8AB.]

IAMAT directory. Available from IAMAT, 736 Center Street, Lewiston, NY 14092. [Names and addresses of English-speaking doctors abroad.]

Illingworth, R.N. *Expedition medicine: a planning guide.* Blackwell, 1984. [For expedition organisers and members.]

Jenkins, B.M. *Terrorism.* Butterworth Publishers, Stoneham Massachusetts.

Jolly, H. *Book of child care: the complete guide for today's parents.* George Allen and Unwin, 1985. [Excellent section on the sick child.]

Kirby, N.G. *Field surgery pocket book*. HMSO, 1980. [A useful companion for expedition doctors.] *

Lucas, A.O. and Gilles, H.M. *A short textbook of preventative medicine for the tropics*. Hodder & Stoughton, 1984.*

Manson-Bahr, P.E.C. and Bell, D.R. *Manson's tropical diseases* 19th edn. Baillière Tindall, 1987.

Melville, K.E.M. *Stay alive in the desert*. Roger Lascelles, London, 1984.

Money, K.E. Motion sickness. *Physiological Reviews*, **50**, 1–38, 1972.

Morley, D. *The care of young children and babies in the tropics*. National Association for Maternal and Child Welfare (1 South Audley Street, London WIY 6JS). [Also available from TALC, address below.]

National Council for Civil Liberties. *Body searches at customs—What the law says and your rights*. Available from NCCL, 21 Tabard St, London SE1 Tel. 01 403 3888

Nicholson, A.N. Hypnotics: their place in therapeutics. *Drugs*, **31**, 164–176, 1986.

Nicholson, A.N. and others. Sleep after transmeridian flights. *Lancet*, **22**, November, 1205–8.

Norton, A.L. (ed.) *Family-Travel*. St John's Wood Press, 1987.

Peters, W. and Gilles, H.M. *Colour atlas of tropical medicine*. Wolfe Medical Atlases, 1986.*

Readers Digest *What to do in an emergency*. Readers Digest Publications, 1986. [Covers almost every conceivable emergency, and even some inconceivable ones.]

Reason, J.T. and Brand, J.J. *Motion sickness*. Academic Press, London, 1975.

Royal College of Physicians, London. *Links between exposure to ultraviolet radiation and skin cancer** and *The sun on your skin*. Special reports, available from The Royal College of Physicians, 11 St Andrew's Place, London NW1 4LE

Scotti, A.J. *Executive safety and international terrorism: a guide for travellers*. Prentice-Hall, New Jersey 1986.

Smith, T. (ed.) *British Medical Association Family Doctor*. Home Adviser, Dorling Kindersley, 1986. [A wide-ranging guide to symptoms and self-diagnosis.]

Sperryn, P. N. *Sport and Medicine*. Butterworth, 1983.*

St John's Ambulance, St Andrew's Association, British Red Cross Society. *First aid manual*. 1982.

Steele, R. *Medical care for mountain climbers*. Heinemann, 1976.

Strickland, G.T. *Hunter's tropical medicine*.* Saunders, 1984

Sutherland S.K. *Australian animal toxins: the creatures, their toxins, and care of the poisoned patient*. Oxford University Press, Melbourne, 1983.

US Dept. of Health, Education and Welfare. *The ship's medicine chest and medical aid at sea*. 1984. Available from the Superintendent of Documents, US Govt. Printing Office, Washington DC 20402.

US Dept. of State, Bureau of Consular Affairs. Issues many publications of interest to prospective travellers, including: *Your trip abroad; A safe trip abroad; Tips for travelers: the Caribbean, Cuba, Eastern Europe & Yugoslavia, Mexico, Middle East, People's Republic of China, Saudi Arabia, USSR; Travel warning on drugs abroad; Travel tips for senior citizens; Tips for Americans residing abroad; Key officers of foreign service posts* (names of key US officers abroad with addresses of all US embassies and consulates); *Background notes, Country information notices*, and *Travel advisory memoranda*. Available from the Superintendent of Documents, US Govt. Printing Office, Washington DC 20402; some of these are also available from passport offices; in case of difficulty, write to the Bureau of Consular Affairs, Dept. of State, Washington DC 20402.

Warrell, D.A. Venomous and poisonous animals. In *Tropical and geographical medicine*. (ed. K.S. Warren and A.A.F. Mahmoud) McGraw Hill, New York, 1984.*

Weiss, L. *Access to the world*. Henry Holt, New York, 1986. [Access guide for the disabled.]

Werner, D. *Where there is no doctor*. Macmillan 1985. [Available also from TALC, 30 Guilford Street, London WC1N 1EH, and the Hesperian Foundation, PO Box 1692, Palo Alto, Ca 94302, USA—intended for people in developing countries with little education, but contains much useful advice on management of common tropical conditions. Also available on microfiche.]

Wiseman, J. *The SAS survival handbook*. Collins Harvill, 1986.

World AIDS, Panos Institute, 8 Alfred Place, London WC1E 7EB, UK. 1409 King Street, Alexandria, VA 22314 USA. [Worldwide news about AIDS.]

World Health Organization, Geneva. *International travel and health: Vaccination requirements and health advice*. Published annually in the spring, available from HMSO, London; the UN Bookshop, NY; and Govt. Publishing Service Bookshops in Australia. [The official WHO listing of requirements and recommendations for travel, including global distribution of malaria and chloroquine resistance.] * *World health statistical quarterly* and WHO *weekly epidemiological record* periodically publish updated maps and assessments of the world malaria situation.* *Atlas of the global distribution of Schistosomiasis* (1987) shows all known geography of this disease, often listing cases by village. The ultimate reference.

Yaffé, M. *Taking the fear out of flying*. David and Charles Publishers (UK) and Sterling Publishing Co, New York, 1987.

Glossary

Acute: An acute illness is one that is sudden in onset, regardless of severity.

Antibody: A protein made by the body in response to anything that it recognises as 'foreign'—such as components of bacteria and viruses called antigens. Antibodies bind to antigens and inactivate them, and are 'tailor-made' for each antigen. The principle of 'active' immunization is based on the fact that exposure to a small amount of harmless antigen—present in a vaccine—stimulates the production of antibodies that remain ready for action when infection threatens. (Vaccines fool the immune system that they are 'the real thing'.) (See also immunoglobulin.)

Antigen: Any substance capable of triggering an immune response. They include components of bacteria, viruses, toxins, and vaccines. Hepatitis B surface antigen (HBsAg) is an antigen present in the blood of people who have had hepatitis B, and can be detected by laboratory tests.

Bacillus: 'Rod-shaped' bacteria. Anthrax, leprosy, and TB are examples of diseases caused by bacilli.

Bacteria: Tiny organisms that consist of a single cell, and have a cell wall but no nucleus. There are a great many types, not all of which cause disease.

Chemoprophylaxis: The use of drugs to *prevent* disease.

Chronic: A chronic disease process is one that develops gradually, or lasts a long time.

Contra-indication: Any disease or condition that renders a proposed form of treatment or course of action undesirable.

Culture: Growth of micro-organisms in the laboratory for testing and identification.

Cutaneous: Of the skin.

Diuretic: A drug that increases urine production.

Dysentery: Severe diarrhoea with blood, mucus, and abdominal cramps.

Embolism: The sudden blockage of an artery, usually by a blood clot that has travelled in the bloodstream from elsewhere in the body. Clot, or 'thrombus', sometimes forms in the veins of the legs; 'pulmonary embolism' occurs when it travels to, and blocks, the arteries of the lungs. Gas entering the bloodstream can have a similar effect—'gas embolism'.

Endemic: A disease that is constantly present to a greater or lesser degree, in a particular area.

Enterocytes: The cells that line the intestinal wall.

Host: Man, or any animal that harbours a parasite.

Immunity: A state in which the individual is resistant to specific infections.

Immunoglobulin: A protein possessing antibody activity. Most immunoglobulins circulate in the bloodstream, and 'gamma globulin' is a preparation of 'ready-made' antibodies from donated blood. 'Passive' immunization consists simply of injecting such ready-made antibody into someone who does not have it, and is the principle on which protection of travellers against hepatitis A is based.

Incidence: The number of new cases of a disease in a given period.

Incubation period: The time between exposure to an infection and the first symptoms.

Intradermal, Intramuscular, Intravenous: These terms refer to the position of the tip of the needle during an injection. An intradermal injection is given as close to the skin surface as possible. An intramuscular injection is given deep into a muscle—usually in the buttock. An intravenous injection is given into a vein, directly into the bloodstream.

Jaundice: Yellow discolouration of the skin and whites of the eyes, due to the presence in the blood of excess amounts of a substance called bilirubin, which is normally excreted by the liver into the bile. It occurs in hepatitis, other liver diseases, and sometimes malaria, and is a sign of reduced liver function. Lay people sometimes use this term to mean hepatitis.

Lesion: Sore, wound, ulcer, or area of tissue damage.

Lymph nodes (glands): Part of the immune system. Some can normally be felt as small lumps close to the skin in the neck, groin, and armpit. They may enlarge or become inflamed during an infection.

Micro-organism: Any microscopic organism, including viruses, bacteria, funguses and yeasts, protozoa, and rickettsiae.

Narcosis: Depression of the nervous system—by a drug, or other agent such as an excess of dissolved nitrogen in the blood (the latter is called nitrogen narcosis, which may occur in divers).

Oedema (edema): Fluid in the tissues, causing swelling.

Oesophagus (esophagus): The gullet, or food passage from mouth to stomach.

Papule: A small, circumscribed, solid elevation of the skin.

Parasite: An animal that lives within or upon man or any other animal (its host), and upon which it depends for nutrition and shelter—sometimes at the detriment of the host.

Pathogen, enteropathogen: Any disease-producing micro-organism. Enteropathogens produce intestinal disease.

Physiological: Normal, or related to the way the body functions in health rather than in disease. Physiology is the science of the mechanisms of normal body function.

Prevalence: The total number of cases of a disease at a certain time in a given area.

Prophylaxis: A word that doctors use when they mean prevention!

Protozoa: The simplest organisms in the animal kingdom, consisting each of a single nucleated cell. Some of them cause disease. Malaria, amoebic dysentery, sleeping sickness, trichomoniasis, and giardiasis are all caused by protozoa.

Psychotropic: Mind or mood-altering.

Rickettsiae: A group of micro-organisms that have many similarities to bacteria. They include the micro-organisms that cause typhus.

Sputum: Phlegm; mucus secretions from the lung and respiratory passages.

Subcutaneous: Under all layers of the skin. Many immunizations are injected subcutaneously.

Thrombosis: Clotting of blood within a vein.

Toxin: A specific chemical produced by a living organism that damages or poisons another organism (e.g. man).

Trophozoite: The active, feeding, growing, disease-producing form of a protozoan parasite.

Ulcer: An inflamed defect following damage, at the surface of the skin, the stomach lining, or any other tissue surface.

Vector: A carrier of infection or of a parasite, from one host to the next.

Viruses: Tiny, particulate micro-organisms, much smaller than bacteria and too small to be seen without the aid of the electron microscope. They live inside our cells, multiplying within them, and it is this characteristic which protects them from antibodies and drugs, and makes viral infections so difficult to treat.

Vitiligo: Patches of white, de-pigmented skin.

Index

Drug names in *italics* are brand names, i.e. the name most prominent on the label or packaging of a preparation. These names may vary from country to country. Drugs are also listed here under their generic or scientific names (see note on pp. 489–90) — each of these drugs may be available under a variety of brand names.

Selected reviews of *Travellers' Health*

'If you travel overseas, pick up a copy of TRAVELLERS' HEALTH/HOW TO STAY HEALTHY ABROAD—it covers everything . . . .'
Forbes Magazine.

'TRAVELLERS' HEALTH/HOW TO STAY HEALTHY ABROAD is the only guide of its kind that you will ever need. It covers the full range of health problems faced by travellers. It is especially useful for pregnant travellers, travellers with children, diabetics, and other special groups . . . .'
Travel Smart Newsletter USA.

'Each chapter is written by a specialist. The premise that unites them all is that most health problems on the road CAN be avoided.'
San Francisco Examiner.

'TRAVELLERS' HEALTH is the most comprehensive rundown of the subject. We strongly recommend it to all travellers, but especially to the intrepid who go to out-of-the-way places.'
The South American Handbook.

'The author and contributors have impeccable qualifications and experience for writing this detailed but readable book on illness abroad. As a preventive measure against tropical disease. Richard Dawood's book ranks alongside immunizations.'
MDU Review.

'This book fills a gaping hole in the literature on helping travellers cope with a daunting range of diseases, viruses, parasites and venomous creatures waiting to strike anyone adventuring far afield. Clearly written, this book provides straight forward suggestions for preventing, diagnosing and treating various ailments.'
Vancouver Sun.

'I would recommend this inexpensive paperback to all student health doctors, medical officers of expeditions, and small groups travelling to any medically isolated location.'
British Student Health Association Bulletin.

'Not only is this book packed full of useful information and common-sense advice, it is also enjoyable to read.'
Occupational Health.

'Filled with all sorts of practical advice, explaining how diseases are spread, what precautions to take, and how to treat yourself in an emergency. A Bible no traveller should be without.'
The Diplomat.

'An excellent book, practical and strongly recommended.'
Travel Medicine International.

'Well written, useful and readable. Recommended for every serious, sensible traveller, his family and friends, as well as to every medical and nursing library. Forgo a couple of whodunits to make room for this in your luggage.'
Nursing Standard (Official Newspaper of The Royal College of Nursing).

'Everything you need to know to keep fit abroad is in TRAVELLERS' HEALTH. It covers all aspects. Easy to understand, no traveller should be without this book.'
Woman.

'Admirably comprehensive and delightfully written.'
Hospital Doctor.

'Avid readers of medical journals now have the perfect inflight paperback. It covers everything from dust under your contact lenses and an appraisal of contraceptives, to what to do if you are bitten, gored or mauled by a member of another species.'
Vogue Australia.

'A useful guide to staying healthy on the move.'
The Australian.

'Highly recommended.'
The Reinsurance Market Report.

'Covers everything from malaria in South East Asia to hook-worm in Florida.'
Family Circle.

'If you have the itch to travel, TRAVELLERS' HEALTH should cure you; gruesome detail and sound advice custom made for that long flight or slow train. A wonderful, juicy book that will help people cope with different environments, and warn the truly intrepid about local pathologies.'
Marxism Today.

'Thoroughly fascinating.'
International Management.

'I would pack Richard Dawood's updated TRAVELLERS' HEALTH, for obvious reasons.'
Elisabeth De Stroumillo, Daily Telegraph.